AF772450

E-Government Diffusion, Policy, and Impact: Advanced Issues and Practices

Mehdi Khosrow-Pour
Information Resources Management Association, USA

Information Science REFERENCE

INFORMATION SCIENCE REFERENCE

Hershey · New York

Director of Editorial Content: Kristin Klinger
Director of Production: Jennifer Neidig
Managing Editor: Jamie Snavely
Assistant Managing Editor: Carole Coulson
Typesetter: Sean Woznicki
Cover Design: Lisa Tosheff
Printed at: Yurchak Printing Inc.

Published in the United States of America by
Information Science Reference (an imprint of IGI Global)
701 E. Chocolate Avenue, Suite 200
Hershey PA 17033
Tel: 717-533-8845
Fax: 717-533-8661
E-mail: cust@igi-global.com
Web site: http://www.igi-global.com

and in the United Kingdom by
Information Science Reference (an imprint of IGI Global)
3 Henrietta Street
Covent Garden
London WC2E 8LU
Tel: 44 20 7240 0856
Fax: 44 20 7379 0609
Web site: http://www.eurospanbookstore.com

Copyright © 2009 by IGI Global. All rights reserved. No part of this publication may be reproduced, stored or distributed in any form or by any means, electronic or mechanical, including photocopying, without written permission from the publisher.

Product or company names used in this set are for identification purposes only. Inclusion of the names of the products or companies does not indicate a claim of ownership by IGI Global of the trademark or registered trademark.

Library of Congress Cataloging-in-Publication Data

E-government diffusion, policy and impact : advanced issues and practices / Mehdi Khosrow-Pour, editor.
p. cm. -- (Advances in electronic government)

Includes bibliographical references and index.
Summary: "This book sheds light on how e-government technologies are shaping today's knowledge society from the ground roots of the citizen experience to the supreme level of policy and decision making"--Provided by publisher.

ISBN 978-1-60566-130-8 (hardcover) -- ISBN 978-1-60566-131-5 (ebook)
1. Internet in public administration. 2. Political participation--Technological innovations. I. Khosrowpour, Mehdi, 1951-
JF1525.A8E199 2008
352.3'802854678--dc22

2008022542

British Cataloguing in Publication Data
A Cataloguing in Publication record for this book is available from the British Library.

All work contributed to this book set is original material. The views expressed in this book are those of the authors, but not necessarily of the publisher.

E-Government Diffusion, Policy, and Impact: Advanced Issues and Practices is part of the IGI Global series named *Advances in Electronic Research (AEGR) Series*, ISBN: 1935-3073

If a library purchased a print copy of this publication, please go to http://www.igi-global.com/agreement for information on activating the library's complimentary electronic access to this publication.

Advances in Electronic Government Research Series (AEGR)

ISBN: 1935-3073

Editor-in-Chief: Mehdi Khosrow-Pour, D.B.A.

E-Government Research: Policy and Management
Donald Norris; University of Maryland Baltimore County, USA
IGI Publishing • copyright 2007 • 300+ pp • H/C (ISBN: 978-1-59904-913-7) • US $99.95 (our price)

Virtual technology is increasingly prevalent in all spheres of daily life, including infiltration into governmental policies, processes, infrastructures, and frameworks. E-Government Research: Policy and Management provides scholars and practitioners with a critical mass of research on the integration, management, implications, and application of e-government. Covering such issues as e-government adoption and diffusion; social and performance issues of e-government; and information security, privacy, and policy, this book is an essential resource to any library collection.

Current Issues and Trends in E-Government Research
Donald Norris; University of Maryland Baltimore County
CyberTech Publishing • copyright 2007 • 319 pp • H/C (ISBN: 1-59904-283-5) • US $85.46 (our price)

As emerging trends and research threads surface in the area of e-government, academicians, practitioners, and students face the challenge of keeping up-to-date with new and innovative practices. Current Issues and Trends in E-Government Research provides a complete synopsis of the latest technologies in information policy, security, privacy, and access, as well as the best practices in e-government applications and measurement. Current Issues and Trends in E-Government Research presents the most current issues in e-government hardware and software technology, adoption and diffusion, planning and management, and philosophy.

E-Government Diffusion, Policy, and Impact: Advanced Issues and Practices
Mehdi Khosrow-Pour, Information Resources Management Association, USA
Information Science Reference • copyright 2008 • 306 pp • H/C (ISBN: 978-1-60566-130-8) • US $195.00 (our price)

As governmental entities face accelerating public demand for electronic services and the internal need to utilize technology to achieve superior outcomes and operational efficiency, traditional techniques and tools are radically reshaping and evolving into innovative electronic methods of conducting governmental activities. E-Government Diffusion, Policy, and Impact: Advanced Issues and Practices sheds light on how e-government technologies are shaping today's knowledge society from the ground roots of the citizen experience to the supreme level of policy and decision making. With chapters providing insights into such critical topics as public service delivery, technological diffusion, and e-readiness, this publication offers researchers, students, policy makers, and practitioners a quality depiction of worldwide social practice and how advancements within the realm of technology will affect all corners of the globe.

The Advances in Electronic Government Research (AEGR) Book Series is a multi-disciplinary international book series that publishes high-quality, original research about electronic government. Electronic government is broadly defined within topics such as but not limited to the hardware and software technology, e-government adoption and diffusion, e-government policy, e-government planning and management, e-government applications and e-government impacts. The AEGR Book Series also serves as a forum for scholars and practitioners to present theoretical and philosophical discussions on current issues relating to the practice of electronic government. AEGR aims to supply academicians, practitioners, and professionals with quality applied research results in the field of electronic/digital government, its applications and impacts on governmental organizations around the world. It is the intention of this book series to effectively and positively provide organizational and managerial directions with greater use and management of electronic/digital government technologies in organizations.

IGI GLOBAL
DISSEMINATOR OF KNOWLEDGE

Hershey • New York

Order online at www.igi-global.com or call 717-533-8845 x100 –
Mon-Fri 8:30 am - 5:00 pm (est) or fax 24 hours a day 717-533-8661

Associate Editors

Ari-Veikko Anttiroiko, *University of Tampere, Finland*
Mila Gascó-Hernández, *International Institute on Governance of Catalonia, Spain*
Marijn Janssen, *Delft University of Technology, The Netherlands*
Lawrence Pratchett, *Montfort University, UK*
Jeffrey Roy, *University of Ottawa, Canada*
Spiros Sirmakessis, *Technological Educational Institution of Messolongi, Greece*
Genie Stowers, *San Francisco State University, USA*
Arthur Tatnall, *Victoria University, Australia*
Veluchamy Venkatakrishnan, *Addis Ababa University, Africa*
Vishanth Weerakkody, *KIIT School of Rural Management, India*

Editorial Review Board

Rodrigo Sandoval Almazán, *Business School of the Tecnológico de Monterrey Campus, Mexico*
Kim Viborg Anderson, *Copenhagen Business School, Denmark*
Yigal Arens, *University of Southern California, USA*
Subhajit Basu, *Queen's University, UK*
Stuart I. Bretschneider, *Syracuse University, USA*
Colette R. Brunschwig, *University of Zurich, Switzerland*
Stephen Burgess, *Victoria University, Australia*
Jorge Cardoso, *Universidade da Madeira, Portugal*
Dr. Jyoti Choudrie, *University of Hertfordshire, Hatfield, UK*
Stephen Coleman, *University of Leeds, UK*
Isabel Cruz, *University of Illinois at Chicago, USA*
Keith Culver, *University of New Brunswick, Canada*
William Dutton, *Oxford University, UK*
Mohamed Elbannan, *Cairo University, Egypt*
Ephrem Eyob, *Virginia State University, USA*
Jon Gant, *Syracuse University, USA*
Germanakos Panagiotis, *National & Kapodistrian University of Athens, Greece*
Stephen H. Holden, *University of Maryland, Baltimore County, USA*
Tommi Inkinen, *University of Helsinki, Finland*

Lech Janczewski, *The University of Auckland, New Zealand*
Marijn Janssen, *Delft University of Technology, The Netherlands*
Ralf Klischewski, *Germany University in Cairo, Egypt*
Robert Krimmer, *Vienna University of Economics and Business Administration, Austria*
Herbert Kubicek, *Universität Bremen, Germany*
Marlyn Kemper Littman, *Nova Southeastern University, USA*
David McClure, *The Gartner Group, USA*
M. Jae Moon, *Texas A&M University, USA*
Alf Neumann, *Siemens, Head of Business Development, Tunisia*
Pippa Norris, *Harvard University, USA*
Alana Northrop, *California State University, Fullerton, USA*
John O'Looney, *University of Georgia, USA*
Sangin Park, *Seoul National University, South Korea*
Lise Préfontaine, *University of Quebec, Canada*
Hakikur Rahman, *Bangladesh Open University, Bangladesh*
Priscilla M. Regan, *George Mason University, USA*
Harold Relyea, *Congressional Research Service, USA*
Juan D. Rogers, *Georgia Institute of Technology, USA*
Hans Jochen Scholl, *University of Washington, USA*
Carlos Nunes Silva, *University of Lisbon, Portugal*
Spiros Sirmakessis, *Patras University, Greece*
Reima Suomi, *Turku School of Economics, Finland*
Panayiotis Tahinakis, *University of Macedonia, Greece*
Maurizio Talamo, *University of Rome, Tor Vergata, Italy*
Costas Vassilakis, *University of Peloponnese, Greece*
Lucas Walsh, *Deakin University, Australia*

Table of Contents

Detailed Table of Contents

Stimulated by the need to reduce cost and improve service provisioning and client involvement at the same time, the concept of business models has gained attention in the e-government domain over the last few years. Business models can appear at the individual organization and network level and describes how an entity plans to provide services. The basic premise of business models is that it helps to understand the relation between service offering and other elements and can be used as an instrument to improve service provisioning and lowering cost at the same time. In this chapter an overview of the state-of-the-art of e-government business models, a theory integrating the various elements and research challenges and issues are presented. There is ample need for research and overcoming these challenges result in better leveraging the advantages of business models.

In this chapter we provide an overview of electronic government as it pertains to national security and defense within the Department of Defense (DoD) and Department of Homeland Security (DHS). We discuss the adoption of web services and service oriented architectures to aid in information sharing and reduction of Information Technology (IT) costs. We also discuss the networks on which services and resources are being deployed and explain the efforts being made to manage the infrastructure of available services. This chapter provides an overview of e-government for national security and defense and provides insight to current initiatives and future directions.

The emergence of new doctrine is enabling Security, Stabilization, Transition and Reconstruction (SSTR) operations to become a core U.S. military mission. These operations are now given equal priority to combat operations. The immediate goal in SSTR is to provide the local populace with security, restore essential services, and meet humanitarian needs. The long-term goal is to help develop indigenous capacity for securing and maintaining essential services. Therefore, many SSTR operations are best performed by indigenous groups with support from foreign agencies and professionals. Large scale disasters, however, are an example where military support can improve SSTR operations by providing a much needed boost to foreign governments and nongovernmental organizations which may already be under great stress to respond in a timely and effective manner. However, without the means to effectively coordinate the efforts between many diverse groups across the civil-military boundary during SSTR operations, basic assistance and relief operations may be severely impeded. This chapter will describe a conceptual portal called ShareInfoForPeople, which provides advanced Information and Communication Technology to enable collaboration, coordination and information sharing across the civil-military boundary during SSTR operations.

Recently, there has been increased interest in sharing digitized information between government agencies, with the goals of improving security, reducing costs, and offering better quality service to users of government services. The bulk of previous work in interagency information sharing has focused largely on the sharing of structured information among heterogeneous data sources, whereas government agencies need to share data with varying degrees of structure ranging from free text documents to relational data. In this work, we explore the different technologies available to share information. Specifically, our framework discusses the optional data storage mechanisms required to support a Service Oriented Architecture (SOA). We compare XML document, free text search engine, and relational database technologies and analyze the pros and cons of each approach. We explore these options along the dimensions of information definition, information storage, the access to this information, and finally the maintenance of shared information.

As e-government becomes increasingly pervasive in modern public administrative management, its influence on organizations and individuals has become hard to ignore. It is therefore timely and relevant to examine e-governance—the fundamental mission of e-government. By adopting a stakeholder perspective and coming from the strategic orientation of control and collaboration management philosophy, this study approaches the topic of e-governance in e-government from the three critical aspects of stakeholder management: (1) identification of stakeholders, (2) recognition of differing interests among stakeholders, and (3) how an organization caters to and furthers these interests. Findings from the case study allow us to identify four important groups of stakeholders known as the Engineers, Dissidents, Seasoners, and Skeptics who possess vastly different characteristics and varying levels of acceptance of and commitment towards the e-filing paradigm. Accordingly, four corresponding management strategies with varying degrees of collaboration and control mechanisms are devised in the bid to align these stakeholder interests such that their participation in e-government can be leveraged by public organizations to achieve competitive advantage.

Over the last decade, the Internet has become one of the most important means of communication in all social areas. The success of Web technology adoption in the private sector has put pressures on the public sector to adopt the Internet to present information and service resources. The concept of creating more efficient and convenient interaction between government and the interacting parties using Internet technology is referred to as electronic government (or digital government). Recent studies have shown an increase in the adoption of electronic government by various countries (Archer, 2005; I-Ways, 2005; Janssen et al. 2004). Nevertheless, the level of implementation diverges from country to country. This study identifies critical success factors of electronic government and proposes an implementation framework. This chapter presents an extensive case study to illustrate how the proposed framework can be used to analyze electronic government strategies in a developed country (United States) and a developing country (China). In conclusion, recommendations are made to developed and developing countries for their implementation of electronic government.

This collaborative action research study reports the experiences in developing e-government innovations in early childhood education context in Finland. While e-government is too often understood as transforming paper documents used in public services into electronic mode, the ultimate objective should be to enhance communication and interaction between citizens and public organizations and thus increase the value of public services. This objective cannot be reached without involvement of service professionals in the eGovernment innovation processes. This research introduces a method for involving service professionals in the process of generating and evaluating alternative ways how new technology can be incorporated in service processes. Amit and Zott's (2001) e-business value creation method was applied to clarify the value of alternative e-government innovations for citizens and for the service organization. The practical result of the study was several business model innovations for the early childhood education. The methodological result was a collaborative method for analyzing and generating business model innovations.

This article examines how horizontal integration between the various departments of a local authority in the United Kingdom (UK) occurs. Following that the aim of this article is to extract the "success factors" in government intervention that support horizontal and vertical integration based on the strategies pursued in the UK in order to render favourable results if applied elsewhere. The research methodology consisted of an in-depth case study that used the research tools of interviews and referring to archival documents. This research is timely as the maturity of e-government increases the issues of integrating processes and systems across various government departments becomes pertinent. The conclusion and lessons that can be learnt from this research is that e-government integration on a horizontal level obtains significant efficiency and effectiveness as more and more public services are being centralized.

As developments in communication technologies impact upon many spheres of public and private life, they influence the way in which the public sector engages citizens. While most governments have an online presence, this is mainly applied to the provision of one-way (i.e. government to citizen) information and services. However, available technologies such as the Internet and mobile telephony provide opportunities for governments to enter into a two-way dialogue with citizens, increase transparency of their operations, and encourage democratic participation outside election time. As the government closest to the people, local government is particularly well placed to use online technologies to enhance and expand participatory democracy through strategies such as e-consultation.

Due to compulsory voting, Australia's turnout rate is among the highest and most socially-even in the industrialised world. Nevertheless, some voters are still left behind on election day. In this chapter we examine the potential for E-technologies to address the problem of political exclusion among some currently excluded groups of voters. We canvas known and suspected patterns of such exclusion and, in some cases, suggest possible reasons for it. We review the capacity for electronic forms of voting and registration to address: Low voting and registration levels among indigenous Australians; declining registration levels among the young; restricted access to the secret ballot caused by disability; informal voting among minority language speakers and people with low literacy and numeracy competence; low voting participation among people who experience difficulty in attending a polling place on election day and low voting participation among the Australian diaspora. We begin by providing some technical background, after which we report briefly on the E-voting state of play in Australia today.

This chapter analyses local government's response to the pressure to modernise its structures through its use of Information Communication Technologies (ICT) to execute its broad range of tasks. The chapter begins by discussing Chadwick and May's (2003) three basic models of e-government; managerial, consultative and participatory. Using data collected from an analysis of 658 local government websites in Australia together with existing survey research the chapter then analyses the extent to which local government sites fit into the three models. The chapter concludes with a discussion of the issues and problems faced by local government in its attempt to develop e-governance as both an extension of administrative as well as democratic functions.

This chapter examines the spread of Information and Communication Technologies (ICTs) in South Australia. It starts by assessing South Australia's leading role in the adoption of democratic reforms in

are ambiguity and data misinterpretation. This is due to the diversity of ontology creators, differences in linguistics and ontological overlapping. Users may also knowingly or unknowingly add incorrect information to ontologies. Ontological Mediation tries to address such collaboration issues relating to ambiguous and unfamiliar information arising due to various reasons. We propose a communication based approach for ontological mediation. In the process, we also present a classification model for ontological mediation.

With the proliferation of the Internet and rapid development of information and communication infrastructure, E-governance has become a viable option for effective deployment of government services and programs. Areas of E-governance such as Homeland security and disaster relief have to deal with vast amounts of dynamic heterogeneous data. Providing rapid real-time search capabilities for such databases/sources is a challenge. Intelligent Foraging, Gathering, and Matching (I-FGM) is an established framework developed to assist analysts to find information quickly and effectively by incrementally collecting, processing and matching information nuggets. This framework has previously been used to develop a distributed, free text information retrieval application. In this chapter, we provide a comprehensive solution for the E-GOV analyst by extending the I-FGM framework to image collections and creating a "live" version of I-FGM deployable for real-world use. We present a CBIR based image retrieval technique that incrementally processes the images, extracts low-level features and map them to higher level concepts. Our empirical evaluation of the algorithm shows that our approach performs competitively compared to some existing approaches in terms of retrieving relevant images while offering the speed advantages of a distributed and incremental process, and unified framework for both text and images. We describe our production level prototype that has a sophisticated user interface which can also deal with multiple queries from multiple users. The interface provides real-time updating of the search results and provides "under the hood" details of I-FGM processes as the queries are being processed.

Data dissemination and information management technologies for tactical environments are quickly becoming major areas of research for both military and civilian applications. Critical to the problem is the need for fully distributed information management technologies that are efficient, adaptive and resilient. In this paper, we introduce and discuss a new strategy for tactical data dissemination and processing

Preface

In its formative years, the concept of e-government was typically seen as a new process with unlimited potential in the rapidly expanding global environment. In today's society, processes are no longer new and we find ourselves in the phase of refining and redeveloping the foundation upon which the concept of e-government was first introduced to improve the efficiency and effectiveness of government. If models continue to be improved upon, e-government in our knowledge society will be an open and transparent institution that provides a maximum amount of services as well as limited intrusion into the lives and privacy of its citizens.

E-Government Diffusion, Policy, and Impact: Advanced Issues and Practices, part of the *Advances in Electronic Government Research Book Series*, includes many contributions from researchers covering the important topics in e-government, and is intended to elicit comments, raise concerns and open dialogue as we continue to implement e-government programs in mainstream society. Further, the book responds to e-government's present shortcomings, while exploring a renewed understanding of e-government's visions and responsiveness.

Chapter I, *E-Government Business Models: Theory, Challenges and Research Issues* by Marijn Janssen, Delft University of Technology (The Netherlands) and George Kuk, Nottingham University Business School (UK) defines the concept of business models, which can appear at the individual organization and network level and describe how an entity plans to provide services. The basic premise of business models is that they help to understand the relation between service offering and other elements and can be used as an instrument to improve service provisioning and lowering cost at the same time. This chapter provides an overview of the state-of-the-art of e-government business models and presents a theory integrating the various elements and research challenges and issues.

Chapter II, *Electronic Government: Overview and Issues for National Security Interests* by Roy Ladner and Frederick E. Petry , Stennis Space Center (USA) offers a description of electronic government as it pertains to national security and defense within the Department of Defense (DoD) and Department of Homeland Security (DHS). The authors discuss the adoption of web services and service oriented architectures to aid in information sharing and reduction of Information Technology (IT) costs. They also discuss the networks on which services and resources are being deployed and explain the efforts being made to manage the infrastructure of available services. This paper provides an overview of e-government for national security and defense and provides insight to current initiatives and future directions.

Chapter III, *Towards Civil-Military Coordination During Security, Stabilization, Transition and Reconstruction Efforts* by Ranjeev Mittu, U.S. Naval Research Laboratory (USA), Suleyman Guleyupoglu, ITT Corporation (USA), William Barlow, Office of Secretary of Defense Networks and Information Integration (USA), Michael Dowdy, Femme Comp, Inc. (USA), and Sean McCarthy, Femme Comp, Inc. (USA) describes a conceptual portal called ShareInfoForPeople, which provides advanced Information and Communication Technology to enable collaboration, coordination and information sharing across the civil-military boundary during Security, Stabilization, Transition and Reconstruction (SSTR) operations.

Chapter IV, *A Comprehensive Framework Towards Information Sharing Between Government Agencies* by Akhilesh Bajaj, The University of Tulsa (USA) and Sudha Ram, The University of Arizona (USA) explores the different technologies available to share information. Specifically, the authors' framework discusses the data storage mechanisms required to support a Service Oriented Architecture (SOA). The chapter compares XML document, free text search engines, and relational database technologies and analyzes the pros and cons of each approach. These options are explored along the dimensions of information definition, information storage, the access to this information and, finally, the maintenance of shared information.

Chapter V, *E-Government Implementation: Balancing Collaboration and Control in Stakeholder Management* by Eric T.K. Lim, National University of Singapore (Singapore), Chee-Wee Tan, University of British Columbia (Canada), and Shan-Lin Pan, National University of Singapore (Singapore) approaches the topic of e-governance in e-government from the three critical aspects of stakeholder management: (1) identification of stakeholders; (2) recognition of differing interests among stakeholders; and (3) how an organization caters to and furthers these interests. Findings from the case study allow the authors to identify four important groups of stakeholders, who possess vastly different characteristics and varying level of acceptance of and commitment towards the e-filing paradigm. Accordingly, four corresponding management strategies with varying degrees of collaboration and control mechanisms are devised.

Chapter VI, *Electronic Government Implementation: A Comparison Between Developed and Developing Countries* by Yining Chen, Western Kentucky University (USA), H.M. Chen, Shanghai Jiaotong University (China), Russell K.H. Ching, California State University (USA), and Wayne W. Huang, Ohio University (USA) identifies critical success factors of electronic government and proposes an implementation framework. An extensive case study is presented to illustrate how the proposed framework can be used to analyze electronic government strategies in a developed country (United States) and a developing country (China). In conclusion, recommendations are made to developed and developing countries for their implementation of electronic government.

Chapter VII, *Involving Service Professionals in E-Government Innovation: The Case of Finnish Early Childhood Education* by Jonna Järveläinen, Turku School of Economics (Finland), Eija Koskivaara, Turku School of Economics (Finland), Päivi Pihlaja, University of Turku (Finland), Hannu Salmela, Turku School of Economics (Finland), Jarmo Tähkäpää, Turku School of Economics (Finland), Timo Kestilä, Turku School of Economics (Finland), and Jarmo Kinos, University of Turku (Finland) reports the experiences in developing e-government innovations in an early childhood education context in Finland. While e-government is too often understood as transforming paper documents used in public services into electronic documents, the ultimate objective should be to enhance communication and interaction between citizens and public organizations and thus increase the value of public services. This objective cannot be reached without the involvement of service professionals. This research introduces a method for involving service professionals in the process of generating and evaluating alternative ways to incorporate technology in service processes.

Chapter VIII, *Horizontal Process Integration in E-Government: The Perspective of a UK Local Authority* by Jyoti Choudrie, University of Hertfordshire (UK) and Vishanth Weerakkody, Brunel University (UK) examines how horizontal integration between the various departments of a local authority in the United Kingdom (UK) occurs in order to deliver e-services to the citizens in the vicinity. The research question guiding this paper is: What can be learnt about the achievement of horizontal integration between local authorities in the e-government context in order to better deliver e-services to citizens? The aim of this paper is to extract the "success factors" in government intervention that support horizontal and vertical integration.

Chapter IX, *Online Policy Consultation: A Case Study of Local Government* by Lucas Walsh, Deakin University (Australia) draws from an external evaluation of an Australian local government initiative, Darebin eForum. Conducted in 2007, this evaluation included a survey of e-consultation participants and interviews with Council Officers responsible for moderating the site. The findings provide a snapshot of some of these challenges. Though modest in size and ambition, the experiences of Darebin eForum provide valuable insight into the challenges faced by the government's seeking to use ICTs to engage in dialogue with their constituents.

Chapter X, *Electronic Conduits to Electoral Inclusion in an Atypical Constituency: The Australian Case* by Lisa Hill and Kate Alport, University of Adelaide (Australia) examines the potential for e-technologies to address the problem of political exclusion among some currently excluded groups of voters. The authors canvas known and suspected patterns of such exclusion and, in some cases, suggest possible reasons for it. This chapter reviews the capacity for electronic forms of voting and registration to address: Low voting and registration levels among indigenous Australians; declining registration levels among the young; restricted access to the secret ballot caused by disability; informal voting among minority language speakers and people with low literacy and numeracy competence; low voting participation among people who experience difficulty in attending a polling place on election day and low voting participation among the Australian *diaspora*.

Chapter XI, *Australia Local Government and E-Governance: From Administration to Citizen Participation?* by Kevin O'Toole, Deakin University (Australia) analyses local government's response to the pressure to modernise its structures through its use of Information Communication Technologies (ICT) to execute its broad range of tasks. The chapter begins by discussing Chadwick and May's (2003) three basic models of e-government—managerial, consultative and participatory. Using data collected from an analysis of 658 local government web-sites in Australia together with existing survey research, the chapter then analyses the extent to which local government sites fit into the three models. The chapter concludes with a discussion of the issues and problems faced by local government in its attempt to develop e-governance as an extension of both administrative and democratic functions.

Chapter XII, *Engaging the Community Through E-Democracy in South Australia* by Kate Alport and Clement Macintyre, University of Adelaide (Australia) assesses the spread of Information and Communication Technologies (ICTs) in South Australia. It starts by examining South Australia's leading role in the adoption of democratic reforms in the nineteenth century. The paper draws from an appraisal of Internet based initiatives by government, non-profit, and private agencies and compares these to best practice models for community engagement. Based on this research, the authors conclude that there is little originality and initiative in the formal State Government sites and that there is little designed to foster e-democracy. Existing innovation can be found in more local and specific community based applications of ICT.

Chapter XIII, *Users' Acceptance of E-Government: A Study of Indian Central Excise* by G.P. Sahu, M. N. National Institute of Technology (India) and M. P. Gupta, Indian Institute of Technology Delhi (India) seeks to highlight the key variables affecting the usage of e-government by internal users of Indian Central Excise. An e-government acceptance model is developed and empirically tested using the 163 usable questionnaire responses from internal users of the Indian Central Excise. A priority of the variables is set by calculating the "total effect" of each variable on "intention to use e-government." Further the "total effect" is compared with "Ratio of Acceptance" and clear recommendations for the Central Excise are generated for increasing the usage of e-government among its users. The model developed here can be applied in other similar e-government projects to test the users' intention to accept the system.

Chapter XIV, *A Multi Agent Service Oriented Modeling of E-Government Initiatives* by Tagelsir Mohamed Gasmelseid, King Faisal University (Saudi Arabia) reviews the e-government project in Sudan, whose goal is to build a society based on a strong base of industry knowledge in which all segments of the media have access to information that leads to the distribution, publication and use of information and, in turn, economic growth, increased employment, higher rates and quality of production in all sectors, and poverty eradication. However, the project has been based on the use of a client-server architecture that has many limitations. This paper provides a multiagent service oriented architecture for the implementation of the project based on a thorough review of project documents and implementation reports.

Chapter XV, *A Methodology for Ontological Mediation in Multi-Agent Systems* by Shahram Rahimi, Bidyut Gupta, and Pravab J. Rana, Southern Illinois University (USA) provides an overview of current search and retrieval systems, contending that their effectiveness is restricted because they do not use the semantics of the data but mainly utilize keywords. Multi-agent systems in which agents gather information and organize it, by creating ontologies, are being utilized to improve the performance and quality of the data gathering and integrating systems. Major difficulties that arise during collaboration among such agents are ambiguity and data misinterpretation. This is due to the diversity of ontology creators, differences in linguistics and ontological overlapping. Users may also knowingly or unknowingly add incorrect information to ontologies. Ontological Mediation tries to address such collaboration issues relating to ambiguous and unfamiliar information arising due to various reasons. The authors of this chapter propose a communication based approach for ontological mediation.

Chapter XVI, *Analyst-Ready Large Scale Real Time Information Retrieval Tool for E-Governance* by Eugene Santos, Jr., Dartmouth College (USA), Eunice E. Santos, Virginia Polytechnic Institute & State University (USA), Hien Nguyen, University of Wisconsin (USA), Long Pan, Virginia Polytechnic Institute & State University (USA), John Korah, Virginia Polytechnic Institute & State University (USA), Huadong Xia, Virginia Polytechnic Institute & State University (USA), Fei Yu, Dartmouth College (USA), and Deqing Li, Dartmouth College (USA) introduces a comprehensive solution for the e-government analyst by extending the Intelligent Foraging, Gathering, and Matching (I-FGM) framework to image collections and creating a "live" version of I-FGM deployable for real-world use. A CBIR based image retrieval technique that incrementally processes the images, extracts low-level features and maps them to higher level concepts is presented. An empirical evaluation of the algorithm shows that the current approach performs competitively compared to some existing approaches in terms of retrieving relevant images while offering the speed advantages of a distributed and incremental process, and unified framework for both text and images.

Chapter XVII, *In-Stream Data Processing for Tactical Environments* by Marco Carvalho, Institute for Human and Machine Cognition (USA) re-introduces and discusses a new strategy for tactical data dissemination and processing based on distributed online learning. The concept was first proposed in Carvalho (2006) for the kinds of environments envisioned by the Army's Future Combat Systems program. In this work, the authors revisit, summarize and discuss the proposed approach. Starting from a formal description of the problem, the proposed solution and its theoretical properties are discussed. A number of simulation experiments for different data dissemination scenarios are also presented, and the work concludes with a discussion on how such techniques may be applied to critical e-government environments under different assumptions of service availability and information release policy constraints.

Chapter XVIII, *AJAX in Development of Web-Based Architecture for Implementation of E-Governance* by Dilip Kumar Sharma, G.L.A. Institute of Technology and Management (India), Gopalji Varshneya, G.L.A. Institute of Technology and Management (India), and Ashwani Kumar Upadhyay, M. N. National Institute of Technology (India) analyzes the diffusion of a web technology named AJAX in facilitating an e-government architecture and enhancing its potential by enabling modern web features such as democracy and collaboration. This chapter emphasizes that proper collaboration between private, public and government entities can only be achieved by proper information dissemination and acceptance of competent web technologies such as AJAX. Features of AJAX, which include sectional processing ability, speed, bridging, portability and compatibility are viewed in terms of their practicality.

As the concepts of practices of e-government become more common around the world, the need to explore newer opportunities and applications based on sound practices will become more important and necessary. This book is a collaborative effort between many researchers around the world, who share their knowledge of best e-government practices and discuss the current issues in e-government in an effort to expand the body of literature in the field and continue to enhance the frameworks that encourage innovation and adoption, moving e-government toward its goal of easy access for the masses. My hope is that this valuable collection of contributions will be instrumental in broadening our understanding of e-government technologies and their potential in reshaping society.

Mehdi Khosrow-Pour, D.B.A.
Editor-in-Chief
E-Government Diffusion, Policy, and Impact: Advanced Issues and Practices
Advances in Electronic Government Research Series

Chapter I
E-Government Business Models:
Theory, Challenges and Research Issues

Marijn Janssen
Delft University of Technology, The Netherlands

George Kuk
Nottingham University Business School, UK

ABSTRACT

Stimulated by the need to reduce cost and improve service provisioning and client involvement at the same time, the concept of business models has gained attention in the e-government domain over the last few years. Business models can appear at the individual organization and network level and describes how an entity plans to provide services. The basic premise of business models is that it helps to understand the relation between service offering and other elements and can be used as an instrument to improve service provisioning and lowering cost at the same time. In this chapter an overview of the state-of-the-art of e-government business models, a theory integrating the various elements and research challenges and issues are presented. There is ample need for research and overcoming these challenges result in better leveraging the advantages of business models.

INTRODUCTION

Countries worldwide are developing towards online service provisioning as a logical response to technology advances. Delivering government services to the public electronically requires innovation which entails the adaptation of policy and strategy, and the associated changes in technologies and infrastructures. Often governments are imitating each other and pursuing a similar set of novel business models without careful examination of the hidden challenges. The business models is aimed at describing how organization entities plan their service provisioning and depicts the relationship among the elements (Janssen & Kuk, 2007). This chapter aims to provide an overview of e-government business models and

Copyright © 2009, IGI Global, distributing in print or electronic forms without written permission of IGI Global is prohibited.

described the background, a theory and research challenges and issues

The business model concept has become a popular and important strand within the field of information systems and strategic management (Hedman & Kalling, 2003), specifically its application to the electronic business environment (e.g. Afuah & Tucci, 2000; e.g. Timmers, 1998; Weill & Vitale, 2001). Initially, different types of business models were experimented with and tested. The ones contributing to the financial success are widely promoted by the e-commerce and e-business practitioners. Despite the lack of a universal definition (Alt & Zimmerman, 2001) and the fact that the theory often lags behind the practice it attempts to describe and explain (Hedman & Kalling, 2003), there is little difficulty for direct adoption and transfer of the business model concept across domains and from the private to the public sector. The latter underscores the mentality that the practical rationality will compensate for the lack of theoretical underpinnings (Kuk, 2003).

The concept of business models developed and tested in the network economy cannot be translated to the public sector in a one-to-one manager. One of the notable differences is the level of inter-firm rivalry and mistrust which can limit resources and knowledge sharing in private networks (Adner, 2006). Whereas public networks which are often grounded on the non-exclusive and non-rival properties of public goods can facilitate a greater extent of resources and knowledge sharing among governmental agencies. Yet increased sharing will also lead to an increase in the coordination challenges comprising of how to route and reuse the existing silo-based types of functions and resources which are developed and resided within a public agency to a network arrangement; and crucially, how to generate new capabilities in support of developing new service offerings.

New types of service offering are made possible due to the cross-agency collaboration in form of a public service network (Provan & Milward, 2001). Different networked business models tackle different coordination challenges and will likely have other benefits. When it comes to the decision of which business models to adopt, consideration should be given to what coordination challenges that different business models may engender. Organizations should consider which ones are worthwhile to invest their resources. And by successfully tackling these challenges, organizations can acquire a new and useful set of knowledge which in turn improves the business and coordination logics of offering new web-based services.

Whilst there is a small but growing body of research on using Internet-based models as a front-end proxy of e-government business models, the concept of business models in the context of e-government is relatively unexplored. Janssen, Kuk and Wagenaar (2008) developed eight atomic business models based on e-commerce literature and existing governmental Web sites in the Netherlands. They found that a most web sites could be described using the atomic business models and the type of atomic business models found were predominantly non-interactive and non-deliberative. Janssen and Kuk (2007) explored the components of a business model, intermediate variables and processes that translate an e-government business model into new service offerings. They developed a business model framework based on resource-based view, dynamic capability and coordination theory to provide insights into the coordination challenges and the potential benefits that accrued to a government as a result of adopting a particular business model. The rest of the chapter is structured as follows. In the next section we discuss the concept of business models as found in literature. In section three, we to present a framework for analyzing, and ultimately designing, the logic of service provisioning. In section four, three main research challenges and issues are discussed. Finally, we draw conclusions and recommend further research.

THE BUSINESS MODEL CONCEPT

The concept of business model is originated in the field of e-commerce in which firms tried to copy the successful business models. New types of web-based businesses often create new business models and new forms of organizations. In e-commerce the concept of business model is ill-defined, and there is no consensus regarding what comprises the key elements of a successful business model (Alt & Zimmerman, 2001; Rappa, 2002). Furthermore, the concept has been interpreted variedly. Timmers (1998) regards a business model as "an architecture for a product, service and information flows including various actors and their roles". Wand et al. (1999) state that a business model reflects the core business of an organization from the perspective of its main functions, products and services. Mahadevan (2000) defines a business model as a unique blend for three critical streams to the business comprising of the value stream for the business partners and the buyers, the revenue stream, and the logistical stream.

There are a large number of *business model taxonomies* available in e-commerce literature (Afuah & Tucci, 2000; Mahadevan, 2000; Rappa, 2002; Timmers, 1998; Weill & Vitale, 2001). Taxonomies are developed to identify the core aspects of each model, whereas each model tackles other challenges. There is no established general classification, which means that there is as yet little theoretical base for business model research and application in e-government. Rappa (2002) provides a detailed overview of Internet business models aimed at describing and defining the underlying components. Weill and Vitale (2001) offer eight *atomic* business models. Instead of trying to specify a comprehensive list, as Rappa has done, these authors define eight "atomic" models. Specific models can be constructed by combining the atomic business models, in analogy with atoms that can be combined to form molecules. All these taxonomies of business models tend to be more oriented towards the front-end, visible to the customer but bear no relationship to the back-end logic. The strategy, customer, services quality come before technological concerns. These models can be criticized for only depicting the elements adding value and neglecting the business and coordination logics for new service offerings. For example, business processes may need streamlining and change, and even replacement in order to become more citizen-centric; and also increase government internal effectiveness and efficiency (e.g. Scholl, 2006). Furthermore, value is not created by a single actor in the networked economy, instead it is created by coordinating organizations in value networks (Bouwman & MacInnes, 2006).

The *level of detail and the components* that should be captured by business models is subject of discussion (Bouwman & MacInnes, 2006; Chesbrough & Rosenbloom, 2002; Wand, Woo, & Hui, 1999). Wand et al. (1999) describe business models at a very high strategic level, of how organizations behave, independent of the actual organizational structure and the implementation of the business processes. For this reason, they assert that a business model is usually very stable over time and even under major changes as it is not necessary to restructure a business model. They argue that it will only change if the basic nature of the products and services changes. In their perspective a business model should be used to drive the evolution of information systems and guide the re-use of existing components. Other scholars offer a more detailed description in terms of the implementation of a business model. For example, Chesbrough and Rosenbloom create a heuristic logic that connects technical potential with the realization of economic value. Afuah and Tucci (2000) argue that a business model should come with a detailed description of how a firm builds and uses its resources. Yet the detailed approach is criticized for neglecting the customer aspect, as it details what the model does for the business, but not for the customers (Dubusson-Torbay, Osterwalder, & Pigneur, 2002). Others attempt to depict the various elements of a business models. Hedman and Kalling (2003) propose a generic business model which includes seven causally related components. They are customers, competitors, offering, activities and organization, resources, supply of factor and production inputs and the longitudinal process to cover the dynamics of the business model. Yet which component constitutes a business model for e-government is unclear as the focus of the public networks is on neither profit nor competition, some of the aforementioned components such as competitors and the regulation and market aspects that govern the dynamics of a business model are inapplicable to e-government.

Most of the literature in e-commerce has been focused on producing taxonomies or categorizations; and on stating which components should be included or excluded. Also there is a considerable ways of interpreting the term 'business model' in the context of e-commerce. The business model concept can be used in a narrow sense to refer to a model of business processes, either within a single organization or among closely-linked business partners. In a network arrangement, the focus is on coordinating interdependent relationships among independent actors and cross-organizational business processes. This implies that to analyze networked business models, at least these elements should be taken into account. The interdependence among actors impose coordination challenges but at the same time offer potential benefits when actors can effectively leverage the advantages of each other resources and capabilities. Lastly, the concept of business model is primarily on firm-based resources and capabilities, hence a business model in the context of e-government needs to encompass the network aspects of coordination both within and between organizations.

A THEORY OF E-GOVERNMENT BUSINESS MODELS

In this section, we seek to identify the key components of a business model. E-commerce business models often focus on maximizing profit and differentiating from competitors whereas the primary interests of governments are in gaining more efficiency, enhancing the existing and/or developing new public services. Against this backdrop, we equate the value creation elements of an e-government business model to the improved service offering including improved efficiency, and offers of new types of services. This might be a narrower view than often meant with the value concept, yet logical considering that our focus is on the business models in public service networks. We ground the development of our framework primarily on the coordination theory to examine different types of interdependences; resource-based view, to understand challenges in managing shared resources in a network arrangement; and dynamic capabilities to examine the role of IT in leveraging intra and inter-agency resources and knowledge.

We start with examining the logics of a business model in the creation of a specific service offering. Hedman and Kalling (2003) provide a framework for this by drawing upon the perspectives of industrial organizations (I/O), resource-based view (RBV), and the strategy process. The I/O perspective which concerns the explanations of firm performance in a competitive environment is not relevant to e-government, simply because there are no competitors or product substitutes. The resource based view is useful as it draws the attention to dual goals of managing the public administration's resources efficiently and at the same time achieving high levels of service. The strategy process perspective refers to the process by which a business model evolves. This process is heavily influenced by dynamic capabilities, the ability to integrate, build, and reconfigure to address rapidly changing environments. As we are dealing with public service networks this implies that the interdependencies among organizations need to be coordinated.

First, business processes in public service networks consist of a sequence of activities that need to be managed. *Coordination* of the interdependent activities of the organizations is essential for collaboration. Organizations use human resources and consume goods for performing their activities. The limited capacity and goods, and the corresponding problems and the possibilities to overcome the problems caused by the division of tasks and labour, form the core of organizational design (Galbraith, 1977). Malone and Crowston (1990) found that the need for coordination arises from constraints imposed on the performance of tasks by the interdependent nature of these tasks. These interdependencies arise from the mutual use of common resources to carry out a task.

Public networks are quite different from organizational hierarchies, as they require autonomous organizations to work with each other in a collaborative, non-bureaucratic structure. In this regard, the business models and the coordination challenges associated with public networks can be very different from that of managing individual organizations. In a public network, actors with varying resources and capabilities often need to engage in a reciprocal relationship to benefit from each other unique resources and capabilities. The focus is one of managing the interdependencies among activities (Malone and Crowston 1994). Essentially, each type of interdependency relates the actors own and others' resource contributions to the performance of service provisioning. Interdependence arises as no single actor has total control of all the conditions necessary for the achievement of an action or for obtaining the desired outcome based on a singular action (Pfeffer & Salancik, 1978).

Since the service provisioning in the context of e-government typically require collaboration among a range of actors across different agencies, the interdependent activities of these different actors need to be coordinated in a network. Thompson (1967) uses interdependencies between activities to describe coordination mechanisms. He distinguishes three types of interdependencies: pooled, sequential and reciprocal. *Pooled interdependence* is the situation where each activity contributes to the whole system, without the need for interaction between activities. *Sequential interdependence* is the situation where the output of one activity forms the input for another activity. *Reciprocal interdependence* occurs when two activities are interdependent.

Executing the business processes to provide service offerings requires resources. The *resource-based view* suggests that the rationale for coordination is in the value-creation potential of organizational resources when they are pooled together (Das & Teng, 2000). This theory states that idiosyncratic and organizational specific sets of imperfectly mobile resources determine the performance that can be reached (Barney, 1991). Resources can have a tangible or intangible nature, some examples of resources are budget, equipment, proprietary technology, skills and expertise of technology experts and managers. Although resources are limited, the cross-agency collaboration encourages shared resources which through better coordination offer agencies better ways of utilizing and expanding their resources and long-term capabilities.

Consider that agencies in the network are potential partners in all aspects of the business model in the bundling of products, in activities and in the configuration of resources. Each organization might have different expertise, budgets and other capabilities to profit from the resources. Apart from contributing to the business models, the agencies limit the potential of business models due to their limited capabilities to adopt new business models.

Dynamic Capability Theory describes the organization's ability to integrate, build, and reconfigure internal and external competences to address rapidly changing environments (Teece,

Pisano, & Shuen, 1997). Dynamic capabilities help a firm adjusting its resource mix and thereby maintaining the sustainability of the organization. Dynamic capabilities are need to adjust the resource mix to profit from collaboration in public service networks. Each organization might have different strategic objectives, capabilities and resources available. Moreover, potential partners may have different processes and levels of IT sophistication that needs to be synchronized before services can be shared. This leads to an examination of the role of IT, and how it provides the needed coordination mechanism which facilitates the creation of shared resources and additional capabilities.

There is a growing body of literature on the relationships among IT, knowledge management capability and firm performance (e.g. Eisenhardt & Santos, 2002; Teece, 1998). Essentially, the role of IT is one of informing and sharing knowledge and notably promoting effective reuse of knowledge resources (Tanriverdi, 2005). Using IT relatedness as a second-order construct (comprising of relatedness of IT infrastructure, IT strategy-making processes, IT vendor management processes and IT-human resources management processes), Tanriverdi (2005) empirically tested its significance to firm performance, and found that IT relatedness which promoted knowledge reuse contributed significantly to the financial performance of multi-business firms. This is particularly relevant to the creation of service offering within the setting of cross-agency collaboration as IT increase knowledge management capability, allows better reuse and avoids wastage due to duplication of activities.

Melville et al. (2004) provide a similar finding regarding the role of IT in business value creation. They suggest that IT impacts organizational performance via intermediate business processes; that other organizational resources such as workplace practices interact with IT, whether as mediator or moderator, in the attainment of organizational performance; that the external environment also plays a role in IT business value generation; and that it is important to disaggregate the IT construct into meaningful subcomponents.

In summary, business models of public service networks are aimed at better leveraging the unique resources of each agency, and in turn better provision of service offerings. To enable the public networks to adjust and expand their resource mix to create a better service offering and meet the ever-changing business requirements, we need to consider the dynamic capabilities by harnessing IT to realize the logic of a business model. The role of IT will depend on whether the business model emphasizes more on exploiting the existing knowledge and/or generating additional capabilities. In addition, the longitudinal dimensions should be considered, as business models likely evolve over time.

Against the importance of the public networks and the cross-agency coordination through, leveraging the shared resources and creating network capabilities through effective applications of IT, we create a framework for designing and analyzing e-government business models. The *logic* of the service offering is captured by the following elements of the business model framework (based on Janssen & Kuk, 2007):

1. *Organizational entities involved in the service delivery.* Governmental agencies need to collaborate with each other to form a network and effectively coordinated the pools of resources and adjusting them using their pooled capabilities. The latter is likely to be enhanced when the public networks include agencies with unique resources and capabilities.
2. *Service offerings.* Better bundling of the existing and new services is likely to by enhancing and modifying the existing service offerings and to improve the perceived quality of the service offering.
3. *Coordination.* Mechanisms comprising of managerial and organizational structures

have to be in place to facilitate coordination and overcome problems caused by the division of tasks and labor.

4. *Business processes.* In a public service network, which involves the coordination among actors and infrastructures, the focus is on managing the intermediary processes and defining interfaces to enhance inter- and intra-organizational information flows; and enabling new levels of emphasis on coordination across agencies via workflow management, project management, and supply chain management.
5. *Shared resources.* The role of all kinds of resources, including IT-infrastructures, humans and technologies should aim at supporting the business models, including streamlining through system integration and standardization.
6. *Dynamic capabilities.* The adaptation of IT aims to better reuse of the existing knowledge and expertise dispersed in a public network through building interfaces among management, operation, and the design and development of the infrastructures.
7. *Longitudinal dimension:* The framework is largely static because the business model is described in a discrete point in time and does not include anything about what happens in the face of change. Consequently, the longitudinal elements should be included, aimed at capturing the evolvement over time. This dimension captures the change processes that should enable the move towards a new or improved business model.

Figure 1 shows the causal relationship among the elements numbered 1 to 6. Each organization (1) has a distinct set of business processes (4), resources (5) and dynamic capabilities (6) that need to be coordinated (3) to create a service offering (2). In the service provisioning processes (4), resources (5) are consumed in business processes, (6) dynamic capabilities are needed to transform and deploy the (IT) resources in an efficient and effective way and (7) this results in

Figure 1. E-government business models framework

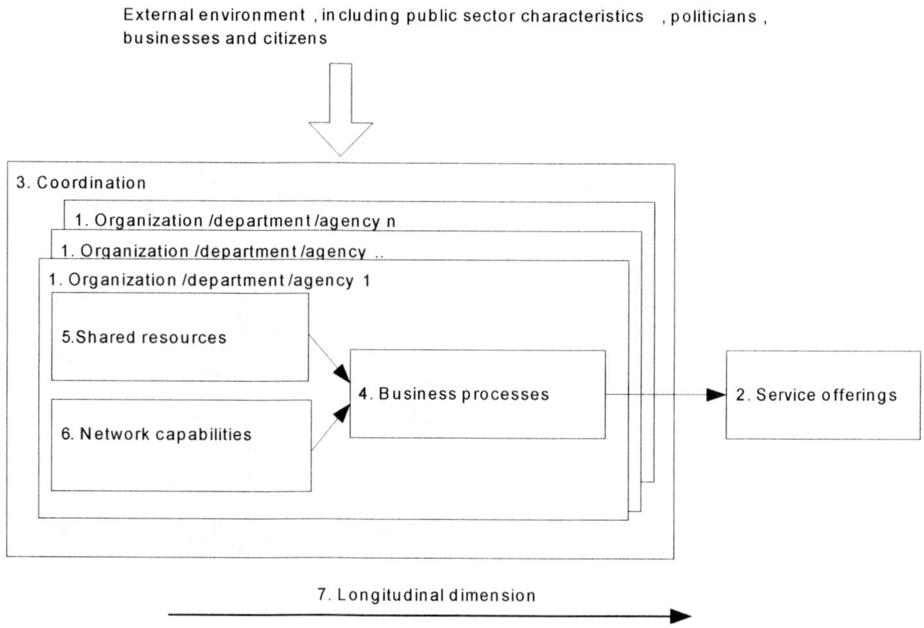

change of business models over time. Business processes are the vehicle for creating services and coordination mechanisms manage the interdependencies among the activities executed by the various network members. Melville et al. (2004) found that external environment also influences the underlying dynamics of the business model. Therefore external environment is also included in the figure. The external environment concerns public sector characteristics, the institutional pressures and incentives from the politicians and the expectation of businesses and citizens.

The bottom line is that the service offering is determined by public organizations' ability to coordinate the interdependencies among network members by minimizing resource consumption and adapting to these situations using their intra and inter-agency capabilities.

RESEARCH CHALLENGES

The current use of business models is often focused on taxonomies or identifying the main components aimed at generalizing business models to other domains and countries, hoping that it should help to design better models in enhancing service delivery .This brings us to our first two categories of research challenges, the development of e-government business model taxonomies and the development of business models frameworks. The last category of research challenges considered linking the business model concept to enterprise architecture and is aimed at further operationalizing the business models and in this way helping government agencies not only to copy each other business models, but also design improved models and translating it to their own organizations.

Business Model Taxonomies

There are several types of e-government business models, which often focus on website and external behavior. There are some that link the service offerings to the organization, however, provided limited support. Especially atomic business models seems to be useful, which are aimed at specifying business models by combining atomic business models, in analogy with atoms that can be combined to form molecules. There are no established or generalized classification of business models in e-government (Janssen, Kuk, & Wagenaar, 2008) and more research into this direction is needed.

In addition, classification might be dependent on the country, the culture and political climate and might not be transferred from one country to another country. The state-of-the-art of technology developments might prevent the inclusion of innovative ideas and concepts which will only be enabled by further technology. As a result, taxonomies of atomic business models should be periodically updated and evaluated.

These (atomic) taxonomies and classifications are very useful and can help other organizations to learn from other and try to copy good elements. This stimulates comparison and learning from each other, which should be supported by the taxonomy. For this purposes it should be clear which business models are useful to apply in which situation and under what conditions can this model be copied. The use of taxonomies might result in simple copying of each other elements without considering the situation and context and how these results in better service provisioning. As a result, critical success factors contributing to success and constraints that prevent copying need to be investigated.

Many governmental organizations fail to create a business models matching their ambitions and visions. Typologies of business models can be used to assess their current situation and might help to identify opportunities, but are not enough for the actual translating of these concepts to the organization, which brings us to our second category.

Elements of E-Government Business Model

There is no consensus about what constitutes a business models and what elements should be addressed. Business models are directly related to the mission, visions and strategy of the government organizations and are an abstraction from a certain point of view focused on a particular aspect under study specifying the logic for creating customer orientation by governments. Designing business models requires that different elements are addressed in balance with the other elements. Yet little theoretical base for business model research and application in the e-government field (Janssen, Kuk, & Wagenaar, 2008). Addressing a number of elements is useful when applying the concept of e-government business models. These elements include that a business model (based on Janssen, Kuk, & Wagenaar, 2008):

- A business model is derived from the main mission of the public organization, often founded in law, policies, regulations and in strategy statements and descriptions.
- The model should contain the logic and elements to fulfill the mission and strategy successfully using the Internet, and to satisfy citizens and/or businesses. It addresses these elements at a high level of abstraction and depicts what is needed in the long term. As such it is prescriptive in nature and contains the ambitions that need to be realized.
- The products, services and mix of channels should be described in the business model.
- Addresses the relationship between an agencies' strategy and enterprise architecture and implementations.
- Describes the position of the organizational entity within a larger context and the relationships with other entities that target the same audiences.
- Describes future evolvement and help to evolve to improve business models.
- Is ideally independent of temporary technology and takes a long term view.

These elements show that there is much more to adopting new business models than just analyzing which atomic business models are not supported by an agency's website, and then copying and integrating the missing business model into the website. Considering these elements should help public managers to gain more insight into the need for adopting new business models to improve customer orientation. These elements show the need for starting with specifying the logic for creating additional customer-orientation based on the agency's mission. As such, the term e-government business model does add to our descriptive understanding of public organizations. It draws the attention to the creation of constituents-value by improving customer-orientation and to the elements and logic that can be used to produce this value.

Developing Business Models and Enterprise Architecture

The business model concept should help governmental agencies to improve their business models, by ensuring that the service offerings and organization are coordinated. This is directly linked to enterprise architecture, in which the organizing logic of IT assets and the relationship with business model and strategy is addressed. In this sense IT can follow business strategy, but viable business strategies depends on the underlying ICT (Ross, 2003). It is this mix of issues that need to be addressed. Although the framework discussed above takes these relationships into account, there are no design methods, theories and tools addressing the relationship and providing support. Due to the diversity of the architecture in terms of systems, processes and the number of actors it is becoming increasingly difficult to manage enterprise architecture. The enterprise architecture concept should be broadened and should not only provide an overview of dependencies between systems. Instead it should also act as a communication vehicle, address the link to strategy and in this way support decision-making.

Both business models and enterprise architectures serve as a communication means and as a result should be understandable for stakeholders having different interests and objectives and knowledge. Business models remain more at a strategic level and can remain at another level of abstraction than enterprise architecture. The business model describes how to do business, whereas enterprise architecture addresses the foundation for execution and capturing detailed assets and in this way can bridge the gap between business models and execution. Business models are more stable, whereas enterprise architecture addresses the design of ICT-infrastructure, systems and processes for the current and future operation. In this sense business models are more prescriptive and enterprise architecture contains both descriptive and prescriptive part, including a migration path to move from the current situation to the desired situation. In this way, a business model can be used as an instrument to create a joint understanding and vision that is shared by the stakeholders and enterprise architecture can in turn be used to translate the business model to the organizational realities.

CONCLUSION

Our review of the extant literature on e-commerce business models suggests that the business model concept is fuzzy and abstract; and based on several different ideas without having sound theoretical underpinnings. The use of business models is often focused on taxonomies or identifying the main components aimed at generalizing business models to other domains and countries, aimed at helping to design better models in enhancing service delivery. Apart from extending atomic business model classifications, we plea for developing models capturing the logic and main elements of business models, instead of providing taxonomies which are subject to change over time and often technology dependent.

This chapter draws upon the literature on resource-based view, dynamic capabilities and coordination theory to develop a framework for studying e-government business models that require the setup of a public service network. We argue that a business model should describe both the business and the coordination logics of creating the new service offerings. The logics are captured by six elements; 1) organizations in the public service network, 2) service offerings, 3) network coordination, 4) business processes, 5) shared resources, 6) network capabilities and 7) time-aspects to capture the evolvement of the model. We drafted a theory for capturing the main elements describing the relationship between service offering and coordination challenges. More e-government business model research is needed to extend the present framework and refine the elements further, especially other types of public service networks and their underlying business and coordination logics. In addition, the business model concept needs to be operationalized and linked to the enterprise architecture. A business model can guide enterprise architecture efforts and the architecture might constrain potential business model. The link between business models and enterprise architecture should be addressed in further research.

REFERENCES

Adner, R. (2006). Match your innovation strategy to your innovation ecosystem. *Harvard Business Review, 84*(4), 98-107.

Afuah, A., & Tucci, C. L. (2000). *Internet Business Models and Strategies.* Boston: McGraw-Hill, Irwin.

Alt, R., & Zimmerman, H. D. (2001). Introduction to Special Section: Business models. *Electronic Markets, 11*(1), 3-9.

Barney, J. B. (1991). Firm resources and sustained competitive advantage. *Journal of Management, 17*(1), 99-120.

Bouwman, H., & MacInnes, I. (2006). *Dynamic Business Model Framework for Value Webs.* Paper presented at the 39th Annual Hawaii International Conference on System Sciences (HICSS2006), Hawaii.

Chesbrough, H., & Rosenbloom, R. S. (2002). The role of the business model in capturing value from innovation: evidence from Xerox Corporation's technology spin-off companies. *Industrial and Corporate Change, 11*(3), 529-555.

Das, T. K., & Teng, B. S. (2000). A Resource-based Theory of Strategic Alliances. *Journal of Management, 26*(1), 31-61.

Dubusson-Torbay, M., Osterwalder, A., & Pigneur, Y. (2002). E-business model design, classification, and measurements. *Thunderbird International Business Review, 44*(1), 5-23.

Eisenhardt, K. M., & Santos, F. M. (2002). Knowledge- Based View: A New Theory of Strategy? In A. Pettigrew, H. Thomas & R. Whittington (Eds.), *Handbook of Strategy and Management* (pp. 139-164). London: Sage Publications.

Galbraith, J. R. (1977). *Organization Design.* Reading, Massachusetts: Addison-Wesley.

Hedman, J., & Kalling, T. (2003). The business model concept: Theoretical underpinnings and empirical illustrations. *European Journal of Information Systems, 12*(1), 49-59.

Janssen, M., & Kuk, G. (2007). E-Government Business Models for Public Service Networks. *International Journal of E-government Research (IJEGR), 3*(3), 54-71.

Janssen, M., Kuk, G., & Wagenaar, R. W. (2008). A survey of web-based business models for e-government in the Netherlands. *Government Information Quarterly, 25*(2), 202-220.

Kuk, G. (2003). Digital divide and quality of electronic service delivery in UK local government. *Government Information Quarterly, 20*(4), 353-363.

Mahadevan, B. (2000). Business Models for Internet-based E-commerce. *California Management Review, 42*(4), 55-69.

Malone, T. W., & Crowston, K. (1990). *What is coordination theory and how can it help design cooperative work systems?* Paper presented at the Proceedings of the Conference on Computer-Supported Cooperative Work CSCW'90, , Los Angelos, California.

Melville, N., Kraemer, K., & Gurbaxani, V. (2004). Information technology and organizational performance: an integrative model of it business value. *MIS Quarterly, 28*(2), 283-322.

Pfeffer, J., & Salancik, G. R. (1978). *The External Control of Organizations - A Resource Dependence Perspective.* New York: Harper & Row.

Provan, K. G., & Milward, H. B. (2001). Do Networks Really Work? A Framework for Evaluating Public-Sector Organizational Networks. *Public Administration Review, 61*(4), 414–423.

Rappa, M. (2002). *Business Models on the Web* [Electronic Version]. Retrieved 25 October 2006 from http://digitalenterprise.org/models/models.html.

Ross, J. (2003). Creating a strategic IT architecture competency: Learning in stages. *MISQ Quarterly Executive, 2*(1), 31-43.

Scholl, H. J. (2006). Electronic government: Information management capacity, Organizational capabilities, and the sourcing mix. *Government Information Quarterly, 23*, 73-96.

Tanriverdi, H. (2005). Information technology relatedness, knowledge management capability and performance of multibusiness firms. *MIS Quarterly, 29*(2), 311-334.

Teece, D. J. (1998). Capturing Value from Knowledge Assets: the New Economy, Markets for Know-How, and Intangible Asset. *California Management Review, 40*(3), 55-79.

Teece, D. J., Pisano, G., & Shuen, A. (1997). Dynamic capabilities and strategic management. *Strategic Management Journal, 18*(7), 509-533.

Thompson, J. D. (1967). *Organizations in Action*. New York: McGraw-Hill.

Timmers, P. (1998). Business Models for Electronic Markets. *Electronic Markets, 8*(2), 3-8.

Wand, Y., Woo, C., & Hui, S. (1999, 11-12 December). *Developing Business models to Support information System Evolution*. Paper presented at the Ninth Workshop on Information Technologies and systems.

Weill, P., & Vitale, M. (2001). *Place to Space: Migrating to E-Business Models*: Harvard: Harvard Business Press.

Chapter II
Electronic Government:
Overview and Issues for National Security Interests

Roy Ladner
Stennis Space Center, USA

Frederick E. Petry
Stennis Space Center, USA

ABSTRACT

In this chapter we provide an overview of electronic government as it pertains to national security and defense within the Department of Defense (DoD) and Department of Homeland Security (DHS). We discuss the adoption of web services and service oriented architectures to aid in information sharing and reduction of Information Technology (IT) costs. We also discuss the networks on which services and resources are being deployed and explain the efforts being made to manage the infrastructure of available services. This chapter provides an overview of e-government for national security and defense and provides insight to current initiatives and future directions.

INTRODUCTION

With the growth of the Internet, electronic commerce has become prevalent for the exchange of information, goods and services. Electronic government or e-government refers to the government's utilization of the tools of electronic commerce in order to accomplish its mission. Typical e-government services include online driver's license renewal, federal income disbursement, and even filing federal or state income tax returns. In this chapter we provide an overview of electronic government as it pertains to national security and defense within the Department of Defense (DoD) and Department of Homeland Security (DHS). The DoD is the lead federal agency for homeland defense and includes military departments such as the Navy, Air Force and Army as well as defense agencies such as Defense Information Systems Agency (DISA) and the Defense Threat Reduction

Copyright © 2009, IGI Global, distributing in print or electronic forms without written permission of IGI Global is prohibited.

Agency. (Department of Defense, 2000) The DHS is the lead federal agency for homeland security and includes the US Coast Guard, Customs & Border Protection, US Secret Service, Federal Emergency Management Agency, Transportation Security Administration, etc. (Department of Homeland Security History, 2006) (O'Rourke, 2005) We describe how the capabilities available through electronic government are changing the way these agencies provide homeland defense and homeland security.

This chapter is organized as follows. We begin with a general description of electronic government. We then describe the functional components of web services. Following this we show how service oriented computing is being adopted for homeland security and defense. We describe the Global Information Grid (GIG) and other networks on which services and resources are being deployed and explain the efforts being made to manage the infrastructure of available services. We conclude with a description of the Integrated Web Services Broker (IWB) being developed by the Naval Research Laboratory as an example of how web services can be efficiently identified, selected and used in service oriented environments such as the GIG.

E-GOVERNMENT OVERVIEW

Electronic government or e-government is also known as e-gov, digital government, and online government. E-government deals mostly with Internet applications to assist in government functionality. Although not a focus of this chapter, the term has also been applied to some non-Internet applications such as citizen tracking systems that deal with omnipresent surveillance and biometric identification (What is e-Government, 2007).

The overall objective of e-government may be characterized as streamlining government operations in some form. This can take a number of forms, including those listed in a 2002 e-government implementation strategy (United States Office of Management and Business[OMB], 2002, p.4), as:

- "Eliminating layers of government management."
- "Making it possible for citizens, businesses, other levels of government and federal employees to easily find information and get service from the federal government."
- "Simplifying agencies' business processes and reducing costs through integrating and eliminating redundant systems."
- "Enabling achievement of the other elements of the President's Management Agenda."
- "Streamlining government operations to guarantee rapid response to citizen needs."

In the course of achieving e-government, delivery of services may follow a number of models similar to those found in electronic commerce; namely, Government-to-Citizen, Government-to-Business, Government-to-Government and Intra-governmental: Internal Efficiency and Effectiveness (IEE) (OMB, 2002).

The E-Government Handbook (InfoDev and The Center for Democracy and Technology, 2002) organizes the functions of e-Government into three categories: publish, interact and transact.

Publish

Publish web sites are structured to make widely available information both about government and compiled by government. The idea of providing such information can be greatly effective in developing nations which would otherwise often require travel to government offices, tedious waits and even bribery. Some specific recommendations and guidelines include among others:

- "Post information of value to people in their daily lives..."

- "..mandate that all agencies publish a specified range of information online"
- " ..support goals such as economic development, anti-corruption, ..."

Interact

The step following the publication of information on web sites is to provide for two-way interaction with citizens. This enhances citizen trust in government by knowing they can be more directly engaged in the governmental process. In recent presidential campaigns, several candidates have made very effective use of Internet fund raisings. This was very prominent in the campaigns of candidates Howard Dean in 2004 and Barack Obama in 2008. A further example of interaction is the possibility of voting in elections over the Internet. Because this will represent one of the most important and widespread interactions of ordinary citizens with government, the security and integrity of such systems is crucial (Beroggi, 2008). Some of the suggested guidelines for interaction sites from the Handbook are:

- "Show citizens their engagement matters, by informing them of the outcomes of their online comments."
- "Break down complex policy issues into easy-to-understand components."
- "Be proactive about soliciting participation; use traditional media to publicize..."

Transact

Transaction capability has been largely developed based on e-commerce capabilities that now are so commonly used by the public and businesses. This model can be used in providing such services in an e-government context. Some recommendations for such transaction sites from the E-Government Handbook are:

- "Integrate e-government with process reform, streamlining and consolidating processes before putting them online."
- "...investments in transact systems can pay off over time in terms of cost savings and increased revenue"
- "Create a portal for transact services"

E-Government capabilities can become particularly important during major disasters. Indeed a new DOD doctrine is that enabling security, stabilization, transition and reconstruction is now a core U.S. military mission (US DOD, 2007). In support of this activity a variety of systems are being developed such as the ShareInfoForPeople portal which allows sharing of information and collaboration and coordination of efforts between civilian and military organizational structures (Mittu et.al., 2008)

As a concrete example of the need for information disaster management, consider the effects of Hurricane Katrina in the Gulf Coast areas and especially in the city of New Orleans. Indeed the Federal Emergency Management Agency (FEMA) Director has stated that it was the most catastrophic natural disaster in the nation's history and that it effectively altered the structure of the entire emergency management community, from the international and federal levels to state and local levels (FEMA, 2006). Many levels of government interacted to provide recovery services. These were often disjointed and confusing to average citizens struggling with recovery and rebuilding efforts. The local government established several websites to provide information and centralize disparate efforts. This was done in conjunction with local neighborhood organizations that developed after the storm often in response to ineffectiveness of governmental efforts – in effect government from the bottom-up. One of the most effective websites (Carrolton Technology Partners, 2006) provides an organized portal with information and links to government programs, housing, child care, health resources, etc. Particularly effective are the links to 13 city neighborhoods, each with one or more neighborhood organizations, many of which evolved in response to the storm-related conditions.

The United States government has established an e-government office having online presence at http://www.whitehouse.gov/omb/egov/. The following statement on this web site indicates the significance of the transformation taking place , "E-Gov does not mean putting scores of government forms on the Internet. It is about using technology to its fullest to provide services and information that is centered around citizen groups." In order to facilitate access to federal, state and local e-government, the federal government has also established a web portal, http://www.usa.gov/. Additionally, recent developments in e-government news are routinely published in Federal Computing Week and available on-line at the following web site: http://www.fcw.com/e_government.asp?topic=egov.

The Geospatial One-Stop is an example of a presidential initiative that provides federal and state agencies with Web portal access to mapping related data. This single point of access allows the sharing of data in a way that makes better use of resources. The portal is found at geodata.gov and includes the tools for finding and analyzing the multiple sources of information that are available. These tools support functions such as search, interactive mapping and metadata publishing. Mapping data available through the Geospatial One-Stop is accessible via the Open Geospatial Consortium's Web Mapping Service (WMS) specification. The Geospatial One-Stop can also make use of other portals to maximize available data. One example of how it makes non WMS data available is seen in its access to the Geospatial Information Database (GIDB) portal system developed at the Naval Research Laboratory. The GIDB provides a portal to over 1,500 data servers. Many of these servers are not WMS compliant. In order to enable non-WMS compliant data to be accessible together with WMS compliant data on the Geospatial One-Stop, the GIDB portal provides a WMS entry point to its portal. This is illustrated in Figure 1.

An example of e-government within the DoD is the Air Force Innovation and Technology Knowledge Management web site. This site was launched in April 2006 in order to coordinate knowledge sharing among many innovation communities that are working on new technology and solutions. The Air Force Knowledge Now (AFKN) service is accessed through the Air Force portal and is pictured in Figure 2. Other agencies, such as the US Navy, and Army also have web portals that are similar in nature.

One example of DHS e-government is the Homeland Security Digital Library (HSDL). This web-based service is an online library that provides access to several hundred thousand documents pertaining to U.S. policy, presidential directives, and national strategy. It also includes specialized resources such as theses, reports from various universities, organizations and local and state agencies. The library is intended to help federal, state and local government agencies develop

Figure 1. Geospatial One-Stop access to data via GIDB portal

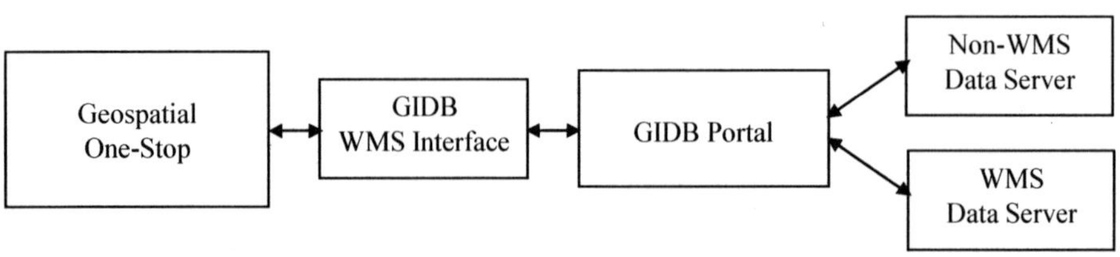

future policies as well as assist students/faculty to research the decision-making processes since the September 11 terrorists attack. It would have been difficult for each government official, student or faculty member to individually obtain a copy of these documents. It also would have been a duplication of efforts. (Department of Homeland Security at Naval Post Graduate School, n.d.) The goals of e-government are achieved here by providing the information in a speedy manner and eliminating redundant efforts (Lamont, 2006).

WEB SERVICES IN ELECTRONIC GOVERNMENT

E-government is aimed at "simplified and timely delivery of services to the citizens" (OMB, 2002) of a community. In its simplest form, this may involve e-government solutions that make government services conveniently available via web pages as shown through the e-government solutions mentioned above. In contrast, many DoD and DHS application areas call for more complex machine-to-machine interaction with electronic government services and even data interoperability across multiple communities. E-government solutions in these cases utilize web services technology.

Web Services provide data and services to applications and users over a network via a set of standards and protocols. Commonly used standards and protocols include, but are not limited to, the Extensible Markup Language (XML), Simple Object Access Protocol (SOAP), the Web Services Description Language (WSDL) and Universal Discovery Description and Integration (UDDI) (Cerami, 2002).

XML is a language that provides a means to describe data in a platform and programming language independent manner; thus providing a means of decoupling client and server applica-

Figure 2. Air Force Portal (Adkins, R , n.d.)

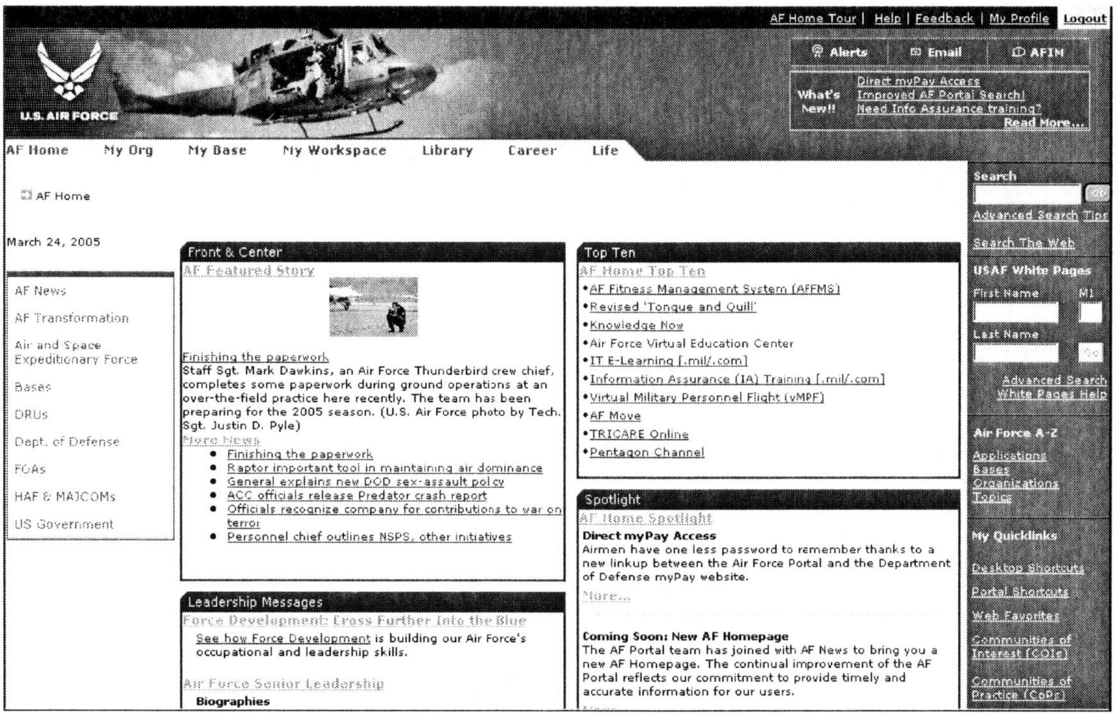

tions. A WSDL file is a document that uses XML to define a web service interface or "contract" for a web service. The "contract" details the syntax and structure of requests that a web service will accept and responses that the web service will generate. In addition, the "contract" defines the XML messaging mechanism of the service. SOAP will most likely be the messaging mechanism identified in the WSDL file as SOAP allows for the exchange of information between computers regardless of platform or language. The WSDL or web service contract may be registered in a UDDI web service registry much like a phone number is published in a phone book. Figure 3 illustrates the use cycle of web services.

A web service registry provides a way for consumers to find data providers and desired services. A registry provides a means for data providers to advertise their Web Services. Registering or publishing a web service with a registry is optional; however, not registering a web service with a registry is comparable to not publishing a phone number in the phone book. It will be difficult for a potential consumer to locate the web service. Not publishing a web service may be a desired security measure for the providers of some web services such as those involved in the nation's security and defense.

There are applications on the Internet that provide services to consumers without using the commonly used web service standards and protocols. These applications are "Web-based services" and they employ diverse methods for discovery, description, messaging and transport. (International Journal of Web Services Research, 2006). In this chapter, the use of the term "web services" refers to the services that employ at least XML, WSDL and SOAP standards and protocols.

SERVICE ORIENTED COMPUTING

The significance of web services and web-based services for electronic government is found in the service oriented computing paradigm. Service oriented computing is a means of organizing web services and web-based services around a conceptual Service Oriented Architecture (SOA). The SOA has been technically described as (Marks & Bell, 2006 p. 1) "a conceptual business architecture where business functionality or application logic is made available to users or consumers as shared reusable services on an IT network. Services in an SOA are modules of business application functionality with exposed interfaces and are

Figure 3. Illustrated use of Web services

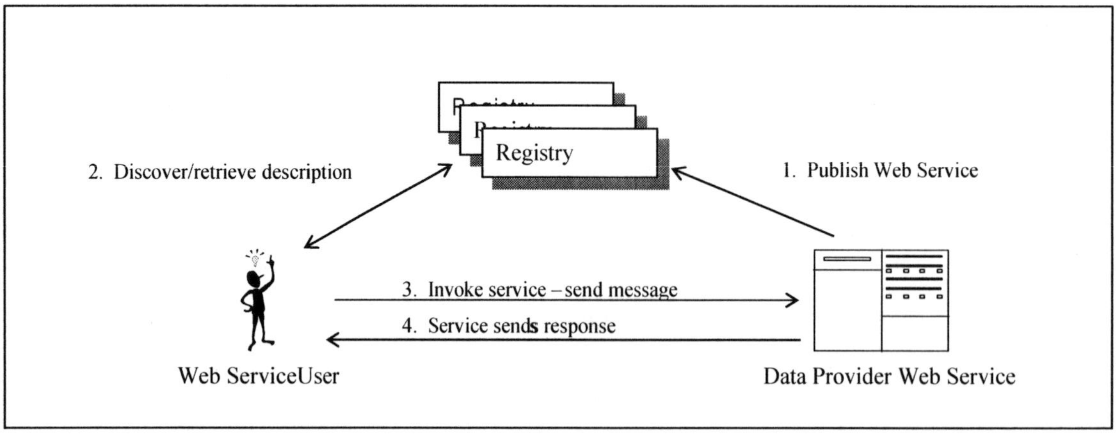

invoked by messages." The SOA is the means by which business functionality is published, discovered and consumed on a network. Services offer resources in a loosely coupled manner and users are able to build composite applications that draw on multiple sources.

DoD Service Oriented Computing

Service oriented computing is being embraced by major DoD initiatives such as the Global Information Grid, Net-Centric Enterprise Services, the Navy's ForceNet, the Army's Future Combat System and the Air Force's Joint Battlespace Infosphere and Joint Battle Management/Command & Control (Paul, 2005). The following sections explain some of these initiatives in more detail and reveal some of the challenges associated with the DoD's service oriented e-government for its internal customers.

Global Information Grid

In short, the GIG proposes to provide the framework in which to connect all technology within the Department of Defense and outside the DoD as needed. The GIG can be thought of as a global network that will support data and service needs to all DoD functions at all times (in war, in crisis, and in peace). By providing a global network with connectivity and resources available to all DoD users, a free flow of information will be established that will provide a significant edge over adversaries. (National Security Agency, n.d.)

However, the GIG must allow this free flow of information to authorized users only. Security of this system is of utmost concern. This same free flow of information in the hands of an adversary could prove to be detrimental.

Net-Centric Enterprise Services (NCES)

The GIG is the global network on which DOD services and resources can be deployed. These deployed services and resources should have an over arching organization on the global network in order to prevent information overload and chaos for users. NCES, which was created by Defense Information Systems Agency (DISA), is an attempt to organize and manage the proliferation of resources available on the GIG.

Any user within the DoD community who needs to share and retrieve information is considered to be an NCES customer. This includes Warfighters. Resources on the GIG should be available 24/7/365 and the information available should be of the highest quality. In addition, the user should have the capability to pull data with minimum latency to support time critical decisions. (Defense Information Systems Agency | Core Services, 2006).

The NCES Program has four product lines of services: Enterprise Service-Oriented Architecture Foundation, DoD Enterprise Collaboration, Content Discovery and Delivery, and Portal. Enterprise Service-Oriented Architecture Foundation enables the reusability of services and helps to reduce the complexity of the DoD's information technology environment. Foundation services include, for example, the NCES Mediation Service, which provides for eXtensible Markup Language (XML) translations using eXtensible Stylesheet Language Translation (XSLT) stylesheets. Enterprise Collaboration provides collaboration tools such as conferencing and white board sessions. Content Discovery & Delivery supports efficient information advertisement, discovery, and delivery.

The Portal provides secure Web access to NCES services and the capability to leverage an application throughout the GIG thereby reducing creation of redundant functionality. The portal to the GIG, named Defense Online, is pictured in Figure 4. (Defense Information Systems Agency - Net-Centric Enterprise Services [DISA-NCES], 2006)

NCES describes users of the program as either end users, service providers, service consumers or

Figure 4. Portal to the Global Information Grid

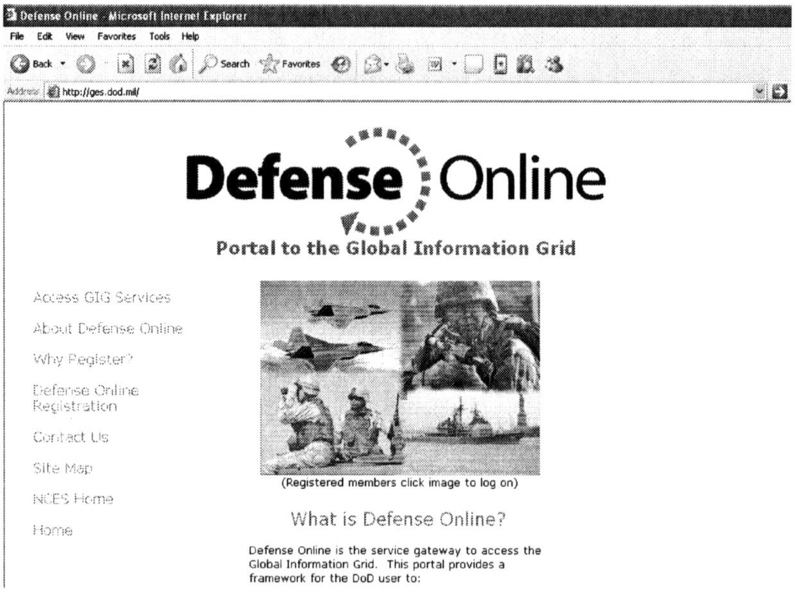

data providers. End users directly access services via a portal environment. Accessible services include the portal, messaging, search and service discovery. Service providers make services available through NCES. Service consumers support programs of record through applications that make use of NCES services. For example, a developer may integrate an application with NCES mediation services (described above). Sample applications are made available to assist developers with writing their own applications to make use of the mediation services for specific needs. Data providers support programs of record by making data available via NCES. Users learn about and retrieve this data using Content Discovery and Delivery services.

Net-Centric Enterprise Solutions for Interoperability (NESI)

Currently, NESI is a joint effort between Defense Information Systems Agency (DISA), Air Force and Navy. NESI provides concrete guidance for the life cycle management of a service to be deployed on the GIG. NESI brings to life the concepts and ideas expressed in higher level abstract directives, policies and mandates regarding net-centric warfare. (Netcentric Enterprise Solutions for Interoperabilty, 2006) While NESI provides lifecycle guidance, NCES provides a registry in which to publish a service along with other tools which enhance the reusability of the service. A service that has been created using NESI guidance and registered with NCES is deployed on the GIG. This net-centric enterprise is depicted in Figure 5 (Navy PEO C4I, 2004). End-users at various nodes on the GIG access needed services that may be co-located or located at other nodes. Among the core enterprise services offered through NCES are data discovery, service discovery, mediation, security and enterprise service management. Through this core services, for example, a warfighter at Node C may be able to discover a source of needed data that is available from a service at Node B and then use the NCES mediation service to retrieve the data. The same warfighter may then transmit the same data to a service offered by Node A that provides defensive strike power.

Figure 5. Net-centric DoD enterprise

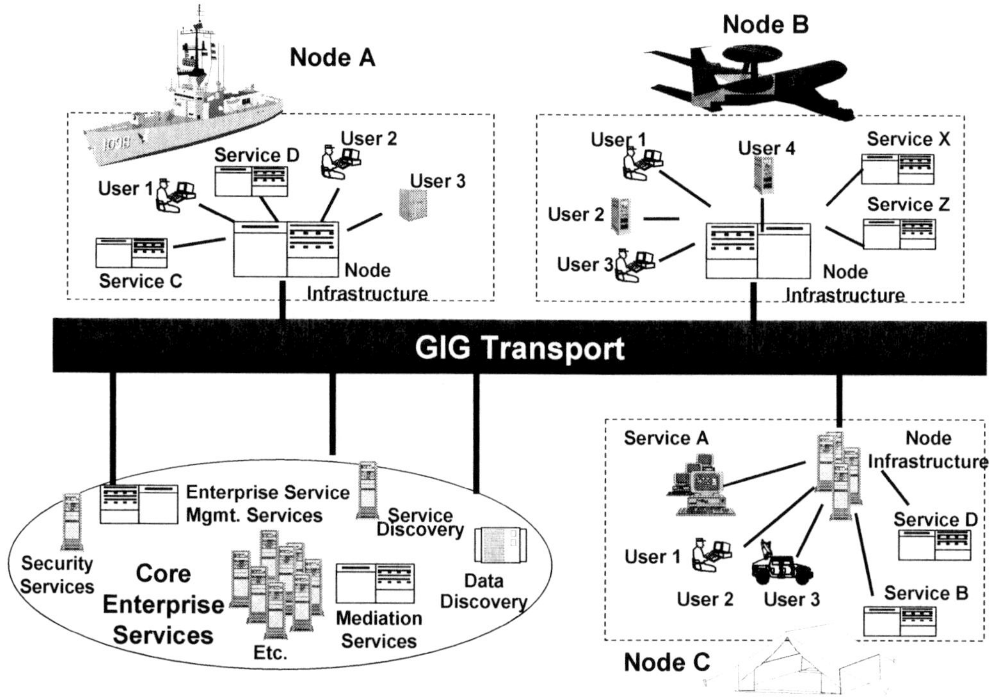

DHS Service Oriented Computing

The DHS, like the DoD, is moving toward service oriented computing. (Stevens, 2007) Through an effort called "OnetNet" DHS is seeking to achieve maximum data sharing and service reuse by connecting the various networks that were put under the DHS umbrella when the department was formed (DHS Special Report | Component Approach, 2006). OneNet is distinct from DoD's Global Information Grid and is focused on sharing unclassified but sensitive data. (Magnuson, 2006) (DHS Special Report | Forward Motion, 2006) However, the need for DHS to collaborate with DoD agencies is obvious and communication bridges are being established so that multiple components from the two departments can share information over a network.(DISA DMZ, 2006) One example of this is the Maritime Domain Awareness project in which the US Navy, the US Coast Guard and the Office of Naval Intelligence share information over a network.

The Integrated Common Analytical Viewer (iCAV) is a noteworthy service oriented effort within DHS. Using an integrated geographic information system and Services Oriented Architecture, this software provides web-based dissemination, analysis and visualization of shared data. The effort connects systems that previously could not share information so that a consistent, mission-specific common operating picture is provided to DHS and its mission partners. The intent of this geospatial-intelligence analytic tool is to enable better preparation, prevention, response and recovery from natural and man-made disasters. (SOAWorld Magazine News Desk, 2006)

E-GOVERNMENT AND THE SEMANTIC WEB

With the growth of electronic government much more relevant data is available for decision-making. Within DoD, for example, the proliferation of service oriented computing on the GIG means that services must be effectively and efficiently identified, selected and used. Yet the identification and retrieval of data from heterogeneous sources in such a distributed system poses many difficulties. Assimilation of data from heterogeneous sources means that differences in notation, terminology, usage, etc. prevent simple querying and retrieval of data. Approaches utilizing manual translations or interface mappings as with XSLT stylesheets (an approach taken by NCES Mediation Services) require an application developer to write new software or prepare new stylesheets.

The recognition of such integration difficulties has influenced many of the concepts that are embodied in the Semantic Web. Semantic technologies such as ontologies have been developed to support the goal of sharing knowledge for various domains of interest. An ontology captures terms, concepts and relationships within a domain to provide a model and the semantics of a domain. Part of the power of an ontology is that it can capture the semantics of a single domain as shared by different communities (Korotkiy and Top, 2006).

The Knowledge Management Working Group and the Semantic Interoperability Community of Practice are two federal working groups that are focused on semantic technologies and the promise they hold for information sharing challenges within electronic government. Additionally, various methodologies for applying ontologies to exploit the semantics of Web services have been explored. (Ladner et al., 2006) (Medjahed and Bouguettaya, 2005) (Korotkiy and Top,2006). One approach being developed by the Naval Research Laboratory is the Integrated Web Services Broker.

Integrated Web Services Broker

The Integrated Web Services Broker (IWB) is an example of middleware for use in a services oriented environment such as the GIG to achieve semantic interoperability between clients and web services. The goal of the IWB is to give client applications net-centric plug-and-play capabilities with regard to retrieving needed data.

To accomplish this goal, the IWB is being engineered to independently decompose and analyze ad hoc Web services interface descriptions in order to identify Web services of interest and then cache information about each service in order to support an autonomous mediation process. The mediation process does not require a priori knowledge of any particular service for specialized code development, pre-prepared taxonomies of available services or end-user resolution of structural and syntactic differences inherent in varying Web services interfaces. The approach is intended to avoid the necessity of client application software enhancements to address changes in services' interfaces as the service evolves.

The IWB utilizes semantic web technologies (ontologies) and artificial intelligence techniques (classifiers) in order to carry out its functions. Although the IWB is being prototyped for the meteorological and oceanographic (METOC) domain. The techniques employed are generic enough to apply to many other domains.

The approach followed in the IWB is in contrast to other approaches to web service data brokers that assume that web service providers will deploy an ontological description of their web service (Paolucci et al., 2004). The IWB assumes that ontological descriptions of web services have not been provided by the service provider; the IWB instead assumes that only the web service WSDL and associated schemas have been provided. Through the use of ontologies and classifiers, the IWB seeks to avoid the need for web service providers to supply an ontological description of their service (Ladner et al., 2006).

The primary functions of the IWB can be described as web service discovery and client request mediation. These functions are depicted in Figures 6 and 7. The IWB first discovers web services that supply data for the domain of interest by searching web service registries and the Internet for WSDLs. It then classifies the WSDLs and methods contained therein using classifiers that have been trained on the domain of interest.

Upon finding WSDL operations that provide the desired domain data, the IWB then caches information about the web service interface needed to support mediation of client requests. In this process, the IWB uses its own domain ontology to create critical on-the-fly XML schema to ontology concept mapping that the software records during this phase. This is similar to an ontology alignment or schema mapping task. Additionally, the software determines and records instructions for composing a valid request to this web service. All of this information is used to populate an index of web services within the dynamic knowledge base. In doing so, an additional classifier is used to identify data specializations within the domain

Figure 6. Autonomous Web service discovery

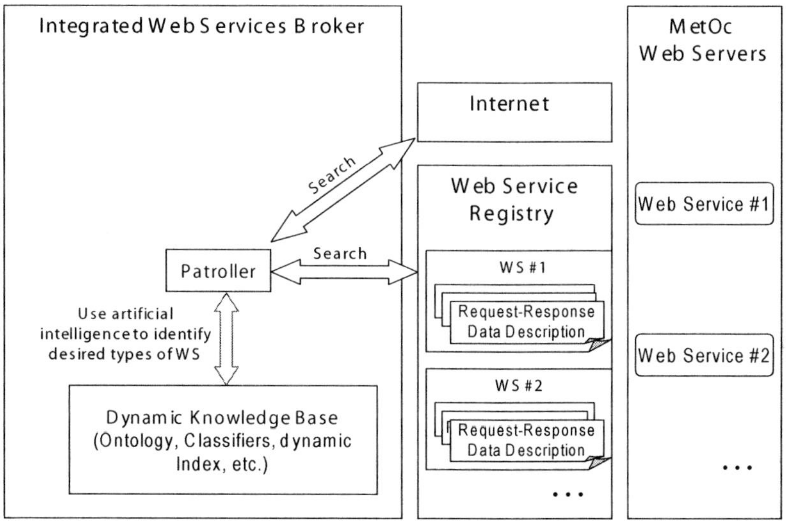

Figure 7. Autonomous mediation

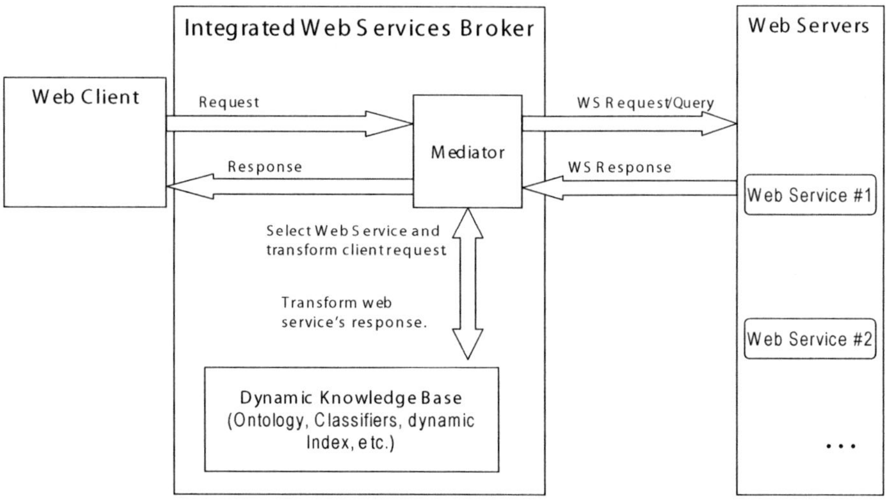

for which the web service supplies data. The cached information allows the IWB to select the web service as an appropriate target for filling a client application request, to invoke the web service when selected and also to transform the client application's XML terminology and structure to that of the web service.

In the mediation process, the IWB receives and decomposes client application requests to determine the data that is being requested. The software consults the domain ontology to determine key concepts in the current decomposed request. A list of appropriate web services are selected based on the intersect of web services providing the key concepts. The selected web services are ordered by confidence ranking. The web service with the highest confidence ranking will be contacted first in attempt to fill the client request.

Mediating a data request to a web service requires the IWB to compose a valid request for the selected web service operation. To do this the IWB must resolve terminology and structure differences between the client request and the selected web service operation. If the highest ranked web service does not supply an answer, then the IWB moves on to contact the next highest ranked web service in the list. This continues until the desired data is received or until there are no more web services to contact to fill that particular client request. Upon receiving a response from a web service, the IWB must perform a reverse transform of XML terminology and structure from that of the web service to the client.

The IWB should not be confused with middleware that provides composite Web services, that is Web services composed of at least two other web services to form a business process. IWB can be thought of as a "façade" as defined in NESI implementation guidance in that provides a unified interface to a dynamically changing set of interfaces in a subsystem (Netcentric Enterprise Solutions for Interoperabilty, 2006). However, "façade" is simplistic and does not disclose the real power of the IWB. The IWB is a run-time discovery and mediation engine. The set of interfaces that it represents are undetermined at the startup of the IWB software. The IWB educates itself on the topic of which web service interfaces to represent by finding web services and then using artificial intelligence to determine if these services are within the desired domain. The IWB then uses knowledge management techniques to record instructions for itself regarding how to construct valid XML messages to those web services which includes resolving terminology and XML structure differences between the client XML and the web service XML. During mediation, the IWB provides a smart dynamic reconfiguration mechanism (Paul, 2005). The IWB is charged with representing the web service interface that has the highest confidence score to fulfill an individual user request. However, when the service with the highest confidence score does not return an answer (for whatever reason) another service will contacted by the IWB to fill the client request. This will be the service with the next highest confidence score. The IWB will again resolve terminology and structure differences; this time between the client request and the newly substituted web service. It will also construct an appropriate XML message using instructions that it determined and recorded for itself previously. This dynamic reconfiguration allows for mission critical client applications to proceed without interruption. (Paul, 2005) The ontology is key in the mediation process as it acts a pivot device for terminology mapping between client web service requests.

Case-Based Classification Approach

Because of the complexity in the development of domain ontologies, IWB also used case-based classification for web service discovery. Specifically, this complements the ontologies to support the automated discovery of meteorological and oceanographic Web Services. Case-based reasoning (CBR) is a problem solving methodology that retrieves and reuses decisions from stored cases to solve new problems (Kolodner, 1992), and case-based classification focuses on applying CBR to supervised classification tasks. Identifying whether a given web service supplies data for a particular domain can be framed as a classification or categorization task, which involves assigning one or more predefined labels to an unlabelled object. Thus, the Web Services classification task for the MetOc domain will involve assigning the label "MetOc" or "Non-MetOc" to a given web service.

Case-based classification proceeds as follows. To classify a new object, the classification decision from previously classified objects is reused. Objects that have characteristics similar to the new object are called cases. To assess the similarity of one case with another, the classifier uses a similarity metric or a matching function such as the Euclidean distance metric used as a similarity function. The cases that are most similar to the unclassified object are called the nearest neighbors. The decisions from the *k* nearest neighbors from the case base are used in assigning the class label to a new object. Training the classifier typically implies estimating the weights or parameters applicable to the similarity metric.

SUMMARY

We have described how the DoD and DHS are expanding e-government capabilities through several major initiatives to support security and defense. These initiatives are centered on service oriented computing to support the internal customers and partners of DoD and DHS. The adoption of service oriented computing provides the DoD and the DHS with the opportunity to better leverage information and data to provide enhanced protection for United States assets while reducing the long term IT budget. However, moving toward service oriented computing also provides challenges such as managing a massive service oriented architecture, like the GIG, so that information overload does not negate the possible gain from such an architecture. The strategies and full benefits of utilizing a Service Oriented Architecture are a field of much research interest. The application of the semantic web through work such as the Integrated Web Services Broker should bring new methodologies that will most likely play a significant role in realizing the full benefits of this Service Oriented Architecture.

ACKNOWLEDGMENT

The authors would like to thank the Naval Research Laboratory's Base Program, Program Element No. 0602435N for sponsoring this research. The authors also acknowledge Frank McCreedy who was a co-author of an earlier publication on which this extended version is based.

REFERENCES

Adkins, R. (2005). *Air Force Knowledge Now.* http://www.e-gov.com/events/2005/km/downloads/KM05_2-3_Adkins.pdf

Beroggi, G. (2008). Secure and Easy Internet Voting. *IEEE Computer*, 41(2), 52-56.

Carrolton Technology Partners. (2006). http://www.louisianarebuilds.info

Cerami, E. (2002). *Web Services Essentials.* California: O Reilly & Associates.

Defense Information Systems Agency, Department of Defense. (2006). *Core Services - Net-Centric Enterprise Services.* http://www.disa.mil/main/prodsol/cs_nces.html

Defense Information Systems Agency- Net-Centric Enterprise Services. (2006). *Net-Centric Enterprise Services User Guide, Version 1.0/ECB 1.2.* http://www.disa.mil/nces /NCES_UG_Final_v1_0.pdf

Department of Defense. (2000). *Organizational Chart*. http://www.defenselink.mil/odam/omp/pubs/GuideBook/Pdf/DoD.PDF

Department of Homeland Security. (2006). *History: Who Became Part of the Department?* http://www.dhs.gov/xabout/history/editorial_0133.shtm

Department of Homeland Security at Naval Post Graduate School. (n.d.). *Homeland Security Digital Library*. https://www.hsdl.org/

Department of Homeland Security. (2006). *Special Report | Component approach aiding IT infrastructure consolidation*. http://www.gcn.com/print/25_17/41104-1.html

Department of Homeland Security. (2006). *Special Report | Forward Motion, Amid widely documented IT failures, security advances and infrastructure upgrades are gaining traction at DHS*. http://www.gcn.com/print/25_16/41076-1.html

Federal Emergency Management Agency. (2006). http://www.fema.gov/hazard/hurricane/2005katrina/ anniversary.shtm

InfoDev and The Center for Democracy and Technology. (2002). *E-Government Handbook*. www.cdt.org/egov/handbook/

Kolodner J. (1992). An Introduction to Case-Based Reasoning. *Artificial Intelligence Review*, 6(2), 3-24.

Korotkiy, S. and Top L. (2006). Onto SOA: From Ontology-enabled SOA to Service-enabled Ontologies. *IEEE International Conference on Internet and Web Applications and Services*, 347-353.

Ladner, R., Petry, F. Gupta, K., Warner, E., Moore, P., & Aha ,D.(2008). Soft Computing Techniques for Web Services Brokering. *Soft Computing*, 12(11), 299-308.

Lamont, J. (2006). *E-government: enhancing national security*. http://www.kmworld.com/Articles/ReadArticle.aspx?ArticleID=15806 (review)

Magnuson, S. (2006). Homeland Security Mission Creates More Complications. *National Defense Magazine*. http://www.nationaldefensemagazine.org/issues/2006/August/HomelandSecurity.htm

Marks, E. & Bell, M. (2006). *Executives' Guide to Service-Oriented Architecture (SOA): A Planning and Implementation Guide for Business and Technology*. Wiley.

Medjahed, B. & Bouguettaya, A. (2005). Customized Delivery of E-Government Web Services. *IEEE Intelligent Systems*, 20(6), 77-84.

Mittu R., Guleyupoglu, S. Chang, C. Johnson, A. Dowdy, M. & Barlow, W. (2008). Unclassified Information Sharing in Stability, Security, Transition and Reconstruction Efforts. *International Journal of Electronic Government Research*, 4(1) , 36-48.

National Security Agency. (n.d.). *Global Information Grid, Scope and Objectives*. http://www.nsa.gov/ia/industry/gigscope.cfm?MenuID=10.3.2.2

Navy PEO C4I & Space RAPIDS Team & Air Force ESC C2ERA Team. (2004). *Net-Centric Enterprise Solutions for Interoperability*. http://nesipublic.spawar.navy.mil/files/NESI-Overview-v1e.ppt

Netcentric Enterprise Solutions for Interoperabilty (2006). *Netcentric Enterprise Solutions for Interoperability Part 5: Developer Guidance Version 1.3*. http://nesipublic.spawar.navy.mil/part5/releases/1.3.0/WebHelp/nesi_part5_v1_3.htm

O'Rourke, R.(2005). *Homeland Security: Navy Operations -- Background and Issues for Congress*. http://www.history.navy.mil/library/online/homeland_security.htm

Paolucci, M., Soudry, J., Srinivasan, N., and Sycara, K. (2004). A Broker for OWL-S Web services. *Proceedings of the AAAI Spring Symposium on Semantic Web Services*, 562-567.

Paul, R. A.(2005). DoD Towards Software Services. *Proceedings of the 10th IEEE International Workshop on Object-Oriented Real-Time Dependable Systems* (WORDS'05), 3-6.

SOAWorld Magazine News Desk. (2006). *ManTech Awarded Disaster-Mapping Contract From DHS*. http://webservices.sys-con.com/read/299259.htm

Stevens, L (2007). *The In and Out of SOA, FedTech Technology Insights for leaders in Federal Government*. http://www.fedtechmagazine.com/article.asp?item_id=257

United States Office of Management and Business. (2002). *Implementing the President's Management Agenda for E-Government*. http://www.usa.gov/Topics/Includes/Reference/egov_strategy.pdf

U.S. DoD. (2007). *U.S. Department of Defense: DoD Directive 3000.05-Military Support for Stability, Security, Transition, and Reconstruction (SSTR) Operations*. http://www.dtic.mil/whs/directives /corres/html/300005.htm

What is e-Government? (2007). http://www.wisegeek.com/what-is-e-government.htm

Chapter III
Towards Civil-Military Coordination During Security, Stabilization, Transition and Reconstruction Efforts[1]

Ranjeev Mittu
U.S. Naval Research Laboratory, USA

Suleyman Guleyupoglu
ITT Corporation, USA

William Barlow
Office of Secretary of Defense Networks and Information Integration, USA

Michael Dowdy
Femme Comp, Inc. (FCI), USA

Sean McCarthy
Femme Comp, Inc. (FCI), USA

ABSTRACT

The emergence of new doctrine is enabling Security, Stabilization, Transition and Reconstruction (SSTR) operations to become a core U.S. military mission. These operations are now given equal priority to combat operations. The immediate goal in SSTR is to provide the local populace with security, restore essential services, and meet humanitarian needs. The long-term goal is to help develop indigenous capacity for securing and maintaining essential services. Therefore, many SSTR operations are best performed by indigenous groups with support from foreign agencies and professionals. Large scale disasters, however, are an example where military support can improve SSTR operations by providing a much needed boost to foreign governments and nongovernmental organizations which may already be under great stress to respond in a timely and effective manner. However, without the means to effectively coordinate the efforts between many diverse groups across the civil-military boundary during SSTR operations, basic assistance and relief operations may be severely impeded. This chapter will describe a conceptual portal called ShareInfoForPeople, which provides advanced Information and Communication Technology to enable collaboration, coordination and information sharing across the civil-military boundary during SSTR operations.

Copyright © 2009, IGI Global, distributing in print or electronic forms without written permission of IGI Global is prohibited.

INTRODUCTION

With the signing of the Department of Defense Directive (DoDD) 3000.05, *Military Support for Security, Stabilization, Transition and Reconstruction (SSTR) Operations* into policy (U.S. DoD, 2007), SSTR operations have become a core U.S. military mission that the Department of Defense (DoD) must be prepared to conduct and support. These operations are now given equal priority to combat operations. The immediate goal is to provide the local populace with security, restore essential services, and meet humanitarian needs. The long-term goal is to help develop and maintain: indigenous capacity for securing essential services, a viable market economy, rule-of-law, democratic institutions, and a robust civil society. These operations are conducted to help establish order, while promoting U.S. interests and values.

SSTR operations are best performed by indigenous groups with support from foreign agencies and professionals. Large scale disasters, however, are an example where military support can improve SSTR operations by providing a much needed boost to foreign governments and nongovernmental organizations which may already be under great stress to respond in a timely and effective manner. Therefore, the ability to coordinate the response across the civil-military boundary during such operations is essential.

This chapter will begin by briefly describing SSTR operations and provide notional examples. Next, we will describe the capabilities of the ShareInfoForPeople portal (https://www.ShareInfoForPeople.org) which provides the necessary tools to enable coordination and information sharing across the civil-military boundary during SSTR operations. We will then discuss the utilization of this portal in the Navy's Trident Warrior experiment. Lastly, we describe future development activities and technical challenges that remain to be investigated within our portal environment. We will conclude with a brief summary.

SECURITY, STABILIZATION, TRANSITION AND RECONSTRUCTION

SSTR operations are conducted outside the boundaries of U.S. lands and territories, and Information and Communication Technology (ICT) capabilities are critical enablers for the conduct of these missions. While there are similarities within the ICT systems for the employment of automated information systems between domestic and international partners, policy and structural frameworks create a different workflow for each side with regard to information dissemination and coordination. We will limit our scope to examples of military operations outside of U.S. borders.

Many SSTR operational tasks are best performed by indigenous groups, with support from foreign or U.S. civilian professionals. Complex disasters are an example where military involvement and support for SSTR operations can provide significant value to foreign governments and non-governmental organizations (NGOs) which may already be under great stress to respond in a timely and effective manner. The command and control structure, resources and assets that the military can offer in such situations can shorten the response timeline. However, without the means to properly coordinate the efforts of such a large and diverse group which spans the civil-military boundary, basic assistance and relief operations may be severely impacted, leading to delays or waste in the overall response cycle.

In SSTR operations, the U.S. military supports the Department of State and works with non-DoD partners, which may include select military units of other nations NGOs, International Organizations (IO) and private volunteer organizations. Large scale disasters are one example where proper coordination between participating organizations can increase the effectiveness of the overall response. A key element in the success of SSTR operations is the ability of the U.S. (or other lead activity) to obtain and process information about the situation and status of participating partners, while disseminating (or making accessible), the widest amount of relevant information to the partners in the ad-hoc coalition. Through the sharing of unclassified information via an appropriate ICT framework, the goal is to increase the level of coordinated activity among all of the participants. As illustrated in the following notional scenarios, SSTR operations are also subjected to non-traditional and unanticipated partners:

- **Disaster Relief:** Following a tsunami in the western Pacific, the U.S. Navy has been designated Combined/Joint Task Force Commander for U.S. military disaster relief operations involving an island nation that experienced severe destruction from several 50-foot waves. Coalition partners include naval elements from various Pacific Rim nations e.g., Australia, Thailand, Japan, China, South Korea, and India. Ground/air elements from these same countries are involved in delivering relief supplies and distribution of those supplies is being managed by a combination of efforts by the host nation, the United Nations, USAID, and international relief organizations e.g., Red Cross.
- **Humanitarian Assistance:** Following a period of severe drought and dislocation of local peoples, the U.S. Army is designated Combined/Joint Task Force Commander for humanitarian assistance operations in a region of sub-Saharan Africa. Coalition partners include the United Nations, Doctors without Borders, and the International Red Cross.

While these are notional examples, recent history reveals that the initial years of the 21st century have witnessed numerous large-scale crises such as the Indian Ocean tsunami and Kashmir earthquake. There have also been longer-term, multi-faceted emergencies such as those in Sudan. The United States has been involved as a part of multinational coalition missions, including the Balkan states, Afghanistan, and Iraq. The U.S. has also provided humanitarian assistance in response to devastating natural disasters around the world. Increasingly, the scale and scope of such events involve both civilian and military components.

The next section will describe the ShareInfo-ForPeople portal that is being developed to enable collaboration and information sharing across the civil-military boundary during SSTR operations. The purpose is to enable non-traditional and unanticipated partners to share information (situational awareness) and better coordinate with the civil and military components.

INFORMATION AND COMMUNICATIONS TECHNOLOGIES FOR SSTR

The Internet is driving emergent behavior in personal and group communications, and is leading to new forms of interaction, as witnessed through many social network websites that are growing in popularity such as MySpace.com, Flickr.com, Craigslist.org, Wikimapia.com, etc. These, and similar web sites, are leveraging new trends in collaboration such as Web 2.0 (e.g., mashups) to enable social networking. A few characteristics of the Web 2.0 may include the use of Real Simple Syndication (RSS), weblogs (aka blogs), wiki's and social book marking which enables web sites to be highly interactive (at a personal level). Some of the capabilities associated with mashups may include the ability to aggregate or transform content from remote sites through web browser-based applications. These applications generally provide simple and convenient programming interfaces to easily ingest or interact with new content. The benefits of aggregating, transforming or creating new content enables new ideas and concepts to emerge, which then become discoverable and accessible from within the site, or to other sites through mechanisms such as RSS.

The DoD is also beginning to embrace Web 2.0, and is actively leveraging these technologies in order to understand their value for improving collaboration and helping to achieve coordinated action during SSTR operations. This chapter will describe a specific implementation of such a system called ShareInfoForPeople that is being funded by the *Office of Secretary of Defense - Networks and Information Integration* to explore the methodologies for unclassified information sharing capabilities across the civil-military boundary during SSTR operations.

As can be seen in Figure 1, ShareInfoForPeople (SIFP) provides a set of tools through a web browser interface to enable real time coordination and information sharing (shared situational awareness view) based on open standards and frameworks. The infrastructure is implemented using the Drupal (2007) Content Management System (CMS) and many of the baseline information sharing and collaboration tools have been contributed through the Drupal open source community. Drupal is a very modular open source software written in PHP Hypertext Processor language. It was chosen due to the very broad development community and user-base, as well for its many "off-the-shelf" modules which can be extended as needed to suit the particular problem domain. While other frameworks have the potential to provide similar advantages (Ruby, 2007), Drupal was chosen as the framework since it is already a complete CMS, without requiring additional programming effort to build CMS functionality. In addition, the fact that it is a community driven open

Figure 1. The ShareInfoForPeople.org opening screen

source project means that it is easier to transition the system to the partner organizations without imposing an investment burden on them for expensive software licenses. Furthermore, the use of open source software has been approved in IT systems within the Department of the Navy, which also demonstrates a paradigm shift within DoD towards the acceptance and use of open source software (Rendleman, 2007). This should lead to an opportunity to improve collaboration and coordination between the civil groups and military components as both are migrating towards open source software, and our portal may be able to serve as a baseline. The primary capabilities of SIFP include the following:

- **Fully Indexed Site:** Content is indexed based on user-specified meta-data tags to enable search of local content. When a user creates and uploads content to the site such as images, audio, blogs, etc., there is an opportunity for the user to specify meta-data tags that serve as an index mechanism, in order to facilitate searching from within the site.
- **Real Simple Syndication (RSS) and GeoRSS Feeds:** RSS and GeoRSS technology is utilized to incorporate the latest content from TRITON and Information Management and Mine Action Programs (iMAPP) as well as from other sites that support such feeds. The use of GeoRSS enables the coding of geospatial information within traditional RSS feeds, and allows SIFP to display these feeds using its local mapping interface.
    - o TRITON (https://maps.nswc.navy.mil) is a scalable web application architecture engineered to integrate and visualize geospatial data. It can be linked to databases or information and near real-time data feeds. It integrates imagery on-the-fly and dynamic map services from other organizations. TRITON is currently serving static images via GeoRSS to SIFP to demonstrate the initial proof-of-concept. User feedback on desired future capabilities within SIFP will enable us to expand our interactions with TRITON.
    - o The iMMAP focuses on the larger concerns of war including the realities of an overstretched military; how America goes to war; and the civilian casualties of war. The iMMAP is involved in public education / news gathering and supports distribution of such information. Similar to TRITON, iMMAP is providing GeoRSS feeds to SIFP to demonstrate proof-of-concept.
- **Collaborative Authoring:** SIFP supports a wiki capability (Figure 2) to promote collaboration and dissemination of shared knowledge. A community-driven approach should enable convergence towards accurate and reliable information being shared.
- **Upload or Create Content:** SIFP provides tools to upload content such as video, audio (Figure 3) and images within a group-based structure. Users can provide a title to what is being uploaded, upload the files by browsing their local directory, provide a description of the content, define keyword tags describing the content so that the tags can be indexed and used to facilitate search. The user can specify the group in which to make that content visible, and can also place the content on a map by specifying a latitude and longitude coordinate (or by clicking directly on the map). Only a few of these items are mandatory during the upload process. Additional content such as forums, polls, blogs, events and disaster assessment reports can be created and shared within the site.
- **Image annotation capability:** SIFP permits users to annotate images as well as describe the annotation through free-form comments. A user can click on a particular

Figure 2. The ShareInfoForPeople Wiki pages

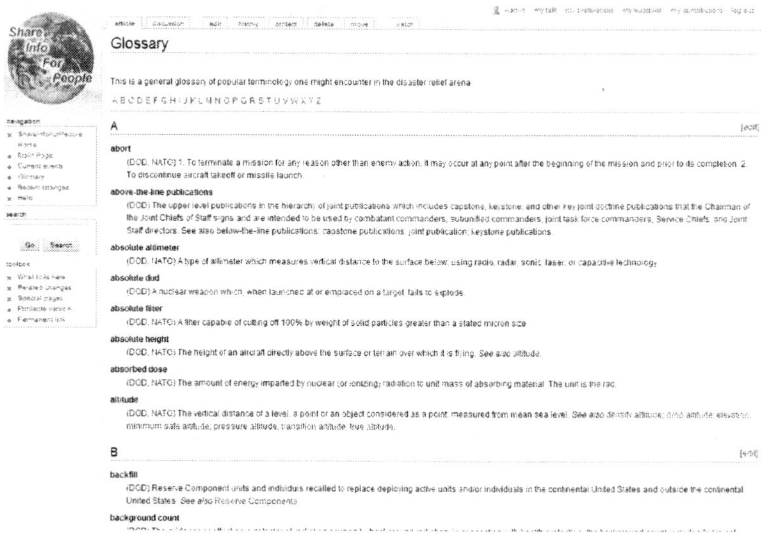

Figure 3. Screenshots showing how to upload audio content

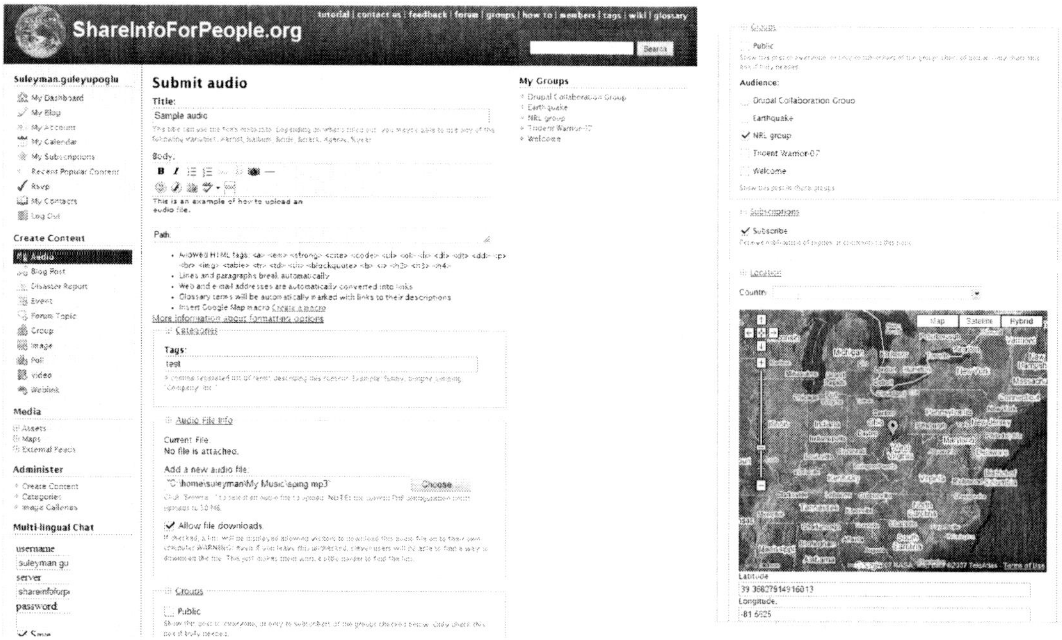

image that is stored within the site, which will subsequently reveal an interface as shown in Figure 4. This interface permits the user to add, edit, delete or hide notes. After the user clicks on “add note”, a note is created by drawing a bounding box over the area of interest on the image, which can be moved or resized by the user. These notes can contain a subject and free form comments (which can facilitate search) describing the area over which the note is overlaid. Furthermore if geospatial coordinates are specified for the

Figure 4. Image-annotation capability

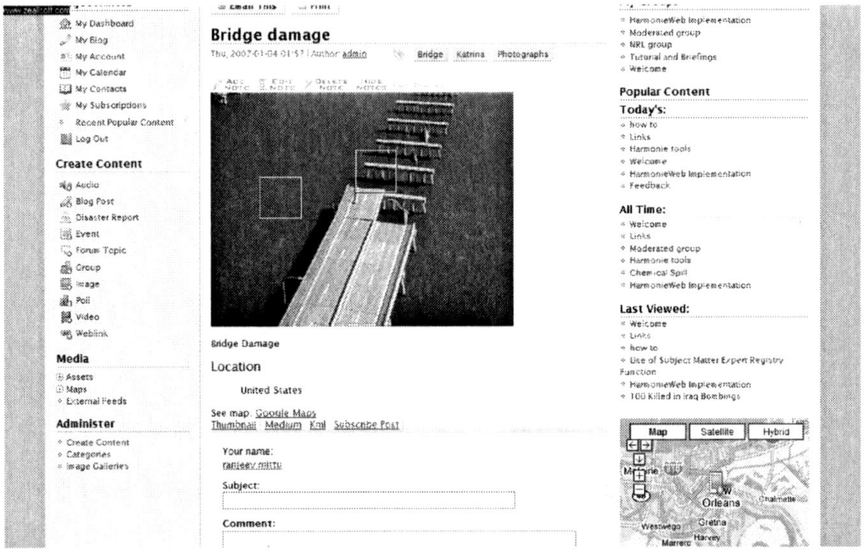

image, it can be displayed on corresponding map (seen at the lower right corner of Figure 4).

- **Content can be geo-tagged and displayed on a map:** The mapping capability leverages COTS solutions to maximize interoperability (e.g., Google Maps). Figure 5 shows the Google Map interface within SIFP. The content on the map can be clicked, and a pop-up area will appear that provides additional description.
- **Subscription-based Email Notifications:** All *subscribed-to* content generates email alerts. For example, one can enable email notifications through the user account settings. This will allow users to receive email notification when new content has been posted to a group. Furthermore, email notifications can also be provided when a user has replied to a particular discussion thread within a group.
- **Searchable Subject Matter Expert (SME) registry:** When users complete their personal information such as expertise or skill sets through the account preferences area, this information gets indexed. This will facilitate searching, so that users can easily find individuals who are able to offer specific services, support or other assistance during a crisis situation. People publish as much information about themselves as they are comfortable in sharing with other users of the site.
- **Multi-lingual Chat:** In addition to the typical asynchronous mode of communication associated with Web portals, the site offers a multi-lingual chat capability. Each user is assigned a Jabber ("What is Jabber", 2007) chat account that can be used with a locally installed application or through the web-based interface. This allows on-the-fly translation and communication between users who do not share a common language.
- **JPEG Metadata Discovery Tool (JMDT):** As a means of discovering additional information, SIFP interfaces with JMDT (2007). This allows users to run keyword queries to search for images indexed within JMDT. In addition, GeoRSS feeds can update the site users on any new image indexed by JMDT.

Figure 5. ShareInfoForPeople Map Display

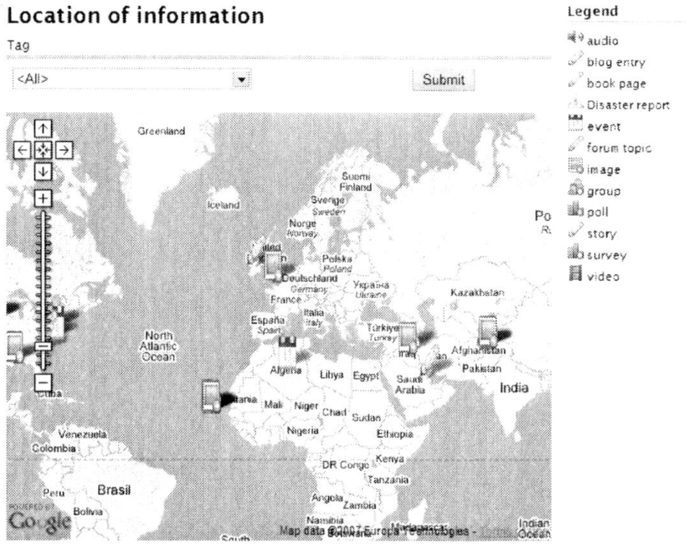

These feeds can be filtered by keywords to provide only relevant images.

The current implementation of SIFP provides the foundation on which to build more sophisticated capabilities, as specific requirements emerge from experimentation and other forms of user feedback. Furthermore, the philosophy of SIFP has been to use free and open software and standards to enable interoperability with other systems. We envision this approach will offer an increased opportunity to instantiate an enterprise-wide capability composed of loosely-coupled, agile systems that provide synergistic capabilities. The next section discusses our involvement in experimentation, followed by a discussion of near term development activities.

EXPERIMENTATION IN TRIDENT WARRIOR 2007

The SIFP portal underwent user experimentation during the Trident Warrior experimentation in March 2007. Trident Warrior is a yearly exercise designed to provide a venue for technology experimentation that supports the Navy's FORCEnet vision. The focus of the experimentation in March addressed Maritime Domain Awareness (MDA). However, there were additional and related scenarios as a complement to MDA.

The portal was used by various civil and military groups to coordinate and share information in response to a hypothetical scenario consisting of a bird-flu outbreak on the Cape Verde Islands off the coast of West Africa. The portal was used by various groups from the NGO medical communities as well as those from Commander, Second Fleet in response to the events in the scenario to discuss medical logistics issues, post information on status of activities, share images on local geography, etc. Through participation in this experiment, we were afforded an opportunity to collect valuable feedback from the civil and military communities in order to improve the future capabilities of our portal. Future experiments are also being planned in the Joint Forces Command's Noble Resolve experiment series which also focuses on civil-military information sharing.

NEAR TERM DEVELOPMENT ACTIVITIES

While the current implementation of SIFP provides a basic set of capabilities and functionality needed for collaboration and information sharing, there are still a number of areas to investigate and further prototype. Since our system is architected using the Drupal framework, we expect to leverage modules already being developed by the Drupal community, and modify those as needed to meet the requirements of our user community. In addition, three primary areas for future exploration include Social Network Analysis (SNA), OpenID and task management capabilities.

Social Network Analysis (SNA)

The current capabilities of SIFP provide a mechanism to search for users based on their skill set or expertise. The emerging concepts and ideas associated with SNA have the potential to add significant value within the information sharing environment. Research and tools from the SNA community may allow users to understand who the experts are in the SSTR community and to whom and how they are linked. As a simple example, social maps that depict connectivity between users in the context of their discussion threads, and ability to filter the content within a social map based on specific keywords are likely to provide the foundation to enable the community to identify service providers or those that may offer similar services or capabilities. The ability to rate individuals within the social network may also be an important aspect in building trust within the community of users. This is particularly important during pre-deployment prior to any crisis situation so that some level of trust and common understanding can be achieved. Furthermore, pre-deployment interactions can help in the development of concept of operations or doctrine to provide guidance during real life situations by helping people or organizations form the bonds of working together. One of the challenges, however, will be to effectively visualize such a network or efficiently filter through the various dimensions of information contained in the social network.

With the growing popularity of social networking websites as described earlier in this chapter, the Drupal community has also realized the potential benefits of applying social network analysis techniques and, therefore, has contributed the "Social Network Analysis Tool" module (http://drupal.org/project/sna) funded by the Google Summer of Code (http://code.google.com/soc) project (Figure 6). This early SNA tool has been incorporated within SIFP. This module is an initial implementation of several of the features described above but is not actively supported. The current features include finding the shortest path from one user to another, visualizing linkages between users, distribution of edges, and estimation of the clustering coefficient. The module is a first step in building more sophisticated capabilities. For instance, an example of additional capabilities that may be useful and worth exploring is the identification of relationships in the social network based on the various forms of posted information content, and subsequently computing the network statistics (e.g., eigenvector centrality, clustering coefficient) in aggregate form across the various dimensions of information space. This may lead to a more efficient mechanism for information discovery and exchange.

Identity and Site Access Management

The need to protect sites from malicious behavior and limit participation to those actually involved in responding to a crisis, in addition to the large number of sites that one needs to interface with to gather information in order to respond during complex emergencies drives users to have multiple accounts/passwords to accomplish their work. The ability to get timely access to new sites, as well as remember and manage passwords can be

Figure 6. Social Network Analysis Tool

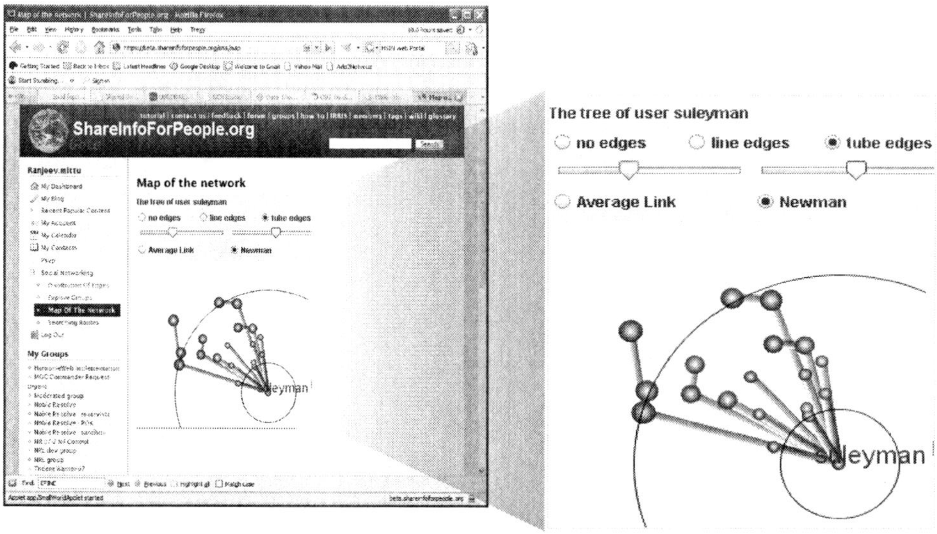

a significant obstacle in gaining access to critical information in real-life emergency situations. Having a single-sign-on access to a federation of sites that have agreed to common security criteria would improve tremendously the user's ability to discover and access the appropriate information. An ability to logon to the site using, for example, the OpenID (2007) standard will likely provide those advantages and benefits. This will enable users to log on once, and seamlessly navigate to and from sites that must be password protected by relying on the OpenID service provider to verify user identities.

Task Management

Task management is a key area that is currently being explored through the application of techniques to coordinate tasks across a large and diverse group of users such as first responders and those in command centers. While information sharing capabilities are a necessary first step, in a real disaster or crisis situation it is very likely that there will be thousands of groups containing hundreds of different discussion threads. The discussion threads are likely to evolve to contain descriptions of who can offer services such as shelter (service providers) or who may need shelter and where they are currently situated (service requestors). The biggest challenge will be to automatically extract such information from the discussion threads. Manual processes are likely to be slow and inefficient. Therefore, techniques to automatically extract these descriptions from the on-line discussions and translate those into representations that can be manipulated by tools will be required. This is an area where we expect to leverage other work from text or natural language processing. Capturing such information could also be achieved by users completing structured templates or forms, and it is likely that some combination of free text extraction and forms would be used or available to the users.

Once information can be extracted and translated into a more structured representation (or is already available in a structured form) then it becomes easier to manipulate and use that information to match service providers to service requestors. We expect to develop algorithms to provide the underlying capabilities to enable such a matching. As an example, in related research we have developed several approaches for the global

Figure 7. Task management

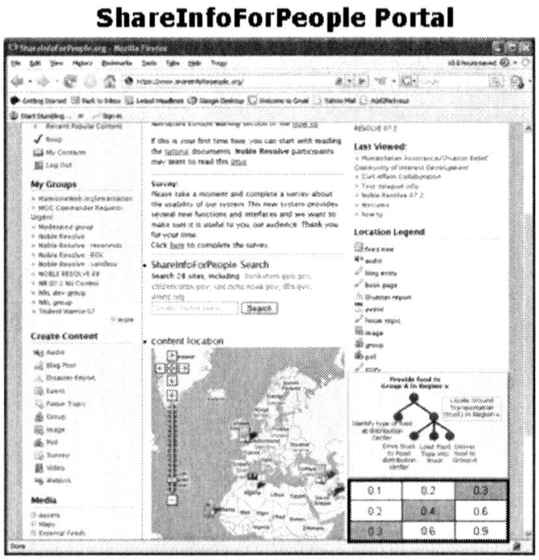

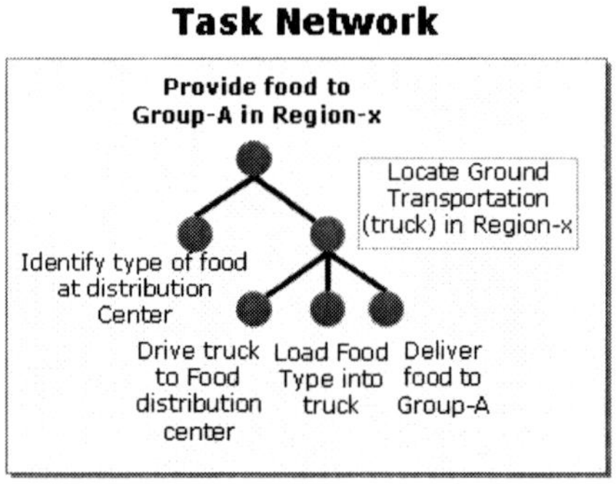

Assignment Matrix

Tasks	Performers NGO-1	NGO-2	NGO-3
Drive Truck	0.1	0.2	0.3
Load Food Truck	0.2	0.4	0.6
Deliver Food	0.3	0.6	0.9

optimal assignment of resources, such as people or organizations, to activities based on the *Hungarian Algorithm* (2007). These algorithms will be further enhanced to enable users or organizations to negotiate between the allocated assignments (e.g., accept, decline, etc).

The task delegation and management concept is depicted notionally in Figure 7 as a set of interactive tools in the portal environment. As potential service providers (i.e., task performers) are identified from the site's content using forms or text extraction, additional techniques will need to be developed and applied to transform and map the services that are being requested into appropriate tasks. The tasks may be hierarchical or peer-to-peer. For instance, hierarchical tasks may be appropriate for the military as protocols tend to be very structured and organized, while tasks for the civilian side may be peer-to-peer. However, the determination and selection of the appropriate task representation is best handled locally and there is no strict requirement that organizations use one representation or the other.

In order to automate task scheduling and assignment to a degree, the tasks and potential task performers will be organized into an assignment matrix, and the entries in the matrix will be numerical values that represent the cost for doing each of the tasks across each of the performers. The costs may be monetary or may be based on a more complex cost function and it is up the participants to agree upon and choose the appropriate cost model. The computation of the cost functions across performers may vary, so some normalization techniques may need to be applied. Once these costs are determined, the goal of the matching algorithm is to find a set of assignments between tasks and performers in the matrix that globally minimizes the total cost across all of the performers. Alternatively, numerical values for preference could be included instead of cost in the assignment matrix, and the objective would be to find a set of assignments that globally maximize the preference.

The task network provides a visualization of the tasks and would allow the user to modify the tasks or include new tasks, which would be subsequently reflected in the assignment matrix. The task network would also allow the specification of preconditions that need to be true before a task or subtask can be executed. The assignments that are calculated based on the algorithm would update the task network to show which performers have been assigned to various tasks. Lastly, the tools would support a negotiation process, to allow the performers to interact with each other to change their tasks assignments for various reasons that might not have been accurately reflected in the cost functions. Such a negotiation would be pursued until task equilibrium is reached. Once equilibrium is reached, the passing of appropriate messages using any method chosen by the user (e.g., instant messaging, SMS, e-mail, etc.) would permit the transmission of the assignments to potential responders for action or renegotiation.

TECHNICAL CHALLENGES

On one end of the spectrum, activities may be (re) allocated or negotiated at emergency command centers, which have a reliable communications backbone, and promulgated to those in the field. However, at the other end of the spectrum, where actual users are likely to negotiate activities with each other, the communications environment may be unreliable. These "disadvantaged users", however, may be able to access a mobile version of the SIFP portal, and maintain minimal functionality for uploading or creating content, annotating images, participating in discussion threads as well as negotiating activities between each other. However, given the chaotic and communications-challenged environments in which these types of systems will likely operate, it is conceivable that there may be users who get disconnected from each other in the field or with those at some remote command centers. There is a real challenge, from a network perspective, to ensure connectivity. This presents an opportunity to leverage research from the field of mobile wireless networking and intelligent agent-based applications to help alleviate these problems.

Mobile Ad-Hoc Network Environments

Critically damaged areas with degraded or no infrastructure (e.g., transportation, communication, etc) provide a challenge in SSTR operations. We focus our discussion on the communications infrastructure. The ability to coordinate a large and diverse group of first responders begins with the ability to communicate guidance or orders, while receiving situation reports from those in the field. The lack of a stable communications infrastructure will negatively impact the efforts of those that need to coordinate and share information. Recent technological advances in Mobile Ad-Hoc Networks (MANET) are key enablers in the deployment of net-centric cooperative multi-agent systems in disaster areas. MANET technology holds the promise of enabling communications between first responders when the local communications infrastructure is unusable. These networks support mobile entities, connected through a wireless network which supports discovery and self-organization through peer-to-peer message exchanges, leading to an increase in the robustness of the overall network. Figure 8 shows a comparison of MANET with high performance networks and the mainstream internet.

Although MANET technology is advancing to enable connectivity between mobile users, there still may be circumstances in which users get disconnected (examples such as distance between users or the affects of the environment on signal propagation). In order to improve the overall success of the deployment of MANET, new approaches and techniques that enable users to communicate to the maximum extent possible utilizing whatever network bandwidth is available will be needed.

The concept of "NETwork-Aware" Coordination and Adaptation (NETACA) is emerging, and is depicted in Figure 9. In such an approach, the users or application are aware of the state of the network, thereby allowing the applications to

Figure 8. Communications and networking issues

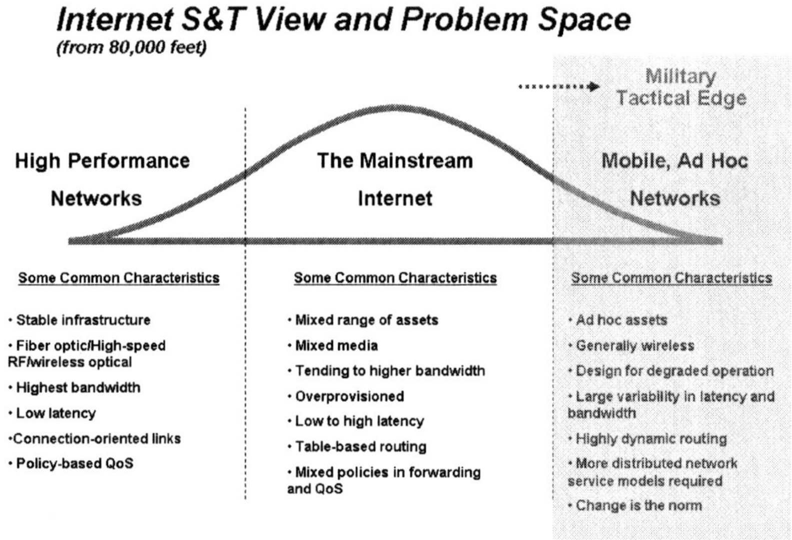

Figure 9. Network-aware coordination

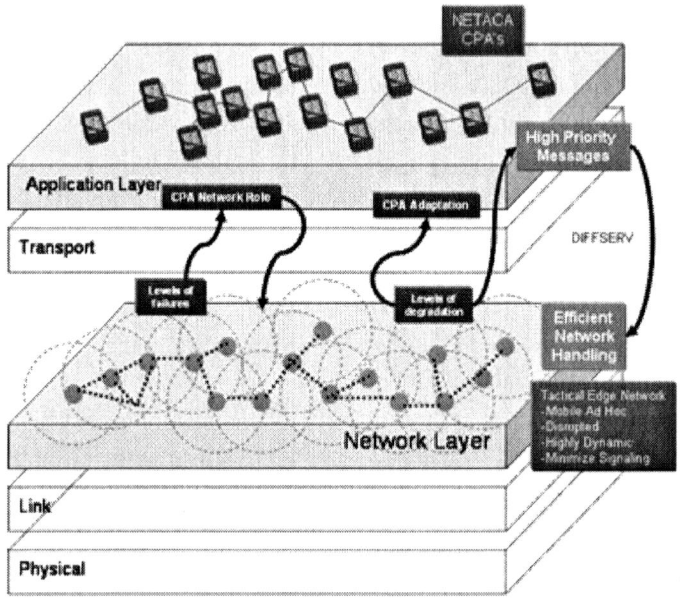

adapt in order to "work around" network constraints, while the network is aware of the state of the applications or mission needs in order to better handle traffic flows. Such cross-layer information exchange is important to enable a more robust communication strategy for the first responders in order to support their coordination activities. To the extent possible, coordination strategies also have to be robust against message loss and equipment failures.

A few of the research issues in network-aware coordination include defining measures for determining network congestion or other types of failures such as loss of connectivity within the network, in order to provide such measures and parameters to the application layer. The key challenges for the application layer include how to best utilize that information in order to adapt communication strategies (e.g., sharing images that are smaller in size, prioritizing certain information, or identifying certain nodes to act as communications relays). Such a feedback loop may be continuous, so that the network could support larger bandwidth exchanges as congestion is proactively alleviated in the network.

Distributed Planning and Multi-Agent Systems

Research may also be leveraged from the field of multiagent planning, replanning and scheduling between heterogeneous coordination entities. Distributed techniques such as automated plan merging and negotiation tools between responders may resolve local conflicts and issues without an entire replanning effort. While coordination tools have been directed towards assisting human-to-human collaboration, software agents can be introduced to reduce interdependence by providing fast and robust solutions bypassing delays in human response such as information gathering tasks. Specifically, coordination software agents may help incident commanders in directing large-scale teams and to gather information for situational awareness.

SUMMARY AND CONCLUSION

This chapter has described the SIFP portal to enable coordination and information sharing between the civil and military communities in support of SSTR operations. The architecture is based on the Drupal framework, an open source CMS being managed under General Public License (GPL). Furthermore, the philosophy of SIFP is to embrace free and open source software and standards as much as possible to enable future interoperability with other portals that provide similar or complementary capabilities. We have also briefly described how SIFP was used at the Trident Warrior 2007 experiment in order to gather user requirements.

The chapter has also described future development activities such as the planned leverage of modules already being developed by the Drupal community, which will be tailored to meet the needs of the SIFP users. In addition, technologies such as social maps will be investigated, as well as single-sign-on to enable users to seamlessly interact with other sites and portals. Because the latter technology is in its infancy, the challenge will be to find supporting hubs or portals that will be prepared to integrate with our portal using this capability. The ability to manage and negotiate tasks across the civil-military boundary are also worthy of exploration in order to improve coordination. Lastly, we have described some of the open challenges that remain such as network aware coordination, to enable SIFP to be robust in response to an increase in the number of mobile users during a real crisis situation.

REFERENCES

DHS (2007). U.S. Department of Homeland Security, *National Response Plan*. http://www.dhs.gov/xprepresp/publications, last accessed July 23, 2007.

U.S. DoD (2007). U.S. Department of Defense, *DoD Directive 3000.05-Military Support for Stability, Security, Transition, and Reconstruction (SSTR) Operations*, http://www.dtic.mil/whs/directives/corres/html/300005.htm, last accessed July 23, 2007.

Drupal (2007). http://www.drupal.org, last accessed July 23, 2007.

Hungarian Algorithm (2007). http://en.wikipedia.org/wiki/Hungarian_algorithm, last accessed July 23, 2007.

What is Jabber? (2007). http://www.jabber.org/about/overview.shtml, last accessed July 23, 2007

JMDT (2007). *JPEG Metadata Discovery Tool.* http://metadata.solers.com, last accessed July 23, 2007.

OpenID (2007). *Open ID – Free Secure Identity.* http://www.openid.org, last accessed July 23, 2007.

Rendleman, John (2007). Navy CIO approves open-source software use. *Government Computer News.* http://www.gcn.com/print/26_14/44462-1.html, last accessed July 23, 2007.

Ruby (2007). http://groups.drupal.org/node/2176, last accessed July 23, 2007.

ENDNOTE

1 The original version of this chapter, entitled "Unclassified Information Sharing and coordination in Security, Stabilization, Transition and reconstruction Efforts" by Ranjeev Mittu, Suleyman Guleyupoglu, Al Johnson, William Barlow, Michael Dowdy, and Sean McCarthy appeared in the International Journal of Electronic Government Research, Volume 4, Issue 1.

Chapter IV
A Comprehensive Framework Towards Information Sharing Between Government Agencies

Akhilesh Bajaj
The University of Tulsa, USA

Sudha Ram
The University of Arizona, USA

ABSTRACT

Recently, there has been increased interest in sharing digitized information between government agencies, with the goals of improving security, reducing costs, and offering better quality service to users of government services. The bulk of previous work in interagency information sharing has focused largely on the sharing of structured information among heterogeneous data sources, whereas government agencies need to share data with varying degrees of structure ranging from free text documents to relational data. In this work, we explore the different technologies available to share information. Specifically, our framework discusses the optional data storage mechanisms required to support a Service Oriented Architecture (SOA). We compare XML document, free text search engine, and relational database technologies and analyze the pros and cons of each approach. We explore these options along the dimensions of information definition, information storage, the access to this information, and finally the maintenance of shared information.

INTRODUCTION

The digitization of information has fundamentally altered the environment in which government agencies conduct their missions and deliver services. Recently, there has been considerable interest in exploring how emerging technologies can be used to promote information sharing among different governmental agencies (Bajaj & Ram, 2003). Such information sharing is desirable for

Copyright © 2009, IGI Global, distributing in print or electronic forms without written permission of IGI Global is prohibited.

several reasons. First, increased levels of security can be achieved if different government agencies share information. These effects can be felt in areas as diverse as global counter-terrorism (Goodman, 2001) and the war on drugs (Forsythe, 1990). Several recent articles, for example,(Dizard, 2002), strongly endorse the view that the sharing of intelligence information amongst different law enforcement agencies will enhance their ability to fulfill their required functions. Second, there has been a growing need to streamline inter-agency communication from a financial savings perspective. For example, Minahan (1995) shows how the lack of information sharing between different government organizations considerably hampered the establishment of an import-export database that would have streamlined the flow of goods into and out of the US and potentially saved billions of dollars. As pointed out in (Stampiglia, 1997), data sharing between health care agencies can also result in significant cost savings. Third, inter-agency information sharing results in offering fewer contact points for end-users of public services, thereby leading to more efficiencies in the delivery of these services to the end-users. For example, allowing agencies to share geographic information systems (GIS) information improves the quality of customer service afforded to end-users of these services (Hinton, 2001). Other common examples of activities that can benefit from information sharing include: the application for licenses and permits and the ability of aid workers to provide essential services.

Much work has been done in the area of the integration of *structured* information between heterogeneous databases (Hayne & Ram, 1990; Reddy, Prasad, Reddy, & Gupta, 1994; Larson, Navathe, & Elmasri, 1989; Batini, M.Lenzerini, & Navathe, 1986; Hearst, 1998; Ram & Park, 2004; Ram & Zhao, 2001). The two broad approaches in this area are a) the creation of *virtual* federated schemas for query integration (Zhao, 1997; Chiang, Lim, & Storey, 2000; Yan, Ng, & Lim, 2002) and b) the creation of actual *materialized* integrated warehouses for integration of both queries and updates (Vaduva & Dittrich, 2001; Hearst, 1998). While the area of structured information integration is relatively well researched, considerably less attention has been paid to the area of the integration of **unstructured** information (e.g., free text documents) between heterogeneous information sources. Recently, several researchers (Khare & Rifkin, 1997; Sneed, 2002; Glavinic, 2002) have pointed out the advantages of the XML (extensible markup language) standard as a means of adding varying degrees of structure to information, and as a standard for exchanging information over the Internet.

As pointed out in (Dizard, 2002; Minahan, 1995; Stampiglia, 1997), much of the information that government organizations share is at least somewhat unstructured. The primary contribution of this work is a comprehensive framework in the service oriented architecture (SOA) context, that explores three diverse technologies that exist to enable information sharing: digitized free text documents with related search engines, relational database management systems, and XML document repositories. We explore how SOA allows for a) the ability to provide varying degrees of structure to the information that needs to be shared, by sharing all information in the form of XML documents and b) the inclusion of various groups' viewpoints when determining what information should be shared and how long it should be shared. We also compare methods of *storing* and *accessing* the information under the different technologies. We compare the three technologies using well-understood criteria such as ease of information definition and storage, ease of information access, and ease of system maintenance.

The rest of this paper is organized as follows. In the second section, we discuss prior research in the area of information integration. In the third section, we describe SOA and data integration, and describe the potential conflicts that would need to be resolved in order to arrive at common data definitions. In the fourth section, we present alternative strategies for information definition as well as mechanisms for information storage and retrieval and compare these alternate methodologies. The fifth section contains the conclusion and future research directions.

PREVIOUS WORK

Much of the work in the area of information integration has focused primarily on integrating *structured* data from heterogeneous sources. Excellent surveys of data integration strategies are presented in (Batini et al. 1986; Hearst, 1998; Chiang et al. 2000). There have been primarily two broad strategies used to integrate structured data: a) retain the materialized data in the original stores, but use a unified federated schema to allow the querying of heterogeneous sources or b) actually materialize the combined data into a unified repository to allow for faster query response and also allow updates. Note that b) requires a unified federated schema also, but the schema in this case is not virtual, as in a).

Work in the area of unified federated schema generation is well established (e.g., Batini et al. 1986, has an excellent survey of early work in the area). Several issues have been addressed in this area. First, Blaha & Premerlani (1995) highlight the commonly observed errors in the design of the underlying heterogeneous relational databases, which often need to be resolved before integration is possible. Second, the issue of semantic inconsistencies between database object names (such as attribute names) has been widely addressed. Strategies to resolve semantic conflicts have ranged from utilizing expert systems (Hayne & Ram, 1990) to neural networks (Li & Clifton, 1994). Recently, several researchers have recognized this problem to be only partially automatable (Chiang et al. 2000). A recent solution to partially automate semantic resolution (Yan et al. 2002) utilizes synonym sets, with similarity measures. A set of potential unified federated schemas is generated using algorithms proposed in this work, and final selection of the unified schema is done manually. As an alternate solution, a schema coordination methodology is proposed (Zhao, 1997), where the minimal mapping is done only at the semantic level (rather than at the logical level) and overheads are lower than in traditional schema integration. However the tradeoff is that this methodology can only be used for querying, and the query resolution process is more complex than with a federated schema.

In the area of materialized data integration, a federated schema is required as a first step. However, there are several additional issues such as the retention of legacy systems, the coordination and refresh rate of information in the materialized warehouse, and the resolution of data quality issues (Chiang et al. 2000; Vaduva & Dittrich, 2001). Chiang et al. (2000) highlight possible problems that can arise when integrating actual data, after the schema integration has taken place. Examples of these problems include entity identification, relationship conflicts, and attribute value discrepancies between data from heterogeneous sources. Even though much work has been done in the area of the integration of structured information, Silberschatz, Stonebraker, & Ullman (1996) highlight it as one of the major research directions for database research in the future, and work continues in this area.

Unlike the integration of structured information, considerably less work has been done in the area of unstructured information integration. The domain of interest in our work is the sharing of information between government organizations. This raises several new issues. First, while traditional integration work has considered domains where there are heterogeneous structured database schemas, much of the information shared between government organizations tends be unstructured (Dizard, 2002; Minahan, 1995; Stampiglia, 1997). As such, structured data integration methodologies are insufficient to allow data sharing between government organizations. Second, since information in government organizations is often sensitive from a policy and privacy perspective, the actual definition of the information that needs to be shared is often performed by several parties. Thus, applicable methodologies in our domain of interest should allow various groups to flexibly structure information at varying degrees of structural rigidity. Thus, for example, certain information (such as names and addresses) can be structured down to the same detail as relational database columns are structured, while other information (such as descriptive comments, rules, and regulations) should be retained as free text.

Recently, several researchers have pointed out the advantages of the XML standard as a means of adding varying degrees of structure to information and as a standard for exchanging information in different domains. For example, Sneed (2002) points out how XML can be used to pass data between different software programs in batch or real-time mode. Glavinic (2002) describes how XML can be used to integrate applications within an organization. Next, we explore the different options for data integration within an SOA context, in order to allow the sharing of information between heterogeneous information sources. This is useful since information sources in a government organization can range in structure from repositories of text documents to relational databases.

DATA INTEGRATION OPTIONS

Core Design Criteria Behind SOA

The goal of SOA is to achieve loose coupling among interacting software programs. A service is a unit of work performed by a service-provider software for a consumer software (He, 2003; Pazoglou and Georgakopoulos, 2003). Services are invoked by consumers or client applications via messages that conform to descriptive schemas. Service descriptions are usually exported by providers to registries. Consumers contact a broker software that helps discover the service. SOA is different from standard client/server architecture in that a schema defines the functionality for each service and registries are available for lookup and binding without knowledge before the execution (Vetere and Lenzerini, 2005). One example of a service provider may be a relational DBMS that provides read and write access to its fields, with consumers using these services to actually make changes to the data. In SOA, the semantic layer is used to ensure that the data embedded within messages are interpreted in a similar fashion by consumers and producers. For example, attribute *customer_id* may be a unique identifier in one database, whereas *customer_name* and *customer_address* together may be the identifiers in another database. If a client supplies the *customer_id*, *name* and *address*, and asks for all the customer service conversations related to a certain customer, from two different databases, different web services may be needed to be run on the two databases.

As pointed out in (Vetere and Lenzerini, 2005), the semantic layer includes operational aspects that characterize the provider's service. It covers events and states, in effect the overall ontology of the application. Figure 1 shows a web services framework for data visibility, that utilizes an ontology layer for semantic resolution. A service request can be translated into appropriate requests based on each target database, based on the ontology layer.

Components of a Data Services Infrastructure

We consider three major components important to defining data services: a) an information definition component, b) an information storage component, and c) an information retrieval component.

Figure 1. Web Service Layers for data services, adapted from Ceccola (2006)

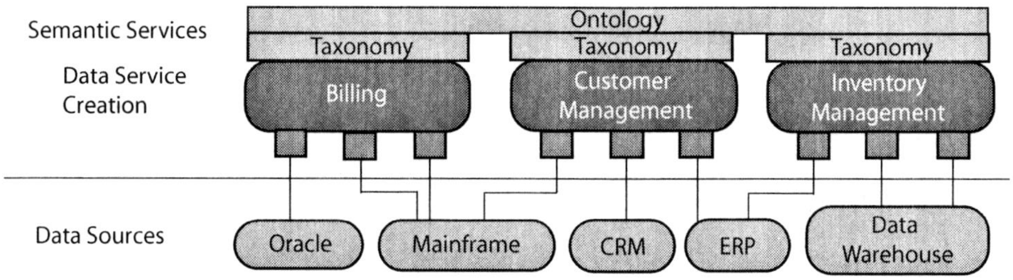

Information Definition

Several choices are available for specifying how the information to be shared among government agencies can be defined. We list three commonly used standards here. The first and most obvious is free text documents, where the name of the document along with other fields such as keywords can be used to structure information about the document. This standard includes documents in pure text markup languages such as HTML (hypertext markup language). Free text documents are appropriate when storing records of proceedings, hearings, rules and regulations, or memoranda. A significant portion of government information is in this format (Dizard, 2002; Minahan, 1995; Stampiglia, 1997).

The second standard is using a relational database structure (Codd, 1970), and it involves storing information in the form of relations, where each table has attributes and the tuples contain the actual data. Relations are linked to each other using common attributes that usually uniquely identify a tuple in one table. The relational model has well-accepted rules for eliminating data redundancy using the concept of data normalization. Most commercial database management systems (DBMSs) support this standard. This option is useful if the information to be shared consists of clearly defined attributes such as: the name, address, physical description and attributes describing immigration entries and exits for individuals.

The third standard for structuring information is the use of XML document type definitions (DTDs)[2]. XML DTDs allow information to be structured, using tags to differentiate elements and sub-elements. This is analogous to tables and columns in the relational model. Several researchers believe that XML will allow the Web to become more semantic in nature, such that software agents will be able to access information and understand what it means (Berners-Lee, Hendler, & Lassila, 2001). The main advantage of XML are a) it is a platform independent standard where the data does not need to be read by a proprietary product (as it would in a relational DBMS) and b) it allows for variable structuring of information, where some parts can be free text and others can be more structured.

When creating an XML DTD, the first step is for the players involved to create fields in each DTD, and also set limits on the amount of time information items are shared. For example, if a county's police and treasury departments wish to share information, they will first collaborate and create DTDs of the information items they wish to share. These DTDs will be discussed and agreed upon by the various players described earlier, until a settlement is reached. An example of two such DTDs is shown in Figure 2. The DTD in Figure 2a shows information that the police agrees to provide to the treasury department if the latter desires to verify if a specific business license applicant has been convicted of a felony. The information on each felon contains the name

Figure 2. Example of DTDs created to share information between Police and Treasurer

```
<?XML version = “1.0” ?>
<!DOCTYPE DOCUMENT [
<!ELEMENT DOCUMENT (FELON)*>
<!ELEMENT FELON (NAME, SSN, CONVICTIONS,EXPIRATIONDATE)>
<!ELEMENT NAME (LASTNAME,FIRSTNAME)>
<!ELEMENT LASTNAME (#PCDATA)>
<!ELEMENT FIRSTNAME (#PCDATA)>
<!ELEMENT SSN(#PCDATA)>
<!ELEMENT CONVICTIONS (CONVICTIONITEM)*>
<!ELEMENT CONVICTIONITEM (CONVICTIONDATE,CONVICTIONDESCRIPTION,
   CONVICTIONSENTENCE)>
<!ELEMENT CONVICTIONDATE (#PCDATA)>
<!ELEMENT CONVICTIONDESCRIPTION (#PCDATA)>
<!ELEMENT CONVICTIONSENTENCE (#PCDATA)>
<!ELEMENT EXPIRATIONDATE (#PCDATA)>
]>
```

a) DTD of Information Shared from Police to Treasurer.

```
<?XML version = “1.0” ?>
<!DOCTYPE DOCUMENT [
<!ELEMENT DOCUMENT (APPLICANT)*>
<!ELEMENT FELON (NAME, SSN, APPLICATIONS,EXPIRATIONDATE)>
<!ELEMENT NAME (LASTNAME,FIRSTNAME)>
<!ELEMENT LASTNAME (#PCDATA)>
<!ELEMENT FIRSTNAME (#PCDATA)>
<!ELEMENT SSN(#PCDATA)>
<!ELEMENT APPLICATIONS (APPLICATIONITEM)*>
<!ELEMENT APPLICATIONITEM (APPLICATIONDATE,APPLICATIONDESCRIPTION,
   APPLICATIONDECISION)>
<!ELEMENT APPLICATIONDATE (#PCDATA)>
<!ELEMENT APPLICATIONDESCRIPTION (#PCDATA)>
<!ELEMENT APPLICATIONSENTENCE (#PCDATA)>
<!ELEMENT EXPIRATIONDATE (#PCDATA)>
]>
```

b) DTD of Information Shared from Treasurer to Police

(first and last), the social security number, a list of convictions, and an expiry date. The convictions list has repeatable conviction items. PCDATA stands for parsed character data (text) while the * symbol indicates that the item can be repeated. The DTD in figure 2b is information that the treasury department agrees to share with the police to notify them of business applications that are being processed. The *expiration date* tag allows a software program to delete elements whose expiration date has passed.

Data and Schema Conflict Resolution Strategies

A major impediment to creating DTDs that span agencies, as well as populating the actual XML pages that contain data gathered from databases in different agencies, is the resolution of conflicts that exist between the data and data-definitions that resides in the different databases. In this section, we identify several types of conflicts that can occur.

Based on work presented in (Ram, Park et al. 1999), we divide conflicts into two main types:

data-level and *schema-level*. Data-level conflicts are due to differences in data domain and storage decisions, while schema-level conflicts occur because of differences at the logical definition (schema) level. Next, we describe the different sub-types of these conflicts.

a. *Data-Level Conflicts*

1. **Value conflicts:** These occur because the same data values (for the same attributes) can have different meanings that are context dependent. For example, the value "excellent" in one context for a convict's rating may mean the convict did nothing negative, while in another database, the value "excellent" may mean they were proactive in good behavior.
2. **Representation Conflicts:** These arise when similar real-world objects are described using different data types or format representations. For example, the *expiration date* for a conviction record may have different formats in different databases.
3. **Unit Conflicts:** These are due to different units being used to represent the same data. For example, if data on the length of parole of a felon was being shared, it could be weeks in one database, and months in another.
4. **Precision Conflicts:** These occur when data is represented using different scales or granularities. For example, the population of prisoners may be stored in tens in one database, and in hundreds in another. Similarly, the satisfaction rating of parole boards with a prisoner may be captured using a 3 point scale in one database and a 5 point scale in another, leading to different granularities of information.

b. *Schema-Level Conflicts*

1. **Naming Conflicts:** These are due to assignment of different labels for schema objects such as attributes, entity sets, and relationships sets. Homonyms occur when the same word is used for two different meanings in different databases. For example, "Inspector" in the police database versus "inspector" in the treasury database. Synonyms are two or more words, used to describe the same concept. For example, "prisoner" in one database and "inmate" in another database. Homonyms and synonyms can also occur at the entity and relationship levels.
2. **Primary Key Conflicts:** These arise when the same set of objects is identified using different sets of properties across databases. For example, a prisoner may be identified by his social security number in one database, and his prison_id in another database.
3. **Generalization Conflicts:** These occur when different generalization choices are made across databases. For example, one database may have an entity set called "prisoners" that includes all prisoners. Another database may have three different entity sub-classes called "maximum security prisoners", "medium security prisoners", and "minimum security prisoners".
4. **Schematic Discrepancies:** These occur when a different schema is used to represent the same information. For example, a citizen's application for a business license can be either an entity by itself, or a relationship between the applicants entity set and the business_license_types entity set. In other words, the same information can be structured differently across databases, based on the schema designs.

The different types of conflicts described need to be resolved as part of the information definition phase. Two options exist to accomplish this. First, recent work on automated conflict resolution such as in (Ram and Park 2004) can be used to automate a large portion of conflict resolution. Second, a one-time manual walk-through can be used to understand the conflicts between different databases, after which translation programs can be written so that the databases deliver information in the form of XML pages conforming to the DTDs that are finalized in the information definition phase.

Information Storage

Based on the three alternate standards of information definition described, there are alternate methods of storing the structured information as well. If the information is structured in the form of free text or HTML files, then storage on a file server (usually a component of the operating system) is a first alternative. Another option is third party document management tools such as Documentum (www.documentum.com), that facilitate the creation and management of these pages. Most of these systems use the existing file system to store the applications, but store additional information that makes it easier to retrieve the files. Finally, it is possible to use object-relational features of current commercial DBMSs to store and retrieve these files.

For information stored in the form of free text, search engines, for example, Google and AltaVista, offer one method of accessing information. This is similar to a search on the Internet, except that instead of searching across numerous web sites, the search in our case is on a repository of free text or HTML documents. A second method is to use directory based search engines such as Yahoo (www.yahoo.com). If a third party application is used for storage, the search capabilities are limited to the capabilities of the tools offered by that application. Finally, if object-relational DBMSs are used, the ease of access depends on extensions to the structured query language supported by the DBMS.

If the information is structured in a relational database, a commercial DBMS can be used to store this information. Commercial relational DBMSs are a tested technology that allow for concurrent access by multiple users. They provide good throughput, recovery and reliability for most applications. The structured query language (SQL) standard allows easy access to information. Results can be served on the Internet using a number of available technologies such as active server pages (ASP) or JSP.

If the information is structured in XML, it consists of text files, though the text is now structured with tags. Storage alternatives for XML files are similar to free text, that is, file systems, third party applications, and object relational DBMSs. However, there is an important difference between free text and XML formats, when accessing the information. For XML files, the methodology of using conventional search engines with key word searches either breaks down, or at the very least, negates the whole purpose of structuring the information as an XML document. Similarly, directory based search engines do not allow the search and retrieval of portions of XML pages. To overcome these problems, two standards have been proposed by the WWW consortium (www.w3c.org) to search XML files. These are the XPATH standard, and the more recent XQUERY standard, which is still evolving. As of now, these standards allow the querying of a single XML page, not a repository of XML pages.

In order to create an XML repository, first, a one-time effort is required to create reports from the local databases or document repositories (of the police and the treasury) in the form of XML pages. Since most commercial DBMSs currently offer the ability to create scheduled reports in XML, this task is possible without adding to existing

IS systems and personnel. Next, a repository is created to store these pages. This repository is a directory structure with an IP (internet protocol) address that consists of interlinked HTML and/or XML pages. Finally, procedures are implemented to affect the periodic transfer of pages to this repository, and purging of these pages from the repository.

Figure 3 summarizes the different methods of information storage (in each column), and the alternate methods available to access them (along the rows).

Information Retrieval

Information retrieval of free text documents can be performed with text search engines such as www.google.com or www.yahoo.com. Information stored in relational databases can be retrieved using SQL. For XML document repositories, one example of a search agent is XSAR (XML search agent for information retrieval) that searches for information from the repository (Bajaj, Tanabe, & Wang, 2002; Bajaj and Ram, 2003). XSAR can dynamically query large information repositories of XML documents. It is **DTD independent**, so the same agent can be used to query documents consisting of multiple DTDs. XSAR is also a dynamic agent, in that it does not use an underlying database or directory scheme of information on pages. Rather, it dynamically queries the repository on behalf of a user. There is no requirement for the repository site to have any special software or hardware; the only assumption is that it is a site that contains a mixture of HTML and XML pages.

XSAR does require the user to be aware of the underlying DTD, insofar as being aware of which fields the user needs to search. Essentially, XSAR reformulates the query as an XQL expression, and then launches a spider that traverses the information repository and executes the XQL query against each XML page found in the repository. Figure 4 shows the operational flow of XSAR.

Choice of XML Query Language

Currently, there is no standard query language for XML designated by the WWW Consortium (W3C). However, several query languages for XML documents have already been proposed, for example, *XQL*, *XML-QL*, and *Quilt* (all accessible via http://www.w3c.org). XQL was utilized when implementing XSAR because a) its grammar is based on *Xpath*, which has already been standardized by W3C and b) application programming interfaces (API) for XQL are available in Java.

Figure 3. Information formats and their possible methods of search

Information Format →	Free text /HTML Pages	Relational Alphanumeric Data	XML Pages
Search Mechanisms ↓			
Search Engines using Key Words	X	NA	NA
Directory Based Search Engines	X	NA	NA
Third party applications for storing and searching pages	X	NA	X
Structured Query Language	NA	X	NA
XPATH, Xquery for single XML pages	NA	NA	X

Figure 4. Operational flow of XSAR

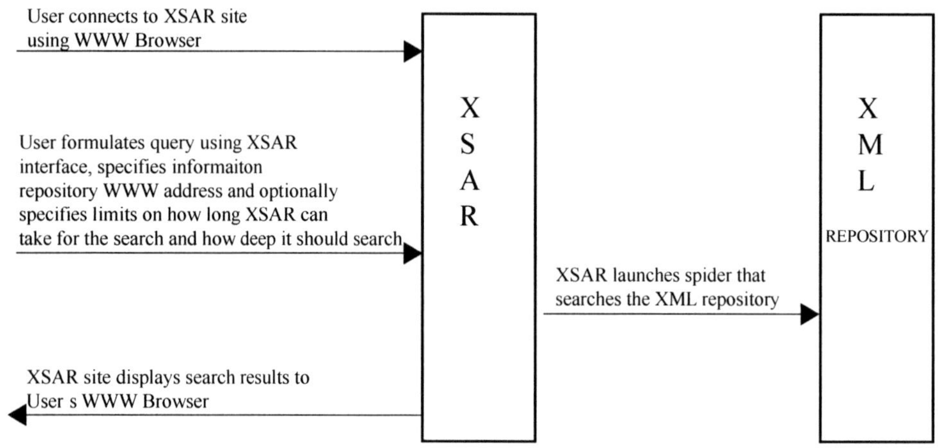

COMPARING THE POTENTIAL METHODOLOGIES

Ease of Information Definition and Storage

In the *free text* methodology, unstructured information such as agency documents can be identified and shared. However, it is not possible to define specific, structured information that can be shared. Since most agencies have a collection of documents, the information definition step will in general be the easiest in this phase, and consist of a relatively simple identification of documents that can be shared, without any in-depth study of the actual data elements in the agencies. In the *database schema* methodology, the schema of each government agency will have to be prepared for review by the different parties. Different data items can then be identified for sharing. A similar process can be followed for XML document repositories, where the data elements will need to be defined and then a DTD created. Thus, both the *database schema* methodology and the XML repository methodology require an examination of the actual data elements used by the agencies.

From the storage standpoint, the *free text* methodology requires that the pages be stored on a server's file system. A coordination mechanism is needed in place so that changes to documents in the organizations' internal repositories are reflected in the shared repository. In the *database schema* methodology there is no need for additional storage of data, since information is obtained *dynamically* from the underlying databases within each organization. With XML repositories, storage is similar to the *free text* methodology, with a coordination mechanism to ensure that the pages are refreshed periodically to reflect the structured information within the internal databases. Thus, the *database schema* methodology requires less implementation effort from a storage perspective, than with *free text* and XML repositories.

From this discussion, in general, we see that the *free text* methodology offers the easiest data definition while the *database schema* methodology offers the easiest information storage.

Ease Of Information Access

Web search engines that search files on different web sites have their origin in the information retrieval (IR) systems developed during the last 50 years. IR methods include Boolean search methods, vector space methods, probabilistic methods, and clustering methods (Belkin & Croft, 1987). All these methods are aimed at finding documents relevant for a given query. For evaluating such systems, *recall* (ratio of the number of relevant retrieved documents to the total number of available relevant documents) and *precision* (ratio of the number of relevant retrieved documents to the number of total retrieved documents) are the most commonly used measures (Billsus & Pazzani, 1998). Finally, *response time* (time taken for the user to get the information she desires) has been found to be a useful metric (Anderson, Bajaj, & Gorr, 2002).

Furthermore, the performance of each search tool is directly influenced by the user's ability to narrowly define the nature of the query, for example, in the form of precise key-word strings or correct specification of a search condition. For the sake of the discussion below, we assume that the search specificity is held constant.

Recall

For the *free text* methodology, recall is the ratio of the number of pages identified correctly as matching to the total number that should have been identified as matching. This ratio is clearly dependent on the algorithms used to perform the matching, with most current algorithms based on weighted indices. In general the ratio will be less than one. Also, as the number of pages increases, all else being equal, the recall drops.

For the *database schema* methodology, the recall of a search is determined by the accuracy of translation of the user's query into the underlying database language (usually SQL) query. If the query translation is accurate, and the underlying database is searched completely, the recall will be one.

For agents like XSAR that search XML repositories, the recall is dependent on the accuracy of translation of the user query into the underlying XML query language, and the existence of a path from the specified starting point to all the XML pages that exist in the repository. For a well-connected repository where every page is reachable from a starting node, the recall will be one. From this discussion, we can see that in general, the recall for the free text methodology would be lower than for the other two methodologies.

Precision

For the *free text* methodology, precision is determined by a) the features offered to the user to specify a query to a desired level of precision (e.g., concatenated strings, wild card characters, boolean operators), b) a the extent to which precision can be sacrificed for response time, and c) the extent of information captured in the underlying search engine database about the real pages. All else being equal, a search engine that offers more options for searching should have greater precision, as compared to one where response time is secondary to precision. For c), a search engine that captures only the title of each page will have less precision than one that captures the title and the META tags of each page. As the number of pages increases, all else being equal, the precision drops.

When using the *database schema* methodology, the precision of an information repository that uses an underlying database depends on a) the features provided by the user query interface and b) the maximum precision allowed by the underlying query language of the database. If a relational database is used, then the underlying query language is SQL, which provides excellent precision.

If an agent like XSAR is utilized, the query interface fully supports XQL. Thus, the precision of XSAR is identical to the precision of XQL, which supports *XPath* (http://www.w3c.org), the W3C standard for precision.

Response Time[3]

The response time in the *free text* methodology depends on: a) the algorithm used to perform the key word match with the database that has information on each page in the repository and b) the extent to which the designers are willing to sacrifice precision for response time.

When using the *database schema* methodology, the response time depends on the complexity of the specified query and the extent to which the database is optimized for that query. Thus, for a relational database, a range query on non-indexed attributes with several joins is likely to take significantly more time than a simple SELECT query. Thus, these repositories would need a database administrator to keep track of most frequent queries, and ensure proper tuning access optimizations.

For agents that search XML repositories, response time is determined by the time taken by the agent to crawl through the target repository. This depends on exogenous factors such as network speed, performance of the web server of the target repository, and the size of the target repository. In designing XSAR, we used three endogenous strategies to minimize this time, for given values of exogenous factors: a) a multi-threaded agent, b) a proxy server for caching, and c) providing the user the ability to specify response time threshold. We next describe each of these strategies.

As the agent program fetches new pages from the target repository, it spawns threads to parse these fetched pages. HTML pages are only parsed for links, while XML pages are parsed and searched for the query. One design trade-off here is that spawning a new thread is expensive if the pages being parsed and/or searched are small, while increasing the number of threads pays off is the size of each page in the repository increases.

Finally, XSAR allows the user to set the threshold response time and maximum depth to which the agent should search the target repository. This allows XSAR to be used by different classes of users, for example, one class of users may want to search large repositories comprehensively and leave the agent running, say, overnight, while another class of users may want quicker responses for searches where the maximum depth of the search is set to a finite number.

We tested the performance of XSAR using three experiments described in Appendix 1. In our experiments, a multi-threaded program had the maximum impact in reducing response time, with a proxy cache playing a secondary role. The results (see Appendix 1) indicate that XSAR is clearly slower than the other mechanisms available for searching, which is to be expected, since it searches a target repository dynamically. XSAR trades off faster response time for the ability to search a changing information repository in real time.

Figure 5 summarizes the performance comparison between search mechanisms for the three different methodologies.

Figure 5. Comparison of methods for information access

Metrics → **Methods** ↓	**Recall**	**Precision**	**Response Time**
Free Text Method	Low	Low	Fast
Database Schema Method	100%	High	Fast
XML repositories	100%	High	Slow

Ease Of System Maintenance

In the *free text* methodology, the major maintenance issues include the upkeep of the document repository, the search engine and the coordination software required to maintain consistency between the internal pages within the organization, and the pages in the information repository. In the *database schema* methodology, there is a need to track changes to the underlying database schema. Whenever these changes to the schema occur, appropriate changes are needed in the application code that directly queries the database. Furthermore, the organizations have to *reveal their schemas* to the team maintaining the application code in the system used for information sharing. With XML document repositories, there is an added layer of transparency, since each organization promises to deliver information in the form of XML pages conforming to the DTDs. This allows each organization to *hide* their internal database schemas and to make schema changes independent of the information sharing process, as long as each organization delivers its required pages. The maintenance issues for the IAIS information sharing system include refreshing pages from each organization and maintenance of the search agent (such as XSAR).

From the above discussion, we can see that in general the database schema method requires the most maintenance, while the free text and IAIS methods require less maintenance.

The results of our comparison of these three methodologies are shown in Figure 6.

From Figure 6, it is clear that the main advantages of using XML documents over the *free text* methodology are a) the ability to share structured information and b) the ability to search a repository dynamically with greater precision and recall. The main advantages of IAIS over the *database schema* methodology are a) the former is in general easier to maintain and precludes the need for making database schemas available across organizations, because of the increased layer of indirection provided by DTDs and b) the ability to share unstructured as well as structured information in IAIS. The tradeoff is that queries on XML document repositories require more response time than in the other methodologies.

Figure 6. Overall comparison results for the three methods

Metrics → **Methods↓**	**Information Definition**	**Information Storage**	**Information Access**	**Information Maintenance**
Free Text Method	Easy but structured information cannot be defined	Difficult	Low recall and precision, fast response	Easy
Database Schema Method	Difficult but structured information can be defined %	Easy	High recall and precision, fast response	Difficult. Subsets of data schemas need to be made visible across organizations.
XML Document Repository	Difficult but structured information can be defined	Difficult	High recall and precision, slow response	Easy

CONCLUSION AND FUTURE RESEARCH

This chapter proposed a comprehensive framework consisting of three different data integration options in an SOA context, to facilitate sharing of information among government agencies. Information in this domain tends to be both structured and unstructured. This article analyzed the pros and cons of each of the three options, so as to enable decision makers to make better choices when developing inter-agency information sharing plans.

Recently, there has been significantly increased activity in deploying XML in the government. The portal Web site accessible at http://xml.gov, indicates various XML registries that are in progress. The Global Justice XML Data Model (Global JXDM), accessible at http://www.IACPtechnology.org, is one example of interagency cooperation between the US Department of Justice, US Attorney, and the American Association of Motor Vehicle Administrators. In this dictionary, common data definitions are used to support information sharing among prosecutors, law enforcement, courts, and related private and public bodies. As another example, the enactment of the Health Insurance Portability and Accountability Act (HIPAA) of 1996 has also led to a strong motivation to develop a healthcare XML standard.

A new area of research that is emerging is the automatic generation of glossaries from government free text repositories, leading to an ontology layer, as discussed in this article. For example, as pointed out in (Reed, 2003) recent research has resulted in a crawler that sifts through government Web pages that are in free text format and attempts to construct a glossary. Once the glossary is built, the pages are parsed into a large common representation format in XML.

For future work, we plan on a) prototyping a tool to facilitate the information definition aspect by allowing different parties to collaborate on producing XML DTDs and b) validating the usefulness of our framework in real world case studies of inter-agency information sharing, and c) exploring ways to incorporate automated conflict resolution into our framework, to assist agencies in the critical phase of information definition.

REFERENCES

Bajaj, A. and Ram, S. (2003). IAIS: A methodology to enable inter-agency information sharing in e-government. *Journal of Database Management, 14*(4), 59-80.

Anderson, B. B., Bajaj, A., & Gorr, W. (2002). An estimation of the relative effects of external software quality factors on senior is managers' evaluation of computing architectures. *Journal of Systems and Software, 61*(1), 59-75.

Bajaj, A., Tanabe, H., & Wang, C.-C. (2002). *XSAR: XML based search agent for information retrieval.* Paper presented at the AMerica's Conference on Information Systems, AMCIS, Dallas, TX.

Batini, C., M.Lenzerini, & Navathe, S. B. (1986). A comparative analysis of methodologies for database schema integration. *ACM Computing Surveys, 18*(4), 323-364.

Belkin, N. J., & Croft, W. B. (1987). Retrieval techniques. *Annual Review of Information Science and Technology, 22*, 109-145.

Berners-Lee, T., Hendler, J., & Lassila, O. (2001). The Semantic Web. *Scientific American, September.*

Billsus, D., & Pazzani, M. (1998). *Learning collaborative information filters.* Paper presented at the Machine Learning: Proceedings of the Fifteenth International Conference.

Blaha, M. R., & Premerlani, W. J. (1995). *Observed idosyncrasies of relational database designs.* Paper presented at the Second Working Conference on Reverse Engineering, Toronto, Canada.

Ceccola, S. (2006). Defining service oriented architecture and examining semantic SOA. Web Report Accessed at: colab.cim3.net/file/work/SOACoP/2006_05_2324/SCeccola205242006.ppt, 2006.

Chiang, R. H. L., Lim, E.-P., & Storey, V. C. (2000). A framework for acquiring domain semantics and knowledge for database integration. *The DATA BASE for Advances in Information Systems, 31*(2), 46-62.

Codd, E. F. (1970). A relational model for large shared databanks. *Communications of the ACM, 13*, 377-387.

Dizard, W. P. (2002). White House promotes data sharing. *Government Computer News, 21*(25), 12.

Foley, M., & McCulley, M. (1998). *JFC unleashed.* SAMS Publishing.

Forsythe, J. (1990). New weapons in drug wars. *Information Week, 278*, 26-30.

Gelman, R. S. (1999). Confidentiality of social work records in the computer age. *Social Work, 44*(3), 243-252.

Glavinic, V. (2002). *Introducing XML to integrate applications within a company.* Paper presented at the 24th International Conference on Information Technology Interfaces, Zagreb, Croatia.

Goodman, M. A. (2001). CIA: The need for reform. *Foreign Policy in Focus, Special Report 13 F 2001*, 1-8.

Hayne, S., & Ram, S. (1990). *Multi-user view integration system (muvis)-an expert system for view integration.* Paper presented at the IEEE International Conference on Data Engineering (ICDE).

He, H. (2003). *What is service oriented architecture?* Retrieved from http://www.xml.com/pub/a/ws/2003/09/30/soa.html, 2006.

Hearst, M. (1998). Trends and controversies: information integration. *IEEE Intelligent Systems Journal* (Sept-Oct), 12-24.

Hinton, C. (2001). *Seven keys to a successful enterprise GIS* (Report IQ Service Report, vol. 33, no. 3). Washington, DC: International City/County Management Association.

Hunter, C. D. (2002). Political privacy and online politics: How e-campaigning threatens voter privacy. *First Monday, 2*(4).

Khare, R., & Rifkin, A. (1997). XML: A door to automated web applications. *IEEE Internet Computing, 1*(4), 78-87.

Larson, J. A., Navathe, S. B., & Elmasri, R. (1989). A theory of attribute equivalence in databases with application to schema integration. *IEEE Transactions on Software Engineering, 15*(4), 449-463.

Li, W.-S., & Clifton, C. (1994). *Semantic integration in heterogeneous databases using neural networks.* Paper presented at the International Conference on Very Large Databases (VLDB).

Minahan, T. (1995). Lack of interoperability delays import-export database. *Government and Computer News, 14*(10), 72.

Papazoglou, M.P, & Georgakopoulos, D. Service oriented computing. *Communications of the ACM, 46*(10), 25-28.

Ram, S., & Park, J. (2004). Semantic conflict resolution ontology (SCROL): An ontology for detecting and resolving data and schema-level semantic conflicts. *IEEE Transactions on Knowledge and Data Engineering, 16*(2), 189-202.

Ram, S., Park, J., Kim, K. and Hwang, Y. (1999). *A comprehensive framework for classifying data- and schema-level semantic conflicts in geographic and non-geographic databases.* Ninth Workshop On Information Technologies And Systems (WITS), Dallas, TX.

Ram, S., & Zhao, H. (2001). *Detecting both schema-level and instance level correspondences for the integration of e-catalogs.* Paper presented at the Workshop on Information Technology and Systems (WITS).

Raul, C. A. (2002). *Privacy and the digital state: balancing public information and personal privacy.* Norwell, MA: Kluwer Academic Publishers.

Reddy, M. P., Prasad, B. E., Reddy, P. G., & Gupta, A. (1994). A methodology for integration of heterogeneous databases. *IEEE Transactions on Knowledge and Data Engineering, 6*(6), 920-933.

Reed, M. (2003). *Bridging the data gap.* Retrieved from http://www.digitalgovernment.org/news/stories/2002/1102/1102_dgrc_reed.jsp, 2006.

Rights., U. S. H. C. o. t. J. S. o. C. a. C. (1984). *Domestic security measures relating to terrorism: Hearings* (Congressional Hearings 98th Cong., 2nd sess.; Serial no. 51). Washington, DC: US Congress.

Silberschatz, A., Stonebraker, M., & Ullman, J. (1996). Database research: Achievements and opportunities into the 21st Century. *SIGMOD Record, 25*(1), 52-63.

Sneed, H. M. (2002). *Using XML to integrate exisitng software systems into the web.* Paper presented at the 26th Annual International Computer Software and Applications Conference, Los Alamitos, CA.

Stampiglia, T. (1997). Converging technologies and increased productivity. *Health Management Technology, 18*(7), 66.

Vaduva, A., & Dittrich, K. R. (2001). *Metadata Management For Data Warehousing: Between Vision and Reality.* Paper presented at the International Database Engineering and Applications Symposium (IDEAS), Grenoble, France.

Vetere, G. and Lenzerini, M. (2005). Models for Semantic Interoperability in Service-Oriented Architectures. *IBM Systems Journal, 44*(4), 887-904.

Yan, G., Ng, W. K., & Lim, E.-P. (2002). Product Schema Integration for Electronic Commerce-A Synonym Comparison Approach. *IEEE Transactions on Knowledge and Data Engineering, 14*(3), 583-598.

Zhao, J. L. (1997). Schema Coordination in Federated Database Management: A Comparison with Schema Integration. *Decision Support Systems, 20*, 243-257.

ENDNOTES

1. Xerces is available at xml.apache.org, the GMD-IPSI XQl engine is available at: xml.darmstadt.gmd.de/xql/ and tomcat is available at jakarta.apache.org.
2. While alternatives to DTDs such as XML schemas (www.xml.org) do exist, this article focuses on XML DTDs since they are the predominant standard for structuring data on the World Wide Web.
3. This chapter assumes a given size of the universe of pages.

APPENDIX A

Performance Results of Test Cases

This article presents the results of three test cases that illustrate the performance of XSAR.

The first case was a repository created inside the same network as XSAR. Therefore, the target Web site and the agent server were connected by Ethernet, 10Mbps. The contents of the repository were small HTML files and XML files, less than 4Kbytes each.

The second case was a real XML repository (http://www.xml-cml.org/), which has the conclusive resource for Chemical Markup Language which is used to exchange chemical information and data via the Internet.

The third case was also a real-world case: the Dublin Core Metadata site (http://purl.org/dc/) which is a specification for describing library materials.

Table A1-1 shows the search time for the cases mentioned. The search time results clearly depend on exogenous variables like network conditions, PC hardware specifications, and load status. In order to eliminate at least some variation in these factors, we tested each case five times, and present the mean values in Table 1.

Table A1-1.Comparison among experiment cases

	Local experimental Environment	CML	Dublin Core
Number / Average size of HTML	16 / 458 [bytes]	1 / 10490 [bytes]	34 / 16966 [bytes]
Number / Average size of XML	16 / 2756 [bytes]	173 / 10314 [bytes]	27 / 974 [bytes]
Direct access	2545[ms]	19291[ms]	44637[ms]
Via cache server	1772[ms]	14577[ms]	40305[ms]
Ratio of (w/ Cache) / (w/o Cache)	0.696	0.756	0.903

This work was previously published in the International Journal of Electronic Government Research, Vol. 3, Issue 2, edited by M. Khosrow-Pour, pp. 29-44, copyright 2007 by IGI Publishing, formerly known as Idea Group Publishing (an imprint of IGI Global).

Chapter V
E-Government Implementation: Balancing Collaboration and Control in Stakeholder Management

Eric T.K. Lim
National University of Singapore, Singapore

Chee-Wee Tan
University of British Columbia, Canada

Shan-Ling Pan
National University of Singapore, Singapore

ABSTRACT

As e-government becomes increasingly pervasive in modern public administrative management, its influence on organizations and individuals has become hard to ignore. It is therefore timely and relevant to examine e-governance—the fundamental mission of e-government. By adopting a stakeholder perspective and coming from the strategic orientation of control and collaboration management philosophy, this study approaches the topic of e-governance in e-government from the three critical aspects of stakeholder management: (1) identification of stakeholders, (2) recognition of differing interests among stakeholders, and (3) how an organization caters to and furthers these interests. Findings from the case study allow us to identify four important groups of stakeholders known as the Engineers, Dissidents, Seasoners, and Skeptics who possess vastly different characteristics and varying levels of acceptance of and commitment towards the e-filing paradigm. Accordingly, four corresponding management strategies with varying degrees of collaboration and control mechanisms are devised in the bid to align these stakeholder interests such that their participation in e-government can be leveraged by public organizations to achieve competitive advantage.

Copyright © 2009, IGI Global, distributing in print or electronic forms without written permission of IGI Global is prohibited.

INTRODUCTION

Corporate governance is intensely debated within strategic management literature (Sundaramurthy and Lewis, 2003). Disputes have persisted over the optimal configuration of power in an organization to exploit the collective strength of its stakeholders (see Demb and Neubauer, 1992; Sundaramurthy, 2000; Westphal, 1999).

Strategic management scholars, such as Eisenhardt (1989), Hawley and Williams (1996), have argued for procedural controls to curtail the manifestation of self-serving opportunism prevalent among stakeholders. Yet, sociologists suggested that because stakeholders may share an intrinsic desire for self-actualization, they should be empowered to exercise autonomous judgments and be cherished as partners of the governance system (Davis et al. 1997; Donaldson and Davis, 1994). Not surprisingly, these conflicting viewpoints have prompted researchers to seek alternative theoretical approaches that go beyond either direction (see Audia et al. 2000). Among them, Demb and Neubauer (1992) advocate a paradoxical and provocative strategy to corporate governance—one that encapsulates the simultaneous demand for both stakeholder control and cooperation.

Advances in Information Technology (IT) in business processes further complicate corporate governance. Allen et al. (2001) postulated that the emergence of *electronic governance* (*e-governance*) goes beyond the mere infusion of technologies to encompass novel patterns of managerial decision-making, power-sharing, and resource-coordination. Changes include the induction of adaptive corporate structures, innovative leadership styles, and even a redefinition of business purpose—the entirety of which are made possible and necessary through IT (Allen et al. 2001). Arguably, this study deems e-governance as the embodiment of challenges confronting corporate governance in the realization of an optimal mix strategy of control and collaboration for the maximization of organizational stakeholder value. Aptly, we conceive e-governance as the ***effective leverage of IT to strategically manage stakeholders for competitive sustainability***. This definition builds upon scholarly predictions that foresee the future of organizations as intimately dependent on their capabilities to exploit technological innovations in harnessing competencies within an enhanced network of stakeholder interdependencies (Guillaume, 1999; Prahalad and Ramaswamy, 2000).

These managerial implications of e-governance are not exclusive to the private sector (Allen et al. 2001; Seavey, 1996). Pablo and Pan (2002) noted similar IT-induced reformations in public administration. With a renewed strategic focus on external stakeholders as partners in the governing process (Wimmer and Traunmuller, 2000), this modernized strategy to public management promises expanded citizen-centric functionalities through IT integration, and has been popularly termed "*Electronic Government* (*e-government*)" (Stratford and Stratford, 2000). This promoted Aichholzer and Schmutzer (2000) to maintain that the appreciation of e-transformation in public administration should entail a corresponding reconceptualization of the underpinning governance system.

The study of e-governance in e-governments thus offers an excellent opportunity to explore efforts by public institutions to redefine their tactics in IT-enabled stakeholder management. We adopt an e-governance perspective to examine the Electronic Tax Filing (e-filing) system, a pioneering e-government initiative of the Singapore government. By means of a case study, we seek to unveil the strategic elements of effective e-governance that will promote economical and efficacious elicitation of stakeholder value. Furthermore, we considered the significance of an e-governance vision in developing e-government initiatives and in structuring policy decisions within the public administration.

This chapter comprises seven sections.The second section offers a conceptual overview of the current status of research in the domains of e-government and corporate governance. It underlines our theoretical impetus for synthesizing knowledge from these domains to better understand stakeholder management in developing e-government initiatives.The third section discusses the rationale and considerations behind the choice of the research methodology utilized in this study. It covers the reasoning behind the case study method, the research techniques as well as the data collection, and analysis process. The fourth section continues with a breakdown of the events and decisions leading to the conceptualization, development, and implementation of the e-filing system. The fifth section focuses on the analytical discussion of core findings from the case that contribute to the appreciation and management of stakeholders within e-government initiatives. The sixth section emphasizes some implications for managerial practice to be gleaned from this study and highlights future research directions, which manifest from our case findings. Finally, the seventh section concludes with the limitations of this study.

LITERATURE REVIEW

The impact of IT on public administration is immense as governments worldwide rapidly embrace emerging technologies to restructure archaic bureaucratic procedures (Moon, 2002). By redeploying conventional public services through new communication media (Ho, 2002; Milford, 2000), recent IT-driven advancements in civil administration are more than mere cosmetic changes. Rather, they represent a paradigmatic shift in basic government functioning (Wimmer et al. 2001) as public management is restructured to steer away from conventional book-keeping functions (Norris, 1999). Increasingly, this phenomenon of adapting IT for the modernization of public administration has been commonly referred to as the dawn of the e-government era.

Definitions of E-Government

To arrive at an intuitive working definition for e-government, it is helpful to get acquainted with the various terminologies offered by researchers. From a technological angle, Milford (2000) considered e-government to be the means by which IT is utilized to simplify and to automate transactions between public organizations and its external constituent entities such as citizens, businesses, or even foreign governmental agencies (see also Marchionini et al. 2003). It is no different from that of pursuing "*electronic commerce*" within the context of public administration (Stratford and Stratford, 2000). Tapscott (1996) however, provided an alternative appraisal of the role of IT in revamping public administration. He visualized an "*inter-networked government*" in which public agencies thrive on the collaborative potential of networking technologies in forging virtual alliances to create strategic value for collaborators (Tapscott, 1996). Yet, there are still other scholars who subscribed to a more societal outlook on its mission. Embracing a citizens' perspective, Lawson (1998) put forward the idea that e-government is the provision of public services in a "*one-stop, non-stop*" manner where "*power is transferred to the people*".

Summarizing these discourses, Wimmer and Traunmuller (2000) hypothesized that e-government exists as the guiding vision toward a modern genre of public administration and democracy where citizens are substantially empowered to contribute toward policy formulation and legislation. From above, three major characterizations of e-government have emerged (see Table 1).

To reconcile the positions undertaken by either the technical or the sociological emphasis on e-government, Aichholzer and Schmutzer (2000) conceive the function of e-government as "covering the changes of governance in a twofold manner: (1) the transformation of the business of governance, that is, improving service quality delivery, reducing costs, and renewing admin-

Table 1. E-government definitions and their implications

Definitions of e-government (e-government is envisioned as...)	Implications for Citizens' Involvement (Citizens are deemed as...)
IT Artefacts employed by public institutions to achieve cost-effective business transactions	Customers of governmental transactions and the objective of e-government is the delivery of improved products and services through electronic media.
Virtual Value Chains of public institutions and their transactional partners to enhance virtual transacting experience	Business partners of governmental agencies and the purpose of e-government is the creation of additional value in any given transaction by exploiting the collective strengths of participants through digital alliances.
The ***Virtual Socialization Process*** between public institutions and citizens to create responsive governments	Pillars of the democratic system and the aim of e-government is to amplify citizens' voice in the process of governance through easily accessible virtual communication channels.

istrative processes and (2) the transformation of governance itself, that is, re-examining the functioning of democratic practices and processes" (p. 379). This conceptualization aptly captures the duality of e-government and will be thus espoused as the working definition for this paper. Based on this definition, the participation of citizens in e-government occurs on two distinct levels: (1) citizens as consumers of public goods and services (Fernandes et al. 2001; Newcombe, 2000) and (2) citizens as members of a democratic system (Cumming, 2001; Elgarah and Courtney, 2002; Webler and Tuler, 2000).

It should be noted that e-government is distinguishable from e-governance, even if the interchangeability of both theoretical constructs pervaded in some existing empirical studies has blurred their conceptual boundaries (see Allen et al. 2001; Tan et al. 2005a). E-governance is the broader definition of the two and symbolizes the adaptation of technologies to give rise to innovative managerial approaches in public-private organizations whereas e-government, on the other hand, is reserved solely for the manifestation of e-governance in the realm of public administration.

Pablo and Pan (2002) hence postulated that e-governance materializes in e-governments along four separate dimensions: (1) a transformation in the operational principles of governance by shifting towards enhanced communication, participation, integrity, and transparency (Schiavo-Ocampo and Sundaram, 2001), (2) a transformation in the internal functions of government by automating public transactions and administrative processes (Backus, 2001; IADB, 2002), (3) a transformation in the interactions between governments and their citizenries (Csetenyi, 2000; Heeks, 2002; Stiglitz et al. 2000), and finally, (4) a transformation of society itself by crafting and sustaining networks of social relationships through electronic means (IADB, 2002). The advent of e-governance within public administration denotes a major overhaul of traditional stakeholder management practices to revitalize the estranged relationship between governmental agencies and citizens, which in turn warrants an in-depth investigation. Unless stated otherwise, this paper is more attuned towards the appreciation of e-governance in public administration or simply, e-government.

Collaboration versus Control in E-Governance

Despite the benefits of infusing e-governance into public administration, scholars have questioned the impact of business-like transformations embodied in the drive towards e-government. Gregory (1999) and Haque (2001) hypothesized that the transplant of business norms onto public administration would undermine the role of government agencies in representing and fulfilling public interest. In response, some articles have emphasized the need for e-governments to realign their developmental objectives with stakeholder determinants (see Pardo et al. 2000; Pardo and Scholl, 2002; Scholl, 2001; Tennert and Schroeder, 1999). They espouse the view that the success of e-government initiatives hinges on the capacity of public institutions to effectively leverage IT in managing stakeholder expectations (Allen et al. 2001).

It is clear that effective e-governance translates to competitive advantages for the organization in the form of improved operational efficacies (e.g., reduced production costs, enhanced services, higher levels of customer satisfaction, and reengineered decision-making processes). These operational gains in turn, generate substantial financial profits, political returns, and more significantly, relational rewards in terms of new and more intimate connections with stakeholders (Aichhlozer and Schmutzer, 2000; Allen, et al. 2001; Backus, 2001; Csetenyi, 2000; Heeks, 2002; Lenk and Traunmuller, 2000; Stiglitz, et al. 2000; von Hoffman, 1999).

Nevertheless, granting stakeholders direct access to government transactions via electronic media removes human intermediaries, which may transfer certain transactional burden (e.g., the interpretation of and search for additional information) onto citizen-clients. Such a shift often requires the establishment of adaptive architectures, coordinated change efforts, and unanimous cooperation among government units, businesses, and citizen partners (Aichhlozer & Schmutzer, 2000; Csetenyi, 2000; Wescott, 2002). It is precisely because of this increasingly sophisticated web of government-stakeholder relations embedded within the governance system of e-governments that prompted Pardo et al. (2000) to allude to the importance of identifying stakeholders and incorporating their requirements into the delivery and maintenance of public e-services.

Unfortunately, strategic management theorists are divided over the most effective mode of governance from which to maximize stakeholders' contributions. Those who support the agency theory emphasize the enforcement of procedures to curb the opportunistic behavior of managers (agents) and align their actions to the wishes of principals (owners) within an organized atmosphere (Eisenhardt, 1989; Hawley and Williams, 1996). Excessive control however, has been contested to be counterproductive to corporate missions as it transmits a strong signal of distrust towards organizational stakeholders (Ghoshal and Moran, 1996). As reinforced by Frey (1997), "the agent may perceive more intensive monitoring by the principal as an indication of distrust, or as a unilateral break of the contract built on mutual trust" (p. 664). In this sense, structural regulations may fuel growing suspicion among stakeholders, which in turn undermines the quality of participation by triggering defensive postures and self-censorship behaviors (Davis et al. 1997; Lim and Tan, 2005; Tan et al. 2005b).

Alternatively, departing from the agency approach, stewardship theory details an opposite collaborative stance on stakeholder management (Davis et al. 1997). Drawing on insights from social psychology, proponents of the stewardship theory postulate that managers are "good stewards of the organizations and diligently work to attain high levels of corporate profit and shareholder returns" (Donaldson and Davis, 1994). Organizations may thus be better served by freeing managers from subservience to non-executive director dominated boards (Donaldson and Davis, 1994). Yet, critics have also denounced an over-emphasis on collaboration. Sundaramurthy and Lewis (2003) highlighted that a blind focus on cooperative decision-making and goal alignment could lead to the suppression of competitive tensions which are necessary for the systematic monitoring and critiquing of collective decisions (Janis, 1982; Kisfalvi, 2000). Over time, such biased confidence in supporting collaborative resolutions will lead to rigid mental maps in stakeholders by inducing complacency and constricting the flow of constructive feedback (Audia et al. 2000; Lindsley et al. 1995).

These contradictory positions on corporate governance may be traced to an oversimplification of stakeholder management. By forcing the spectrum of organizational stakeholders into extremities in the role of either the shareholders or the managers, the agency and stewardship ideologies conveniently discount the interplay of broader stakeholder dependencies in shaping corporate performance (Demb and Neubauer, 1992).

Consequently, these two pyramidal governance models may not be applicable to the public sphere as governments exist to fulfill obligations pertaining to a larger social community as opposed to a selective group of shareholders (Coursey and Bozeman, 1990). Indeed, the developmental cycle of e-government reveals patterns of evolution, which emphasize the steady empowerment of traditionally neglected citizens while preserving the administrative ethos of public institutions (von Hoffman, 1999; Traunmuller and Wimmer, 2000). Audia et al. (2000) appeal for the re-conceptualization of governance thus lends weight to the viability of our research objectives for this study.

Stakeholder Theory

Stakeholder theory, with its emphasis on realistic corporate circumstances (Freeman, 1984), offers a logical first step in the search for a viable theoretical alternative for the study of e-government. Stakeholder theory posits that an organization encompasses a sophisticated network of stakeholders operating within the broader framework of the host society that offers the necessary market infrastructure for its business activities (Clarkson 1995). From this aspect, stakeholder dynamics may extend beyond the narrow dimensions of principals and agents with each identifiable stakeholder segment warranting a matching relational stratagem.

As Carroll (1989) defined, a stake is "an interest or a share in an undertaking" (p. 56). Therefore, a stakeholder is "any individual or group who can affect or is affected by the actions, decisions, policies, practices, or goals of the organization" (Freeman, 1984, p. 25; see also Greenley and Foxall, 1998; Scott and Lane, 2000). Intuitively, it can be inferred that stakeholders are specific to a firm (Berman et al. 1999) and the first stage in strategic stakeholder management is the listing of all entities which have a stake in the establishment—what Freeman (1984) referred to as the stakeholder map of an organization.

Once stakeholders have been identified, Pfeffer and Salancik (1978) recommended that managers "rank or assign weights to them in order to indicate their impact on the organization or the extent to which the organization believes it should moderate its consequences on them" (p. 52), that is, stakeholders should be segmented according to their priorities or impacts on the organization. This will facilitate the efficient allocation of limited corporate resources to cater to the relational requirements of the most salient stakeholders (Frooman, 1999). A noteworthy framework developed by Mitchell et al. (1997) for demarcating stakeholders is founded on the notion that the extent of stakeholders' influence on an organization is subjected to the interplay of the three attributes of power, legitimacy, and urgency (Agle et al. 1999; Scott and Lane 2000). And depending on the configuration of power attributes possessed by a particular stakeholder, appropriate managerial actions are necessary (Mitchell et al. 1997). This imperative nature of power-oriented saliency in stakeholder management is further reinforced through the seminal work of Frooman (1999), who devised what is known as the "Typology of Relationships between Stakeholders and Firm". Frooman's (1999) typology is represented as a 2 x 2 matrix where each axis reflects the extent of resource dependency or level of power symmetry between the firm and its stakeholders (see Figure 1). Essentially, strategic stakeholder management in commercial enterprises manifests as three basic principles:

1. **Identification of Salient Stakeholders:** Firms should always seek to isolate their most powerful partners as these stakeholders have the capacity to sway the survival of the organization (Blair, 1995; Freeman, 1984; Greenley and Foxall, 1998; Scott and Lane, 2000).
2. **Categorization of Salient Stakeholders:** Firms should always been mindful of their most influential partners and prioritize them according to their impact on the organization so as to devise business strategies that align with the interests of these crucial stakeholders (Blair, 1995; Boatright, 2002, Donaldson and Preston 1995; Porter, 1992).
3. **Management of Salient Stakeholders:** As long as stakeholders do not acquire the capability to exert sufficient influence to obstruct organizational functions, there is no necessity to allocate resources to accommodate their requirements (Frooman *et* al, 1999; Mitchell et al. 1997). Conversely, if the balance of power is tilted towards stakeholders, firms should concoct means by which to manoeuvre these stakeholders into mutually dependent relationships so as to level the playing field for both parties (Frooman, 1999; Lawler and Yoon, 1995).

Undeniably, these guidelines in stakeholder management are well-formulated and tailored exclusively to commercialized businesses, which operate to optimize their responses to deserving stakeholders (Boatright, 2002; Donaldson and Preston, 1995; Schneiderman and Rose, 1996) within a relatively smaller resource scarcity perimeter (Greenley and Foxall, 1998; Scott and Lane, 2000). However, given the socio-political distinctions between public-private organizations such as a lower degree of market exposure, the

<table>
<tr><td colspan="2" rowspan="2"></td><td colspan="2">Is the Stakeholder Dependent on the Firm?</td></tr>
<tr><td>No</td><td>Yes</td></tr>
<tr><td rowspan="4">Is the Firm Dependent on the Stakeholder?</td><td rowspan="2">No</td><td>Low Interdependence
Neither the firm nor the stakeholder depends on each other.</td><td>Firm Power
The stakeholder is dependent on the firm, but the firm is not dependent on the stakeholder.</td></tr>
<tr><td colspan="2">Management Strategy
Since the firm is not dependent on the stakeholder for resources, it is likely to be indifferent towards stakeholders' concerns, that is, the firm should be almost oblivious to their needs and expectations.</td></tr>
<tr><td rowspan="2">Yes</td><td>Stakeholder Power
The firm is dependent on the stakeholder, but the stakeholder is not dependent on the firm.</td><td>High Interdependence
Both the firm and the stakeholder depend on each other.</td></tr>
<tr><td>Management Strategy
Since stakeholders control resources pivotal to the survival of the firm, the firm has an immediate mandate to attend their needs and whenever possible, manoeuvre them into interdependent relationships.</td><td>Management Strategy
Since both the firm and the stakeholder are reliant on each other for resources, the firm will attempt to negotiate with stakeholders to arrive at mutually acceptable solutions.</td></tr>
</table>

prevalent centralization of power and a wider range of constituents (Rainey et al. 1976), we contend that commercial principles of stakeholder management are not entirely transferable to the public domain. On the contrary, it may be prudent to re-evaluate the concept of stakeholders in IT-enabled public administration by exploring how e-governance is realized in e-governmental systems through the assimilation of control and collaborative mechanisms. More specifically, this study endeavors to address the following research questions:

1. Who are the stakeholders of an e-government initiative and how are they identified?
2. Since the function of e-government is synonymous to that of a sponge in soliciting stakeholders' opinions, is there a need for stakeholder segmentation? If so, how are stakeholders differentiated and for what purpose?
3. As a follow-up to the previous question, what is the relational strategy employed by public administration in developing e-government initiatives? Is it a one-solution-fits-all or are there multiple strategies corresponding to different stakeholder categories?

METHODOLOGY

This study adopts an in-depth case research methodology for data collection and analysis (Strauss and Corbin, 1990). According to Yin (1994), a case study is "an empirical inquiry that: investigates a contemporary phenomenon within its real-life context, when the boundaries between phenomenon and context are not clearly evident, and in which multiple sources of evidence are used" (p. 23). It is most pertinent in scenarios where the research question is exploratory in nature and focuses on the examination of current events that occur beyond the control of the investigator (Yin, 1994). Moreover, case studies offer a chance to engage in theory-building in an area where there is relatively little prior knowledge (Eisenhardt, 1991; Parkhe, 1993). Therefore, through the case research methodology, we hope to reveal unforeseen relationships and generate deeper insights into the interdependencies among the themes uncovered over the course of this investigation (Benbasat et al. 1987). Inspired by Markus' (1994) articulation of individuals as conscious beings existing in a shared social context, we further postulate that stakeholders are not passive receptacles of corporate actions, and that they participate actively in shaping government-stakeholder relations. Consequently, a holistic comprehension of the socio-political environment through the triangulation of multiple perspectives is an explicit undertaking for this study.

Maintaining strict objectivity in data collection is impossible for case studies since the researcher interacts with the human subjects involved in the enquiry, and in the process, alters the perceptions of both parties (Walsham, 1995). Also, taking into account the unique circumstances of this investigation where everybody, including the investigator, is a target audience of the e-government initiative, an interpretivistic perspective of the data collected can be perceived as a logical decision, that is, the experience and contextual understanding of the researcher impart complementary background information that is invaluable to the interpretation of the evidence gathered (Lacity and Janson, 1994).

The research was conducted at the Inland Revenue Authority of Singapore (IRAS) over a period of 6 months with several methods of data collection (Benbasat et al.1987). A series of focused interviews (Merton et al. 1990) were conducted with the Chief Information Officer (CIO), the e-filing system design team, the e-filing system implementation team, and the e-filing administrative group to solicit data on the intra-organizational considerations behind the implementation of the e-filing project. The data was triangulated with interviews with perspectives provided through interviews with taxpayers (Orlikowski, 1993). Additionally, supplementary data from other sources including meeting minutes, press statements, and a huge compilation of archival records was also solicited. From the 30 hours of interviews and the pool of secondary data, we built an in-depth collection of qualitative data points within the study environment (Lacity and Janson, 1994), which focus exclusively on developmental issues pertaining to the e-filing system (Eisenhardt, 1991).

In conjunction with data collection, thematic analysis (Boyatiz, 1998) was employed for the coding and interpretation of the raw information. Patterns from the transcribed interviews were first identified and then combined and catalogued into sub-themes (Taylor and Bogan, 1984) that were eventually coded to derive the main themes for this investigation. The research concluded when thematic information appeared to have reached saturation.

CASE DESCRIPTION

The Singapore government faced an escalating amount of uncollected revenue during 1980s. Unprocessed tax returns accumulated in the Singapore Income Tax Department (SITD) and resulted in administrative backlogs leading to widespread dissatisfaction among departmental staff and taxpaying citizens. The Inland Revenue Authority of Singapore (IRAS) was hence inaugurated in 1992 to remove the bureaucratic red tape by restructuring the taxation system. This responsibility became the corporate vision guiding the IRAS over the next eight years when the tax administrative process was reengineered into an integrated system that saw a decrease in staff turnover rate and a general rise in public satisfaction.

The introduction of direct taxpayer services (phone filing) in 1995 was a milestone in the IRAS' drive towards revolutionizing the taxation system. Forty-three percent of tax inquiries could be handled by the automated voice response system, with the remaining 400,000 calls being left to the care of tax officers. The Internet provided an opportunity for the IRAS to further expand the user base of its phone filing services. With the launch of the e-filing system on February 16, 1998, taxpayers are now capable of filing their income returns electronically through the Internet. This new $1.90 million e-filing system is even accessible to citizens overseas. Since filed returns are entered directly into the IRAS' centralized digital database, the e-filing process is paperless other than the issue of a verification receipt. The desirability of the e-filing system was reflected in a 2001 survey where 94.1% of individual taxpayers, 89.6% of corporate taxpayers, and 94.6% of goods and services taxpayers expressed high levels of satisfaction with the refurnished tax services. Another recent customer service evaluation study conducted by Forbes in October 2003 also echoed identical sentiments for which 2,466 respondents admitted to being pleased with the e-filing system.

A deciding factor behind the accomplishments of the e-filing initiative is its fusion of both control and collaborative mechanisms such that the collective strength of stakeholders (i.e. taxpayers and employers) can be harnessed without an over-reliance on checks and balances. Before the installation of the e-filing system, physical paper returns were the norm in reporting employment figures. This physical tax filing practice places an overwhelming demand on both manpower (to sift through tax documents) and storage capacity (to archive the accumulating tax returns). Moreover, cumulating paper folders limits the capacity of tax officials to concurrently access and process tax returns while greatly boosting the chances of misplacing important documents.

The e-filing system was conceptualized as an IT-inspired paperless solution to the problems inherent in its labor-intensive predecessor. Exploiting an integrated back-end infrastructure to incorporate tax calculations and legislative regulations, the e-filing system automates taxation processes according to an 80/20 rule, that is, it is crafted on the assumption that 80% of tax returns are 'normal' and do not require further validation by tax officers. The remaining 20% of tax returns are then automatically routed to the appropriate tax official with the matching skill proficiency for verification.

The e-filing system grants two points of data entry. If tax returns are filed through the e-filing service web-portal, transmitted information will be directly entered into the centralized database. But whenever paper returns are submitted, relevant data fields must be extracted and keyed into the database while the document is scanned as a digitized image for archiving purposes. Basically, through such design specifications, the premise of the e-filing system lies in granting a consolidated one-stop electronic tax filing option for taxpayers' convenience. The structure of the e-filing system is depicted in Figure 2.

The revamped e-filing system not only boasts of synchronous communication channels for stakeholders to participate in service development and enhancement, it also inherits the exact same rigorous administrative controls imposed by its paper-based predecessor. As highlighted by a system engineer:

By integrating the front-end data capturing process with back-end tax processing functions, the e-filing system basically represents a whole new perspective on how we interact with our taxpayers... However, in designing the e-filing system, we have also made sure that the new system does not compromise the integrity of the tax filing process by retaining the same level of control as the previous paper [-based] system.

In an extra bid to make e-filing effortless for taxpayers, the IRAS established close ties with numerous government agencies and business organizations to allow relevant tax information for their employees to be directly transferable to the IRAS' central database during each tax cycle. Once the information for a particular taxpayer has been uploaded into the system, he/she has only to submit a series of "zero" returns through the e-filing system. To date, this auto-inclusion scheme has clinched data transfer agreements with 2,509 business organizations in Singapore. These companies account for an approximate figure of 550,000 or 46% of all employees in the country. The direct transmission of tax information reduces data capturing efforts and enables structure controls to be built into the e-filing system to validate the accuracy of taxpayers'

Figure 2. Illustration of the contemporary e-filing system of the IRAS

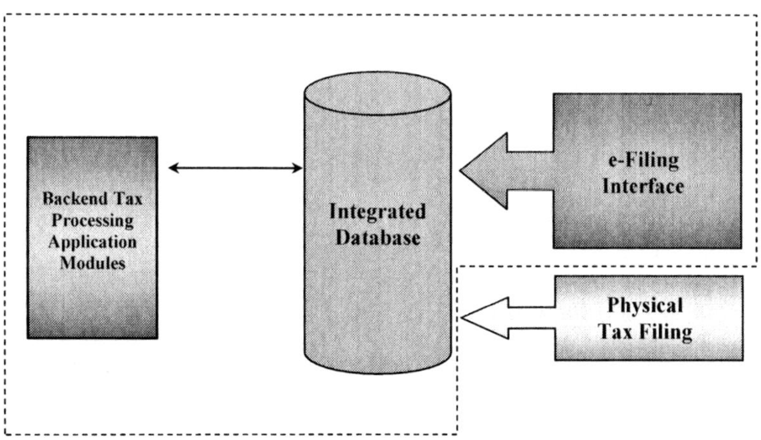

financial portfolio. Through the solicitation of data directly from third-party employers, the IRAS is assured of the veracity of employees' income information.

CASE ANALYSIS AND DISCUSSION

The IRAS' e-filing system demonstrates how a public agency unleashes the capabilities of IT to craft a robust e-government architecture that acts as a common denominator between the establishment and its salient stakeholders. Given the success of the e-filing system, the case could offer invaluable insights into the strategic elements constituting an efficacious governance system, which unravels the sophisticated interdependencies among governmental goals, stakeholder involvement and IT-enabled public service acceptance. By analyzing the case of the IRAS guided by the three managerial principles of stakeholder theory, we attempt to formulate guidelines for the marriage of control and collaboration in strategic stakeholder management.

Identifying Crucial Stakeholders

The identification of critical stakeholders has been described as an indispensable step in effective corporate governance (Demb and Neubauer, 1992; Monks and Minow, 1995). Scholars have argued this step to identify strategic stakeholders, whose presence directly determines a firm's survival capability (Donaldson and Preston, 1995; Turnbull, 1997), and to concentrate corporate resources on these specific niches of stakeholders (Blair, 1995; Freeman, 1984).

In this case, the stigma typically associated with being the governmental 'tax collector' coupled with an escalating problem of uncollected tax revenue due to inefficient manual tax processing procedures, have prompted the inauguration of the IRAS. The IRAS was tasked with the responsibility of reinventing the bureaucratic tax processes and repairing the tarnished public image inherited from its predecessor, the SITD. To accomplish its designated duty, the IRAS embarked on an extensive e-transformation campaign devised to cut across archaic business functions and revitalize its obsolete governance system.

Armed with a forward-looking managerial philosophy, acute sensitivity and improved receptivity towards the potential of emerging technologies, the IRAS has triumphed in sculpting a cutting-edge and responsive e-filing system that integrates its complete range of tax processing activities into a homogeneous informational architecture. With its relentless drive towards strategic and operational reformations, the IRAS, unlike its bureaucratic predecessor, acknowledged the value of mutually beneficial cooperative networks and methodically assimilated various stakeholder constituencies in constructing seamless partnerships that uphold the ideals of its business reengineering objectives.

Under the revamped taxation system, taxpayers are no longer dismissed as mere subjects in the eyes of ritualistic bureaucracies (Moon and Bretschneider, 2002), but are respected as peers in the pursuit of collaborative alliances. This dose of customer-centrism was aptly surmised in IRAS' corporate motto of "I Respond And Serve" (IRAS, 2000). A tax official recalled the initial psychological barriers associated with such antonymous mental conversions from past attitudes:

In the past, taxpayers were like people who owed us money. To be honest, we actually needed [to learn] to see taxpayers as customers...and not simply people bound by law to pay taxes.

Through such enterprise-wide rectification exercises, the IRAS managed to inculcate an organizational culture that installs citizens as rightful partners of the taxation system (Cumming, 2001; Webler and Tuler, 2000). A testimony of such explicit stakeholder empowerment is evidenced from the IRAS' continued emphasis on placing consumer interest in parallel priority with corporate concerns during the conceptualization of the e-filing system. As observed by an e-filing system engineer:

We want to gather taxpayers' opinions. It is important to place ourselves in taxpayers' shoes and incorporate their views in whatever we do, so that we can deliver new systems or procedures that are receptive to taxpayers.

Interestingly, the involvement of both internal and external stakeholders plays a pivotal role in the eventual success of the e-filing system. First, by bringing on-board a fair representation of crucial stakeholders during the system planning process, the IRAS was able to compensate for the absence of exemplary tax governance models which could be utilized to benchmark the design blueprint for its envisioned e-filing paradigm (Oliver, 1999). The CIO confessed to the dearth of pragmatic examples for the e-filing system to be modelled after:

For the e-filing system, we did not have anybody to learn from; nobody. When we conceptualized the system at that time, there were no other models to look at.

Moreover, while the inception of the e-filing system has been premeditated as the technological imperative bridging front-end customer transactions with backend business processes (Calista, 1986; Ho, 2002; Rainey and Rainey, 1986), a primary corporate concern was the adequate retention of knowledge assets or proficiencies in mapping the functional routines of the physical tax structure onto the new informational architecture (Wimmer and Traunmuller; 2000). The recruitment of internal 'experts' into the system development team hence acted as a precautionary measure to preserve localized knowledge resources that have been acquired through specialization in existing work processes (Pan et al. 2001).

A cross-functional project committee of 'power-users' was handpicked to create a wellspring of knowledge reflecting the range of business requirements that corresponds to the spectrum of tax processing functions in the public agency. The feedback garnered was then infused into the exoskeleton of the e-filing system to cater to diverse expectations across the IRAS' internal business divisions. This in turn reduced the probability of incompatibilities or even outright rejection by core staff members. Furthermore, to enhance the appeal of the e-filing system among its targeted audience, the design and implementation schematics were further refined through regular focus group gatherings where candid and dialogic interactions between designers and taxpayers helped to reinforce bidirectional appreciation of systemic components. As explained by one of the system engineers:

We need to go through the whole process and let the taxpayers see it the way we do. If we find that we have placed something there that two persons interpret differently, we will request for input. When we perform testing, we will involve the taxpayers and then observe the result. Whenever we obtain unexpected results, we ask them why they interpret it in that manner.

With extensive involvement of stakeholders in defining the techno-structure of the e-filing system, the end product was delivered as a holistic solution for the efficacious and seamless management of value chain networks. The embedded functionalities of the e-filing system are welcomed by its various recipients as a fresh change from its conventional administrative practices. As professed by one of the e-filers:

It [e-filing system] is a convenient system because it is quite reliable and I don't need to send any tax filing application such as the employer income form.

Furthermore, through ingenious inspirations such as the EF Pin (i.e. a unique identification number for each e-filing taxpayer), the IRAS has succeeded in capturing a loyal threshold of e-filers that increases exponentially with each passing tax cycle. This constitutes significant cost savings for the tax agency:

We have a lot of repeat users and we discovered that there are benefits to be gained for the e-filing system. Previously, when we have to send you a tax package, we wasted a lot of effort but now once you e-file, we only need to send you a letter together with the [EF] pin number for subsequent years. There is no necessity to send forms and as a result, we become more cost efficient.

Arguably, the crux of the e-government challenge resides in eliciting proactive participation and continuous support from stakeholders in conceptualizing, implementing, maintaining, and strategizing public e-services (Elgarah and Courtney, 2002; Lowndes et al. 2001). This tendency of public agencies to reach out to concerned parties (e.g. citizens) contradicts commercial applications of stakeholder theory whereby the influence of stakeholders is deliberately manipulated through countermeasures aimed at diminishing firms' dependency on external entities (see Frooman et al. 1999; Mitchell et al. 1997).

Nevertheless, despite the IRAS' intensive efforts to reach out to the general taxpaying population, a sizeable portion of this community still chooses to distance themselves from the prospect of a fully automated tax filing system. Discounting the fraction of taxpayers who has adamantly insisted on traditional paper filing procedures due to security or privacy concerns (McNaughton, 1999); resistance was also met from internal project players. The most noteworthy trepidation expressed by these vanguards was the unprecedented shift away from the conservative mentality of viewing taxpayers as legally-binding and unwilling participants of the tax filing process.

Not surprisingly, the business logic embodied within the e-filing system to permit taxpayers to assume their civic responsibilities in submitting reliable income figures [80/20 rule] has proven to be a source of tension between officials vying for control versus those appealing for collaboration. Generally, disapproving voices tend to demand that the e-filing system came equipped with control mechanisms to validate the accuracy of self-declared tax information. As recollected by the CIO:

The principal concept is that we must accept the new tax filing model [80/20 rule] and so there must be a change in mindset. Of course, with the change in mindset, there are a lot of obstacles when you have to throw the old thinking out. A number of tax officers will argue that: "No, this [manual tax return verification process] is the right way. We must still check and things like that.

Such disparities in perceptions contribute to a seemingly contradictory scenario where certain categories of stakeholders may not be receptive towards the technical propositions of the e-government initiative even though they may identify with the direction of its strategic vision. From above, we hypothesize that stakeholders, in the context of e-governments, may be distinguishable along two separate dimensions. The majority of employees from the IRAS, together with the class of public members who has participated actively in public consultation sessions, share a strong sense of ***commitment*** towards the strategization of the e-filing system as a synchronous and bilateral channel for fostering permanent transactional relationships between the tax agency and its targeted audience (Cutlip et al. 1994; Taylor and Kent, 1999). The acquirement of commitment, as advocated by Nelson and Winter (1982), is vital in change management because it determines the extent to which reformed business capabilities are likely to be acknowledged by employees and thus infused into their existing work routines.

Conceivably, commitment is a decisive virtue of e-government initiatives as it defines the psychological attachment or desire among various factions of the stakeholder community to voluntarily contribute to the best of their abilities in shaping public e-services.

Conversely, *acceptance* presents another deterministic aspect of stakeholder identification for e-governments. Consistent with contemporary extant literature on Information Systems (IS) development, the concept of system acceptance has been broadly depicted as an implicit connotation for the measurable success of IS implementation (see Davis et al. 1989; DeLone and McLean, 1992; Markus et al. 2000; Seddon, 1997). Existing studies have accumulated a mixture of technical and sociological factors that influence operators' acceptance of installed technological applications. Within this list are features such as system quality (Hamilton and Chervany, 1981), information quality (Ahituv, 1980; Bailey and Pearson, 1983), amount of usage (Kim and Lee, 1986), user satisfaction (DeLone and McLean, 1992), and perceived usefulness (Davis, 1989, 1993; Seddon, 1997), which collectively, encapsulate the socio-technical forces driving system utilization. Acceptance of any e-government initiative can therefore be perceived to be tantamount to the alignment of stakeholders' anticipations with the inherent attributes of its corresponding functional manifestation. And often, such psychological receptivity towards delivered technological features, serve to perpetuate stakeholders' behaviour in fulfilling pre-assigned roles and duties within the e-government arrangement. Referencing our above description, acceptance thus refers to the behaviour exhibited by the general taxpaying population whereby an e-filer may demonstrate recurring usage of the e-filing system but does so with neither questions nor options.

It is hence our primary contention that commitment and acceptance exists as distinct constructs in the identification of stakeholders for any e-government initiative, that is, the commitment of stakeholders towards an e-government initiative does not guarantee an automatic acceptance of its actual manifestation. As depicted in the circumstances surrounding the e-filing system, veteran tax officials, having gone through a chaotic and unstable era under the IRAS' predecessor, can be presumed to be highly committed or even anticipative towards the construction of an efficacious, customer-centric tax filing system. Nonetheless, the merger of this vision into the e-filing system opens up disputes over its mechanistic structure. Clearly, the case substantiates our delineation of commitment and acceptance in that the acceptance of the e-filing system can be understood to be founded on an attraction to its tangible elements (i.e. service functionalities) whereas its commitment is analogous to that of a psychological affinity for its strategic vision. Because commitment denotes stakeholders' willingness to go beyond symbolic participation in advancing the mission of the e-filing system, stakeholders who display high levels of commitment should be more open to collaboration. Acceptance, on the other hand, pertains only to stakeholders' affirmative appraisal of the functional properties of the e-filing system such that a certain degree of control is probably necessary to ensure compliance in system utilization. Prior research on IS Critical Success Factors (CSF) is also lined with paradoxical evidence (Markus and Robey, 1988), which parallels our postulation that the progress of e-governments cannot be based solely in mere technological acceptance but instead, should also include considerations for the intangible aspect of sociological commitment.

Recognizing Differing Stakeholder Interests

The recognition and prioritization of differing interests among stakeholders is another essential component of corporate governance. According to Demb and Neubauer (1992), "governance is the process by which organizations are made responsible to the rights and wishes of stakeholders". Hence, Tricker (1994) proposed that effective governance hinges on the ability of the organization to address the issues raised by different interest groups associated with the firm. Similarly, Monks and Minow (1995) highlighted that the relational interests among various partners would ultimately dictate the agenda and performance of the organization.

Embracing an identical emphasis on the importance of segmenting stakeholders in accordance to their impacts on the e-filing system, the investigators notice that the case classification can be derived from the interplay of the two aforementioned dimensions of acceptance and commitment. Even though both factors are representative of cognitive spectrums ranging from low to high, but for parsimony, they have been reduced to a dichotomy of positive or negative dimensions (e.g. Frooman, 1999).

Evidently, from the interactions of these two vectors, four main categories of stakeholders can be labeled as deterministic to the adoption and strategization of the e-filing system. The first group of stakeholders is characteristic of individuals who are both receptive and committed towards the strategic momentum of the e-filing system. It is clear from preceding discourses that this category of stakeholders would comprise the vast majority of corporate employees for which the IRAS has undertaken precautions to obtain their allegiance as well as solicit their feedback through broad functional representation during system conceptualization. Support from this wide-ranging base of internal agents throughout various phases of project development has eased implicit transition barriers (Pan et al. 2001) during the installation of the e-filing system. Strategically, this facilitates the tax agency to advance synchronously with the e-filing system, thereby reinforcing the reins on acceptance and commitment within its own administrative body.

Furthermore, the initiation of the Taxpayer Feedback Panel (TFP) marks an alternative but novel approach by the IRAS to extract responses from the relatively nebulous composition of the tax-paying population. Specifically, the invitation of e-filers to partake in quarterly dialogue sessions has evolved into an indispensable source of exclusive consumer insights that frequently translates into consecutive improvement options for the e-filing system:

The [taxpayer feedback] panel has a regular meeting on a quarterly basis. If they should gather any feedback, they will come back to us. And on our part, if we are launching any new services, we will let them know and have a look at the new system. They are like our source of feedback; our eyes and ears among the taxpayer population. In fact, some of the system changes were actually initiated by them. (Manager, IRAS)

In view of the time and effort invested by this category of stakeholders to continuously familiarize themselves with the facilities of the e-filing system before passing judgment, they can be deemed as the true Engineers of the e-government initiative by offering discerning and constructive critiques whenever appropriate.

There is however another segment of stakeholders, who, despite a strong commitment towards the strategic vision of the e-filing system, may frown upon the directional bearings of its technical implementation. As highlighted earlier, there was a specific cluster of tax officials who opposed the fundamental presumption of the e-filing system that regards taxpayers as dependable participants of the taxation procedures. Such a stance of disagreement is comprehensible for these long-serving employees because it is not unusual for them to feel uncomfortable with the loss of stringent controls inbuilt within the manual tax filing model such that they found it hard to come to terms with the business process modification embedded in the e-filing system.

Similarly, within the ranks of the taxpayers, there are also individuals who contribute actively in focus groups and forums but disapprove of the e-filing system's current mechanical architecture. One primary concern raised by these taxpayers was the inadequacy of information transparency in the e-filing system. Apparently, these taxpayers expressed doubts over their limited knowledge of what went on behind the e-filing system. In particular, questions were raised pertaining to the confidentiality and security of transmitted personal data to the agency with one of them suggesting that the IRAS should lay down "explicit rules and guidelines" governing sensitive tax-related information (McNaughton, 1999). Such innate reservations over the e-filing system protocols imply a certain degree of mistrust among taxpayers of the control mechanisms erected through information regulation (Foucault, 1991; Tannenbaum, 1967).

The launch of the auto-inclusion scheme has also compounded this misconception through its opaque data transmission agreements. Under the auto-inclusion scheme, income figures are transferred directly via electronic media from the employers to the IRAS and taxpayers will not get a chance to review these numbers even with the e-filing interface. Naturally, a standard call by taxpayers for prospective system enhancements is for the transmitted employment information to be verifiable by its tax paying owner. As commented by one of the taxpayers:

I don't see any differences between they [the employers] filing it for you versus they sending the information for you file it yourself. However, since they have access your income information, I suppose if there is anything to note here is how accurate this information is ... how much we actually make this year. If they can show the numbers when you e-file, then it would be even better.

The non-disclosure of the transmitted employment information also worries taxpayers in that it may comprise data integrity. As remarked by a taxpayer:

I suppose if there is anything to note here, it is the accuracy of the information. If the employer files it for you, the implication or interpretation may be a bit different.

These apprehensions over data management discourage this category of stakeholders from accepting the e-filing system. But as clarified by the CIO, there are strategic considerations and tactical limitations in meeting such an expectation. The IRAS noted that acceding to taxpayers' request to show the resultant tax computations during the e-filing process would mean disseminating sensitive tax information over the public medium of the Internet. Such a step might trigger the possibility of data interceptions, which in turn would impose unnecessary expenditure in implementing security measures within the channel of data transfer. The IRAS maintains that in enforcing a non-transfer policy where data transmission is unidirectional from the taxpayer to the agency, it is in fact looking after the interests of the broader community:

A lot of information is already captured by the system, so what we need for e-filing is just asking you to complete the remaining portion. As such, the information [available via the Internet] of the taxpayer is never a complete picture; it would be meaningless to a [hacker] without the rest of the information [kept by the IRAS]. (CIO, IRAS)

The group of stakeholders who are committed to the strategic objectives of the e-filing system but expressed dissatisfaction over the existing technical configuration can be considered to be *Dissidents* whom the public organization should make a conscious effort to engage because as illustrated in this case, such disagreeing sentiments may simply arise from conflicting perspectives of the same issue despite being rooted in identical well-placed intentions.

A third group of stakeholders are those who unenthusiastically accepts the e-filing system in its current state without giving due attention to any possible avenues of improvement. This class of stakeholders is characteristically representative of the general taxpaying population where the electronic tax filing process is perceived merely as an annual event that takes up less than an hour with the installation of the e-filing system. Due to the infrequent and cyclical pattern in which these stakeholders come into contact with the e-filing system, they are usually only attentive to its operational performance within the short timeframe of the tax filing period. The CIO highlighted one prominent example of this seasonal frenzy during the tax filing cycles:

The taxpayer just keeps sending [emails] during the e-filing period. Basically, they treat it like a chat room. They keep sending and then complain of late or failure to respond. They believe that there is a person there all the time and they expect instant replies.

The term, *Seasoners*, is thus appropriately reserved for this specific segment of stakeholders who accepts the e-filing system solely as a mechanical tool to carry out mundane seasonal chores and has no desire to get involved beyond the fulfillment of their tax filing duties. A feasible explanation for this dispassionate stand, as put forward by Lowndes et al. (2001), is the longstanding mistaken mindset of social exclusion among citizens, which mislead them to believe that they are detached from the process of decision making in public institutions. These citizenries assume that they do not hold sway over the legislation of governmental policies and as a direct consequence, choose to remain passive to the governance system. Any feedback and suggestions put forward to IRAS by these seasoners are thus normally short-term frustrations and criticisms targeted at systemic failures rather than long-term strategically-oriented recommendations.

Finally, the last category of stakeholders comprises individuals who are neither comfortable nor committed to the e-filing system. Undeniably, the paper tax filers are clearly representative of this stakeholder classification. Despite the IRAS' efforts to reach out to this population of paper filers through extensive promotional events and easy access to assisted PC terminals, there is still a considerable fragment of the taxpaying community who is obdurately unmoved. This lot of non-believers or *Skeptics* is therefore one of the most arduous hurdles that must be overcome by the IRAS in institutionalizing the e-filing system.

To summarize, the concept of stakeholder segmentation in e-government development can be deduced as the combination and interdependence between the cognitive facets of commitment versus acceptance in arriving at a two-dimensional theoretical framework (see Figure 3).

A crucial lesson to be learnt is that governments, despite a mounting emphasis on citizens' empowerment and involvement, do indeed shoulder a great responsibility in safeguarding the general welfare of the society (see Haque, 2001). The case of the e-filing system illustrates that although the IRAS values taxpayers' participation in developing the e-initiative, it neither foregoes nor compromises on the integrity expected of public services. Indeed, the infusion of IT into governmental services may create grey areas of contention where the discharge of public duty comes into conflict with the need for congenial collaborative ties between government agencies and their direct service recipients

As Foucault (1991) observed, the challenge is to attain equilibrium between individual expectations and the interests of the wider community such that the organization may avert progress-inhibiting squabbles (Kruckeberb and Starck, 1998). Therefore, in merging IT with government processes, it is necessary for public institutions to evaluate the technological limitations of the e-government services before designing and implementing control and collaboration mechanisms in the system. Specifically, at no time should e-governments be pursuing along the extremities

Figure 3. A proposed framework of stakeholder segmentation in e-government projects

		Is the operationalization of the e-governmental initiative acceptable to the stakeholder?	
		Yes	**No**
Is the stakeholder committed to the strategization of the e-government initiative?	**Yes**	**Engineers** Stakeholders who are both receptive towards the technical propositions of the e-government initiative and committed towards its strategization.	**Dissidents** Stakeholders who are committed towards the strategization of the e-government initiative even though they may not be receptive towards its technical propositions.
	No	**Seasoners** Stakeholders who are receptive towards the technical propositions of the e-government initiative even though they may not be committed towards its strategization.	**Skeptics** Stakeholders who are neither receptive towards the technical propositions of the e-government initiative nor committed towards its strategization.

of either pure control or unconditional collaboration in satisfying stakeholders' wishes. Rather, it demands a delicate balance in accommodating differing expectations of stakeholders in the anticipated functionalities of the e-government system.

Catering to and Furthering Stakeholder Interests

Indisputably, the eventual objective of sound governance is to enable organizations to formulate plans and management strategies that cater to and further the interests of their stakeholders (Clarkson, 1995; Blair, 1995). Alternatively, if stakeholders can behave independently to further partisan interests, organizations may be hindered from maximizing its potential (Jensen and Meckling, 1976; Shleifer and Vishny, 1996). And with an expanding stakeholder base in the digital economy, organizations face a more steeply uphill task in catering to the diverse interests of multiple players.

Based on the proposed model of stakeholder segmentation, the researcher observed the concoction of various relational strategies by the IRAS to cope with the expectations of multiple stakeholder groups in achieving the vision of a communal e-filing system. Beginning with the engineers from whom the IRAS derives its readily accessible and inexpensive concentration of support behind the e-filing system, the expertise of these voluntary contributors can be easily leveraged to coordinate a conducive application environment and to sketch out plans for prospective system enhancements. The establishment of periodic dialogic interactive sessions with this team of stakeholders provides a structural means by which the public agency and its partners can interact with the ultimate aim of maintaining continuous and productive dialogues (Cutlip et al. 1994; Taylor and Kent, 1999).

The IRAS practices a ritual of conducting a post-mortem after every tax cycle to serve as a cardinal foundation of knowledge to gather input from internal staff members based on issues that cropped up during the e-filing duration. As for the harder-to-reach external taxpayers, it is evident that the sponsorship of the TFP tenders the much needed platform for the IRAS to socialize with its extrinsic engineers for cooperative rumination on the developmental progress and strategic direction of the e-filing system (Wimmer and Traunmuller, 2000).

Conversely, dissidents are often deemed to be "unwelcome" as they emit a disruptive tone to the smooth operationalization of management strategies. However, it is foolhardy to discount any form of dissatisfaction in the public sphere as it compromises the publicness of the governmental institution (Haque, 2001). Moreover, this category of stakeholders, given their full backing to the strategization of a customer-centric taxation paradigm, may manifest as an alternative knowledge resource of disagreeing voices. In fact, at times, it may prove to be favorable for the organization to take into account conflicting comments and mull over the motivations behind these criticisms in order to appreciate the e-government initiative from multiple facets. To this end, the IRAS tries its best to be accommodative of deviating opinions from stakeholders and readily incorporates their opposing views in future system enhancements.

The auto-inclusion scheme is an example born out of intense deliberations with dissenting tax officials clamoring for a revolutionary paradigm to ensure the veracity of the tax information that is submitted by the e-filers. Such an outcome represents an exemplification of the immense benefits that can be reaped by maintaining an open and receptive culture that inadvertently led to the discovery of previously unexplored sources of strategic value for the e-government initiative. On the other hand, it is not the case that any proposals from dissents will necessarily be entertained.

For instance, as explained in the previous section, while the IRAS has cautiously explored the viability of deploying the e-filing system for the digital presentation of transmitted employment information under the auto-inclusion scheme, the danger of probable data interceptions when transferring information across public domain such as the Internet has induced the IRAS to maintain its non-transfer policy, where data transfer is unidirectional from the taxpayers to the agency.

In such scenarios, the IRAS chose to exploit communication opportunities in the likes of seminars to address the concerns of these dissents, that is, the IRAS attempts to induct these individuals to the rationale behind some of the more controversial characteristics of the e-government initiative through education and familiarization courses in hope of co-opting these members by boosting their level of acceptance to match that of their commitment.

Furthermore, the tax agency has wisely devised a comprehensive knowledge repository archiving records of past comments, opinions from taxpayers as well as any corresponding remedies undertaken by tax officials (Kankanhalli et al. 2001). This trail of historical experiences forms a large part of the IRAS' environmental surveillance efforts to uncover any disputes taxpayers may have had with the e-filing system in order to arrive at ways to integrate their suggestions. Moreover, by making use of IRIS' integrated framework, this information within the database is transliterated dynamically throughout the organizational operations, thereby allowing knowledge to be shared and assimilated within the IRAS' strategization effort (Alavi and Tiwana, 2002, Nonaka et al. 1998; Pfeffer and Sutton, 2000; von Krogh, 1998). One of the corporate communication officers verified:

Whenever we answer phone calls from taxpayers, we have a template whereby we can keep a log on the problems raised by them. Through such records, we will know the percentage of calls registered for any particular problem. There is also a remark column whereby we are able to type in comments for similar queries so that when we refer to the template, we will be able see from the remark column if taxpayers are having a recurring problem...Basically, our template is quite well designed because it is equipped with all possible options available from the e-filing Web site.

For the seasoners, even though they may be receptive to the e-filing system, they demonstrate only fleeting commitment towards the strategization of the e-filing system. In most cases, they are primarily concerned with ironing out immediate software problems that stymied them during the tax filing process. These stakeholders derive no gratification from spending time and effort to work hand in hand with the public agency to enhance the e-filing system. As highlighted, such apathetic disposition from them stems frequently from their antipathy towards dealings with the government and their cynicism of ever significantly influencing the direction of public administration (Lowndes et al. 2001). This mentality and its aftermath undoubtedly prove to be counter-productive to such a heavily-invested initiative that is meant to form the perdurable national taxation understructure. From the stance of the IRAS, it is hence important to increase the level of commitment of these stakeholders.

In line with e-government and public management literature, the IRAS has ventured zealously to fashion a corporate persona that is transparent and ingenuous in its bid to aspire to greater strategic heights with the e-filing paradigm (Aichholzer and Schmutzer, 2000). For instance, the availability of e-mail addresses and telephone numbers of relevant tax officials on the e-filing website effectively communicates a flat hierarchical structure atypical of traditional bureaucratic, procedural-driven governmental image (Bozeman and Kingsley, 1998) and sends a strong signal to taxpayers of the IRAS' resolve to initiate dialogic relationships with them. Likewise, the IRAS is constantly on the move to explore new channels for bilateral exchanges or improve existing communication options in order to reduce the cost of communication to increase the intensity of dedication to these stakeholders.

Finally, the last group of skeptics poses one of the greatest challenges to the e-filing system as they are most likely to shrug off any relational gimmicks directed at them to tempt them aboard. Recognizing this constraint, the IRAS believes that it is more realistic to secure acceptance of the system before it can harness their commitment. Particularly, the auto-inclusion scheme, apart from being a stopper of dissenting voices, doubles as a key relational strategy to persuade these stakeholders into accepting the e-filing system. From a strategic management perspective, the auto-inclusion scheme represents an innovative application of IT to preserve or even strengthen the level of control in e-government services without undermining taxpayers' perception of the organization's collaborative position. An IRAS manager commented:

We prefer it that way [auto-inclusion] because first of all it is very accurate. In fact, sometimes the taxpayers themselves enter the thing wrongly.

More importantly, the auto-inclusion scheme enabled the IRAS to employ imperceptible but effective controls in ensuring the reliability of the tax filing system. The CIO commented:

By getting the information directly from the employer and automatically into the system...I have no worries about whether there is an understatement of income because [now] I source it directly from a third party. I can accept tax information from third parties without worries because it is not in their interest to lie.

Interesting enough, to encourage adoption of the auto-inclusion scheme, the IRAS relied on the promotion of mutual benefits through regular dialogue with taxpayers. By strengthening collaborative bonds with different stakeholders, the cooperative benefits to be derived from the auto-inclusion scheme could be better appreciated and more readily accepted by all parties involved. In fact, individual taxpayers sometimes became the primary promotional means of the IRAS in encouraging employer participation. As verified by the CIO:

We encourage a lot of them to get their employers to join the auto inclusion scheme because whether an item is taxable or non-taxable, we can arrange with the employer. So taxpayers don't have to crack their heads.

On the part of the employers, participation in the auto inclusion scheme also translates into greater efficiency. Rather than catering to the requests of individual employees who may approach the company separately for documentation in support of their personal tax filing needs, it is simpler for the company to transmit the tax information directly to the IRAS. For the employees, they are spared the hassle of sifting through and supplying the details of their employment information for their tax returns. For the IRAS, direct access to taxpayer information at its source – that is from the employers who are paying the salaries of the taxpayers – means a reduction to the tremendous costs of data capturing and safeguarding against erroneous and fraudulent tax declarations. Eventually, the IRAS believes, the auto inclusion scheme can be converted into a paperless tax filing paradigm where all relevant tax information is automatically channeled into the e-filing system, without any form of physical intervention. As explained by the CIO:

Doing auto inclusion means we can reduce our tremendous data capture efforts because we capture so much of the tax information. That's why when you do e-filing, it is not as tedious as if you were to file all the different forms; you only have to complete the part that is necessary...Since we started the auto inclusion scheme, we have been systematically trying to auto include as much tax information as possible. And, hopefully one day, we will reach the stage where taxpayers do not have to do anything anymore (in the filing of their tax returns). That's our ultimate goal.

The case illustrates that e-government offers a novel alternative of blending the ideals of control and cooperation into strategic stakeholder management. In the case study, the IRAS employs an integrated e-government solution to fashion a strategic convergence of interests among stakeholders such that a mentality of self-governance becomes the intrinsic motivational driver in e-government service adoption. Specifically, the integrated e-government solution enables the co-existence of control and collaboration by allowing control mechanisms to assume a more discreet nature while giving more prominence to the agency's collaborative intent in encouraging citizen participation. The case of the e-filing

Table 2. A summary of implications on stakeholder relationship management

Types of Stakeholders	Implications for Stakeholder Management in E-Governments
Engineers	Establishment of a leveled platform to facilitate symmetrical communications and dialogic relations
Dissents	Cultivation of an open and receptive culture to accommodate and consider dissenting opinions
Seasoners	Promotion of a transparent and approachable organizational structure to dismiss socially exclusive behavior
Skeptics	Induction of strategic value networks to provide mediating relational elements or incentives to induce psychological conversions

system demonstrates that e-governance in e-government can adopt a less intrusive and more engaging approach in stakeholder management by keeping controls subtle and making collaborative intentions more explicit.

Essentially, the budding strategic value network underlines the presence of mediating relational elements or incentives among stakeholders, which may be leveraged to compel certain segments of this network to modify their stances towards the e-filing system. The case of the IRAS offers a preliminary glimpse into the strategic management of stakeholders for e-government initiatives as tabulated below:

E-GOVERNANCE IN E-GOVERNMENT: IMPLICATIONS FOR PRACTICE AND RESEARCH

Case findings point to the dawn of a technologically-driven era in public administration where governance is guided by a constant search for the optimal blend of control interjected with increasing emphasis on the element of collaboration (Demb and Neubauer, 1992). This phenomenon, driven partially by the increasing emancipation of citizens from over-relying on authorities for information access, demands refinements to the principles of stakeholder management in corporate governance so that they may remain relevant in an e-governance system of e-government. The revised principles are:

1. Stakeholders can no longer be left out of the development of e-government initiatives and public organizations should be proactive in identifying all relevant parties. Depending on the level of commitment versus acceptance for involved parties, governments may consider giving up their conventional preference for punitive controls to pursue more cooperative ventures to systematically engage their stakeholders (Pardo et al. 2000; Pardo and Scholl, 2002; Scholl, 2001; Tennert and Schroeder, 1999).
2. In acknowledging stakeholders' expectations, e-government practitioners should not simply give in entirely to stakeholders' demands. Rather, they should meticulously distinguish among probable stakeholder categories and cautiously assess the technological restrictions underlying the IT-transformed public service so as to map out the boundary for devising and implementing control and collaboration mechanisms in the system. Most importantly, as noted by Haque (2001), the mandate of any governmental modernization efforts should not omit the responsibility of catering to a broader public community. The choice of technological improvements should be weighed against the larger social cost brought on by their implementations.
3. Instead of relying on futile attempts to integrate the expectations of every stakeholder, government agencies should develop corresponding strategies to align the interests of different stakeholder categories such that participation in e-government becomes self-governing (Turnbull, 1997). Specifically, to be less invasive and more accommodating to the social community, controls should be subsumed into the back-end infrastructure of the e-government initiative while collaboration is given more prominence in front-end contact.

The proposed requirements of e-governance in e-governments must be investigated further for an understanding of their implications for e-government project development. Future research in e-governance could progress along the following three streams/trajectories:

1. Since information accessibility is a crucial determinant of an organizational stakeholder, studies could be conducted to uncover

the means by which desirable behavior of stakeholders can be encouraged through information regulation within e-governance processes.
2. Considering that the success of e-government is governed by the accurate evaluation of technical limitations surrounding IT-inspired public services, subsequent studies could focus on how metrics can be constructed to improve the accuracy of such evaluations.
3. Due to the complexities associated with stakeholder alignment, future research in the area could focus on the discovery of barriers to stakeholder convergence in e-government and how IT can be utilized to overcome these obstacles.

LIMITATIONS AND CONCLUSION

This study has approached the topic of e-governance in e-government from the three critical aspects of stakeholder management in corporate governance: (1) identification of stakeholders, (2) recognition of differing interests among stakeholders, and (3) how an organization caters to and furthers these interests. In the case study, the impetus for e-governance in e-government has manifested as an impending need for the public organization to strategize its relationship with stakeholders in order to achieve a convergence of interests for the creation of an ever-expanding IT-driven value network (see Guillaume, 1999; Prahalad and Ramaswamy, 2000; Stratford and Stratford, 2000; Wimmer and Traunmuller, 2000). And the case of the e-filing system provides evidence supporting the integration of IT into government processes as a vital facilitator in the fusion of control and collaborative mechanisms into e-government activities.

While our single case study has supplied empirical evidence pointing to the importance of balancing control and collaboration in the understanding of e-governance within e-government, we acknowledge the limitations of our study in providing statistical extrapolation across the board. Nevertheless, the actual value of case-based research, as clarified by Yin (1994), lies in the ability to provide "analytical generalization" as opposed to that of survey research to present "statistical generalization". In analytical generalization, the investigator is "striving to generalize a particular set of results to some broader theory" (p. 36). As such, our study undertaken from this perspective should provide a vocabulary that e-government researchers and practitioners may employ during their examination of e-governance within other public organizations, allowing future public e-transformations to be compared and be benchmarked.

In sum, the emergence of organizational e-governance has made obsolete, old administrative wisdom about power distribution in public institutions. In its place, there is a rising need to view strategic stakeholder management as an important competitive imperative of e-government. As such, business-IT integration in public administration should evolve along the direction of a strategic convergence of stakeholder interests.

REFERENCES

Agle, B.R., Mitchell, R.K., & Sonnenfeld, J.A. (1999). Who matters to ceos? An investigation of stakeholder attributes and salience, corporate performance, and ceo values. *Academy of Management Journal, 42*(5), 507-525.

Ahituv, N. (1980). A systematic approach towards assessing the value of an information system. *MIS Quarterly, 4*(4), 61-75.

Aichholzer, G., & Schmutzer, R. (2000, September 6-8). Organizational challenges to the development of electronic government. In *Proceedings of 11th International Workshop on Database and Expert Systems Applications* (DEXA'00), Greenwich, London, UK, pp. 379-383.

Alavi, M., & Tiwana, A. (2002). Knowledge integration in virtual teams: The potential role of kms. *Journal of the American Society for Information Science and Technology, 53*(12), 1029-1037.

Allen, B.A., Juillet, L., Paquet, G., & Roy, J. (2001). E-governance & government on-line in Canada: partnerships, people & prospects. *Government Information Quarterly, 18*(1), 93-104.

Audia, P.G., Locke, E.A., & Smith, K.G. (2000). The paradox of success: an archival and a laboratory study of strategic persistence following radical environmental change. *Academy of Management Journal, 43*(5), 837-853.

Backus, M. (2001). E-governance in developing countries. *IICD Research Brief – No 1.*

Bailey, J.E., & Pearson, S.W. (1983). Development of a tool for measuring and analyzing computer user satisfaction. *Management Science, 29*(5), 530-545.

Benbasat, I., Goldstein, D.K., & Mead, M. (1987). The case research strategy in studies of information systems. *MIS Quarterly, 11*(3), 369-386.

Berman, S.L., Wicks, A.C., Kotha, S., & Jones, T.M. (1999). Does stakeholder orientation matter? The relationship between stakeholder management models and firm financial performance. *Academy of Management Journal, 42*(5), 488-506.

Blair, M.M. (1995). *Ownership and control.* Washington DC: The Brookings Institution.

Boatright, J.R. (2002). Contractors as stakeholders: Reconciling stakeholder theory with the nexus-of-contracts firm. *Journal of Banking and Finance, 26*(9), 1837-1852.

Boyatzis, R.E. (1998). *Transforming qualitative information: Thematic analysis and code development.* CA: Sage Publication.

Bozeman, B., & Kingsley, G. (1998). Risk culture in public and private organizations. *Public Administration Review, 58*(2), 109-118.

Calista, D.J. (1986). Reorganization as reform: the implementation of integrated human services agencies. In D.J. Calista (Ed.), *Bureaucratic and Governmental Reform*,(pp. 197-214). Greenwich, CT: JAI Press.

Caroll, A.B. (1989). *Business and society.* Cincinnati: South-Western.

Clarkson, M.B.E. (1995). *A risk based model of stakeholder theory.* The Centre for Corporate Social Performance & Ethics, University of Toronto.

Coursey, D., & Bozeman, B. (1990). Decision making in public and private organizations: A test of alternative concepts of "publicness". *Public Administrative Review, 50*(5), 525-35.

Csetenyi, A. (2000, September 6-8). Electronic government: perspectives from e-commerce. *Proceedings of the 11th International Workshop on Database and Expert Systems Applications* (DEXA'00), (pp. 294-298). Greenwich, London, UK.

Cumming, J.F. (2001). Engaging stakeholders in corporate accountability programmes: A cross-sectoral analysis of UK and transnational experience. *Business Ethics: A European Review, 10*(1), 45-52.

Cutlip, S.C., Center, A.H., & Broom, G.M. (1994). *Effective public relations.* Englewood Cliffs, NJ: Prentice-Hall, Inc.

Davis, F.D. (1989). Perceived usefulness, perceived ease of use, and user acceptance of information technology. *MIS Quarterly, 13*(3), 319-340.

Davis, J.H., Schoorman, F.D., & Donaldson, L. (1997). Toward a stewardship theory of management. *Academy of Management Review, 22*(1), 20-47.

DeLone, W.H., & McLean, E.R. (1992). Information system success: the quest for the dependent variable. *Information Systems Research, 3*(1), 60-95.

Demb, A., & Neubauer, F.F. (1992). The corporate board: Confronting the paradoxes. *Long Range Planning, 25*(3), 9-20.

Donaldson, L., & Davis, J.H. (1994). Boards and company performance – research challenges the conventional wisdom. *Corporate Governance: An International Review, 2*(3), 151-160.

Donaldson, T., & Preston, L.E. (1995). The stakeholder theory of the corporation: Concepts, evidence and implications. *Academy of Management Review, 20*(1), 65-91.

Eisenhardt, K.M. (1989). Agency theory: An assessment and review. *Academy of Management Review, 14*(1), 57-74.

Eisenhardt, K.M. (1991). Better stories and better constructs. *Academy of Management Review, 16*(3), 620-627.

Elgarah, W., & Courtney J.F. (2002, August 9-11). Enhancing the G2C relationship through new channels of communication: Web-based citizen input. In *Proceedings of 8th Americas Conference on Information Systems* (AMCIS 2002), (pp. 564-568). Dallas, TX.

Fernandes, D., Gorr, W., & Krishnan, R. (2001, August 3-5,). ServiceNet: An agent-based framework for one-stop e-government services. In *Proceedings of the 7th Americas Conference on Information System* (AMCIS 2001), (pp. 1590-1594). Boston.

Foucault, M. (1991). Governmentality. In G. Burchell, C. Gordon, & P. Miller (Eds.), *The foucault effect: studies in governmentality* (pp. 87-104). Chicago: University of Chicago Press.

Freeman, R.E. (1984). *Strategic management: a stakeholder approach.* Boston: Harper Collins.

Frey, B.S. (1997). On the relationship between intrinsic and extrinsic work motivation. *International Journal of Industrial Organizations, 15*(4), 427-439.

Frooman, J. (1999). Stakeholder influence strategies. *Academy of Management Review, 24*(2), 191-205.

Ghoshal, S., & Moran, P. (1996). Bad for practice: A critique of the transaction cost theory. *Academy of Management Review, 21*(1), 13-47.

Greenley, G.E., & Foxall, G.R. (1998). External moderation of associations among stakeholder orientations and company performance. *International Journal of Research in Marketing, 15*(1), 51-69.

Gregory, R.J. (1999). Social capital theory and administrative reform: Maintaining ethical theory in public service. *Public Administration Review, 59*(1), 63-75.

Guillaume, G. (1999). *L'empire de Réseaux.* Paris, France: Descartes & Cie.

Hamilton, S., & Chervany, N.L. (1981). evaluating information system effectiveness - Part I: comparing evaluation approaches. *MIS Quarterly, 5*(3), 55-69.

Haque, M.S. (2001). The diminishing publicness of public service under the current mode of governance. *Public Administration Review, 61*(1), 65-82.

Hawley, J.P., & Williams, A.T. (1996). Corporate governance in the United States: The rise of fiduciary capitalism, a review of the literature. *Prepared for the Organization for Economic Cooperation and Development,* Paris, France.

Heeks, R. (2002). *Understanding e-governance for development, i-government working paper Series.* Retrieved March 25, 2002, from http://idpm.man.ac.uk/ idpm/igov11.htm

Ho, A.T-K. (2002). Reinventing local governments and the e-government initiative. *Public Administration Review, 62*(4), 434-44.

IADB (Inter-American Development Bank) (2002). *E-governance; e-government. ICT for development*. Retrieved June 20, 2004, from http://www.iadb.org/ict4dev/governance.htm

IRAS (2002). *Realizing our vision*. Singapore: Inland Revenue Authority of Singapore.

Janis, I.L. (1982). *Groupthink*. Boston: Houghton, Mifflin.

Jensen, M.C., & Meckling, W.H. (1976). Theory of the firm: Managerial behavior, agency costs and ownership structure. *Journal of Financial Economics, 3*, 305–360.

Kankanhalli, A., Tan, B.C.Y., & Wei, K.K. (2001, December 16-19). Seeking knowledge in electronic knowledge repositories: An exploratory study. In *Proceedings of the 22nd International Conference on Information Systems* (ICIS 2001)(pp. 123-134). New Orleans, LA.

Kim, E., & Lee, J. (1986). An exploratory contingency model of user participation and mis use. *Information and Management, 11*(2), 87-97.

Kisfalvi, V. (2000). The threat of failure, the perils of success and ceo character: sources of strategic persistence. *Organization Studies, 21*(3), 611-639.

Kruckeberg, D., & Starck, K. (1998). *Public relations and community: a reconstructed theory*. New York: Praeger, 52.

Lacity, M., & Janson, M.A. (1994). Understanding qualitative data: A framework of text analysis methods. *Journal of Management Information System, 11*(2), 137-155.

Lawler, E.J., & Yoon, J. (1995). Structural power and emotional processes in negotiation: A social exchange approach. In R.M. Kramer, & D.M. Messick (Eds.), *Negotiation as a Social Process* (pp. 143-165). Thousand Oaks, CA: Sage.

Lawson, G. (1998). *NetState*. London: Demos.

Lenk, K., & Traunmuller, R. (2000, September 6-8).A framework for electronic government. In *Proceedings of the 11th International Workshop on Database and Expert Systems Applications* (DEXA'00),(pp. 71-277). Greenwich, London, U.K.

Lim, E.T.K., & Tan, C.W. (2005, August 5-10). *What you think others think: Influence of presumed influence in e-collaborations*. Paper presented at the 65th Annual Meeting of the Academy of Management, OCIS Division, Honolulu, Hawaii.

Lindsey, D.H., Brass, D.J., & Thomas, J.B. (1995). Efficacy-performance spirals: A multilevel perspective. *Academy of Management Review, 20*(3), 645-378.

Lowndes, V., Pratchett, L., & Stoker, G. (2001). Trends in public participation: part 2 - citizen's perspectives. *Public Administration, 79*(2), 445-455.

Marchionini, G., Samet, H., & Brandt, L. (2003). Digital government. *Communications of ACM, 46*(1), 25-27.

Markus, M.L. (1994). Electronic mail as the medium of managerial choice. *Organizational Science, 5*(4), 502-527.

Markus, M.L., & Robey, D. (1988). Information technology and organizational change: casual structure in theory and research. *Management Science, 34*(5), 583-598.

Markus, M.L., Tanis, C., & Fenema, P.C. (2000). Multi-site ERP implementation. *Communications of the ACM, 43*(4), 42-46.

McNaughton, K. (1999). *Taxpayers reluctant to file over web, cnet.com*. Retrieved May 2, 2003, from http://news.com.com/2100-1017-223215.html?legacy=cnet

Merton, R.K., Fiske, M., & Kendall, P.L. (1990). *The focused interview: a manual of problems and procedures* (2nd ed.). New York: Free Press.

Milford, H.S. (2000). Racing to e-government: Using the internet for citizen service delivery. *Government Finance Review, 16*(5), 21-22.

Mitchell, R.K., Agle, B.R., & Wood, D.J. (1997). Toward a theory of stakeholder identification and salience: defining the principle of who and what really counts. *Academy of Management Review 22*(4), 853-886.

Monks, R.A.G., & Minow, N. (1995). *Corporate governance*. Blackwell, Cambridge, MA.

Moon, M.J. (2002). The evolution of e-government among municipalities: rhetoric or reality? *Public Administration Review, 62*(4), 424-33.

Moon, M.J., and Bretschneider S. (2002). Does the perception of red tape constrain it innovativeness in organizations? Unexpected results from simultaneous equation model and implications. *Journal of Public Administration Research and Theory, 11*(3), 327-52.

Nelson, R.R., & Winter, S.J. (1982). *An evolutionary theory of economic change*. Cambridge, MA: Harvard University Press.

Newcombe, T. (2000). Customer is king. *NetGov - Supplement to Government Technology*, 8-11.

Nonaka, I., Reinmoeller, P., & Senoo, D. (1998). The "ART" of knowledge: Systems to capitalize on market knowledge. *European Management Journal, 16*(6), 673-684.

Norris, P. (1999). Who surfs? New technology, old voters, and virtual democracy. In E.C. Kamarck, & J.S. Nye (Eds.), *Democracy.com? governance in networked world* (pp. 71-94). Hollis, NH: Hollis Publishing Company.

Oliver, C. (1997). Sustainable competitive advantage: combining institutional and resource-based views. *Strategic Management Journal, 18*(9), 697-713.

Orlikowski, W. (1993). Case told as organizational change: Investigating incremental and radical changes in system development. *MIS Quarterly, 7*(3), 309-40.

Pablo, Z.D., & Pan, S.L. (2002, September, 2-4). A multi-disciplinary analysis of e-governance: Where do we start? In *Proceedings of the 6th Pacific Conference on Information Systems* (PACIS 2002), Tokyo, Japan.

Pan, S.L., Newell, S., Huang, J., & Wan, K.C. (2001, December 16-19). Knowledge integration as a key problem in an ERP implementation. In *Proceeding for the 22nd Annual International Conference on Information Systems* (ICIS 2001), (pp. 321-328). New Orleans, LA.

Pardo, T.A., & Scholl, H.J. (2002, January 7-10). Walking atop the cliffs: Avoiding failure and reducing risk in large scale e-government projects. In *Proceedings of the 35th Hawaii International Conference on System Sciences (HICSS 2002)*. HI.

Pardo, T.A., Scholl, H.J., Cook, M.E., Connelly, D.R., & Dawes, S.S. (2000). *New York Atate central accounting system stakeholder need analysis*. Albany, NY: Central for Technology in Government.

Parkhe, A. (1993). Messy research, methodological predispositions, and theory development in international joint ventures. *Academy of Management Review, 8*(2), 227-268.

Pfeffer, J., & Salancik, G.R. (1978). *The knowledge-doing gap: How smart companies turn knowledge into action*. Boston: Harvard Business School Press.

Pfeffer, J., & Sutton, R.I. (2000). *The knowledge-doing gap: How smart companies turn knowledge into action*. Boston: Harvard Business School Press.

Porter, M.E. (1992). Capital choices: Changing the way america invests in industry. *Research Report Presented to the Council on Competitiveness*, Co–sponsored by The Harvard Business School, Boston.

Prahalad, C.K., and Ramaswamy, V. (2000). Co-opting customer competence. *Harvard Business Review, 78*(1), 79-87.

Rainey, G.W., & Rainey, H.G. (1986). Breaching the hierarchical imperative: The modularization of the social security claims process. In D.J. Calista (Ed.), *Bureaucratic and governmental reform*, (pp. 171-196). Greenwich, CT: JAI Press.

Rainey, H.G., Backoff, R.W., & Levine, C.H. (1976). Comparing public and private organizations. *Public Administration Review, 36*(2), 233-244.

Schiavo-Ocampo, S., and Sundaram, P. (2001). *To serve and preserve: improving public administration in a competitive world.* Manila, Philippines: Asian Development Bank.

Schneiderman, B., & Rose, A. (1996). Social impact statements: Engaging public participation in information technology design. In *Proceedings of The Symposium On Computers and The Quality Of Life*, (pp. 90-96).

Scholl, H. (2001). Applying stakeholder theory to e-government. In B. Schmid, K. Stanoevska-Slabeva, & V. Tschammer (Eds.), *Towards the e-society: e-commerce, e-business, and e-government* (pp. 735-747). MA: Kluwer Academic Publishers.

Scott, S.G., & Lane, V.R. (2000). A stakeholder approach to organizational identity. *Academy Of Management Review, 25*(1), 43-62.

Seavey, A.C. (1996). Final thoughts on interesting times. *Journal of Government Information, 23*(4), 515-520.

Seddon, P.B. (1997). A respecification and extension of the delone and mclean model of IS success. *Information Systems Research 8*(3), 240-253.

Shleifer, A., & Vishny, R.W. (1996). *A survey of corporate governance, national bureau of economic research.* Working Paper 5554, Cambridge, MA.

Stiglitz, J., Orszag, P., & Orszag, J. (2000). *The role of government in a digital age.* Retrieved April 16, 2002, from http://www.ccianet.org/digital_age/report.pdf

Stratford, J.S., & Stratford, J. (2000). Computerized and networked government information. *Journal of Government Information, 27*(3), 385-389.

Strauss, A.L., & Corbin, J. (1990). *Basics of qualitative research: Grounded theory procedures and techniques.* London: Sage.

Sundaramurthy, C. (2000). Antitakeover provisions and shareholder value implications: A review and a contingency framework. *Journal of Management, 25*(5), 1005-1030.

Sundaramurthy, C., & Lewis, M. (2003). Control and collaboration: Paradoxes of governances. *Academy of Management Review, 28*(3), 397-415.

Tan, C.W., Pan, S.L., & Lim, E.T.K. (2005a). Managing stakeholder interests in e-government implementation: Lessons learned from a singapore e-government project. *Journal of Global Information Management, 13*(1), 31-53.

Tan, C.W., Pan, S.L., Lim, E.T.K., & Chan, C.M.L. (2005b). Managing knowledge conflicts in inter-organizational project: an exploratory study of the infocomm development authority of singapore. *Journal of the American Society for Information Science and Technology, 56*(11), 1187-1199.

Tannenbaum, A.S. (1967).*Control in organizations.* New York: McGraw–Hill.

Tapscott, D. (1996). *Digital economy: Promise and peril in the age of networked intelligence.* New York: McGraw-Hill.

Taylor, M., & Kent, M.L. (1999). Challenging assumptions of international public relations. *Public Relations Review 25*(2), 131-144.

Taylor, S., & Bogdan, R. (1984). *Introduction to qualitative research methods.* New York: John Wiley & Sons.

Tennert, J.B., & Schroeder, A.D. (1999). Stakeholder analysis. *Presentation at the 60th Annual Meeting of the American Society of Pubic Administration.*

Traunmuller, R., & Wimmer, M. (2000, September 6-8). Process – collaboration – norms – knowledge: signposts for administrative application development. In *Proceedings of the 11th International Workshop on Database and Expert Systems Applications* (DEXA'00),(pp. 1141-1145). Greenwich, London, UK.

Tricker, R.I. (1994). *International corporate governance.* Singapore: Simon & Schuster.

Turnbull, S. (1997). Stakeholder co-operation. *Journal of Co-operative Studies, 29*(3), 18-52.

von Hoffman, C. (1999). The making of e-government. *COI Enterprise Magazine* (November 15).

von Krogh, G. (1998). Care in knowledge creation. *California Management Review, 40*(3), 133-153.

Walsham, G. (1995). Interpretive case studies in is research: Nature and method. *European Journal of Information Systems, 4,* 74-81.

Webler, T., & Tuler, S. (2000). Fairness and competence in citizen participation – theoretical reflections from a case study. *Administration & Society, 32*(5), 566-595.

Wescott, C. (2002). *E-government in the Asia Pacific Region.* Retrieved March, 27, 2002, from http://www.adb.org/ Documents/Papers/E_Government/default.asp

Westphal, J. D. (1999). Collaboration in the boardroom: Behavioral and performance consequences of CEO-board social ties. *Academy of Management Journal, 42*(1), 7-24.

Wimmer, M., & Traunmuller, R. (2000, September 6-8). Trends in electronic government: managing distributed knowledge. In *Proceedings of the 11th International Workshop on Database and Expert Systems Applications* (DEXA'00), (pp. 340-345) Greenwich, London, UK.

Wimmer, M., Traunmuller, R., & Lenk, K. (2001, January 3-6). Electronic business invading the public sector: Considerations on change and design. In *Proceedings of 34th Hawaii International Conference on System Sciences. (HICSS 2002),* HI.

Yin, R.K. (1994). *Case study research: design and methods.* London: Sage.

This work was previously published in the International Journal of Electronic Government Research, Vol. 3, Issue 2, edited by M. Khosrow-Pour, pp. 1-28, copyright 2007 by IGI Publishing, formerly known as Idea Group Publishing (an imprint of IGI Global).

Chapter VI
Electronic Government Implementation:
A Comparison Between Developed and Developing Countries

Yining Chen
Western Kentucky University, USA

H.M. Chen
Shanghai Jiaotong University, China

Russell K.H. Ching
California State University - Sacramento, USA

Wayne W. Huang
Ohio University, USA

ABSTRACT

Over the last decade, the Internet has become one of the most important means of communication in all social areas. The success of Web technology adoption in the private sector has put pressures on the public sector to adopt the Internet to present information and service resources. The concept of creating more efficient and convenient interaction between government and the interacting parties using Internet technology is referred to as electronic government (or digital government). Recent studies have shown an increase in the adoption of electronic government by various countries (Archer, 2005; I-Ways, 2005; Janssen et al. 2004). Nevertheless, the level of implementation diverges from country to country. This study identifies critical success factors of electronic government and proposes an implementation framework. This chapter presents an extensive case study to illustrate how the proposed framework can be used to analyze electronic government strategies in a developed country (United States) and a developing country (China). In conclusion, recommendations are made to developed and developing countries for their implementation of electronic government.

Copyright © 2009, IGI Global, distributing in print or electronic forms without written permission of IGI Global is prohibited.

INTRODUCTION

"Electronic government" or "digital government" refers to the initiative taken by governmental agencies and organizations to use the Internet technology in increasing their working effectiveness and efficiency. It is a permanent commitment made by the government to improve the relationship between the private citizen and the public sector through enhanced, cost-effective, and efficient delivery of services, information, and knowledge. Broadly defined, electronic government includes the use of all information and communication technologies, from fax machines to wireless palm pilots, to facilitate the daily administration of government, exclusively as an Internet driven activity that improves citizen's access to government information, services and expertise to ensure citizen's participation in, and satisfaction with government process (UN and ASPA, 2001). Narrowly defined, electronic government is the production and delivery of government services through IT applications; used to simplify and improve transactions between governments and constituents, businesses, and other government agencies (Sprecher, 2000).

Electronic government can improve communication between government agencies and their constituents by providing access to information and services online at relatively low cost, and provide public services through Web sites. The Economist magazine estimates that the potential savings of implementing electronic government could be as much as $110 billion and 144 billion English Pounds in the US and Europe respectively (Symonds, 2000). In recent years, electronic government has attracted more and more research interest and focus from industries, national governments, and universities (Barnes and Vidgen, 2006; Bertot and Jaeger, 2006; Chen et al. 2006;

Table 1. Benefits of electronic government

Removed Boundaries
Electronic government will help break down agency and jurisdictional barriers to allow more integrated whole-of-government services across the three tiers of government (Federal, State, and Local). With electronic government, the provision of seamless access will be taken much further and will make government much more approachable.
Enhanced Accessibility
Government in the off-line environment can be difficult to access. While some business can be conducted by phone, it often requires a visit to a government office. This can be problematic for people in regional and remote locations. Electronic government offers the potential to dramatically increase access to information and services.
Improved Service Quality
The underlying goal of electronic government is to improve service quality for all citizens. Electronic government represents convenient and reliable services, with lower compliance costs as well as higher quality and value.
Integrated Agencies
Cross-agency initiatives can lead to high value services that provide efficiency benefits for both citizens and government. Scope for cross-agency initiatives exists where several services are closely related – that is, where information needs to be acquired from more than one agency (e.g., business services).
Improved Reputation
Electronic government helps build an image of a country as a modern nation, an attractive location for people to visit, and businesses to invest.
Greater Citizen Participation
Electronic government makes it easier for those who wish to contribute.

Carter and Belanger, 2005; Grönlund and Horan 2004; Chircu and Lee, 2003; Huang, D'Ambra and Bhalla, 2002; Huang, Siau and Wei, 2004; Jaeger, 2006; Jain and Patnayakuni, 2003; Moon and Norris, 2005; Navarra and Cornford, 2003).

Benefits of Electronic Government

The development and implementation of electronic government brings about impacts and changes to the structure and functioning of the public administration (Snellen, 2000). Unlike the traditional bureaucratic model where information flows only vertically and rarely between departments, electronic government links new technology with legacy systems internally, and in turn, links government information infrastructures externally with everything digital (Tapscott, 1995). Electronic government offers a potential to dramatically increase access to information and services and makes it easier for citizens to participate in and contribute to governmental issues. Table 1 lists benefits of electronic government.

Stages of Electronic Government Implementation

Table 2 lists five stages of electronic government that reflect the degree of technical sophistication and interaction with users (Hiller and Belanger, 2001).

DEVELOPED VERSUS DEVELOPING COUNTRIES

Every year the United Nations releases a report on the least developed countries (LDC) and compares their economic conditions in several different categories. For 2002, 49 countries were designated as the least developed. These countries were decided based on their low GDP per capita, their weak human assets, and their high degree of economic vulnerability (UNCTAD, 2002). Electronic government implementation and development is a high-priority issue on various countries' agenda. Some countries have surpassed others in online services that they offer to their citizens. Indicators on education and literacy show that in Mozambique, only 7% of the total population was enrolled in secondary school. Indicators on communications and media show that in Bangladesh, only 3.4% of the population has a telephone, while 9.3% are in the circulation of daily newspapers (UNCTAD, 2002).

Although electronic government technologies have a potential to improve the lives of 80% of the world's population that lives in developing countries, the developed countries such as USA, Canada, UK, and Australia are so far the leaders in electronic government (Annual Global Accenture Study, 2002), reaping the vast majority of initial gains of electronic government implementation. Actually, the gap between developed and developing countries in Internet technological

Table 2. Stages of electronic government

Stage 1	The most basic form of electronic government; uses IT for disseminating information by posting data on the web sites that is viewable
Stage 2	Two-way communication between government and constituents; e-mail systems are incorporated as well as data-transfer technologies
Stage 3	Web-based self services where online service and financial transactions are available
Stage 4	Various government services are connected internally and externally for enhanced efficiency, user-friendliness, and effectiveness
Stage 5	The promotion of web-based political participation, including online voting; highlights Web-based political activities by citizens

infrastructures, practices, and usage has been wider rather than narrower over recent years. Besides the lack of sufficient capital to build up an expensive national information infrastructure (NII) on which electronic government is based, developing countries also lack the sufficient knowledge and skill to develop suitable and effective strategies for establishing and promoting electronic government.

An estimated 500 electronic government programs were launched in the year 2001 by governments worldwide (Palmer, 2002). Electronic government strategies have had a tremendous impact on the way governments interact with their citizens. More than 75% of Australians file income taxes online, while the mayor of Minnesota receives about 13,000 e-mails from the public each week (Palmer, 2002). According to the 2002 Annual Global Accenture (former Anderson Consulting: AC) Study, Canada is the leader in electronic government implementation. The remaining top 10 countries are (in order): Singapore, the United States, Australia, Denmark, the United Kingdom, Finland, Hong Kong, Germany, and Ireland. A survey by the United Nations found that of its 190 member states, only 36 out of the 169 available Web sites had one-stop portals and less than 20 offered online transactions (Jackson, 2002). This clearly shows a big gap in current electronic government implementation status in different countries. A more recent study using United Nations data to empirically prove that electronic

Table 3. Main differences between developed and developing countries

	Developed Countries	Developing Countries
History and Culture	• Government and economy developed early, immediately after independence • Economy growing at a constant rate, productivity increasing, high standard of living • Relatively long history of democracy and more transparent government policy and rule	• Government usually not specifically defined; economy not increasing in productivity • Economy not growing or increasing productivity; low standard of living • Relatively short history of democracy and less transparent government policy and rule
Technical Staff	• Has a current staff, needs to increase technical abilities and hire younger professionals • Has outsourcing abilities and financial resources to outsource; current staff would be able to define requirements for development	• Does not have a staff, or has very limited in-house staff • Does not have local outsourcing abilities and rarely has the financial ability to outsource; current staff may be unable to define specific requirements
Infrastructure	• Superior current infrastructure • High internet access for employees and citizens	• Inferior current infrastructure • Low Internet access for employees and citizens
Citizens	• High Internet access and computer literacy; still has digital divide and privacy issues • Relatively more experienced in democratic system and more actively participate in governmental policy-making process	• Low Internet access and citizens are reluctant to trust online services; few citizens know how to operate computers • Relatively less experienced in democratic system and less actively participate in governmental policy-making process
Government Officers	• Decent computer literacy and dedication of resources; many do not place electronic government at a high priority	• Low computer literacy and dedication of resources; many do not place electronic government at a high priority due to lack of knowledge on the issue

government development and implementation differ in three areas: income level, development status, and region (Siau and Long, 2005).

In comparison with other countries, the United States along with Australia, Singapore, and Canada are the early leaders in the march toward electronic government. Governments in the United Kingdom, France, Germany, Spain, Norway, Hong Kong, and New Zealand have vowed to change their policies towards the implementation of electronic government in order to take the full advantage of the digital information age. Other cautious implementers include Italy, Japan, Netherlands, and South Africa. Though there has been significant progress made in developed countries in electronic government implementation, many developing countries have been left behind with a long way to catch up. Table 3 summarizes differences between developed and developing countries in various aspects of government.

AN IMPLEMENTATION FRAMEWORK

Most, if not all electronic government strategies and implementation plans in developing countries have been based on theories and experiences of developed countries (Huang, D'Ambra and Bhalla, 2002). Feeling the pressure and demand from citizens to provide electronic government services online, many developing countries have no choice but to hastily jump into the electronic government implementation wagon by following electronic government development strategies proposed and carried out by developed countries. However, due to substantial differences in many key aspects of electronic government related technological and social conditions between developed and developing countries, electronic government development strategies and experiences from developed countries may not be directly applicable to developing countries. Even in developed countries, about 20-25% of electronic government projects are either never implemented or abandoned immediately after implementation, and a further 33% fail partially in terms of falling short of major goals, causing significant undesirable outcomes or both (Heeks, 2000).

National E-Government Infrastructure (NeI) Factors

The Center for International Development at Harvard University, USA, supported by IBM, identified four key factors describing differences between developing and developed countries in terms of implementing e-commerce (Kirkman, Osorio and Sachs, 2002). These four factors, presented in Table 4, are adapted to study electronic government in this research, and are termed as National e-government Infrastructure (NeI) factors.

Culture and Society Factors

E-commerce largely deals with business transactions in private sector whereas electronic government deals with services in public sector. Due to key differences between private and public sectors (e.g., Bozeman and Bretschneider, 1986; Caudle, Gorr and Newcomer, 1991; Rainey, Backoff and Levine, 1976), factors other than the ones identified by the Harvard University e-commerce research project may also be important to electronic government strategies and implementations. Prior relevant research suggested some key factors for electronic government strategies and implementations, which can be used to identify differences in electronic government between developed and developing countries. Those suggested factors include society factors like *history, citizens* (Huang, D'Ambra and Bhalla, 2002), *government staff and governance* (Wimmer, Traunmuller and Lenk, 2001), *organizational structure* (Baligh, 1994), and cultural factors like *national culture* (Hoftstede, 1980; Hofstede, 1991), *organizational culture* (Hoftstede, 1980; Schein, 1993), and *social norms* (Ajzen, 1988). Other than those suggested by literature, society

Table 4. NeI Factors

	NeI Factor 1: Network Access
Key Question	What are the availability, cost and quality of Information & Communication Technology (ICTs) networks, services, and equipment?
Key Issues	• Infrastructure Development Infrastructure development is a necessity before countries can consider any large projects dedicated to electronic government. Citizens must have access to services before any of the cost saving benefits will apply. Also, with a lack of back-end infrastructure, governments and their employees will be unable to move into transactional process and further stages of electronic government implementation. • Resources and IT Support Outsourcing can be an option for countries to implement electronic government. The private sector has an obligation to support governments throughout the world in their dedication to electronic government. Developing countries need financial discounts and support from the private sector to successfully develop applications due to their lack of resources and staff. • Utilization The citizen utilization of the Internet is based on the access to the Internet and the Web site. Technical support must provide 24/7 access, in addition to providing a better infrastructure so that more citizens can utilize the Internet. Much like in developed countries, citizen utilization is an important part of the cost savings for countries.
	NeI Factor 2: Network Learning
Key Question	• Does an educational system integrate ICTs into its processes to improve learning? • Are there technical training programs in the community that can train and prepare an ICT workforce?
Key Issues	Technical staffing and training In developing countries, the problems lie in the lack of financial resources to hire full time in-house support and in the inability to find such support due to the lack of education in these countries. Outsourcing is an alternative; however, affordable and competent companies may not be available. Even if a country can find the finances to support an outsourcing project, stability and maintenance of the application are often difficult.
	NeI Factor 3: Network Economy
Key Question	How do businesses and governments use information and communication technologies to interact with the public and with each other?
Key Issues	Boundary removal, collaboration, partnership, public-private sector partnership, e-community creation. In many developing countries, government structure is undefined and destabilized by corruption and communism. War and terrorism can be a constant threat that disrupts government operations on a daily basis. Consequently, boundary removal and department collaboration is a difficult and slow process. Government departments must collaborate with each other, private sectors, and related communities in order for electronic government to be implemented in an efficient way. Due to the low computer literacy and high cost of online access, long and unnecessary transactions need to be cut down in processes to allow users to quickly access documents and print them or fill them out online.

continued on the following page

Table 4. continued

	NeI Factor 4: Network Policy
Key Question	To what extent does the policy environment promote or hinder the growth of ICT adoption and use?
Key Issues	Legislations, laws, strategies (visions and missions), and accountability Government agencies and departments must be accountable for their information and processes they support. It is essential for processes and duties to be segregated and responsibilities to be assigned to appropriate agencies and departments. These agencies and departments then need to work together to design their Web pages and IT flows. After implementation, they must have the abilities and be held accountable to support the web pages and troubleshoot them. Governments must also be accountable for their financial and accounting systems. Many developing countries have issues and economic problems due to their lack of reliable accounting systems.

Figure 1. A conceptual research framework

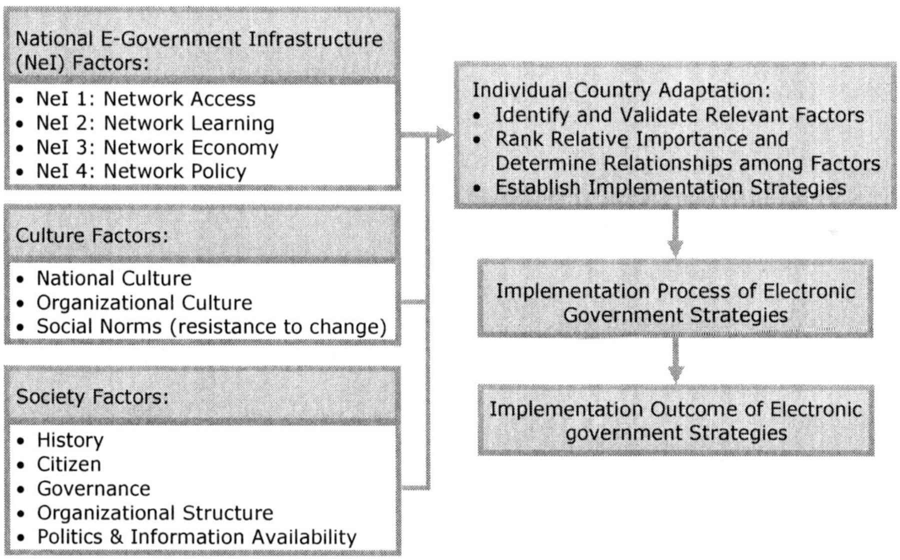

factors like *politics* and *information availability* should also be considered. Developing countries are often less democratized with underdeveloped press communication resulting in unbalanced and deficient information availability. These politics and information factors have significant impact on the speed of infrastructure establishment in developing countries, thus should be considered in creating electronic government strategies.

Based upon the literature review and discussion, a research framework incorporating critical success factors (CSFs) that influence electronic government strategies and implementations, is proposed and shown in Figure 1. Some CSFs identified in proposed framework could be more important to developed countries than to developing countries, or vice versa. The framework can also be used to assess and guide the strategic development of electronic government implementation in developed and developing countries.

Use the Proposed Framework to Analyze Electronic Government Implementation in Developed and Developing Countries

The proposed electronic government implementation framework can be used to analyze different electronic government implementation strategies adopted in developed and developing countries. The snapshot of two big countries in electronic government implementation is analyzed using the proposed framework: USA (the largest developed country) and China (the largest developing country, with a focus on Shanghai - the biggest city and economic center of China).

Though China has maintained its position as the fastest growing economy in the world in recent years, there still exists a big gap in terms of National e-government Infrastructure (NeI) between China and other developed countries like the USA. China is still in the process of transitioning from a centrally controlled planned economy to a market-based capitalist economy. Using the proposed framework, we assess the electronic government implementation status in China with a focus in Shanghai, the economic centre and the most developed regions/cities in China. Given the scale of difference between the US and Shanghai in terms of NeIs and other factors of electronic government implementation identified in the proposed framework, one can envision the even greater difference between the US and China as a whole. Table 5 presents the differences in NeI and other factors between the US and Shanghai.

In summary, due to the differences discussed in NeIs and other social issues, it may not be feasible for the private sector to play a leading role in electronic government implementation; instead it may be governments to drive the progress of electronic government implementation. Therefore, the electronic government implementation strategy between the US and China are largely different, which will be discussed.

Electronic Government Implementation Strategy in the United States

The United States, as the largest developed country, has one of the most advanced National electronic government Infrastructures (NeIs) in the world, and it also has a long history and culture of democratic government structure and capitalist economic system. As a result, the USA government adopted the following three strategic principles in the implementation of electronic government: (1) citizen-centered, not bureaucracy-centered; (2) results-oriented; and (3) market-based, actively promoting innovation (source: www.firstgov.gov). In short, electronic government implementation strategy of the USA is market-based with the aim of serving and supporting citizens' specific requirements, which is assessed by clear and specific results.

The policy environment in the United States is an important consideration in understanding the strategy for electronic government implementation. A complete set of laws relating to the development of electronic government has been in place already, including Privacy Act, Computer Matching and Privacy Protection Act, Electronic Freedom of Information Amendments, Computer Security Act, Critical Infrastructure Protection, Government Paperwork Elimination Act, and Electronic Government Act (Relyea, 2002).

According to the white paper of US federal government's electronic government strategy (2002 and 2003), more than 60% of all Internet users interact with government Web sites. Moreover, by leveraging information technology (IT) spending across federal agencies, the US federal government will make available over $1 billion in savings from aligning redundant investments. Federal IT spending in the United States exceeded $48 billion in 2002 and $52 billion in 2003. That level of IT spending provides enormous opportunities for making the transformation government into a citizen-centered electronic government.

Table 5. Comparison of NeI and other factors between the US and Shanghai

NeI Factor 1: Network Access

The information infrastructures in Shanghai have undergone mega changes and made some big progresses in recent years: Up to the beginning of year 2002,

- The bandwidth Internet connection to the outside world was expended to 2.5G;
- The network cable lines were stretched out for more than 550 kilometers that covered more than 99% of the whole city;
- The number of broadband Internet users reached 125 thousand that year;
- The number of fixed phone users exceeded 6 million while mobile phone users exceeded fixed phone users; and
- More than 3.1 million families had access to the Internet, which almost doubled the number of the previous year.

However, even in Shanghai, one of the most advanced cities in China, subscribing to Internet service is still more costly in China than in developed countries such as the United States. In China, the charge of ISP (Internet Service Provider) is bi-directional; users pay for not only sending but also receiving information.

NeI Factor 2: Network Learning

According to the *Human Development Report in 2001* by the United Nations Development Program (UNDP), which first publishes Technical Achievements Index (TAI) in the world, China is listed as the 45th among the 72 Countries; whereas the US is ranked as the No. 2 in the list. The development of the network learning is speeding up in Shanghai.

- The broadband of the main network of Shanghai Science & Education Network (SSEN) was expanded to 1.25G from the 64k in its budding stage.
- The fibro-cable connecting the educational institutions in Shanghai was longer than 200 kilometers in Year 2001.
- More than 19 universities in Shanghai made their effects to launch a common-shared database of the book information in the above 19 universities' libraries. In this system, people could also search for the key academic periodicals and borrow through the Remote Borrowing/Lending Service.
- Up to Year 2001, the SSEN had a sea-sized collection of materials including: 12 thousand periodical databases, 200 thousand e-book resources, business sub-databases, science and technology sub-databases, digital periodical system database, and so forth.
- More than 100 multifunctional databases provided a wide range of selections to the students' content. Furthermore, several universities in Shanghai have received permission from the government to develop their "net-school" projects, which made the e-learning in Shanghai more professional and orderly.

NeI Factor 3: Network Economy

The information industry in Shanghai is keeping a fast developing momentum in recent years. It has maintained the top three throughout the whole country in terms of its scale that it also draws the attention from the worldwide. The network economy is thus greatly enhanced by the strategy Shanghai adopted—"To promote the Industrialization by Informationization".

- The turnover was 130.225 billion Yuan by its growth rate of 24.4%, which maintained its strategic position as Shanghai's first pillar industry.
- The proportion of the added value in this industry in the GDP amounted to 8.1% that was 0.7% more than the previous year.
- The turnover of the information product manufacturing industry reached 101.3 billion Yuan, 37.4% increase from the precious year.
- The product sales percentage was increased by 1.8% and summed up to 97.5%.
- The information services and software in Shanghai achieved an output of 28.8 billion Yuan, 52.2% increase from the previous year.

Among the 1500 industry companies,

- Eighty percent of them have set up IT department;
- Ninety-seven percent of them have popularized the use of computer;
- Eighty-nine percent of them have become familiar with common software;
- Twelve percent of them have conducted ERP; and
- Eight percent of them have implanted CRM.

More than 500 marketplaces have adopted their MIS. Most Convenient chain stores and supermarkets have launched POS and also got them linked with each other to form a value added network system. As a whole, China's e-commerce turnover is relatively small in size, accounting for only 0.23% of US' annual e-commerce turnover.

Table 5. continued

NeI Factor 4: Network Policy
Network policy might be the weakest part of the four NeI factors for China. China has been transforming its economic system from the old Soviet Union's "planned economy" model to the capitalist's "market economy". The transition period, though seems to be on the right track, is painful and far from completion. The legal systems, laws, and regulations have been gradually established, yet they are far from maturity in managing the big developing economy, not to mention the completeness of its network economy policy and related laws. Due to its relatively short history of modernized society and long history of feudal governmental system, China's democratic system and policy still has a long way to go even though it has achieved much more progress in the last decade.
Culture and Society Factors
Developed countries have a long history and culture of democratic governmental structure and capitalist economic system, with many governments forming in the 1500's. Many developing countries have not completed its process of establishing an effective and transparent governmental structure as well as an efficient capitalist economic system. China has only started its "open door" policy since the late 1970s and "market-driven economy" in the 1990s. The differences in history and culture, citizens, government officers, and technical staff between China and other developed countries like USA are also noticeably large.
For example, China was under the feudal government system for nearly 5000 years, where the dictator of the country, the emperor, has absolute power and possesses absolute wealth in the country. Only until the early 1910s, such a governmental structure was overturned. Such a long history of ruling by an absolute powerful emperor has a prolong impact on modern governmental structure and system. Even now, national and provincial governments still have certain privileges to access and use valuable resources, such as financial, human, and production resources. Governmental agencies and organizations are generally more effective/powerful than private sectors in carrying out electronic government implementations. The level of transparency of governmental management mechanism and decision-making process is relatively low. Because of those historical reasons and practically some advantages existing in governments, many university graduates and talents favor to work for governments. As a result, governmental officers and/or technical staff in governments are generally more knowledgeable than those in private sector in using information technologies and systems in their daily work.

Indeed, a good portion of current federal IT spending is devoted to Internet initiatives, yielding over 35 million Web pages online at over 22,000 Web sites. However, past agency-centered IT approaches have limited the government's productivity gains and ability to serve citizens. As a result, the federal government is determined to transform the way it does business with citizens through the use of electronic government.

In 2003 and 2004, the overall electronic government strategy addressed the following areas:

- **Driving results and productivity growth:** IT and management reform investments that create an order of magnitude improvement in value to the citizen, especially in the areas of homeland security information sharing and knowledge flow;
- **Controlling IT costs:** consolidating redundant and overlapping investments, enterprise licensing, fixing cost overruns, and competing away excess IT services charges;
- **Implementing the e-government Act of 2002:** including government-wide architecture governance and Web-based strategies for improving access to high quality information and services; and
- **Improving cyber security:** desktop, data, applications, networks, threat and vulnerability-focused, business continuity, and privacy protection.

In summary, due to the relatively long history of a democratic system, the main goals of US electronic government focuses on increasing effectiveness and efficiency of government work and at the same time, reducing costs.

Electronic Government Implementation Strategy in China

The first electronic government implementation project in China began in 1994. According to the 11th Report of the Statistic of China National

Network Development (RSCNND) by China National Network Information Centre (CNNIC), up to the first half of 2006, the Internet users had achieved 123 million, only second to the users of USA. There were 780,000 Web sites. Among 200 million of high school and middle school students, the Internet users were more than 30 million.

Due to the substantial differences in all four key aspects/factors of NeI and other CSFs between China and developed countries like the US, instead of adopting the electronic government implementation strategies developed in the US directly, China should adopt a strategy that fits well with its current position in terms of the four aspects of NeI and other CSFs as specified in the proposed assessment framework. For example, as the center of China's economy development, Shanghai's electronic government implementation can function as a role model for other cities and provinces in China to follow by. Three specific electronic government implementation strategies of Shanghai are specified. They are (1) to increase the transparency of government work, (2) to provide the convenience and better services to citizens and enterprises, and (3) to improve the efficiency of the government administration.

Compared with the U.S.'s electronic government strategic principles—"citizen-centered", "results-oriented" and "market-based" (E-government Strategy, 2003), Shanghai has largely different strategic goals. The ultimate goal of electronic government implementation could be quite similar, which is to improve the performance and efficiency of the government work and lead to better interactions/cooperation between the government and the public and between the government and private enterprises. The unique feature of Shanghai's electronic government strategy is to "increase the transparency of the government work". Other than achieving its usual goals, electronic government in Shanghai is used as an instrument in expediting government transformation and conformity. Via the implementation of electronic government, civil rights are concretized, bribability is minimized, and governance by law and democracy are enhanced.

The electronic government implementation in China as a whole is aiming to serve its overall economic development goal, which is to completely transform China's former Soviet Union style "planning economy" to "market economy". Such changes in the overall mechanism of the country will definitely have profound effects on electronic government implementation strategy and practice. On the other hand, the US has a long history of market-economy and democratic system. The government work is relatively much more transparent than that in China. Therefore, "increasing the transparency of government work" may not seem to be important as it is to China.

In fact, based upon the successful experience of electronic government implementation strategies in developed countries, China adopted a different electronic government implementation strategy, which could be characterized as "government-driven and partnership with private sector". In this strategy, governmental departments consolidate all forces and resources available in a society (a city or a province) to lead the implementation of electronic government while establishing partnership with the private sector for the implementation purpose. So far, China's electronic government implementation is still at stage one with some features in stages two, three, and four in some economically more developed cities and provinces, whereas the US may already be at stage three, according to the five stage model (Hiller and Belanger, 2001), and it has achieved some initial results. Chinese government perceived that the rapid development of the Internet in the USA resulted from effective and significant direct support and sponsorship from the government through the military, education, and government procurement policies, which has been regarded as a good example and effective means for driving the development of electronic government in China by Chinese government.

The dominant role played by Chinese government generally fits well with the historical and cultural characteristics as well as the NeI of China. In fact, the Chinese government could be the only possible entity in society that has enough power and capability to coordinate all related government agencies, organizations, and private sectors as well as consolidate all available resources to effectively implement electronic government. The government has also had successful experience in playing the leading role in modernizing its previous out-dated telecommunication industry, which is perhaps the most successful contemporary example of China's interventionist economic strategy. By mid-2001, China's public switching capacity was 300 million circuits, which is the world's largest. This was largely due to the supply-driven program of network rollout by the government, with the growth rate of double digits through the 1990s (Lovelock and Ure, 2001).

In summary, while China has achieved its fast economic development in the late decade, it has also started to move to a more democratic and transparent government system and mechanism. Electronic government has become one key implementation mechanism for the government to achieve its goal of a more transparent government. China, different from the US, adopted a different electronic government implementation strategy. Based on its own economic, historic and social factors, China's electronic government implementation is so far largely driven by government, rather than by market forces. In a relatively short time period, it has achieved some noticeable results although there is still a long way to go.

DISCUSSIONS AND CONCLUSION

Due to the substantial differences in four aspects of NeI and other CSFs as specified in the proposed framework, the electronic government implementation strategies adopted in developed countries may not be directly applicable to developing countries. Developing countries may need to use governments' administrative and legislative power to consolidate and better make use of limited available resources to implement electronic government. The proposed framework provides a clear structure and guideline for developing suitable electronic government implementation strategy. Developing countries should consider their own positions in terms of CSFs as specified in the proposed electronic government strategy framework and learn from other countries' successful electronic government implementation strategies, and then work out their electronic government implementation strategies that fit with their countries' characteristics and conditions. Table 6 presents recommendations for developed and developing countries in their implementation of electronic government.

Although there are some prior studies published on electronic government strategies and implementation (e.g., Carter and Belanger, 2005; Chircu and Lee, 2003; Glassey, 2001; Greunz, Schopp and Haes, 2001; Huang, D'Ambra and Bhalla, 2002; Wimmer, Traunmuller and Lenk 2001), to our knowledge, most, if not all, published electronic government strategies are from the perspective of developed countries, not from the perspective of developing countries. Due to the considerable differences between developed and developing countries, the latter cannot directly adopt electronic government strategies used in developed countries. As a result, the current study is an initial work to bridge this gap.

Future Research in Electronic Government

The proposed framework and the relationships of the critical success factors (CSFs) in the framework can be tested and validated by collecting national data in both developed and developing countries in future studies. In addition, security and cross-cultural issues in electronic government implementation are noteworthy.

Table 6. Recommendations for developed and developing countries in electronic government implementation

	Recommendations for Developed Countries
Technical Staff	The current staff of the government IT departments are older and inexperienced in highly technical fields. This is true for the United States and many other developed countries. To correct this problem, the federal governments must offer highly competitive benefits packages and salary compensation. Governments must compete with the private sector IT departments that exist in their countries. College and entry level recruiting is also necessary to bring in young staff. In addition, training programs need to be improved to allow for inexperienced staff to be technically able to support the existing applications and to deliver enhancements.
Stabilization and Support	About half of the existing US Federal IT workers will be eligible to retire within the next three years, with less than 1% of the workforce under 25 and only 10% is under 32 (Ledford, 2002). As mentioned earlier, that limits the in-house abilities of the government. In-house ability and stability is critical especially for electronic government applications. Without 24 hour availability, it is unlikely that citizens will continue to visit the site if the site is down when they first visit it. The Web site must be stable and up at least 99% of the time. Specific goals must be set for each IT department and if there is downtime on any application, logs and documentation must be provided on why the outage occurred and what steps are being taken to prevent this from a repeat occurrence. Whether the support is outsourced or completed in house, IT management and project leads must offer support to internal applications through support phones and assigned IT employees.
Collaboration	In the shift to a Weberian bureaucracy, government departments will stay individualized and make decisions on their own. However, it is important that there is effective communication between departments and agencies. To do this, internal applications need to be developed and utilized by employees to share information and improve communication. E-mail is the most obvious success story for improved communications, but other applications can be enhanced to improve communications.
Resource Allocation	A government Web site takes time, money, and professional talent to achieve maximum quality. All of these resources are hard to come by, depending on budget criteria and government official's dedication to the project. Governments must budget and plan ahead for electronic government resources and allocate them. A specific analysis of the benefits of electronic government must be estimated to determine the anticipated savings and the length of delay time in those savings. By examining that, governments can appropriately budget for that return on investment.
	Recommendations for Developing Countries
Internal Support	Financial problems are the most prevalent among developing countries. The finances needed for implementation of electronic government can be drawn from a stricter tax structure and a concentrated effort on formal business transactions. Developing countries need to build upon their retail market for their citizens' necessities, like grocery and clothing outlets. This will generate additional taxes to bring the country out of its economic demise.
External Financial Support	In an effort to assist developing countries in coming out of the economic demise, external financial support from non-profit groups and other government agencies can help to implement electronic government. Not only can the developing countries designate money into IT budget, they can also use external financial assistance to assist them in the aforementioned step of internally cleaning up their retail industry. For example, Italy and the United Nations have already started this initiative with their Palmero Conference of electronic government by assisting several developing countries financially.
Infrastructure Develop-ment	Infrastructure development is a necessity before countries can consider any large projects dedicated to electronic government. Throughout the world, 63 countries have less than 1% access to the Internet (ICeGD, 2002). To improve infrastructure, developing countries must have the financial resources mentioned above to build upon their existing infrastructure and to pay for the technical support. Outsourcing is an option that needs to be carefully considered due to the lack of internal technical staff.

continued on following page

Table 6. continued

Technical Staffing	Technical staffing is a major issue in electronic government implementation in developing countries. In developing countries, the problems lie in the lack of financial resources to hire full time in-house support and in the inability to find such support, due to the lack of education in these countries. Outsourcing would be recommended for many countries that do not have the proper education and training to hire in-house staff. However, it is detrimental for outsourcing to be successful that a minimum of in-house staff be present to understand maintenance issues and support.
Collaboration	Boundary removal between different agencies in the government is a major issue in electronic government. In several developing countries, their government structure is undefined and unstable due to corruption and communism. However, government departments in developing countries must strive to obtain a specific structure and boundary between themselves before the departments can align. With the disorganization that most developing countries have in their government system, it is important that tasks are accounted for and distributed among the departments before electronic government implementation can be successful.
Accountability	Departments and governmental divisions must be accountable for their information and the processes they support. They must be able to separate processes and information so that the appropriate department is responsible for that part of the Web site. They must also work together to make their pages and IT flow together. After the implementation, they must have the abilities to support the site and troubleshoot it. By being accountable for the appropriate segments of the site, it will make troubleshooting easier if problems occur. Governments must also be accountable for their financial and accounting systems. This can happen through the use of IT for their accounting systems; however, they too need to generate funds to support building an automated accounting system.
Simplification of Transactions	Long and unnecessary transactions need to be cut down in processes to allow users to quickly access documents and print them or fill them out online. To do this, the government departments must first define their structure and accountability as mentioned. After the departments are determined and structure is in place, the transactions need to be simplified and a decision making process must be determined. By simplifying transactions, citizens will be more likely to access the site.

Kalloniatis, Kavakli and Gritzalis (2004) commend that the need for keeping information secure is increasingly important in modem electronic government environments. This holds because personally identifiable information can be electronically transmitted and disseminated over insecure open networks and the Internet. Some key security issues of electronic government implementation include: (1) how to develop quality requirements engineering (RE) framework for eliciting and managing security requirements (SR) and then develop an effective security system for electronic government services? (2) What are key restrictions and difficulties while building up a secure electronic government system?

Denman-Maier and Parycek (2003) pointed out the importance of cross-cultural issues in global electronic government development and implementation. As shown in the implementation framework proposed earlier in this study, there exist big differences between developed and developing countries in terms of national cultures. Even within developed countries where most electronic government initiatives are being launched, many can not be characterized as culturally homogeneous political entities. They have large minorities that may not only speak different languages, but also have different religions, use different scripts, and differ in their cultural values, traditions, and attitudes. It is essential for future study to examine how these cross-cultural factors influence peoples' understanding of information distributed by public authorities and their cognitive approach to knowledge representation so that they can use electronic government services more effectively in a more satisfactory way.

REFERENCES

Ajzen, I. (1988). *Attitudes, personality and behavior*. Milton Keynes: Open University Press.

Annual Global Accenture (former Anderson Consulting: AC) Study Report, 2002.

Archer, N.P. (2005). An overview of the change management process. *E-government, International Journal of Electronic Business, 3*(1), 1.

Baligh, H.H. (1994). Components of culture: nature, interconnections, and relevance to the decisions on the organization structure.*Management Science, 40*(1), 14-28.

Barnes, S.J., & Vidgen, R.T. (2006). Data triangulation and web quality metrics: A case study in e-government. *Information & Management, 43*(6), 767-777.

Bertot, J.C., & Jaeger, P.T. (2006). User-centered e-government: Challenges and benefits for government Websites. *Government Information Quarterly, 23*(2), 163-168.

Bozeman, B., & Bretschneider S. (1986). Public management information systems: theory and prescription. *Public Administration Review*, Special Issue, *47*-487.

Carter, L., & Belanger, F. (2005). The utilization of e-government services: Citizen trust, innovation and acceptance factors. *Information Systems Journal, 15*(1), 5-25.

Caudle, S.L., Gorr, W.L., & Newcomer, K.E. (1991). Key information systems management issues for the public sector. *MIS Quarterly, 15*(2), 171-188.

Chen, Y.N., Huang, W., Chen, H M., & Ching, R.K.H. (2006). E-government strategies in developed and developing countries – an implementation framework and a case study. *Journal of Global Information Management 14*(1), January-March, 25-48.

Chircu, A.M., & Lee, H.D. (2003). Understanding it investments in the public sector: The case of e-government. In *Proceeding of American Conference on Information Systems (AMCIS)*, Florida, USA.

Denman-Maier, E. & Parycek, P. (2003). Cross-cultural factors in global e-government. In Proceedings Of Electronic Government, (LNCS, Vol. 2739, 456-459). Berlin: Springer-Verlag.

Dooley, B.L. (2002). Telecommunications in India: State of the marketplace, *Faulkner Information Services* (February), Docid 00016872.

E-government Strategy. (2002 and 2003). US Federal Government, www.firstgov.gov.

Glassey, O. (2001, June 27-29). Model and architecture for a virtual one-stop public administration. *The 9th European Conferences on Information Systems*,(pp. 969-976).

Greunz, M., Schopp, B., & Haes, J. (2001). Integrating e-government infrastructures through secure XML document containers. In *Proceedings of the 34th Hawaii International Conference on System Sciences.*

Grönlund, A., & Horan, T. A. (2004). Introducing e-gov: History, definitions, and issues. *Communications of the Association for Information Systems, 15*, 713-729.

Heeks, R. (2000). *Reinventing government in the information age*. London: Roultedge Press.

Hiller, J., & Belanger, F. (2001). *Privacy strategies for electronic government e-government series.* Arlington, VA: PricewaterhouseCoopers Endowment for the Business of Government.

Hofstede, G. (1980). *Culture's consequences: international differences in work-related values.* Newbury Park, CA: Sage Press.

Hofstede, G. (1991). *Cultures and organizations: Software of the mind.* London: McGraw Hill.

Huang, W., D'Ambra, J., & Bhalla, V. (2002). An empirical investigation of the adoption of egovernment in australian citizens: some unexpected research findings. *Journal of Computer Information Systems, 43*(1), 15-22.

Huang, W., Siau, K. and Wei, K.K. (2004). *Electronic government: Strategic and implementations*. Hershey, PA: Idea Group Publishing.

International Conference on E-government for Development (IceGD). Retrieved September 25, 2002, from http://www.palermoconference2002.org/en/home_a.htm.

I-Ways (2005). E-government in the European union: online availability of public services. *I-WAYS, Digest of Electronic Commerce Policy and Regulation*, *28*, 92–95.

Jackson, N. (2002). State of the marketplace: e-government gateways. *Faulkner Information Services* (February), Docid 00018296.

Jaeger, P.T. Assessing Section 508 compliance on federal e-government Web sites: A multi-method, user-centered, evaluation of accessibility for persons with disabilities. *Government Information Quarterly*, *23*(2), 2006, pp.169-190.

Jain, A. and Patnayakuni, R. (2003). Public expectations and public scrutiny: an agenda for research in the context of e-government. In *Proceeding of American Conference on Information Systems (AMCIS)*, August 2003, Florida, USA.

Janssen, D., Rotthier. S., & Snijkers K. (2004). If you measure it they will score: An assessment of international eGovernment benchmarking. *Information Polity*, *9*,121–130.

Kalloniatis, C, Kavakli, E, & Gritzalis, S. (2004). Security requirements engineering for e-government applications: Analysis of current frameworks. In *Proceedings Of Electronic Government*, (LNCS 3183, pp. 66-71).

Kirkman, G.S., Osorio, C.A. and Sachs, J.D. (2002). The networked readiness index: measuring the preparedness of nations for the networked world. In *The global information technology report: readiness for the networked world* (pp. 10-30). Oxford University Press.

Ledford, J. L. (2002). Establishing Best Practices for e-Government within the U.S. *Faulkner Information Services* (February), Docld: 00018275.

Lovelock, and Ure. (2001). E-government in China. Retrieved from http://www.trp.hku.hk/publications/e_gov_china.pdf.

Moon, J.M. (2002). The evolution of e-government among municipalities: Rhetoric or reality? *Public Administration Review, 62*(4), 424-433.

Moon, M.J. and Norris, D.F. (2005). Does managerial orientation matter? The adoption of reinventing government and e-government at the municipal level. *Information Systems Journal*, *15*(1), 43-60.

Navarra, D.D., & Cornford, R. (2003). A policy making view of e-government innovations in public governance. In *Proceeding of American Conference on Information Systems (AMCIS)*, Florida.

Palmer, I. (2002). State of the world: E-government implementation. *Faulkner Information Services* (January), Docid 00018297.

Quinn, J.B., Anderson, P., & Finkelstein, S. (1996). Leveraging intellect. *Academy of Management Executive*, *10*(3), 7-27.

Rainey, H.G., Backoff, R.W., & Levine, C.H., (1976). Comparing public and private organizations. *Public Administration Review*, March/April, 233- 243.

Relyea, H.C. (2002). E-gov: Introduction and overview. *Government Information Quarterly*, *19*, 9-35.

Schein, E.H. (1993). On dialogue, culture, and organizational learning. *Organizational Dynamics*, Autumn, 40-51.

Siau, K. and Long, Y. (2005). Using social development lenses to understand e-government development. *Journal of Global Information Management*, (in press).

Symonds, M. (2000). The next revolution: After e-commerce, get ready for e-government. *The Economist.* Retrieved June 24, 2000, from http://www.economist.com/l.cgi?f=20000624/index_survey.

Snellen, I. (2000). Electronic commerce and bureaucracies. In *Proceedings of the 11th International Workshops on Database and Expert System Application*, (pp. 285-288).

Sprecher, M. (2000). Racing to e-government: using the internet for citizen service delivery. *Government Finance Review, 16*, 21-22.

Tapscott, D. (1995). *Digital economy: promise and peril in the age of networked intelligence.* New York: McGraw-Hill.

UN (United Nations) and ASPA (American Society for Public Administration). (2001). *Global Survey of E-government.*

UNCTAD (2002). *Least developed countries at a glance.* United Nation Information Communication Technology Task Force.

U.S. Census Bureau. Government Organization: 1997 Census of Governments, Washington, D.C., 1999. Retrieved from http://www.census.gov/prod/www/abs/gc97org.html.

Watson & Mundy (2000). Electronic democracy: A strategic perspective. *Communications of ACM.*

Wimmer, M., Traunmuller, R., & Lenk, K. (2001). Electronic business invading the public sector: considerations on change and design. In *Proceedings of the 34th Hawaii International Conference on System Sciences.*

This work was previously published in the International Journal of Electronic Government Research, Vol. 3, Issue 2, edited by M. Khosrow-Pour, pp. 45-61, copyright 2007 by IGI Publishing, formerly known as Idea Group Publishing (an imprint of IGI Global).

Chapter VII
Involving Service Professionals in eGovernment Innovation:
The Case of Finnish Early Childhood Education

Jonna Järveläinen
Turku School of Economics, Finland

Jarmo Tähkäpää
Turku School of Economics, Finland

Eija Koskivaara
Turku School of Economics, Finland

Timo Kestilä
Turku School of Economics, Finland

Päivi Pihlaja
University of Turku, Finland

Jarmo Kinos
University of Turku, Finland

Hannu Salmela
Turku School of Economics, Finland

ABSTRACT

This collaborative action research study reports the experiences in developing e-government innovations in early childhood education context in Finland. While e-government is too often understood as transforming paper documents used in public services into electronic mode, the ultimate objective should be to enhance communication and interaction between citizens and public organizations and thus increase the value of public services. This objective cannot be reached without involvement of service professionals in the eGovernment innovation processes. This research introduces a method for involving service professionals in the process of generating and evaluating alternative ways how new technology can be incorporated in service processes. Amit and Zott's (2001) e-business value creation method was applied to clarify the value of alternative e-government innovations for citizens and for the service organization. The practical result of the study was several business model innovations for the early childhood education. The methodological result was a collaborative method for analyzing and generating business model innovations.

Copyright © 2009, IGI Global, distributing in print or electronic forms without written permission of IGI Global is prohibited.

INTRODUCTION

The diffusion of e-government has been slower than the diffusion of e-business and many applications are designed from an organization centric view not from customer- or citizen-centric view (Marche & McNiven, 2003). In some public sectors usage of information and communication technology is quite a recent development and they do not have therefore capabilities to fully utilize it. One of these public sectors in Finland is the state and municipality controlled early childhood education (ECE), the environment for this research.

E-government is often perceived as a channel for government to offer information intensive public services in electronic form. Janssen, Kuk and Wagenaar (2005) have studied and categorized e-government business models in Netherlands. According to their research, most of the e-services in the content and direct-to-customer (e-government) business models were intended to make existing information and services available. They recommended that value creation should become an essential part of e-government.

Identifying ways to improve the value of public services requires involvement of service professionals. The problem in many sectors of public services, including early childhood education, is that the professionals have a narrow or even negative view of information technology. Hence, a prerequisite for any eGovernent innovation is to invite these professionals in rethinking the role of IT in their field. Amit and Zott (2001) have presented value creation methods for e-business. We will extend the scope of their model to the area of e-government. The new model has been applied in this action research study in Finland. The context of this chapter is ECE service provided by a public organization and the purpose is to study how e-government creates value for customers or citizens.

In the research area of e-business, customer is in a central role. In the field of e-government the concept of "customer" is more complex. As users of public services we are customers, but at the same time we are citizens, who have more power than an ordinary business customer. As tax payers, we are also owners of the public service provider and as citizens we are also subjects with obligations (Mintzberg, 1996). One of our obligations is to rear our children to be good citizens. Early childhood education shares this educational responsibility with us; therefore the relationship between parents and ECE-professionals should be viewed as a long-term partnership.

This chapter is organized as follows. In the next section, we outline the theoretical basis of the study. Section 3 describes the case, ECE in Finland, which is followed by presentation of the collaborative research method used in this study. Section 5 highlights the results against the theoretical framework. Finally, discussion and conclusions section conclude the chapter.

THEORETICAL BACKGROUND

One of the various definitions of a business model "is a method and a set of assumptions that explains how a business creates value and earns profits in a competitive environment" (Lumpkin & Dess, 2004). In Finland public organizations´ the financing comes from the tax payers, the business model for government should therefore be a method and a set of assumptions that explains how a public organization creates value.

According to Lee, Tan & Trimi (2005) the purpose of e-government is to offer citizens valuable and quality public services and information on the Internet. Although it is possible just to digitize the services for example returning a tax form, the best value from public e-services is gained when different public organizations horizontally integrate their processes in order to provide a "one-stop" e-service point for citizen (Lee et al., 2005).

Referring to Lumpkin & Dess's (2004) definition, the idea of a e-business model is to gain profit and create value to customers by using the organization's existing resources on the Internet. Value creation in e-business has been studied by many authors in recent years. Lumpkin & Dess (2004) themselves discovered that search, evaluation, problem-solving, transaction activities, as well as different types of content may create value for a customer online. Zhu and Kraemer (2005) define that value is created in e-business with transactional efficiencies, market expansion, and information sharing and integration. Barua, Konana, Whinston, & Yin (2001) argue that operational excellence is a key element in e-business value creation. Porter (2001) explains that Internet can create value for buyers by increasing consumers ability to negotiate with traditional channels and thus eliminating them.

One of the most used value creation model is by Amit & Zott (2001), who have presented four possible sources of value creation, specifically *efficiency, complementarities, lock-in,* and *novelty.* Since public organizations should also be focusing on creating value for the citizens these value creation methods could be applied into e-government context.

Amit & Zott (2001) define efficiency based on transaction cost theory (see Williamson, 1975) namely "transaction efficiency increases when the costs per transaction decrease". In e-business, the transaction efficiency can be measured by comparing transaction costs between different web shopping sites or online and offline channels. In e-government the transaction costs could also be measured by comparing transaction costs between online and offline channels, for example returning an application for early childhood education in the traditional way by mail or electronically via the Internet. Transaction efficiency can also be improved by reducing information asymmetry between customers and providers as well as streamlining transactions (Amit & Zott, 2001).

The second value creation method in e-business introduced by Amit & Zott (2001) is to offer complementary products and services. In e-government this can be realized using vertical or horizontal information systems and process integration. Vertical complementaries could be for example after transaction services (after registering as a student in a university, it provides the access to electronic libraries and other online resources to the new student). Horizontal complementaries could be e.g. one-stop e-service point (the early childhood education web pages containing all child related services offered in the municipality also by the private organizations and associations).

Lock-in is the third value creation means in e-business according to Amit & Zott (2001). Lock-in refers to customers' unwillingness to transact business with other service providers. In e-government, customers or citizens seldom are able to choose between service providers, unless they either move to another municipality or country or there are public and private service providers to choose from. Therefore the lock-in could refer here unwillingness to change transaction channel from offline to online or vice versa. If citizens are offered for example benefits (loyalty programs) from using online services, or customization options on the Internet, they might be locked-in to using the online channel. Another lock-in strategy for e-government could be to empower the citizens, namely offer them means to interact with and influence the public organization.

Novelty is the last value creation method in e-business suggested by Amit & Zott (2001). E-businesses and public organizations may introduce new services on the Internet, such as eBay introduced the customer-to-customer Internet auction or a small Finnish IT firm introduced an online service for parents, who during their working day may look at pictures of their children taken with a multimedia mobile phone by the day care teachers.

CASE: EARLY CHILDHOOD EDUCATION IN FINLAND

Finish public sector have long history about utilizing IS in their internal use. Same information sharing between public agency and well developed bank network are corn stone for many e-government initiatives. Finland has been ranked quite well (2nd to 9th) in five different international e-government rankings published in 2004-2005 Andersen, Grönlund, Moe, & Sein (2005)

However, there are public sectors where e-government does not ring a bell and information technology is considered to complicate the daily routines. Ministry of Social Affairs and Health has launched in 2005 an Information Technology Project for Social Sector, which aims to integrate existing information systems and create new service conventions and process structures In the course of IT Project for Social Sector child protection services, distant interpretation services for deaf persons, virtual communities for alcoholics etc. have been developed. This research group chose Early Childhood Education (ECE) services, the users of which are young parents, who are familiar with information and Internet technology. The difficulties in adopting new technological innovations into ECE had been noticed in previous studies of the research group; therefore we are aiming to contribute to the practical daily routines of ECE as well as theory with collaborative action research.

In Finland the concept Early Childhood Education refers both to the research as well as education and care of children under compulsory school age (seven years). Day-care is a public and official place where latter comes true. The significance of early childhood education has been eloquently summarized by Blenkin, Rose & Yue (1996) who state that "early years is arguably the most significant period of children's education and their first encounters with education are, therefore, of fundamental importance".

ECE has different levels in Finland. State has central role by steering system. States′ instruments are guiding by norms or rules, financial resources and steering by information. Day-care Act had more importance before, when there were for example limits to amount of children in child groups. After decentralization and legislative changes state gave more power to municipalities at the beginning of 1990. Nowadays municipal authorities are in charge at local level of how to organize services. Like in other Nordic countries the share of the private day-care in Finland is very low.

Since the establishment of the Day-care Act in 1973 the debate has been around whether the task of day care system is nursing or education. (comp. OECD, 2006; Ojala, 1993). It can be said that the pedagogical and developmental needs of children have been ignored and the culture of day care is based on adult-centered values. However, every now and then the focus of day-care has also been directed to children, for example in 1980 when Committee of Educational Objectives (1980:31) gave directions for public day-care. Lately, after the Council of State gave definition of policy to early childhood education in 2002 the focus of ECE has definitively changed more to education (Valtioneuvoston periaatepäätös varhaiskasvatuksen valtakunnallisista linjauksista, 2002). As a summary, it can be said that Finnish system has long traditions of separating education and care. There is even a bit left of this incoherent approach in current state of ECE in Finland, one reason for this is that day care can be in municipalities under social services or educational system. (c.f. OECD, 2001, 14, 164).

Nowadays every child has a statutory subjective right to receive public day-care and the municipalities are responsible to organize a placement according to demand. Day-care takes place mostly in day-care centers or in family day-care. Early childhood education is offered for children between ages 0 and 6. Group size can vary in day care centers from 18 to 38 children in whole day-care groups (Pihlaja & Junttila 2001). Early childhood education emphasizes the qualitative (developmental) outcomes of day-care. The main objective in day-care is to promote child's healthy growth, development and learning skills. The social task of ECE includes the promotion of child's social, intellectual and emotional development and offer a favorable context and activities. (Day care Act 117/1983.) Central values in ECE are - in addition to right to live and fully develop - non-discrimination and equal treatment, the child's best interest and giving due weight to the views of the child (Stakes, 2005). Day-care should also support parents raising their children (Day-care Act 36/1973). Parents are seen as partners, but their influence or participation for example to group education is not very significant. There is no formal Parent Teacher Association in Finland and parents do not work as volunteers in day-care centers. There is a need for larger participation of parents.

In Finland day care system is administered in state level by The Ministry of Social – and Health Care. Despite of this more than 15 % of the local and municipal day-care is connected to the educational administration. In all neighboring countries of Finland (Sweden, Norway, Russian, Estonia) day-care system is already administered by the Ministry of Education. (OECD, 2006).

The ECE in Finland has faced many challenges or threats recently. Simultaneously as the number of children in groups has risen and the number of employees has decreased, the quality of the pedagogical context has declined. The proportion of teachers in day-care among all employees has decreased, which is one reason for why the pedagogical competence has lost its value (Kauppinen, 1995; Kinos & Laakkonen, 2006; Pihlaja & Junttila, 2001). Since there are fewer teachers in proportion to larger number of children, teachers have less time to educate and have to spend more time for operative care work as well as administrative tasks. The economical depression of the 1990s has left its marks on services directed to children and families, as it was these services that suffered the most cut-offs (Hermansson, Karvonen & Sauli 1998). The day-care educators had hard times for a number of years, and some municipalities complain that "saving money" seems to have come to stay. Work-related stress, emotional pressures, and the pace and intensity of work increases with the growing demands of efficiency (Seddon 2000). This is apparent in the case of day-care personnel as well (Pihlaja & Junttila 2001).

Of staff working directly with children, about 30% have a tertiary degree (bachelor or master of education or bachelor of social science), and the rest an upper secondary level education. According to OECD (2006), this percentage of tertiary trained pedagogues is low compared to Denmark (60%) or Sweden (51%). As a result of teachers proportion has decreased, perhaps, municipalities' net cost for a one child has decreased from 390 € in 1997 to 329 in 2004 (Kangasharju & Aaltonen, 2006). Despite such changes, the political pressure to improve the quality of ECE has increased, which calls for effective systems and high quality ECE competence.

Current educational challenges and needs for improvements are linked to competence and teamwork with multi-professional educational teams and with parents. The growth of tertiary trained staff, the administrational clarity and integration to the educational system are the main macro level objectives in the nearest future. (e.g. Kinos, 2006)

RESEARCH METHOD AND DATA COLLECTION

The action research definition of Rapoport (1970, 499) is mostly cited in the literature: "Action research aims to contribute both to the practical concerns of people in an immediate problematic situation and to the goals of social science by joint collaboration within a mutually acceptable ethical framework." The action research aims at promoting simultaneously both the theoretical conceptualization and the practical command of the phenomena it studies which is, perhaps, the most fundamental feature of action research (Baskerville & Wood-Harper, 1998; Susman & Evered, 1978). Indeed, the action research is widely used also in the field of education (Carr & Kemmis, 1983; Stringer, 2004) and information systems, and was therefore familiar to both IS and ECE researchers, the authors of this chapter. Collaborative action research emphasizes the interdependence of the activities of university academics and educators to converge practical and theoretical knowledge between research and field work (Kemmis & McTaggart, 2000).

Accumulation of information during the research process and new ideas for service development in ECE with the help of IT was essential for this research. Figure 1 shows how the collaborative action research in this case accumulated the information. The role of the multiprofessional ECE professionals was to bring into the research project the challenges of the daily ECE work. The ECE researchers were responsible for introducing the newest research results in their field. The IT researchers' role was to introduce the possible IT innovations that might be suitable for ECE purposes. Furthermore, both ECE and IT researchers worked as "interpreters" for the process of adaptation of IT in ECE.

This collaborative aspect and teamwork between the scientists and professionals in ECE as well as the scientists of information systems and software providers has been the backbone of our research. The collaboration was based on small groups of people, clusters, interacting with each other to seek information on a focused number of issues. Furthermore, in the beginning of the research project, the software providers provided many valuable viewpoints of ECE software for the researchers. The authors participated as facilitators to establish the ECE network in Southwest Finland during the period of May 2005 to April 2006. Our practical objective was to establish a collaborative network of small groups and to produce an initiative for the development of early childhood education practices and information systems. More deeply this process has been described in previous publication (Järveläinen, Kestilä, Koskivaara, Pihlaja, & Salmela, 2006).

After producing the initiative, the decision makers in four municipalities in Southwest Finland decided that ECE in each municipality needed both collaboration and efficiency in developing

Figure 1. Collaborative knowledge creation in the ECE project

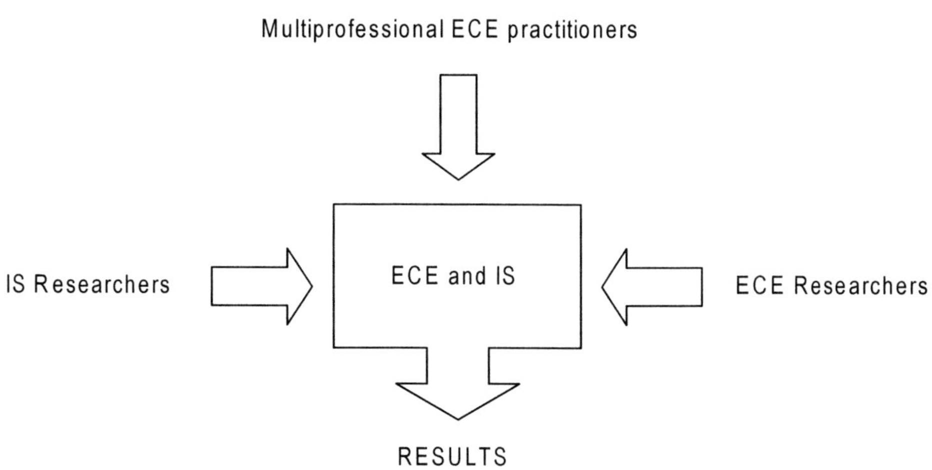

processes and the content of e-services. The directors of ECE in the municipalities presented the forthcoming research project (described in this chapter) to their subordinates and appointed them to the project based on their area of expertise and/or interest. The altogether 50 ECE professionals involved in the research project had different professional backgrounds, varying from the director of ECE to the day-care teachers and administrative officers. To facilitate the smooth flow of the research, the whole research project had a steering committee, combining of the directors of ECE in each municipality and ECE and IS academics.

Before the actual research process started, the researchers divided themselves into three interest clusters.[1] The three interest cluster were based on previous research results (Järveläinen et al., 2006): A) municipal planning and e-guidance of services, B) ECE processes, C) every day content of ECE (Figure 2). The academic researchers were divided into the clusters so that the A and C interest cluster had both ECE and IS academics, and B cluster only IS researchers.

In planning and supply of services (A) interest cluster, there were three primary research questions: what kind of information is required to forecast the demand of ECE e-services, and how the overall guidance of the ECE services and the entrance into the ECE services is managed.

Figure 2. Division of clusters and working groups in the research project

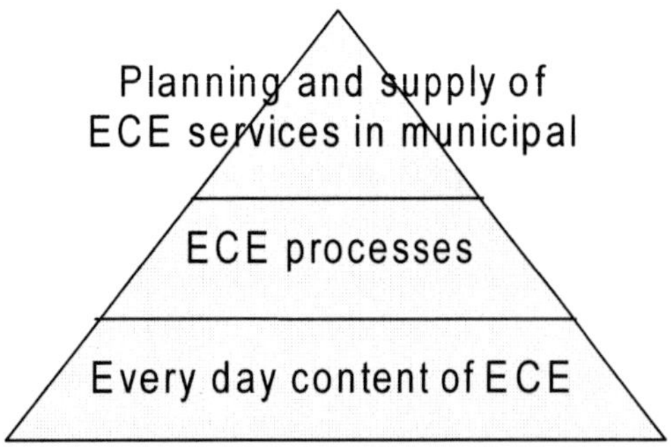

At the moment, the forecasting of ECE service demand is very challenging, because either the required information is missing or it is hidden somewhere in the organization or in the society. The guidance of ECE services and the entry process varies a lot in municipalities and neither of these is supported with web-based technologies. If these tasks would be supported with decision support systems, the scarce resources could better be allocated and families as well as children could get better services.

In the ECE processes (B) interest cluster, the work focused on recognizing routine work in day-care centers, which has been done manually and then attempting to find a technological solution which would transform the manual work automatic. If repetitive manual work would be converted into automatic tasks, the day-care teachers could spend the saved time for education, since they are professional educators.

The interest cluster C had initially four main themes, which were integrated into two main areas. The first main area under these themes was to develop the day-care planning process in yearly, monthly and weekly level and integrate this planning to communication with parents. The planning process would generate for example information for parents about the timetables and the content of the activities. Second main area was to integrate the purchase of games and tests which support the growth and detection of learning problems to one regional and jointly owned professional organization. The integration should solve the problem of choosing a usable and evaluated material to their use from the pile of possibilities for day-care staff.

The research reported in this chapter had altogether six phases (Table 1). These phases varied from lectures to group and team works as well as individual work between workshops. The process started with an orientation meeting, which included short lectures of the challenges and opportunities of adoption of information technology (IT) in the Finnish ECE. This orientation

Table 1. Research process from top to down

Phase I	Orientation lecture and briefing of group and team homework		
Phase II	Homework in municipals and in research community		
Phase III	Workshop A/1	Workshop B/1	Workshop C/1
Phase IV	Intermediate assignments per teams in groups and in research community		
Phase V	Workshop A/2	Workshop B/2	Workshop C/2
Phase VI	Ideas for service development in ECE		

session was followed by dividing the participants into three working groups, based on the interest clusters. Before the orientation meeting, some rough group divisions were already made in the municipalities in advance based on the interests and professional background of the participants. However, some of the professionals switched over to the other groups during the process, since their expertise would benefit other groups better.

During the orientation meeting, a short briefing of the focus of each working group was given in a form of interactive lecture to the ECE professionals. The professionals were given homework related to the focus, for example in municipal planning and the guidance of services group the tasks were to consider the current processes of: 1) municipal planning and supply of ECE services, 2) overall guidance of the ECE service and the guidance of the entrance into ECE services both from the family's point of view and from the child's point of view. After the briefing, the research process continued with two group meetings, i.e. workshops, for all three individual working groups.

In the first workshop the homework was discussed. For instance, in the A and B working groups the "learning café" method was used to facilitate the discussion.[2] The working group C had a different approach because the larger number of participants. Four team leaders were selected amongst the working group participants, one from each municipality, and they discussed the issues with the members from their own municipality and communicated the results to the researchers. In addition, the team leaders engaged in planning the workshops and the issues which were discussed during the workshops.

Before the second workshop, the working group participants were assigned new homework, such as "In the first workshop, you recognized that you spend much time for calculating wages for family day-care teachers. How do the family day-care teachers communicate their working hours in your municipality?" In the second workshop the selected developments ideas and the IT solution innovations were presented to the practitioners, who considered the benefits, risks and costs of the ideas and were able to abandon unpractical IT solutions. After the second workshop the remaining development ideas were discussed and presented to the steering committee.

RESULTS

Each working group generated several IT solutions for different ECE development problems, which mirror the value creation methods presented by Amit and Zott (2001). The below presented problems and IT solutions were accepted by the working groups and were discussed in the steering committee and municipalities. While all proposals were not possible and sensible to implement on same time two, solutions were decided to implement just after this development project. In the following paragraphs the problems and solution is presented in our e-government focused framework which is divided to efficiency, complementarities, lock-in and novelty.

Efficiency

One of the problems recognized in working group B, ECE process, was that the billing information was gathered manually in both day-care centers (by marking up in a paper diary if a single child was present or not each day) and family day-care (by filling up a paper diary the exact time when a single child arrived and was picked up), and these manually filled diaries were then entered into the billing system by a administrative officer. In addition to entering errors, the billing process was slow and inefficient. The presence/absence and arrival/departure information could be gathered automatically with RFID technology; each child could have a RFID transponder which would enter the correct information directly to the administrative information system used in billing, improving the transaction speed. It would also help in forecasting the service needs in each day-care center, since the data could be analyzed to focus human resources better based on service need of families.

Another problem recognized in working group A, was that customers should be better informed about all the ECE service alternatives. Furthermore, the guidance of the ECE services as well as the entry processes vary a lot in municipalities. The guidance could easily be supported with web-based technologies. There should also be access to complementary information from partner or private firms and societies. This would reduce asymmetry of information and provide parents with accurate information.

The major problem in planning and forecasting the ECE service demand was that there was no systematic way of gather the information. IS researchers recommended that first should study what information really is needed. Thereafter, data warehousing and data marts could be built e.g. on municipal or some district level to provide information for decision support. In the long run, this would help decision makers focus resources efficiently and effectively.

The problem in communication between parents and day-care has been that the information about day-care center has not always been unambiguous and available when it is needed. The solution for this could be a portal, where the information about weekly activities, electronic notebook, e-mail would be provided for parents. One feature of the portal could be a possibility to inform child's absence etc. 24/7, thus the information sharing would improve both ways. Parents and staff could discuss the situation of a single child in a trusted part of the portal, if necessary. Another part in portal is public information where all the parents and staff would have access.

Complementarities

In internet there was only a little or nothing information about other services (for exc. private or third sector) meant to children or child families. It would be good for parents to know other possibilities in local level when thinking how to organize child care after parent allowance.

The information portal would offer also complementary services in a form of an e-portfolio of the growth of a child. For example photos, drawings, and other productions of a child made during her/his day-care time could be included in the e-portfolio. From the portfolio the staff, parents and a child himself could follow his/her development during years.

Lock-In

Electronic notebook could also be used in locking in the parents. The use of manual notebook for the communication between home and day-care has been difficult in some cases, since the information of the notebook cannot be checked if the book is in a wrong place. The information on the Internet portal enables for parent to check information for example in work or at home.

Amit & Zott (2001) describe that one strategy for locking the customers into the system is to provide them loyalty programs. One kind of loyalty program in ECE could resolve the problem of resource focusing. Nowadays, if a child becomes ill during the evening or night, parents have to wait until morning to call day-care about the child's absence that day. Often the absence information is received late, which is especially inconvenient if the child has a special diet and his/her meal has to be customized. Calls force a teacher or manager to be in the office and the parents should wake up early to make the call also after staying up all night. The parents could also send a standardized SMS message or use the information portal to inform about their child's absence 24/7 and this information could be shown at the manager's and kitchen's desktop in the morning. The parents who inform about the absence in time, for example before 7 o'clock, could be given a discount. This kind of loyalty program could have a lock-in effect according to the ECE professionals, but this could also be seen as a complementary service, since it integrates the different parts gathering the billing information, one kind of supply chain integration.

The information portal could also create a lock-in effect, if it would be used for parent empowerment. As described, the parents could have a virtual community for sharing contact information and event photographs with each other, but parent's association could also use the portal for information sharing, communication and surveys which could be used for communicating with the day-care center or the municipality.

Novelty

The novelty of the information centralization is concretized in combining the different products in one location. In addition to offering services to parents, the centralization could produce benefits from integrating portal into the planning process of yearly, monthly and weekly activities.

Parents have seldom possibility to discuss with other parents because they might not see each during in the mornings and evenings. A virtual community for parents would offer a possibility to change experiences, phone numbers, arrange child's visits to a friend, distributing photos of events etc. This kind of novelty incentive would improve the communication and for example for new parents it would offer a way to get information about daily routines or habits in day-care.

DISCUSSION

The initial situation where the eGovernment innovation started can be characterized as very difficult. Majority of the ECE professionals had very limited knowledge about information technology and many perceived it merely as a bureaucratic tool or even a threat for children. Hence, the organizational setting for eGovernment initiative can be characterized as very challenging. The changing nature of the service (from day-care to education), shortage of resources, large number of different projects, lack of information systems management skills and resources, monopoly position of few software vendors, etc. all makes it very difficult to general a positive atmosphere for "yet another project".

Nevertheless, the experiences of the process are positive. Practitioners were very committed to the project and discussion in the workshops was very active. The process has also assisted the workshop participants to differentiate between viable and non-viable ideas and to prepare business cases for those that seem most promising.

The discussion of potential applications in workshops appeared to have many beneficial impacts for the municipalities involved. The possibility to discuss potential benefits within a group of other professionals appeared to change the attitudes of the participants about IT. Furthermore, the ECE managers, who were also involved, received information about the benefits as perceived by the service professionals. The immediate feedback from the municipalities concerning the working methods has been positive.

The process has also resulted to several service improvement proposals containing an explicit description of the business model. These proposals were distributed to decision makers, both in that local and national level. This paved way for more concrete projects that were initiated soon after the completion of the workshop phase. The participating municipalities have continued to collaborate in three different projects: providing IT education for ECE professionals, using IT to improve communication between ECE-professionals and parents, and automating the daily routines of collecting hours when children have entered and left day care.

The Amit and Zott's (2001) e-business value creation method was used as means to foster comprehensiveness of discussions during workshops. The method appeared to fit well in illustrating the variety of possibilities to improve day-care services with information technologies. Such technologies can improve the management of services, facilitate the implementation of day-to-day routines, and contribute to early childhood education objectives.

All four value creation types represent e-government business models. Automation of service invoicing represents an efficiency type of model. Complementary products and services are represented by adding information from several partner organizations to day-care web pages. Lock-in type of value creation is perhaps not so obvious in the public sector. However, applications that support e.g. parent-teacher interaction can be seen as increasing parents' commitment. Even if parent lock-in is not needed in a similar manner as in private businesses, such commitment will bring several benefits during the customer relationship. Finally, fostering parent to parent communication in the web would meet the criteria of adding novelty to the service (see Table 2).

The case does, however, also illustrate problems related to implementing these business models. State has central role in the development of early childhood education. States' coordinating instruments are norms, economic steering and steering by information. In some sectors, such as healthcare, state level authorities have taken responsibility for building a national IT infrastructure to support service delivery. In the day-care sector, this work is just started. . Furthermore, the implementation will be based on laws that require state, key software vendors and municipalities to implement the required systems.

Municipal authorities are in charge of developing the services at the local level. Hence, another approach to realizing the potential of web based systems is voluntary implementation by municipalities. Here, the need to support investment decisions with explicit business model is a prerequisite for making any progress. In a difficult financial situation, decision makers in municipalities will not be using money to build new systems, unless there is evidence about clear and immediate benefits.

This research used collaborative action research to investigate and document potential business models for different innovations. Following the principles of collaborative action research, university academics and educators converged practical and theoretical knowledge to produce realistic business models. The method for analyzing and generating business models comprised six phases, and the methods of interaction varied from lectures to group and team work as well as individual work between workshops.

Because action research is a qualitative research method with a small sample size, it is vulnerable to positivist critics (Checkland, 1991). Because it attempts to contribute to practical concerns, it is sometimes confused with applied research or consulting (Jönsson, 1991). However, action research can follow rigorous guidelines. One of the principal guidelines for conducting action research is that researchers should make

Table 2. Summary of e-Government business models in early childhood education

Value creation method	Foundation of business model	Value created for customer by the business model
Efficiency	Increasing transaction speed	Service bills are generated more quickly (B)
	Reducing asymmetry of information	Customers are informed better about the service alternatives (A)
	Focusing the resources better	Electronically gathered information can be used for forecasting the service need in the future (A + B)
	Improving information centralization	Portal for the communication and information sharing between parents and daycare (C)
Complementarities	Combining online and offline resources and capabilities	E-Portfolio about the phases of growth of the child for the use of staff, parents and child (C)
	Access to information from (partner) firms and customers	Information from partner organizations such as parents association (A)
	Supply chain integration	Real time information about amount of children (B + C)
Lock-in	Customized and/or personalized offerings and features	Electronic Notebook as parent-teacher communication channel in daily use to ease the information flow about the everyday activities in day care (C)
	Loyalty programs	Customers get discount of informing the service providers of absence in time (B)
	Empowerment	Web pages for the parents association (C)
Novelty	New combinations of products, services, information	Weekly program and other information in electronic form, can be integrated with parent's calendar (C)
	New incentives (e.g. customers can create content)	Community for parents for discussion, sharing phone numbers, distributing photos, coordinating play dates etc. (C)

their reasoning explicit and organize it in such a way that it is testable (Argyris, 1982; Checkland, 1991).

Action research cycle consists of five stages: diagnosing, action planning, action taking, evaluating, and specifying learning (Susman & Evered, 1978). The diagnosis of ECE organizations studied in this reported study is that at least three problems have emerged in recent years:

1. "Net generation" parents demand services on the Internet
2. The work load of ECE professionals has increased
3. Advancements in information technology should be taken into account also in early childhood education

Action planning stage of this study took place in the orientation lecture and homework phases when the diagnosed problem areas were defined in more detail. Based on the feedback from practitioners, detailed plans for different workshops were formulated. The planning stage identified potential business models to be addressed in the three workshops and the working methods to be used. In action taking stage, the feasibility and benefits of selected business models were discussed in the workshops and in the meetings of steering group. Evaluation and specifying learning stages materialized, when business models were continuously evaluated at the same time as ECE professionals learned how IT solutions could assist them in their daily work and were able to give feedback about suggested business models.

Contributions for Research

Prior conceptual research on e-business business models has primarily focused on the context of the private sector. The focus of this research is in the use of business models in the public sector. The chapter reviewed literature on business models, selected one framework and adapted it to the context of e-Government. The use of the framework is illustrated through the analysis of business models in one sector of public services, e.g. early childhood education.

The chapter contributes also the literature on methods for designing business models. The method used in the case emphasized inter-organizational collaboration in analyzing the business rationale behind different ideas. The process consisted of workshops where practitioners and researchers could discuss about potential applications, associated service process changes and the benefits that implementing new processes and systems could bring. In particular, the work focused on the early stages of the innovation process and in an organizational setting, where innovation capacity of the organizations involved was limited.

Summary

Early phases in the adoption of new uses of information technology are often the most challenging and critical. Only too often, public sector organizations start using new technologies as separate pilot projects and with little understanding of the wider business model and the organizational and process changes required. This research illustrates a different approach, where a lot of emphasis is placed on the early phases of organizational innovation adoption. Immediate feedback from the participating municipalities has been positive. This is, however, only one project implemented in one network organization. While the actual implementation process is still ahead, the research method can, and should, be applied and improved in further research in new organizational settings.

REFERENCES

Amit, R., & Zott, C. (2001). Value creation in e-business. *Strategic Management Journal, 22*(6/7), 493.

Andersen, K. V., Grönlund, Å., Moe, C. E., & Sein, M. K. (2005). Introduction to the Special Issue - E-Government in Scandinavia. *Scandinavian Journal of Information Systems, 17*(2), 3-10.

Argyris, C. (1982). *Reasoning, Learning and Action: Individual and Organiational.* San Francisco: Jossey-Bass Publishers.

Barua, A., Konana, P., Whinston, A. B., & Yin, F. (2001). Driving E-Business Excellence. *MIT Sloan Management Review, 43*(1), 36-44.

Baskerville, R. L., & Wood-Harper, T. (1998). Diversity in information systems action research methods. *European Journal of Information Systems, 7*(2), 90-107.

Blenkin, M., Rose, J., & Yue, N. (1996). Government Policies and Early Education: Perspectives from Practioners. *European Early Childhood Education Research Journal, 4*(2), 5-19.

Carr, W., & Kemmis, S. (1983). *Becoming Critical: Knowing through action research.* Victoria: Deaking University.

Checkland, P. (1991). From Framework through Experience to Learning: The Essential Nature of Action Research. Discussant's comments. In H.-E. Nissen & H. K. Klein & R. Hirscheim (Eds.), *Information Systems Research: Contemporary Approaches & Emergent Traditions.* Amsterdam: Elsevier.

Janssen, M., Kuk, G., & Wagenaar, R. W. (2005). *A Survey of e-Government Business Models in the Netherlands.* Paper presented at the 7th International conference on Electronic commerce, Xi'an, China.

Järveläinen, J., Kestilä, T., Koskivaara, E., Pihlaja, P., & Salmela, H. (2006). *Adoption of IT in The Finnish Early Childhood Education.* Paper presented at the Well-being in the Information Society -seminar (WIS 2006) May 11-12, 2006, Turku School of Economics.

Kangasharju, A., & Aaltonen, J. (2006). *Kunnallisen päivähoidon yksikkökustannukset: Miksi kunnat ovat niin erilaisia?* Government Institute for Economic Research. Available: <http://en.vatt.fi/file/vatt_publication_pdf/t119.pdf13.12.2006>

Kauppinen, S. (1995). *Päivähoidon ryhmäkokoselvitys [Group size evaluation of Day-care].* Helsinki: Stakes [The National Research and Development Centre for Welfare and Health].

Kemmis, S., & McTaggart, R. (2000). Participatory Action Research. In N. K. Denzin & Y. S. Lincoln (Eds.), *Handbook of Qualitative Research* (Second ed.). Thousand Oaks, California: Sage Publications, Inc.

Kinos, J. (2006). Varhaiskasvatuksen keskeiset kehittämiskohteet ja -haasteet, *Puheenvuoroja varhaiskasvatuksen kehittämisestä.* (pp. 13-18): Opetusalan Ammattijärjestö OAJ.

Kinos, J., & Laakkonen, E. (2006). *Pienten lasten opettajat Varsinais-Suomessa. Selvitys lastentarhanopettajatilanteesta Varsinais-Suomen maakunnassa.* Turun yliopisto. Kasvatustieteiden tiedekunta. Available: <http://vanha.edu.utu.fi/tokl/LTO2006/LTO_VS_web.pdf13.12.2006>

Lee, S. M., Tan, X., & Trimi, S. (2005). Current Practices of Leading e-Government Countries. *Communications of the ACM, 48*(10), 99-104.

Lumpkin, G. T., & Dess, G. G. (2004). E-Business Strategies and Internet Business Models: How the Internet Adds Value. *Organizational Dynamics, 33*(2), 161-173.

Marche, S., & McNiven, J. D. (2003). E-Government and E-Governance: The Future Isn't What It Used To Be. *Canadian Journal of Administrative Sciences, 20*(1), 74.

Mintzberg, H. (1996). Managing Government Governing Management. *Harvard Business Review, 74*(3), 75-83.

OECD. (2001). *Starting Strong. Early Childhood Education and Care. Education and Skills.* OECD. Available: <http://caliban.sourceoecd.org/vl=9220233/cl=12/nw=1/rpsv/cgi-bin/fulltextew.pl?prpsv=/ij/oecdthemes/ 99980029/v2001n7/s1/p1l.idx13.12.2006>

OECD. (2006). *Starting Strong II. Early Childhood Education and Care.* OECD Publishing. Available: <http://caliban.sourceoecd.org/vl=9220233/cl=12/nw=1/rpsv/cgi-bin/fulltextew.pl?prpsv=/ij/oecdthemes/99980029/v2006n13/s1/p1l.idx13.12.2006>

Ojala, M. (1993). *IEA Preprimary Study in Finland 2. The use of early childhood settings.* Joensuu: University of Joensuu.

Opetushallitus. (2000). *Esiopetuksen opetussuunnitelman perusteet [Core Curriculum for Pre-School Education].* Opetushallitus [The National Board of Education]. Available: <http://www.edu.fi/julkaisut/maaraykset/ops/esiops.pdf13.12.2006>

Pihlaja, P., & Junttila, N. (2001). Julkishallinnon hajauttaminen - miltä päiväkodin lapsiryhmät näyttävät muutosten jälkeen? [Decentralisation of Public administration - how do child groups look like after changes in Day-care Centres]. *Varhaiskasvatuksen ammattilehti Lastentarha.*

Porter, M. E. (2001). Strategy and the Internet. *Harvard Business Review, 79*(3), 62-78.

Rapoport, R. N. (1970). Three Dilemmas of Action Research. *Human Relations, 23*, 499-513.

Stakes. (2005). *Varhaiskasvatussuunnitelman perusteet [National Curriculum Guidelines on Early Childhood Education and Care].* Stakes.

Available: <http://www2.stakes.fi/varttua/vasu_/VASU-toinen%20painos.pdf13.12.2006>

Stringer, E. (2004). *Action Research in Education*: Prentice Hall.

Susman, G. I., & Evered, R. D. (1978). An Assesment of the Scientific Merits of Action Research. *Administrative Science Quarterly, 23*(4), 582-603.

Valtioneuvoston periaatepäätös varhaiskasvatuksen valtakunnallisista linjauksista. (2002). Sosiaali- ja terveysministeriö. Available: <http://pre20031103.stm.fi/suomi/pao/varhais2/kasvatus.pdf13.12.2006>

Zhu, K., & Kraemer, K. L. (2005). Post-Adoption Variations in Usage and Value of E-Business by Organizations: Cross-Country Evidence from the Retail Industry. *Information Systems Research, 16*(1), 61-84.

ENDNOTES

1 The interest clusters have the following population. The planning and supply of services (A) working group participants were 10 early childhood education professionals – including day-care center managers, day-care teachers, and day-care services area managers and four scientist - three from ECE field and one from information systems field. The ECE process (B) working group participants were 15 early childhood education professionals – including day-care center managers, day-care teachers, day-care coordinators and administrative officers – as well as 4 information systems scientists. The every day content of ECE (C) working group participants were altogether 21 ECE professionals, namely day-care center managers, consultative special teachers as well as day-care teachers, and two IS researchers and a ECE researcher.

2 The learning café method proceeds as follows in the workshops. The workshop participants were divided into three small groups and were given problems, such as in ECE processes working group "What kind of time consuming, repetitive tasks you do daily/weekly/monthly?" In the method, the problems are written on large papers and put on so called coffee tables, and a group of four ECE professionals discusses a problem for 10-15 minutes. After this, one participant stays in the coffee table as the other group members move to the next table. The remaining member reviews the issues which have been discussed so far for the new members, and then they discuss the problem for another 10 minutes and possibly generate new ideas.
After the moving members have been in each table, the whole group was collected together and each idea was reviewed and discussed shortly in order to pass the tacit knowledge from the ECE professionals to academics. Then the further development ideas were selected, based on how much time the task consumes and was the task a problem in at least two municipalities, and could a technological solution be generated for the task. This learning café method proved to be very useful, firstly because the ECE professionals had not been able to generate these ideas as part of their homework, secondly especially the IS researchers were unfamiliar with the everyday life in day-care centers and thirdly since the ECE professionals were used to handle problems by discussing them. However, in this first workshop meeting the participants of working group A argued that the municipal level of planning was too demanding and therefore this task was passed to the steering committee of the project.

Chapter VIII
Horizontal Process Integration in E-Government:
The Perspective of a UK Local Authority

Jyoti Choudrie
University of Hertfordshire, UK

Vishanth Weerakkody
Brunel University, UK

ABSTRACT

This article examines how horizontal integration between the various departments of a local authority in the United Kingdom (UK) occurs. Following that the aim of this article is to extract the "success factors" in government intervention that support horizontal and vertical integration based on the strategies pursued in the UK in order to render favourable results if applied elsewhere. The research methodology consisted of an in-depth case study that used the research tools of interviews and referring to archival documents. This research is timely as the maturity of e-government increases the issues of integrating processes and systems across various government departments becomes pertinent. The conclusion and lessons that can be learnt from this research is that e-government integration on a horizontal level obtains significant efficiency and effectiveness as more and more public services are being centralized.

INTRODUCTION

Due to the advent of the Internet, business opportunities involving information and communication technologies (ICTs) have multiplied, persuading not only commercial enterprises, but also governments around the globe to invest profoundly into e-services. However, now the potential of a clear link between the use of ICTs and economic growth has become apparent, thereby urging numerous organisations and governments to invest profoundly into it (OECD, 2002). The e-services offered by governments are aimed at relaying information and public services to citizens over the Internet

Copyright © 2009, IGI Global, distributing in print or electronic forms without written permission of IGI Global is prohibited.

and is referred to in general as "e-government." E-government encompasses a broad spectrum of activities that are offered using ICTs and allows an improved service of the government to citizens (Northrup & Thorson, 2003). There are many varying definitions of e-government, but for the purposes of this paper, the following definition is offered. *E-government is an electronic technology that has the ability to transform relations within general government and between government bodies, citizens and businesses to better deliver its services and ultimately improve efficiency (World Bank, 2005).*

According to Lee, Tan, and Trimi (2005), various countries adopting the e-government initiative are at different levels of development, and to date very few governments have initiated the collaboration of government agencies across horizontal and vertical levels. With reference to the United Kingdom (UK), which is the backdrop of this research, in 1997 the Prime Minister announced that a quarter of all government services in the UK will be electronically delivered within five years (Phythian & Taylor, 2001). However, by the end of 2005 the deadline for providing 100% of the government services online had to be extended as most local authorities failed to meet the cut-off date; thereby causing the deadline to be extended to 2008 (www.computing.co.uk). It has been recognized as pertinent to offer services according to users' needs, as this enhances cooperation among agencies, which is categorically required in order to provide central services and present an enhanced user experience for citizens using the services (Traunmuller, 2004). Furthermore, Jaeger (2002) argues that e-government will need to promote horizontal and vertical integration of the various governmental branches in order to satisfy the citizens' need for a 24 hours and 7 days service.

Bearing in mind the importance of providing online public sector services, generally governments across the globe are considering ways of amalgamating back office systems, horizontally integrating Web applications across government agencies, and vertically combining levels in order to provide portals, seamless services, and information delivery to citizens more efficiently and effectively (Varshney, 2005). It has also been found that there is no local UK government Web site that can offer users the sophisticated functionalities and interactions associated with online private sector equivalents, such as banks and supermarket Web sites (www.computing.co.uk). Furthermore, many governmental agencies are affording only basic online services such as downloadable forms and transactions; whereas horizontal integration grants real-time systems offering a one-stop-shop for all e-services (Layne & Lee, 2001). Consequently, according to Norris and Moon (2005), very few governments offer much in the way of two- way transactional e-government or provide horizontal e-government integration.

In this article we undertake an examination of the horizontal integration among the various departments of a local authority that occurs in order to deliver e-services to the citizens in a particular vicinity. Therefore, the research question guiding this paper is: What can be learnt about the achievement of horizontal integration among local authorities in the e-government context in order to better deliver e-services to citizens? In line with that, the aim of this paper is to extract the "success factors" in government intervention that support horizontal and vertical integration based on the strategies pursued in the UK in order to render favourable results if applied elsewhere.

This research is timely since currently governments around the globe are becoming technically savvy and the issues of integrating various and diverse departments are becoming important. Subsequently, we intend to examine the possibilities of generalizing our findings to other geographical and/or cultural settings. We believe that our analysis will be useful to policy makers seeking to promote the use of online products and services to communities in a country in an equitable manner. Researchers in the area of process changes can also benefit by obtaining insights into the application of ICT policies at local levels.

Having offered an overview of the main issues regarding this paper the next section offers a literature review of the theory surrounding the framework and e-government and e-governance. Thereafter, a description and explanation of the research methodology is provided. Thereafter, the findings and analysis followed by a conclusion to the paper are provided.

STAGES OF GROWTH AND E-GOVERNMENT

When considering the e-government growth models there are several within the information systems (IS) literature, but in this section a brief description of some of them is provided and a reasoning for utilizing the main model of Layne and Lee is offered.

The development of information technology (IT) within organizations has been studied extensively in organizational research and IS literature, where it has been found that it can occur in a number of phases or stages (Janssen & Veenstra, 2005). Some of the more prominent growth models include Grover and Segars (2005), Layne and Lee (2001), Chandler and Emanuels (2002), UN (2002), Deloitte Research (2000), and Nolan (1979). Nolan (1979) was amongst the foremost to emphasize and publicise the stages of growth model by accentuating the intuitive appeal of the model. The stage model aims to deconstruct IS development into a series of stages, and development occurs from one stage to another. However, a drawback of the stage model is that it does not focus upon change management and organizational development strategies. This disadvantage implies that stage models should not be employed on their own but with a carefully selected change management strategy. This is because change management strategies require the addressing of various types of business management issues, such as the creation of a shared vision, dealing with resistance to change, obtaining political support, intervention strategies, or team building skills (Bruijn, ten Heuvelhof, & int Veld, 2002). However, in the e-government area many academics and researchers have proposed stages of e-government development. According to Siau and Long (2005) research conducted on existing e-government stage models, comparisons between models helped to develop a new e-government stage model with five stages: Web presence, interaction, transaction, transformation, and e-democracy. Therefore, the growth stage models of Gibson and Nolan (1974), the revised model of Nolan (1979) and Layne and Lee (2001) have been identified to be most appropriate for studying the changes. Gibson and Nolan (1974) and Nolan (1979) also describe stages of growth but offer much more detail, for instance, an investigation into initiation, formalization, and control, which is further broken into dimensions: (a) computer applications, (b) IT expert specialization, and (c) formal management and organization (Gibson & Nolan, 1974). The e-government area is still in the growth stages and is much more generic and does not follow a temporal continuum, thereby limiting the application of Gibson and Nolan (1974) and Nolan (1979) frameworks. Layne and Lee's model (2001) offers some similarities and synergies to Gibson and Nolan's (1974) models and Gibson's (1979) model by distinguishing the degree of development; however, the difference lies in the model not representing a temporal continuum, where one stage follows the other (Scholl, 2005). For the purpose of this paper and for the cited reasons the researchers selected the four-stage (cataloguing, transactions-based, vertical integration and horizontal integration) growth model by Layne and Lee (2001).

The four stage model above offers a way to map the evolution, maturity, and sophistication of e-government services both in terms of the organization and technical aspects. Furthermore, as illustrated in Figure 1 it outlines the multi-perspective transformation needed within government structures and functions for the exploitation of a one stop e-government Web portal.

The aforementioned discussion has offered the justifications for employing the four-stage growth model, which is the main framework of this research. However, the implementation of e-government impinges upon the information and communication technologies (ICTs) sector. Therefore, the next section describes the problems existent within the public sector and why and how ICTs could and may afford a solution.

Addressing Information and Communication Problems in the Public Sector

There are also many instances where information is clearly not available locally (within the organisation) to execute processes and service specific customer demands (Saxena & Wadhwa, 2003). This further complicates the process, as the required information may now need to be obtained from an external source outside the organisational boundaries of local government/councils (ibid). As in e-business, access to this information is also needed at a rapid speed in e-government, and thus demands instant communication and integration between processes and information systems in different agencies (ibid). This information communication and access process is illustrated in Figure 2 (which is a modification of the work by Saxena & Wadhwa, 2003).

As indicated in Figure 2, when a citizen requests information from a central government or local authority (council) Web portal, this information may always not be available within their respective internal systems. In this case, the internal systems of the respective government agency will need to request and interact with other organizations' (i.e., local government agencies, central government, local businesses, etc.) information systems to extract the required information to service the citizen's need. As mentioned before this demands the interaction between processes and IS/IT systems at both internal and external levels and thus needs an environment

Figure 1. Dimensions and stages of e-government development (Adapted from Layne & Lee, 2001)

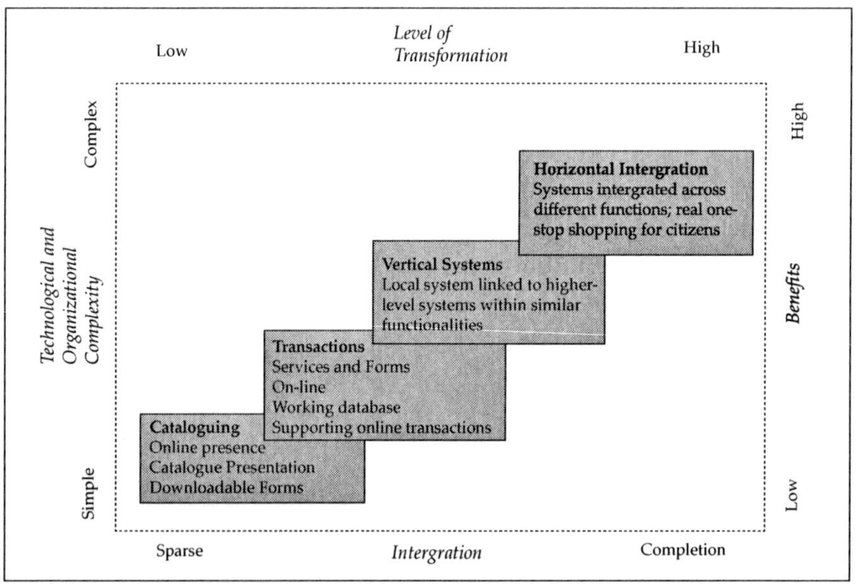

where integration and interoperability between disparate ICT systems is seamless. It is fair to suggest that realising this type of environment using traditional modes of enterprise application integration (EAI) is inconceivable given the nature of the diverse hardware and software systems that span government IT infrastructures (as in Figure 2). Given this context, the emerging concept of Web services cannot be ignored.

Web services breakdown applications into reusable components or services and enable the linking of these services within and across the enterprise using standards based on extensible mark up language (XML) (Fustes, 2003). It uses three XML-based standards: SOAP (simple object access protocol) for transmitting XML-encoded data and remotely accessing services in a platform independent way; UDDI (universal description and discovery language) for registering and discovering services; and WSDL (Web services description language) to provide an XML grammar for describing available Web services

Figure 2. Information and communication infrastructure in e-government source (Adapted from Saxena & Wadhwa, 2003, p. 130)

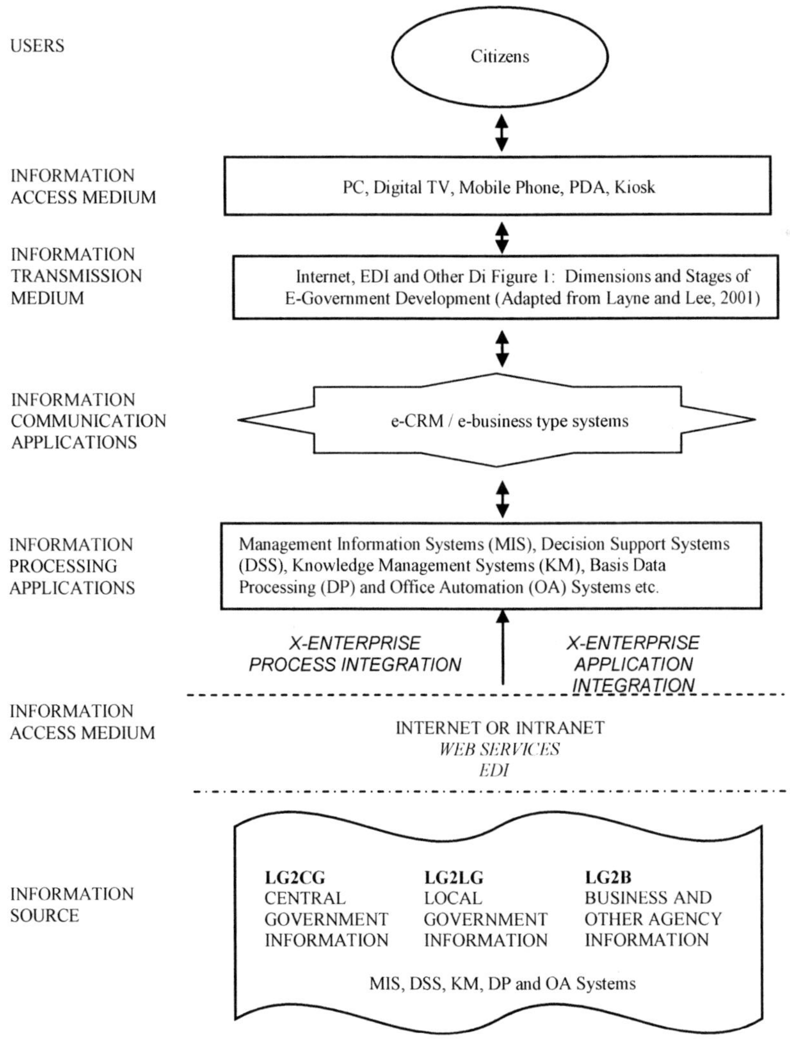

(Monson-Haefel, 2004). In comparison to the most common traditional EAI method, electronic data interchange (EDI), XML is specifically designed to use the Internet as the data transfer mechanism whereby business documents and services can be freely exchanged electronically, whereas the latter needs point-to-point connection between each participating system (Thompson, 2002).

Web services help EAI by providing the tools needed to manage end-to-end extended processes independently of the execution platform (Masood, 2002; Monson-Haefel, 2004). This is enabled through the use of SOAs, where, when the business needs to automate a business function or process, it merely plugs into a service like logging onto a Web site irrespective of whether this may be an internal application, or an external application that may be accessed over the Internet (Lawrence, 2004). Already organisations in the US such as DaimlerChrysler (Information Age, 2004b) and Jersey Post (Information Age, 2004b) and UK supermarket chains Sainsbury's (Information Age, 2004a) and Tesco's (Mclever, 2002) have used the Web services-SOA model to integrate their supply chains. Given this context, it is fair to suggest that government can draw from these successful cases of supply chain integration in their efforts to implement e-government.

In the context of e-government, as shown in Figure 2, an SOA/Web services environment could potentially replace EDI, Intranets, e-mails, and other forms of communication used to exchange information among government agencies. Also, XML can provide the common bridge between the various backend MIS, DSS, KM, DP, OA, as well as front-end CRM, ERP, and e-business type systems. In relation to Figure 1 (Layne and Lee's 2001 e-government development model), Figure 2 then illustrates some of the essential ICT concepts that need to work in synchrony to move from basic information delivery to vertical and horizontally integrated e-government services.

Having offered a theoretical overview of the main issues impinging upon this research, the next section describes and details the research methodology that was utilized for this research.

RESEARCH METHODOLOGY

Before stating the data collection a brief description of the local authority, the main context of this research, is offered. This will allow readers to obtain an understanding of the setting of this research.

Describing Council X

Case studies are viewed to fulfill three roles in research, exploratory, explanatory, or descriptive, depending upon the purpose (Yin, 1984). In the case of this research, a case study was considered to offer all three aspects as the case allowed us to explore the impacts of a process change. Then it allowed us to explain the changes that were obtained as a result of online products and services and finally, the findings following this section describe the undertaken changes. For the purposes of this research and to ensure that our pledge to the research organization was kept, anonymity of the case study had to be ensured and for this purpose we refer to our case study as Council X. Council X is an outer-London borough that is the second largest borough in the London region. The Council is currently home to 248,000 residents, which are vastly ranging in cultures and nationalities (Council Report, 2005). From the archival documentation and references from the Internet the following information regarding Council X was obtained. Council X was formed in 1965 and is London's second largest unitary borough covering 42 square miles. It covers the north-west corner of the former county of Middlesex and is the westernmost London borough. The borough also includes Heathrow airport and Northolt aerodrome. From the Census 2001 statistics it was found that of the resident population, 48% were male and 52% female. The average age of the population was 36.9 years in comparison to 38.6 years in England and Wales (Census, 2001).

Data Collection

As this research examined process changes, it was necessary to determine the reaction and opinions of various individuals. For this it was pertinent to collect data that focused upon words, and thus the data collection was a qualitative research approach (Miles & Huberman, 1994). The data was collected using face-to-face interviews with the main stakeholders involved in the process of the abandonment of motor vehicles at Council X during the period November 2005 to February 2006. According to Hellingsworth et al. (2001) it is necessary to conduct interviews with several members of the organisation as a comprehensive picture of requirements is gathered. The interviews (total of 10 were open-ended and contained semi-structured questions, as this allowed flexibility with the responses and allowed the researchers to probe further into matters related to e-government. As seen in Table 1 the questions do not require responses that are short and detailed. Rather they can allow the researcher to probe into the questions and yet not establish too stringent a boundary.

Before interviewing began, the participants were e-mailed with the interview questions so that the participants could familiarize themselves with the questions, and also to arrange a suitable date and time convenient for the participants (Smith, 2004). Furthermore, the participants were given a consent form regarding ethical considerations and their rights to withdraw from the study anytime without any prior notice or explanation. The interviews lasted approximately 30 to 45 minutes, and were undertaken in a meeting room of the council buildings. This allowed the researchers and respondents to build the necessary rapport and privacy for the required questions. The interviews were audio recorded with the consent of participants as this allowed an easier analysis of the information and allowed the participants to be quoted when writing the results of the research (Crane, 2005). Further, to validate and verify that the results were true and accurate, transcripts of the interviews were sent back to the respondents. This was done using the postal service and e-mail. The information was then transcribed onto a document and later analysed using coding and mainly, themes. That is, a thematic analysis process was utilized. This involved a process that involved encoding the qualitative information in order to identify a particular theme with the information; that is, if some sort of pattern is identified within the information that may have some relevance to the area of research (Boyatzis, 1998).

These explanations of the data collection and analysis are crucial, not only for this research, but for any research. The key findings obtained

Table 1. Snapshot of questions used for the data collection

	Questions for the Operations Development Manager
1.	What role does the customer contact centre provide to citizens?
2.	What is the procedure for a citizen to report an abandoned vehicle?
3.	What information do you require from the citizen to make a report of an abandoned vehicle?
	Questions for the Parking Services Support Manager
1.	What role does the abandonment of vehicles section provide to the overall service of removing abandoned vehicles?
2.	What is the procedure when the abandonment of vehicles section receives a report from the contact centre?
3.	What information is required for an Inspector to arrange the removal of an abandoned vehicle?

from the data collection phase are discussed in the next section.

THE NEED FOR PROCESS IMPROVEMENT AND INTEGRATION IN LOCAL GOVERNMENT: A CASE STUDY AT COUNCIL X

In section two a literature review identified numerous challenges that governments may face when e-enabling public sector processes. In this section we explore the impact of these issues in real life. Consequently, we examine the execution of a key public service process and related process management and integration issues in one of the largest local councils in the UK (identified as X). Since the aim of this research was to explore process management and integration aspects in local government, as said above, the researchers chose to focus on a key service provided by the council, the abandonment of motor vehicles. Given this context, interviews were conducted primarily at Council X's abandoned vehicles division (AMD). These interviews identified a scenario where lack of harmonisation and integration between business processes and underlying IS/IT systems has resulted in inefficient and ineffective process execution and service delivery in local government (LG). Based upon the information gathered from interviewing the service area participants from the abandoned vehicles division, the data flow diagram in Figure 3 illustrates the overall procedures of the entire service of reporting and removing abandoned vehicles.

The AMV process operates in the following manner: The citizen needs to report to the local authority the abandoned vehicle using telephone, fax, e-mail, or an online report form. The enquiry is sent to the central CRM (customer relationship management) system at the contact centre. The citizen's enquiry is automatically logged

Figure 3. Data flow diagram for abandonment of vehicles

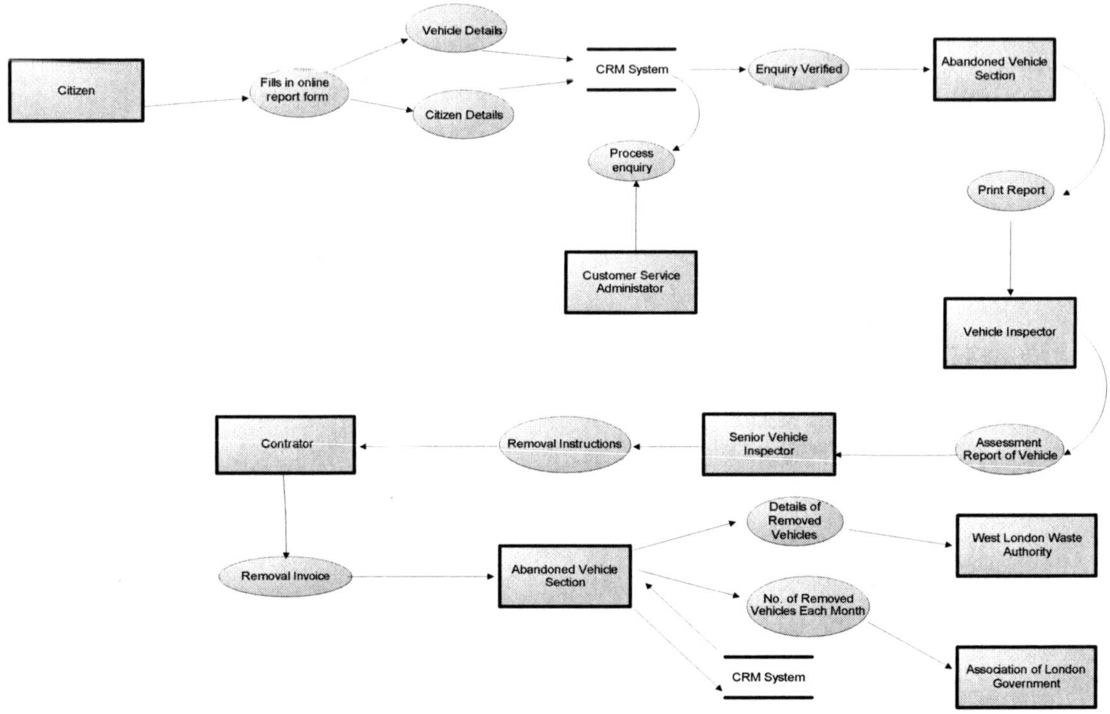

onto the system and a CSA (customer service administrator) is alerted about the enquiry via an e-mail system. Thereafter, the CSA determines whether the provided information by the citizen is accurate and correct by checking the system to see if the vehicle has been reported prior to the enquiry. If the vehicle is established as taxed, then the process must end. However, if the vehicle is untaxed then the enquiry is processed and marked onto the CRM system. The information is then sent to the abandoned vehicle section that has the responsibility to print out details of the enquiry and give it to an inspector. The inspector then must make a visit to the location and assess the condition of the vehicle and document the assessment. If the vehicle is taxed and does not look abandoned then the council cannot remove the vehicle and the process ends. However, if the vehicle is determined abandoned then the inspector will affix a message onto the vehicle stating that the council is aware of the vehicle. If the vehicle still remains after two days then the inspector revisits the vehicle and once again affixes a notice stating that the vehicle will be removed in 24 hours. Once the assessment report has been completed it is given to the senior vehicle inspector, who has the final decision to remove the vehicle. If the senior inspector decides to remove the vehicle then a legal document to remove the vehicle is sent through to the contractor. The contractor is responsible for the actual removal and disposal of the vehicle. The removal instructions are physically delivered to the contractor. Once the vehicle has been removed all the details are logged onto the CRM system and also statistical information is distributed to the West London Waste Authority and the Association of London Government.

The scenario above clearly contradicts Council X's vision for improved services in the context of e-government and highlights a number of process management problems in a key public service process. The key problems lie in delays caused when retrieving and exchanging information between different internal departments as well as external entities. This is further compounded by delays that occur when physically delivering or handing over documentation from one employee (vehicle inspector) to another (senior inspector) as well as when information and documents are passed to the external contractors.

Levels of Process and Systems Integration Required at Council X for Improved Service Delivery

Given the above context, moving from cataloguing to the horizontal integration stage in the e-government service delivery structure as outlined in the second section (see Figure 1: Layne & Lee, 2001) will require cross-functional as well as cross-organisational redesign of business processes and supporting software applications (Champy, 2002) in government institutions, at both local and national levels. Given the communication and information exchange problems at Council X, the primary focus therefore needs to be the integration and improved communication between internal as well as external processes and IT systems. Figure 4 maps the various problems encountered at Council X against Layne and Lee's (2001) framework for e-government development (see Figure 1) and the information processing and communication infrastructure model of (Saxena & Wadhwa, 2003) (see Figure 2). It is fair to suggest that this diagram outlines the kind of challenges that not only Council X, but many other local government agencies will face when implementing e-government services. Figure 4 also illustrates the link between the various information systems and the level of integration required among these systems to overcome the challenges faced by local councils in general in the context of delivering efficient and effective local government services to citizens. As revealed before in the previous section and outlined in Figure 4 below, the main challenges that Council X faces revolve around integration and communication problems between various

Figure 4. The levels of systems integration necessary to facilitate better LG services

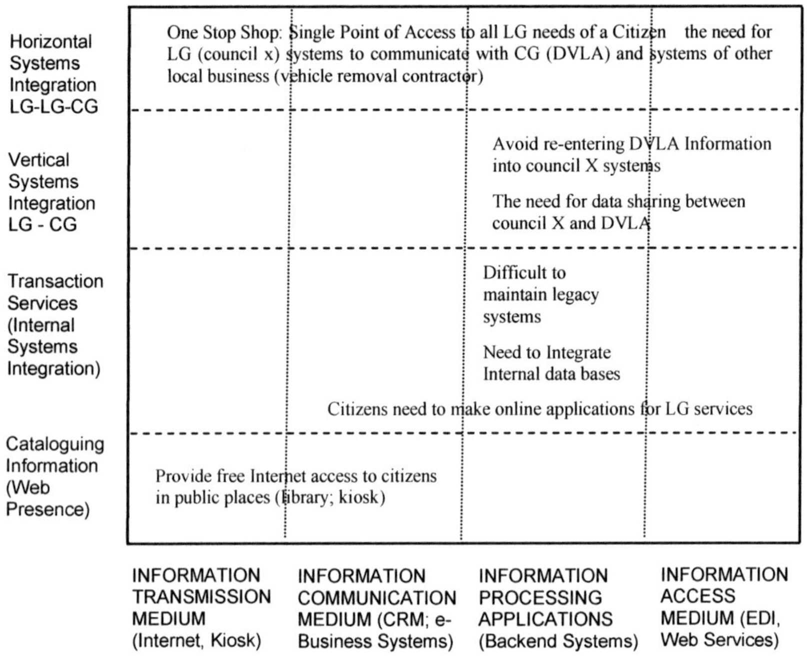

systems (such as internal data bases, ERP/CRM systems, Web-based systems, etc.) at both vertical and horizontal levels.

As outlined in Figure 4 the higher levels of e-service delivery required the harmonisation and integration of business processes and supporting ICT systems between the main stakeholders. In this case, the main stakeholders are the citizens, government agencies (Department of Vehicle License Applications-DVLA), employees (vehicle inspectors, administrators, and CSA in this instance), and business partners (contractors). Champy (2002) supported the view that harmonisation and integration of the processes and supporting ICT systems between the main stakeholders is imperative. While the integration between two or more of these entities may allow governments to deliver e-services at the cataloguing stage, in order to offer fully integrated e-services, the overall integration and harmonisation of all the above elements is imperative. However, this requires a high level of enterprise application integration (EAI) and this is where emerging technologies such as Web services can offer a fast and effective solution to councils (such as X) by helping to retain many existing (functional) applications in the council. However, instead of sojourning in relative isolation from each other, they can be integrated to create new services that are more attuned to the needs of the citizens.

At this point, it can be noted that the above description outlines the problems that are inherent within the existing process and systems. However, as mentioned before we propose a Web-based system portal (at a conceptual level) to overcome these issues and the following section details this.

A Proposal for Process Change and Integration Using a Web Portal

Currently, the business processes and supporting systems that make up the abandonment of motor vehicles (AMV) service were operating in isola-

Figure 5. Associations between actors and the redesigned Web system

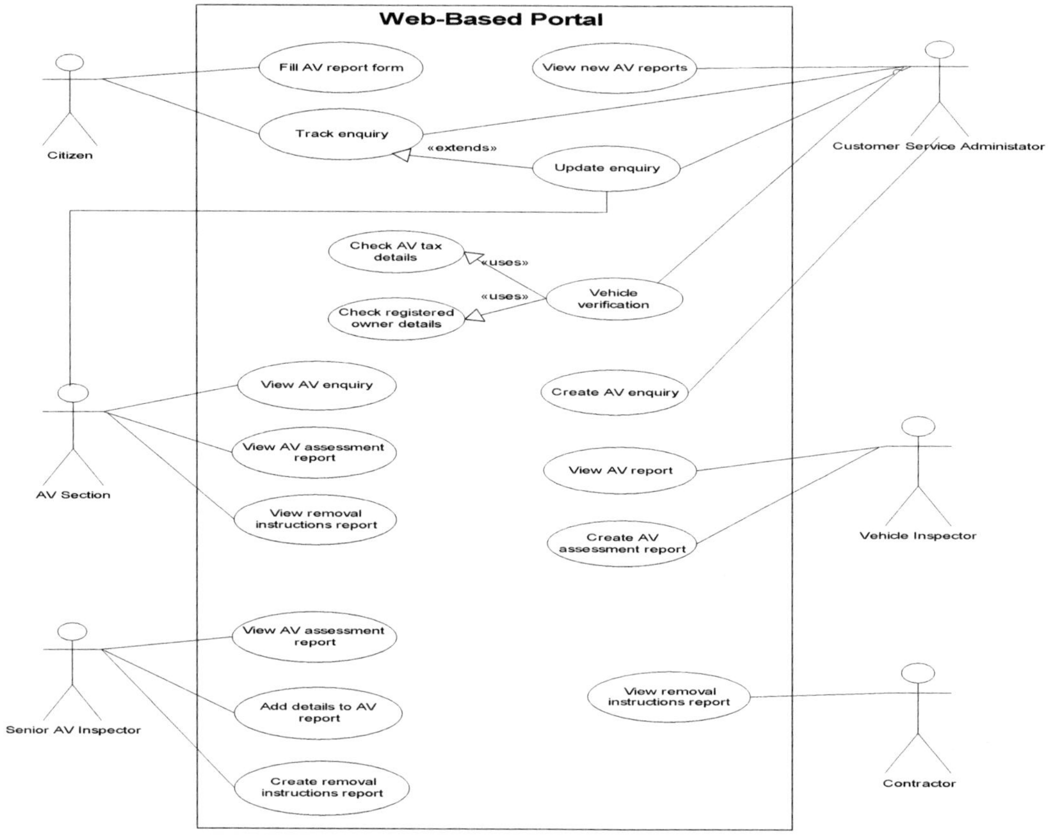

tion from each other resulting in several problems, more specifically in terms of communication. For example, a citizen was not aware of the outcome of his/her enquiry and the CSA in turn was not aware of the whole cycle. However, following the interviews and observations of the current system, a description of the newly designed integrated process for abandonment of vehicles in terms of a use case is offered. The use case below (Figure 5) describes the associations between actors and what is happening in the proposed redesigned web based system for processing abandoned vehicles at Council X.

The collaboration diagram in Figure 6 demonstrates the tasks carried out by a citizen in the new redesigned AMV process and the collaboration of each object in the system in order to perform tasks. The new process begins with the citizen logging into the main security user interface. From the new system a prompt is sent to the user for the provision of a username and password so that the services can be accessed. Once the username and password are verified by the system the main menu control appears. The main menu control allows the citizen to fill out an abandoned vehicle report form and the information captured in the form will be stored in a class named AV reports. The main menu control automatically assigns the AV report with a unique ID number so that the report is classified as an individual enquiry. Once the citizen has completed the report form, then the system obtains the AV details from the AV reports class and allows the user to view the submitted report via the track enquiry facility.

Figure 6. Collaboration diagram for citizen interaction with new Web-based portal

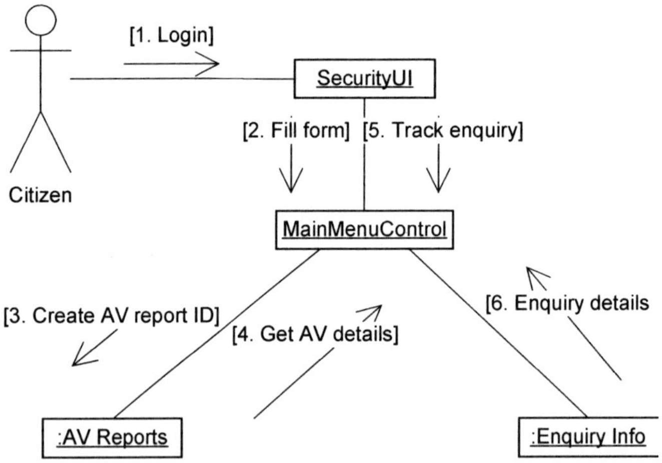

When the user selects the track enquiry facility from the main menu control the AV details are taken from the AV reports class and also the enquiry details are taken from the enquiry info class. The enquiry info class is updated by the customer service administrator with information regarding the progress of the investigation of the suspected abandoned vehicle.

The collaboration diagram in Figure 7 demonstrates how a customer service administrator will interact with the new system when attempting to perform tasks, in which objects in the system will need to collaborate together in order to perform those tasks. The process begins when the customer service administrator logs into a new system using a secure user interface. The secure user interface prompts the user to provide a username and password. The system then verifies the details and if the details are correct then access is granted. Once the CSA has successfully logged onto the system, the main menu control appears. At this point, the system alerts the CSA of recently received reports. Further, details of the reports are displayed to the user via the interaction of the class named AV reports. In order to verify the information from the AV report such as the vehicle tax and keeper details, the user needs to search the DVLA Database. Once the user selects the option to search the DVLA Database, the main menu control interacts with the class named DVLA DBase in order to get the TAX and AV keeper details to the CSA. Once the CSA has verified and checked the information the CSA needs to create an AV enquiry, which is stored in the class named AV inspection report. Once the CSA has sent the AV enquiry then the user is required to update the AV info, whereby details of the progress of the abandoned vehicle are presented for the viewing of the citizens.

Whilst this section has offered a practical outlook to this research, there is little known about whether this is a suitable system and also whether the issues identified in practice will be overcome by our proposed Web portal. In the next section we evaluate this further.

DISCUSSION AND ANALYSIS

As a result of the inefficiencies identified with the AMV service a new Web portal-based solution was proposed to provide a more integrated service to the citizen in the previous section. The new working model proposes to integrate the IS/IT systems of the contact centre, AV Section, DVLA and contractor horizontally with the aid

Figure 7. Collaboration diagrams for CSA interaction with the new Web-based portal

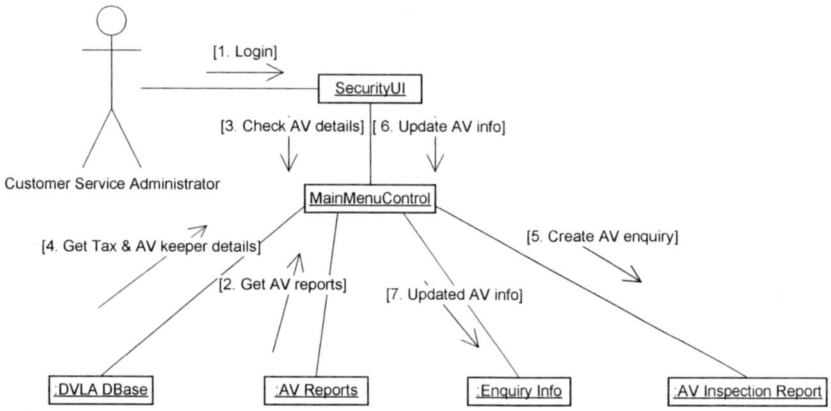

of XML technology and a Web services model as proposed conceptually in Figure 2. This allows the sharing of information through one single Web-based portal.

In the new redesigned solution a number of new features have been incorporated into the design of the Web-based system for Council X. In particular, a citizen can report and also track the progress of an abandoned vehicle through one single Web-based portal. In the previous working model no such feature was available for citizens to track the progress of an enquiry electronically. Further, the Web-based portal also allows the administrators involved in the service of abandonment of vehicles to update the progress of an abandoned vehicle through the portal, which was also not possible in the previous working model. Equally, the Web-based portal provides a new feature, in which the CSAs can carry out a check on a suspected abandoned vehicle, in which tax and keeper details of the vehicle are directly viewable through the portal. However, in the existing working model Council X relied on the vehicle inspectors and citizens to physically check if the vehicle is taxed or not.

With the new portal the Abandoned Vehicle Section administrators have been offered a new horizontal process that can provide feedback to citizens regarding the abandoned vehicle at each stage of the investigation. In the current working model this feature is not available to the AV Section administrators or citizens. Vehicle inspectors are directly alerted through the portal and can also fill out an electronic assessment report form of an abandoned vehicle, which will be directly sent through to the senior vehicle inspector via the portal. The current working model offers the AV Section administrators a facility of printing out a copy of the initial report and giving it to an inspector. The inspector in turn would then physically visit the location, manually fill out an assessment report form and bring the report back for the viewing of the senior inspector. In the new system the senior inspector can view the assessment report directly through the portal and also create a removal instructions report electronically and send it through directly to the vehicle removal contractor. In contrast these features are not possible in the current process as the entire process relied on extended communication among the stakeholders involved in the process of abandonment of vehicles. With the new portal the vehicle removal contractor can also access the portal to view the instructions electronically and also print out the report. However, in the current process the AV Section administrators would physically visit the removal contractor's office to deliver the report for removal by hand.

Overall, with the new system information and communication dissemination among entities involved in the service of removing abandoned vehicles at Council X was improved as the new working model demonstrates greater efficiency in delivering the service to citizens. Furthermore, duplication of information disseminated among entities is reduced in the new process model. Equally, the cycle time for removing a vehicle from the street is reduced as information is centralised and can be passed to various stakeholders a lot faster, thus the abandoned vehicle can be removed faster than the previously identified 10 working days for the current process.

Whilst the above discussion illustrates that the newly designed Web-based portal can work in theory, it was difficult to determine whether the new system does indeed satisfy the citizens' requirements. Although it was not possible to implement and test the proposed solution in practice, the system prototype was valuated using citizens. From the evaluation (summative evaluation method) it was learnt that there is greater efficiency of information flow and communication amongst the various stakeholders involved in the service of removing and reporting abandoned vehicles at Council X. As a rejoinder to this section. The observation and think-aloud protocol methods were used. Alongside the think-aloud approach a set of evaluation heuristics devised by Jakob Neilson were utilised in order to target usability problems with the interfaces (Mack & Neilson, 1993). There were eight respondents used for this purpose. This included a local authority system's administrator, citizens (working)-3 and 4 citizens (mature students).

As an example of the problems that were inherent in the new system and some of the citizens' views of the new system, Table 2 is provided.

In terms of horizontal integration and efficiency it became evident that it is significantly a vision of efficiency and effectiveness as public services will be centralized and public agencies and businesses can share information in a seamless fashion. Stoltzfus (2004) identified that increased participation with citizens can make them feel that they have more of a voice in the policies and functions of government, are able to access information that may have once seemed inaccessible and are able to conduct business with government in a more understandable and effective manner. However, very few countries have

Table 2. Evaluation results

Result No.	Usability Problem Description
1	Two participants pointed out that the main menu tabs need to be highlighted in a different colour as they found it difficult to distinguish what Web page they were viewing. Therefore, the usability problem distinguished was related to the heuristic named visibility of system status, which will be improved in order to allow users to navigate the system more efficiently and effectively. "However, we like the way that the information is all in one place. We do not have to go to different pages or go to different desk (if we go to the offices of the council)."
2	One participant suggested that in the interface named abandoned vehicle report form (Figure 5.14) the citizen details such as name, address, and so on should automatically appear without inputting them.
3	One participant noticed that the track enquiry interface (Figure 5.15) has a button named 'E-mail Us,' which confused the participant as the user thought that there is a need to e-mail the council for some reason or another, therefore the system needs to be adjusted so that users are clearly notified with a message underneath explaining the intention of each control.
4	One participant pointed out that on the main login menu (Figure 5.13) the button named 'Logon' needs to be changed to 'Login', which relates to the heuristic named visibility of system status. Overall, both citizens found the system to be consistent and very informative for information that they required.

excelled in the context of horizontal and vertical levels of integration in e-government (Weerakkody et al., 2007). Therefore, many academics and researchers have highlighted the need to collaborate and integrate IS/IT systems, processes across horizontal and vertical levels of government. According to Bekkers and Homburg, (2005) transaction level e-government services require a degree of integration and this can be achieved through vertical and horizontal integration of information systems. Furthermore, literature has distinguished that governments must utilize business process redesign initiatives in order to streamline processes and also integrate IS/IT systems using available standards such as XML and EAI techniques.

However, horizontal integration of IS/IT systems pose a number of barriers for governments and businesses trying to collaborate, such as participating organisations requiring compatible IS/IT infrastructures and standardised data definitions. Governmental agencies are surrounding by bureaucracy and red tape policies that discourage the change in governmental procedures (Weerakkody et al., 2006). Equally, organisations and people resist sharing information due to structural conflicts, managerial practices that discourage the sharing and integration of IS/IT systems. Conversely, according to Government Computing (2005) the UK public sector is looking upon making public services more efficient; many governmental agencies are considering shared services as a probable solution. However, the same article distinguished that issues regarding trust among governmental agencies and businesses are seen as a potential barrier and also smaller district councils have less funding to spend on such plans for sharing (Government Computing, 2005).

Having discussed and analyzed the results of this research in terms of theory and practice, the next section provides some conclusions and future directions to this research.

CONCLUSION

The main question driving this research was: What can be learnt about the achievement of horizontal integration among local authorities in the e-government context in order to better deliver e-services to citizens? The e-government context in this instance is the local authority; Council X. This research has demonstrated that horizontal integration between local authorities when implemented removes the perceived inefficiencies of an e-service (removal and reporting of abandoned vehicles) to the citizen. In this instance, the inefficiency existed in the entire process of removing and reporting abandoned vehicles. However, it was also learnt that the key service providers, for example the operations development manager, within the local authority did not think that there were any inefficiencies. In fact they thought the processes were efficient.

It was also learnt that due to the success of horizontal integration initiatives such as the removal and reporting of abandoned vehicles there were future plans to eventually integrate all the processes with the IS/IT systems. However, whilst integration of processes and IS/IT is important, another issue that is vital for any process change, which includes the horizontal integration of processes and systems is that the people aspect needs to be carefully considered and that is something that the e-government programme manager at Council X commented upon: "In terms of achieving a one-stop-shop service with integrated IS/IT systems, there are no problems from a technological viewpoint; however, it will require a change in people's attitude to accept technological changes."

Another aspect of horizontal integration within the e-government context that needs to be emphasized is the awareness of government policies. Although the DVLA database was integrated with the council Web-portal for this research, from a practical sense such an action cannot be undertaken as there are limitations-the DVLA discourages and prevents the sharing of information due to the Data Protection Act. However, as demonstrated in this research governmental agencies, central government and organisations need to be linked together in order to provide a one-stop-shop environment. For the success of a one-stop-shop environment each one of the parties must give up some power in order to truly reap the benefits of sharing across horizontal and vertical levels (Gupta & Jana, 2003).

In the above context, however, we can not ignore the progress made towards integrated service delivery by the UK government, where links to all 388 English local councils have now been implemented through the "direct.gov" Web portal (Government Computing, 2006). Using the address http://local.direct.gov.uk/mycouncil/ citizens can now link to access their respective local council services. However, we argue that this is merely a Web link and therefore only provides access to the same cataloguing and basic transaction level services that are already available through the local council Web sites. On the contrary, the evidence in Council X suggests that there are still a number of deeper process and systems integration issues that need to be addressed at both local and central government levels before fully integrated services are offered to citizens through a single point of access.

This research also proposed a Web-based solution incorporating process changes and better information exchange for the AMV process. Although theoretical in nature, there is no reason why such a solution cannot be implemented. In our proposed solution, due to the centralized Web site that is available for the AMV process, the local authority (Council X) can offer information to the central government departments about abandoned vehicles. This will prevent double counting or avoid cars being collected from sites. For the citizen this will ensure that residents are satisfied in the knowledge that their vicinities are being looked after and that their tax money is being utilized in an efficient and effective manner. Further, Stoltzfus (2004) identified that increased participation with citizens can make them feel that they have more of a voice in the policies and functions of government, are able to access information that may have once seemed inaccessible, and are able to conduct business with government in a more understandable and effective manner. However, a limitation that organizations, whether public or private should be aware of is that education, training, pre-preparation, and awareness is necessary when any substantial change such as this is being undertaken.

As with every research, there is always a future direction. This research focused upon only one local authority and one public sector service. Therefore, in future this research could be focused upon horizontal integration and ultimately a one-stop-shop environment on a national and even global aspect. Although some technological issues such as the application of XML were examined in this research, there are pertinent issues such as security and the impacts of the Data Protection Act that could be examined in the future. Further issues that can be explored upon such a topic are vertical levels of integration, the impacts of integration upon organizational change and the usability of the new services and portals for citizens.

ACKNOWLEDGMENT

The empirical study used in this paper was conducted by Mr. Gurjit Dhillon as part of his final year project/dissertation for the award of BSc (Honors) in computer science at the School of Information Systems, Computing and Mathematics at Brunel University. The authors wish to thank Gurjit for his contribution.

REFERENCES

Bekkers, V., & Homburg, V. (2005). *The information ecology of e-government.* Amsterdam: IOS Press.

Bruijn, H. de, Heuvelhof, E. ten, & Veld, R., int (2002). *Process management: Why project management fails in complex decision making processes*. Boston: Kluwer.

Boyatzis, R. (1998). *Transforming qualitative information*. Sage Publications.

Champy, J. (2002). *X-engineering the corporation: Reinventing your business in the digital age*. Warner Books.

Chandler, S., & Emanuels, S. (2002). Transformation not automation. In *Proceedings on the 2nd European Conference on E-Government*, Oxford, UK, (pp. 99-102).

Crane, J. (2005). *Qualitative research methods*. Retrieved December 6, 2005, from http://web.isp.cz

Deloitte Research (2000). *At the dawn of e-government: The citizen as customer*. Deloitte Consulting and Deloitte and Touche, New York.

Fustes, M. (2003). The unconstrained business. *Insight*, 3, 15-17.

Gibson, C. F., & Nolan, R. L. (1974). Managing the four stages of EDP growth. *Harvard Business Review*, *52*(1), 76-88.

Government Computing Publication: March (2005)

Government Computing Publication: November (2005)

Government Computing (2006), A New Era Dawns: Local Directgov Programme, May 2006

Grover, V., & Segars, A. H. (2005). An empirical evaluation of stages of strategic information systems planning: Patterns of process design and effectiveness. *Information & Management*, 42, 461-479.

Gupta, M., & Jana, D. (2003). E-government evaluation: A framework and case study. *Government Information Quarterly*, 365-387.

Hazlett, S. A., & Hill, F. (2003). E-government: The realities of using IT to transform the public sector. *Managing Service Quality*, *13*(6), 445-452.

Information Age (2004a). SeeBeyond empowers Sainsbury's transfomation. *Information Age*, B10-B11.

Information Age (2004b). Understanding, implementing and managing core technologies, Information Age advisory series. *Information Age*, *1*(3), 26.

Janssen, M., & van Veenstra, A. F. (2005). Stages of growth in e-government: An architectural approach. *The Electronic Journal of E-Government*, *3*(4), 193-200. Retreived from www.ejeg.com

Lawrence, A. (2004). From EAI to SOA. *Information Age, Infoconomy*, B8-B9.

Miles, M. B., & Huberman, A. M. (1994). *Qualitative data analysis: An expanded sourcebook*. Thousand Oaks, CA: Sage.

Jaeger, P. (2002). Constitutional principles and e-government: An opinion about possible effects of federalism and the separation of powers on e-government policies. *Government Information Quarterly*, 357-368.

Layne, K., & Lee, J. (2001). Developing fully functional e-government: A four-stage model. *Government Information Quarterly*, 18, 122-136.

Lee, S. M., Tan, X., Trimi, S., (2005). Current practices of leading e-government countries. *Communications of the ACM*, *48*(10), 99-104.

Mack, R., & Neilson, J. (1993). Usability inspection methods. *SIGCHI*, *25*(1), 28-33.

Masood, S. (2002). The missing link. November 2002, 31-32.

Monson-Haefel, R. (2004). *J2EE Web services*. Boston: Addison Wesley.

Nolan, R. L. (1979). Managing the crisis in data processing. *Harvard Business Review, 57*(2), 115-126.

Norris, D., & Moon, M. (2005). Advancing e-government at the grassroots: Tortoise or hare? *Public Administration Review, 65*(1), 64-72.

Phythian, M., & Taylor, W. (2001). Progress in electronic service delivery by English District Councils. *The International Journal of Public Sector Management, 14*(7), 569-584.

Saxena, A., & Wadhawa, S. (2004). E-business perspective of e-governance. In M. D. Gupta (Ed.), *Promise of e-governance: Operational challenges* (pp. 128-135). New Delhi: Tata-McGraw-Hill.

Scholl, H. J., Klischewski, R., & Moon, J. M. (2005). Minitrack: E-government infrastructure and interoperability. Proceedings of the 38th Hawaii International Conference on System Science, IEEE.

UN (2002). *Benchmarking e-government: A global perspective, assessing the progress of the UN member states*. Division of Public Economics and Public Administration (DPEPA). Nettelafrica.org/doc/NetTel%20Safari@the%20Equator%20(Uganda%202003)/Benchmarkingegovt.pdf

Varshney, A. (2005). New frontiers of social policy. Proceedings of Arusha Conference. December 12-15, 2005. Retrieved December 1, 2006, from http://siteresources.worldbank.org/INTRANET-SOCIALDEVELOPMENT/Resources/Varshney_Formatted.pdf

Weerakkody, V., Baire, S., & Choudrie, J. (2006). *E-government: A case for process improvement in the public sector*. Proceedings of the Hawaii International Conference on Systems Sciences (Hicss-39), January 2006.

Weerakkody, V., Janssen, M., & Hjort-Madsen, K. (2006). Realising integrated e-government services: A European perspective. *Journal of Cases in Electronic Commerce, 3*(2), 14-38.

World Bank (2005). *Definition of e-government*. www1.worldbank.org/publicsector/egov/definition.htm

Yin, R. K. (1984). *Case study research: Design and methods*. Beverley Hills, CA: Sage Publications.

This work was previously published in the International Journal of Electronic Government Research, Vol. 3, Issue 3, edited by M. Khosrow-Pour, pp. 22-39, copyright 2007 by IGI Publishing, formerly known as Idea Group Publishing (an imprint of IGI Global).

Chapter IX
Online Policy Consultation:
A Case Study of Local Government

Lucas Walsh
Deakin University, Australia

INTRODUCTION

As developments in communication technologies impact upon many spheres of public and private life, they influence the way in which the public sector engages citizens. While most governments have an online presence, this is mainly applied to the provision of one-way (i.e. government to citizen) information and services. However, available technologies such as the Internet and mobile telephony provide opportunities for governments to enter into a two-way dialogue with citizens, increase transparency of their operations, and encourage democratic participation outside election time. As the government closest to the people, local government is particularly well placed to use online technologies to enhance and expand participatory democracy through strategies such as e-consultation.

The implementation of an e-consultation strategy by local government presents a number of challenges to local governments seeking to enhance their dialogue with constituents using information and communication technologies (ICTs). This chapter draws from an external evaluation of an Australian local government initiative, Darebin eForum.[1] Conducted in 2007, this evaluation included a survey of e-consultation participants[2] and interviews with Council Officers responsible for moderating the site.[3] The findings provide a snapshot of some of these challenges.[4] Though modest in size and ambition, the experiences of Darebin eForum provide valuable insight into the challenges faced by governments seeking to use ICTs to engage in dialogue with their constituents.

E-Consultation

E-consultation is seen as a valuable channel through which a two-way relationship can be developed and enhanced between citizens and elected representatives. It involves the use of ICTs such as the Internet, interactive broadcasting, and digital telephony, to extend and/or enhance political democracy through access to information, and to facilitate participation in democratic communities, processes, and institutions (Balnaves, Walsh & Shoesmith, 2006; Hacker & van Dijk, 2000; Walsh, 2006).

Copyright © 2009, IGI Global, distributing in print or electronic forms without written permission of IGI Global is prohibited.

Governments typically use consultation to develop a two-way relationship with citizens by inviting them to provide feedback on a specified issue. Governments typically set the questions, provide related information and manage the process (OECD, 2001). The OECD defines consultation as:

a two-way relationship in which citizens provide feedback to government. It is based on the prior definition of the issue on which citizens' views are being sought and requires the provision of information. Governments define the issues for consultation, set the questions and manage the process, while citizens are invited to contribute their views and opinions. (2001 p. 23)

E-consultancy combines the electronic delivery of government services with:

the direct use of new technologies to provide members of the public with access to the decision-making process. This type of programmatic behavior, electronic consultation, or participation can be seen as a direct means by which elements of the public service and executive can engage directly with the community or relevant stakeholders to develop policy. (Chen, Gibson & Geiselhart, 2006 p. 101)

One type of e-consultation, online consultation, uses the Internet to enable citizens to provide feedback to government based on information and issues defined and facilitated by government (OECD, 2003). Governments may draw from a variety of electronic media to conduct e-consultation, such as online forums, surveys, feedback forms, and polls, electronic voting, webinars and podcasts (Bailey, 2007). Distinguished from the "push-down" delivery of government information and services, online consultation uses the Internet to enable interactive communication (Hacker & van Dijk, 2000 p. 40). This dialogue can take place vertically between elected representatives, public servants, and the public or horizontally between members of the public and/or civil society representatives and stakeholders. Governments may draw from a variety of electronic media to conduct e-consultation, ranging from informal engagements, such as non-binding discussions facilitated online and "electronic suggestion boxes," to more structured and formal activities, such as online collaboration and report development, structured online discussion forums, surveys, feedback forms, and polls, electronic voting, webinars, podcasts, planning simulations and games (Bailey, 2007; Chen et al., 2006 p. 101).

Drawing from a case study, this chapter will focus on how e-consultation has been adopted and adapted at the level of local government in Australia. The experience of the Darebin eForum provides some interesting insights into the development and implementation of online consultation. The following examination of online policy consultation is divided into five parts: following a brief overview of Darebin eForum (http://eforum.darebin.vic.gov.au), some of the ways in which e-consultation challenges the roles of the public service, elected representatives, and citizens are identified. Following this, the author identifies the need to situate e-consultation within a continuum of citizen engagement that is essentially ongoing, deliberative, educative, and inclusive.

Darebin eForum

Launched in March 2006, the rationale of the Darebin eForum was to provide an additional mechanism for councillors in local government to consult members of their constituency "and make local politics a more meaningful part of people's lives" (Merkes, 2004). Specific aims of the online forum included: the extension of pathways to democratic discussion, consultation, and decision-making by citizens, councillors, and council officers in a local government area; the offer of greater government transparency and accountability; the facilitation of easy access to councillors and council officers; the demonstration of the potential of e-democracy in local government; and the promotion of lifelong learning (Merkes).

Located in Melbourne's inner north, the Darebin Council serves a wide diversity of constituents. The southern part of the city is populated mainly by young professionals, whereas the northern region has a high degree of cultural and socio-economic diversity, and is more socially disadvantaged. In 2005, one in three of Darebin's population was born overseas, with the highest proportion coming from southern and eastern Europe (mainly Italy, Greece, and Macedonia) (Darebin City Council, 2006). It also has a high indigenous population (ABS, 2007).

Darebin eForum began as a pilot project in 2004 with a fairly simple e-mail-based format that ran for four months. A topic of local interest was proposed for discussion each fortnight. At the conclusion of the trial, Darebin Council decided to continue the forum on an ongoing basis. Over the course of the next 12 months, a reference group consisting of internal eForum stakeholders decided what the topics would be and what form the moderation would take (Interview 2, July 27, 2006). A more technologically advanced open source platform was also developed for the eForum.

The advanced eForum, which was launched in 2006 and ran until 2007, hosted a publicly open discussion on a given topic of local concern for two-week periods (Darebin City Council, 2006). Topics ranged from issues such as transport and community harmony to developing sustainable approaches to the environment. Each topic had one permanent moderator and one to two comoderators acting as a subject specialist on the given topic. Once the topic was posted, the moderators tended to check for issues of legal liability but avoided moderation of the content. While Darebin eForum moderators developed general guidelines for their roles and expectations outlining appropriate use of language and basic issues of legal liability, they did not adopt formal procedures for e-moderation (Interview 1, July 27, 2006). At the end of the discussion period for each topic, the discussion was summarized and posted on the council's Web site. The moderators then disseminated the feedback to the relevant area of local government, which in turn determined how that information would be used.

Darebin eForum was, significantly, motivated by a public servant (Walsh, 2007b) as part of a broader "Governing Darebin" initiative. This Council Officer became the main moderator responsible for approval of posts and the clarification of issues. Subject specialist comoderators were responsible for providing specific questions for debate, specific topic-relevant information and feedback to eForum participants (Interview 1, July 27, 2006).

Implementation of this e-consultation created new demands on Council Officers' time and resources and required specific skills and expertise (Interview 1, July 27, 2006; Richard, 2004; Bailey, 2007).

The experience of public officials in Darebin echoed those of colleagues in other parts of the world such as Canada, who have noted the profound impact of online policy consultation on the public service, creating new demands of time, resources, and expertise, while perhaps most importantly challenging notions of accountability within contemporary governance (Interview 1, July 27, 2006; Richard, 2004). In the Canadian context, Richard notes that "Consultations with the public, other levels of government and other parties for the purposes of policy development ... affects government-to-citizen and citizen-to-government relationships at all levels of the bureaucracy" (Richard p. 7). Moderation of online discussion (e-moderation) requires interpersonal skills, technical proficiency, skills in time management and may draw upon methodologies and strategies developed in areas such as e-learning (e.g. Salmon, 2000).

The following explores the challenges faced by public servants responsible for moderating online forums in both Australia and Canada and discusses the ways in which these challenges are inextricably linked to the changing roles of elected representatives and citizens engaged in online consultation.

THE CHANGING ROLE OF THE PUBLIC SERVANTS

In her reflection on the processes and models underlying the practice of e-consultation in the Canadian public service, Richard (2004) outlines three roles for public servants involved in the consultative process: (1) as subject-matter experts; (2) as educators; and (3) as moderators. Moderators in turn can undertake three types of tasks: as moderator-facilitators who administer online discussions with stakeholder groups of various sizes on an ongoing basis, or within a specific area of policy development (Darragh, 2003); as comoderators; and/or as "e-tivity" team captains (Richard, 2004 pp. 9-11).

As moderator-facilitators acting within a specific area of policy development, Darebin eForum moderators served three roles identified by Richard.[5] The main moderator was responsible for approval of posts and the clarification of issues, but generally deferred responsibility for providing specific topic-relevant information and feedback to the subject specialist comoderators. These comoderators generated questions for debate, provided brief background information, responded to postings, and attempted to stimulate discussion (Interview 1, July 27, 2006). Comoderators also provided introductory comments about the topic, specific questions, and links to relevant documents (Interview 2, July 27, 2006).

As a subject-matter specialist, the comoderator's role is similar to other initiatives, such as the U.K.'s *DialogueByDesign* and Finland's *Share Your Views With Us* online forum (www.otakantaa.fi), which include public servants as subject-matter experts. Discussions conducted by the Finland Ministry of Finance within the *Share Your Views With Us* forum, for example, have been initiated by the public servant responsible for the issue who is expected to be active in the dialogue as a subject-matter specialist. The forum has provided an open arena for Finnish citizens to freely discuss, comment, and share views on government projects. Contributions from public servants have been highly valued by participants (Holkeri, 2003; Richard, 2004).

Darebin eForum moderators faced two overarching challenges: resourcing and responsibility. They were constrained by the limited funding and time that they could dedicate to the forum. Similarly, Richard observes in the Canadian context that additional coordination of consultations between stakeholders' other departments and jurisdictions is required to match the new bureaucratic networks emerging from e-consultation. The expanded role of public servants outlined above creates new demands on time, expertise, and resourcing: "In all models of consultation, whether online or off-line, public servants ... develop the objectives of the consultation, as well as the timetable, content, questions, and evaluation. Online applications multiply the roles of public servants in the background" (Richard, 2004 p. 12).

Public servants also enter the consultative process as participants. In New-Brunswick, Canada, Deputy Ministers are urged to "actively encourage public servants to... make a contribution on a personal basis, as concerned and involved citizens. At the municipal or regional levels, there are a number of examples of municipal public servants involved in discussions" (Richard, 2004 p. 7). Darebin moderators also had considerable autonomy in determining what took place within the topic, occasionally offering personal as well as professional suggestions to users of the site. Personal suggestions were well received by users, extending and enhancing discussion (Interview 1,

July 27, 2006). According to one moderator, "it's also good that the community sees that we are councillor officers yes, but we are also humans … and have opinions about things too" (Interview 1, July 27, 2006). But because they provided opinions as well as information, moderators sometimes encountered challenges as to how they could respond to potentially sensitive political issues (Interview 1, July 27, 2006).

As in the Canadian context, Darebin eForum moderators experienced uncertainty about the extent to which they as public servants could respond. In the *Digital Commons E-Democracy Pilot*, which commenced in 2002 to explore the respective roles of public servants and elected officials, public servants in Canada expressed concern over their ability to participate freely in discussions as employees of the Crown (Center for Collaborative Government, 2002). Richard notes that Canadian public servants, while recognizing the valuable potential of e-consultation, "feel uneasy transcending their role as a *faceless bureaucrat* when in a position to facilitate an online discussion on service improvement or when developing a policy." Some Canadian public servants "see their role as supporting the government agenda, which restricts their ability to participate freely in a discussion and forces them into the position of observers, unless they are official spokespeople" (2004 p. 1).

Echoing Richard's observations, Darebin moderators sometimes experienced awkwardness about their role as public facilitators. One Darebin eForum moderator cited a specific example of where a participant's concerns could not be addressed via the online forum because the moderator was concerned about breaching a politically sensitive area. The concern was then forwarded to the relevant council personnel who chose to contact the citizen directly (and in private). The need for council personnel to be responsive is critical here. From the users' viewpoint, a lack of response from public officials and/or representatives can lead to lack of credibility in the consultative process.

Sometimes, information cannot be shared because it may damage a relationship or offend, so moderators "have to be strategic." As with the Canadian experience outlined earlier, this is a difficult area for the moderator because they remain public officials and employees of the council (Interview 2, July 27, 2006).

Another challenge to moderators was the management of behaviors and expectations of those who *were* able and willing to participate online. Coleman and Gøtze (2002) identify the potential problem of citizens expecting too much of the online consultative process. Ensuring representation has, as its corollary, the danger that online consultation may yield unrepresentative extreme views or abuse of the process. General managers at the Darebin City Council expressed concern over the possibility that some eForum users may flood the site with posts or with messages of a controversial nature (Interview, 27 July 2006).[6] This concern was not unfounded. In February 2004, for example, Finland's *Share Your Views With Us* forum was shut down after it was spammed with some 4000 nationalist messages demanding a monolingual Finland and modifications to the official status of the Swedish language (Richard, 2004 p. 6). Given the cultural and socio-economic diversity of the Darebin City community, the Darebin eForum also received a diversity of views (Walsh, 2007a); indeed, its first discussion topic on Community Harmony was politically charged and potentially controversial (Darebin City Council, 2006; Interview 1, July 27, 2006).

CONSULTING AT A DISTANCE: THE ROLE OF ELECTED REPRESENTATIVES

Though endorsed by the Darebin City Council as part of the "Governing Darebin" strategy, the eForum was developed with "cautious support from senior management and councillors … as long as nothing goes wrong" (Merkes, 2004).

As mentioned above, it is significant to note that the Darebin eForum was initiated by a member of the public service and that Darebin Councillors tended not to take a direct interest in the eForum discussions (Interview 2, July 27, 2006).[7] Historically, Australian political representatives have been reluctant to use ICTs to facilitate greater and more direct participation in democratic processes and institutions. This trend may be attributable to at least two broad factors: an emergent political conservatism and a lack of adequate skills by representatives to develop the potential of the online medium to enhance representative capabilities.

Magarey's (1999) study of the Internet and Australian parliamentary democracy during the late 1990s identified reluctance on the part of parliamentarians towards the use of technology to enable greater public input into policy formation. The attitude of many parliamentarians is in turn attributable to a broader political conservatism towards more participatory modes of democracy and the use of technology to create greater opportunities to facilitate participation in general (Davidson, 1997; Magarey, 1999).

This attitude appears to be shifting in Australia. A 2002 survey of Australian elected representatives by Chen (2002) found that the generalized use of online services by elected representatives has in recent years been substantially higher in comparison to the wider Australian population. Interest in the use of online consultation by parliamentarians is "quite high," however, while elected representatives generally see the Internet as an important vehicle for consultation, it did not rank highly against other "off-line" media forms as a communications channel. Chen found that parliamentarians were twice as likely (64%) to engage in online consultation than their peers in local government. Parliamentarians were likely to rate e-consultation as more important than councillors. Nevertheless, a significant proportion of parliamentarians and councillors expressed indifference or wariness. Approximately 45% of councillors and 20% of parliamentarians saw online consultation as "neither important nor unimportant," "unimportant," or "having a negative impact on democratic consultation." Perhaps most significantly, only 3% of representatives could name a specific example of online consultation among their peer-network (Chen, 2002). These findings echo those in the U.K., where elected politicians are "conspicuous by their absence" from policy engagement or consultation initiatives in general (Coleman & Gøtze, 2002 p. 20).

A lack of resources and skills may have restricted the uptake of e-consultation by representatives; representatives who rated themselves as having "very competent" and "highly capable" computer skills were more than 10 times more likely to undertake online consultation. The need for appropriate technological and political skills and literacy among public servant moderators and political representatives also applies to the citizens to whom the e-consultations are addressed.

THE CORE CHALLENGE? THE ROLE OF CITIZENS

Moderators of the eForum were very aware of the particular benefits to users who were "time-poor" and wanted to participate in Council from home (Interview 2, July 27 2006). Users tended to reside locally, although occasionally the forum was accessed internationally. Nearly 90% of survey respondents accessed the Internet daily. The Darebin eForum website required registration to post responses to topics. Personal information that users were expected to provide was deliberately kept to a minimum, including the person's real name and post code. (Users had the option of providing additional information but tended not to (Walsh, 2007a). While participants could use email or a web-based text box to post to the eForum, email was by far the preferred mode of posting.

In 2007, users of the Darebin eForum were asked to respond to a user-survey which sought responses from eForum users to questions in three areas: (1) motivations for using the forum; (2) response to the design of the forum; and (3) demographic questions about users (Walsh, 2007a). Some of the key findings of the survey were as follows: 84.6% of survey respondents accessed the Internet daily. The gender of respondents was fairly balanced. 50% were male, 42% female while just under 8% declined to answer. The majority of respondents were aged between 46-55 years (34.6%), while the next highest age bracket was 26-35 years (26.9%). A range of age groups were represented in the survey.

The user survey indicated that people joined the eForum for work/official duties, general curiosity, to become more informed about local issues, and to have their voice heard. Around one in five survey respondents joined for political debate. But, notably, few respondents joined the eForum to change Council decisions. Furthermore, no survey respondents accessed the forum to meet like minded people, suggesting a preference for vertical interactions with government rather than horizontal communications with each other (Walsh, 2007a).

Just under half of survey respondents (42%) posted a message, while the same number declined to post a message. Respondents gave a number of reasons as to why they looked at the site but did not post a message. Lack of time was a factor. One moderator observed the forum often seemed to be dominated by those "confident enough to be posting", while many users lacked the confidence to submit their views (Interview 1, July 27, 2006). For example, one respondent indicated that "At present the discussion is relevant [and] interesting, but I feel those sharing are far more experienced in this topic than I am, so at present I'm just benefiting from their shared knowledge. In future I may post questions or comments, if the discussion evolves." Similarly, another suggested that "There's only recently been any real discussion of issues. Some recent views were interesting [and] relevant to my work, but I felt I had less experience of the topic than those who posted, so I didn't post myself. In future if the discussion continues I may post questions or comments." Others did not feel that they could make a valid contribution. For example, one user indicated that she "didn't have any valid input on the topic." Another survey respondent "[d]id not feel it was appropriate." Similarly, one user did not feel that she "had time to formulate thoughts worthy of posting" (Walsh, 2007a).

The need for Darebin consultations to be inclusive continues to be particularly important in Darebin City, whose population is characterized by socio-economic, cultural and linguistic diversity. The language barrier is identified by one eForum moderator as being particularly significant because many members of the local community are either new migrants and refugees or settled migrants who prefer to communicate in their heritage language (Interview 1, July 27, 2006). Many community members also experience physical impairment, such as mobility and vision (Walsh, 2007a).

Users felt that the eForum encouraged some good debate on subjects both directly related to local citizens of Darebin, and issues of broader significance. One user felt that the eForum is a "great two-way consultative facility with lots of potential." However, some users were conscious of the lack of any explicit involvement of Council members in the e-consultation process and were thus sceptical of its effectiveness (Walsh, 2007a).

Of concern to some survey respondents was the need to foster wider membership. On the other hand, some users suggested that the eForum should include discussion on "more issues that are confronting the community like poverty, petrol, Iraq War, Industrial Relations, issues that affect our lives." Perhaps most importantly, some users questioned if Councillors actually read and responded to concerns raised on the eForum (Walsh, 2007a).

For e-consultation to be democratically effective, a number of key overlapping factors need to be taken into consideration with respect to the engagement of citizens in the consultation process. First, the provision of technological access provides a critical foundation to e-consultation. By 2005, around 58% of households in Darebin had Internet access from home. This rate of household access has increased by over 39% since 1999 (over 60% have a computer at home). A 2005 Household Survey of Darebin City draws a connection between this trend and the proportion of households in Darebin preferring to receive information from this council via Web site or e-mail. Between 2001 and 2005, the proportion of households in Darebin visiting the Darebin City Council Web site increased over threefold (Darebin City Council, 2006). But, as one of the moderators pointed out, Internet access was higher in the southern, more affluent region of Darebin, thus presenting the possibility that moderators are getting a biased (or at least limited) view of the residents' feedback (Interview 1, July 27, 2006). Use of the Internet among Darebin households was quite high when compared to Australians in general. By 2005, less than one-third (5.98 million) of Australians subscribed to the Internet (ABS, 2005). Moreover, in international terms, Australia's rate of overall technological access has arguably declined in recent years when compared to other developed nations (Muir, 2004 p. 5). Any form of online engagement risks digital exclusion wherein a relative minority of the population has access to the Internet at home.

Second, the process must ensure informed representation of interests. Darebin eForum participants were recruited through advertisements in local newspapers, printed book marks, a formal face-to-face launch, through viral marketing on e-mail lists, newsletters on related networks, and media-releases for each topic.[8] The typical user to post a message was male (although, interestingly, during the pilot the typical poster was female, middle-aged, professional, and working full-time).[9] While the developers of the eForum were, on one hand, surprised by the high weekend usage of the site (as it was expected that users would be engaged in other activities on the weekend), they also were very aware of the particular benefits to users who are "time-poor" and may prefer to participate in council from home (Interview 2, July 27 2006).[10]

Not of all Darebin's eForum users lived locally – some users were based internationally. The moderators were aware that the relatively small number of current eForum users was not necessarily representative of views and "isn't a big consultation by any means." While it is acknowledged that the eForum does not give a broad consultation:

it gives a detailed consultation from a few, those who are confident enough to be posting, I know a lot of people were following the posts but not posting and I think there is a confidence that is needed to actually ... submit your views. (Interview 1, July 27, 2006)

Third, beyond merely having access to information, it is necessary for citizens to have access to the capacity and resources to be able to use the technology in an informed and effective way. One report published by Australian community organisation The Smith Family urged a more complex understanding of how ICTs can be used to promote social inclusion:

Technological inclusion is far more complex than the black and white descriptive term "digital divide." Education levels, opportunities, and motivations to learn are strongly tied to a person's ability to access and utilize technology to its fullest capacity; and the extent of access and usage exists on a continuous scale, not merely as a two way split. (Muir, 2004 p. 4)

The issue of inclusion is particularly significant in Darebin City, where the population is characterized by socio-economic extremes, as well as cultural and linguistic diversity. For example, one eForum moderator identified the language barrier as being particularly significant – especially because of high levels of new migrants and refugees and older migrants who prefer to communicate in their heritage languages (e.g., Greek and Italian) (Interview 1, July 27, 2006). Forty percent of the population is characterized as Culturally and Linguistically Diverse (CALD), and as many as 140 languages are spoken across the Darebin City area. While the main Web site for Darebin Council featured a multilingual component, the eForum resided as a separate site and did not have a translation service.

While respondents to the eForum evaluation survey indicated that English was the main language spoken at home, some respondents spoke Mandarin and Indonesian. Some respondents were of Aboriginal or Torres Strait Islander background and around 15% had some form of impairment (e.g. vision and mobility) (Walsh, 2007a).

Fourth, it is crucial that good deliberation can take place. While it has been noted that Darebin eForum did not have a representative proportion of users, the moderators suggested that the type of discussion taking place featured good quality deliberation, including informed debate between users and refinement of views that provided useful feedback to council (Interview 1 & 2, July 27, 2006). Some users agreed, stating, for example, that the eForum "encouraged some good debate on some very important subjects." Other users, however, expressed a more critical view. Just over half of survey respondents indicated that the eForum did not encourage debate and interest in public issues relevant to the Darebin community (Walsh, 2007a).

Toward a Continuum of Citizen Engagement

Ultimately, e-consultation needs to be understood as part of a continuum of citizen engagement. Three overlapping stages of public engagement have been identified by the OECD. The first stage involves the one-way provision of government information to citizens and stakeholders including both "passive" access to information on demand by citizens and the "active" dissemination of information and services to citizens by government. An example of this is the Citizenscape Web site in Western Australia (Department of Premier & Cabinet, 2006).

The second stage introduces the two-way consultative process, in which citizens provide feedback to government. Examples of e-consultation in Australia include the use of polling and short, directed questions to elicit feedback on specific issues. In the U.K., the Hansard Society has facilitated e-consultations for the British Parliament on areas ranging from taxation, to Parliament's use of computers, to domestic violence (www.hansardsociety.org.uk). *TellParliament* used online discussions to gather anecdotal feedback from citizens (Richard, 2004 p. 15). Local governments, such as Porto Alegre, Brazil, have used ICTs to enable citizens to discuss and vote on local issues (Hobsbawn, 2003). The most prominent initiative in Australia is the Queensland Government's e-Democracy Unit, which has conducted e-consultations to enhance access to government and participation in government decision-making (Hogarth, 2004).

During the third stage of engagement, citizens actively participate in the policy-making process in partnership with government in a policy dialogue (OECD, as cited in Coleman and Gøtze, 2002 p. 13). In Estonia (http://tom.riik.ee), for example, citizens have been invited to discuss draft laws and suggest new ones (Parliament of Victoria, 2004; Ronaghan, 2002).

Coleman and Gøtze cite the importance of moderation and mediation, arguing that "deliberation requires trusted facilitation" (2002 p. 17). E-moderating requires new understandings and techniques specific to online delivery (Salmon, 2000). E-moderation adds value to the e-consultation process by drawing on a number of strategies for participation and interaction. For example, an e-moderator weaves discussion forum messages with other messages, related materials, issue-specific resources, external Web sites, and face-to-face practice. The e-moderator then summarizes after 10 to 20 messages and compiles information into a summary that is then fed back to users to discuss on the forum.

Essentially, these skills are required to convert information into knowledge in ways that are deliberative and that engender political efficacy. Strategies for moderation in e-learning have been applied to e-consultation, providing frameworks that maximize the functional and educational potential of the Internet (Collis, 1999; Collis & Moonen, 2001). Some Web-based e-learning frameworks use a "learning object approach," in which online information is developed as learning objects, which can be reassembled and reused in a variety of ways.

As an interactive tool, the potential for learning is optimized when the interactive capacity of the Internet is used for communication and interactive purposes to foster knowledge construction. Knowledge products are created by integrating these resources into an explicit learning outcome, which can be fed back to users as a resource. Discussion forums are potentially useful means of developing these knowledge products by explicitly using the online discussion process to enhance knowledge sharing and knowledge construction. E-moderators play a central role in this process using a series of skills that focus on the facilitation of discussion forums. These skills seek to enable users of a forum to engage in effective communication, networking, content management, and knowledge construction. In the context of Canadian e-democracy initiatives, it has been observed that public servants need to develop these kinds of skills as facilitators and moderators (Richard, 2004 p. 13).

Consider the following example: during the first phase of policy development, an online survey of specific issues (or group of related issues) may be presented to the general public to define the issue at hand and the agenda of development. During the next stage of development, discussion forums directly addressing these issues are moderated by subject area experts, the feedback from which may then be used to refine the policy under deliberation. These discussions are then summarized and fed back to the public as knowledge products. In the final phases of policy development, online discussion groups (consisting of key citizens and stakeholders affected by the policy) may then work in partnership with government on an effective method of delivery using these knowledge products as the basis for decision-making. While the Darebin eForum followed the first basic steps of this framework, topics tended not to focus on a policy area under consideration. Moderators acknowledged the general nature of consultation taking place on the Darebin eForum, suggesting that "we were interested in peoples' views and finding out what they thought, but we weren't consulting on something in particular" and that the eForum could be focused on a particular policy area or set of recommendations within a given government strategy (e.g., local transport services); "for example a particular action plan, where there is 30 actions to be done by council over the next five to ten years and people could comment on that by eForum" (Interview 1, July 27, 2006).

As a strategic process of gathering feedback about a given area of policy development, the potential value of online policy consultation is increased when located within a broader continuum of citizen engagement in which consultation is just one phase of an iterative, developmental process. Education plays an important role in this engagement continuum. Richard suggests that in Canada, "multi-directional dialogues enabled by ICTs are seen as an important factor in creating an environment of continuous learning: learning from citizens and contributing to their knowledge, so that Canadians are fully engaged in shaping government" (Richard, 2004 p. 4).

Consultation Across Vertical and Horizontal Networks

Online policy consultation involves more than an exchange of information; it is also about the cultivation of important social relationships across horizontal and vertical networks. E-consultation opens significant possibilities for collaborative work and partnership – both vertically between citizen and government, and across horizontal networks of individuals, communities, agencies, NGOs, and so forth.

Other citizen-based organizations, such as Minnesota E-democracy in the U.S., have developed online public spaces for citizen interaction on public issues (http://www.e-democracy.org/). Communitybuilders.nsw provides a similar horizontal network in the form of an interactive online clearing house and discussion network concerned with community-level social, economic, and environmental renewal (New South Wales Government, 2005). The Darebin eForum also promoted a limited degree of horizontal exchange. Many questions on the Darebin eForum were open-ended and sought to promote horizontal community dialogue. For example, for the "Community Harmony" topic, local citizens were asked whether the Cronulla race riots of 2005 could happen in Darebin (Darebin City Council, 2006).

Horizontal networks transcend borders and provide powerful opportunities for knowledge sharing and collaboration, as exemplified by the work of Steven Clift (2004). Richard (2004) observes that:

inexpensive access to information and the ability to communicate rapidly from many points across time zones has led to an explosive growth of civic organisations with the potential to influence policy-making. These online communities take advantage of the fact that volunteerism and information sharing are natural community behaviors .... As the Internet enables deeper and wider networks, the process of online policy consultation is no longer a matter of consultation with a limited group. (Richard, 2004 p. 4)

The Darebin eForum explicitly sought to connect to broader community development and related initiatives, such as the "Going Places" online travel reward scheme to promote sustainable travel for commuters travelling from home to work. This Web site (established in 2006) featured a message board allowing for horizontal postings by members of the site (Interview 1, July 27, 2006). This site was also moderated, but the moderators took a very "hands off" approach, preferring members to exchange their own ideas and tips for travel (Interview 1, July 27, 2006).

Above all, political efficacy is the important dimension of the participation continuum. Citizens need to know that their efforts will influence an outcome. For instance, participants in the public dialogues organized by Canadian Policy Research Networks do so on the condition that their contribution is firmly embedded within concrete policy development processes (Richard, 2004 p. 5).

CONCLUSION

Other local councils across Australia have shown interest in the e-consultation model employed by Darebin City Council (Brisbane City Council, 2007; Surf Coast Shire, 2007). In response, Darebin developed the Local Council e-Consultation Guide (Bailey, 2007) to assist local governments to develop their own e-Consultation strategies. The modest experience of the Darebin eForum provides a number of instructional lessons of interest to local governments seeking to develop an e-consultation strategy. Firstly, Darebin eForum was not linked to formal consultation or policy-making processes within council. Nevertheless, there was an explicit effort to link the discussion topics to policy initiatives. For example, the first topic on Community Harmony was aligned to policy development within the council's Multicultural Unit.

Council members were not actively involved in the Darebin eForum. A lack of engagement from political representatives reflects a more general challenge to e-consultation across Australia. As Chen (2002) suggests:

limited levels of "policy learning" exist between representatives ... (exacerbated by partisan competition, the part-time nature of local government representation, and time constraints), which should be addressed if successful and valuable online consultation and stakeholder interaction is to occur at the individual level.

That said, the eForum consultation process was driven by local government. The site did not accept topics suggested by users. The framework for continuous engagement above suggests that citizens and community stakeholders must take a more proactive role in the dialogue with government. Council Officers acknowledged the value of providing more focussed online consultations linked to formal processes of policy development, decision-making and representation. One moderator suggested that the eForum could be focused on a particular policy area or action plan (Interview 1, July 27, 2006).

Furthermore, the eForum, as with the pilot, did not reach the wider community in any significant manner. The challenges of cultural and linguistic diversity, access to computers, and low computer literacy levels were undoubtedly important factors – although access to computers and Internet is significantly increasing. Furthermore, one moderator rightly acknowledged a general "anxiety about change" amongst citizens and local government alike (Interview 2, July 27, 2006).

But the technological environment in Australia is rapidly changing. General uptake of the Internet in Australia has been slow, but accelerating during the last several years. Whereas a minority of Australians had internet access in 2001, by 2006, 63% of the population had internet access (ABS, 2007 p.18). Equally significant has been the rapid replacement of slow dial-up connections with "always on" faster services accessed by 40% of the population (ABS, 2007 p. 9).

Online consultation is best perhaps applied as part of a group of engagement strategies. As one eForum moderator suggested, the type of e-consultation that would ideally take place in future "would have to be within a suite of consultation methods ... Just as we do now, we try not to just to do a survey ... but we also have a public meeting, and we have a focus group as well ..." (Interview 1, July 27, 2006). Furthermore, these suites of consultation methods should explicitly seek to address vertical and horizontal forms of consultation. One government-hosted open forum in Fujisawa, Japan, offered both government-led topics and citizen-led discussions (Richard, 2004 p. 6). As Coleman and Gøtze suggest, "it is important to select the right model of participation for the right situation" (2002 p. 20).

As only one form of consultation, e-consultation should be deployed as part of a suite of electronic, hard-copy and face-to-face methods, and thus integrated into traditional consultation methods to achieve maximum impact (OECD, 2003). The developers of Darebin eForum intend that future e-consultation will be conducted as one of a suite of consultation methods, alongside conventional tools such as surveys, focus groups and public meetings (Interview 1, July 27, 2006). Other initiatives, such as Connecting Bristol in the UK, have further explored the use of convergent media such as podcasting, vodcasting, SMS and interactive television (O'Malley et al., 2007).

Collaborative websites, such as wikis, provide opportunities for governments to incorporate community-based and deliberative forms of engagement into the e-consultation process. Widespread adoption of Web 2.0 collaborative media have exposed publics to the possibilities for sharing and developing community-based forms of horizontal and vertical dialogue. As the use of these media become an unobtrusive part of human interaction, it is possible for governments to engage more people as part of daily life. Similarly, online social networking services extend the possibility for viral forms of communication which in turn may make the process of e-consultation more inclusive.

The collaborative and social networking possibilities of e-consultation provide enhanced capacities for horizontal forms of engagement initiated and driven by citizens, using a range of media. One Darebin eForum user suggested that the eForum could be improved by encouraging further debate on topics raised by the community, such as letters to the local newspaper (Walsh, 2007a). In this environment, e-consultation involves more than the exchange of information: it is also concerned with fostering community development and cultivating important social relationships across vertical and horizontal networks.

Aside from the broader political issues identified in this discussion, there were more specific technical issues, such as navigability and interoperability. For example, one moderator has noticed that "you only have a certain number of headings up there ... but there other headings you can respond to, but they are sort of hidden back under another click" (Interview 1, July 27, 2006). With regards to interoperability, the Darebin eForum site used open-source software, whereas the main Darebin Council Web site used a proprietary Microsoft platform. While housed within the council buildings, IT support for the eForum was externally sourced. This lack of technical integration of e-government services with the discussion forums is characteristic of many government Web sites throughout the world. A more seamless and secure flow of ICT services, as well as economies of scale within the council itself would provide a more technically viable foundation for future e-consultation.

The idea of elected representatives being able to collect direct and instant feedback from their constituents is both powerful and potentially transformative. A comprehensive move forward for a local government strategy like the Darebin eForum would require a more holistic approach to consultation which has a clearly stated set of objectives and a framework within an articulated vision of e-democracy. This framework takes into consideration the benefits (and limitations) of convergent media (such as the Web, e-mail, podcasting and interactive television) and seek to foster the required technological skills and political literacy among representatives, constituents and the public service to effectively engage the development of policy. This framework also explores how consultation can take place across both vertical and horizontal networks in which individuals, community groups, and other stakeholders have an opportunity to deliberate and contribute to policy development and become involved in the ongoing development of democracy.

Taking a more deliberative approach to citizen engagement involves encouraging citizens "to scrutinize, discuss, and weigh up competing values and policy options. Such methods encourage preference formation rather than simple preference assertion" (Coleman & Gøtze, 2002 p. 6). Fostering greater deliberation requires a rethinking of the processes by which e-consultation takes place. As Coleman and Gøtze (2002) point out:

government consultations do not require respondents to have access to any information before they state an opinion. Deliberative exercises are primarily concerned to discover what citizens think about issues once they have become reasonably informed about them. The provision of information to deliberating citizens needs to be comprehensive, balanced and accessible. (p. 6)

For public servants, new responsibilities for administration, facilitation, and participation required for e-consultation are imbued with political issues of accountability and responsibility. The fundamental question here is this: to what extent should bureaucracy be empowered to engage in a dialogue between citizens and elected representatives (Coleman & Gøtze, 2002)? Defining the role of public servants in e-consultation is also crucial, given the importance of citizen trust in them as subject-matter experts and facilitators through the often complex dialogue with representatives and each other.

A holistic approach to consultation features a clearly stated framework and objectives. Such a holistic approach may require a movement beyond thinking about e-consultation as a special form of electronic democracy, to a notion in which e-consultation is simply regarded as another functional dimension of democracy. The technology needs to be understood as something that services and enhances good practise, not as particularly novel or as some kind of panacea.

ACKNOWLEDGMENT

The author is grateful to Dr Monika Merkes for her generous contribution to this research, and to Emma Rujevic for her editorial feedback.

REFERENCES

Adams, D. (2003, November 25). Democracy without sound grabs. *The Age*. Retrieved May 24, 2007, from http://www.theage.com.au

Australian Bureau of Statistics [ABS] (2003). *Socio-economic indexes for areas Australia 2001* (2039.0). Canberra: Commonwealth of Australia.

Australian Bureau of Statistics [ABS]. (2005, March 31). Internet activity survey [IAS]. Retrieved May 24, 2007, from http://www.abs.gov.au

Australian Bureau of Statistics [ABS] (2007). *2006 Census of Population and Housing*, ABS, Canberra. Retrieved July 16, 2007, from http://abs.gov.au/websitedbs/d3310114.nsf/Home/census

Australian Bureau of Statistics [ABS] (2007b). *Patterns of Internet Access in Australia*, Australian Bureau of Statistics, Canberra.

Bailey, J. (2007). *Local Council e-Consultation Guide*. Australia: Darebin City Council. Retrieved June 28, 2007, from http://www.darebin.vic.gov.au/Files/local_council_e-consultation_guide_2007.pdf

Balnaves, M., Walsh, L., & Shoesmith, B. (2006). E-Democracy: Media-liminal space in the era of age compression. In J. Weiss, J. Nolan, J. Hunsinger & P. Trifonas (Eds.), *International handbook of virtual learning environments* (pp. 1007 – 1023). Springer International Handbooks of Education, 14.

Brisbane City Council (2007) *Participation Guidelines*. Brisbane City Council Website. Retrieved November 14, 2007, at http://www.brisbane.qld.gov.au/BCC:BASE:1190883272:pc=PC_1

Center for Collaborative Government. (2002, April). *Digital commons e-democracy, pilot-final report*. Canada: CEG.

Chen, P. (2002). Virtual representation: Australian elected representatives and the impact of the Internet. *The Journal of Information, Law and Technology, 3*. Retrieved May 24, 2007, from http://www2-test.warwick.ac.uk/fac/soc/law/elj/jilt/2002_3/chen/

Chen, P. (2007) *Electronic Engagement: A Guide for Public Sector Managers* ANZSOG Monograph. Retrieved July 20, 2007, from http://epress.anu.edu.au/anzsog/engage/mobile_devices/index.html

Chen, P., Gibson, R., & Geiselhart, K. (2006). *Electronic democracy? The impact of new communications technologies on Australian democracy*. Report No. 6 for the Democratic Audit of Australia. Canberra, Australia: The Australian National University.

Clift, S. (2004). *DoWire - Democracies online newswire*. Retrieved May 24, 2007, from http://www.dowire.org/

Coleman, S., & Gøtze, J. (2002). *Bowling together: Online public engagement in policy deliberation*. London: Hansard Society.

Collis, B. (1999). Designing for differences: Cultural issues in the design of WWW-based course-support sites. *British Journal of Educational Technology, 30*(3), 201-215.

Collis, B., & Moonen, J. (2001). *Flexible learning in a digital world*. London: Kogan Page.

Darebin City Council (2006) 2005 *Household survey. Summary Report*. Retrieved 25 June, 2007, from http://www.darebin.vic.gov.au/Files/2005_Household_survey_summary_report.pdf

Darebin City Council (2005) 2005-2006 *Annual Report*. Retrieved 25 June 2007 from http://www.darebin.vic.gov.au/Files/Annual_Report.pdf

Darebin City Council. (2007). *Darebin eForum*. Retrieved May 24, 2007, from http://eforum.darebin.vic.gov.au/

Darragh, I. (2003). *A step-by-step guide to successful Web consultations*. Canadian International Development Agency. Retrieved May 24, 2007, from http://www.pwgsc.gc.ca/econsultation/text/tools-e.html

Davidson, A. (1997). *From subject to citizen: Australian citizenship in the twentieth century*. Cambridge, UK: Cambridge University Press.

Department of Premier & Cabinet (Western Australia). (2006). *Citizenscape*. Retrieved May 24, 2007, from http://www.citizenscape.wa.gov.au/

Hacker, K.L., & van Dijk, J. (Eds.). (2000). *Digital democracy: Issues of theory and practice*. London: Sage Publications.

Hobsbawn, A. (2003, December 10). Phone a foreigner. *The Guardian*. Retrieved May 24, 2007, from http://society.guardian.co.uk/e-public/story/0,,1103283,00.html

Hogarth, F. (2004, November 17-18). *Engaging communities online - A Queensland perspective*. Paper presented at the Australian Government Information Management Office [AGIMO] Seminar Enabling Government, Engaging Communities: An Online Perspective, Brisbane, Australia. Retrieved May 24, 2007, from http://www.agimo.gov.au/resources/events/2004/engage

Holkeri, K. (2003). *Case study – Citizen consultation and engagement: Share your views with US*. OECD. Retrieved May 24, 2007, from ccnm/gf/gov/pubg, 2

Merkes, M. (2004, November 17-18). *Darebin eForum*. Paper presented at the Australian Government Information Management Office [AGIMO] Seminar Enabling Government, Engaging Communities: An Online Perspective. Brisbane, Australia. Retrieved May 24, 2007, from http://www.agimo.gov.au/resources/events/2004/engage

Merkes, M., Walsh, L. and Bailey, J. (2007). *Building Community Capacity Through eConsultation: Darebin eForum*. Paper presented at the Australian Social Policy Conference: Social Policy through the Life Course: Building Community Capacity and Social Resilience, 11-13 July 2007, Sydney NSW.

Minnesota E-Democracy. (2004). *Minnesota e-democracy Web site*. Retrieved May 24, 2007, from http://www.e-democracy.org/

Muir, K. (2004, June). *Connecting communities with CTLCs: From the digital divide to social inclusion*. Report by the Smith Family. Sydney: the Smith Family.

New South Wales Government. (2005). *Communitybuilders.nsw*. Retrieved May 24, 2007, from www.communitybuilders.nsw.gov.au

OECD. (2001). *Engaging citizens in policy-making: Information, consultation and public participation.* PUMA Policy Brief No. 10. Retrieved May 24, 2007, from http://www.oecd.org/dataoecd/45/25/35063274.pdf

OECD. (2003). *Promise and problems of e-democracy: Challenges of online engagement.* OECD Report. France: OECD.

O'Malley, K., Higgins, P., Hayward, C., Watson, K., and Hilton, S. (2007). *E-Democracy in Bristol.* UK: Bristol City Council.

Parliament of Victoria. (2004). *Inquiry into electronic democracy* (Discussion Paper). Scrutiny of Acts and Regulations Committee, State of Victoria. Melbourne, Australia: Parliament of Victoria.

Richard, E. (2004, August 4-6). *E-consultation: New roles for public servants.* Paper presented at the International Colloquium, Communication and Democracy: Technology and Citizen Engagement, Fredericton, New Brunswick, Canada.

Ronaghan, S.A. (2002). *Benchmarking e-government: A global perspective-assessing the progress of the UN member states.* Report by the American Society for Public Administration [ASPA] and the United Nations Division for Public Economics and Public Administration [UNDPEPA]. New York: ASPA & UNDPEPA. Retrieved May 24, 2007, from http://unpan1.un.org/intradoc/groups/public/documents/UN/UNPAN021547.pdf#search=%22%22Benchmarking%20E-government%3A%20A%20Global%20Perspective%22%22

Salmon, G. (2000). *E-Moderating: The key to teaching and learning online.* London: Kogan Page.

SurfCoast Shire (2007). SurfCoast Shire Eforum. Retrieved October 5, 2007, from http://eforum.surfcoastdirectories.com/

Walsh, L. (2006). The use of technology to extend e-government and citizen participation in Australia. In A. Anttiroiko & M. Malkia (Eds.), *Encyclopaedia of digital government.* Hershey, PA: Idea Group Reference.

Walsh, L. (2007a). *Darebin eForum Evaluation Report.* Report commissioned by Darebin City Council. Centre for Citizenship & Human Rights, Deakin University, Melbourne Australia. Retrieved September 5, 2007, from http://www.darebin.vic.gov.au/Files/Darebin_eForum_Evaluation_090807.pdf

Walsh, L. (2007b). A Case Study of Public Servants Engaged in E-Consultation in Australia. *The International Journal of Electronic Government Research* (IJEGR), 3(4), pp. 20-37.

ENDNOTES

1. This chapter draws from research conducted in 2006 as part of a research project at Deakin University, Australia, into the use of online policy consultation and discussion forums as a means of seeking greater citizen participation in Australia. The overall findings were presented at the Australian Social Policy Conference, 11-13 July 2007, Sydney, Australia (Merkes, Walsh, and Bailey, 2007).
2. This survey sought responses from eForum users to questions in three areas: motivations for using the forum; response to the design of the forum; and demographic questions about the users (Walsh, 2007a).
3. Interviews with eForum moderators were conducted on 27 July 2006 and are designated accordingly (e.g., Interview 1, 27 July 2006). For a more detailed analysis of these interviews in the context of public servants in general, see Walsh, 2007b.
4. This discussion of Darebin eForum focuses on its operation between March 2006 and July 2007.
5. With the exception of the e-tivity captain.
6. The Darebin eForum did not have a rule about how many posts could be made per day as

the number of posts were not high enough to introduce such a rule (unlike Minnesota e-Democracy, for example, which restricts the number of posts per user, per day).

7 Councillors from other local councils have, however, expressed an interest in what is taking place. One coastal shire is considering setting up their own forum to enable many of their seasonal residents to maintain maintaining an ongoing relationship with the council (Interview 2, July 27, 2006).

8 It was not Darebin City Council policy to contact individual journalists, unlike other forums such as Minnesota eDemocracy (2004).

9 Little demographic information is known about users, who only had to provide a real name, their suburb/postcode of residence and valid e-mail address. This minimal requirement for participation was a conscious decision of the part of the eForum developers to minimize the discouragement of potential users who may have been reluctant to provide personal information. (Some users did, however, volunteer information such as their age).

10 Usage of the site was in part measured by a comparison of the number of posts and the regularity of the posts (Interview 1, July 27, 2006).

Chapter X
Electronic Conduits to Electoral Inclusion in an Atypical Constituency:
The Australian Case[1]

Lisa Hill
University of Adelaide, Australia

Kate Alport
University of Adelaide, Australia

ABSTRACT

Due to compulsory voting, Australia's turnout rate is among the highest and most socially-even in the industrialised world. Nevertheless, some voters are still left behind on election day. In this chapter we examine the potential for E-technologies to address the problem of political exclusion among some currently excluded groups of voters. We canvas known and suspected patterns of such exclusion and, in some cases, suggest possible reasons for it. We review the capacity for electronic forms of voting and registration to address: Low voting and registration levels among indigenous Australians; declining registration levels among the young; restricted access to the secret ballot caused by disability; informal voting among minority language speakers and people with low literacy and numeracy competence; low voting participation among people who experience difficulty in attending a polling place on election day and low voting participation among the Australian diaspora. We begin by providing some technical background, after which we report briefly on the E-voting state of play in Australia today.

Copyright © 2009, IGI Global, distributing in print or electronic forms without written permission of IGI Global is prohibited.

AN ATYPICAL CONSTITUENCY

Australia is one of those rare settings where voting is compulsory. The introduction of compulsory voting 'elevated the status of the franchise from a privilege to a duty' and thereby encouraged 'electoral commissions to treat every vote as sacred' (Orr *et al*, 2002 p. 389). The advent of compulsory registration and voting triggered the development of many democratic innovations to achieve maximum voting participation (Sawer, 2001 pp. 24-5) and Australia's State and Federal electoral offices take enormous care to ensure that the vast majority of Australian voters, regardless of contingent status, and obstacles experienced, is included in the voting process (Hill, 2002). In fact Australia's voting system is one of the most accessible and 'user friendly' in the world (Mackerras and McAllister, 1999 p. 223) with minimal opportunity and transacation costs to voters. The net effect is that, despite the persistent disenfranchisement of some potential voters, few systems are able to boast such consistently high and socially-even voter turnout rates (usually around 95% Voting Age Population –VAP).

Australia's exemplary record on voting inclusion should not, however, be cause for complacency; rather, when almost everyone votes, the exclusion of the non-participating few is greatly magnified and exacerbated. This is especially so where the non-participators in question have a distinct ethnic or socio-demographic profile because their exclusion cannot be discounted as random or anomalous. Neither should it be assumed that such voters will spontaneously begin to vote at some point in the future because, if voting is to become a habit, it should commence as soon as a citizen is enfranchised (Fotos *et al.* 2002). Further, propensity to vote seems to be partly norm-driven (Hasen, 1996; Hill, 2002) and if non-voting is the norm in any subculture, members may never break the habit. It is therefore important to be pro-active in identifying any technical, practical, or cultural barriers to the establishment of the voting habit among members of social groups where abstention is routine.[2] In a rare constituency like Australia's where voting is a mainstream activity we canvass potential means for embracing those few who remain outside this mainstream.

Specifically, we explore how E-technologies might help to engage some currently excluded groups of voters. It should be stressed that, at this stage, the use of E-voting (and related technologies) is regarded purely as a potential supplement to paper ballots and not as a replacement; this is partly because Australia is an atypical constituency where getting the majority of citizens out to vote is not a major issue. But it is also because the authors are mindful of the fact that widespread use of E-technologies has the potential to drain Australian elections of their prized festive and solidary character: As a shared experience for almost all Australian adults, universal voting gives rise, temporarily at least, to a powerful, non-particularistic, moral and political community. In the lead up to, and on election day itself, politics in Australia is, literally, everybody's business.

Before continuing, let us clarify what is meant by electronic voting for the purposes of this chapter.

ELECTRONIC VOTING

By definition, electronic voting is any electronic means by which votes are cast or data transferred for counting, collation and reporting (Orr, 2004 28). Misunderstandings persist about computer assisted E-voting because many associate it exclusively with computers connected to each other through the Internet. However, not all E-voting technologies are Internet-connected; rather E-voting is defined here as computer-assisted (but not punchcard) voting, vote counting, data transfer and reporting of results. The two main forms of E-voting dealt with here are Internet-enabled voting - which encompasses Full Internet Voting (FIV) and Partial Internet Voting (PIV) - and

Non-Internet Electronic Voting (NIEV). Full Internet Voting can take place from any computer anywhere; voter identification, vote casting and counting and transmission of results all take place on the Internet. Partial Internet Voting involves connection with the Internet at one or more stages of the process but limits the casting of votes to a designated polling place. Non-Internet Electronic Voting uses portable voting machines or kiosks that are electronic but at no point are connected to the Internet.

Specific Technologies

Direct Recording Electronic Voting (DRE) machines are used in both PIV and NIEV forms of E-voting which take place at a polling place on a computer terminal, by means of a mouse to direct the cursor to the desired candidate's name, touching a facsimile of a ballot on a vertical or horizontal (tablet) touch screen or pushing a button against a candidate's name on an electronic panel (Fischer, 2001). Similar to touch screens used to search databases in public libraries, these electronic machines are activated by voters swiping special purpose identity cards distributed by polling officials. The cards are normally designed for single-use only. Votes are not recorded until the 'vote' button is pushed, so that voters can review her/his choices before finishing, thus safeguarding against accidental errors. The votes are then stored within the computer on a memory device (hard drive, floppy disk or CD) and collected by officials at the close of polling. This reduces the time required for vote counting, as the votes are immediately available in a computer-readable form. The technology is therefore totally computerized without necessarily being connected to the Internet. The successful use of this Direct Recording Electronic technology is increasing globally, although it remains subject to a high level of scrutiny by both election authorities and computing professionals.

Voting on computers (not connected to the Internet) from a polling place is generally recognized as being more secure than Internet voting. In addition, voters are less resistant to using this method. Such machines also offer faster and more accurate vote counting than conventional paper and even punch-card methods (Fischer, 2001).

Internet Voting (used in FIV and PIV): Voting over the Internet from one's home or a remote location using a security code issued by the electoral authority to activate the process is a technology currently being evaluated in many countries (for example, Estonia, Switzerland, The Netherlands, Great Britain, France and Slovakia). Sometimes referred to as 'I-voting,' to distinguish it from other forms of electronically-assisted voting, Internet voting may also be used in the supervised environment of a polling place. In most trials, the remote Internet voting process is adapted to existing technology - usually personal computers - and uses a format based on the paper ballot. The vote is submitted via the Internet to a centralized (and supposedly secure) master computer, housed in a government or otherwise secure facility, for collation and counting.

ELECTRONIC VOTING IN AUSTRALIA SO FAR

Australia is moving slowly and conservatively towards the use of E-voting technologies. Some initial trials have proved positive. For example, in response to 'a close election in 1998 [that] exposed errors in the state's hand-counting system' (Zetter, 2003), the Australian Capital Territory (ACT) Electoral Commission conducted two (PIV) trials of electronic voting machines. In these trials of Internet enabled elections[3] the paper ballot alternative was still offered to voters. A total of 8% of people in 2001 and 13% in 2004 chose to vote electronically (Green, 2005). In the latter trial, voter satisfaction was high, with less than ten complaints from the 28,169 people who cast electronic votes (ACT Electoral Commission, 2005). First used in the ACT's Legislative Assembly election in October of that 2001, the system, called eVACS (Electronic Voting and Counting System) is based on using keypads and standard personal computers housed in polling booths and linked to a computer server at the same polling station. It operates with open source (Linux) software within a local area network (LAN). This means that, as well as the source code being available for outside assessment, security is enhanced by each polling location being independent; thus there is no permanent or long-term Internet connection that could be subject to security breaches.[4] Logistically, voters reported to polling officials to have their names crossed off the printed electoral roll; then, if they chose to vote electronically, they were given a randomly selected bar-coded card to insert in the machine and activate the voting process. This is a single-use card that precludes multiple voting (Green, 2004) and has a code identifying the electorate encrypted on it as well as a digital signature for security purposes. Instructions were placed in each polling booth and the same card was used to confirm the vote, after which it was posted in a box. These E-voting trials were judged successful, partly because of the authorities' conservative approach, incremental take up and considerable efforts at community consultation about the preferred technology.

Other trials have been conducted for specific constituencies, namely, those with a visual disability and Australian military personnel serving abroad. In response to submissions from peak advocate groups acting for blind and vision-impaired electors the Victorian State Government passed legislation in July 2006 to clear the way for E-voting trials at the 2006 November election (VEC, 2007 p. 66). The technology was trialled at six polling centres using locally networked E-voting machines and a system similar to the ACT's eVACS, but with the added feature of a voter verification paper ballot for audits and recounting (Parliament of Victoria, 2005). This 'paper trail' offers greater levels of authenticity, accuracy and therefore trust and is widely advocated by IT academics and professionals.[5] An electronic voting system, developed by Hewlett-Packard and Scytl Secure Electronic Voting was used in this NIEV system; voters' names were crossed off the roll in the traditional way, after which they were issued with a single-use Smart-card containing their electoral details. Instructions were relayed through headphones after the card was inserted into a card-reader attached to the voting terminal.[6]

Significantly, the legislation drafted to permit the trials provided that the voter should 'be able to cast an informal vote'(VEC, 2007 p. 66). This condition seems to reflect an awareness of two features peculiar to the Australian system: First, Australia has an unusually high rate of informal voting that is related to the fact that the vast majority of eligible citizens -including minority language speakers and people with low literacy and numeracy competence – do vote, something that does not happen in voluntary systems; therefore the legislation is designed to ensure that the vision-impaired have the same 'opportunity' to vote as informally as the rest of the population. Second, this legislative condition embodies a recognition of the fact that the compulsion to attend a polling booth does not, in practical terms, include the compulsion to record a *formal* vote. Around one quarter of informal votes in Australia are intentional (Hill and Young, 2007) and the informal voting provision in the E-voting legislation ensures that blind and vision impaired voters have the same opportunity as anyone else in the electorate to deliberately spoil their ballots if they so wish to. (This is ironic considering that a key benefit of E-voting is its ability to *reduce* the unintentional informal vote. See below).

Only 199 voters statewide participated in the trial despite heavy media promotion (VEC 2007)[7] but the numbers participating in future elections is likely to grow as the electorate becomes accustomed to the idea of E-voting (the fact that over a third of participants in a national trial undertaken in 2007 were Victorians suggests that this is probable). In any case, the Victorian trial was deemed extremely successful by voters and electoral authorities alike. Voters providing feedback reported 'high levels of satisfaction with the software' and were particularly appreciative of being able to vote in secret for the first time. From the VEC's perspective, the technology was 'proven to work' and to be 'appropriate in a real election environment'. Further, there was a general consensus that the 'integrity, accuracy' and 'authenticity' of the votes cast was assured (VEC, 2007 pp. 73-4).

The Australian Electoral Commission (AEC) also trialled E-voting (on EVM machines) for vision-impaired and blind voters in the two-week pre-polling period leading up to the November 2007 Federal Election and on Election Day. At 29 polling places Australia-wide 800 electors participated in the trial. Prior to the election the machines were independently audited by BMM Australia and were declared to be secure, accurate and capable of providing secrecy (BMM, 2007).

The Human Rights and Equal Opportunity Commissioner responsible for Disability Discrimination, Graeme Innes, (himself able to cast a secret vote for the first time) was an enthusiastic promoter of the trials. He noted that 'with 20 percent of Australians living with some form of disability, this issue [of voting in secret] will touch most families in some way'. He also surmised that '[t]he success of this trial is an integral step toward ensuring that *all* Australians, whether living with a disability or not, will have the option to vote in secret in all future elections.'(HREOC, 18 November 2007).

As well as providing the estimated 300,000 blind or vision-impaired Australians with the opportunity to cast a secret (NIEV) vote, the Federal government also introduced at the 2007 Federal election remote (FIV) E-voting for Australian Defence Force (ADF) personnel on operational duty in Iraq, Afghanistan, Timor Leste and Solomon Islands. At these locations, there is access to the secure ADF 'satellite and ground-based telecommunication infrastructure' that meets national security and privacy standards (AEC 2007). Defence personnel who had previously registered as remote Electronic Voters with the Australian Electoral Commission voted using an on-line computer that issues a personal receipt to enable them to check that their vote has been correctly recorded (AEC 2007). The votes were encrypted and transmitted directly to the tally room by the Defence intranet. The technology involved was also independently audited by BMM Australia who reported that it complied with established secrecy, accuracy and security criteria (BMM 2007a). It is not clear whether this trial will be continued and/or extended at the next Federal election since the legislation clearing the way for it (*The Electoral and Referendum Legislation Amendment Act, 2007*) referred only to the 2007 election (AEC 2007a).

Australians seem cautiously positive about E-voting technologies but the level of acceptance appears to be tied to the nature of the technology in question. A 2002 survey of 1,000 A.C.T. voters conducted after a by-election, found that 76 per cent of respondents showed an interest in at least one electronic voting method. Although many reported that they liked the idea of voting on the Internet from home, when asked what voting system they were most likely to actually *use*, voting on a computer in a polling booth on polling day was preferred to Internet voting (Pearce, 2002). Similar results were obtained in Northern Territory polls, namely, that while many respondents 'indicated their willingness to trial electronic voting in schools and the like on the basis of the ACT experience...[v]ery few...indicated a willingness to consider voting on the Internet' (Pullen *et. al.*, 2003).

Future plans include the AEC's intention to spend $17 million on upgrading its computing system so that it is capable of handling a better electronically managed electoral roll; it will also be able to handle electronic voting on the Internet (Mitchell, 2005).

MINORITY LANGUAGE VOTERS AND LOW LITERACY/NUMERACY VOTERS

Because of compulsory voting - and against the pattern of participation in voluntary voting systems - Australian minority language voters and citizens with lower than average levels of education generally turn out to vote. Nevertheless many remain excluded due to the fact that their votes are often informal, thereby nullifying their attempts at political engagement. Australia 'has one of the highest levels of spoiled or informal ballots among the established democracies' (McAllister and Makkai, 1993 p.23) yet, as we have noted, the majority of informal votes in Australia are unintentional (Hill and Young, 2007).

Being a voter from a non-English speaking background is *the* major predictor of informal voting in Australian elections (Dario, 2005). In the 2004 and 2001 federal elections informal voting was highest in divisions that had the highest proportion of voters of non-English speaking backgrounds. Rates of informal voting are also high in electorates dominated by the less well educated. In 2004 in affluent electorates like Higgins the rate was as low as 3% but as high as 12% in Greenway which is a working class electorate with a high proportion of voters from non-English speaking households (Dario, 2005). Australia has a complex electoral system which, coupled with universal participation and a large immigrant population, exacerbates its informal vote rate (McAllister and Makkai, 1993).[8]

E-technologies can potentially alleviate this problem and the effective political exclusion of those affected by it. As Jerry Kang notes (2001, p.1167), E-voting technology 'can be used to decrease linguistic barriers to voting [because of its capacity to] offer language translation services at the click of a button'. Two ACT electronic voting and counting trials (PIV) conducted in 2001 and 2004 were described in a subsequent review as successful partly because of E-voting's superior capacity to accommodate minority language voters (ACTEC 2005). Further, eVACS systems are able to provide instructions on how to vote through headphones if the voter is unable to read. Such a facility reduces the rate of invalid voting: The ACT Electoral Commission's 2005 report on its trials highlighted the significant reduction in informal votes (1% for E-voting compared to 3% for paper ballots) and unintentional voter errors (ACTEC, 2005). Even more dramatic was the effect in the 2006 Victorian State election trial, whereby out of 199 votes cast by vision-impaired and blind voters only 1 was informal (VEC, 2007). Though this was a small sample, an informal vote rate of only .5 per cent in an electorate where the average rate hovers at about 5 per cent is a considerable achievement. DRE machines can thus not only improve the accuracy of election results dramatically (due to their superior counting capacities) but more 'clearly record voter intent' (Green, 2004). So, to those who argue that E-voting will only exacerbate the digital divide it is worth noting that it can also reduce it, especially when its use is restricted to citizens who are currently excluded by traditional methods or to technologies that do not depend on private ownership of computers.

ABORIGINAL VOTERS

There is evidence that despite the considerable efforts of electoral officials some of the most isolated and vulnerable of Australian citizens - Indigenous Australians - continue to exist outside mainstream civic life. Our research here is so far limited to the South Australian context and especially remote regions. In Australia, people living in remote areas, specifically anyone who does not live within 8 km of a polling station, are automatically excused from voting. We know that in any election, up to 5% of South Australians fail to attend a Polling Booth, cast a postal vote or make a declaration vote. Turnout in such remote regions as the seat of Giles is depressed by a further 5 percentage points below the SA average.

It is hard to determine precise or even approximate figures for SA Aboriginal electoral participation. The State Electoral Office estimates that as many as 50% of the eligible Aboriginal population in some remote areas fail to either enrol or vote in first order (i.e., State and Federal) elections. In the Federal electorate of Grey, which includes rural and remote areas in the north and west of this state, and which has the greatest number of Aboriginal citizens, the official voting deficit of eligible citizens in 2004 was calculated at 5.8% of enrolled voters (AEC, 2004), but when the 2001 Census figures for citizens over the age of 18 years in that electorate are compared with the number of enrolees, the voting deficit rises considerably to 27%. Even when using Census figures the full extent of Aboriginal non-voting is still likely to be masked by the problem of undercounting in indigenous communities. For example, the ABS 'acknowledges that enumeration procedures failed in particular localities in 1996, such as in the Anangu Pitjantjatjara Lands (Ross 1999 pp. 62-4, cited in Martin, *et al*, 2003). Similarly, Martin and Taylor (1995, 1996, cited in Martin, et al 2003, p. 9) estimate that there was a 'census undercount of 17 per cent in the Cape York Peninsula community of Aurukun', with those not counted being 'the young, the more mobile and the more socially marginal'.

One of the authors has conducted some preliminary fieldwork on this segment of the population by observing voting with the Far West Remote Polling Team for the Federal election and the Anangu Pitjantjatjara Yankunytjatjara Council elections (both held in 2004) and by interviewing people who have lived and worked with Anangu for many years.[9] Her research so far seems to contradict Aboriginal lawyer, Michael Mansell's claim that Aboriginal people do not, in fact, wish to vote (Mansell, 1993). Rather, it appears that their voting abstention has a number of sources; it may be a form of protest but it may also be a function of lack of interest; low external political efficacy; lack of electoral salience; cultural difficulties; under-enrolment; language literacy problems; practical or ergonomic obstacles (such as remoteness) or the result of insufficient civic education. Our preliminary research suggests that many Aboriginal people do, in fact, want to vote and if distance, low literacy levels and cultural factors (like the intervention of Sorry Business)[10] are barriers, E-solutions that optimise the opportunities for voting engagement may be apposite and welcome.

The system described above, (eVACS) being self-contained, could be used in any area with a reliable power source, because the votes are written to two CDs in a local machine and can be tallied and read on a PC. As occurs with the present paper-voting systems, vote counting occurs locally and the results are phoned in to a Tally Room. This simple technology is available with satellite and broadband telecommunications connections now available to the outback, so there is every reason to believe that this form of electronic voting would be possible in the remote Aboriginal lands. In particular, using local languages through an ear piece, or by playing a CD, in voting conducted by trained local election officials who understand cultural issues this technology is likely to be more successful than the current method of mobile remote polling that does not offer language translation *with secrecy* and has tight time restrictions, with, on average, only two hours at each location (a window of time that is often too narrow for many Aboriginal people). Appropriately fitted kiosks situated at community centres and schools, ideally with a window of up to a week (as opposed to 1 day, or in the case of mobile polling, two hours), might conceivably capture more Aboriginal votes. Broadband connections also open up opportunities to enrol voters at remote locations on a continuous basis and could be used to inform and engage potential voters at community functions such as annual sports events. Electronic enrolment and access to the Electoral Roll also allows the generation of lists of voters for each Remote Polling location to be available to assist Electoral Officials find the voter's correct details in a culturally appropriate way, that is, by pointing at the name instead of speaking it.[11] Furthermore, kiosks fitted with earphones could provide instructions in local languages, thereby overcoming any minority language and literacy/numeracy issues currently impeding participation.

Another available option that may be suitable for local government elections, such as regional council elections in remote areas, is the Electronic Voting Machine (EVM) developed for totally electronic Indian elections. The two-unit EVM replicated the Indian ballot paper on the face of one unit, with a push-button beside the symbol for each candidate to record the (single) vote and activate the vote recording and tallying software in the second sealable unit. Although a 2002 nationwide survey (Caldow, 2004) had found that 'fewer than one per cent of Indian adults had used the Internet in the preceding three months', nevertheless the election was deemed successful. This indicates that computer literacy is not necessary to operate such a unit. Such machines are secure and can allow for faster vote counting and transmission of results. This would benefit voters living in remote areas where postal voting can be problematic because it depends on a reliable and accessible postal system, both for the posting out of the papers and their collection. A short timeline between the election announcement and polling day makes postal voting difficult because citizens need to register their current postal details in order to get a voting paper, so registering on-line as a preliminary step towards on-line voting would be an advantage to such voters. Enrolment forms are downloadable from the Australian Electoral Commission (AEC) website, although they have to be signed and witnessed, then posted in. If they could first be faxed to the AEC, receipt of the posted form would confirm the provisional enrolment. These technologies, computers and fax machines exist in all Community Centres in remote regions. It would be ideal if Aboriginal people were permitted to enrol and vote online, thereby overcoming problems of distance, a slow postal service and the complexities introduced by local cultural practices.

E-technologies can also aid electoral education. In outback South Australia, on-line TAFE education[12] and online Community meetings[13] are now being used to train isolated people in computer usage and to connect remotely located citizens. South Australian Electoral Commissioner, Kay Mousley (2006), in her Submission to the Commonwealth Parliamentary Inquiry Into Civics and Electoral Education has proposed that electoral education be delivered on-line, in partnership with Aboriginal education specialists and Anangu communities. Interactive web broadcasts, CDs and innovative web pages designed by indigenous students, all have the potential to engage outback communities.[14]

PEOPLE WITH DISABILITIES

Recent research conducted by Scope Victoria (2004), indicates that people with disabilities voted in lower than average numbers in the most recent national election (91% compared with an average of 95%), with half of those who failed to vote stating 'that they were not listed on the Electoral Roll'. According to a third of the respondents, the following difficulties were experienced, most of which were considered 'disincentive[s] for participation': Limited access to the polling booth including a lack of ramps; a lack of disabled parking; 'pain in walking'; standing in line and standing for too long; crowds; lack of shade and 'claustrophobic or room atmospherics problems (lighting)' (Scope, 2004 p. 2). Especially where postal voting and registration is a problem for such citizens (and more so where short time-lines are involved) FIV could potentially stimulate their participation. Security could be secured via Smart Cards and PINs.

The Secret Ballot and People with Disabilities

The secret ballot, first developed in South Australia and included in the South Australian Electoral Act of 1855-6, is now universally embedded in electoral procedures, where it is known as the 'Australian Ballot'. But until recently, voters who needed assistance to vote for whatever reason, be it illiteracy, disability or any other impairment, tacitly relinquished their right to a secret vote. Commissioner Graeme Innes, in a recent interview on Radio National, described how his blindness meant that he had never been able to cast a secret ballot. Apart from this loss of secrecy, blind voters could never be sure of the authenticity of their vote. As Innes noted: 'I am never sure, absolutely sure, that the vote I want to cast is cast.' Innes estimated that 'there are 150 electorates in Australia with 1500-2000 people in each electorate who don't have access to a secret ballot and that could mean the difference between winning or losing an election' (Innes, 2006).

As the previously discussed trials indicate E-voting can not only address the authenticity problem but make the waiving of this important democratic right unnecessary. Both Internet voting and Kiosks (NIEV and PIV) equipped with the capacity to provide verbal instructions in any language through headphones to protect the secrecy of the ballot for these voters (as well as those of low literacy and minority language voters). For this to work well the voting machine must give no publicly audible indication of the voters' choices or errors (IRCEV, 2004), should make it impossible 'to ascertain the vote of a particular elector' (VEC, 2007) and should be enabled so that individual voters can verify their choices.

Aside from the 2007 Federal election and 2006 Victorian State election trials mentioned previously, the 2001 and 2004 ACT electronic voting and counting (PIV) trials also successfully enabled people with disabilities to enjoy unassisted (secret) voting (ACTEC 2005).

EXPATRIATE AUSTRALIANS

The Australian *diaspora* is significantly disadvantaged by current electoral arrangements. Although Australian electoral offices try to service the needs of the itinerant, the homeless, prisoners and even Australians living in the Antarctic, the diaspora's extensive exclusion persists. Speaking on behalf of the Southern Cross Group[15] Anne MacGregor has expressed concern at the disenfranchisement of significant numbers of adult Australian citizens resident overseas, estimating that of the approximately 700,000 adult Australian citizens currently living abroad, 'only about 15,000 Eligible Overseas Electors [are] on the electoral roll'. Expatriate disenfranchisement is related to limitations on enrolment under the *Commonwealth Electoral Act 1918*. Although it is not compulsory to vote once out of Australia, failure to vote will likely result in having one's name struck off the electoral roll. Once this has happened (and provided the person concerned has been out of the country for 3 years) Australian expatriates have no legal right to re-enrol from overseas and can only do so on their return to Australia (and after having resided at an address for one month or more). The Southern Cross group is asking for current 'enrolment restrictions in the Electoral Act to be removed' while still advocating that voting should remain non-compulsory for the *diaspora* (McGregor, 2006).

Whether or not this legal barrier is overcome, FIV and registration technologies could help re-connect the Australia *diaspora* to civic life at home. Internet voting has been useful elsewhere in servicing expatriate voters who still retain their voting rights in their country of origin. For some of these citizens, remote voting by attendance at a consulate (PIV) is available but the inconvenience to the voter of consulate attendance (or reliance on the postal service) makes FIV an attractive alternative. 'External' or 'remote' voting is currently available for citizens of Belgium, Estonia, Germany, Finland, the UK, Spain, Poland, Portugal, Denmark, Luxemburg, the Netherlands, Austria, Slovenia, Sweden, Czech Republic, Italy and Hungary (Buchsbaum, 2005). For example, in 2003, the French government instituted legally binding remote E-voting (FIV) for French citizens living in the US to elect the representatives of the Assembly of the French Citizens Abroad, who in turn elect twelve members to the Upper House of the French Parliament (Buschbaum, 2005). In this landmark remote voting event, 61% of voters cast their vote over the Internet (ACE 2004). Along similar lines a pilot program has been developed to enable expatriate US citizens to enrol to vote from any overseas location. The registration tool, called RAVA is an electronic program that takes 5-10 minutes to complete and replaces a cumbersome 462- page instruction booklet and Federal Post Card Application voter registration form that covers the fifty-five different state and territory requirements in the Unites States. Information entered on the form is encrypted for security and once the form is printed out for posting or e-mailed, the personal information is destroyed (Knowlton, 2006).

The Internet could be used by expatriate Australians for enrolment purposes, provided security and authenticity could be ensured, probably by use of PIN numbers and separately delivered access codes (Knowlton, 2006)[16] - in the case of FIV [17] - or Smart Cards - in the case of PIV. This could be invaluable in alerting voters to the threats to their voting rights occasioned by leaving the country. The Southern Cross Group has recommended encouraging departing Australians to sign up to an AEC electronic mailing list for the purposes of keeping them informed of any matters relevant to their interests (Southern Cross Group, 2006 pp. 50-1). We would recommend that such a service be used to email to expatriates impending election alerts and enrolment forms with appropriate security measures put in place to enable them to both register and vote online.

Expatriates who currently do attempt to vote while overseas experience a number of other problems that E-voting technologies could conceivably ameliorate. For example, '[l]ong waiting times were experienced in London, the busiest overseas polling station, with people queued up around the block outside, sometimes in inclement weather.' According to the Southern Cross Group (2006 p. 52), '[s]everal Australians in the UK endured the long wait only to find that they had no legal entitlement to vote when they got to the front of the queue'. Other obstacles to participation recorded at the 2004 Federal election include the following: Many pre-poll votes failed to be counted because they arrived late in the enrolled division; many postal ballots failed to arrive due to postal delays or difficulties in the country of origin; poor levels of service were experienced at DFAT and the Austrade Post; and there was inadequate adherence to proper voting procedure at the designated polling place (AEC, 2004-5 p.197).

Australian governments, electoral authorities and their advisors all seem receptive to E-solutions for the *diaspora*. In a status report for the Australian Electoral Commission, Barry *et al* suggest that Internet voting may be a viable alternative to postal voting in Australian elections, but only in certain circumstances. For example, voters living in Antarctica are suitable candidates because their numbers are very small and 'the identity of each elector can be verified' therefore 'the risk of fraud or impersonation' can be contained. Similarly, citizens about to travel overseas could, prior to departure, apply 'to register as an Internet voter' (Barry *et. al.*, 2004). In the case of these voters, electronic voting over the Internet would replace postal voting. The advantage of this is that the votes are available for counting much sooner. It also offers the assurance that voting information will arrive on time. As this form of electronic voting is conducted in a fixed location such as a research base or an embassy it is possible to institute a greater level of security through surveillance and equipment checks than is achievable when voting is conducted from personal computers. *The Electoral Reform and Referendum Legislation Act (2007*) that passed into law in March 2007, allowed Defence personnel to vote online at the last Federal election 'in certain locations where there is access to secure Defence computing and communications facilities' (AEC, 2007 p. 70). (Online voting for Australians living in the Antarctic was not implemented for the 2007 election (AEC 2007)).

One in twenty Australians is presently overseas, almost half of whom are young voters.[18] Given what we know about the long-term effects of failure to get into the voting pattern early (see below), capturing the vote of this constituency is vital. According to the Southern Cross Group (2006, p. 64) 'Internet voting would in all likelihood contribute to not only greater levels of electoral participation among youth in Australia, but also Australians of all ages abroad.'

YOUTH

Reliable figures on voting abstention among Australian youth are not available (Hallett, 2006) but Print *et al* (2005 p. 2) estimate that around 300,000 voters aged 18-24 fail to vote in elections. The lower voting participation of the young does not seem to be related to protest or disaffection about compulsory voting (as per the suggestion of some critics) because we know that approval for the institution is just as high in this cohort as in others. It may, however, be related to disaffection with other aspects of politics. There are also important mechanical factors at play here such as youth under-registration which is, in turn, largely related to the over-representation in the Australian *diaspora* of young people (who become deregistered due to legal restrictions).

The AEC has estimated that at the time of the 2004 electoral roll close only 82% of young Australians between 17 and 25 years of age were enrolled compared with a national average of 95%. This lower-than-average registration and turnout has recently worsened due to the changes made by the former Howard Liberal Government to voter registration procedures under the *Electoral and Referendum Amendment (Electoral Integrity and Other Measures) Act 2006.* This legislation has introduced barriers to registration (such as the early closure of the rolls and more stringent identity requirements) that have had a disproportionate effect on younger voters. Though some claim that the number of young people enrolled jumped since the last election, according to Simon Jackman and Peter Brent 'the 18-24 subset' had actually 'shrunk' marginally (Jackman and Brent, 2007).

The Youth Electoral Survey (Print *et. al.* 2004 p.15) reports that 45% of their sample of year 12 students considered voting 'a waste of a Saturday'. In other Western democracies youth disengagement is a more or less universal phenomenon. But E-technologies have the potential to both engage and re-engage young citizens.

One notable effect of a (FIV) Swiss national referendum trial in 2004 was that although only a small increase in turnout of several percentage points above the five-year average was recorded (European Communities, 2004b), this improvement was concentrated among the young (European Communities, 2004a). There is every reason to suspect that the same effect would be felt in Australia. In an AEC-commissioned survey of 1000 voters in the ACT (Pearce 2002) it was found that those who were more comfortable with the idea of electronic voting were also the early adopters of Internet technology, namely, the young adult demographic who do business online and have Internet access at home. Nationwide surveys of over 4,000 Swiss citizens in 2003 and 2004 (Braendli 2005, 13) found that young adult voting abstainers considered being able to vote online an incentive to vote. Similar polling of US voters indicates that 'Internet voting is attractive to...younger voters.' The researchers concluded that '[i]f Internet voting is shown to bring young voters into the electoral process, then significant, long term, cohort effects could follow' (Solop 2001 p. 292).

Whereas the low voting participation of the young was once dismissed (correctly) as a life-cycle phenomenon, evidence is emerging that the civic disengagement of the young could signal a pattern of disengagement that is likely to persist (Jowell and Park 1998; Fotos and Franklin 2002; Hill and Louth, 2006). Getting young people into the voting habit early seems to be crucial for the future of vital (i.e. participatory) democracies. Thus, one good reason for pursuing E-voting is the potential it holds for democratic renewal and political inclusion, particularly among high abstention groups like the young who are less resistant to the idea of voting on the Internet. This, indeed, is the belief of recently surveyed French Internet users, the majority of whom indicated that they believed the Internet 'could lead to a better democracy...fight abstention [and]...contribute to more transparency in politics'. Significantly, when French Internet users were polled on their receptiveness to online voting non-voters and occasional voters were those most interested in using FIV. As habitual Internet users the young are more open to the idea of voting online than those who aren't (European Communities, 2004b). At face value, this finding seems to be a predictable one but it is noteworthy because those most familiar with cyber-crime and cyber-interference are also the least resistant to FIV.

Though FIV would, of course, be of more benefit to the more prosperous young (due to the digital divide) this could still be of value were it granted that greater numbers of involved citizens is better than lower numbers. But granting this may be too problematic. Will I-voting merely raise the voting inclusion of even more majority group voters? For example, in the Arizona Democratic primary of 2000 (the first binding Internet election of public office), almost half the votes were cast over the Internet but most of them were cast by white, high-income citizens (Solop, 2001 p.291. See also Salkowski, 2000). On the other hand, socially marginalised groups like aging and physically immobile voters, for whom even postal voting is a problem, could significantly benefit from FIV technologies thereby reducing their exclusion in at least one area of life.

CONCLUDING REMARKS

It could be argued by E-voting sceptics (eg. Nockleby 2001 p.1029) that in a period allegedly characterized by declining social capital, E-voting (and especially FIV) would deprive societies of one of the few remaining occasions for solidary participation, namely election day. This would (and should) be cause for regret, especially in a setting where voting is such a social and festive activity. As noted, E-technologies can express and exacerbate the digital divide. However, if E-voting were restricted to the high-abstention and risk-of-abstention groups identified in this chapter, and did not depend exclusively on private ownership of Internet-connected computers, this effect could be minimised and Australian democracy deepened. As Tony Clark and Peter Abbinga suggest (2004), E-voting could 'revolutionise' the access and participation of groups who are traditionally and increasingly disconnected from politics, namely, 'the elderly, people with disabilities and from culturally and linguistically diverse backgrounds, Indigenous Australians and people with literacy problems'.

E-voting has the potential to enhance political inclusion in a number of ways: Firstly, FIV may stimulate turnout particularly among the young, a traditionally (and increasingly) high-abstention voting group. Secondly, E-voting technology is now available to enable blind and vision-impaired citizens to vote without having to waive a most important democratic right, namely the right to vote in secret. Similarly, E-voting can incorporate technology to facilitate voting participation among Aboriginal, physically immobile, isolated, minority language and low literacy voters. Internet voting could also replace postal, consulate and mobile voting for people in remote regions, for citizens temporarily resident overseas, and for people with a disability who experience difficulty in attending polling booths.

REFERENCES

ACE Project. (2004). 'Focus on E-voting.' *Electoral Knowledge Network*. URL: http://aceproject.org/ace-en/focus/e-voting/ (Consulted 8/02/2008).

Australian Capital Territory Electoral Commission (ACTEC). (2005). *Electronic Voting and Counting System Review.* Elections ACT, 2005 URL: http//www.elections.act.gov.au/pdfs/election_04/2004electionreviewcomputervoting.pdf (Consulted 8/02/08).

Australian Electoral Commission (AEC). (2005). *Australian Electoral Commission Annual Report 2004-5,* http://www.aec.gov.au/_content/What/publications/annual_report/2005/index.htm (Consulted 8-02-08).

AEC (2007). *Remote Electronic Voting for Overseas Australian Defence Force personnel.* Consulted at URL: http://www.aec.gov.au/Voting/e-voting/adf.htm (Consulted 8/02/2008).

AEC (2007a). *Electronic Voting Trial for Electors who are Blind or Have Low Vision.* http://www.aec.gov.au/Voting/e_voting/low_vision.htm (Consulted 20-8-08).

BMM Australia (2007). *Audit of AEC's Electronic Voting Machine for Blind and Vision Impaired Voters.* http://www.aec.gov.au/Voting/e_voting/bvi_audit.htm (Consulted 20-2-08).

BMM Australia (2007a). *Audit and Certification of a Remote Electronic Voting System for Overseas Defence Force Personnel.* http://www.aec.gov.au/Voting/e_voting/adf_audit.htm (Consulted 20/02/08).

Braendli, D. (2005). *The Scope of E-voting in Switzerland* [Conference paper, E-voting and Electronic Democracy: Present and the Future. An International Conference, Seoul, South Korea, March 17-18, 2005. URL: http://www.hallym.ac.kr/~icat/evoting2005/81ppt/braendli_paper.pdf (Consulted 25/08/05).

Broughton, C. (2005). *Democracy and voting.* White Paper. Software Improvements, Australia, http://www.softwareimp.com.au/Common%20content/White%20Papers/voting-Democracy.pdf (Consulted 8/02/2008).

Buchsbaum, T. M. (2005). *E-voting: Lessons Learnt from recent pilots.* Conference paper, E-voting and Electronic Democracy: Present and the Future. An International Conference, Seoul, South Korea, March 17-18, 2005. URL: http://www.hallym.ac.kr/~icat/e-voting2005/b-speakers.html. (Consulted 25/08/2005).

Caldow, J. (2004). *E-Democracy: Putting Down Global Roots.* Institute for Electronic Government, IBM Corporation. URL: http://www-1.ibm.com/industries/government/ieg/pdf/e-democracy%20putting%20down%roots.pdf (Consulted 8/02/2008).

Chong, A.(2004). Personal comment. Senior Research and Ethics Officer, Aboriginal Health Council of South Australia, September 2004.

Clark, T. and Abbinga, P. (2004). *Enabling Independent and Empowered Participation in the Electronic Democratic Process by People with Disabilities.* [Conference paper]. E-Governance Conference, University of Melbourne. URL:

http://www.visionaustralia.org.au/docs/services/jscelectoral.doc (Consulted 8/02/2008).

Dario, G. (2005). *Research Report No. 7: Analysis of Informal Voting During the 2004 House of Representatives Election*. Canberra: AEC.

European Communities. (2004a). *Second Successful Use of Internet Voting During Swiss Federal Referendum* [newsletter]. European Commission, 02 December 2004 URL: http://europa.eu.int/idabc/en/document/3607/358. (Consulted 8/02/2008).

European Communities. (2004b). *Internet Referendum Successfully Held in Switzerland* [newsletter]. European Commission, 28 September 2004. URL: http://europa.eu.int/idabc/en/document/3311/358. (Consulted 18/02/2008).

Fischer, E. A. (2001). *RL30773: Voting Technologies in the United States: Overview and Issues for Congress*. CRS Report for Congress, URL: http://www.ncseonline.org?NLE?CRSreports/Risk/rsk-55.cfm?&CFID=8946853&CFTOKEN=5583815 (Consulted 5/05/2005).

Fotos, M. and Franklin, M. (2002). *Naïve political science and the paradox of voting*. Paper Prepared for the Annual Meeting of the Midwest Political Science Association, Palmer House Hilton, Chicago, April 25-28, 2002.

Green, P. (2004). *Electronic voting underway for ACT election*. Australian Capital Territory Electoral Commission. URL: http://www.elections.act.gov.au/media/media0413.html. (Consulted 8/08/2008)

Green, P. (2005). *Electronic voting and counting for elections for the Australian Capital Territory*. Paper presented at an International Conference on E-voting and Electronic Democracy: Present and the Future. March 17-18, Seoul [conference paper on line]. URL: http://www.hallym.ac.kr/%Eicat/e-voting2006/index.html (Consulted 8/02/2008).

Hasen, R. L.(1996). Voting without law. *Pennsylvania Law Review*. 144 (5), 2135-2179.

Hill, L. (2001). A great leveller: Compulsory voting as a democratic innovation. In Marian Sawer (ed), *Elections Full Free and Fair*. Federation Press, Sydney.

Hill, L. (2002). On the reasonableness of compelling citizens to vote: The Australian case. *Political Studies*. 50(1), 80-101.

Hill, L. and Young, S.(2007). Protest or error? Informal voting and compulsory voting. *Australian Journal of Political Science*, 42 (3), 515-521.

Hill, L. and Louth, J. (2006). Mobilising the youth vote and the future of British democracy. *Proceedings of the Australasian Political Studies Association Conference 2006*, University of Newcastle, http://www.newcastle.edu.au/school/ept/politics/apsa/PapersFV/Panel_Youth/Hill,%20Lisa%20&%20Louth,%20Jonathon.pdf

Human Rights and Equal Opportunities Commission. (2007). *Electronic voting could decide election*. (Media Release). http://www.hreoc.gov.au/about/media/media_releases/2007/91_07.html (Consulted 8/02/2008).

Innes, G. (2006). *In the National Interest*, interview with Peter Mares, 7 May 2006, Radio National. URL: http://www.abc.net.au/rn/nationalinterest/stories/2006/1 630942.htm. (Consulted 8/02/2008).

Interim Report of the Commission on Electronic Voting (IRCEV) (2004). *20-24, 29*. URL: http://www.cev.ie/. (Consulted 8/02/2008).

Jackman S. and P. Brent. (2007). Rolls Close, Young People Still Under Represented. *Crikey*, October 29, 2007, http://www.mumble.com.au/misc/20071029_crikey_electoralroll.htm (Consulted 2-11-07

Jenkins, C. 2006. Blind to lead way in E-voting. *Australian IT, The Australian*. July 25, 2006.

Joint Standing Committee on Electoral Matters (JSCEM). (2005). *The 2004 Federal Election: Report of the Inquiry into the Conduct of the 2004 Federal Election and Matters Related Thereto*, Canberra: The Parliament of Australia. URL: http://www.aec.gov.au/_content/why/committee/jscem/ (Consulted 8/02/2008).

Jowell, R.and A. Park. (1998). *Young People, Politics and Citizenship: A Disengaged Generation*. London: Citizenship Foundation.

Kang, G. (2001). E-Racing E-Elections. *Loyola of Los Angeles Law Review*. 34 (3), 1155-1170.

Knowlton, Brian. (2006). US voters overseas get a computerized helper. *International Herald Tribune*. Friday, February 3. URL: http://www.iht.com/articles/2006/02/03news/vote.php. (Consulted 8/02/2008).

Mackerras, M., and McAllister, I. (1999). Compulsory Voting, Party Stability and Electoral Advantage in Australia. *Electoral Studies*, 18, 217-233.

McAllister, I and T. Makkai. (1993). Institutions or protest? Explaining invalid votes in Australian elections. *Electoral Studies* 12(1), 23-40.

McGregor, A. (2006). Personal email communication between Lisa Hill and Ms Anne MacGregor, Co-founder Southern Cross Group, 06/06/2006.

Mansell, M. (1993). Aborigines and the Constitution. *Human Rights Defender*. 2 (4), 27-28.

Martin, D.F., F. Morphy, W.G. Sanders and J. Taylor (2002). *Making Sense of the Census: Observations of the 2001 Enumeration in Remote Aboriginal Australia*. Research Monograph No.22, Centre for Aboriginal Economic Policy Research, Australian National University, Canberra: ANU E Press, available at http://www.anu.edu.au/caper_series/no_22/frames.php (Consulted on 8/02/2008).

Mitchell, S. (2005). Step towards having our say electronically. *The Australian* 17/05/2005. URL: http://global.factiva.com/en/arch/display.asp (Consulted 8/02/2008).

Mousley, K. (2006). *Submission 84*. Submission to the Commonwealth Parliamentary Inquiry into Civics and Electoral Education, 16 June 2006. URL: http://www.aph.gov.au/house/committee/em/education/subs/sub084.pdf(Consulted 8/02/2008).

Nockleby, J. (2001). Why internet voting? *Loyola of Los Angeles Law Review*. 34(3), 1023-1032.

Orr, G., Mercurio, B. and Williams, G. (2002). Australian Electoral Law: A Stocktake. *Election Law Journal*, 2 (3) 383-402.

Orr, G. (2004). *Australian Electoral Systems: How Well Do They Serve Political Equality?* Report prepared for the Democratic Audit of Australia. Report No.2, Australian National University.

Parliament of Victoria. (2005). *Scrutiny of Acts and Regulations Committee, Inquiry into Electronic Democracy, Final Report, April 2005*. URL http://www.parliament.vic.gov.au/SARC/E-Democracy/Final_Report/ToC.htm (Consulted 8/05/06).

Pearce, J. (2002). Aussies vote for electronic polling: survey. *ZDNet Australia*. 17/12/2002. URL: http://www.zdnet.com.au/news/business/Soa/Aussies-vote-for-electronic-vouing-survey/0,139023166,120270740,00.htm (Consulted 8/2/2008).

Pickering, B.C. T., Dacey, P.,and Byrne, D. (2004). *Electronic Voting and Electronic Counting of Votes: A Status Report* [report]. AEC, 15 April 2004. URL: http://www.aec.gov.au/_content/what/voting/electronic_report/ (Consulted 8/02/2008).

Poundstone, William (2008). A Paper Trail for Voting Machines. *New York Times*. URL: http://www.nytimes.com/2008/01/07/opinion/07poundstone.html, 7/01/2008 (Consulted 8/02/2008)

Pullen, S. and Minter Ellison Consulting. (2005). *Independent Review of the Northern Territory Electoral System: Final report and Recommendations*. Canberra: Scope.

Print, M, L. Saha, and K Edwards. (2004). *Youth Electoral Study: Report 1: Enrolment and Voting*. December 2004. URL: http://www.aec.gov.au/AboutAECPublications/youth_study_1/index.htm (Consulted 8/02/08.)

Salkowski, J. (2000). Thumbs down on E-voting until minorities go online. *Los Angeles Business Journal* via LookSmart's. URL: FindArticles@http://www.findarticles.com/p/articles/mi_m5072/is_17_22/ai_61894523/ (Consulted 8/08/2008).

Sawer, M. (2001). Pacemakers for the world. In Sawer, M. (ed.) *Elections Full, Free and Fair*, Leichhardt: The Federation Press.

Scope, (2004). Cited in *Scrutiny of Acts and Regulations Committee Victorian Electronic Democracy*, Final Report, May 2005. URL: http://www.parliament.vic.gov.au/sarc/E-Democracy/Final_Report/PartIII.htm, (Consulted 8/02/2008).

Solop, F. I. (2001). Digital democracy comes of age: Internet voting and the 2000 Arizona election. *PS: Political Science and Politics*. 34(2), 289-93.

Southern Cross Group. (2006). *Primary Submission to the Joint Standing Committee on Electoral Matters Inquiry into Civics and Electoral Education*, 2006. 1.22. URL: http://www.aph.gov.au/house/committee/em/education/subs.htm. (Consulted 01/06/2006).

Timson, Lia (2006). Victoria puts blind faith in electronic voting. *The Age*, November 14, 2006. Consulted at http://www.the age.com.au/news/technology/victoria-puts-blind-faith-in-electronic-voting/ on 8/02/2008

Victorian Electoral Commission (VEC), 2007. *Report to Parliament on the 2006 Victorian State Election*, Section 6, Electronic Voting. http://www.vec.vic.gov.au/files/2006stateelectionreportSection6.pdf

Zetter, K. (2003). Aussies do it right: E-voting. *Wired News*. 3/11/2003. URL: http://www.wired.com/news/ebiz/0,1272,61045,00.html. (Consulted 8/2/2008).

ENDNOTES

1 The authors wish to thank Paul Thornton-Smith and Chris Gribben of the VEC for their help in clarifying some of the technical aspects of this paper.

2 In fact, it happens to be the case that Australia's various state and federal electoral officers have been unusually proactive in the pursuit of the goal of full electoral inclusion.

3 Ballot machines were connected to a local area network (LAN) rather than the Internet but final count results were transmitted via the Internet on computers at a polling place.

4 For a detailed description of the eVACS system, see Broughton (2005).

5 In the United States, where concerns about voting fraud have escalated in the approach to their upcoming Presidential election, an innovative suggestion by computer scientist, Ronald Rivest, and mathematician, Warren Smith combines E-technologies with the paper-trails that are almost universally advocated by E-voting specialists. In this scheme '[p]aper ballots would be tallied by optical scanners or even by hand [and] ...results would then be posted on a Web site. Using a serial number assigned to each ballot, voters could check the site to make sure that their random ballots were posted and had not been altered or misread. [Voters] could take home a photocopy of a randomly

selected ballot cast by someone else...and could check [the Web site] to make sure that their random ballots were posted and had not been altered or misread. ....Rivest and Smith demonstrate mathematically that it takes only a tiny number of people checking the Web site to catch any substantial fraud with near certainty. For instance, to have 95 percent assurance of detecting a fraud involving 6 percent of ballots, only 50 voters would have to check, and this is true no matter how large the electorate. If the margin of victory is less than 6 percent, then more people would surely check' (Poundstone 2008).

6 'Once a vote is cast, the card is locked and cannot be used again...[V]oting preferences [are] recorded on a hard disk and a removable back-up USB key inside each terminal. When polling closes, the ecrypted data [is] burnt on to a CD and transported to the central VEC office for printing...At the VEC the data [is] decrypted by two officials using individual key cards and passwords. Votes [are] then printed on to paper ballots and returned to their electorate centres to be counted by hand' (Timson, 2006).

7 The AEC, via Vision Australia's emailing list, sent out messages to 7000 visually impaired people in Victoria prior to the election. The trial was also extensively advertised on 3RPH Radio, a station dedicated to serving the needs of print-handicapped people.

8 Though the reasons have yet to be determined, the informal voting rate dropped slightly at the 2007 Federal Election.

9 In the Anangu Pitjanjtjatjara Lands, 3,000 indigenous people live in a dozen communities and 70 scattered homelands on the country granted to them when the State government signed the land-mark AP Land Rights Bill in 1981.

10 When a person dies in a community, a 'Sorry Meeting' is held and relatives travel from other communities to make enquiries about the death.The whole community may shut down for 'Sorry Business' and go to a 'Sorry Camp' held away from the main community. Close relatives will not talk for a period of time that varies between communities, and for a significant community member, the deceased person's name will not be used; this latter prohibition may continue for many years.

11 For example, many Anagnu people are reticent to utter their legal names out loud. This is related to the cultural practice whereby when a relation has died, many change their names completely, including their surnames. This means that the name recorded on the roll will not match their new name. Further, it is taboo to utter the name of a deceased person so when a relation has died it is not proper to mention a surname if it is in common with that relative. In any case, it is usual for an indigenous person to say her/his name quietly so any measure that prevents errors occurring because of this are apposite.

12 For example, the Australian Flexible Learning Framework program funds a cultural awareness program, *'Interactive Ochre'*, through Spencer TAFE, whereby indigenous trainers use digital technology to transfer cultural information through music, and stories to service professionals who work with Aboriginal people.

13 An example is the *Outback Connect* project which connects about eighty communities in the remote region using webcams and instant messaging software to encourage community members to interact.

14 One software package that has the potential to engage Aboriginal people is the multimedia animation software program, MARVIN (Messaging Architecture for the Retrieval of Versatile Information and News), developed in the Northern Territory. It is enabled to speak the language of the audience and

is used in the Northern Territory for client service delivery and health education.

15 Which describes itself as 'an international volunteer-run, non-profit advocacy and support organisation for the Australian Diaspora'.

16 As used by the Australian Taxation Department for Tax File Numbers.

17 Varying from a four to six letter/digit password to one that combines letters, numbers and symbols of up to fifteen characters.

18 A survey conducted in 2006 by the Southern Cross Group in collaboration with Professor Graeme Hugo, University of Adelaide, found that 47% of eligible voters living overseas at the time of the last Federal Election were aged between 20-34. The full results of this survey are yet to be released.

Chapter XI
Australia Local Government and E-Governance:
From Administration to Citizen Participation?

Kevin O'Toole
Deakin University, Australia

ABSTRACT

This chapter analyses local government's response to the pressure to modernise its structures through its use of Information Communication Technologies (ICT) to execute its broad range of tasks. The chapter begins by discussing Chadwick and May's (2003) three basic models of e-government; managerial, consultative and participatory. Using data collected from an analysis of 658 local government websites in Australia together with existing survey research the chapter then analyses the extent to which local government sites fit into the three models. The chapter concludes with a discussion of the issues and problems faced by local government in its attempt to develop e-governance as both an extension of administrative as well as democratic functions.

INTRODUCTION

Like many other institutions of governance around the world, Australia's local governments are facing new challenges in the 21st century. The pressure for reform has seen major structural changes as state and federal governments seek to impose a new economic and political agenda upon the local institutions of governance (Baker, 2003). The result has seen a renewed focus on way that local government does business especially in areas such as statutory service obligations, financial accountability, local economic development and to a lesser extent democratic representation (Dollery, Marshall, & Worthington, 2003).

In more recent times local governments have adopted Information Communication Technologies (ICT) in the form of websites in the hope of

Copyright © 2009, IGI Global, distributing in print or electronic forms without written permission of IGI Global is prohibited.

expanding their role in the new world of e-government. With large cash injections from the Federal government's *Networking the Nation* program and local state programs to improve the reach of ICT, local governments have set about the task of relocating much of their activity online (Macdonald, 2001). The first wave of websites established on the internet and local governments are now in the process of learning how to work in the world of e-government.

As this chapter demonstrates, the first rush of e-government, and for that matter e-governance, has brought mixed results for local government across Australia. Websites exist for most local governments but the types of e-government vary from place to place both within and between the state systems. Following an outline of an analytical framework for understanding e-government the chapter explores the approaches to e-governance adopted across local government in Australia and discusses the major issues that face any future developments.

E-GOVERNMENT

Australian local governments have adopted the Australian Local Government Association's (ALGA) definition of e-government as 'the structured use of electronic technology to pursue the traditional goals of government in areas such as:

- The interface with government
- Service relationships with people and businesses
- Commercial relationships with business partners
- Implementing sectoral and community based policy
- Enhancing the role of citizens in democratic processes (i.e. e-democracy)
- Interacting with other public institutions
- The conduct of government's own 'back-office' operations' (Australian Local Government Association, 2004, p. 10)

What this list does is reaffirm the fundamental role of 'government' in interfacing, implementing, conducting and servicing. For all intents and purposes it is business as usual for 'government' without a lot of thought about increasing the reach of local democracy (Crabtree, 2001).

On the other hand there are those that consider the shift to e-government as a change to the way that the government and its citizens interact. Chadwick and May (2003) argue that there are three basic models of interaction between the state and its citizens that underpin the notion of e-government: managerial, consultative and participatory. The first approach is akin to the ALGA definition as a managerialist focus. Chadwick and May (2003) argue that the managerialist approach has a number of features:

- "A concern for the 'efficient' delivery of services" of government information to citizens and other groups of users.
- The use of ICTs to improve flows of information within and around government.
- A recognition of the importance of 'service delivery' to 'customers'.
- The view that speeding up information provision is, *by itself*, 'opening up government'.
- A general absence of user resources issues, such as the ability to receive and interpret information.
- And 'control' and presentational professionalism (often termed spin) as defining logics. (Chadwick & May, 2003, p. 272).

The Chief Information Officer for the Government of Canada sums up the managerialist position as:

The ultimate goal is to use technology to strengthen Canada's economy and society; reduce the cost and burden of government processes and transactions; encourage innovation with government as a strategic procurer and model user of new technologies; and, optimize the effective and efficient delivery of government programs and services. (d'Auray, 2003, p. 36)

What governments have sought to emulate is the commercial world by developing a form of e-government that includes four types of interaction; 1) simple information; 2) access by citizens and businesses (even update particulars) – weak form of interactivity; 3) online transactions and purchases, or electronic sending of tender information; integrated portal of all government services and information (Symonds, 2000). The only difference between government and commercial sites using information and services online is that the types of information and activity of e-government relate to services located in the public sector.

Under these conditions people mainly go online to government sites 'to download forms, find out about processes and rules, and generally to run their private affairs' (Rennie & Hartley, 2004, p. 10). E-government in this sense becomes a top-down governing process using online information and services that are often thought to be apolitical or more uninvolved (Griffiths, 2002).

Chadwick and May's (2003) second model of e-government – consultative -facilitates the communication of citizen opinion to government. This model embraces a 'continuum of consultation, stretching from low-level information gathering towards (but not finally reaching) a fuller, quasideliberative level of interaction and consultation' (Chadwick & May, 2003, p. 279). While citizens remain the passive recipients of information there is some encouragement to engage with government.

There are those that consider this engagement to be a shift to e-governance or 'a technology-mediated relationship between citizens and their governments from the perspective of potential electronic deliberation over civic communication, over policy evolution, and in democratic expression of citizen will' (Marche & McNiven, 2003, p. 75). The emphasis is more on democratic governance where citizens are engaged in an active process of governing apart from their place as clients and consumers of state services. This is an extension of e-government where all forms of ICT are used by governments and their agents to broaden the reach of public information and services, and engage citizens in some form of public engagement (Curtain, Sommer, & Vis-Sommer, 2003, p. 2).

Chadwick and May's (2003) third model - participation -, 'conceives of a more complex horizontal and multidirectional interactivity' (Chadwick & May, 2003, p. 280). Citizens are enjoined to play a more active role in governing at all levels of government though greater ICT interactivity (Coe, Paquet, & Roy, 2001). The use of ICT becomes not merely a means of communication but a way of facilitating interactivity between multiple sites in the political process (Geiselhart, Griffiths, & Fitzgerald, 2003: p. 216). Through the use of bulletin boards, chat rooms, file sharing, and peer to peer networking citizens can be involved in forms of deliberative democracy around opinion formation and political action in a new 'cyber civil society' (Chadwick & May, 2003, p. 281).

This final model shifts the e-governance approach from one of top-down government to one where citizens can 'gather without the need for propinquity to politically organize, discuss and collectively resolve issues of the day' (Lim, 2002, p.383). There is sense here that new forms of e-democracy can enable citizens to propose, discuss and vote upon new policy decisions directly. However there are those who doubt that electronic direct democracy will be anything other than 'politics as usual' (Barney, 2000; Crabtree, 2001; Moore, 1999; Norris, 2001). Their argument is that while some governments have experimented with various forms of deliberative e-democracy they are largely ephemeral and have not led to any longer lasting changes to participation in the political process. This is an especially important question for local governments and in the next sections we will explore the ways that local governments have developed their web sites across Australia.

LOCAL GOVERNMENT: BACKGROUND

There are 721 local government bodies in Australia, including 97 indigenous community councils in Queensland, the NT and WA and all come under the constitutional authority of the States and Territories. Virtually all of Victoria, Queensland, WA and Tasmania come under the jurisdiction of some local government authority, unlike NSW, SA and the NT where there are large unincorporated areas. Uniquely in Australia, the Government of the Australian Capital Territory combines both state and local government functions but it will not be treated as local government in this instance.

The legal framework for local government differs from state to state but generally the functions and services of local government can include engineering, recreation, health, welfare, security, building, planning and development, administration, culture and education. However as a recent federal government enquiry found local government has been taking on responsibility for a wide range of social functions that include management of health, alcohol and drug problems, community safety and improved planning and accessible transport. Furthermore the regulatory functions of local government have increased in areas like development and planning, public health and environmental management (House of Representatives Standing Committee on Economics Finance and Public Administration, 2003).

However the expansion of these services is far from uniform across Australia, even within State and Territory Boundaries. For example local government in Queensland, New South Wales and Tasmania have local responsibility for water while in other states water is the role of State government agencies. Local government in the Northern Territory does not have responsibility for planning whereas in other states local governments have a significant yet differential role to play in the area (May, 2003).

Overall local governments across Australia exhibit a wide variety of characteristics. Besides differences in population and geographic area, the range of functions they perform and their legislative frameworks local governments also vary markedly in income and expenditure, the skills of employees, and physical, economic, cultural and social environments. One significant differential is the ratios of elected members to their populations and way the electorates are organised (Burdess & O'Toole, 2004; Kiss, 2003). The average population per councillor ranges from 258 in the Northern Territory to 8,122 in the state of Victoria (May, 2003). Electorates can be divided into wards or unsubdivided and voting in local government elections is compulsory in three states (New South Wales, Victoria and Queensland) while the rest are voluntary (Kiss, 2003). There are also differences in voting procedures with many local governments opting for postal voting where it is either allowed or mandated as in Tasmania (Kiss, 2003).

With such differences in the way that local government organises itself in the different jurisdictions any shift to new forms of communication such as ICT will most probably reflect those variations. The next section begins that process by outlining the results from research into ICT in Australia local government.

AUSTRALIAN LOCAL GOVERNMENTS AND ICT

To ascertain whether the degree to which local government in Australia was embracing any of the three models of e-government at an analysis of all available local government web-sites in Australia together with existing survey research was undertaken. A small number of case studies that exhibited any advanced forms of e-government were also undertaken.

Local government's capacity for e-government is related to two issues; 1) local government's connection to communication networks; and 2) its ability to take advantage of the available technology. This is especially the case for rural and remote municipalities where fast communication networks are either non-existent or reasonably expensive.

In many instances the physical capacity for the adoption of e-government across all municipalities in Australia is still problematic. In 2004 a survey of 200 councils across Australia, found that all councils had Internet access (Rural Industries Research and Development Corporation, 2004). However, 89% of urban councils were on broadband compared to 59% of those in rural areas. Across the country as a whole, 68% of councils were on broadband and 32% on dial up. Nearly 40% of councils not on broadband (equivalent to 10% of all councils) said they had no plans to upgrade nor did they indicate when they would do so. There were three main reasons given for remaining on dial-up: broadband was not available (62%); dial up was perceived to be cheaper (15%); and 'dial up was best for their needs' (11%) (Rural Industries Research and Development Corporation, 2004, p. 31).

Beyond access to the broadband is the construction of websites themselves and across Australia there are no common bench marks. A report entitled *Services and Metadata on Local Government Websites* found that the websites are not very consistent in what constitutes a service, what service information is important to convey, how services are grouped on websites and how to name these groupings (Farkus, 2004). The report also found that the information provided on local government websites fell into three categories:

- **Council promotion:** All sites provide detailed information about the Council, its role, structure, councillors, departments, sometimes meeting minutes and history and other information about the Council and its functions.
- **Regional promotion:** Most sites provide some information about the region, its major centre(s), tourist attractions and sometimes economic development potential. Some sites include details of commercial tourist accommodation and venues; some provide or support local business directories.
- **Services information:** Everything else on most of the sites could loosely be described as 'service-oriented' information, in the sense that it is not commercial, not advertising, not local news items' (Farkus, 2004).

Many local governments do have interactive online services especially the payment of rates and it appears that where online capabilities are available ratepayers are using the Internet to make payments to councils (Rural Industries Research and Development Corporation, 2004). In states like Victoria this is almost uniform whereas in Western Australia there are only 28% of councils across Western Australia that have the capacity to offer the payment of rates online

When it comes to the application of more extended models of e-government to include consultation and participation there is even less capacity on local government sites. A review of local government websites was conducted in October 2005 to better understand the way that local governments had positioned themselves with regard to consultation and participation. All available websites (658 in total) were scanned in each state and territory to discover the interactivity of sites especially with regard to citizen consultation and participation (See Tables 1 & 2). The overall percentage of local governments who had some form of online feedback mechanism on their sites was 40 percent. The types of feedback were usually contained in an online form that allowed people to post complaints, compliments, suggestions, comments or 'customer requests'. Sometimes the forms were available on the home page under such headings as 'have your say' or 'feedback'. At other times the forms were found in the contacts area or attached to the council activities part of the site. Most local government sites also included email addresses but for the purposes of this research it was the capacity to reach the council online that was used as the criterion for electronic feedback. Furthermore those websites that had feed back mechanisms asking for comment about the site itself were also excluded.

The types and placement of feedback forms varied from state to state and across the four categories of municipality (Department of Transport and Regional Services, 2005):

- Metropolitan developed or part of an urban centre of more than 1,000,000 or population density more than 600/sq km.
- Regional Towns/City or part of an urban centre with population less than 1,000,000 and predominantly urban in nature.
- Fringe or a developing LGA on the margin of a developed or regional urban centre.
- Rural incorporating the agricultural and remote LGAs.

The metropolitan and fringe municipalities accounted for the highest proportion of municipalities to have feedback mechanisms online (See Table 1). The size of metropolitan and fringe local governments and their proximity to better e-resources makes it easier for them to produce more sophisticated sites. However, even though the proportion was only 25%, the actual number of rural municipalities that had some form of online feedback mechanism was much higher than that of the metropolitan and fringe councils. Victoria's rural category had a high proportion at 70% although with fewer and larger rural councils this is to be expected (Barlow, Chen, Chimonyo, Lyon, & O'Loughlin, 2004). While the proportions in New South Wales and Western Australia were relatively low the actual number was reasonably high considering the size and technical difficulties of electronic delivery in those states.

Beyond the feedback mechanisms there were few examples of councils (5%) supplying specific online facilities for comments on policy or planning proposals (See Table 2). While proposals for policy and planning changes were often posted on websites the method of relaying comments was either by post or email. Directions on these types of websites never included the use of the online feedback forms even if they existed. To that extent any feedback loop took place outside of the internet.

Table 1. Number and percentage of state category for online feedback mechanism

	Metro	Regional	Fringe	Rural	Total
New South Wales	18 (53%)	19 (53%)	9 (82%)	29 (41%)	75 (50%)
Victoria	19 (86%)	20 (77%)	8 (80%)	14 (70%)	61 (78%)
Queensland	3 (100%)	12 (33%0	7 (64%)	18 (21%)	40 (29%)
Western Australia	11 (58%)	7 (64%)	7 (70%)	14 (31%)	39 (31%)
South Australia	15 (100%0	4 (57%)	3 (75%)	14 (49%)	36 (49%)
Tasmania	0	3 (38%)	0	7 (34%)	10 (34%)
Northern Territory	1 (100%)	3 (75%)	0	0	4 (6%)
Total	67 (71%)	68 (53%)	34 (71%)	96 (25%)	265 (40%)

However there were some quite advanced examples of online consultation and participation. The Perth Council's *City Interactive* site includes a range of functions including online consultation and participation. The Melbourne City Council website contains a 'have your say' section on its home page that includes three parts; consultation, feedback and ideas. The consultation section gives residents the chance to read the documentation online as well as supply online comment via web communication. It also helps to target the response to specific policy issues rather than being lost in the more general feedback mechanisms.

Some municipalities attempt to involve people in dialogue about policy issues. The Bayside Municipality in Victoria includes an online form that gives residents the opportunity to request 'to be heard' at committee meetings of the Council. While the actual presentation is not online the fact that the council has an easy to complete online form gives residents a chance to have their opinions heard. There is also evidence that some Councils use websites to gather support for submissions to other levels of government. The Sutherland Shire in New South Wales has a permanent section on its site entitled online surveys and petitions. When the site was accessed in October 2005 there was a petition seeking support against a desalinisation plant in its region. These types of petitions are rare on local council sites at present but they do extend the reach of local council engagement with their residents

There were very few councils that took the further step of supplying a more participative model of e-governance where discussion forums could be both horizontal and well as vertical in natures. Besides large urban municipalities like Leichhardt Municipal Council in New South Wales and the Brisbane City Council there were also a smaller municipalities like the Chapman Valley Shire located north of Geraldton in Western Australia. The Brisbane and Leichardt examples are instructive in that the dialogue is monitored with feedback from the council about the issues raised. Brisbane also has a community reference panel made up of Brisbane residents who receive information on local issues and have a say about important decisions affecting the city. Currently there are more than 7,000 members of the *Your City, Your Say* community reference panel.

LOCAL GOVERNMENT IN THE DIGITAL AGE

Local government has followed the general trend of e-government by establishing internet sites that offer a means of doing more of its business online through services such as paying rates, licenses and charges or offering tender specifications

Table 2. Number and percentage of state category for online consultation

	Metro	Regional	Fringe	Rural	Total
New South Wales	7 (21%)	4 (11%)	3 (27%)	0	14 (9%)
Victoria	3 (14%	3 (13%)	0	0	6 (8%)
Queensland	2 (67%)	4 (11%)	2 (18%)	0	8 (6%)
Western Australia	3 16%)	0	0	0	3 (2%)
South Australia	1 (7%)	0	1 (25%)	2 (4%)	4 (5%)
Tasmania	0	0	0	0	0
Northern Territory	0	0	0	0	0
Total	16 (17%)	11 (9%)	6 (13%)	2 (1%)	35 (5%)

as well as communicating to the world at large about the benefits of business investment in the municipality. Most local governments in Australia now have at minimum an internet presence but the extent to which local government has developed its capacity for moving to more consultative and participatory models of e-governance is not as certain. The tension between what some term the 'local democracy model' and the 'structural efficiency model' (May, 2003) will spill over into the direction that local governments will take in the development of, and more importantly the use of their web sites.

To begin with local governments in rural and remote areas face a 'digital divide'. While access to broadband is becoming more widespread across Australia there are still large areas that are still limited to dial up facilities to service their local area (Rural Industries Research and Development Corporation, 2004). However the digital divide is not restricted to access to the technical infrastructure but also to the social infrastructure that supports ICT (Rooksby, Weckert, & Lucas, 2002). This includes socio-demographic factors such as income, gender, race, ethnicity, education, age and location as well as the availability of ICT support services. Furthermore there are other local issues that are significant barriers to the expansion of e-democracy is local government. Firstly language and literacy are two interdependent issues in terms of the present communication channels to local government. Learning to participate in chat rooms, file sharing, and peer to peer networking not only involves language proficiency but also the confidence to want to be included (Barry, 2002). At present some local government websites include languages other than English but none provide the capacity for non-English participatory mechanisms (Geiselhart et al., 2003). Secondly, education and training for engaging with local issues on the web are fundamental for participation. In framing the way policy and planning issues appear on the web local officials will need to be aware to make the content readily accessible but also to motivate 'underserved groups' to want to participate (Kretchmer & Carveth, 2001). Thirdly, there is the issue of access for other disadvantaged groups whether that is through disability or location.

Federal and state governments have provided a good deal of the infrastructure costs over recent years for ICT development especially through the *Networking the Nation* program. However like other government infrastructure programs there is an initial outlay for the costs of development but then the ongoing maintenance is left to local government. Accordingly ICT is not a high priority in many local governments especially when there is significant 'cost shifting' from other levels of government which the ALGA estimated could be between $500 million and $1.1 billion per annum (House of Representatives Standing Committee on Economics Finance and Public Administration, 2003, p. 29). Whether the cost shifting is purely in dollar terms, through the imposition of new service or through costly compliance activity, local governments have become more cash strapped and thus looking to fund their basic requirements.

The ability of local governments to generate more local income is also thwarted by state government compliance requirements. For example in NSW rate-capping severely limits the capacity of local government to raise local revenues (House of Representatives Standing Committee on Economics Finance and Public Administration, 2003). In this environment the marked differences in the uses of ICT in the local government system across Australia are not unexpected. The size of local governments that range from approximately 900,000 to around 160 indicates the differences in the economies of scale and thus the ability to supply and maintain an appropriate ICT system. As it stands local Government investment in electronic technology falls within a range of 1 to 3% of its own revenues (Australian Local Government Association, 2004).

There are also issues of on-going ICT support in some areas such as access to qualified professionals. As the Mayor of Barraba Shire Council in rural NSW stated:

In the rural areas ... you have great difficulty in attracting quality people to apply for positions, whether they are in police, health, education or any professional service, such as banking. It is not just in government areas, it is also in private enterprise. It is the professional services. ... So the responsibility of meeting the community expectation to attract those people there falls back on local government. ... Local government are then forced to spend their rate dollars on providing housing, incentives, rent subsidies or some other form of attraction. (House of Representatives Standing Committee on Economics Finance and Public Administration, 2003, p. 8)

This poses a major problem for rural and remote areas in supporting and maintaining ICT services especially if there are significant demands upon local revenues to supply the basic infrastructure services like roads.

In such a climate a 'local democracy model' that is more akin to the collaborative and participatory approaches to e-governance, is likely to be subordinate to a 'structural efficiency model' that focuses on a more managerial approach. The structure of the majority of local council websites indicates the dominance of a managerial mentality. The flow of communication is more often than not in one direction; from the Council to their residents. Further the major interactivity of most sites between a Council and its constituents is through the available rates and charges mechanisms. Consultative models are available through feedback mechanisms on a small minority of sites but participation in the form of some online dialogue is very rare. Overall it is fair to say that e-government at local level is dominated by a managerial model.

CONCLUSION

While it is apparent that local government in Australia has made some significant advances in its use of ICT in recent years the results are far from uniform. Nearly all local governments have a website with basic information about the local area, minutes of council meetings, some access to public documents and minimum contact details. A few others have developed interactive capacities that give citizens access to online payment of rates and charges or the ability to download forms. The 'managerial model' is consistent with local government's role as a service provider. There are also a sizeable number of municipalities that give citizens some form of feedback mechanism thus relaying their concerns directly to the local council. This is a weak form of the 'consultative model' where citizens engage directly with local government through expression of their complaints, compliments, suggestions, comments or 'customer requests'. Finally there are a few local governments that allow their citizens to engage in conversations across and between other citizens as well the local council itself. Such engagement emulates a participative model of horizontal and multidirectional interactivity.

The next phase in the development of e-government at local level will be a test of whether local governments continue to develop their websites towards more participatory models of e-governance. To retain websites merely as places where local governments can develop their commercial and in-house functions would be to miss an opportunity to increase the participation of their residents in a broader more inclusive fashion. If local government claims to be the government nearest to the community it would be appropriate that it be the leader in development of more participatory models of e-governance.

REFERENCES

Australian Local Government Association. (2004). *A Directional Roadmap for the Use of Electronic Technology by Councils*. Deakin, ACT: Australian Local Government Association.

Baker, G. (2003). Management Reform in Local Government. In B. Dollery, N. Marshall & A. Worthington (Eds.), *Reshaping Australian Local Government: Finance, governance and reform*. Sydney: UNSW Press.

Barlow, S., Chen, P., Chimonyo, J., Lyon, A., & O'Loughlin, B. (2004). *eGovernance Practice and Potential in the Local Government Sector*. Paper presented at the The Australian Electronic Governance Conference, Centre for Public Policy, Melbourne University, http://www.public-policy.unimelb.edu.au/egovernance/ConferenceContent.html#nancyotis.

Barney, D. (2000). *Prometheus Wired: The hope For Democracy in the Age of Network Technology*. Chicago: University of Chicago Press.

Barry, B. (2002). Social Exclusion, Social Isolation, and the Distribution of Income. In J. Hills, J. Le Grand & D. Piachaud (Eds.), *Understanding Social Exclusion*. Oxford: Oxford University Press.

Burdess, N., & O'Toole, K. (2004). Elections and representation in local government: A Victorian case study. *Australian Journal of Public Administration*, 63(2), 66-78.

Chadwick, A., & May, C. (2003). Interaction between States and Citizens in the Age of the Internet: e-Government in the United States, Britain and the European Union. *Governance: An International Journal of Policy Administration and Institutions*, 16(2), 271-300.

Coe, A., Paquet, G., & Roy, J. (2001). E-Governance and Smart Communities. *Social Science Computer Review*, 19(1), 80-93.

Crabtree, J. (2001). *Whatever Happened to the E-lection: A survey of Voter Attitudes Towards new Technology During the 2001 Election*. http://www.egov.vic.gov.au/pdfs/electiondesigned1.pdf: iSociety

Curtain, G., Sommer, M., & Vis-Sommer, V. (2003). The World of E-Government. In G. Curtain, M. Sommer & V. Vis-Sommer (Eds.), *The World of E-Government*. New York: The Haworth Press.

d'Auray, M. (2003). The Dual Challenge of Integration and Inclusion: Canada's Experience with Government Online. In G. Curtain, M. Sommer & V. Vis-Sommer (Eds.), *The World of E-Government*. New York: The Haworth Press.

Department of Transport and Regional Services. (2005). *Local Government National Report*. Canberra: Department of Transport and Regional Services.

Dollery, B., Marshall, N., & Worthington, A. (2003). Introduction. In B. Dollery, N. Marshall & A. Worthington (Eds.), *Reshaping Australian Local Government: Finance, governance and reform*. Sydney: UNSW Press.

Farkus, L. (2004). *Services and Metadata on Local Government Websites*. Canberra: Australian Local Government Association.

Geiselhart, K., Griffiths, M., & Fitzgerald, B. (2003). What Lies Beyond Service Delivery - An Australian Perspective. In G. Curtain, M. Sommer & V. Vis-Sommer (Eds.), *The World of E-Government*. New York: The Haworth Press.

Griffiths, M. (2002). *Forming Audiences for E-Democracy: Government Policies, Portals and Pilots - and Citizen Literacies*. Paper presented at the 2nd European Conference on e-Government, St Catherine's College, Oxford.

House of Representatives Standing Committee on Economics Finance and Public Administration. (2003). *Rates and Taxes: A Fair Share for*

Responsible Local Government. Canberra: Commonwealth Government.

Kiss, R. (2003). Reasserting Local Democracy. In B. Dollery, N. Marshall & A. Worthington (Eds.), *Reshaping Australian Local Government: Finance, governance and reform*. Sydney: UNSW Press.

Kretchmer, S., & Carveth, R. (2001). The color of the Net: African Americans, race and cyberspace. *Computers and Society,* September, 9-14.

Lim, M. (2002). Cyber-civic space in Indonesia: from panopticon to pandemonium? *International Development Planning Review,* 24(4), 383-400.

Macdonald, I. (2001). *Local Government Receives Massive Networking the Nation Funding*. http://www.ministers.dotars.gov.au/im/releases/2001/july/m197_2001.htm: Media Release, Department for Regional Services, Territories and Local Government.

Marche, S., & McNiven, J. D. (2003). E-Government and E-Governance: The Future Isn't What It Used To Be. *Candian Journal of Administrative Sciences,* 20(1), 74-86.

May, P. (2003). Amalgamation and Virtual Local Government. In B. Dollery, N. Marshall & A. Worthington (Eds.), *Reshaping Australian Local Government: Finance, governance and reform*. Sydney: UNSW Press.

Moore, R. (1999). Democracy and Cyberspace. In B. Hague & B. Loader (Eds.), *Digital Democracy: Discourse and Decision Making in the Information Age*. London: Routledge.

Norris, P. (2001). *Digital Divide: Civic Engagement, Information Poverty and the Internet Worldwide*. Cambridge & New York: Cambridge University Press.

Rennie, G., & Hartley, J. (2004). *Show-Business for Ugly People? Media Politics and E-Democracy.* Paper presented at the The Australian Electronic Governance Conference, Centre for Public Policy, Melbourne University, http://www.public-policy.unimelb.edu.au/egovernance/ConferenceContent.html#nancyotis

Rooksby, E., Weckert, J., & Lucas, R. (2002). The Rural Digital Divide. *Rural Society,* 12(3), 197-209.

Rural Industries Research and Development Corporation. (2004). *Broadband adoption by agriculture and local government councils: Australia and the USA*. Barton, ACT: Rural Insustries Research and Development Corporation.

Symonds, M. (2000). Government and the Internet - The Next Revolution. *The Economist,* June 24.

Chapter XII
Engaging the Community Through E-Democracy in South Australia

Kate Alport
University of Adelaide, Australia

Clement Macintyre
University of Adelaide, Australia

ABSTRACT

This chapter examines the spread of Information and Communication Technologies (ICTs) in South Australia. It starts by assessing South Australia's leading role in the adoption of democratic reforms in the nineteenth century. It then suggests that there is not the same enthusiasm for the more contemporary reforms found in the implementation of e-democracy. The chapter draws from an appraisal of internet based initiatives by government, not for profit and private agencies and sets these against best practice models for community engagement. Based on this research it concludes that there is little originality and initiative in the formal State Government sites and that there is little designed to foster e-democracy. What innovation there is can be found in more local and specific community based applications of ICT.

INTRODUCTION

The relationship between citizens and the agencies of government has been transformed by recent developments in information and communication technology (ICT). Just as in business, education and entertainment – indeed, in almost every aspect of our lives – the way we interact with the institutions of government has been reordered by exposure to rapidly changing technology. This change has affected the way that we, as citizens, express our views and respond to government initiatives as much as it has changed the way that information and the delivery of government services are provided. The growth and the extent of 'e-democracy' and the consequences of this

Copyright © 2009, IGI Global, distributing in print or electronic forms without written permission of IGI Global is prohibited.

transformation in the relationship between governments and those who are governed are difficult to over-estimate. In many respects the impact of e-democratic initiatives may be as significant a reform as the initial spread of democratic institutions in the nineteenth century.

If this is the case, then it is likely that South Australia will not be at the forefront of current reform in the way that it was in the past. There can be no doubt that South Australia has a long record of reform and that it was a leader in the early implementation of democratic initiatives. There is, however, less evidence that this pace of reform has been sustained in more recent years. So, while there have been a number of (commendable) developments that, on their own have been significant, there has been little overall embrace of broad and co-ordinated reform based on new developments in ICT and there has been no clear recent commitment to e-democracy.

Even a brief summary of South Australia's colonial history shows that it led the way in introducing many of the democratic acts and initiatives that became common elsewhere. In contrast to all other former British colonies, South Australia's foundation was a product of legislation rather than direct settlement. The *South Australia Act 1834* (UK) laid the foundations for the democratic style of governance that the new colony would eventually adopt and established many of the key institutions that shaped its democratic culture. The fact that the structures of government were laid out by statute rather than emerging from conflict meant that South Australia avoided many of the tensions that accompanied democratic reforms elsewhere. Accordingly, by 1857 South Australia had a bi-cameral Parliament that included a House of Assembly (lower house) with suffrage extended to all adult male British subjects (included Aboriginal men). Similarly, South Australia was either the first or among the first to use secret voting, have an elected Town Council, to separate Church and State, to introduce industrial reforms and to legalise Trade Unions. In 1894, the South Australian Parliament was the first parliament in the world to give women the right to stand as candidates for election, and one of the first few to give women the right to vote. As Chris Sumner has argued, South Australia's early political initiatives placed it 'at the forefront of democratic reform' (Sumner, 2003, p.22), with a Constitution among the most democratic in the contemporary world.

Despite these initiatives, through the twentieth century the passion for democratic reform in South Australia became less evident. For much of this time, political initiatives were focussed principally upon securing economic growth through periods of war and depression. Most of the first 60 years of the twentieth century were dominated by conservative political groups that saw little need for further reform. Then, while the governments of the final four decades reflected the more progressive social mood of the times and introduced a range of overdue social reforms, there was no more than piecemeal attention given to democratic and constitutional reforms. There were changes to the electoral laws that saw the end of a property qualification to vote for the Legislative Council (the upper house of the State Parliament), the introduction of proportional representation in the Legislative Council, and the ensuring of one-vote-one-value for House of Assembly elections, but beyond these, there is little that any government could point to as constituting significant reform to the institutions of government or to the character of the democratic culture. Rather, the changes that did emerge came from the broader revolutions that were occurring across society. These reflected both the changing nature of the relationship between citizen and state and the transformed role of the media and, in time, new communication technologies.

Among the most significant of the early communication revolutions were the growing use and influence of broadcast technology. The penetration of the market by radio and subsequently television changed the way that many South Australians saw their political leaders and institutions. Of course, this phenomenon was not restricted to South Australia. In the latter half of the twentieth century the connection between politics and the mass media was researched extensively across the globe as social scientists investigated the extent to which politicians' use of these media had an influence on democracy and on the public's perception of the contenders for political office. This was a dynamic period in political communications as candidates sought to use radio and television to communicate directly with voters and to engage political opponents in debating the issues in real time. Candidates received feedback from their constituents about their performance in the media, and not all of it was encouraging. (For an overview, see Nimmo and Sanders, 1981).

In more recent years, distinguished by the rapid rise of accessibility to Internet communication and the World Wide Web, the emphasis has moved to be more concentrated on the potential of ICT. This development has meant that governments can both inform citizens (in a much more tailored and direct way than was previously possible) as well as give the community a direct channel to voice their opinions to their political representatives through interactive web sites and direct communication. The enthusiasm for ICT has rapidly spread throughout the world and its potential for eradicating the barriers to universal equality was enshrined in a declaration from Geneva's World Summit on the Information Society in December 2003:

our common desire and commitment [is] to build a people-centred, inclusive and development-oriented Information Society, where everyone can create, access, utilize and share information and knowledge, enabling individuals, communities and peoples to achieve their full potential in promoting their sustainable development and improving their quality of life, premised on the purposes and principles of the Charter of the United Nations and respecting fully and upholding the Universal Declaration of Human Rights. (World Summit of the Information Society, 2003)

This utopian declaration, by emphasising the right of the individual to control their own destiny, invites an examination of the controversial movement for Direct Democracy. Direct Democracy advocate and President of *Vote.com*, Dick Morris, (Morris, 1999 and 2000-1) argued that: '[t]he Internet offers a potential for direct democracy so profound that it may well transform not only our system of politics but also our very form of government' (Morris, 2001-2, p.1033). Morris's model foresaw greater use by citizens of the Internet that will force politicians to use the Internet (in preference to earlier communication technologies) for campaigning and so reduce the influence of big financial contributors to the campaign. One of the most obvious consequences of this would be to limit the power of those contributors and so improve democracy. In turn this will flow on to other forms of governance because: '[I]t will likely usher in a new era of more direct control of public decisions by the voters themselves and will probably further constrain the discretion of our elected officials in making decisions adverse to those sanctioned by public approval'(Morris, 2001-2, p.1046). Morris believes that citizen-initiated on-line referenda will be the means to enable citizens to increase their participation in democratic processes. In Switzerland, where this form of e-democracy is used, citizens vote on-line for three levels of government, local, cantonal and federal. Citizen-initiated referenda are encouraged as well, under controlled conditions, and a popular ballot is held if enough people request it within a set time (Braendli, 2005). Normal participation rates vary from 30 per cent to 50 per cent and, as well as trials of e-voting, the government is keeping a close watch on participation rates to determine citizens' responses to such easy access to democratic processes. Along with the rest of Australia, South Australia has compulsory voting and it is difficult to know what local participation rates would be under voluntary voting, but it is likely that participation rates would match other voluntary voting systems and be regarded as worryingly low. If voluntary participation in existing democratic models and the associated rates of voting are low, then this leads us to examine responses to Morris' direct democracy model by other scholars.

Opposition to the direct democracy model is based on an argument that the one-way communication of such media as television advertisements and face-to-face debates is still effective. Elizabeth Garrett denies the inevitability that Morris proposes:

Realistically, most citizens will never participate in online referendums. The few who are willing to spend some of their limited time in that way will do so infrequently and only answer policy questions posed at a very high level of generality. (Garrett, 2001)

Ellen Hume is equally critical of the ubiquity of television and argues that frequent political communication and sensation-driven 'news' bulletins about politicians is harming democracy. She suggests that '[a]ppearances have become more important than facts. Heaven help the policymaker who doesn't know how to surf the airwaves; officials' effectiveness these days is measured by their media performance' (Hume, 2003, p.332). Despite the advent of Broadband Internet, television is still favoured for political campaigns. For Philip Agre, the Clinton campaign of the 1990s ushered in an era of political duelling on television. As he says, '[t]he 24-hour news cycle constantly required these [privately funded research] organizations to come up with facts that served specific rhetorical purposes, such as defusing an opponent's accusation by unearthing examples of comparable actions by others.' (Agre, 2002). Information technologies help the dissemination of political information but are still only a small part of the process of informing the public about political issues. Opinions on the usefulness of the Direct Democracy model vary and it seems unlikely that there will be general acceptance of it in the near future, regardless of the ubiquity of information and communications technology. However, the use of ICT in informing and connecting people with the several levels of government, is likely to increase if politicians are seen to be listening to their electorates, even though the one-way information flow from the government to the citizen is always likely to dominate.

One significant obstacle to the spread of Direct Democracy is that political communication that depends on Internet connections further disadvantages the poor, illiterate, physically disabled and technology-resistant members of the community. There is also a clear barrier facing those citizens who live in regions where there is little or no connectivity to the Internet. This situation of social inequality, sometimes termed the digital divide, is not confined to the United States, where studies have been conducted. A paper by Korupp and Szydlik (2005) discusses the European research on this issue. Interestingly, the Australian government recently changed the terminology, so that they now discuss 'digital inclusion', rather than the 'digital divide', focusing attention on the broader aspects of 'social, cultural, economic, educational and material factors that continue to exclude people from participating in society generally and specifically the information economy' (DCITA 2006). Accordingly, when considering South Australia, it is worth examining both the infrastructure in place, as well as the practice of political information dissemination and interaction in order to determine whether there is, or should be, any greater engagement in direct democracy via the form of e-democracy.

HISTORY OF ADOPTION AND IMPLEMENTATION OF INFORMATION AND COMMUNICATION TECHNOLOGIES IN SOUTH AUSTRALIA

The adoption of ICT in South Australia has lacked the degree of co-ordination and coherence that has been seen in some of the other Australian States. What limited initiatives there have been have lacked an over-arching plan designed to deliver a consistent and predictable set of outcomes. If e-democracy is going to enable a revision of the relationship between citizen and state and contribute to better outcomes, then a broad take up of opportunities is needed. Whether initiated at community or government level, the opening of diverse avenues of interactivity can begin to break the top-down provision of services and information. In fact, if the range of projects being sponsored by the State government, its agencies and more local organisations is examined, a pattern characterised by piecemeal and limited actions emerges. As a study of these initiatives shows, there is evidence of worthwhile endeavours and it is less clear that this constitutes the beginnings of a radical reformation of the democratic spirit of South Australia. Indeed, most of the developments in ICT are based on priorities designed to secure better communications and more secure economic outcomes with the State and any e-democratic 'benefits' are almost incidental.

Under the terms of the *Networking the Nation* (NTN) project, launched in 1997, South Australia secured slightly more than $49m dollars of the total $696m available (Australian Department of Communications, Information Technology and the Arts (DCITA), 2005). This funding of telecommunications infrastructure was partially supported by the sale of Telstra and represented an opportunity for the State to support a range of local initiatives. Among other projects, the money was used to provide information technology infrastructure for CDMA mobile phone base stations and Internet access across remote regional local government areas, local personal, community and business communications, inter-community video conferencing for on-line education TAFE centres and the SA Virtual Health Network, community library access to the Internet, digital archiving for Aboriginal communities in the remote north-west (Ara Iritija, n.d.) and community access centres for computer training and Internet access (ibid).

The State's Strategic Plan

The South Australian Government released a State Strategic Plan in March 2004. This Plan clearly sets out the vital role that ICT will make to the economic growth of the State. While the fact that the State's internet usage was acknowledged to lag behind the Australian average, (Government of South Australia, 2004 p.42), the Government recognised that future industrial and employment growth will be heavily reliant upon science and technology and that 'ICT will be one of the key factors' in this (White, 2004). For its part, business has similarly recognised the role that government should play in working closely with industry to remove barriers to the taking up of ICT (O'Neill, 2005). The Government has argued that collaboration between public and private sectors is the best means to bring this about (White, 2004). This collaboration may be easier for South Australia than other parts of Australia as the relatively small population may be an asset that will facilitate 'common use infrastructure' as part of this policy (Crespigny, 2006). The State government's support of the creative industries, particularly the film, digital effects and computer games companies, recognises the dynamism of this private sector and their economic potential. This is reflected in a new target for 'Objective 4: Fostering Creativity and Innovation' in the 2007 update to the Strategic Plan, namely to '[to] double the number of feature films produced in South Australia by 2014.'(Rann 2007b)

There is no doubt that the full roll-out of government-supplied broad-band IT infrastructure, at least, is critical to the State's continued growth. To achieve this, the Government will need to play a crucial part working with education and specific IT trainers to enable the State to prosper in a competitive global environment. In the face of falling computer science enrolments, the State government can demonstrate its enthusiasm and support for an increase in the number of students enrolling in ICT courses by opening up ICT positions in government departments, encouraging ICT-related businesses and generally emphasising the benefit of information and communications technology to the future of the State.

Public Service Institutions

Not surprisingly, the State government organisations that have a strong web presence, provide information for the public and invite feedback, are, in the main, also the organisations that open their doors to the public: the cultural centres. However, they vary in their expertise with technology, from little more than internet provision of on-line information services to full virtual gallery tours. A brief survey of some of the current initiatives will illustrate the range of recent government developments. Key cultural sites include the History Trust Museums, the South Australian Museum and Art Gallery of South Australia, with several other specialised centres. These contain detailed information about bookings, permanent and temporary exhibitions, special events and some 'virtual tours' as well as links to international galleries and art museums.

Collaborative research between educational groups is managed by the South Australian Consortium for Information Technology and Telecommunications (SACITT). This comprises the three SA Universities and is supported by an Advisory Board with industry and government representatives. SACITT's brief is 'to explore and develop collaborative information technology and telecommunications opportunities for South Australia's research community and its high performance computing facility users' (SACITT, n.d.). SACITT is well positioned to oversee research initiatives, such as the South Australian Broadband Research and Education Network (SABRENet), which is implementing high speed fibre-optic broadband connections to allow very fast downloads for the defence and education network throughout metropolitan Adelaide.

The Defence Science and Technology Organisation (DSTO), situated in Edinburgh, north of Adelaide, is 'the largest defence research facility in Australia', employing upwards of 1200 staff in six Divisions (DSTO, n.d.) 'Its role is to ensure the expert, independent and innovative application of science and technology for the defence of Australia' (ibid). In 2003, DSTO and National ICT Australia Ltd (NICTA) entered into a partnership by signing the *Umbrella Collaborative Research and Commercialisation Agreement* (National ICT Australia, 2003), ensuring the protection of intellectual property for DSTO research into ICT applications in the defence field. The South Australian Government places considerable emphasis on its participation in defence industries' research and development and the South Australian-based construction of defence military systems. For its part, DSTO has positioned itself well within the State's established tertiary education institutions, so that a symbiotic relationship with all three Universities provides post-graduates attuned to the needs of the defence industry and research funding for the Universities. In late 2007, DSTO and the University of Adelaide signed a new Strategic Alliance Agreement that will expand research capabilities and encourage students to 'engage in the study of future technologies for defence and national security applications' (DSTO, 2007).

Similar research arrangements exist between the Commonwealth Scientific and Industrial Research Organisation (CSIRO) and South Australian government agencies and research organisations of the University of Adelaide and Flinders University. This has resulted in such initiatives as management strategies for the fragile lower Murray River wetlands, the CLAMMecology project. The CSIRO web site has links to all CSIRO projects and water ecology sites, digital images, related topics and on-line publications (CSIRO n.d.).

Debates over public policy are also supported at tertiary educational institutions. South Australian Policy Online (SAPO) is 'an interactive public policy website linking researchers and public policy makers in South Australia' hosted by the Australian Institute for Social Research at the University of Adelaide (http://www.sapo.org.au/about). It aims to offer an interactive forum between the academic institutions, the wider South Australian community and government. Together with notices of seminars, conferences and workshops, it posts research reports, news and opinion pieces. Papers dealing with key socio-economic, environmental, political and cultural trends in South Australia are regularly revised and are posted in a special section called *State of South Australia*.

The Outback Areas Community Development Trust (OACDT) provides both a statutory governance body and an informative web site for the 36 South Australian communities that qualify for out-of-council status because they are rural and remote, have small populations and are non-Aboriginal. The Trust provides good Internet access (accessible to more than half of the community), six video-conferencing/telecentre facilities and five further internal access points to these telecentres, but only limited mobile phone coverage (State Government of South Australia, OACDT, 2005). The trust provides residents of these remote regions with an umbrella local governance body for infrastructure, special purpose grants, a youth advisory group and community planning workshops, with frequent information updated online, through their wide Internet coverage.

For business users, the State government has established ebizSA to facilitate Internet usage by small to medium businesses (SMEs) operating in South Australia (State Government of SA, ebizSA). This site incorporates free business tools such as the 'Website Development Template', Workshops, Seminars and videos, to train business managers in best- practice for on-line communications, procurement and innovation (ibid).

Non-Government Initiatives

Other community and commercial organisations have established 'Strong Community, Healthy State' (South Australian Council of Social Services). This website is the public face of a campaign to secure the future of community services in South Australia. The campaign presents a united approach to government for funding, commentary and the provision of information to politicians and interested citizens.

Community Information Strategies Australia Inc (CISA) is a parallel initiative. It attracts government and private sponsorship for its annual (since 2004) CommunIT Conference for the exchange of information about 'grass roots' and non profit initiatives and projects. These conferences bring international and Australian experts to Adelaide as keynote speakers and encourage local not-for-profit organisations to participate by reporting on their own experiences. The Conference goals include providing a platform for the exchange of experiences and information and supporting people who are disadvantaged in their access to technology. Abstracts and papers from its annual conferences are available in video, audio and paper format and for the first time the CISA 2008 conference, 'Online and Off to the Future', will be held outside of South Australia, in Brisbane, Queensland (CISA 2008) The CISA website also has links to database searching for community services, ICT issues, assistance for community NGOs and event information. In 2006, CISA conducted an online survey of the non profit sector involved in health and community, advocacy, sport and recreation, environment, arts, trade and professional associations and others, with the aim being to discover the best fit of ICT to small and large non profit organizations. The resulting 'Strategic ICT Planning for Nonprofits' report led to a series of workshops to develop resources for ICT Nonprofit organisations freely available at the CISA website (CISA 2008).

In May 2003, the IT Council for South Australia participated in the national Innovation Festival at Adelaide's Festival Centre. The premiering of the *Solution City Adelaide Australia* to enable commercial organisations using ICT to collaborate to pursue development and growth for economic advantage gives an indication of priorities that lie well ahead on e-democracy (O'Neill, 2005). The web site offers membership information, seminars and forums, case studies and investment information and invites business enquiries, as well as 'selling' the State's advantages for lifestyle and accessibility to potential markets. Now known as the 'ICT Council of SA', the body is pursuing the latter goal to 'allow SA Companies to "hit the ground running" in the global export rush to China' (Bawden 2007).

Unions and Online Activism[1]

More direct political initiatives – and ones that are more consistent with e-democratic initiatives elsewhere – can be found in the web pages of trade union branches in South Australia. These give links to further information and to national and international sites, such as LaborNET and Social Change Online. Labour Start, an international activism site, encourages and enables local Union members to be involved in on-line campaigning about global issues. For unions, computerisation and member lists saves money and time spent on mail-outs and creates a cyber community that can be rapidly activated by e-mail to engage in direct political activity and to 'urge boycotts of the products and services of targeted employers, and to do this faster and with far wider coverage than was possible relying on old-fashioned mailings offering "Do Not Buy" lists' (Shostak, 2001). Importantly, as Arthur Shostak, writing on the role of ICT in involving unions in global labour issues, declares, 'Caucuses of like-minded members link together in e-mail list serves or through a shared Web site. Solidarity is built, and the cause of union democracy can receive a strong boost' (ibid).

While the Internet has brought global issues into our homes nearly as well as television has, and with less media selectivity, Capling and Nossal (2000) argue that International 'causes' do not fare so well in Australia. In their investigation of Australian citizens' involvement in recent anti-globalisation movements, they found that, despite the speed and low cost of Internet communication allowing Australians to be included in protests online and local street action, they still considered physical distance from the centres of action an inhibitor to real action. However, when rapid action was required, Australians sent online petitions to protest the Human Rights issue of a woman being sentenced to death by stoning (Thorp, 2004).

There are important implications in this research for regional State governments in Australia that rely on overcoming the 'digital divide' through improving Internet infrastructure and connectivity alone to overcome social exclusion.

Parliamentary Web Sites

The State Parliament of South Australia has a minimal web presence. Hansard is available, there are brief biographical notes about Members of the Parliament and some papers and submissions can be seen on-line – but the web is not utilised to its full capacity. There is no web broadcasting of the proceedings on the Parliament as is the case in a number of other Australian legislatures, though this is currently under consideration. The provision of IT facilities for members is similarly rudimentary and access to modern ICT by the Parliament is limited. For example, members can access the web from laptops in the chambers but neither of the Parliamentary chambers are equipped with fitted data projectors. Individual members of Parliament are free to create their own web sites (though fewer than 10 per cent of the members have sites linked to the official Parliament website). Those that do show individuality and innovation above the level achieved by the official Parliamentary and Party sites. Mark Parnell, MLC has the most comprehensive site and includes podcasts of media contributions and short commentaries on current issues (Parnell, 2008). Liz Penfold, MP has indexed her speeches and includes reports and submissions (Penfold, 2008), Shadow Minister for Science and Information Economy, Duncan McFetridge, MP has a site with useful links to community organisations, a 'Scam Watch', position papers and even a weblog (McFetridge, 2008), and Michelle Lensink, MLC, lists her interests and has a newsletter called, 'Getting on with the Job' (Lensink, 2008). While the 2007 federal election prompted then Prime Minister John Howard to post videos making policy statements on YouTube and both he and then Opposition leader, Kevin Rudd, had social networking website, MySpace, pages, only two of South Australia's eleven federal Members of Parliament used these forms of web-based media (Novak, 2007, p.21). One MP, Christopher Pyne, who admitted having positive public reaction to the videos he posted on YouTube, stated 'When you're an MP you've got to use every option that's available to let people know what you're doing and who you are...YouTube is the latest means to do that... [but] I don't think it's the be all and end all of campaigning' (ibid). State Parliamentarians are not following this example.

All major political parties have a web presence, but the quality of each web site, its relationship to present constituency concerns, the frequency of updates and links to individual elected representative's Home Page, vary widely. Most have a tendency to use the site as an 'information storehouse' as described by Rachel Gibson and Stephen Ward (2002), for generalised party-related information and news items, with hotlinks, transcripts of speeches and frequently asked questions. Most of the State branches of the major political parties use their web sites in a fairly unsophisticated manner. Few have much more than policy statements, links to Members of Parliament, facilities for email exchanges with party activists, copies of press releases and speeches.

Local Government Web Sites

The South Australian Local Government Association (SALGA) developed a software package for Web-based service delivery by regional local government councils (SALGA, 2004). Local Government sites that fit into the 'one-stop-shop' category, with application forms, information sheets and permits available to download, usually in pdf format, sometimes have the capacity for feedback, as this SALGA software does. Others, such as the City of Holdfast Bay's 'State of the Environment Community Survey' (City of Holdfast, 2006) and the Adelaide City Council's Forum weblogs (Adelaide City Council, 2006), encourage greater community engagement. Many also allow residents to make online payments. The Adelaide City Council has also commenced wireless web browsing in the Central Business District (CBD), in partnership with Adelaide-based national broadband Internet Provider, Internode (https://hotspot.internode.on.net/). Free wireless web access, termed 'CityLan Wireless Hotspots', is currently available in more than 90 businesses and public buildings in the CBD and there are plans to increase the access (Mayor, Michael Harbison in Edwards, 2006, p. 96).

Current Status of ICT Initiatives

The history of more direct government engagement with ICT and related technologies is limited. In the late 1990s the then South Australian Liberal Government proposed to dedicate two seats in the Legislative Council (the State upper house) to 'virtual members'. These seats were to be voted for by ex-patriot South Australians. It was felt that the State had lost large numbers of talented citizens who had been drawn to larger and more vibrant markets in Europe and North America, but that communication technology had advanced to the point where an enduring connection with South Australia could be sustained. It was hoped that South Australia might benefit in the short-term from a continuing association and from their perspective that a voting connection might make their eventual return home more attractive (SA Government, 2002 and McEachern, 2000). The idea received some attention – but was not pursued.

Perhaps one way that citizens will change the form of interaction with the State is in connection with one of the most basic of democratic activities: voting. The South Australian State Electoral Office (SEO) 'closely monitors world wide developments' in electronic voting and has noted the concerns expressed in the literature about identity verification, ballot secrecy, security, and equity and access for all eligible voters (State Electoral Office SA, 2003, p.41). Part of the process of investigating the feasibility for such an electronic innovation involves understanding both the capability of the infrastructure to support electronic engagement *per se*, whether or not voting is conducted on-line, and the willingness of prospective e-voters to accept using computers to replace paper voting. Electronic voting, in a Voting Centre, was trialled for people with sight impairment and blindness in the 2007 federal election and for the Defence Forces stationed overseas, but it is unlikely to be adopted in South Australia in the foreseeable future. The widespread use of electronic voting in South Australia will depend upon the spread of appropriate technology. There is a very slow rollout of Broadband in regions outside of the metropolitan area and the onus is now on the rural communities themselves to demonstrate to a potential Internet Provider that it is worth the expense and commitment to provide the infrastructure. Few remote communities are able to make this case, in a state where roughly 10% of the population live outside the greater Adelaide region and its near environs. These remote communities are located in pockets of population in rural towns and small cities or scattered in low-density districts. In the Far North-West, the Pitjantjatjara and Maralinga-Tjaruta Aboriginal lands have a denser population of Aboriginal people than any other region in the State. Helen Coonan (former Commonwealth Minister for Communications, Information Technology and the Arts) announced the federally funded *Backing Indigenous Ability* program, a $36.6 million component of the $3.1billion *Connect Australia* program launched in 2005. ICT infrastructure for local governance as well as health and economic programs, with the emphasis on community ownership and partnership with businesses, are expected to be among the projects to be funded. With sound and constructive submissions from indigenous communities, South Australia's Aboriginal communities in remote areas are expected to benefit both socially and economically from such initiatives. Benefits from the extension of infrastructure and the utilisation of ICT in these regions are likely to flow on to neighbouring non-indigenous communities.

The State government is advancing a few projects on electronic inclusion in rural and remote regions. The principal focus of these is not directly connected to e-democracy, but the infrastructure required will mean that it could easily be used for this purpose. The most advanced programs are being introduced in the Education sector and the Technology School of the Future managed projects specifically designed for e-learning for all sectors of the education community. The programs targeted increasing teacher's skills and extending the skills of students in Information Technology and robotics. The Jason Expedition project, incorporating the skills of partner NASA, introduced visiting classes to an exciting educational experience, but in late 2006 the program was replaced by video conferencing for teacher education and on-line programs for students (Kleinig, 2006)

The Digital Bridge Unit (DBU) is a State government ICT initiative through the Information Economy Directorate, of the Department of Further Education Employment, Science and Technology (DFEEST). The unit's role is to write policies for further government action to address the digital divide, establishing Online Access Centres (OACs) that supplement public access to ICT connectivity in local libraries and give remotely located citizens access to government services online (DBU, 2007a). The small team in the DBU has identified that service quality needs to be improved in community sectors such as: employment, indigenous communities, people living with a disability and rural and remote communities. These sectors are the most likely to benefit from programs to improve their ICT-based social inclusion, e-governance in its simplest sense.

The remote community sector, in particular, is targeted by the DBU's *Outback Connect* project that is funded by several Federal and State government departments to facilitate and support ICT training and develop community capacity in the most remote areas of South Australia, covering about eighty communities and numerous homesteads. Participants have access to free computer training and technical support on-line in a 'virtual classroom' and on-line discussion groups. Using 'headsets and microphones, and occasionally webcams, ... participants can interact, ask questions, share applications, enter breakout rooms, make entries on a class whiteboard, even share a joke or applaud (but silently)' (Golder, Cleary and Johnston, 2006). Conferencing software is used for online help, but face- to- face assistance is available at ten centres in the region. Conferencing software is also used for virtual meetings of outback organisations normally inhibited from face-to-face meetings by extreme distances, and workshops to enable remote small business owners to build their skills (Digital Bridge Unit, 'An Award winning project, Outback Connect in action...' 2007b). The accessibility of this innovative program is illustrated by its use by a group of 'Aboriginal footballers with limited computer experience [who] prepare[d] a photo story to showcase their preparation for a football match in Adelaide.' (Digital Bridge Unit, 2007b). However, this project's federal funding finished in September 2007 and its uncertain future depends on short-term funding (Science and Technology Innovation, 2007). The DBU's partnership with the Office of Disability and Client Services (ODACS) targeted the lack of E-Accessibility of South Australian Government Department web sites for the latter's client group and DBU's Project Officer, Alison Kershaw, highlights one of the possible reasons for this deficiency when she states, 'As there is no one department given with overall responsibility for the management of South Australian websites it was difficult to gain a thorough understanding of why minimum international standards [for Web accessibility] were not being met.' (Kershaw, 2007, p 4). The partners developed four strategies to improve South Australian government web site accessibility , including sponsoring online E-Accessibility Forums and an online Community of Practice for Web designers (ibid p.7).

A further innovation recognising the role of new digital technologies for engaging Aboriginal youth in all regions is the 'David Unaipon Innovation Awards', sponsored by the South Australian government, in conjunction with the DBU, as part of the DFEEST Reconciliation Project for indigenous people. Since its inception in 2006, the format is 'Digital Storytelling', a competition for groups of young indigenous people to 'submit a digital story between 2 and 3 minutes long using either MS Photostory or IMovie telling any story.'(State Government of SA, 2006).

Engagement with the whole of the State is seen as one of the key objectives of the State Strategic

Plan. Under the direction of the *Community Connection* unit within the Department of Premier and Cabinet, the Government has conducted a biennial review of the Plan after a series of consultations. These included face-to-face meetings as well as 'Virtual Town Hall' meetings conducted via an existing government website, remodelled to provide a forum to receive feedback and submissions from the public on the Plan's objectives (State Government of SA, 2004). The software:

allows real-time interaction, using audio, video, collaborative spaces (electronic whiteboard etc), real-time text chat, and shared Powerpoint presentations, creating a shared online collaborative space accessed over a standard internet connection. It is also extremely intuitive and simple to use for beginners. (personal communication, 2006)

This platform is robust, works well as an audio system with dial-up connections (although Broadband connectivity allows video links) and has been tested with School of the Air (SOTA) in South Australia's remote regions for four years. Its utilisation for community consultations demonstrates the possibilities for further engagement with people in remote areas and the software's versatility is verified by virtual classroom training in agricultural business for farmers and community training in governance (Science, Technology and Innovation, 2007).

This level of engagement can be seen to be building upon initiatives by earlier governments. In 2001 the then Liberal State Government commissioned an 'Information Economy Plan' that identified 21 goals that had a 'connected society' as its core aim. Government was seen in this plan to have a vital role as the agency that brought educational institutions, business and community groups together to 'build on and reinvigorate existing State assets' and to 'create the climate for new asset creation in the Information Economy' (State Government of SA, 2002). The government also appointed an Information Economy Minister, reflecting the importance of IT as a key force in economic development and negotiated whole-of-government deals with large external suppliers of services.

Not all of these developments were successful. The 'Information Economy Plan' had little long-term impact and the nature of the economic deal concluded when some of the multinational ICT corporations contributed to the political damage suffered by the Liberal Government after inquires into the arrangements negotiated with Motorola helped speed the resignation of John Olsen as Premier (Macintyre, 2005). In the aftermath of this experience, and after seeing significant players step back from their South Australian presence, governments have been more cautious and the present Labor Government has been more restrained in its reliance upon 'quick-fix' IT commitments (King, 2006).

Rather, the current Government's priorities indicate that preference is no longer given to supporting specific partnerships but to the development of industry sectors. This is further evidence of strategic support for economic development rather than the provision of infrastructure with an eye to its application to e-democratic initiatives. Certainly, it is consistent with the government's strategy to move the dependence of the South Australian economy away from the old heavy manufacturing base to greater dependency upon new technology capacity. An example of this can be seen in the considerable resources devoted to support for high level IT research within the defence industry. The Government has recognised 'that the defence industry is a key sector of the State's economy' and has aimed to double the 'defence industry's contribution to the State's economy from $1bn to $2bn over the next decade, while increasing the number of jobs from 16,000 to 28,000' (*Advertiser*, 26 November 2005). Winning the contract to build the air warfare destroyers in May 2005 was described by the Premier, Mike Rann as 'a monumental day for industry, for business, for jobs for the future, for jobs not only down there on the site but high-tech jobs, electronics jobs, jobs for graduates, jobs for apprentices, this is a monumental day in the history of this State' (ABC Radio, 31 May 2005). Whether such initiatives will be enough to shift the economic focus of the State away from the old 'rust-bucket' reputation to one based on high technology that will be enough to insulate the economy in coming years is not yet clear. Certainly, the government sought to stress the employment opportunities found in the defence industries in the aftermath of the closure of the Adelaide based Mitsubishi car plant in 2008 (ABC Radio, 6 February 2008). Moreover, whether the government's priorities will have an impact beyond economic development and begin to alter the nature of the relationship between the state and the citizen (which after all, is what lies at the heart of e-democracy), is even less obvious.

CONCLUSION

In South Australia it appears that the movement towards innovative e-inclusion is driven from the bottom up – from Councils; the arts industries, particularly film; and the education sectors, in the main. The Councils and a few individual politicians are cautiously venturing into e-democracy and the State government supports some of the initiatives evolving because of the roll-out of Broadband connectivity. However, as yet it has not shown a strong leadership role. Robert Champion de Crespigny, then Chairman of the State Economic Development Board cautioned against making excuses for this lag, when he said:

Over the next five to 20 years we must continue to develop and diversify other key industries and services such as information technology and electronics.... What the government can do is offer common-use infrastructure, education, training and moral support. (Crespigny, 2006)

The South Australian Government's innovative use of 'Virtual Community' consultations, as described above, and a few private companies carrying out their own ICT initiatives, with or without government assistance, offer some insight into future directions for on-line engagement with the public. The Australian Bureau of Statistics reported in 2002-03 that, 'ICT accounted for $36.2 billion or 4.6 per cent of GDP, 13.8% of total investment by Government and industry and made a greater contribution to the economy than the agriculture, forestry and fishing, defence and education industries' (Coonan, 2006a). Australian research commissioned by DCITA and released as two papers (Coonan, 2006b), emphasised the critical role played by ICT in the economy. As Senator Helen Coonan stated: 'Understanding the effective use of ICT is adding value and growing productivity, [and] is critical to the ongoing success of a range of industry sectors' (ibid). As a strong economy is also critical to public confidence in the government, we can make a case for improving the government's ICT practice, especially with e-governance. The government's ICT practice is a critical business which requires good business practice. The State government has no clear agenda for managing its services and information portals, probably because there is 'no one department given with overall responsibility for the management of [its] websites' (Kershaw 2007, p4). Kershaw also found that two 'authoritative websites [had] conflicting information, which in turn means that there is no standard Content Management System, design templates, shared resources or even an 'official' network of Government web workers. The lack of a central coordinating body makes it more difficult for any policy or standards to be consistently and completely implemented, leaving the task to individual officers who are required to be aware of and responsible for this implementation (Kershaw, 2007, p.7)

It is clear that the technological developments found in ICT will continue to change the way that governments respond to and interact with their citizens. These changes, if neglected or used in a negative way, may well act to weaken the relationship between citizen and the state. On the other hand, if they are embraced and used creatively they could do much to build the integrity of the State's democratic institutions. In South Australia there are signs that some tentative initiatives hold great promise, but there appears to be little in the way of overall coordination of policy. The next few years will be telling. The task of building and extending the e-democratic infrastructure will be time consuming, costly and demanding, but it is a task that the government will not be able to ignore.

REFERENCES

Adelaide City Council (2006). URL: http://www.adelaidecitycouncil.com/

Advertiser, 26 November 2005

Agre, Philip (2002). Real-Time Politics: The Internet and the Political Process. *Information Society* 18 (5), 2002, pages 311-331.

Ara Irititja (n.d.) Archival Online Project- Stage 2. Consulted at URL: http:// www.irititja.com/ on 25/01/2008

Australian Broadcasting Commission (2005), ABC Radio, 31 May.

Australian Broadcasting Commission (2008), ABC Radio, 6 February.

Australian Department of Communications and the Arts (DCITA) (2005). Networking the Nation Program Project Funding List – South Australia: As at June 2005.

Bawden, Tania (2007). Exports in the digital era. Adelaide Now. *Advertiser,* 11 October 2007.

Capling, Ann and Nossal, Kim Richard (2000). *Death of Distance or Tyranny of Distance? The Internet, Deterritorialisation and the Anti-Globalisation Movement in Australia.* Paper presented at the XVII Triennial World Congress of the International Political Science Association, Quebec City, 1 August 2000. Consulted at URL: http://rspas.anu.edu.au/ir/pubs/ir-cat.php#00/3 on 25/01/2008

City of Holdfast Bay (n.d.) *State of the Environment Community Survey.* Consulted at URL: http://www.holdfast.sa.gov.au/surveys_forms.htm on 25/01/08

Coonan, the Honorable Helen (2006a). *ICT Driving Economic Growth.* DCITA, Media Release 7 March 2006. Consulted at URL: http://www.minister.dcita.gov.au on 8/03/2006

Coonan, the Honorable Helen (2006b) *Estimating Aggregate Productivity Growth for Australia: The Role of Information and Communications Technology* and *ICT and Australian productivity: methodologies and measurement* [report], DCITA. Consulted at URL: http://www.minister.dcita.gov.au on 25/01/2008

Coonan, the Honorable Helen (2006c). *$36.6 million for Backing Indigenous Ability.* DCITA. Consultcd at URL: http://www.minister.dcita.gov.au on 25/01/2008

*Commonwealth Scientific and Industrial Research Organisation (CSIROnd).*Consulted at URL: http://www.csiro.au/csiro/content/standard/ps25q,,.html on 25/02/2008.

Community Information Strategies Australia Inc (CISA). URL: http://www.cisa.asn.au

CISA. CommunITConference. URL: http://www.connectingup.org

CISA (2008). *Nonprofit ICT Strategy Resources.* URL: http://www.communit.info/index.php/

Crespigny, Robert Champion de (2006). Agility to prosper. *SA 2025 – My Vision for South Australia, Sunday Mail,* Feb. 12, 2006

Defence Science and Technology Organisation (DSTO). URL: http://www.defence_sa.com/html/infrastructure/dsto.htm

Defence Science and Technology Organisation (DSTO) (2007). *Adelaide Research Collaboration To Benefit Defence*. News Item, 28 November, 2007. Consulted at URL: http://www.dsto.defence.gov.au/news/5266/?print=true on 29/01/2008

Department of Communications, Information Technology and the Arts (DCITA) (2006). *Digital Inclusion*. Consulted at URL: http://www.dcita.gov.au/ie/community_co...social_impacts_of_ict/digital_inclusion

Department of Communications, Information Technology and the Arts (DCITA) (n.d.). *Networking the Nation: An Australian Government Initiative*. Consulted at URL: http://archive.dcita.gov.au/2006/06/networking_the_nation on 25/01/2008

Digital Bridge Unit (2007a). *Review of Online Access Centres in Regional South Australia*. Information Economy Directorate, Government of South Australia. Consulted at URL: http://www.innovation.sa.gov.au/_data/assets/pdf_file/0006/7539/0706_OAC_Final_Report.pdf on 27/01/2008

Digital Bridge Unit (2007b). *An Award winning project, Outback Connect in action*. Consulted at URL: http://www.innovation.sa.gov.au/ict/dbu/outbackconnect/whats_new on 25/01/2008

Edwards, Grant (2006). Wireless ties up the city, Computers and Technology, p.96. *Advertiser*, 2/09/06

Electronic News, 4 May 2005.

Garrett, Elizabeth. (2001). Political Intermediaries and the Internet Revolution in Symposium, Internet Voting and Democracy, held at Loyola Law School in October, 2000. *Loyola of Los Angeles Law Review*, 34 (3). Consulted at http://llr.lls.edu/volumes/v34-issues3/garrett.pdf on 25/01/2008

Gibson, Rachel and Stephen Ward (2002), Virtual Campaigning: Australian Parties and the Impact of the Internet, *Australian Journal of Political Science*, vol. 37, No.1, pp. 99-129.

Golder, Wendy, Cleary, Jenny and Johnston, Ann (2006). *Outback Connect: Bridging the digital divide*. Refereed paper consulted at URL: http://www.regional.org.au/au/apen/2006/refereed/1/3059_clearyglover.htm?print=1 on 25/01/08

Green, P.(2004). *Electronic voting and counting for elections for the Australian Capital Territory*. Paper presented at the International Conference on E-voting and Electronic Democracy: Present and the Future. March 17-18, Seoul. Consulted at URL: http://www.hallym.ac.kr/~icat/e-voting2005/81ppt/Phil%20Green.doc on 1/10/2005.

History Trust of South Australia. URL: http://www.history.sa.gov.au/

Howell, P (1986). The South Australia Act, 1834. in Jaensch, Dean (ed.) *The Flinders History of South Australia*, 1986, Wakefield, pp. 26-51 and URL: http://www.foundingdocs.gov.au/item.asp?dID=1

Hume, Ellen (2003). Resource Journalism: A Model for New Media. In Jenkins, Henry and Thorburn, David (eds.) *Democracy and new media*, Cambridge, Ma. MIT Press.

Information Technology Council of South Australia. *Solution City Adelaide*. URL: http://www.solutioncity.com.au/

Internode (2008). *Wireless Hotspots*. Consulted at URL: https://hotspot.internode.on.net/coverage/ on 24/02/2008

Kershaw, Alison (2007). *Playing Catch Up with the Digital Divide*. Paper presented at the 13th Australasian World Wide Web Conference (AUSWEB 2007), held at Coffs harbour, New South Wales, 30 June-4 July, 2007. Consulted at URL:

http://ausweb.scu.edu.au/aw07/papers/refereed/kershaw/paper.html on 29 /01/2008

King, Agnes (2006). Yes, Minister, IT needs you. *The Age*, 28 March 2006.

Kleinig, Xanthe (2006). Principals are furious the Technology School of the Future has been scrapped. *Advertiser,* reported at *Adelaide Now.* Consulted at URL: http://www.news.com.au/adelaidenow/story/0,22606,20773414-5006353,00.html on 2/02/2008

Knowlton, Brian (2006). U.S. voters overseas get a computerized helper. *International Herald Tribune*, 3/02/2006. Consulted at URL: http://www.iht.com/articles/2006/02/03news/vote.php

Korupp, Sylvia and Szydlik, Marc (2005). Causes and Trends of the Digital Divide. *European Sociological Review, 21(4)*, pp.409-422.

Labour Start. URL: http://www.labourstart.org/

Lensink, Michelle, MP. URL: http://www.michellelensink.com

Macintyre, Clement (2005). Politics. In Spoehr, John (ed.), *The State of South Australia*, Wakefield, 2005

McEachern, D. (2000). World's First Virtual Electorate. *Legislative Studies*, vol. 15, no. 1, Spring 2000, pp. 59-65

McFetridge, Duncan, MP. URL: http://www.duncanmcfetridge.com

Morris, Dick (1999). *VOTE.COM.* Los Angeles, Renaissance Books

Morris, Dick (2000-1). Direct Democracy and the Internet in Symposium: Internet Voting and Democracy, held at Loyola Law School in October, 2000, and published in *Loyola Law Review*, Vol. 34:3 Consulted at URL:http://llr.lls.edu/volumes/v.34-issue3/morris.pdf on25/01/2008

National ICT Australia Ltd (NICTA). Background: The Defence Science and Technology Organisation (2003) in Joint Media Release, *DSTO and NICTA sign agreement on ICT commercialisation,* Tuesday 9 December 2003. Consulted at URL: http://nicta.com.au/_data/assets/pdf-file/0004/NICTA_DSTO_agreement.pdf on 25/01/2008

Nimmo, Dan and Sanders, Keith R (eds.), (1981). *Handbook of Political Communication,* Beverly Hills, California. Sage Publications

Novak, Lauren (2007). Missing You…as MPs let young slip through Net. *Sunday Mail,* 12 August 2007

O'Neil, Michael (2005). Information reported at the *ICT Breakfast Forum for Solutioncity Adelaide Australia* members, 19 October 2005. Consulted at URL: http://www.solutioncity.com.au/ on 25/01/08

Outback Areas Community Development Trust (OACDT). URL: http://www.oacdt.sa.gov.au/

Pacific Bell (2002), *Pacific Bell/UCLA Initiative for 21st Century Literacies at the UCLA Graduate School of Education and Information Studies Re-evaluating the Bridge! An expanded Framework for Crossing the Digital Divide through Connectivity, Capability and Content, a Public Policy Roundtable*'. Los Angeles

Parnell, Mark, MLC. URL: http://www.markparnell.org.au/

Penfold, Liz, MP. URL: http://www.lizpenfold.com/

Rann, Premier Mike (2007a). *Update.* News Release, 24 January 2007, Government of South Australian. Consulted at URL: http://www.saplan.org.au/ on 24/01/2008

Rann, Premier Mike (2007b). *Update.* News Release, 24 January 2007, Government of South Australian. Consulted at URL: http://www.saplan.org.au/images/TargetFactSheets/t4.2_target%20%fact%20sheet.doc on 23/02/2008

Science, Technology and Innovation (2007a). *Information Economy Directorate Highlights, STI, October 17 2007.* Consulted at URL: http://www.innovation.sa.gov.ay/ie/recent_highlights on 20/02/2008

Science, Technology and Innovation (2007b). Centra Pilot. *STI-What's New,* STI, October 17 2007. Consulted at URL: http://www.innovation.sa.gov.au/ict/dbu/whats_new on 29/01/2008

Shostak, Arthur B. (2001), Today's Unions as Tomorrow's CyberUnions: Labor's Newest Hope. *Journal of Labor Studies*, April,2001. Consulted at URL: http://www.cyberunions.net/articles/article_shostak_1.htm on 25/01/2008

South Australian Consortium for Information Technology and Telecommunications (SACITT). URL: http://www.sacitt.asn.au

South Australian Council of Social Services (SACOSS). *Strong Community, Healthy State*, (n.d.). URL: http://www.sacoss.org.au/strong-community/

South Australian Local Government Association (SALGA), (2004). *Building your Web Site.* Cited in O'Toole, Kevin, 'E-Governance in Australian Local Government: Spinning a Web Around Community?' (2007).Special Issue: E-Democracy in Australia: Practice and Innovation, *International Journal of Electronic Government Research*, Vol.3, No.4, October-December 2007. IGI Publishing, New York.

South Australian Policy Online (SAPO). *About South Australian Policy Online.* Consulted at URL: http://www.sapo.org.au/about/ on 25/01/2008

State Electoral Office, South Australia, (2003). *SEO South Australia, Annual Report 2002-2003.*

State Government of South Australia, Science and Technology Innovation branch, South Australian Broadband Research and Education Network (SABRENet) (2005), *Media Release.* Adelaide, November 17, 2005. Consulted at URL: http://sabrenet.edu.au/ on 25/01/2008.

State Government of South Australia (2004), 'Creating Opportunity: Moving Forward Together'. *South Australian Strategic Plan.* Consulted at URL: http://www.saplan.org.au/images/sa_strategic_plan_volume1a.pdf on 25/01/2008.

State Government of South Australia (n.d.). *ebizSA.* URL: http://www.innovation.sa.gov.au/ie/ebizsa/about_ebizsa consulted on 25/01/2008.

State Government of South Australia (n.d.). *The Virtual Electorate: Giving a voice to SA's 'Global Tribe'.* Consulted at URL: http://www.ie2002sa.gov.au/plan/default.html on 25/01/2008.

State Government of South Australia, Department of Further Education, Employment, Science and Technology (DFEEST), Science, Technology and Innovation Directorate (STI). *Digital Bridge Unit.* URL: http://www.innovation.sa.gov.au/ict/dbu

State Government of South Australia (2002). *Information Economy Policy Office.* URL: http://www.aoq.asn.au/papers/ie2002.pdf

State Government of South Australia (2004). *Strategic Plan, Virtual Town Hall.* URL: http://www.stateplan.sa.gov.au

State Government of South Australia(2006). *David Unaipon Innovation Award.* Consulted at URL: http://www.innovation.sa.gov.au/ict/dbu/david_unaipon/home on 25/01/2008

State Government of South Australia (2006), DFEEST, STI, Digital Bridge Unit. *Outback Connect.* URL: http://www.innovation.sa.gov.au/ie/dbu/outbackconnect

State Parliament of South Australia. URL: http://www.parliament.sa.gov.au

Sumner, Chris, (2003). Constitutional and Parliamentary Reform for South Australia. In Macintyre, Clement and Williams, John (eds.), *Peace, Order and Good Government*, Wakefield Press.

Thorp, Dian (2006). e-Democracy. *IT Alive, The Australian,* May 4 2004.

White, Trish, (2004). The State of ICT in South Australia: Collaborating To Work Fast and Smart. *Information Age,* 17/06/2004. Consulted at URL: http://www.infoage.idg.com.au/index.php on 25/01/2008.

World Summit on the Information Society (2003-5). *Geneva-Tunis, FAQs.* Consulted at http://www.itu.int/wsis/basic/faqs.asp on 25/01/2008.

ENDNOTE

1 The authors are indebted for information in this section generously given by Patrick Wright, Labour Research Director AISR, centre for Labour Research, University of Adelaide.

Chapter XIII
Users' Acceptance of E-Government: A Study of Indian Central Excise

G. P. Sahu
Indian Institute of Technology Delhi, India

M. P. Gupta
Indian Institute of Technology Delhi, India

ABSTRACT

The study seeks to highlight the key variables affecting usage of e-government by internal users of Indian Central Excise. An e-government acceptance model is developed and empirically tested using the 163 usable questionnaire responses from internal users of the Indian Central Excise. A priority of the variables is set by calculating the "total effect" of each variable on "intention to use e-government." Further, the "total effect" is compared with "ratio of acceptance" and clear recommendations for the Central Excise are generated for increasing the usage of e-government among it users. The model developed here can be applied in other similar e-government projects to test the users' intention to accept the system.

INTRODUCTION

Information technologies (IT), comprising of the Internet, e-mail, database, word processing applications, and so forth, have changed the way people work and live, the governments being no exceptions. IT initiatives in government services known as electronic government, or e-government, are changing the way the government works and interacts with citizens, businessmen, its employees, and other governments. E-government is supposed to provide information, services, or products through electronic means, by and from government agencies, at any given moment and place, offering an extra value for all participating players (Gupta, Kumar, & Bhattacharya, 2004). IT has the potential to transform government structures and to improve the quality of

Copyright © 2009, IGI Global, distributing in print or electronic forms without written permission of IGI Global is prohibited.

government services. Technology provides two main opportunities for government: increased operational efficiency by reducing costs and increasing productivity, and the better quality of services provided by government agencies (Garcia & Pardo, 2005).

Being the largest democracy and having one of the largest government set-ups in the world, India offers a vast potential for effective implementation of e-government (Gupta et al., 2004). The number of Internet users in India is constantly on the rise, with the focus shifting on providing more and more government services electronically. The Indian central government and state governments have problems such as delay in processes, uncertainty, lack of transparency, corruption, and so on, in their various processes. In many successful implementations of e-government, the respective governments or government departments are able to get rid of such problems to a great extent (www.mit.gov.in). The e-government market grew by 18% in 2003-2004 and is the highest growing vertical in the domestic IT market (NASSCOM, 2005). In the tenth five-year plan (2002-2007) of India, government has allocated US$4.92 billion to spend on the e-government implementation (www.mit.gov.in).

However, the failure rate of e-government project implementation is up to 85% in developing countries, which is quite high (Heeks, 2003). E-government acceptance by the end users depends on various factors, which are needed to be studied at the pilot stage of implementation and addressed while the project in on rollout. Therefore, acceptance or intention to use e-government of end users should be studied carefully to identify the various factors affecting the acceptance decision of an individual. This will help in reviewing and fine tuning the projects to achieve higher acceptability.

To identify the factors affecting e-government acceptance and also to develop a model for acceptance, literature was surveyed in the area of e-government acceptance and technology acceptance. The literature survey offered the technology acceptance model (TAM) as a proven tool. Researchers within the information systems (IS) community in the past have sought to conceptualize, empirically validate, and also extend TAM to explain IS adoption in a variety of contexts. The important constructs of TAM are "perceived ease of use," "perceived usefulness," and "attitude towards using technology" (Davis, Bagozzi, & Warshaw, 1989). Another model on the same line of TAM is "Unified Theory of Acceptance and Usage of Technology (UTAUT)" (Venkatesh, Morris, Davis, & Davis, 2003); this model is considered to be a robust model in literature. However, this model does not deal with issues related to system security and strength of control, which are critical in e-government domain. This study includes these as added variables in its research model. The motivation for this study stemmed from a desire to lay down such a model, which highlights the factors that lead to acceptance or rejection of information technology by government employees.

Low system acceptance by the end users is one of the major hurdles to the proliferation of e-government projects. Few studies in the e-government acceptance highlights that usage level of an e-government would depend on a number of criteria viz. intention to use, attitude toward using, effort expectancy, performance expectancy, and so forth. In India there is probably no evidence of such research, however there are some studies carried out in other countries. In a study, Chang, Li, Hung, and Hwang (2005) used TAM in the Taiwan government's Internet tax-filers' system to explain the taxpayers' acceptance of the system. Other studies available on the tax system of Taiwan are by Wang (2003) and Fu, Chao, and Farn (2004). Tahinakis, Mylonakis, and Protogeros (2006) studied the Hellenic Taxation System in Greece applying TAM and concluded that increased participation of taxpayers through an electronic system would create a socioeconomic

Table 1. Literature on e-government acceptance using TAM

Study	Objective	Use Context	Conclusion
Wang, 2003	To identify the factors affecting the adoption of electronic tax-filing systems using the technology acceptance model (TAM) as a theoretical framework	The Taiwanese Government Tax Agency	The findings of this study provide important implications for developing effective electronic government services in general and effective electronic tax-filing systems in particular.
Tahinakis et al., 2006	The influence of the e-government to the application of modern information systems that support direct and indirect taxation is examined	Hellenic taxation system, Greece	The function of electronic tax processes (TAXISnet) and the increased participation of taxpayers will create a socioeconomic environment, which was predicted to satisfy both the tax administration and the taxpayers.
Fu et al., 2004	To develop an understanding of the factors that influence citizens' adoption of electronic tax-filing services	Taiwan's electronic tax payment system.	Taxpayers who adopted the manual tax-filing method perceived lowest overall satisfaction level. Internet filing seemed to perform best in most of the sub dimensions of satisfaction and was perceived as the most efficient.
Chang et al., 2005	To examine taxpayers' acceptance of the Internet tax-filing system using TAM	Users Internet tax filing system	TAM proved to be a valid model to explain the taxpayers' acceptance of the Internet tax-filers' system. Meanwhile, perceived usefulness has created more impact than perceived ease of use on taxpayers' intention to use the system.
Hung, Chang, & Yu, 2006	To identify the factors that determine the publics' acceptance of e-government services	Online tax filing and payment system in Taiwan	Theory of planed behaviour with some modifications is proved to be a valid model explaining 72% variations in behaviour intention to use the system.

environment. A brief of these studies is presented in Table 1.

It was chosen to study e-governance applications in the Central Excise of India which is a part of Department of Revenue under the Ministry of Finance and responsible for collection of indirect taxes like excise levies and service tax. The government of India has identified it as one of the mission-mode e-government projects. Since a large section of the government's revenue collections comes through excise, reforms in this department could heavily benefit the Indian government and its citizens. It also has a large base of citizens which includes manufacturing organizations, importers, exporters, service organizations, and so on; thus, increased usage of e-government options in this department could have wide ranging implications for a large base of business organizations.

Considering technology acceptance factors in e-government, a research model is proposed to explain 'intention to use e-government' by the internal users of the Indian Central Excise. The model is empirically validated using 163 questionnaire responses from internal users of the Central Excise. The validated model can be used for other similar e-government projects in India to test and enhance the level of e-government acceptance.

CENTRAL EXCISE AND E-GOVERNMENT THEREIN

Central Excise is a commissionerate under the Central Board of Excise and Customs (CBEC), under the Ministry of Finance, government of India. It deals with the tasks of formulation of policy concerning levy and collection of Central Excise duties. Central Excise duty is an indirect tax levied on goods manufactured in India. Major processes in Excise include: registration of new assesses, processing of returns and refunds, reconciliation of revenue receipts, audit, and so forth.

Computerization in central excise started way back in 1985, on a limited scale, with a centralized feeding of invoices. However, the entire process took a big jump in 1991, when a application named SERMON (System for Excise Revenue Monitoring) was introduced. Brief information about all important information system application in the Central Excise and Service tax is depicted in Figure 1. The applications are classified into three categories with respect to their usage viz. internal users, external users and common for both internal and external users.

The e-government initiatives in Central Excise are guided by two principles: delivering

Figure 1. Central Excise e-government

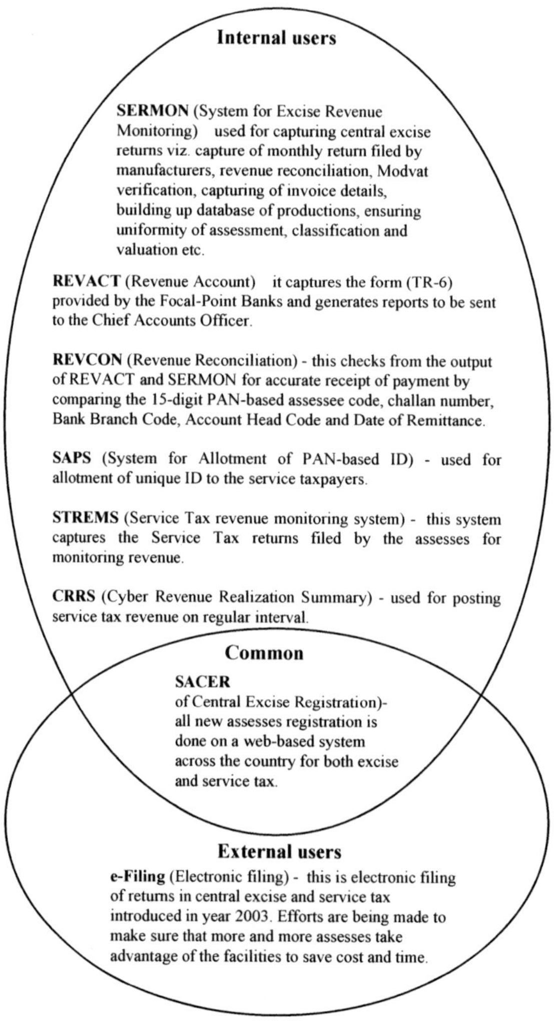

services in ways that reflect what people need or want from the department, and making the department and its services more accessible on an anywhere, anytime basis through its Web site (http://exciseandservicetax.nic.in). This provides a platform for users to transact their work with the department from the comfort of their home or office using the Internet.

STUDY DESIGN

The study is designed with an objective to identify factors that determine acceptance or lead to rejection of e-government by its end users in the Indian Central Excise and to arrive at a model of e-government acceptance for this department. The initial study of the department by interacting with the users identified few issues related to acceptance of e-government. These issues are ease of use, control and security, skill and training, awareness about system usefulness, attitude of government employees towards using e-government, facilitating conditions, top management support, societal concerns, and so on. Many of these issues are similar to the issues of technology acceptance and therefore technology acceptance model and unified theory of acceptance and use of technology (UTAUT) are considered as base models for this study. A research model was designed that incorporates the essential variables of TAM and UTAUT as well as a few other important variables considered relevant for the study. The additional variables are perceived strength of control, self efficacy, attitude towards using e-government, and anxiety. A brief description for all the variables is given. The research model for this study is illustrated in Figure 2.

Figure 2. Research model

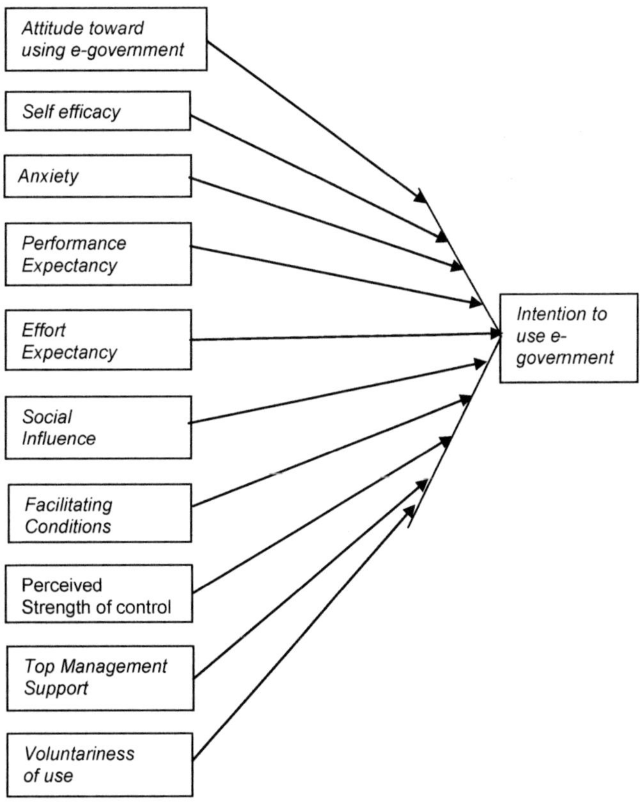

- **Attitude toward using e-government:** This factor measures the individual's positive or negative feelings (evaluative effect) about using the e-government. This factor has been added to the model on the premise that people will use the system they enjoy working on. Originally this factor was used in the "Theory of Reason Action," which is one of the most fundamental and influential theories of human behavior (Hung, et al., 2006; Chang et al., 2005; Sheppard, Hartwick, & Warshaw, 1988; Ajzen, 1991; Chau & Hu, 2001; Taylor & Todd, 1995; Davis, 1989; Mathieson, 1991).
- **Self-efficacy:** Self-efficacy deals with an individual's perception of his or her ability to use the system on his or her own. This factor is considered important as it deals with the level of comfort a person has in working on the e-government. This factor is adapted from the social cognitive theory (SCT), which is one of the important theories of human behavior (Wang, 2003; Hung, 2006; Bandura, 1986; Compeau & Higgins, 1995).
- **Anxiety:** This factor measures anxious and emotional reactions when it comes to performing a behavior. This factor has been added to the model because it was felt that a lot of non-usage issues in government departments could be associated with fear factors relating to various technology options and fear of making mistakes while operating the system. Anxiety is adapted from the social cognitive theory (SCT) (Bandura, 1986) and is subsequently being used by other researchers in the technology acceptance research (Compeau & Higgins 1995).
- **Performance expectancy:** Performance expectancy is defined as the degree to which an individual believes that the e-government will help him or her to gain in job performance. Many users of the government department think that the new system is troublesome and is not helping individuals to improve the performance. Performance expectancy is adapted from the UTAUT model (Venkatesh et al., 2003; Davis, 1989; Compeau & Higgins, 1995; Wang, 2003; Chang et al., 2005; Hung et al., 2006).
- **Effort expectancy:** Effort expectancy is defined as the degree of ease associated with the use of e-government. This factor refers to the perceived amount of effort that the user needs to put to learn and operate the system. Effort expectancy has been adopted from the UTAUT model (Venkatesh et al., 2003; Davis, 1989; Compeau & Higgins, 1995; Wang, 2003; Chang et al., 2005; Hung et al., 2006; Fu et al., 2004).
- **Social influence:** This factor is defined as the degree to which an individual perceives that important others (such as bosses, peers, subordinate, etc.) believe that he or she should use the e-government. In the Indian government departments there is high resistance to change, therefore some initiation is needed by the some employees of the department to form the nucleus and then it percolates to other employees. Social influence construct has been used in UTAUT model (Venkatesh et al., 2003) and model of PC utilization (Thompson, Higgins, & Howell, 1991; Ajzen, 1991; Heintze & Bretschneider, 2000; Ho & Pardo, 2004; LaPorte, Demchak, & de Jong, 2002; Brown & Brudney, 2003; Edmiston, 2003; Holden, Norris, & Fletcher, 2003; Hung et al., 2006).
- **Facilitating conditions:** This is a provision of support for users in terms of computer hardware and software necessary to work on the e-government, the system compatibility with the other systems and the users who are using is also covered. The "facilitating condition" variable has been used in UTAUT model (Venkatesh et al., 2003) and model of

PC utilization (Thompson et al., 1991; Hung et al., 2006).

- **Perceived strength of control:** This is about the system security, which is one of the most challenging problems faced by e-government users who wish to transact with a government online. The problem arises from the vulnerabilities of the Internet, upon which e-government is based. When a user transacts through the Internet, anyone from anywhere around the world will be able to access the information being sent or received if the system is not secured (Suh & Han, 2003; Irvine, 2000; Andersen & Dawes, 1991; Joshi, Ghafor, Aref, & Spafford, 2002; Caffrey, 1998; Milner, 2000; Moon, 2002; Duncan & Roehrig, 2003; Edmiston, 2003; Holden et al., 2003; Hung et al., 2006). The vulnerabilities of the Internet may inhibit users from participating in e-government if they feel that the level of risk is unacceptable (Newell, Goldsmith, & Banzhaf, 1998). Suh and Han (2003) have discussed the basic security control requirements of Internet transaction, which are:
    - *Authentication* ensures that the transaction parties in an electronic transaction or communication are genuine.
    - *Non-repudiation* means that neither of the participating parties should be able to deny having participated in a transaction.
    - *Confidentiality* warrants that all communications between the parties are restricted to the parties involved in the transaction.
    - *Privacy protection* ensures that personal information about the user collected from their electronic transactions is protected from disclosure without permission.
    - *Data integrity* means that data in transmissions are not created, intercepted, modified, or deleted illicitly. These requirements are accomplished by various technologies, such as encryption, third-party certificates, digital signatures, and compliance with privacy policy (Ahuja, 2000; Ratnasigham, 1998).
- **Top management support:** This refers to the extent to which the top management is involved into the planning and implementation of the e-government project. The top management commitment will drive involvement of the top leaders. Gibson (1998) asserted that top management involvement is critical for successful planning of information technology. Most of the government projects in India are bureaucracy driven. Hence "top management" plays an important role in implementations and making the users aware about the benefits of the e-government (Gupta et al., 2004).
- **Voluntariness of use:** This factor deals with the degree to which use of the system is perceived as being voluntary and the users are encouraged to use the system in a non-mandatory environment. Originally this construct was used in innovation diffusion theory (Moore & Benbasat, 1996). Subsequently, Venkatesh et al. (2003) used this construct as a moderating factor for the social influence and behavior intention. In this study, voluntariness of use is considered as a predictor of intention to use e-government; as the e-government are not mandatory for many groups of users. Moreover, the e-government is a new innovation and it is in the process of diffusion among the members of the society.
- **Intention to use e-government:** Intention to use e-government is a measure of the strength of one's intention to perform a specified behaviour. Actual use refers to an individual's actual direct usage of the given system. In this research, "intention to use e-government" is considered as the

surrogate measure of the e-government's actual usages. Actual usage refers to hard facts that have to be ascertained. Since measuring "actual usage" is not the objective of this study, it is therefore prudent to proceed with its surrogate measure.

As shown in the research model (Figure 2), it was hypothesized that all the external variables are predictor of intention to use of e-government. Table 2 depicts the research hypotheses and their supporting studies.

A questionnaire-based approach is used in obtaining data from the e-government users in the Indian Central Excise. The development of a questionnaire involved various phases starting from clear definition of the research topic, issue identification, relationship of variables, and

Table 2. Summary of research hypotheses

Hypothesis		Supporting Studies
H1	Attitude towards using e-government → Intention to use e-government	Sheppard, et al., 1988; Ajzen, 1991; Chau & Hu, 2001; Taylor & Todd, 1995; Mathieson, 1991; Chang, et al., 2005; Hung, et al., 2006; Davis, 1989.
H2	Self-efficacy → Intention to use e-government	Bandura, 1986; Compeau & Higginsm, 1995; Wang, 2003; Hung, et al., 2006.
H3	Anxiety → Intention to use e-government	Bandura, 1986; Compeau & Higgins, 1995.
H4	Performance expectancy → Intention to use e-government	Venkatesh, et al., 2003; Davis, 1989; Compeau & Higgins, 1995; Wang, 2003; Chang, et al., 2005.
H5	Effort expectancy → Intention to use e-government	Venkatesh, et al., 2003; Davis, 1989; Moore & Benbasat, 1996; Fu, et al., 2004; Wang, 2003; Chang, et al., 2005.
H6	Social influence→ Intention to use e-government	Venkatesh, et al., 2003; Ajzen, 1991; Thompson, et al., 1991; Ajzen, 1991; Heintze and Bretschneider, 2000; Ho and Pardo, 2004; LaPorte, et al., 2002; Brown and Brudney, 2003; Edmiston, 2003; Holden, et al., 2003.
H7	Facilitating condition → Intention to use e-government	Venkatesh, et al., 2003; Thompson, et al., 1991; Hung, et al., 2006.
H8	Perception of authentication → Intention to use e-government	Suh & Han, 2003; Irvine, 2000; Andersen & Dawes, 1991; Joshi, et al., 2002; Caffrey, 1998; Milner, 2000; Moon, 2002; Duncan & Roehrig, 2003; Edmiston, 2003; Holden, et al., 2003; Hung, et al., 2006; Newell, et al., 1998, Ahuja, 2000; Ratnasigham, 1998.
H9	Perception of non repudiation → Intention to use e-government	
H10	Perception of confidentiality → Intention to use e-government	
H11	Perception of privacy protection → Intention to use e-government	
H12	Perception of data integration → Intention to use e-government	
H13	Top management support → Intention to use e-government	Gupta, et al., 2004; Gibson, 1998.
H14	Voluntariness of use → Intention to use e-government	Moore & Benbasat, 1996; Venkatesh, et al., 2003.

Note: '→' means 'is a predictor of'

so forth. A precise, structured multiple-choice questionnaire was designed keeping in mind the need for eliciting the requisite information. Likert's scale was used in formulating the questionnaire, in which the respondents were asked to mark their position on the continuum having two extreme ends. The continua were divided into seven intervals of measurement. The intervals were "extremely disagree," "disagree," "partially disagree," "neutral," "partially agree," "agree," and "strongly agree." Questions were also adapted from the previous researches where the same variables were used (Ajzen, 1991; Andersen & Dawes 1991; Brown & Brudney, 2003; Caffrey, 1998; Chau & Hu, 2001; Compeau & Higgins, 1995; Davis, 1989; Duncan & Roehrig, 2003; Edmiston, 2003; Fu et al., 2004; Gibson et. al., 1998; Mathieson, 1991; Moore & Benbasat, 1996; Newell et al., 1998; Sheppard et al. 1988; Suh & Han, 2003; Taylor & Todd, 1995; Venkatesh et al., 2003; Wang, 2003). A rigorous questionnaire validation exercise was undertaken which includes face validity, criterion validity, content validity, and construct validity. Further, the questionnaire was subjected to pretesting through a pilot survey administered to a small sample of respondents and corrective modifications were made.

The final questionnaire contained 87 questions, including sub questions. The questionnaire, along with a covering letter mentioning the objective of the study, was administered across the various offices of Indian Central Excise. Mostly the questionnaires were administered personally and very few through postal services with prior telephonic talk. Many personal visits were made to the offices situated in National Capital Region (NCR) Delhi. Collection of completed questionnaires was very tedious and time consuming. The respondents were very busy in almost all the offices and few of them were ignorant about sharing information besides having prior permission of the senior authority of the office. Total 163 valid questionnaires were collected.

Structural equation modeling (SEM) is used for the multivariate analysis in this study. This allows researchers to perform path analytic modeling with latent variables. Specifically, SEM provides the researcher with the flexibility to: (a) model relationships among multiple predictor and criterion variables, (b) construct unobservable latent variables, (c) model errors in measurements for observed variables, and (d) statistically test a priori substantive/theoretical and measurement of assumptions against empirical data (i.e., confirmatory analysis). The application software used for the SEM was AMOS 5. SPSS (Version 11) was used in this study for data tabulation, descriptive analysis, reliability analysis, and it was used as back-end data support for the AMOS.

The universe of the study is the Indian Central Excise employees using e-government. This selection was made after a primary study of all major Indian e-government projects listed with Department of Information Technology, Government of India. In total a detail of 258 e-government projects were found (www.mit.gov.in). Screening of the projects was done on the basis of its size, life, and government initiatives. Indian Central Excise remained a high priority area. This was further endorsed on June 18, 2006, when the government of India announced eight mission mode projects under National E-governance Plan that includes Indian Customs and Central Excise into the list.

DATA ANALYSIS

The final questionnaire was administered through personal visits among 600 employees working at different capacity ranging from superintendent, inspector, tax assistant, operator, and so on. The number of valid responses received is 163, with a 27.17% of response rate. Reliability measurement has been carried out for the internal consistency of data.

Reliability and Validity of the Instrument

The reliability is assessed using Cronbach's alpha and confirmatory factor analysis (CFA) is used for the convergent validity. High values of Cronbach's alpha indicate high internal consistency of the multiple items measuring each construct, hence indicating high reliability of the individual construct. The reliability coefficients are more than the cut-off value of 0.6 (that is recommended as acceptable for empirical research of similar nature) except "voluntariness of use," which is 0.5732. This is accepted as it is for the further analysis since the cumulative percentage in the CFA is 55.761 (acceptable range). The reliability coefficients of the variables are tabulated in Table 3. Most of the alpha values are highly significant (above 0.75) and others are at a satisfactory level. In this view, it is concluded that the data are found significantly reliable.

CFA was carried out for validation of constructs used in this study. This was performed on all 15 variables to examine the convergent validity of each construct. Table 3 summarizes the results of the CFA. This study validates that the various items used for the variables are converging. The cumulative percentage of variance varies from 55.761 (voluntariness of use) and 93.213 (perception of data integrity). All the individual items have surpassed the recommended value of cumulative percentage of variance 50 (Hair, Tatham, Anderson, & Black, 1998), which demonstrated the convergent validity of the items used for the measurement.

Sample Profile

Questionnaire was distributed among eight different Central Excise Commissionerates in the National Capital Region Delhi and nearby cities. The final acceptable responses collected were 163 in total with a response rate of 27.17%. The majority of the respondents were at the level of superintendent (42.94%) and inspector (24.54%). Majority of the respondents were in age group

Table 3. Reliability validity analysis and confirmatory factor analysis for variables (N = 163)

Sl No	Variable Name	No of Items	Alpha Value	Cumulative (Percentage of the Variance)
1	Attitude toward using e-government	4	.6664	63.858
2	Self efficacy	5	.6471	77.060
3	Anxiety	4	.7934	63.488
4	Performance expectancy	5	.6206	64.742
5	Effort expectancy	4	.6380	67.346
6	Social influence	6	.8273	58.068
7	Facilitating conditions	12	.9074	64.017
8	Intention to use e-government	4	.8647	72.208
9	Perception of authentication	3	.8660	79.940
10	Perception of non repudiation	6	.9196	76.683
11	Perception of confidentiality	4	.8548	65.726
12	Perception of privacy protection	4	.9001	77.347
13	Perception of data integrity	4	.9738	93.213
14	Voluntariness of use	3	.5732	55.761
15	Top management support	4	.8828	74.181

of 36 to 45 (37.4%) and 46 to 55 (36.2%). Of the respondents, 31.9% had postgraduate and 55.2% had graduate degrees. There were 21 (12.88%) respondents who had some diploma courses. All the users had formal qualifications, but most of them were not provided with specific system training.

In the subsequent section structural equation modeling results are discussed.

Structural Model Result

The hypothesized research model (Figure 2) is examined for the model fit index using structural equation modeling (AMOS 5). Table 4 presents the results of the model goodness of fit along with the common recommended criteria for the structural equation modeling. Multiple iterations of path analysis were carried out using AMOS 5. A final model for e-government acceptance for Central Excise—internal user is arrived which is shown in Figure 3 along with the path coefficient. In terms of goodness of fit indicators, chi-square value is 22.22 (degree of freedom = 15) at a probability level of 0.102. This indicates that the probability of getting a chi-square statistics as large as 22.2 is 0.102. In other words, departure of data from the model is significant at the 0.1 level.

The ratio of minimum discrepancy to degree of freedom (CMIN/DF) has been suggested as measure of fit. This ratio should be close to one (Arbuckle, 1996) for correct model. In this model the CMIN/DF ratio is 1.481, indicating a good fit index. It is suggested in the literature that if the ratio of CMIN/DF is more than two, it indicates an inadequate fit of the model (Gillespie & Glisson, 1992). Other fitness indices such as Boolen's relative fit index (RFI), Boolen's incremental fit index (IFI) and the Tucker-Lewis index (TLI) should be close to one for good fit (Arbuckle, 1996). The values of RFI, IFI, and TLI are 0.897, 0.983, and 0.945 respectively. Table 4 shows that the modified model is having good fit index.

The root mean-square residual (RMR) is the square root of the squared amount by which the sample variance and covariance differ from their estimates obtained under the assumption that the model is correct. It is recommended in the literature that the value should be less than 0.05; the smaller the RMR the better it is. In this case the value of RMR is 0.057, which is a slightly higher value.

Further, the significance of each hypothesized path in the research model as well as the variance explained (R^2 value) by each path was examined. The result of the path analysis reports, "raw" and

Table 4. Evaluation of fitness of revised model

Measure of Fitness of Model	Recommended criteria	Results in the study
Chi Square/ Degree of Freedom (CMIN/DF)	<3	1.481
P Value	>0.05	0.102
Goodness of Fit Index (GFI)	>0.9	0.953
Adjusted Goodness of Fit Index (AGFI)	>0.9	0.899
Comparative Fit Index (CFI)	>0.9	0.982
Root Mean square Residual (RMR)	<0.05	0.057
Root mean square error of approximation RMSEA	<0.05	0.049
Boolen's Relative Fit Index (RFI)	Near to 1	0.897
Boolen's Incremental Fit Index (IFI)	Near to 1	0.983
Tucker-Lewis Index (TLI)	Near to 1	0.945

"standardized estimates" for all specified paths along with standard errors and test statistics for each path. Table 5 presents the squared multiple correlations of the various variables in the model. For the "intention to use e-government," the value of R^2 is 0.65, which means the model can explain 65% variations of the "intention to use e-government."

Variance in individual "intention to use e-government" is totally explained 65% by the external variables considered in the model. The external variables includes "attitude toward using e-government," "self efficacy," "anxiety," "performance expectancy," "effort expectancy," "social influence," "perceived strength of control," and "top management support." In this case the "top management support" is having a negative affect on "intention to use e-government," which rejects the hypothesis H13. Regarding total variance of "intention to use e-government"; "social influence" explains 29% variance along with "effort expectancy" (21%), "attitude toward using e-government" (19%), "perceived strength of control" (21%), and "effort expectancy" (8%). There are three variables, which are having negative affect on the variance of "intention to use e-government." They are "anxiety" (-27%), "top management support" (-27%) and "self efficacy" (-17%). Therefore "social influence" "effort expectancy," "perceived strength of control," "attitude toward using e-government," and "top management support" are more important than other determinants of the "intention to use e-government."

Further, the resulting model (Figure 3) of path analysis considers "attitude towards using e-government" and "self efficacy" as intermediary variables. Main determinants of "attitude towards using e-government" are "performance expectancy" (5%), "effort expectancy" (24%),

Table 5. Squared multiple correlations

Variables	Estimate
Self-efficacy	0.24
Attitude toward using e-government	0.54
Intention to use of e-government	0.65

Figure 3. Model along with path co-efficient

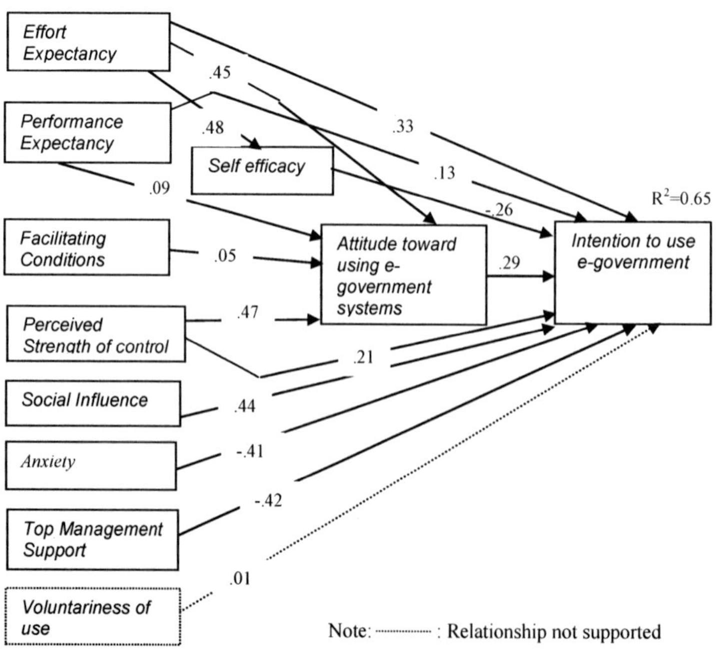

"perceived strength of control" (25%) and "facilitating condition" (3%). Similarly, the "self efficacy" is determined by "effort expectancy" (12%). The next section presents a discussion on hypothesis testing.

Hypothesis Testing

Table 6 illustrates the relationships among the various factors studied; "Critical ratio" is presented for each relation along with the findings. Most of the relations are supported by the statistical analysis except one relation that is between "voluntariness of use" and "intention to use e-government". The hypothesis H14 ("voluntariness of use" is a predictor of "intention to use e-government") could not get support.

Critical ratio (CR) was calculated in the SEM using AMOS 5 software. CR is defined as critical ratio = estimate / standard errors. The CR values greater than 1.96 and 2.32 are statistically significant at 0.05 and 0.01 levels, respectively. The results of SEM are standardized maximum likelihood path coefficients for the hypothesized model.

Using the results of SEM, the hypotheses testing was carried out. Most of the hypotheses set in this study are accepted. Hypotheses H2, H13, and

Table 6. Summary of research findings

Sl No	Relationship	Critical Ratio	Finding
1	Intention to use of e-government ← Attitude toward using e-government	2.959*	Supported
2	Intention to use of e-government ← Effort expectancy	2.361*	Supported
3	Intention to use of e-government ← Performance expectancy	2.007	Supported
4	Intention to use of e-government ← Perceived strength of control	2.051	Supported
5	Intention to use of e-government ← Anxiety	-5.767*	Supported
6	Intention to use of e-government ← Social influence	4.298*	Supported
7	Intention to use of e-government ← Self-efficacy	-3.353*	Supported
8	Intention to use of e-government ← Top Management support	-3.815*	Supported
9	Intention to use of e-government ← Voluntariness of use	0.114	Not Supported
10	Attitude towards using e-government ← Performance expectancy	2.391*	Supported
11	Attitude towards using e-government ← Effort expectancy	8.604*	Supported
12	Attitude towards using e-government ← Facilitating condition	2.067	Supported
13	Attitude towards using e-government ← Social influence	4.756*	Supported
14	Self-efficacy ← Effort expectancy	3.531*	Supported

*Note: * Denotes significance at the $p < 0.01$ level.*

H14 (Table 7) could not get support in this study. The variables self-efficacy and top management support are proven to be the predictors of the intention to use e-government but they are having negative effect. Therefore, the hypothesis H2 and H13 are not supported. voluntariness of use did not prove to be a predictor of intention to use e-government, as this relationship is statistically insignificant, the confidence level is very low ($p = 0.909$). Hypothesis H7 is indirectly supported through an intermediary variable attitude towards using e-government. Table 7 presents the summary of the hypotheses testing.

Self-efficacy was found to be negatively related to intention to use e-government. A possible reason for this is that the system users are not satisfied with the initiatives being taken by the top management, most of the users are concerned about the poor computing infrastructure. There are many places where the systems were either not working or they were outdated, moreover the top management has not taken concrete initiative in improving the situation. The responses were random as respondents were reluctant about saying anything negative about the top management support. In the case of self-efficacy due to the low usage of the system the users are not proficient in using the system. Also there were some problems with the network connectivity of the system. Though 70% of the respondents rated themselves comfortable in using the computer system, the actual usage of the system in the department was poor. These are the possible reason of being the self—efficacy not a significant predictor of intention to use e-government.

Table 7. Hypotheses testing

Hypothesis		Result
H1	Attitude toward using e-government → Intention to use e-government	Supported
H2	Self-efficacy → Intention to use e-government	Not Supported
H3	Anxiety → Intention to use e-government	Supported
H4	Performance expectancy → Intention to use e-government	Supported
H5	Effort expectancy → Intention to use e-government	Supported
H6	Social influence→ Intention to use e-government	Supported
H7	Facilitating condition → Intention to use e-government	Supported *
H8	Perception of authentication → Intention to use e-government	Supported
H9	Perception of non repudiation → Intention to use e-government	Supported
H10	Perception of confidentiality → Intention to use e-government	Supported
H11	Perception of privacy protection → Intention to use e-government	Supported
H12	Perception of data integration → Intention to use e-government	Supported
H13	Top management support → Intention to use e-government	Not Supported
H14	Voluntariness of use → Intention to use e-government	Not Supported

** Indirectly supported through 'attitude towards using e-government'*

This study has given a new empirically validated e-government acceptance model for the Indian Central Excise—internal users. Intention to use e-government is totally explained 65% by the external variables, which includes attitude towards using e-government, anxiety, performance expectancy, effort expectancy, social influence, perceived strength of control, and top management support.

Total Effect of Predictor Variables on Intention to Use E-Government

The total effect of a predictor variable for "intention to use e-government" is calculated using the path coefficient values and R^2 from the SEM results (Figure 3). In the case of direct relation with "intention to use e-government," multiplication of path coefficient and R^2 ($R^2 = 0.65$) is taken as the total effect. In case of indirect relation, the path coefficients are multiplied together and finally multiplied with R^2 value to get the "total effect." The value of "total effect" gives the relative importance of the variable; the higher the value, the higher the importance. The result is presented in Table 8.

The value of total effect equal to or greater than 0.065, is treated as high. This value 0.065 is arrived at by considering an ideal situation where all the ten factors considered have an equal path coefficient of 0.10 (1/10). In this case, the value of R^2 is 0.65, therefore the average value is 0.1*0.65 (i.e., 0.065).

The highest value of total effect on intention to use e-government is of social influence. Other variables having high value of total effect are anxiety, effort expectancy, attitude toward using e-government, perceived strength of control, and performance expectancy.

Table 8. Total effect of predictor variable on intention to use e-government

Sl No	Variable	Total effect on "Intention to use e-government"
1	Attitude toward using e-government	0.1885
2	Self-efficacy	-0.169*
3	Anxiety	-0.2665
4	Performance expectancy	0.0845
5	Effort expectancy	0.2145
6	Social influence	0.286
7	Facilitating conditions	0.009425
8	Perception of authentication	0.1365**
9	Perception of non repudiation	
10	Perception of confidentiality	
11	Perception of privacy protection	
12	Perception of data integrity	
13	Voluntariness of use	0.0065*
14	Top management support	-0.2665*

Note: * *Variables statistically not significant*

***Five sub variables of perceived strength of control are calculated together*

Analysis of Ratio of Acceptance

Ratio of acceptance is calculated for each variable used in this study. Ratio of acceptance is a ratio of the value assigned to the variable by the respondent and the maximum value possible for the factor. For example, the rating scale chosen has values between 1 and 7 therefore the maximum value for any question over the 163 surveys could be 7*163 (i.e., 1141). Further, the highest value for any variable is 1141*n (where "n" is the number of questions relating to that factor in the questionnaire). Thus, for a factor having four questions the maximum value will be 1141*4 i.e. 4564. The actual value for the factor would be the sum of the values given to all the four questions across 163 surveys. A mathematical formula for the calculating the "Ratio of Acceptance" is developed (equation 1). Table 9 gives the values of the "ratio of acceptance" for all the variables. Lower the value of the ratio of acceptance, higher is the scope for improvement.

$$Ratio\ of\ Acceptance(V) = \frac{\sum_{i=1}^{N}\left(\sum_{j=1}^{S_v} R_j^i\right)}{N * M * S_V} \quad (1)$$

V = Variable
S_V = *Number of Subvariables of Variable V*
M = Maximum Rating
R_j^i = *Actual Rating for the jth Subvariable of the ith Response*
N = Maximum Number of Responses

Variables with highest ratio of acceptance are intention to use e-government (0.843) and performance expectancy (0.840). This highlights that most of the users of the system have average intention to use e-government. The score is average as per the scale chosen for analysis. Value of ratio of acceptance less than 0.571 is the negative acceptance (rejection) and average value for acceptance is 0.786. In this study, most of the scores are below average value. The variables, which have ratio of acceptance value above average, are intention to use e-government,

Table 9. Ratio of acceptance

Factor name	Ratio of acceptance
Attitude toward using e-government	0.794
Self-efficacy	0.679
Anxiety (negative predictor)	0.461
Performance expectancy	0.840
Effort expectancy	0.741
Social influence	0.696
Facilitating conditions	0.694
Perception of authentication	0.724
Perception of non-repudiation	0.658
Perception of confidentiality	0.677
Perception of privacy protection	0.713
Perception of data integrity	0.706
Voluntariness of use	0.792
Top management support	0.654
Intention to use e-government	0.843

performance expectancy, and attitude towards using e-government. Therefore, there is a high scope for improvement in almost all the factors to attain a higher acceptance of the e-government. Variables with low ratio of acceptance are top management support (0.654), Perception of non repudiation (0.658), and other security-related factors. Anxiety is a negative predictor of intention to use e-government; therefore its value of ratio of acceptance should be as low as possible. Anxiety is having 0.461 value of ratio of acceptance, which is considered poor. This indicates considerable amount of training and counseling needed for the users to keep their anxiety level low for the use of e-government.

SYNTHESIS AND RECOMMENDATIONS

A comparative study of the ratio of acceptance and total effect gives strategic insight to increase the usage of e-government. A categorization of the factors is done on the basis of high and low value of ratio of acceptance and total effect.

A comparison of ratio of acceptance and total effect is carried out. For total effect, values greater than or equal to 0.065 are treated as high and less than 0.065 are low. In case of ratio of acceptance the value greater than or equal to 0.785 are high and less are treated as low. This value is decided after calculating the average acceptance value. This analysis seeks to prioritize investment of resources and efforts into increasing usage by highlighting whose change will bring about largest positive increase in intention to use e-government and which are right now having a low value leaving a lot of room for leverage and improvement. The comparison of values of ratio of acceptance and total effect is done using Table 8 and Table 9.

Effort expectancy, social influence, and perceived strength of control have low ratio of acceptance and high value of total effect. Therefore these factors are key inhibitors of intention to use e-government. Thus these factors are of high importance and effort should be taken to raise the ratio of acceptance value. Efforts by top management are required in the form of training employees in IT skills as well as motivational training to increase comfort with the systems, which will result in increasing the ratio of acceptance of effort expectancy. Similarly to improve the social influence, it is required to have frequent trainings and improve overall work environment by providing learning ambience. The senior executives should help their subordinates in learning to operate the new system. To improve perceived strength of control it is required to improve the system security features by providing state-of-art security technology, good network connectivity and providing training to the end users to deal with security related issues.

Anxiety is a negative predictor of intention to use e-government; therefore the value of ratio of acceptance should be maintained as low as possible. This can be achieved by keeping low anxiety level of the users.

Attitude towards using e-government and performance expectancy have high ratio of acceptance and high value of total effect. This implies that these two factors are major predictors of the intention to use e-government and simultaneously their values of ratio of acceptance are also high. Further intention to use e-government can be improved by motivating the users to use the e-government and improving the system interface, providing integrated service by clubbing all the modules of Central Excise into one single system, maintaining a central database and online updating and so on. These two factors are of high importance and need to maintain a high ratio of acceptance value.

Facilitating condition has low value of total effect on intention to use e-government and at the same time the value of ratio of acceptance is also low. Still facilitating condition is a predictor of intention to use e-government. Therefore, effort should be put to improve the facilitating condition, which includes computing facility, maintenance, peripheral devices, backup power supply, and so forth in the Central Excise offices.

In brief, the recommendations to increase intention to use e-government by the internal users of Indian Central Excise are summarized here:

- User needs to be trained in IT skills on a regular interval to increase comfort level in operating the systems.
- Improve overall work environment by providing learning ambience. The senior executives should help their subordinates in learning to operate the new system.
- It is required to improve the system security features by providing state-of-the-art security technology, good network connectivity, and providing training to the end users to deal with security related issues.
- Motivate the users to use the e-government.
- Improve the system interface to provide integrated service by clubbing all the modules of Central Excise into one single system; maintain a central database and online updating facility.
- Effort should be put forth to improve the facilitating condition in the Central Excise offices for the e-government users.
- Computing facility, maintenance, peripheral devices, backup power supply, and so forth should be improved.

CONCLUDING REMARKS

The study has identified 15 variables having predictive ability with regard to "intention to use e-government" in Indian Central Excise among their internal users. The study brought out an empirically validated model of e-government acceptance for Indian Central Excise which has helped in developing a strategic insight into various factors for improving e-government acceptance. Relative significance of the variables is also examined. The recommendations of this study would be helpful in developing and implementing new e-government plans. To achieve higher acceptance, apart from the several factors identified, user awareness of e-government services is essential. Also, users' trust depends heavily on increased transparency and therefore organizational reform must follow to ensure users' trust and in turn success. One of the major limitations of this research was that the study has been mostly done in the northern region of India. The other limitation of the research is common to most surveys related to behavioral issues and subjectivity of the questionnaire responses. Suitability of new variables should be tested to increase the overall explanatory power of the model. The e-government acceptance model developed here can be used in other similar studies of e-government acceptance.

REFERENCES

Ahuja, V. (2000). Building trust in electronic commerce. *IT Professional, 2*(3), 61-63.

Ajzen, I. (1991). Theory of planned behavior. *Organizational Behavior and Human Decision Processes, 50*(2), 179-211.

Andersen, D. F., & Dawes, S. S. (1991). *Government information management: A primer and casebook.* Englewood Cliffs, NJ: Prentice Hall.

Arbuckle, J. L. (1996). Structural equation modeling: Amos program. In *Proceedings of Eighth invitational research seminar on advanced issues in research analysis.* Case Western Reserve University.

Bandura, A. (1986). *Social foundations of thought and action: A social cognitive theory.* Englewood Cliffs, NJ: Prentice Hall.

Brown, M. M., & Brudney, J. L. (2003). Learning organizations in the public sector? A study of police agencies employing information and technology to advance knowledge. *Public Administration Review, 63*(1), 30-43.

Brown, S. A., Massey, A. P., Weiss, M. M., & Burkman, J. R. (2002). Do I really have to? User acceptance of mandated technology. *European Journal of Information Systems, 11*(3), 283-295.

Caffrey, L. (1998). Information sharing between and within governments: A study group report. *London7 Commonwealth Secretariat*

Chang, I. C., Li, Y. C., Hung, W. F., & Hwang, H. G. (2005). An empirical study on the impact of quality antecedents on tax payers' acceptance of Internet tax-filing systems. *Government Information Quarterly, 22*(3), 389-410.

Chau, P. Y. K., & Hu, P. J. (2001). Information technology acceptance by individual professionals: A model comparison approach. *Decision Sciences, 32*(4), 699-719.

Compeau, D., Higgins, C. A., & Huff, S. (1999). Social cognitive theory and individual reactions to computing technology: A longitudinal study. *MIS Quarterly, 23*(2), 145-158.

Davis, F. D. (1989). Perceived usefulness, perceived ease of use, and user acceptance of information technology. *MIS Quarterly, 13*(3), 318-340.

Davis, F. D., Bagozzi, P. R., & Warshaw, P. R. (1989). User acceptance of computer technology: A comparison of two theoretical models. *Management Science, 35*(8), 892-1003.

Duncan, G. T., & Roehrig, S. T. (2003). Mediating the tension between information privacy and information access: The role of digital government. In G. D. Garson (Ed.), *Public information technology: Policy and management issues.* Hershey, PA: Idea Group Publishing.

Edmiston, K. D. (2003). State and local e-government: Prospects and challenges. *American Review of Public Administration, 33*(1), 20-45.

Fu, J. R., Chao, W. P., & Farn, C. K. (2004). Determinants of taxpayers' adoption of electronic filing methods in Taiwan: An exploratory study. *Journal of Government Information, 30*(5-6), 658-683.

García, J. R. G., & Pardo, T. A. (2005). E-government success factors: Mapping practical tools to theoretical foundations. *Government Information Quarterly, 22*(2), 187-216.

Gibson, D., Kleinberg, J. M., & Raghavan, P. (1998). Inferring Web communities from link topology. In *Proceedings of ACM Hypertext '98*(pp. 225-234). Pittsburgh.

Gillespie, D. F., & Glisson, C. (1992). *Quantitative methods in social work: State of the art. Binghamton, NY: Haworth Press.*

Gupta, M. P., Kumar, P., & Bhattacharya, J. (2004). *Government online: Opportunities and challenges,* TMH, New Delhi.

Hair, J. F., Tatham, R. L., Anderson, R. E., & Black, W. (1998). *Multivariate data analysis* (5th ed.). Englewood Cliffs, NJ: Prentice Hall.

Heeks, R. (2003). Success and failure rates of e-government in developing/transitional countries: Overview. *E-government for Development,* Institute for Development Policy and Management, University of Manchester, UK.

Heintze, T., & Bretschneider, S. (2000). Information technology and restructuring in public organizations: Does adoption of information technology affect organizational structures, communications, and decision-making? *Journal of Public Administration Research and Theory, 10*(4), 801-830.

Ho, J., & Pardo, T. A. (2004). *Toward the success of e-government initiatives: Mapping known success factors to the design of practical tools.* Paper presented at the 37th Hawaii International Conference on System Sciences (HICSS), organized by the College of Business, University of Hawaii at Manoa.

Holden, S. H., Norris, D. F., & Fletcher, P. D. (2003). Electronic government at the local level: Progress to date and future issues. *Public Performance and Management Review, 26*(4), 325-344.

http://exciseandservicetax.nic.in retrieved during December 2005- July 2006.

Hung, S. Y., Chang, C. M., & Yu, T. J. (2006). Determinants of user acceptance of the e-government services: The case of online tax filing and payment system. *Government Information Quarterly, 23*(1), 97-122.

Irvine, C. E. (2000). Security issues for automated information systems. In G. D. Garson (Ed.), *Handbook of pPublic information systems.* New York: Marcel Dekker, Inc.

Joshi, J. B. D., Ghafor, A., Aref, W. G., & Spafford, E. H. (2002). Security and privacy challenges of a digital government. In W. J. McIver & A. K. Elmagarmid (Eds.), *Advances in digital government, technology, human factors, and policy.* Norwell, MA: Kluwer Academic Publishers.

LaPorte, T. M., Demchak, C. C., & de Jong, M. (2002). Democracy and bureaucracy in the age of the Web: Empirical findings and theoretical speculations. *Administration and Society, 34*(4), 411-446.

Mathieson, K. (1991). Predicting user intentions: Comparing the technology acceptance model with the theory of planned behavior. *Information Systems Research, 2*(3), 173-191.

Milner, E. M. (2000). *Managing information and knowledge in the public sector.* New York: Routledge.

MIT (Department of Information Technology, Government of India), (2005), http://www.mit.gov.in, accessed during May-June 2005

Moon, M. J. (2002). The evolution of e-government among municipalities: Rhetoric or reality? *Public Administration Review, 62*(4), 424-433.

Moore, G. C., & Benbasat, I. (1996). Integrating diffusion of innovations and theory of reasoned action models to predict utilization of information technology by end-users. In K. Kautz & J. Pries-Hege (Eds.), *Diffusion and adoption of information technology* (pp. 132-146). London: Chapman and Hall.

NASSCOM (2005). Retrieved December 3, 2005, from http://www.nasscom.org

Newell, S. J., Goldsmith, R. E., & Banzhaf, E. J. (1998). The effect of misleading environmental claims on consumer perceptions of advertisements. *Journal of Marketing: Theory and Practice, 6*(2), 48-60.

Ratnasingham, P. (1998). The importance of trust in electronic commerce. *Internet Research: Electronic Networking Applications and Policy, 8*(4), 313-321.

Sheppard, B. H., Hartwick, J., & Warshaw, P. R. (1988). The theory of reasoned action: A meta-analysis of past research with recommendations for modifications and future research. *Journal of Consumer Research, 15*(3), 325-343.

Suh, B., & Han, I. (2003). The impact of customer trust and perception of security control on the acceptance of electronic commerce. *International Journal of Electronic Commerce, 7*(3), 135-161.

Tahinakis, P., Mylonakis, J., & Protogeros, N. (2006). The contribution of e-government to the modernisation of the Hellenic taxation system. *Electronic Government, an International Journal (EG), 3*(2), 139-157.

Taylor, S., & Todd, P. A. (1995). Understanding information technology usage: A test of competing models. *Information Systems Research, 6*(2), 144-176.

Thompson, C. S. (2002). Enlisting on-line residents: Expanding the boundaries of e-government in a Japanese rural township. *Government Information Quarterly, 19*(2), 173-188.

Thompson, R. L., Higgins, C. A., & Howell, J. M. (1991). Personal computing: Toward a conceptual model of utilization. *MIS Quarterly, 15*(1), 124-143.

Venkatesh, V. (2000). Determinants of perceived ease of use: Integrating control, intrinsic motivation, and emotion into the technology acceptance model. *Information Systems Research, 11*(4), 342-365.

Venkatesh, V, & Davis, F. D. (1996). A model of the antecedents of perceived ease of use: Development and test. *Decision Science, 27*(3), 451-481.

Venkatesh, V., Morris, M. G., Davis, G. B., & Davis, F. D. (2003). User acceptance of information technology: Toward a unified view. *MIS Quarterly*, 27(3), 425-478.

Wang, Y. S. (2003). The adoption of electronic tax filing systems: An empirical study. *Government Information Quarterly, 20*(4), 333-352.

This work was previously published in the International Journal of Electronic Government Research, Vol. 3, Issue 3, edited by M. Khosrow-Pour, pp. 1-21, copyright 2007 by IGI Publishing, formerly known as Idea Group Publishing (an imprint of IGI Global).

Chapter XIV
A Multi-Agent Service Oriented Modeling of E-Government Initiatives

Tagelsir Mohamed Gasmelseid
King Faisal University, Saudi Arabia

ABSTRACT

The recent economic, organizational and technological transformations are motivating developing countries to adopt electronic government applications. The main objective of the e-government project in Sudan is "to achieve a society based on a strong base of industry knowledge in which all segments of the media access to information that leads to the distribution, publication and use of information as widely as a whole contributes to the achievement of economic growth, increase employment and raise the rates and quality of production in all sectors and poverty eradication. However, the project has been based on the use of a client-server architecture that has many limitations. This chapter provides a multiagent service oriented architecture for the implementation of the project based on a thorough review of project documents and implementation reports.

INTRODUCTION

The use of the internet and other related communication technologies has led to the emergence of multiple business models and dictated new axioms for information acquisition, sharing and utilization. The increasing use of technological platforms is directly related to the emerging organizational transformations, and the growing importance of deploying universally enacted applications to improve the efficiency, effectiveness, and data quality in public and private organizations. Such applications range from electronic document interchange, through e-learning, e-business, e-commerce, e-banking to corporate models of e-government.

Copyright © 2009, IGI Global, distributing in print or electronic forms without written permission of IGI Global is prohibited.

The last couple of years have witnessed an expanding deployment of e-government initiatives and applications at different scales. The emphasis, at the abstract level of analysis, continued to made on the use information and communication technologies in public administrations (following customer-centered perspectives) to strategically enhance accessibility and delivery of government information, public services and democratic processes to citizens, businesses, government employees, and other agencies (Hernon, Reylea, Dugan & Cheverie, 2002; Andersen, 2004; Seifert, 2002; European Community, 2003; Hangen & Kubicek, 2002). The use of such pool of technologies also reflects the existence of a wide range of institutional, structural, technological and personnel-related factors.

The majority of e-government initiatives are aiming at improving government processes by cutting process costs, managing process performance, making strategic connections in government and creating empowerment within the government architecture. Accordingly, connection between governments and citizens (and other stakeholders) can be improved (Hussein, 2006; Richard, 2001). In addition, the interactions associated with the use of such rich pool of organizational and technological platforms in e-governance, creates a "task-oriented" forum of engagement between governments and other stakeholders (Davies, 2002; Paul & Thompson, 2004; Kim & Henriksen, 2006; Traunmüller & Lenk, 2002).

However, the increasing deployment of e-government applications neither means that governments and citizens will gain the "promised" benefits nor the level and magnitude of "downside" risks can be assessed. Estimates about the performance of existing applications in different countries show that almost 85% of the e-government systems are been regarded as "totally or partially" operational failures irrespective of their "technological buildup". Such failure has been attributed to the lack of leadership and strategic thinking, technological infrastructure that facilitate accessibility, connectivity and network readiness, institutional infrastructure that secure an e-business climate, population e-aware, human capital, and legal infrastructure that maintains trust, information security and privacy.

Successful implementation of e-government initiatives depends not only on the availability of "resources" but most importantly on the adoption of appropriate implementation-oriented paradigms that describe the growth and evolution of e-governments. To avoid failures, such modeling paradigms must be practical enough to guide the implementation, monitoring and maintenance of the entire e-government initiative. In addition to the growing percentage of failure of many e-government applications, the importance of focusing on the development of practical models and architectures originates also from the importance of managing the complexity associated with electronic interactions.

The main objective of this chapter is to address the context of e-government modeling by investigating architectural issues taking the e-government initiative in Sudan as a case study. The chapter emphasizes the need for an integrated architectural approach for the management of distributed e-government services by coupling service oriented architectures with multiagent technologies. While section 2 of this chapter presents relevant literature in e-government development architectures, section 3 discusses service oriented concepts. Section 4 reflects on the e-government initiative in Sudan with more focus in section 5 on the process of coupling multiagent technologies with service oriented architecture to be used for the development of the "coupled model" described in section 6. Section 7 addresses the advantages of the coupled model for the case study, potential limitations and modifications with some conclusions provided in section 8.

E-GOVERNMENT DEVELOPMENT ARCHITECTURES: RELATED WORK

The importance of developing appropriate architectures is dictated by their importance for process identification, stakeholders and partners, attitudes and preferential matrix, connection management, resource utilization and monitoring. However, easy access to the Web has created the possibility for new business models and resulted into growth and evolution of multiple computing architectures, programming languages, and development approaches (Crawford et al, 2005). Generally speaking, architecture can be defined as "the fundamental organization of a system embodied in its components, their relationships to each other and to the environment and the principles guiding its design and evolution" (Hillard, 2000). Within this context, the classification of "processes" and "representation of stakeholders" may improve data processing and information communication (Cook, 1996) because it supports improved coordination through the implementation of the principles of "discontinuity" and the definition of the "boundaries" to be articulated among components.

E-Government Modeling Context

The process of modeling e-government applications significantly affects information acquisition and representation. Existing e-government modeling themes address the process of implementation by allowing service providing agencies to be organized around departments that follow the "vertical" lines of command and structures in which each "agency" develops its own information system to publish metadata about the services it provides and enable users to interact electronically to request services. Because this feature leads to the lack of "coordination" and unified theme, there has been a growing concern for the development of architectures that take into account the multiplicity of organizational and structural dimensions "such as line structures, rigidity of standard operating procedures and division of labor", technological factors and legal frameworks. It is only this "invented" architecture which "integrates" all subsystems, subschema and service groupings into service repositories. The information architectures used for the implementation of e-government initiatives need to be in pace with the growing call of citizens for quality, cost effective services and responsiveness in such a dynamic and continuously changing environment (Janseen & Van Veenstra, 2005).

However, despite the contribution of powerful new technologies such as Web services, autonomic and utility computing and grid services (World Wide Web Consortium, 2002; Ganek & Corbi, 2003; Ross & Westerman, 2004; Foster & Kesselman, 2003), the lack of a consistent e-government architecture within which applications can be rapidly developed, integrated, and reused continued to exist. Because of the challenge that e-government solutions face with regards to the integration and interoperability of their applications with other multiple existing systems, emphasis continued to be made on the development of "open architectures".

According to Bernhard, van den Hoven and Igl (2006), e-government architectures show some similar experiences as the domain of enterprise architectures:

1. The level of integration increased with time from rather low integration in early architectures to higher levels in current versions, in pursuit of "independence" and "extensive coverage". Current architectures (like the German SAGA) are focusing on the adoption of technical standards (e.g., interfaces and communication protocols) to ensure interoperability between administrations.
2. The shift of emphasis from "technical issues" to business-driven approaches so as to broaden the scope to incorporate organizational and policy issues. This has led to

the development of "layered architectures" that derive technical requirements and organizational processes from basic principles and a pre-defined policy.

3. A growing emphasis on addressing the dynamic elements of system evolution in e-government architectures because the e-government initiative is viewed as being centered around continued modernization of governments and administrations.

Main E-Government Architectures

Over years, various architectures for e-government are being proposed including, among others, the OSCI platform (Steimke & Hagen, 2003), the SeCo container (Greunz, Schopp & Haes, 2001), the AIPA reference architecture (Arcieri et al., 2002), the eGOV project (Wimmer, 2002), the eMayor project (Kaliontzoglou et al., 2005) and the WebDG architecture (Medjahed et al., 2003). The aim of the eGOV project is to provide an open, extensible, and scalable platform for realizing one stop e-government (Wimmer & Krenner, 2001; Tambouris, 2001; Wimmer & Traunmueller, 2002; Mühl & Krabina, 2003). It includes national and local service repositories and a service creation environment that allows the public sector to provide citizens and other public authorities with information and public services structured around life events, business situations and portals in a customer oriented form. Contrary to the eGOV framework, the e-Service Development Framework (eSDF) is using a service oriented pattern to develop interoperability specifications and standards for e-service to be used in the public sector (Benson, 2002; UK GovTalk, 2004). The Federal Enterprise Architecture aims at facilitating the federal government's transformations towards more citizen "centricity" through five interrelated reference models designed to identify collaboration possibilities across organizational boundaries (Federal Enterprise Architecture, 2005). With the aim of increasing use by stakeholders and reducing cost of ownership, the Enterprise Information Portals (EIPs) use amalgamation of software applications to enable companies to consolidate, manage, analyze, and distribute information across and outside the enterprise (Shilakes & Tylman, 1998). The extended Enterprise Application Integration (eAI) aims at integrating and interconnecting the various databases, platforms, and applications using incompatible technologies to support flexibility, evolutionarity and adaptability (Data Exchanger, 2002; Mediadev, 2002).

The majority of these architectures "structurally" view e-government applications in terms of "entities", transferable objects, service repositories, services, requests, reports, service providers and requesters. They constitute a multiplicity of platforms for "exchanging" electronic requests (for service provision) among multiple "entities" including citizens, businesses enterprises, and government agencies, among others. Entities that provide services (i.e., service providers) act as facilitators that use their own resources or the resources of relevant partners to provide the requested service directly or in collaboration with other entities. They can also direct service requestors to the concerned service providing entities if they are different from the one initially approached for service provision.

The interaction between the service providing entities and the concerned partner service providing entities is usually viewed within the context of "front line" and "back line" offices. If this is the case then all requesting entities must request services through the "front line" office which provides (on behalf of the back line office) the service requesting entity with all relevant information, undertake all types of clearance (both documentary and financial) with the service requesting entity and tracks "service status" (on behalf of the service requesting entity) with the back office. The process continues until the service is provided or the request terminated.

However, the use of the front and back line offices is regarded as a way for reducing the burden on the part of service requestors but in real practice it brings a wide range of internal organizational and institutional complexities. Viewing coordination and interaction within the context of e-government as "back and front offices" is based on the concepts of architectural "classification" and "discontinuity" directed towards the maintenance of a matrix of customers' and interagency interactions. To accommodate the variability that may result from the use of front line and back line offices, the "nature" of the entity (mainly service providing entities) has resulted into some controversy. The main issue is whether it should be left abstract at the model level (as it is the case in centralized e-government deployments) or should be materialized as (fully or partially) automated portal in which human intervention is evident (as it is the case in distributed e-government deployments) (Wimmer, 2002; Kaliontzoglou et al, 2005). However, centralized e-government deployment is best suited for cases where the major focus is on content distribution and searching. It is worth mentioning that it is difficult to implement in a portal services with complex workflow or services with security features such as digital signatures. On the other hand, e-government platforms with distributed components (such as specific applications, portals, application servers, and databases) can handle complex procedures by addressing the general e-government requirements (i.e. interoperability, security and user friendliness) (Kaliontzoglou et al, 2005).

Although the "abstract form" may allow different degrees of technological maturity at the front and back line offices; it may also create some degree of "institutional complexity" and "service instability". Whatever nature is assigned to the entity, there will be some difficulty in identifying how requesting entities will benefit from service repositories in practical terms. Generally speaking, it is only the specification attached to the nature of the service which determines the degree of "dynamism" and "interactivity" associated with cross-organizational and cross-service networking domains.

When considered individually, they fail to address at least some of the following requirements: the full support of a client-centered approach; the integration of both traditional and on-line delivery channels; the support for concurrent access points; versatility; and security (Goncalo & Rafael, 2006). Systems supporting electronic government should expose a high degree of adaptability to change in terms of transparency ease of accommodation and tailorability (Stamoulis et al, 2003; Eardley et al, 2003). According to Vassilakis et al (2005), traditional approaches to service composition, service discovery and service execution exhibit a number of drawbacks related to the following areas: a) a service's availability or lack of it, b) the concurrent execution of services, c) multiple and concurrent invocation of service and d) the a priori knowledge of one or more discrete number of possible compositions that can take place in order to provide a composite service.

SERVICE ORIENTED ARCHITECTURES REVISITED

The migration towards service oriented architectures (SOA) has been advocated by the growing importance of ensuring more flexibility, efficiency and timeliness of reusable government services based on open data standards, procedures and non-proprietary technologies. The aim of SOA is to provide common access points for e-government services using common interface standards, procedures and supporting services, together with the necessary information to make e-government services accessible, affordable and secure. As a result, stakeholders can submit service requests on their own behalf through the standardized mechanisms and procedures of the architecture to allow service providers to interact and provide the service requested.

A service-oriented architecture includes services created in a service layer with published interfaces that support the use of the service in distinct business domains. Because it is made up of interactive components together with their entire interconnections, it emphasizes interoperability and location transparency in a way that shapes both a structural and a behavioral view of the entire system (Michael, 2002). As a result it is possible to leverage application behavior among applications (reusing the same application functionality) without a significant amount of re-coding or integration. In order to accommodate situational changes, the agility of the architecture provides the capability to change "processes" using existing services (single or composite) and information flows. Based on the extended reach features, such "processes" can be exposed to "external entities" or legacy systems (such as Web services, ERP and CRM), to improve collaboration. The concept of modularity in service-oriented architectures increases the range of manageable complexity; allows different parts of a large system to be worked on concurrently and accommodates uncertainty (Baldwin & Clark, 2000). To improve monitoring and reduce complexity, software components are treated as "black boxes" that hide their implementation by providing controlled access to their behavior and data through an interface.

A service is a software component that is described by the meta-data, which can be understood by a program (Schmidt et al, 2005). The distinguishing feature of a service is that the meta-data descriptions are published to enable reuse of the service in loosely coupled systems, frequently interconnected across networks using shared development tools. Service functionalities can be deployed as a part of the entire application (composite service) or as a separate component. By putting the logic and methods necessary for the access and implementation of a particular service into a separate layer, the layer can exist well beyond the lifetime of any system it is composed into. In addition, since location transparency is a property of a service-oriented architecture, the resulting code mobility enables more flexibility in the movement of the service across different machines or providers in a way that make it available irrespective of its location. Because services have published interfaces, they can be easily tested by creating and using test suites that can be run to validate the service independently from any application that uses the service. During the automated building process, services can also be tested independently and accordingly minimizes defects and improves quality.

E-GOVERNMENT INITIATIVE IN SUDAN: FROM VISION TO ACTION

The e-government initiative in Sudan is driven by the need to provide as much government services as possible through an accessible electronic network in pursuit of increasing the "easy-ness" of transactions and rationalizing procedures. Within the context of the 5-years "National Information Strategy", the initiative aims at achieving this objective through the maintenance of transparency in governmental transactions and relationships, improving information dissemination and impartiality, and promoting participation in decision making. However, Sudan is still at the beginning of the road in the field of the computerization of various systems.

E-Government Modeling Perspective

The growth of e-government applications follows a water-fall alike conventional modeling perspective closely related to Layne and Lee model which includes four phases of e-government growth: cataloguing of information on a Web site, transactions on a Web site, vertical and horizontal integration (Layne & Lee, 2001). While the "cataloging of information" phase establishes an online presence for governments, the "transaction phase" aims at building interfaces to enable users to gain universal access to databases and, electronically, perform transactions. Because the e-government project is viewed in a multi-level context, the "vertical integration" phase aims at linking local, state and federal government systems and facilitating information accessibility among them as a prerequisite for the performance of "functions" and the provision of services. The "horizontal integration" phase, on the other hand, enables systems to be integrated across a landscape of different functions and services.

The e-government strategy in Sudan is divided into four phases (Abdorabo, 2004):

a. **Obtaining information about the service:** This is the first step toward the e- government where the provider of the "service" provides information about the services that can be provided by a particular "agency", documentary requirements, fees, and steps to be followed by service requestors such as obtaining forms and applying for service provision. Because considerable effort is being oriented towards G2C applications, emphasis continued to be made on viewing "citizens" as the main "service requestors".
b. **Federal interaction:** Despite the fact that the name of this stage gives the "impression" of cross system interaction, "service requestors" can only download forms from the website of the entire "service providing" agency, print, fill and submit them.
c. **Bilateral interaction:** The aim of this phase is to enable "service requestors" to "electronically" submit their requests for the provision to "service providers", fill and submit forms, get response and (it is hoped) make payment.
d. **Complete interaction:** In this phase, the "service providing" agency follows up the cases (i.e., applications for service provision placed by service requestors); obtain additional information from other governmental agencies to enable "service requestors" to know the "status" of the request submitted. The "process" continues until a decision is taken with regards to service provision.

To move from vision to action, the following e- government executive steps are stated out for implementation: (a) supporting information centers in federal ministries and in the states with computer systems and completion of building of local networks inside these units; (b) establishment of specialized data- bases as an infrastructures to provide electronic services; (c) linking local networks into a broad national network; (d) training of employees in ministries and states; (e) establishment of the governmental services website on the network and (f) establishment of communication centers, in cooperation with the private sector in the urban towns and the rural areas.

The potential types of electronic services to be provided by the e-government project include (a) registration services (certificates of birth & death, marriage and divorce statements, real estate, ownership of vehicles, business names, national ID cards, and Passports); (b) Licensing services (local business Licenses and registration procedures for educational institutions); and (c) payment-based Services (taxes, fines, profits and dividends).

As shown in Figure (1), in addition to the linear modeling approach used, the implementation of the initiative is guided by the centralized e-government deployment approach. In addition to the limitations associated with the modeling approach and architectural orientations adopted, the overall implementation theme of the entire e-government initiative reflects a provider rather than being a client-centric orientation.

Figure 1. E-government centralized implementation architecture

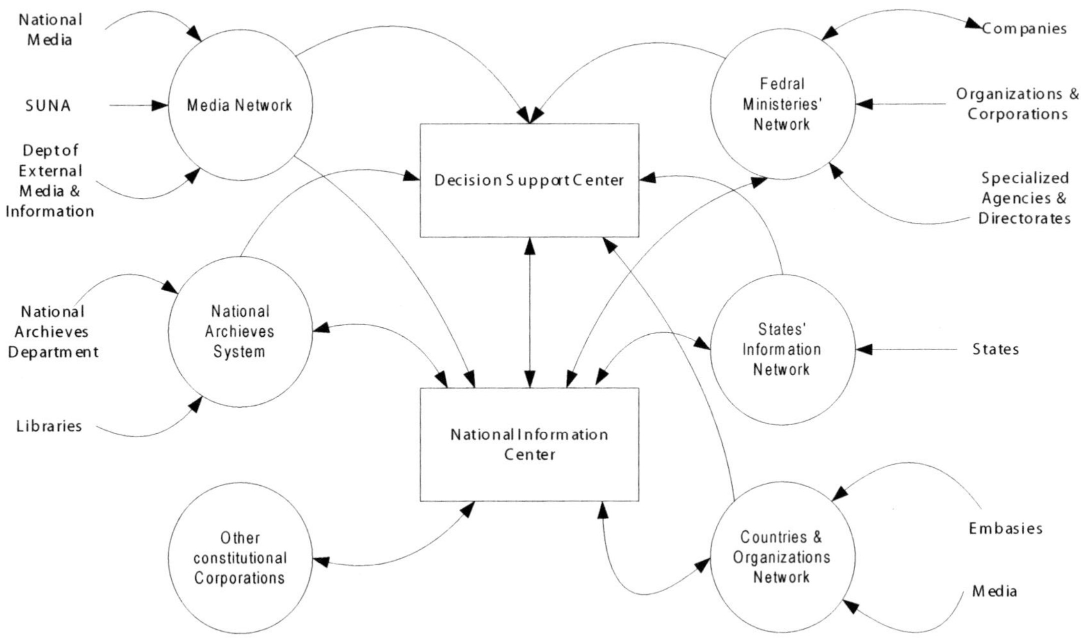

Technological Preparedness and Infrastructure

In addition to the internet and other related web-based platforms, the implementation of e-government applications demands the incorporation of a wide range of hardware, software and telecommunication technologies. This section provides some description of the telecommunication infrastructure used for the implementation of the e-government in Sudan. Figure (2) shows the infrastructure with emphasis on "fixed" telephone lines till the year 2003 which includes a telephone network capacity of 1,738,600 line, switches capacity 1,306,436 port, number of subscriber 936,756, and Tele-density 3.33 %. Figure (3) shows data networks where the first data switched was introduced in 1997. The technologies in use included X.25, Frame Relay, ISDN, ATM and IP backbone. Figure (4) shows the main customers of data communication services which includes about 27 governmental and commercial banks consisting of about 256 branches with the potential to increase the number to 500 branches expected to enact electronically. Together with universities and other institutions, ministries have the potential to be connected to their branches through wide area networks. Figure (5) shows the internet band width where the first internet presence in Sudan was witnessed in 1996. Internet Earth Station maximum capacity is STM-1 up & down link, the STM-1 via submarine cable Port Sudan – Jeddah, and STM-1 via Fiber cable Sudan – Egypt. Figure (6) shows the number of internet service providers (ISP) whose number increased to 20 (till 2004) providing dial up service covering about 75% of cities. Other ISPs are using national calls or VSAT stations to access the Internet and provide service to a network of about 1000 Net cafés. Figure (7) shows internet dial up users using a free internet subscription.

The telecommunication network includes a fiber connection expanding over more than 6500 Km to facilitate the use of the advanced STM-16 & STM-64 rings SDH Technology and Digital

Figure 2. Fixed lines

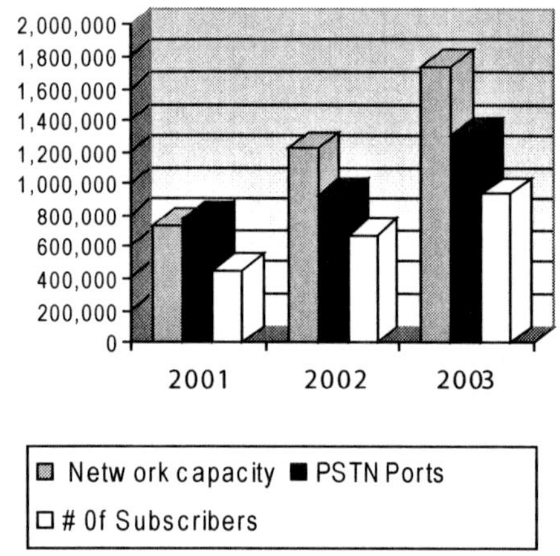

Figure 3. Data networks

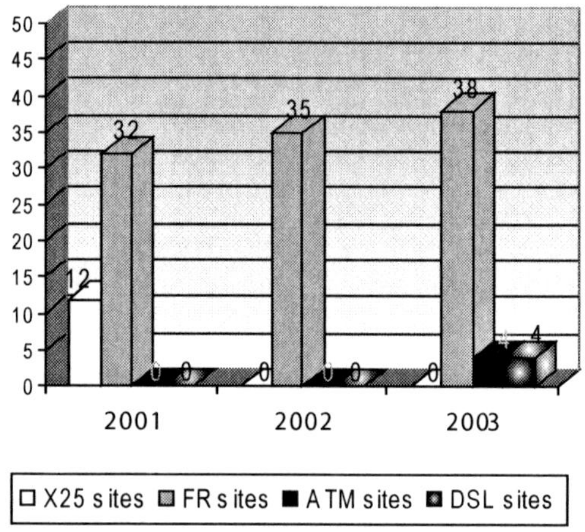

Figure 4. Data communication customers

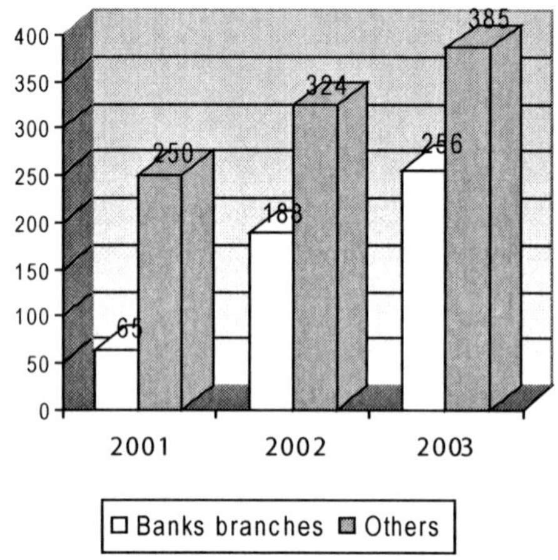

Figure 5. Internet bandwidth

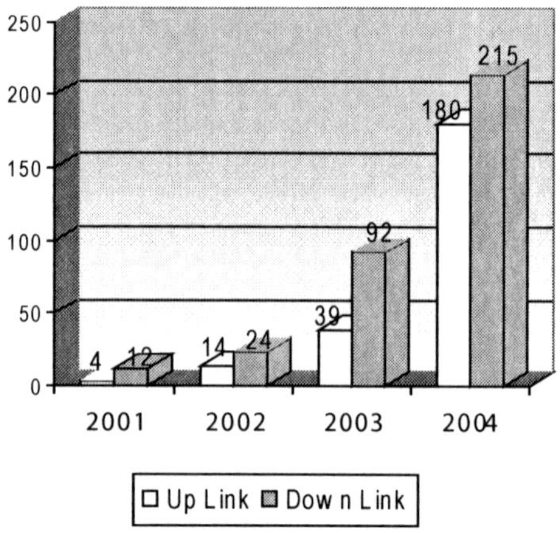

Figure 6. Number of ISPs

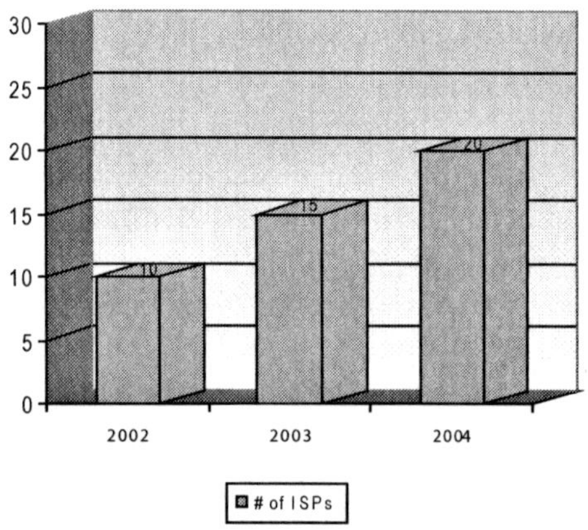

Figure 7. Internet dial-up users

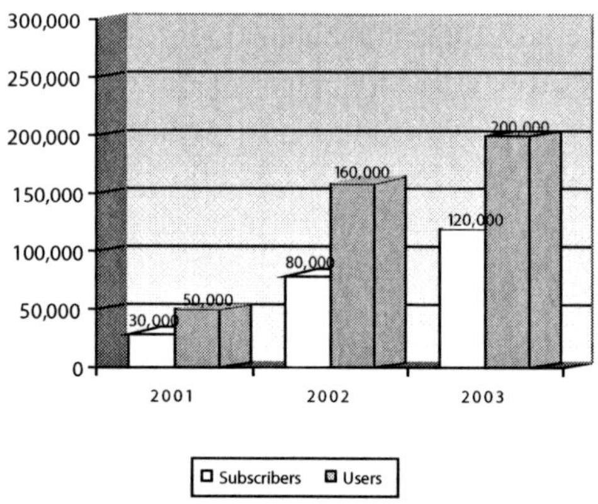

Microwave Links connecting rural areas to the O.F Backbone.

The growing emphasis on improving the technological infrastructure has been accompanied with a remarkable focus on the development and deployment of supporting applications. The last two years have witnessed an increasing emphasis on the adoption of e-banking technologies as the platform for the establishment of e-payment as an enabling architecture for the implementation of e-government initiatives. According to Kamel (2008), the use of electronic cheques clearing across banks is reflected in total value of 236,000, the monthly average number of cheques, settled which amount to 6.6 billion SDG (3.3 billion US $). Table (1) shows some recent operational results.

The work on Sudan's National Switch and Sudapan Payment Network has also gone further. According to Kamel (2008), Sudapan has made a reasonable progress since Feb., 2006, and Table 2 shows the progress. Table 3 provides additional statistics.

Results are depicted into Figure (8) based on the use of ATMs across the electronic payment network.

COUPLING SERVICE ORIENTED ARCHITECTURES AND MULTIAGENT CONCEPTS

The process of coupling alternative computing paradigms is widely used. Different projects have adopted service orientation concepts to address different perspectives by coupling service oriented architectures with other technologies and paradigms. The Terregov Project (2005) adopted

Table 1. Average number of cheques in a Year and % of Rejects. Source: Kamel (2008)

Average No. of Cheques/Month.	No Cheques	%
Accepted For Payments	199,000	82.9%
Insufficient Fund	25,000	10.4%
Closed Account	8,000	3.3%
Inconsistency between Image and Data	2,800	1.1%
End Of Session	550	0.23%
Cheques Paid Before	320	0.13%
	335,670	

Table 2. Sudapan Progress. Source: Kamel (2008)

No.	Sudapan Network Element	No.
1.	ATM	265 Machines
2.	Total No. of transactions on the National Switch for the period: Jan-Nov 2007	3,812,244 Trans
3.	Average Amount of withdrawal	2,500 SGD
4.	Average Number of Transactions per day	20,000 Transactions
5.	Average Growth rate for the Transactions per month.	6%-7%
6.	Number of POS machines Configured on the Switch	295 Machine
7.	Number of POS machines Installed and working	155
8.	Number of Issued cards By EBS	200,000 Cards

the principles of a SOA based on interoperable components with dynamic support for finding services because information, services and administrations are regarded as being spread over several information systems. The architecture contains a set of collaborative tools for e-government web services that are semantically enriched. The Ontogov—Ontology-enabled e-government service configuration project (ONTOGOV, 2006) incorporated service orientation concepts with ontological perspective by developing, testing and validating a semantically enriched (ontology-enabled) platform that will facilitate the consistent composition, re-configuration and evolution of e-government services. Janssen & Van Veenstra (2005) coupled the concepts of "information brokerage" with service-oriented architectures for the composition of new business processes using web services in the context of e-government. Sean & O'Reilly (2004) used Service Oriented Architectures (SOA) and XML representations of data as the basis for service delivery and modernization of e-government in Ireland.

Because this chapter adopts a distributed e-government deployment approach, service oriented architectures are coupled with multiagent

Table 3. Additional statistics

No.	Description	Value.	
1.	% of Total number of Successful Transactions.	70%	
2.	% of Total number of failed Transactions	30%	
3.	Average number of transaction per card in a month.	1.1 trans/card/month	
4.	Total number of cancelled Transactions	15,101	
5.	% of cancelled Transactions	0.35%	
6.	Peak hour (period) number of transactions	58% of Total Trans	
7.	% of the Number of Transaction at 11:00 am	9% of the Transact	
8.	% of number of Transactions during dead period 02:00 am	0.02% of total Transact	
9.	Comparison between a Heavily used ATM and another	191 Trans/day	4 Trans/day

Figure 8. Cross-ATM transactions. Source: Kamel (2008)

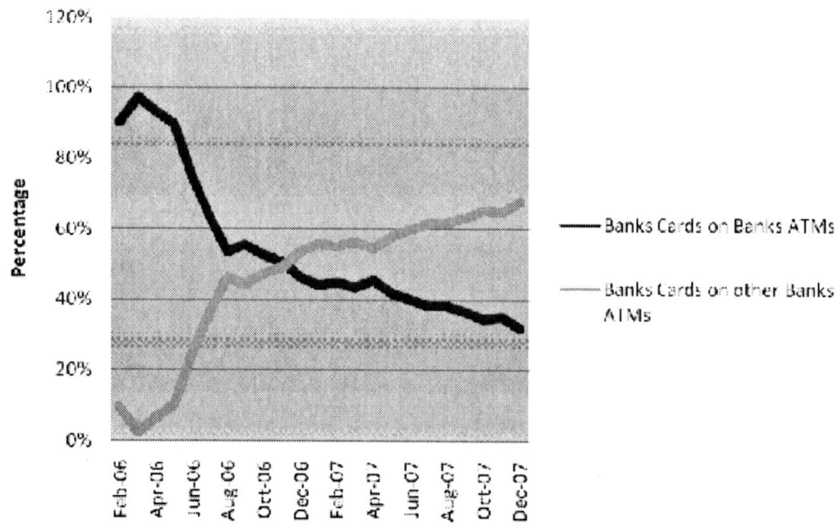

systems' technologies. An intelligent agent is as an autonomous, computational software entity that has access to one or more, heterogeneous and geographically distributed information sources, and which pro-actively acquires, mediates, and maintains relevant information on behalf of users or other agents. The autonomous behavior of these agents is determined by their pro-activeness, reactive and deliberative actions, and social interactions. In a multiagent system, agents jointly use knowledge and resources to solve problems in a context-dependent way (Gasmelseid, 2007a).

Within the context of a distributed work environment software agents can assist in facilitating coordination, cooperation and interaction among government agencies. Accordingly, these agencies can develop effective communication capabilities by benefiting from the resulting horizontally integrated services. Their use would also enhance user interaction and mobility by benefiting from the embedded user, service and physical mobility that support service accessibility and uniformity of service points.

Software agents can also assist with the management of channel conflicts when multiple service providing agencies find themselves operating on a network of front line and back line offices. Channels' conflict exists because e-government services are provided online and accessed by all citizens through multiple channels including computers, kiosks, face-to-face, mail, fax, and new electronic channels like the web, electronic mail, videoconference irrespective of their communication-use attitudes and read-write capabilities. Unless properly managed, channel conflict significantly challenges service interoperability. Software agents could also assist users to avoid a conjugation of different delivery channels that appears when several contacts between the user and the provider of service are necessary with regards to the provision of a single service.

The use of multiagent systems will also reduce the side effects associated with cultural difference that exist among the various government levels and stakeholders. Such differences have their ramifications on the attitudes, preferences and "style" of the user's electronic interactions. The use of multiagent systems can assist in coordinating service provision and limiting the effects of "power struggles" by creating and implementing "service congruence" mechanisms.

The use of multiagent systems can also assist in addressing security issues by enabling the entire system to prevent, avoid, detect or prepare for breaches of security that threaten the confidentiality, integrity or availability of information processed and used electronically (Gasmelseid, 2007a, 2007b). Especially for distributed e-government deployment approaches the importance of security and the use of alternative methods originates from the critical need of improving user confidence and interaction through improved privacy, confidentiality, and authentication (Wimmer & von Bredow, 2002; Lambrinoudakis et al., 2003). Because information will be fed to software agents to act upon, there is a chance to build effective security layers to be adhered to by all agents interacting in the architecture.

However, although security requirements vary with the concrete application, emphasis continued to be made on authentication (the ability to properly and securely identify system users), authorization (the ability to grant access privileges to the resources based on the available user's identities), confidentiality (the capacity to prevent information from being accessed or understood by unauthorized users or systems), integrity (the ability to prevent information from being intentionally or unintentionally corrupted or tampered with), availability (the ability to grant access to resources within a reasonable period of time) and non-repudiation (the ability to prevent any user from later denying his intervention in a given process or transaction) (Lambrinoudakis et al., 2003; Arcieri et al., 2004; Boudriga, 2002; Caloyannides et al., 2003; Joshi et al., 2001).

The relevance of the software agents' paradigm stems from the possibility to use a wide range of object oriented features to conceptualize both the domain and context of e-government applications by "articulating" roles, players and relationships on the one hand and "drawing" road maps for system-wide critical success "technical" factors including security and authentication on the other hand. The context of modeling e-government as "back-line" and "front-line" offices brings to attention the concept of viewing agents as a network of "superior" and "subordinate" agents possessing multiple and heterogeneous, yet related, tasks within the prevailing chain of "relationships" and a set of "verification" and "authentication" processes.

A MULTIAGENT SERVICE-ORIENTED MODEL FOR E-GOVERNMENT IN SUDAN

The architecture described in this chapter follows a distributed e-government deployment. While many authors have classified agents in accordance with their potential capabilities as "information", "internet', "search" and "task" agents, using the concept of "agent sets" as building blocks of a multiagent service oriented organization provides additional insights as shown in Figure (9). The rationale of using "agent sets" stems from the fact that users have no "standardized" mode of "activity-handling" as they can use their agents to "search information" about a "service", implement procedures, browse necessary documentation and locations (service procedures) and request the service through the e-government infrastructure. So, architecturally, users may either have different "agents" to perform different functions or multi-function agents to enable the management of "preferences", "task prioritization" and the balancing of the entire "utility matrix".

The "agent sets" attached to service "requesters" and "providers" reflect the priorities and preferences of service requesters and the dynamics of

Figure 9. Architectural agent sets' perspectives

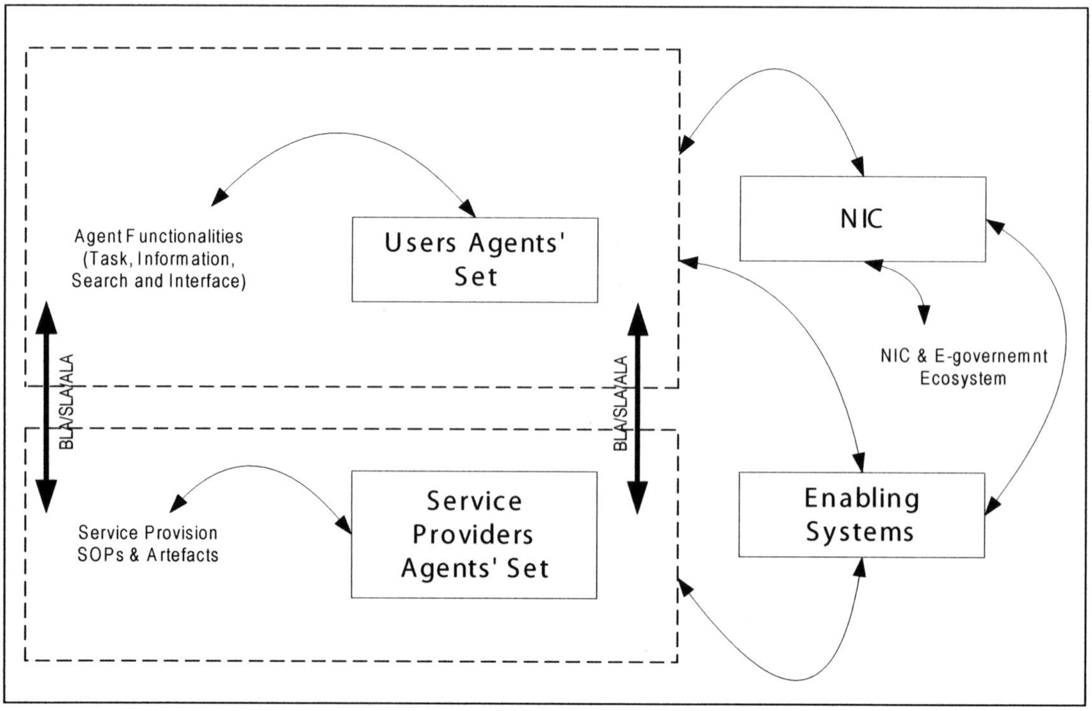

service declaration, assignment or provision. The interaction among different agent sets is governed by standardized service level agreements (SLA), business level agreements (BLA) and agent level agreements (ALA).

As shown in Figure (10), the entire framework is based on the creation, updating and management of the following modules:

a. Service requesting module denoting the framework of interaction between service requestors and the entire e-government infrastructure.
b. Service declaration, publishing, management and provision module in which all entities operating and interacting in the service provision grid state out and implement an agreed upon route of cooperation.
c. Service tracking module concerned with maintaining service logs, service requesting and provision status reports, and update of the qualities of "publishable" services. Requests are instances of services that requesting entities create and upload to providing entities when they need to request a service. To be able to "integrate" the process of service provision, these entities must keep a record of the successive events and results of the requests they receive and, whenever needed, they create reports to describe their state. The importance of such module stems from the fact that when "front-line" and "back-line" structure is adopted, the availability of service requesting and provision reports is essential for "service tracking" and "user notification".

The basic aim of incorporating such modeling modules is to assist in the articulation of the functionalities of agent sets and associating

Figure 10. Coupled distributed e-government architecture

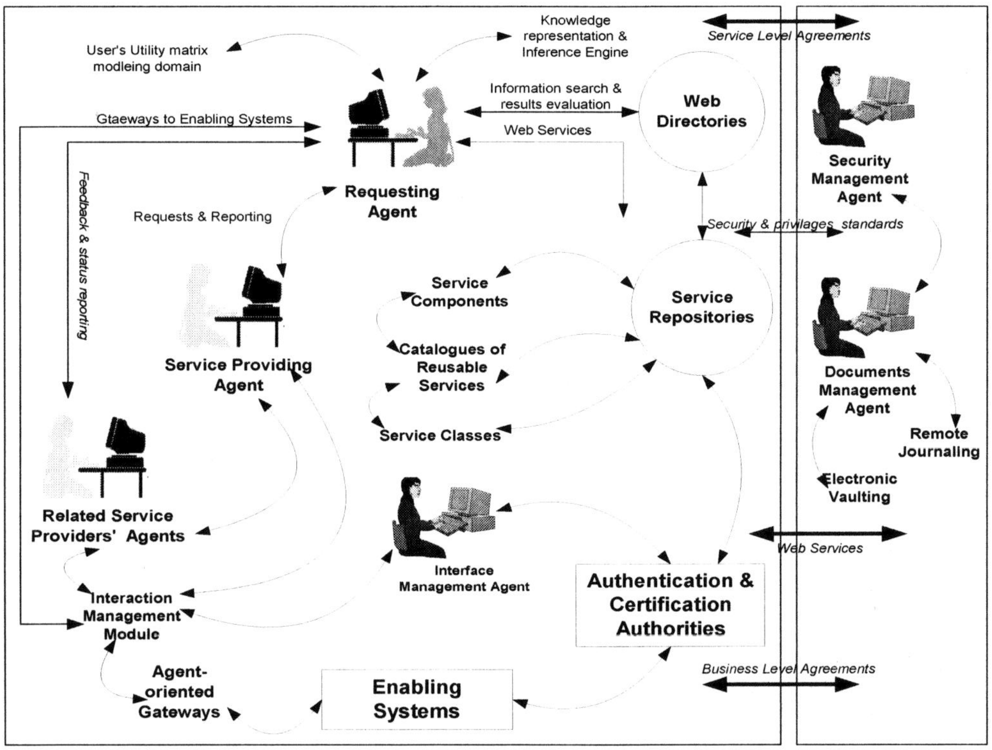

them with the "services" to be offered by the entire multiagent SOA organization. Within the context of the proposed architecture, the concepts of "front-line" and "back-line" offices are left loose and incorporated as "modules" to facilitate "information sharing", "code reusability" and "inter-agent communication" because the entire architecture follows a distributed e-government deployment approach.

The optimization of these modules across the landscapes of the entire e-government project is also affected by agent-specific integrated components (interface engines, knowledge representation algorithm and functionalities) and system-wide ecosystem procedures (security procedures and measures, authorization, authentication and data back up). However, when using software agents such repositories can be shared as they can be a part of the corporate "sharable resources".

However, services are interacted and "transacted" using the "front-line" and "back-line" office paradigm by adopting the concept of "agent sets". The user requests the service from the service providing entity by authorizing his entire agent to do that on behalf of him. If the service is entity-specific then interaction will be limited between the entity, the agent and his owner. If not, then the "front-line" office authorizes it agent set to communicate, on behalf of the user's agent, with the "back-line" office agents' set to request the service. The service providing agent takes the responsibility of collecting necessary documentation from the user's agent and, if necessary, authorize and manage (in collaboration with other agents) electronic payment through "enabling systems". Its roles expand to include user's agent authentication, authorization, and notification. It also tracks the status of the "service requested" and sends feedback to service requestors.

Coupling SOA with "agent sets" provides the possibility to address the potential difficulties associated with the use of the front and back line offices paradigm when integrated large scale e-government applications are being deployed. The implementation of such paradigm is associated with some difficulties that, if not properly managed, will move the whole context into disarray. Generally speaking, the front-back-office paradigm suits situations where services are provided by different organizational units that coordinate and collectively orchestrate their activities and processes within the same "chain of command" i.e., superior-subordinate relationship. In this case, there is a room to challenge and address the difficulties associated with the paradigm within the domain of "information sharing", "work coordination" and "conviviality". However, if the relationship between the "front line" and "back line office" exists outside the unified "chain of command", the process of service management will be affected by the lack of "organizational flexibility" necessary for offering some degree of "transparency", "openness" and "prompt response". In their process to follow their "localized" chain of command, the failure of different "offices" to alter or adapt to existing "structure-based" standard operating procedures to accommodate the need for frequent communication across "multiple" lines of command is another implementation challenge.

The process of communication among organizational units may also be challenged by a wide range of institutional, organizational, and personnel issues. If the service is provided by different entities operating within different chains of command, then each of them must have full knowledge about the services it can provide and accordingly publish metadata to describe it (in a schema-subschema fashion) as a part of relevant service repositories. Within this context, the lack of "standardized" universally accessible communication measures and data formats (together with the failure and/or unwillingness of any entity to adhere to such measures); communication problems will challenge the interactive service requesting-and-provision process and the ability of entities to "share", "load and upload" and access "service objects" using normalized formats.

In addition, even for "entities" operating within the same chain of command, there is a potential of conflict because they are usually organized as "profit", "cost" or "responsibility" centers. Because the process of service provision demands some entities to undertake some functions on behalf of others, the potential "sub-optimization" and "power struggles" significantly affect the quality of service and user satisfaction. Especially when the entities engaged in the process of service provision are enacted in a "value chain", both front line and back line offices must possess reasonable degrees of "technological maturity" and the capacity to manage technology intensive acquisitions. The variety of status on the "technology adoption curve", "technological infusion" and "institutional preparedness" are all, among others, significant change factors.

Using the distributed loose defined entities, connections among service providing entities are viewed as a "value chain" rather than a "chain of commands". The functionality of the entire value chain is governed by multiple service and business level agreements. The failure or lack of adherence to these agreements will result, under practical situations, into different communication and reporting difficulties. Such agreements are backed by a "trust chain" managed by the security agent in collaboration with the document management agent using different security layers.

If the service requesting entity provided its agent sets with advanced context awareness and mobility capabilities, those agents can "sense" and act upon "contextual" information and move across different servers to carry out different functions. Due to the huge amounts of forms, documents and data to be uploaded, downloaded, and exchanged during the service requesting-and-provision process, the question of data back up emerges as an important issue for agents and their migration to "search" for services, service providers, service provision terms, consult with its owner, submit a request for a service and track it through. The architecture proposes the use of remote transaction journaling and electronic vaulting systems to facilitate "data and system mirroring". Electronic vaulting allows effective control of data protection, outsourcing the data backup, offsite storage, archiving and management of recovery tasks. Although electronic vaulting services use a delta backup scheme that transmits only data that has changed, electronic vaulting still requires a good bandwidth in order to do simulations either on specific data presentation applications (such as spreadsheets) or by running its software to find out how long it will take to back up with the user's bandwidth. Remote transaction and server journaling accelerates the recovery time after an unexpected shutdown and significantly improve the availability of data, the capacity of the server and storage systems to maintain a continuous record of these transactions in a separate file (i.e., a journal). Moreover, remote journaling also provides an extremely fast and reliable mechanism for backup by moving critical data-change information to a remote location as it offloads the processor's load required for applying a replication activity to the backup machine, and put the remaining processing load on the production machine beneath the operating system (IBM). It also reduces the latency of replication data and processes, which also increases the transaction integrity of databases.

Implementation of this work will be done using XML and "Concordia" to gain the functionalities of "mobility", "accessibility" and "interoperability".

COUPLING FEATURES AND DEPLOYMENT CONSIDERATIONS

When taken individually, the concepts of agency and service orientations may provide different advantages and limitations with regards to "task accomplishment", user engagement and the rationalization of institutional procedures. The process of coupling has the potential to pool the merits of both concepts and, at the same time, presents some challenges that deserve paramount attention.

Situational Relevance and Advantages

The coupled architecture is relevant for the implementation of distributed e-government initiatives under the following situations:

a. When the service cycle is completely automated and computer based on a network of interconnected legacy systems for service requesting and provision. The process of tax authorization, negotiation, adjustment and settlement, for example can be significantly enhanced by such coupling. Using their entire agent sets, requesting entities (business enterprises) can authorize their tax agent sets to cross reference the internal accounting system and financial statements to get the value of tax due, interface (foreword) through the coupled architecture with the entire service provider (tax administration) to negotiate the amount of tax and interface (backward) with the tax-paying entity to get the final authorization from functional decision makers or their respective agent sets to settle tax through bank transfers or any other electronic method.
b. When there is an environment of orchestrated regulatory domains governing the different levels or scales of service provision. Especially for government service provision, there tend to be different regulations (both procedural and documentational) adopted by different government levels (federal vs. state) that significantly reduces the capacity of the requesting entity to request the service or complete its processing cycle. For the entire coupled model to be of more operational benefit it is preferred that there should exist an integrated, yet orchestrated, regulatory context to enable free mobility of service requesting agent sets otherwise additional effort is needed to modify the overall interface capacity and knowledge engine of service requesting agent sets in pursuit of improving their learning and adaptation skills.

The coupled architecture has the following advantages for the e-government initiative in Sudan:

a. It reduces entry requirements for service requestors and increases the span of implementation by expanding the context and definition of "service requesting entities" from citizens to include business enterprises.
b. Because it is using the concept of "agent sets" it supports the rationalization of procedures and reducing complexities, redundant processes and inefficiencies.
c. It reduces implementation failures associated with the centralized implementation model currently in use.
d. Because the process of coupling is based on the concepts of system integration and multi-dimensionality, it has the potential to provide additional support due to the recent developments witnessed with regards to the deployment of the integrated banking network (the national transactions' exchange facility managed by the Central Bank).

Potential Limitations

Although the majority of e-government initiatives are devoted to the provision of government services to citizens, little has been done to investigate the potential of these initiatives in "re-engineering" government agencies and improving their operational efficiency. The proposed model can be used in the future at a larger scale for the provision of sophisticated services (such as electronic medicine and computer supported collaborative work systems). While this may provide government units with the opportunity to assess their operational capacity to manage electronic processes it also improves operational efficiency through training and enhanced information sharing among different and remote trajectories using different types of data and interfaces. However, the following limitations are expected from the process of coupling agent and service oriented concepts.

In addition to other limitations, the deployment of a coupled framework can be challenged by the difficulty or the lack of willingness to create "learning organizational sets" to support the dimensions of "agents' sets". The functionality of the entire coupled functionality depends exclusively not only on the ability of service providing agencies to provide services but also on the ability of these agencies to operate as "learning organizational sets" each with its own learning capacity that contributes to the overall learning curve. Although the adoption of "agency" concepts support this dimension but in real term service providing agencies must by dynamic enough in preparing and fine-tuning their data sets in a way that allows for mobile agents' navigation and data access.

Foreseen Modifications

However, the following modifications and changes, among others, are expected to improve the potential and capacity of the model to support the implementation of the e-government initiative in Sudan as well as in similar situations:

1. Incorporating additional learning and autonomy dimensions to accommodate multi-channel considerations and shift of customer orientations and preferences. This may not only demand a significant change in the agent sets to be used but it also shifts the context of knowledge acquisition, representation and sharing.
2. To support mobility (user, service and equipment) associated with internet connections and user transactions, the use of the model at a large extent demands the integration of additional powerful mobility, context awareness and ubiquity to support service requestors and enhance the operational efficiency of government units with regards to the provision of sophisticated services. This demands building long term trusted preservation services through the use of service interaction protocols and evidence records to support other sophisticated service.

Therefore, future research might systematically test the interconnections between the effectiveness of e-government initiatives and the dynamics of the social, political, and economic environment. Special emphasis can be made on the effect of resource availability on e-government growth and implementation at different levels of governance. The extent to which the migration to democracy and institutional or political reforms affects the effectiveness of e-government applications is another variable to consider.

Critical research is also important to further address the concerns for interoperability in an open distributed environment, semantic and ontological management issue, standardization of agent-specific and collective processes to maintain an integrated value chain that crosses the boundaries of "command chains", ensuring security and effectiveness of enabling systems such as electronic payment and user authentication and authorization. In addition to the growing number of implementation platforms, taking special care to theses issues, among others, gives an insight about the "transformational" capacity of the entire e-government project to benefit from the unprecedented developments to be exhibited in computing paradigms and user activities and attitudes.

CONCLUSION

The chapter is advocating the use of multiagent systems technology and the concepts of service orientation as a form of coupling multiple e-government implementation paradigms. The proposed agent oriented and service based modeling approach adopted takes basic concepts addressed by previous research and attempted to reduce its merits to the case of the e-government initiative in Sudan. While the use of such research method enriches our understanding about the reasons that lead to the failure of many e-government projects it also provides a testable platform that guides the movement from vision to action especially in developing countries. The architecture proposed in this chapter supports the development and implementation of e-government initiatives by establishing a coupled atmosphere that includes the basic conditions necessary for allowing the entities involved in the provision of governmental services to share resources and cooperate with each other. The architecture supports the implementation of flexibly-enacted agent sets either as single life entities or composite ones by providing the possibility of "concurrent" service provision and access through integrated delivery channels. The proposed architecture is oriented towards relaxing e-government implementation variables by coupling service oriented concepts and the widely spreading and consolidated agents' technologies. The basic aim is to incorporate an effective enabling environment that offers more capabilities to support authentication, authorization, confidentiality, integrity and non-repudiation. Moreover, the architecture follows a distributed pattern where all resources (including knowledge) is accessible to all service providing entities and all channels are open for service requestors. Because of their operational capabilities, the use of agent sets supports such "distribution".

The chapter raised the importance of viewing the implementation of e-government initiative by considering not only technological build ups but also by understanding the variety of institutional, organizational and managerial dimensions. While the benefits and merits of proposed coupled model are based on the use of an integrated approach, its linkage to the case study of the e-government of Sudan has facilitated the articulation of modifications and future work. Addressing the limitations mentioned in this chapter goes hand in hand with the overall effort to strategically manage and implement the entire e-government project in the case studied as well as in similar ones.

REFERENCES

Abdorabo, A. (2004). E-Government and IP Symposium for the Arab Region, UAE – Dubai.

Alexandros, K., Panagiotis, S., Thanos, K., & Despina, P. (2005). A secure e-Government platform architecture for small to medium sized public organizations. Electronic Commerce Research and Applications, 4(2), 174-186.

Arcieri F et al. (2002). Experiences and issues in the realization of e-government services, Proc. of the 12th International Workshop on Research Issues in Data Engineering: Engineering E-Commerce/E-Business Systems, IEEE, New York (2002), pp. 143–148.

Arcieri, F. et al. (2004). A layered IT infrastructure for secure interoperability in Personal Data Registry digital government services, Proc. of the 14th International Workshop on Research Issues on Data Engineering: Web Services for E-Commerce and E-Government Applications (RIDE'04), IEEE, New York, pp. 95–102.

Baldwin, C. Y., & Clark. K. B., (2000). Design Rules, The power of modularity. The MIT Press, Cambridge, Massachusetts.

Benson, T. (2002). E-Service Development Framework Primer. eGIF4 Project, 1.0b version. Office of the e-Envoy, Cabinet Office., UK.

Bernhard, K., Jeroen, H., & Guenther, I. (2005). In principle: Towards an Open Architecture for e-government Identity Management, Working Paper No. 2504, ISSN: 1667-738X, Center for Technology and Innovation Management. Retrieved November 25, 2006 from http://www.cetim.org/wps

Boudriga, N. (2002). Technical issues in securing e-government. Proceedings of the IEEE International Conference on Systems, Man and Cybernetics, (2), pp. 392–397.

Caloyannides, M. et al. (2003). US e-government authentication framework and programs. IT Professional, 5(3), 16–21.

Cook, M.A. (1996) Building Enterprise Information Architectures. Reengineering Information Systems. Prentice Hall, New Jersey, USA.

Crawford, C.H, Bate, G., Cherbakov, L., Holley, K., & Tsocanos, C. (2005). Toward an On Demand Service-Oriented Architecture. IBM Systems Journal, 44(1), 81–108.

DataExchanger (2002). Pierre Audoin Conseil, "Guide comparatif EAI".

Eardley A. et al. (2003) Methods for Developing Flexible Strategic Information Systems: Is the Answer Already Out There? In N. Patel (ed.) Adaptive Evolutionary Information Systems, Idea Group Publishing.

European Community. (2003). The role of e-Government for Europe's future, Communication of the European Commission. Retrieved December 15, 2005 from http://europa.eu.int/information_society/eeurope/2005/doc/all_about/egov_communication_en.pdf

Foster, I and C. Kesselman, (Eds.). (2003). The Grid 2: Blueprint for a New Computing Infrastructure. San Francisco: Morgan Kaufmann Publishing, Inc.

Ganek, A. G., & Corbi, T. A. (2003). The Dawning of the Autonomic Computing Era. IBM Systems Journal, 42(1), 5–18.

Gasmelseid, T. (2007a). From Operational Dash Boards to E-Business: Multiagent Formulation of Electronic Contracts. International Journal of E-Business Research, 3(3), 77-97, July – September 2007.

Gasmelseid, T. (2007b). Engineering multiagent systems. In M. Quigley (Ed.), *Encyclopedia of Information Ethics and Security*, 187-193. Idea Group Publishing, USA.

Gonçalo, P. D., & José, A. R. (2006). A simple model and a distributed architecture for realizing one-stop e-government. Electronic Commerce Research and Applications, doi:10.1016/j.elerap.2006.02.001.

Greunz, M., Schopp, B. & Haes, J. (2004). Integrating e-government infrastructures through secure XML document containers. Proceedings of the 34th Annual Hawaii International Conference on System Sciences (HICSS-34*)*, (2), p. 5004.

Hillard, R. (2000). IEEE-std-1471-2000: Recommended Practice for Architectural Description of Software-Intensive Systems. Retrieved February 15, 2007 from http://standards.ieee.org.

IBM. iTera Echo^2 High Availability for IBM iSeries, http://www.ibm.com

Janssen, M., & Van Veenstra, A. (2005). Stages of Growth in e-Government: An Architectural Approach. The Electronic Journal of e-Government, 3(4), 193-200.

Joshi, J. ct al. (2001). Digital government security infrastructure design challenges. Computer security 34 (2), 66–72.

Kamel, Izzeldin. (2008). E-Banking and its impact on Sudanese Banking sector. Invited lecture, Management Forum, Jan 16, 2008, British Council, Khartoum, Sudan.

Kaliontzoglou, A., et al. (2005). A secure e-government platform architecture for small to medium sized public organizations. Electronic Commerce Research and Applications, 4 (2), 174–186.

Lambrinoudakis, C. et al. (2003). Security requirements for e-government services: a methodological approach for developing a common PKI-based security policy. Computer Communications, 26 (16), 1873–1883.

Layne, K. and Lee, W. (2001). Developing fully functional e-government: A four stage model, Government Information Quarterly 18 (2), pp. 122–136.

Medjahed, B. et al. (2003). Infrastructure for e-government web services. IEEE Internet Computing, 7 (1), 58–65.

Mediadev (2002). Pourquoi et comment faire communiquer les applications. Livre blanc.

Michael Stevens (2002). Service-Oriented Architecture Introduction, Part 1. Retrieved April 26, 2005 from www.developer.com/design/article.php/1010451.

Mühl, F., & Krabina, B. (2003). Online One-Stop Government - Eine Integrierte Plattform: Ergebnisse des EU-Projekts eGOV. In Maria Wimmer (Hrsg.), Quo vadis e-Government? State-of-the-art 2003, Proceedings of eGOV Days 2003 OCG series, 165, pp. 156-165.

ONTOGOV project (2006). Retrieved December 30, 2006 from http://www.sciencedirect.com/science?_ob=RedirectURL&_method=externObjLink&_locator=url&_cdi=6902&_plusSign=%2B&_targetURL=http%253A%252F%252Fwww.ontogov.com%252F

Ross, J.W & Westerman, G. (2004). Preparing for Utility Computing: The Role of IT Architecture and Relationship Management. IBM Systems Journal, 43 (1), 5–19.

Schmidt, M., Hutchison, B., Lambros, P., & Phippen, R. (2005). The Enterprise Service Bus: Making Service-oriented architecture real. IBM Systems Journal, 44 (4), 781-797.

Sean McGrath and Conor O'Reilly (2004), A Service Oriented Approach to e-Government Architecture, Proceedings of the XML-Europe 2004, Amsterdam, The Netherlands. Retrieved November 22, 2006.

Shilakes, C., & Tylman, J. (1988). Enterprise Information Portal. Merill Lynch.

Stamoulis D et al. (2003) A teleological Development of "Design-Decisions-Independent" Information Systems. In N. Patel (ed) Adaptive Evolutionary Information Systems, Idea Group Publishing.

Steimke, F., & Hagen, M. (2003). OSCI: a common communication standard for e-government. Lecture Notes in Computer Science, 2739, 250–255.

Tambouris, E. (2001). An Integrated platform for Realizing Online One-Stop Government: The eGOV Project. In: Proceedings of the DEXA International Workshop "On the Way to Electronic Government", IEEE Computer Society Press, Los Alamitos, CA.

Terregov Project (2005). Retrieved October 20, 2005 from http://www.sciencedirect.com/science?_ob=RedirectURL&_method=externObjLink&_locator=url&_cdi=6902&_plusSign=%2B&_targetURL=http%253A%252F%252Fwww.terregov.eupm.net

The Federal Enterprise Architecture, Program Management Office web site (2005). Retrieved October 29, 2005 from http://www.feapmo.gov.

UK GovTalkTM (2004). Retrieved September 2006 from www.govtalk.gov.uk

UN (2003). World public sector report: E-government at the crossroads, United Nations, New York.

UNPAN, Benchmarking e-government (2002). A global perspective, United Nations Online Network in Public Administration and Finance, New York.

Vassilakis, C., Anya, S., Dimitrios, T., & Dimitris, G. (2005). A Blackboard-Oriented Architecture for e-Government Service Composition. Managing Modern Organizations with Information Technology. 309 – 312.

Web Services, World Wide Web Consortium (2002). Retrieved July 25, 2006 from http://www.w3.org/2002/ws/

Wimmer, M, & Traunmueller, R. (2002). Towards an Integrated Platform for Online One-Stop Government. In: ERCIM News, Special Theme: e-Government, Issue 48, January 2002.

Wimmer, M. (2002). A European perspective towards online one-stop government: the eGOV project. Electronic Commerce Research and Applications 1 (1), 92–103.

Wimmer, M. and Bredow, B. (2002). A holistic approach to security aspects in e-government. Proceedings of the 35th Hawaii International Conference on System Sciences (HICSS-35), (5), p. 128b.

Wimmer, M and Krenner, J. (2001). An Integrated Online One-Stop Government Platform : The Egov Project, 9th Interdisciplinary Information Management Talks. Proceedings of the Schriftenreihe Informatik, Universitätsverlag Trauner, Linz, pp. 329-337.

World Bank. A definition of e-government. Retrieved 25 November 2006 from wwwl.worldbank.org/publicsector/egov

Chapter XV
A Methodology for Ontological Mediation in Multi-Agent Systems[1]

Shahram Rahimi
Southern Illinois University, USA

Bidyut Gupta
Southern Illinois University, USA

Pravab J. Rana
Southern Illinois University, USA

ABSTRACT

The effectiveness of current search and retrieval systems is restricted as they do not use the semantics of the data but mainly utilize keywords. Multi-agent systems in which agents gather information and organize it, by creating ontologies, are being utilized to improve the performance and quality of the data gathering and integrating systems. Major difficulties that arise during collaboration among such agents are ambiguity and data misinterpretation. This is due to the diversity of ontology creators, differences in linguistics and ontological overlapping. Users may also knowingly or unknowingly add incorrect information to ontologies. Ontological Mediation tries to address such collaboration issues relating to ambiguous and unfamiliar information arising due to various reasons. We propose a communication based approach for ontological mediation. In the process, we also present a classification model for ontological mediation.

Copyright © 2009, IGI Global, distributing in print or electronic forms without written permission of IGI Global is prohibited.

INTRODUCTION

The way information is searched and retrieved across vast collections such as the internet is still very raw. Generally, keywords are entered in search engines and documents are searched looking for the keywords. Any such enormous collection can be processed more efficiently if its data is organized. Organization here means data arrangement and representation in such a way that information retrieval is faster, relevant and better, with machines themselves being able to understand the semantics. Creating ontology of terms and forming hierarchy of concepts is one such organization. Such organization of vast sets of data into a well structured ontological representation presents difficulties. The data may be in different formats, using a variety of different languages and with conflicting ideas. Further it is not an easy task to verify the reliability of data, or for that matter, to update or alter any data and make it transparent across the system.

Even after organization of data into ontologies, effectiveness and efficiency are not guaranteed. To be effective the organized information should also form a cohesive interpretation. Without coherence, information will not be useful irrespective of how well it is organized. Uniformity in a multi-agent architecture like ours is not guaranteed without intervention. With different agents gathering and organizing information on different domains, inter agent collaboration is needed. This collaboration with other information providing agents (called information agents for the remainder of this chapter) can unfortunately lead to misunderstandings and ambiguities. Such problems are due to the inherent complexity that arises during automated information exchange, linguistic differences, overlapping information and also due to the diversity of users who create ontological documents. Different information agents may reply with conflicting information for a single query. There can be a variety of reasons for conflicting information. Conflicting information may be the result of a conflicting domain. For example in response to an information request about "OWL", one agent may reply "OWL" as a Web Ontology Language while other agent might respond to the query as a nocturnal bird. Though both agents provide correct information, the information becomes futile as the receiving agent cannot process such ambiguous response.

Conflicts arising from difference in domain are easier to mediate. Few questions relating to where the information is being used can help determine the domain and hence resolve the conflict. Nevertheless, conflicts do not always involve different domains. As different users may be involved in creating the ontology for the information agents, the information itself may be flawed and incorrect. This can result in conflicting information for a same term within the same domain. Linguistic difference can also be one of the causes of such conflicting information. For example, British English uses "first floor" to refer to the first floor above the ground, however in American English, it is another name for the ground floor itself. Among other reasons (discussed later) being able to identify and resolve linguistic difference as in the above example is the goal of ontological mediation. The need for ontological mediation goes beyond the interactions between existing ontologies. It is also desirable that new ontologies bringing in new information are easily incorporated within the system. For this ontological reorganization, reconciliation, merging and update are necessary.

Our model uses techniques suggested in "A Multi-Agent Architecture for Distributed Domain-Specific Information Integration" (Rahimi, Carver & Petry, 2005) as the method for collecting data through knowledge discovery, information gathering and integration from multiple sources. Similar to the Domain Model and the Information Source Model introduced in (Rahimi et al., 2005), our agents have an ontology of terms (its knowledge base) and also partial information about other agents that provide further specialized information on a topic. The following sections present a simple and straight forward communication based ontological mediation approach for efficient collaboration among such information agents. In the process, we also present a classification model of ontological mediation and the viability of our approach.

Previous Works

The field of ontological mediation is active with various past and current researches focusing on different aspects of mediation and negotiation. However, most of these works either cover aspects of mediation or are too specific. Two of the more comprehensive methodologies are introduced in (Campbell & Shapiro, 1998) and (Hexmoor & Sabba, 2006). Campbell's research (Campbell, 1999) focuses on ontological mediation for dialect problem. Whenever a problem in dialect arises, the agents try to find out the ambiguous word by making further queries. The queries may be simple yes or no answer queries. Campbell along with Shapiro, also developed algorithms for ontological mediation (Campbell & Shapiro, 1998). Their approach was used in the WordNet ontology (Miller, 1995) focusing on dialect problem. They however make an assumption that there are no conflicting terms. Their scope of mediation is, therefore, rather restricted.

A more recent approach is presented in "Towards Semantically Coherent Collaboration" (Hexmoor & Sabba, 2006). In this approach each agent has two roles that of an ordinary agent and a mediator. The mediator role is employed when the receiver does not understand some of the terms of the sender. They use functional specification to represent and match concepts. Functional specifications refer to key values or properties of a concept that can uniquely identify it. This approach focuses more on mediation between agents whose lower ontologies differ minimally.

DEVELOPMENT PLATFORM

In our model, a hierarchy of information agents are created following methods introduced in Kenoblock et al. (1997). Similar to the way current information sources are independently constructed, information agents are developed and maintained separately. They draw on other information agents and data repositories to provide a new information source that others can build upon in turn. Each information agent is another information source, but provides an abstraction of the many information sources available. In this network, each agent in addition to having an individual domain ontology, which is a representation of the information it can interpret, includes brief information about other specialized agents in the domain. The hierarchy of agents is built such that in lower levels the agents become more specific in the information (Kenoblock et al., 1997).

Figure 1 illustrates how the ontology of an agent's domain of expertise (domain model) and the model providing information from other agents that can provide relevant information (information source model) are utilized. The model providing information on other agents describes the content of interest available and the relationship between these concepts and the concepts in the domain model. These mappings are useful for inter-agent querying. Such model may not contain a complete description of the other agents, but rather only those portions that are relevant (Kenoblock et al., 1997).

Whenever an information request is issued, every agent initially queries its knowledge base, that is an ontological document, to retrieve information. Agents use query languages such as RDQL (Seaborne, 2004) and SPARQL (Prud'hommeaux & Seaborne, 2007) to retrieve information from their ontological bases. A RDQL query is similar to a SQL query with fields for documents from where information is to be retrieved, conditions that need to be matched for the query and restriction that should be considered. Figure 2 illustrates

Figure 1. Mapping of models

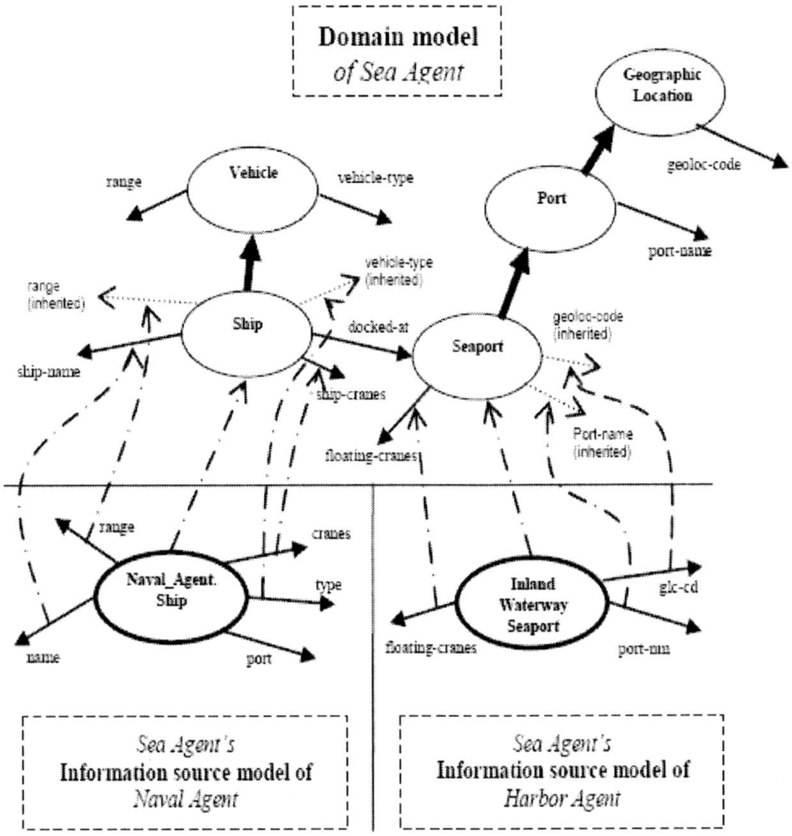

Figure 2. Syntax of a RDQL query

```
SELECT variable
FROM document (optional)
WHERE condition
AND Restriction
USING Namespace
```

the syntax of an RDQL query. The RDQL query is based upon the idea that an RDF document can also be represented as collection of nodes and relationship between nodes. Such collections also known as "triples" have a subject, a predicate and an object. The subject denotes a resource, the predicate denotes traits or characteristics of the resource and the object expresses a value for the trait. The "where" condition specified in an RDQL query is used to match against such triples in the ontological document. If the required information is not available in the agent's ontology, information requests are sent to other agents using an agent communication language (discussed below). Whenever an ambiguous or an unknown response arrives, mediation is required.

Creating ontologies is a fundamental step as these ontologies serve as repositories for our agents. Thus any data we come across is represented and organized using an ontological language. Web Ontological Language (OWL) (McGuinness & Harmelen, 2004) is one such language that is utilized. Editors, similar to SWOOP (Kalyanpur, Parsia, Sirin, Grau & Hendler, 2006) may be used for OWL to create ontologies as well as to write queries for retrieving information from such ontologies. Figure 3 is a screenshot of an OWL class tree created

Figure 3. SWOOP screenshot

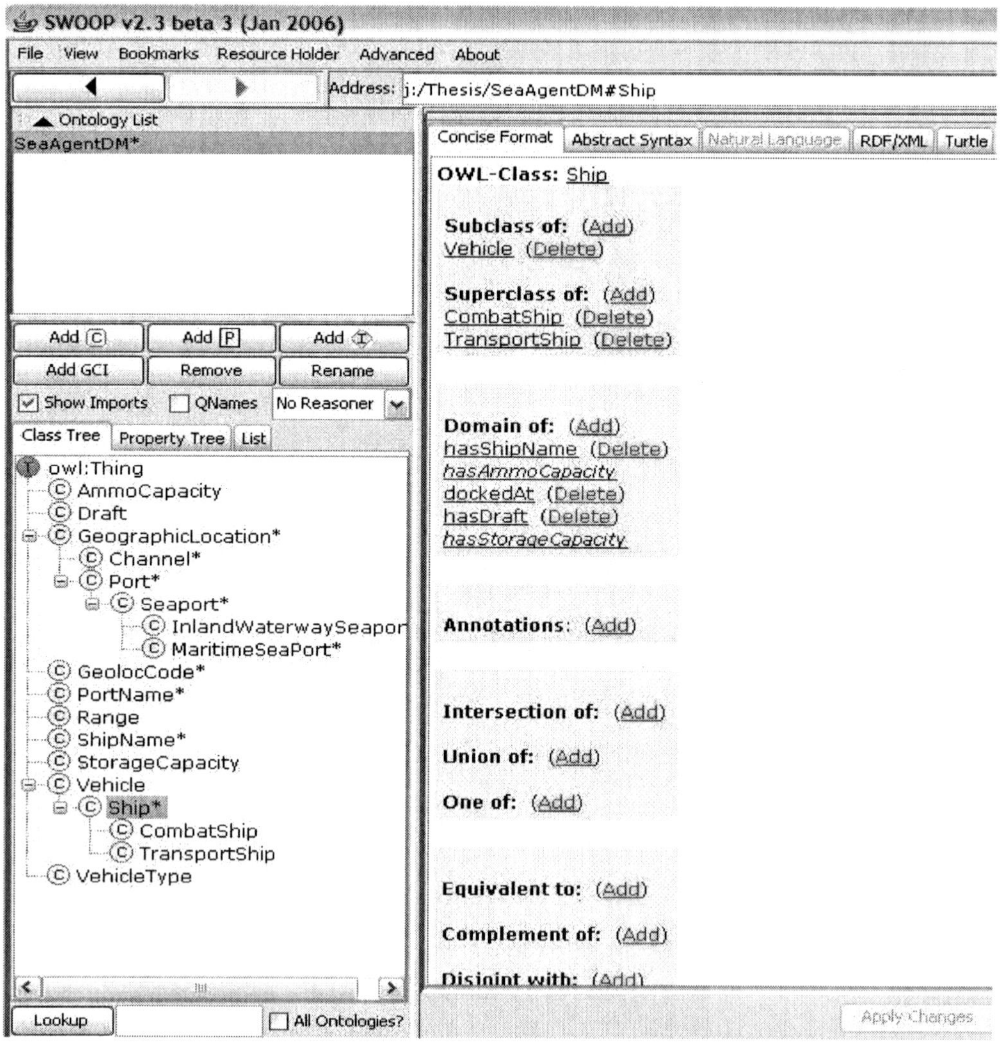

using SWOOP. In our system, OWL is chosen over some of the other existing languages such as RDF (Resource Description Framework) (Bray, 1998), OIL (Ontology Interchange Language) and DAML (Darpa Agent MarkUp Language) (Connolly, Harmelen, Horrocks, McGuinness, Patel-Schneider & Stein, 2001). We selected OWL since much of the work done in OIL and DAML has been included in OWL. Furthermore, every OWL document is also an RDF document. As such OWL provides all the features provided by these languages while adding new tags to better describe classes, properties and relations.

OWL has three sub-languages: OWL-Lite, OWL-DL and OWL-Full. While OWL-Full provides high expressiveness of concepts with a large language vocabulary, OWL-DL supports automated reasoning as it is based on Description Logic. Thus when one requires greater expressiveness, OWL-Full can be selected and if automated reasoning is required OWL-DL may be preferred. Automated reasoning makes automatic inferencing possible. For instance, for basic statements such as (i) Maya is a student, and (ii) All students have student ids, an inference that "Maya has a student id" can be made. Reasoners similar to Pellet (Sirin, Parsai, Grau, Kalyanpur, & Katz, n.d.) and Racer (Haarslev & Moller, 2003) that work with OWL-DL should be able to make inference like this and even more complex ones easily. This is what draws us to choose OWL-DL over other ontological languages.

The agents can be created using Java, and therefore, we require interconnection between Java and the OWL-DL ontologies. The Jena tookit (Jena–A Semantic Web Framework for Java, n.d.) allows Java access to RDF and OWL type languages. Using Jena, it is possible for the agents to create domain and information source models based on OWL-DL documents without losing their semantics. Jena also includes tools that allow the models to be modified and queried through the use of Java code. Reasoners can be accessed and applied to the models by using the DIG interface (Bechhofer, Moller & Crowther, 2003) along with Jena or by using simple, built-in Jena reasoners.

During information retrieval, there is also the need of finding interpretation of unknown terms and making such meanings transparent to other information agents. These issues highlight the need for mechanisms to share information. To be effective the agents need to be able to share information with one another and to use others' services to understand ambiguous and unknown terms. An Agent Communication language is used for this purpose. Knowledge Query and Manipulation Language (KQML) (Finin, Fritzson, McKay & McEntire, 1994) is preferred as the Agent Communication Language in our system. KQML is used by agents to communicate with one another as well as with the mediation agent to report and resolve ambiguity. Figure 4 illustrates a sample KQML query from a weather agent to a temperature agent asking for the current temperature reading at Carbondale. Such queries should be appropriately mapped for information retrieval from ontologies.

MEDIATION METHODOLOGY

As mentioned, even with the same sub-version of OWL, misinterpretations are possible owing to linguistic differences, interpretation differences across domains, faulty and overlapping information and inherent complexity with machine interpretation. In the presented methodology, ontological mediation is carried out by mediation agents. These agents are also information agents. Any information agent possessing sufficient knowledge may act as a mediation agent. In our model, the higher level agents in the information agent hierarchy have brief information about what the agents below them contain (Rahimi et al., 2005). Thus higher level agents can act as mediation agents for the agents below them.

When an information agent comes across an ambiguous or unknown term, it reports to its mediation agent. To answer to an arbitration request, a mediation agent first uses a voting algorithm. It initially sends a message to the manager agent. Manager agent is a specialized agent that performs ontological verification and consistency checking and maintains a list of information agents and brief information about their ontologies so that when required it can provide a directory of agents capable of replying to a particular query. When the system becomes very large, the manager agent can delineate its task to different domain specific manager agents.

Figure 4. A sample KQML query

```
Ask about
    : Content "(Temperature, Carbondale)"
        : Language OWL-DL
    : Ontology Weather Ontology
    : Reply-with "Current Temperature"
    : Sender Weather Agent
    : Receiver Temperature Agent
```

Once the agent's list arrives, a multicast message is sent by the mediation agent to all the agents having information about the subject of the mediation. Using a simple counter, votes are collected for the different interpretations and the interpretation receiving higher than a threshold number of votes (currently 66%) is selected as the correct interpretation. If no clear interpretation emerges from voting, questioning method is used (described later). Any ambiguity or unfamiliarity that cannot be resolved over a long period of time is reported to human experts through the human aid agent. Mediation through voting and questioning mechanism (Figure 5) is described with more details in the following sub-sections.

Voting Based Mediation

When a sender receives multiple interpretations or a response which it cannot understand, it reports to its mediation agent. The mediation agent first sends a message to the manager agent asking for all agents whose ontology has information related to the terms creating ambiguity or unfamiliarity. The mediation agent then sends a message to all the agents that are listed by the manager agent. Each agent receiving the message replies with its interpretation. A counter is maintained and incremented by the mediation agent for each interpretation. The interpretation receiving highest vote (66% or more) is assumed correct. The

Figure 5. Overview of proposed ontological mediation approach

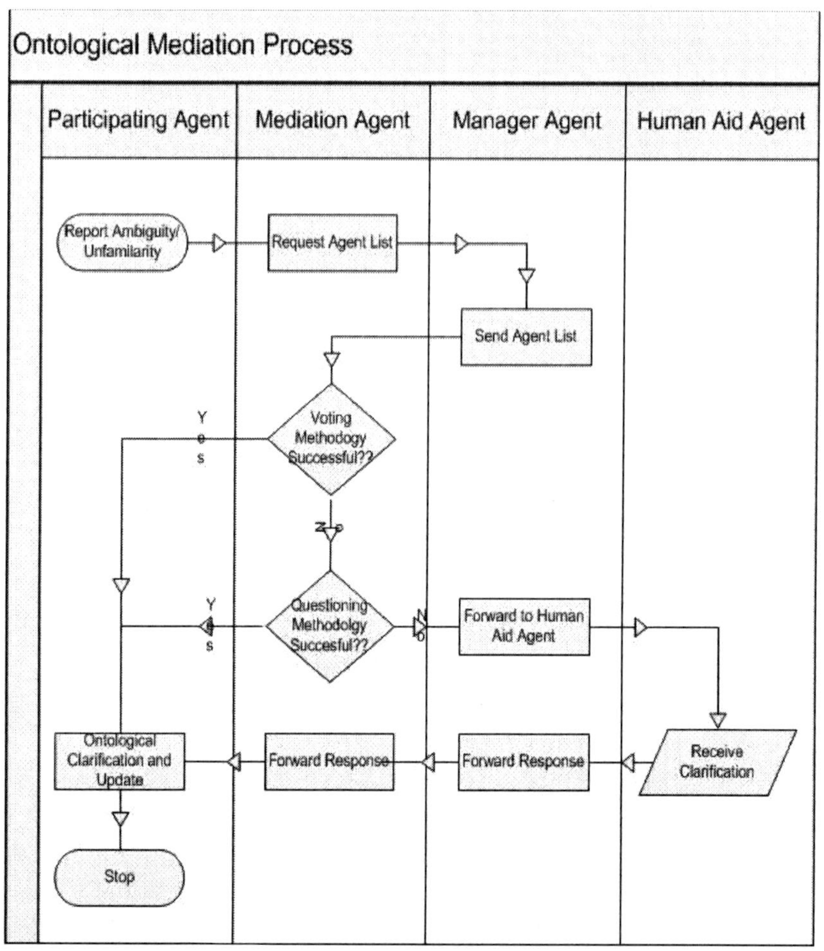

participating agents are informed by mediation agent about the interpretation.

Communication Primitives for Voting Method

The voting based approach uses the following communication primitives for mediation. The sequence of exchange of these communication primitives has been depicted in Figure 6.

- *Request_Agent_List:* The mediation agent asks the manager agent for the list of agents having knowledge on the ambiguous or unknown term. The domain of use is also provided to restrict the search.
- *Request_Term_Information:* The mediation agent sends a "Request_Term_Information" to all agents that are listed in the manager agent's response. "Term" here refers to the word that needs to be interpreted correctly.
- *Term_Information_Response:* Each Agent receiving the request sends its interpretation of the term to the mediation agent.
- *Counter_Update:* "Counter_Update" is an internal communication message used by the mediation agent. It is used for tallying different interpretations.
- *Voting_Success_Term_Interpretation:* This message is used to indicate that voting was successful. Success here means that we

Figure 6. Sequence diagram for voting based mediation

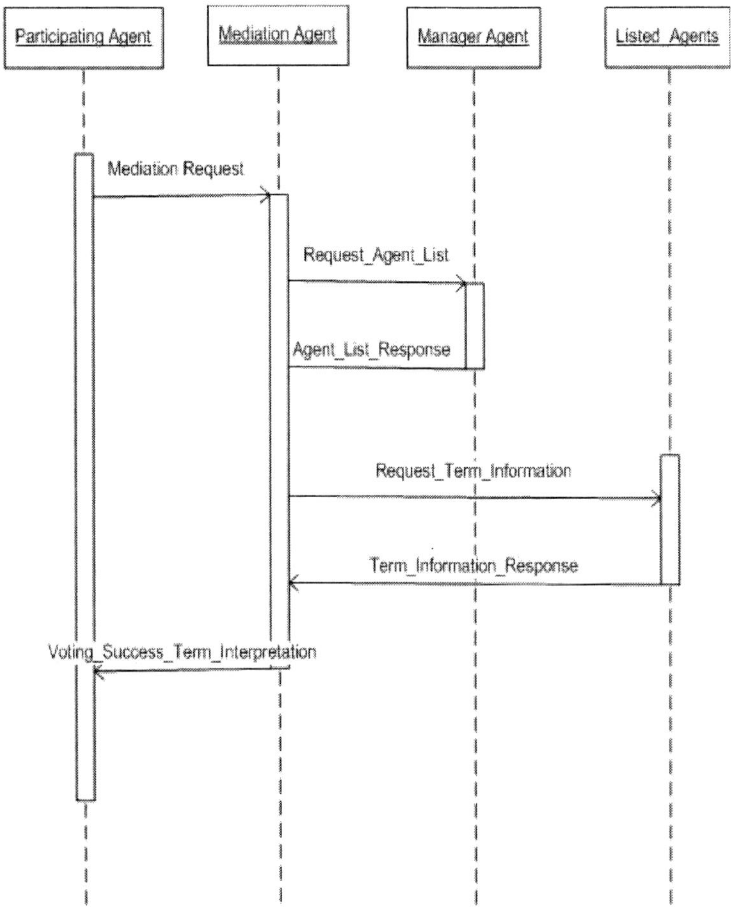

have an interpretation receiving greater than or equal to the threshold number of votes (currently 66%). The correct interpretation is then sent to the agents involved in the ambiguity or trying to interpret an unknown term.

- *Voting_Failure_Term:* This is also an internal communication primitive and is used to indicate that voting could not find a clear interpretation and that questioning method should now be employed.

Questioning Based Mediation

If ambiguous and unknown terms cannot be resolved by voting, mediation agent starts the questioning method. Mediation agent initially inquires about the domain, the higher ontology and the hierarchy of the term among others. If mediation can be achieved through responses to these questions, the participating agents are informed about the correct interpretation. When such information is insufficient to resolve ambiguity, mediation agent asks further questions regarding properties, restrictions, and cardinality. If mediation agent cannot resolve the ambiguity through responses to these questions as well, the data is tagged as ambiguous and passed on to human aid agent for expert human assistance. Once the experts have clarified the ambiguity, all participating agents are informed through the manager agent.

Communication Primitives for Questioning Method

The questioning based approach uses the following communication primitives for mediation. The sequence of exchange of these communication primitives has been depicted in Figure 7.

- *Request_Term_Hierarchy:* This is the initial communication primitive for the questioning method. It is used for requesting clarification on the hierarchy of the term. This message is sent by the mediation agent to the agents involved in the ambiguity inquiring about the super class, the subclass, the domain and any other synonym terms that may be present. For interpretation of an unknown term, this message is sent to the agent from where the request originated as well as agents involved in the earlier voting process.
- *Term_Hierarchy_Response:* Each agent receiving "Request_Term_Hierarchy" responds with a "Term_Hierarchy_Response". The response contains information about the super class, subclass, domain and any other synonyms for the term.
- *Request_Term_Properties:* When mediation agent is unable to clarify the ambiguity or unfamiliarity through "Term_Hierarchy_Response", further information is requested through "Request_Term_Properties". The properties are requested in a manner of increasing significance. The properties that can uniquely identify the term are requested before any other properties. A similar approach has been used in (Hexmoor & Sabba, 2006) for associating concepts and functional specifications.
- *Term_Properties_Response:* This is the message sent in response to the "Request_Term_Properties". It contains the list of properties ordered by increasing significance. One way to find the higher significance of a property is to monitor the associated use of the property in context to the term. It may also be accomplished by adding certain identifying information for the properties that are significant.
- *Request_Term_Cardinalities_Restrictions:* Mediation agent uses this primitive when it is unable to mediate even after receiving the properties list. This is a request to list any cardinalities or restrictions associated with the sent properties.

Figure 7. Sequence diagram for questioning based mediation

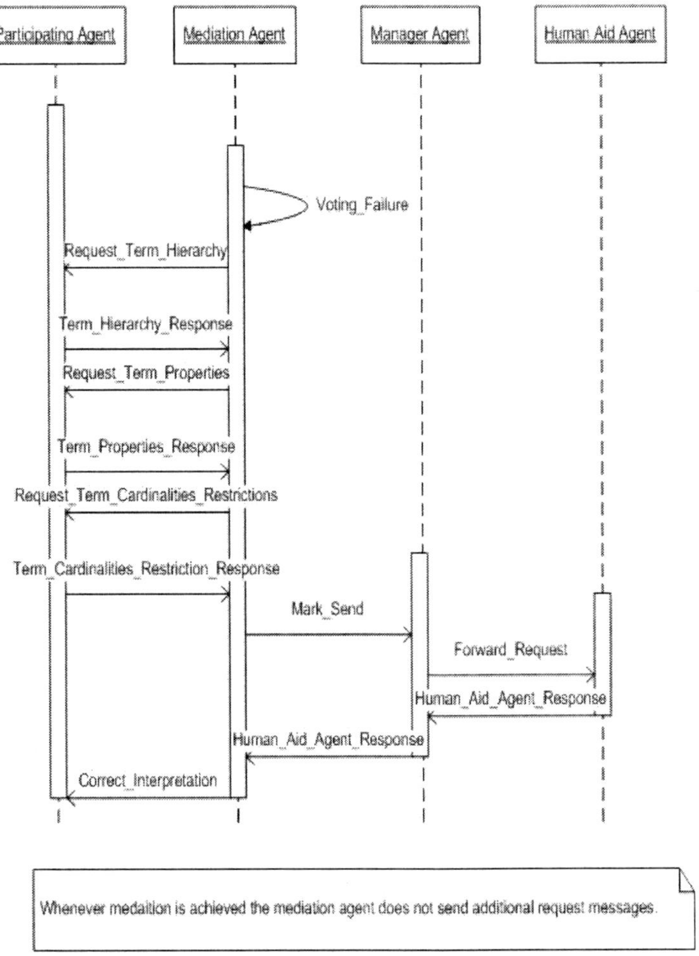

- *Term_Cardinalities_Restrictions_Response:* This is the response for "Request_Term_Cardinalities_Restrictions" and it lists the associated cardinalities and restrictions.
- *Mark_and_Send_to_Manager_Agent:* When the mediation agent is unable to clarify the ambiguity or unfamiliarity through the above mentioned set of communication primitives, it marks it as "currently ambiguous" and passes it on to the manger agent using this message.
- *Forward_Request_Human_Aid_Agent:* Once a term marked as "currently ambiguous" is received by the manager agent, it prepares a data structure to store information relating to the agents involved, the date of reported ambiguity, the mediation agent used and the ambiguous interpretations. It then forwards the term to the human aid agent.
- *Request_Human_Clarification:* This communication primitive is used by the human aid agent to inquire human experts. Human aid agent maintains lists of resource person on various domains. Initially the use of this agent may be more frequent. With time as the system becomes more comprehensive, the role of human aid agent will become insignificant, while agents themselves are

able to mediate the majority of ambiguity and unfamiliarity.

- *Human_Clarification_Response:* When the interpretation of the term has been established by human experts, it is reported to the manager agent through this message.
- *Human_Aid_Agent_Response:* Once human experts have clarified the meaning and sent it to the human aid agent, the human aid agent forwards it. It sends the corrected interpretation to the manager agent, mediation agent and the agents involved in the mediation process.

Addressing Security and Other Issues of Concern

The following sub-sections present security and other issues of concern for the presented methodology. We have to be concerned about security issues such as trust among agents, dealing with malicious users and agents and techniques for maintaining a quantitative measure of such concerns. We keep track of the degree of certainty value that is used as a reflection of percentage match among different concepts. For efficiency purpose, we also make a slight modification to our methodology when dealing with unknown terms.

Trust in Ontological Mediation

Here, we assume that whenever an ontology is created, it is formed as correctly as possible. This assumption helps to reduce the credibility issue regarding information received by an agent. Human experts to some degree also can help to verify the credibility of the ontology, but if such verifications have to be done frequently, the purpose of creating information agents will be futile. If we do not make this assumption, we will have to maintain a trust value for each participating agent that reflects the credibility of the agent and its ontology. When an agent is frequently the cause of ambiguity, its credibility will be reduced. The credibility of an agent not causing ambiguity will be increased as time passes. The trust value of an agent ranges between "0" to "1" with "0" signifying no trust in the agent and "1" signifying that the agent is fully trusted. Initially all agents have trust value of 0.5. Any information sent by an agent having a low trust value is subjected to further questioning by the receiving agent. Over time the trust value increases and the information from an agent with a higher trust value is accepted more readily. The trust value of an agent is decreased if it is found to be sending incorrect information.

History of Mediation

Each mediating agent maintains a log of participants, ambiguity and correct interpretation for all mediations undertaken. With time such information will be helpful in identifying malicious agents in the system. An agent may be termed as malicious if it causes a high number of ambiguities and its interpretations are found to be incorrect most of the time. The history of mediation is also mapped to a value ranging between "0" and "1". A "0" value signifies that the history of the agent is dire while a value "1" represents an ideal history. As with trust value, information originating from agents with low mediation history value is subjected to further questioning and skepticism while information from agents having higher value is accepted readily.

Degree of Certainty

Degree of Certainty is a quantitative scale associated with terms whose meanings are identified through inquiring and property matching. Such terms may be unknown or ambiguous. Degree of certainty is expressed as a numerical value ranging between "0" to "1". This value is also the measure of identical property and property values between two terms. If, for a term "staircase" being interpreted as "ladder", the degree of certainty value associated by an agent is 0.4, it reflects relatively low certainty. It also signifies that property and property values of terms "staircase" and "ladder" match by approximately 40%. On the other hand, a value of "1" expresses highest possible certainty and match. This value is determined by pattern matching properties. As mentioned, any OWL (RDF) type document can also be represented in form of triples and such triples may be matched in the model. Any interpretation having a degree of certainty value less than 0.5 should not be used as a possible synonym. Degree of Certainty value is not used while determining unknown or ambiguous interpretations through existing synonyms.

Dealing with Unknown Terms

When a response is partially or completely unknown, an interpretation is required (an example is provided later). A slightly varied initial approach is undertaken when dealing with such terms. As the first step, the unknown term or terms are marked. The receiving agent then requests the domain in which the term is used. Once the domain is known, a request message is constructed using the unknown term and its domain-of-use information. The requesting agent sends this message to the agent from which it received the initial request asking for any known synonyms. If known synonyms are found, mediation will be simple and computationally very efficient. Figure 8 depicts an abstraction of such an exchange of messages between two agents. If the agent does not receive any known synonym term that can be interpreted, it then uses voting and questioning algorithms.

The domain-of-use information is also used to narrow down the search during execution of

Figure 8. A sample of initial message exchanges for finding unknown term

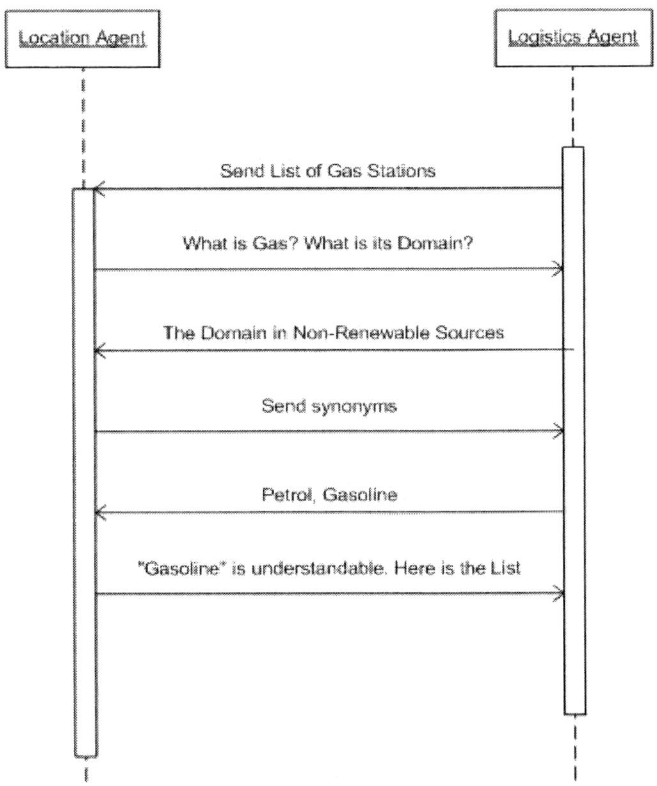

voting algorithm. When the agent is the foremost agent receiving information request (for instance directly from human users) and the sender agent is absent, voting and questioning techniques are directly used.

EVALUATION OF A CLASSIFICATION MODEL FOR ONTOLOGICAL MEDIATION

When discussing ontology and ontological mediation, classification becomes important. Through classification of ontological mediation, not only can we understand its importance and practical enormity, but also can measure the effectiveness of our approach against different realistic scenarios. In this section, we have classified ontological mediation into five categories and discussed how our methodology addresses them.

Mediation of Dialect Problems

This is a classic ontological mediation problem arising from dialect problem. The dialect problem refers to the language differences owing to the region it is spoken. For example what British English refers to as "Lift" and American English as "Elevator", is the same thing. Let us consider another example with two synonyms, "motorbike" and "motorcycle" and see how the presented methodology will handle it. Inquiring about the higher ontology or super domain, the mediation agent will find that both terms refer to a kind of "two wheeler automobile". The mediation agent can now ask questions on properties, restrictions and cardinalities of the terms for further clarification. Questions on properties such as engine, chassis, displacement, and fuel will reveal that in fact both terms refer to the same concept. In this case, the properties and property values are the same and hence it can be concluded that both terms refer to the same concept. The agents can now add a reference for the synonym terms in their individual ontology (Figure 9).

Ontological Reconciliation across Dissimilar Domains

Ontological Mediation is also essential when a term has multiple interpretations across different domains. If a single term has multiple meanings, further questioning about the domain can clarify the context in which it is being used. Considering

Figure 9. Resolving dialect problem

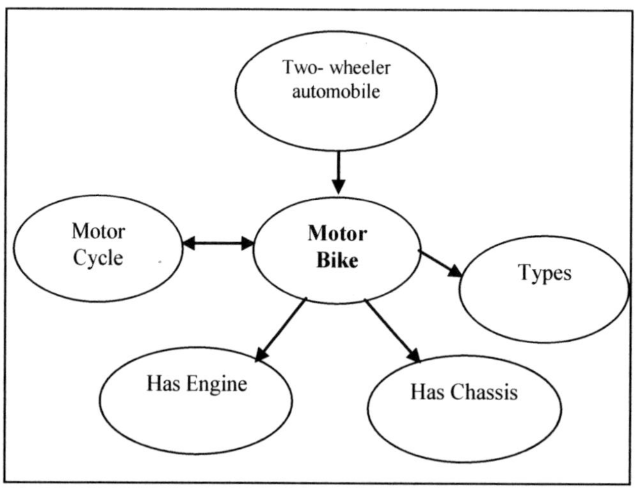

the previous example about "OWL", the mediation agent can ask the participating agents about the domain in which "OWL" is being used. One agent's domain of use is "nocturnal bird", where the other one is "Ontological Language". Since our model is built on a hierarchy of information agents and utilizes KQML (Finin et al., 1994), providing keywords to restrict domains, it can be assumed that we will rarely need to arbitrate such class of ontological mediation. However if we do, a simple question regarding the domain of interest would reveal the right meaning.

Ontological Reconciliation for Faulty Information

This is the most difficult class of mediation to arbitrate. Such ambiguities result from incorrect information or a malicious user. Let us consider an example where knowingly or unknowingly an agent has the term "ladder" listed in its ontological document as "staircase". Whenever any agent is trying to interpret the meaning of "ladder" or "staircase", this agent will propagate incorrect information. The use of standard registration procedures during creation of a new ontology can be utilized to check incorrect and malicious information. Yet, it can not be guaranteed that all the information can be verified. In the above case, two meanings for ladder will exist within the system. First is the actual meaning of ladder and the second is "staircase". It will be very hard to clarify such ambiguities, if a third agent that can interpret "ladder" correctly does not exist. If even after voting and questioning algorithms a clear interpretation does not emerge, the term is marked as ambiguous by the mediation agent. Whenever an agent requests information on an ambiguous data, all meanings and interpretations are returned. Over time as the system grows, by monitoring the history of mediation, such faulty information and agents can be identified. The mediation agent also periodically asks the agents, who are involved in an ambiguity, if through knowledge discovery or from other sources, their interpretations have been modified. The aid of human experts shall be used to resolve long lasting conflicts and ambiguities.

Ontological Merges and Updates

There can be cases when a certain part or a whole response is unfamiliar. When a reply contains unknown terms, they have to be identified and interpreted. Considering the previous example, if the reply to a request asking for "information on motorbike parts" states "a motorbike engine has pistons and cylinders" and the agent cannot interpret what "piston" is, further queries have to be made by the receiving agent. As mentioned earlier, the receiving agent inquiries the sender agent for any synonyms of "pistons" in the domain of "motorbike". Voting and questioning methodologies are used when the unknown term cannot be interpreted through existing synonyms in the senders or receivers ontology. Once the meaning of the unknown term has been determined, the receiving agent can enhance its ontology to contain brief information about what a "piston" is and how it is related in the context of an engine.

One problem with such updates is determining what new information the agent should incorporate and what information it should leave for other agents to add to their ontologies. We should avoid situations where a single agent is burdened with a large volume of information just because it keeps on discovering new terms. The role of mediation agent comes into the picture here, deciding on what information should be passed on to the lower level agents for update and what should not. Any new term that is found unsuitable to be passed onto the lower agents should also be appropriately placed. This can also be accomplished by the mediation agent which itself is a higher level agent in the hierarchy with partial information about the contents of lower level agents. At times it is also suitable to merge two ontologies into a single one. Through the use of automated reasoning, Jena interface (Jena–A Semantic Web Framework for Java, n. d.), and KQML performatives (Finin et al., 1994), our approach permits such necessary merging and updates.

Ontological Reorganizations

Ontological reorganization is necessary as the agents find new terms and concepts. This reorganization is done not only to improve the arrangement of the agents but also for faster and more efficient information exchange.

Suppose initially a logistics agent drew information from agents such as temperature, wind, terrain, altitude and location agents among others. With time as the number of agents and their ontologies grow, reorganization is needed. It may be efficient to reorganize some components of the logistics agent such as terrain, altitude and location agents and place them under another agent say the geographical agent. The geographical agent now draws information from agents such as the terrain, altitude and location agents. The logistics agent, being placed hierarchically above the geographical agent, knows when and for what the geographical agent should be approached. Our model permits such reorganizations.

Performance Analysis

In this section, the performance of the presented methodology is analyzed under some altering parameters. A simulation software was developed to aid the analysis. The software simulates mediation through some specific parameters. It takes into account constraints such as communication delay, agents' response delay, ontological knowledge, system comprehensiveness, and ambiguity level as values between 0 and 1. Ontological mediation algorithms of voting and questioning are simulated on a limited scale. We are mainly trying to analyze the success rate of voting approach, the effect of increasing number of agents on the overall delay (assuming voting fails) and also the effect of increasing levels of ambiguity on mediation time.

Initially, insufficient knowledge in the ontologies or incorrect ontologies can adversely effect voting. Mediation may also be complicated in scenarios where there are only two agents having knowledge on a term and they do not agree on its interpretation. As such, questioning and human intervention can be frequently needed at the beginning. When the individual ontological knowledge grows and the system becomes more inclusive, voting algorithm is able to arbitrate to a greater extent. With time, the comprehensiveness of the system increases, while incorrect ontologies can be marked and corrected. This is due to the dynamic nature of our approach that helps the ontologies to cultivate. Human assistance also aids in this process.

Voting however may never be 100% successful. New, partially incorrect, and ontologies having insufficient knowledge can always play a part in voting. Figure 10 illustrates the mediation success for voting approach against improving ontological knowledge, which is also supported by the simulation program. We based our analysis on the fact that mediation success is mainly a function of ontological knowledge, system comprehensiveness and a randomness factor associated with the information request.

When there is an increase in the number of agents involved in mediation, we expect a symmetrical increase in the overall delay. As Figure 11 depicts, our simulation did support this hypothesis. Our expectation was based on the fact that overall delay for the mediation process is a function of communication delay, agent response delay, number of agents involved, ambiguity level and processing time. Assuming that the number of agents is a factor that varies most often (new agents are added and ontologies are expanded over time), it can act as the prime factor in determining the overall delay. Exceptions can occur if voting methodology is successful and questioning delays are avoided.

Figure 10. Mediation success vs. the quality of ontological knowledge

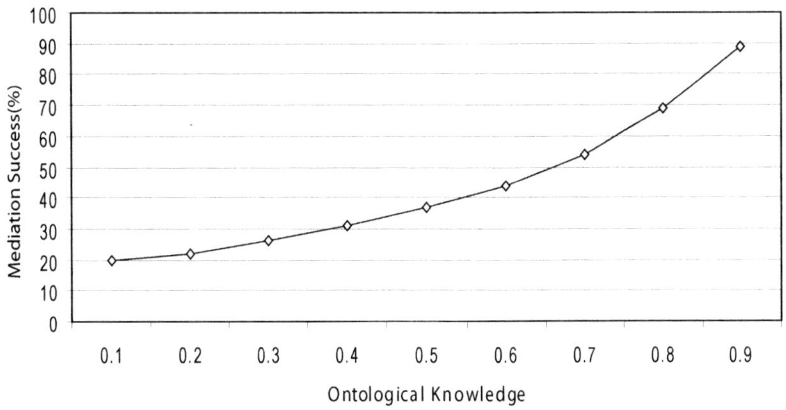

Figure 11. Number of agents vs. delay

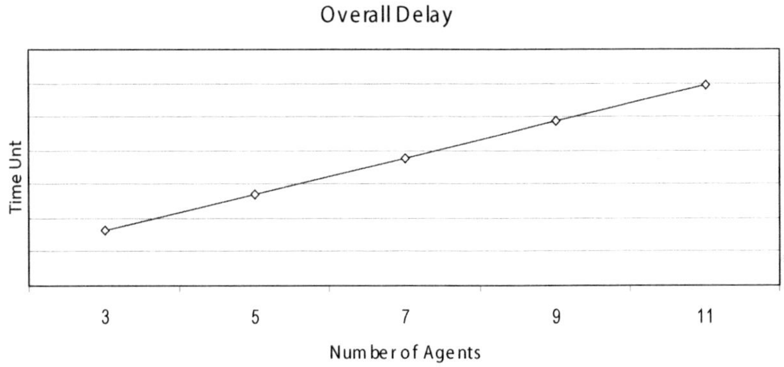

In the proposed approach, the mediation agent requires longer processing time when faced with increasing scales of ambiguity. This is because our methodology uses incremental sub- levels for mediation. For example, if questions on hierarchy cannot resolve ambiguity, further questions on properties are asked, and if questions of properties cannot resolve the ambiguity, questions on cardinalities and restrictions are asked. Therefore, with increasing level of ambiguity, more time will be required for clarifications by the questioning method. When utilized, human aid agent also adds to the mediation time. Figure 12 depicts the expected performance of our approach in this regard. Each sharp increase accounts for utilization of another sub-algorithm within the questioning methodology and for using the human aid agent. Note that in the analysis we have assumed 0.3,0.5 and 0.8 as ambiguity levels that will call for further questioning.

APPLICATION AVENUES IN E-GOVERMENT

Ontology development is finding its way in diverse areas such as semantic web (Ding, Kolari, Ding, Avancha, Finin & Joshi, 2005), peer to peer systems (Parkhomenk, Lee & Park, 2003), automobile projects (Golebiowska, Dieng-Kuntz, Corby & Mousseau, 2001), simulation modeling (Miller, Baramidze, Sheth & Fishwick, 2004), e-commerce

Figure 12. Mediation time vs. ambiguity level

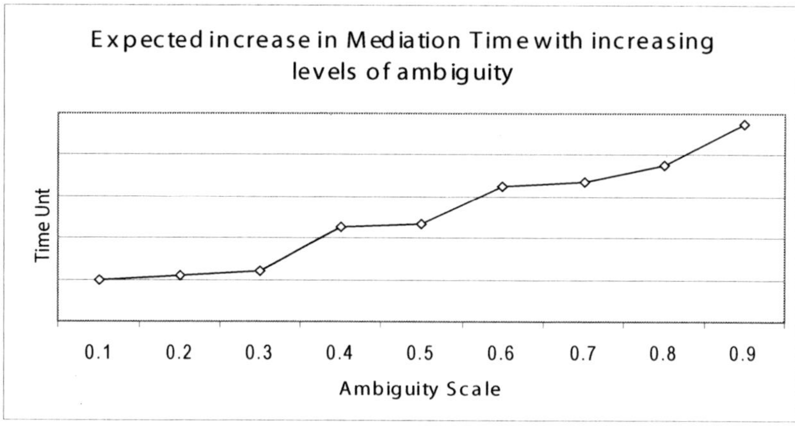

(Obrst, Wray & Liu, 2001), application servers (Oberle, Eberhart, Staab & Volz, 2004) and e-government (Karyda, Balopoulos, Gymnopoulos, Kokolakis, Lambrinoudakis, Gritzalis & Dritsas, 2006). Whatever the avenue for applying ontology may be, ontological mediation is indispensable. In this section, we look into one such avenue that is e-government. E-government is the term used to define a system in which a government uses electronic means for communication. The communication may be with the citizens, other government agencies, internal communication or with foreign governments. Due to its vast and growing nature, E-government itself has been sub-classified into different categories. Some of the categories are Government-to-Citizen or Government-to-Customer (G2C), Government-to-Business (G2B) and Government-to-Government (G2G) (Lee, Tan & Trimi, 2005). Multi-agent systems (MAS) are starting to be applied to different aspects of E-government. Such automated systems are being introduced for applications ranging from online processing and citizen support to matters of security and defense among others.

Data Surveillance

Let us consider a scenario where an e-government is trying to monitor electronic activities of certain individuals. For such a task, an autonomous multi-agent system such as the one introduced in (Rahimi et al., 2005) could be of a great use. Agents are created drawing their knowledge, which in this case is the terms to be monitored, from domain-specific initial lists of terms. Such lists of terms should be organized into ontologies, using tools such as OWL-DL (as mentioned earlier). Via these reference ontologies, the agents can organize electronic data related to a target individual into an ontology. These data may be collected from various communication mediums such as emails, chats, and online search preferences. For such a case, a system based on Rahimi, Carver and Petry (2005), which utilizes the above ontological mediation approach to resolve ambiguity and unfamiliarity would be ideal. The suitability of our approach lies on the fact that with information agents we are not only focusing on keywords to perform search, but also are trying to understand the semantics of the contents. The importance of mediation in such an application is because of the agents' need to communicate with one another to organize the global view of the data being sent or received. During this process, new, ambiguous, or suspicious terms may come up that need clarification. Moreover, as new terms to be monitored are revealed, they are added to the suitable domain-specific lists and the administrative agent of the MAS is informed of them. Other agents can then interact with the administrative agent when needed.

Ontological mediation plays a vital role during the process of data organization as it requires inter-agent communication and knowledge from different ontologies. Our model uses a dynamic mediation methodology which overtime produces comprehensive ontologies to be used by MAS for the purpose of automated monitoring and surveillance.

Viruses and Network Attacks Defense Mechanisms

Malwares are a constant threat to computers and electronic resources. An ontological-based application could be developed to create a comprehensive ontology of malwares with possible solutions and defense mechanisms. Such ontology can be built and maintained as part of an e-government resource. The ontology thus created will not only list the malwares but also provide information regarding its features, possible defend solutions and precautionary steps. Figure 13 illustrates an abstract overview of ontology for malwares with solutions and precautionary steps for each type. Such ontology when completed will be significant for a MAS. Agents can use this knowledge as a reference to check for malwares, and if detected, carry out specified solutions. As with malwares, an ontology of network related attacks and defense mechanisms can also be created. Such ontology will provide comprehensive information on detecting possible network related attacks and appropriate means of defense. With time as these ontologies grow, they can be broken down into different sub-ontologies, each for a type of malware or network related attack or even further into various sub-types. Once we have a network of collaborating ontologies, ontological mediation is indispensable.

Even with a single ontology of malwares or network related attacks, ontological mediation is crucial. The proposed ontological mediation methodology facilitates materializing global knowledge bases and provides for locating and accessing the right resources.

System Logs

To better serve and protect sensitive information in e-government servers, log files can be organized into ontologies. Whatever log files are generated in servers can be transformed into ontology of events, causes and effects (Figure 14). Different ontologies can be created for different events. Ontologies may also be based on servers, server locations or domain of log messages. Agents could be built over such ontologies to automate part of the responsibilities of the system administrators. These ontologies are also valuable for system administrators as references with agents assisting in retrieving required information and monitoring the system efficiently. Here also mediation will be critical when retrieving information as these ontologies are large and may have duplicate or similar terms, events or causes.

Online Profile of Individuals

A central ontology of online profile of individuals could be created by an e-government to better serve citizens and protect their personal data. For such an ontology, the government should have access rights, while the individuals are able to query, retrieve and update their personal information. Such an ontology will serve dual purpose. First it makes it easier for the users themselves to perform tasks such as updating mailing address and profile modification at a single portal with effects reflecting across all areas. Secondly, it would be easier to track and trace frauds and online mischief. With information being placed at a single location, personal data could be better protected. Instead of having multiple online accounts in banks, phone companies, and e-commerce sites, a single account can be created for

Figure 13. An abstract overview of an ontology for malwares

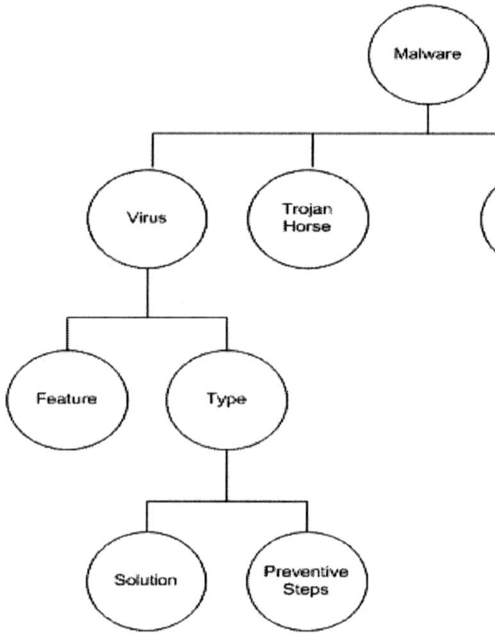

Figure 14. An abstract overview of an ontology for system logs

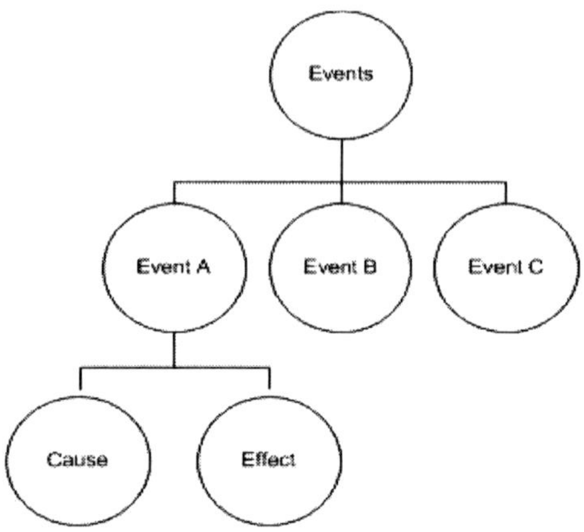

all online activities. The online profiles can be extended to incorporate hotel and travel preferences, airline preferences, shopping preferences etc. External information requests from third party companies could be granted based on predefined policies and access rights.

The proposed mediation methodology is effective in clarifying requests and responses between the central ontology and the agents trying to retrieve information from it. Development of such system would not be possible without mediation capabilities (Ke & Wei, 2004).

In each of the above examples, ontology serves as an excellent tool for information organization. Nevertheless as mentioned earlier, information organization by itself is insufficient. Ontological mediation methodologies become equally important whenever multiple ontologies are involved and inter-agent activities are required (Figure 15). Our methodologies of voting and questioning are simple but versatile enough to be suitable for different ontological applications in areas such as e-government. Saying that, appropriate reasoning tools and well defined inter-agent communication protocols are essential for effective mediation.

CONCLUSION

In the World Wide Web and the major intranets, information is constantly created and modified by thousands of users and hence may not be co-

Figure 15. Block representation of ontological mediation and inter-agent communication

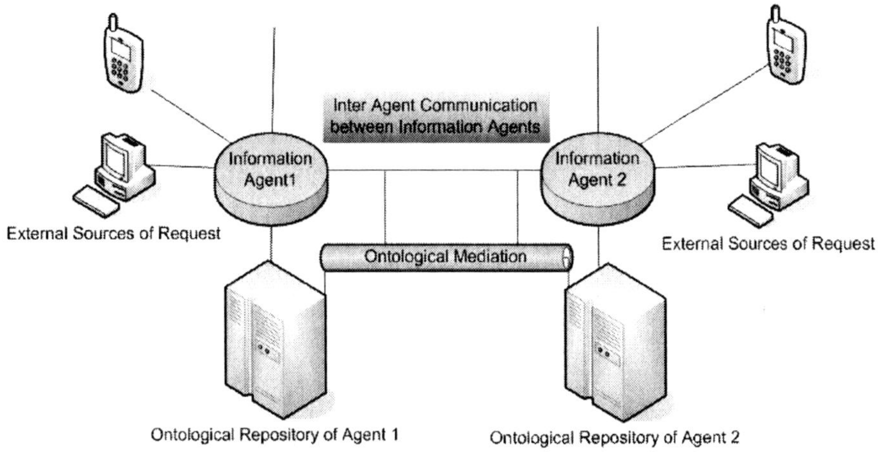

hesive. Multi-agent systems provide an efficient and effective approach for large scale information gathering and dispersion by generating and maintaining ontologies. In this chapter, an ontological mediation methodology was presented for such multi-agent systems.

A collaborative mediation approach is preferred due to its effectiveness and simplicity. In our model, mediation agents are used to resolve ambiguity and unfamiliarity among agents. A mediation agent initially employs a voting algorithm. If voting does not produce a clear interpretation, specific questions are asked to resolve ambiguous or unknown terms. Our methodology also benefits from taking advantage of human experts when an ambiguity or unfamiliarity cannot be resolved by agents over a period of time. We have considered a benevolent environment; nevertheless, trust values and history of mediation are utilized to defend against ill intends and malicious agents. Our approach for mediation is thus simple yet practical and comprehensive which provides for a high degree of mediation success. High mediation success in turn reflects efficiency in information search and retrieval.

This is important to note that automated reasoning is the heart of effective information retrieval as well as the mediation process. How well the semantics of the data can be understood and processed depends on how well the reasoners, working on top of the ontological documents, can make inferences. Although OWL-DL supports automated reasoning, its capability is restricted. With the introduction of more powerful ontology languages and reasoners, the system could perform with greater effectiveness and efficiency. This chapter does not comprehensively cover the implementation issues and is more concern about the mediation framework and methodology.

REFERENCES

Austin, J. L. (1962). *How to do Things with Words*. Cambridge: Harvard University Press.

Bechhofer, S., Moller, R. & Crowther, P. (2003). The DIG Description Logic Interface. *Proceedings of 2003 International Workshop on Description Logic (DL2003), Rome, Italy,* 85–94.

Bray, T. (1998). RDF and Metadata. Retrieved January 20, 2007 from http://www.xml.com/pub/a/98/06/rdf.html

Campbell, A. E. (1999). *Ontological Mediation: Finding Translation Across Dialects by Asking*

Questions. Doctoral dissertation, University at Buffalo, The State University of New York, Department of Computer Science and Engineering.

Campbell, A. E. & Shapiro, S. C. (1998). *Algorithms for ontological mediation* (Technical Report 98-2). University at Buffalo, The State University of New York, Department of Computer Science and Engineering, SNePS Research Group.

Connolly, D., Harmelen, F. V., Horrocks, I., McGuinness, D. L., Patel-Schneider, P. F. & Stein L. A.(2001). DAML+OIL (March 2001). *Reference Description.* Retrieved January 20, 2007 from http://www.w3.org/TR/daml+oil-reference

Ding, L., Kolari, P., Ding, Z., Avancha, S., Finin, T., & Joshi, A. (2005). *Using Ontologies in the Semantic Web: A Survey* (TR-CS-05-07). University of Maryland Baltimore County, Ebiquity Research Group.

Finin, T., Fritzson, R., McKay, D., & McEntire, R. (1994). KQML as an agent communication Language. *Proceedings of the 3rd International Conference on Information and Knowledge Management,* 456 – 463.

Golebiowska, J., Dieng-Kuntz, R., Corby, O. & Mousseau, D. (2001) . Building and exploiting ontologies for an automobile project memory. *Proceedings of the 1st international conference on Knowledge capture K-CAP,* 52 – 59.

Haarslev, V. and Moller, R. (2003). Racer: An OWL Reasoning Agent for the Semantic Web. *Proceedings of the International Workshop on Applications, Products and Services of Web-based Support Systems, in conjunction with the 2003 IEEE/WIC International Conference on Web Intelligence,* 91-95.

Hexmoor, H. & Sabaa, H. (2006) .Towards Semantically Coherent Collaboration. *Proceedings of the International Symposium on Collaborative Technologies and Systems* (pp. 264-269). IEEE Computer Society Washington, DC, USA.

Jena–A Semantic Web Framework for Java. (n.d.). Retrieved December 4, 2006 from http://jena.sourceforge.net/index.html

Lee, S. M., Tan, X. & Trimi, S. (2005) . Current practices of leading e-government countries. *Communications of ACM 48,* 99 - 104.

Kalyanpur, A., Parsia, B., Sirin, E., Grau, B. C. & Hendler J. A. (2006) .Swoop: a web ontology editing browser. *Journal of Web Semantics,* 4(2), 144-153.

Karyda, M. , Balopoulos, T. , Gymnopoulos, L., Kokolakis, S., Lambrinoudakis, C., Gritzalis, S. & Dritsas, S.(2006) An ontology for secure e-government applications. *Proceedings of the first international conference on availability, reliability and security (ARES'06), 00,* 1033-1037.

Ke, W. & Wei, K. K. (2004) . Successful e-government in Singapore. *Commnications of ACM 47,* 95 - 99.

Knoblock, C.A. & Ambite, J.L. (1997). *Agents for Information Gathering,* Software Agents. J. Bradshaw, (Ed.), MIT Press, Metlo Park, CA.

McGuinness, D. L. and Harmelen F. V. (Eds) (2004) .OWL Web Ontology Language Overview. Retrieved, December 4 2006 from http://www.w3.org/TR/owl-features/.

Miller, A. George. (1995). WordNet: A lexical Database for English. *Communications of ACM* 38, 39-41.

Miller, J. A., Baramidze, G. T., Sheth, A. P. & Fishwick, P. A. (2004) . Investigating Ontologies for Simulation Modeling. *Proceedings of the 37th annual symposium on Simulation ANSS,* 55.

Oberle, D., Eberhart, A., Staab, S. & Volz, R. (2004). Application servers, enterprise computing and software engineering: Developing and managing software components in an ontology-based application server. *Proceedings of the 5th ACM/IFIP/USENIX international conference on Middleware,* 459 - 477.

Obrst, L., Wray, R. E. & Liu, H. (2001) .Ontological engineering for B2B E-commerce. *Proceedings of the international conference on formal ontology in Information Systems, 2001*, 117 - 126.

Parkhomenko, O., Lee, Y. & Park, E. K. (2003). Ontology-driven peer profiling in peer-to-peer enabled semantic web. *Proceedings of the twelfth international conference on Information and knowledge management,* 564 – 567.

Prud'hommeaux, E. & Seaborne, A. (Eds.) (2007). *SPARQL Query Language for RDF.* Retrieved June 16, 2007 from http://www.w3.org/TR/rdf-sparql-query/

Rahimi, S., Carver, N. & Petry, F. E. (2005). A Multi-Agent Architecture for Distributed Domain-Specific Information Integration. In Ladner, R. & Petry, F. E., *Net-Centric approaches to intelligence and national security* (pp 129-148). New York: Springer US.

Seaborne, A. (2004) .*RDQL – A Query Language for RDF.* Retrieved December 4, 2006 from http://www.w3.org/Submission/RDQL/

Searle, J. (1969). *Speech Acts: An Essay in the Philosophy of Language.* London: Cambridge University Press.

Sirin, E., Parsai, B., Grau, B. C., Kalyanpur, A. & Katz Y. (n.d.). *Pellet: A Practical OWL-DL Reasoner.* Retrieved December 4, 2006 from http://mindswap.org/papers/PelletJWS.pdf

ENDNOTE

1 The original version of this article, entitled "Ontological Mediation for Multi-agent Systems" by Shahram Rahimi, Pravab J. Rana, Raheel Ahmad, and Bidyut Gupta appeared in the International Journal of Electronic Government Research, Volume 4, Issue 1.

Chapter XVI
Analyst-Ready Large Scale Real Time Information Retrieval Tool for E-Governance

Eugene Santos, Jr.
Dartmouth College, USA

Eunice E. Santos
Virginia Polytechnic Institute & State University, USA

Hien Nguyen
University of Wisconsin, Whitewater, USA

Long Pan
Virginia Polytechnic Institute & State University, USA

John Korah
Virginia Polytechnic Institute & State University, USA

Huadong Xia
Virginia Polytechnic Institute & State University, USA

Fei Yu
Dartmouth College, USA

Deqing Li
Dartmouth College, USA

ABSTRACT

With the proliferation of the Internet and rapid development of information and communication infrastructure, E-governance has become a viable option for effective deployment of government services and programs. Areas of E-governance such as Homeland security and disaster relief have to deal with vast amounts of dynamic heterogeneous data. Providing rapid real-time search capabilities for such databases/sources is a challenge. Intelligent Foraging, Gathering, and Matching (I-FGM) is an established framework developed to assist analysts to find information quickly and effectively by incrementally collecting, processing and matching information nuggets. This framework has previously been used to develop a distributed, free text information retrieval application. In this chapter, we provide a comprehensive solution for the E-GOV analyst by extending the I-FGM framework to image collections and creating a "live" version of I-FGM deployable for real-world use. We present a Content Based Image

Copyright © 2009, IGI Global, distributing in print or electronic forms without written permission of IGI Global is prohibited.

Retrieval (CBIR) technique that incrementally processes the images, extracts low-level features and map them to higher level concepts. Our empirical evaluation of the algorithm shows that our approach performs competitively compared to some existing approaches in terms of retrieving relevant images while offering the speed advantages of a distributed and incremental process, and unified framework for both text and images. We describe our production level prototype that has a sophisticated user interface which can also deal with multiple queries from multiple users. The interface provides real-time updating of the search results and provides "under the hood" details of I-FGM processes as the queries are being processed.

INTRODUCTION

One of the main challenges in E-governance is to effectively and efficiently find relevant information from vast amounts of dynamic heterogeneous sources quickly under the pressures and limitations of time, supporting tools, and resources. For instance, when natural disasters such as Hurricane Katrina (2005) or the Asian Tsunami of 2004 happen, we need to quickly locate the areas that are most affected and collect information in order to estimate the amount of relief items such as medicines, foods, and drinking water. Unfortunately, in such a situation, frontline communications are typically chaotic and/or there are too many channels of information from different sources that make the retrieval of relevant pieces of information a lot harder. For "hot spots" such as disaster relief areas, combat zones, etc., information is changing rapidly and as such, there is only a small window of time during which information remains valid. Additionally, various types of data representation are used such as images, blogs, maps, news reports, audios, and videos. Each type of data format contains important and indispensable information for the various governmental agencies. Therefore, in order to better assist these agencies in addressing these challenges, there is a clear and urgent need to develop a system that rapidly provides real-time retrieval capabilities of heterogeneous sources of information. There are three main issues that we need to address: (i) how to gather and retrieve information quickly in a real-time setting given the limitations of resources and time; (ii) how to address the problem of **heterogeneous data**; and, (iii) how to improve retrieval success.

We address the above issues by developing a **framework** for intelligent foraging, gathering, and matching (I-FGM) that incrementally and distributively gathers, processes, and matches information nuggets to assist users at finding information quickly and effectively. In our previous work (Santos et al, 2005, 2006), I-FGM has been empirically demonstrated to be an effective tool for text retrieval on large and **dynamic search** spaces. Even though unstructured text is a typical format for most databases/sources, images are also popular with significant support from commercialized search engines such as Google, Yahoo!, and MSN. In order to demonstrate that I-FGM is a general framework for information retrieval, it is necessary to study the system's ability at effectively handling such heterogeneous databases which contain at least text and images. In this chapter, we apply the I-FGM framework on image collections by using a Content Based Image Retrieval **(CBIR)** method. We approach this by incrementally processing the images, extracting low-level features, and then mapping them to higher level concepts. The novelties of our approach lie with the distributed storage, and incremental processing and matching of information nuggets extracted from a region-based wavelet image retrieval scheme. We deploy a concept-based image retrieval algorithm that maps low level features of the images to high level concepts. In this way, we are also able to translate the visual information of images into document graphs (Santos et al, 2005) which are used in I-FGM as a common representation of information for heterogeneous data types. Thus, I-FGM provides a seamless integration of text and image through a single unifying semantic representation of content. By implementing and testing our image retrieval algorithm in I-FGM, we can validate the I-FGM framework as a method for future unified rankings of heterogeneous documents.

The prototypes presented in our previous efforts were primarily aimed at validating the I-FGM framework and was not meant to be deployed in the field. In order to fully validate I-FGM as an effective tool for the E-Gov analyst, we implemented a Production-level system. This system uses 79 high end computing nodes versus the 20 nodes in the earlier prototypes. The extensive computing resources enable us to guarantee quick results despite multiple queries from multiple users being processed simultaneously in the system. One notable difference with the previous prototype is that text and image retrievals are performed simultaneously for a given query. Additionally, we provide a set of tools for users to monitor the progress of their search via a graphical user interface. This interface displays the status of the internal processes in the system and allows the user to tailor the framework to his/her needs or area of expertise.

This chapter is organized as follows: In the methodology section, we first provide a brief background on current image retrieval systems. Next, we give an overview of the image retrieval algorithm that was implemented in I-FGM. We then describe the architecture of I-FGM and the implementation details of the current prototype. This section is followed by a description of our system evaluation procedure along with simulation results. We validate the performance of the image algorithm and show that it can be used in I-FGM for faster retrieval of images. Then, in the production system section, we explain in detail about its setup and how it interacts with the users. Finally, we will present our conclusions and future work.

METHODOLOGY

Background and Related Work

The goal of the Intelligent Gathering, Foraging, and Matching (I-FGM) framework is to facilitate real time searches in large and dynamic search spaces. In particular, I-FGM aims to integrate the retrieval of multiple data types; to enable a unified framework to compare heterogeneous documents; and, to employ resource allocation policies facilitated by partial processing to conduct efficient anytime searches. In this chapter, we integrate image retrieval in I-FGM by employing an algorithm based on techniques from Content Based Image Retrieval (**CBIR**). We now present the current state of research in CBIR and the approaches that have been leveraged in I-FGM.

CBIR is an important sub-area of image retrieval that aims to classify, identify, and retrieve images based on its visual content rather than using human generated information such as meta-tags, and annotations. Through the previous decade, there has been significant progress in this field, documented in various surveys (Rui, Huang, & Chang, 1999; Smeulders, M. Worring, Santini, Gupta, & Jain, 2000; Veltkamp & Tanase, 2000). Although, a general solution for image retrieval still eludes researchers due to the difficulties posed by the well-documented phenomena of sensory gap and semantic gap (Enser & Sandom, 2003), CBIR techniques have shown great promise in automating the process of interpreting images. We decided to employ CBIR in I-FGM because other methods require extra-image information such as meta-tags or HTML text from web pages containing the image. In the CBIR methods, the visual content or low-level features of the images have to be converted into an intermediate form or signature before it can be interpreted. Our choice of low-level features and feature signature are important as it has a direct influence on the performance of the system. Examples of low-level features in images are color, texture, and contrast.

Region-based methods are a widely used type of CBIR. In these methods (Carson, Belongie, Greenspan, & Malik, 2002; Li, Wang, & Wiederhold, 2000; Ma & Manjunath, 1997; Natsev, 2001), images are divided into regions, each of which has similar pixel characteristics. This collection of regions forms a signature for the image. The premise behind these methods is that similar images will have similar regions. Methods such as WALRUS (Natsev, Rastogi, & Shim, 2004) and SIMPLIcity (Wang, Li, & Wiederhold, 2001) use wavelets (Daubechies, 1992) to represent the feature signature of regions. Methods such as (Natsev, Rastogi, & Shim, 2004; Wang, Li, & Wiederhold, 2001) generate regions by calculating a feature signature for a part of the image (window) at a time. The window is slid across the image such that every pixel of the image is contained in at least one window. These windows are then clustered based on a distance measure. Each cluster is then considered to be a region. These methods work well even with complex images, containing multiple concepts or objects. One of the drawbacks in these methods is that they take query images, instead of a text query. This is also one of the reasons preventing its direct usage within the I-FGM framework.

We will use the image segmentation and region clustering techniques from WALRUS in our image retrieval algorithm. The feature vector that we use to represent the low level features of the image is similar to the one used in SIMPLIcity. Although SIMPLIcity is a well known regions method, it does only coarse grained classification of images into semantic classes such as "*outdoor*", "*indoor*", "*texture*", "*non-textured*", and "*photographs*". I-FGM on the other hand deals with more fine-grained classifications. Our algorithm seeks to map low level features to high level concepts, by forming regions of similar pixel characteristics and then mapping them to the concepts. Although this is similar to the CAMEL (Natsev, Chadha, Soetarman, & Vitter, 2001) algorithm (a variant of the WALRUS method), there are significant differences. The concepts used in CAMEL are single object concepts such as "apple". It compares the feature vectors for this concept with incoming images and tries to determine if the concept is contained in the image using a distance based similarity measure. We found that CAMEL does not deliver the required performance when implemented with the images that we typically deal with. The main reason is that it is difficult to accurately identify single object concepts in images. Another important reason why we cannot use this method is that it uses a distance based similarity measure that is adversely affected by the presence of non-relevant features in the images. A better option is to use machine learning techniques to match the low level features of concepts and images. ALIPR (Li & Wang, 2006) is another automatic annotation method that tries to map low level features to keywords. ALIPR is an established method that has given good performance. It has also been used commercially. Unfortunately, it cannot be used with the partial processing paradigm of I-FGM. In I-FGM, we incrementally process an image, using each partial step to gain an insight into the relevancy of image and proportionately grant resources. The information gathered from one step has to be reused in successive partial steps so as to minimize the overhead. In ALIPR, the probability distributions associated with its feature vectors cannot be calculated with the incomplete image information available at each partial step in I-FGM.

Another technology that we will leverage in I-FGM is the prevalent WWW image search engine. I-FGM uses the Internet as a search space in this chapter since it is a rich source of images and dynamic in nature. We will use image search engines such as Google and MSN to do a first order filtering on the search space similar to the Internet and narrow down the search space. These search engines cannot be used for **real time retrieval** as they use static indexes that are built offline (Kherfi, Ziou, & Bernardi, 2004). Also, they require human generated information in the form of the html text surrounding the images (Tsymbalenko, & Munson, 2001) or meta-tags. On the other hand, analysts using I-FGM must deal with images from various sources: satellite imagery, aerial reconnaissance images, etc., which may not be accompanied by annotations.

In this chapter, we seek to incorporate image search by implementing a content-based image retrieval algorithm. Our algorithm will extract low level features of images and map to pre-defined concepts. We will show how we can convert images into document graphs which are the common knowledge representation used in I-FGM. By doing so, we will validate our framework for unifying heterogeneous data types.

Image Retrieval for I-FGM

As mentioned earlier, we have validated I-FGM as a credible framework to provide real time search in large and dynamic free text databases. Here, we incorporate image retrieval into the framework. As such, our goal is not about presenting a new method for **image retrieval** but rather a method that is built on principles that have been tested and validated by the image retrieval research community which can be used in the I-FGM framework. We will use our image retrieval algorithm to validate the I-FGM framework on image collections. We also intend to show how smart resource allocation strategies can reduce computational costs and save time when dealing with large and dynamic databases. Furthermore, by representing the information in images as a document graph, we will demonstrate how a unified representation can be applied to multimedia (text and/or image) documents.

As we mentioned earlier, heterogeneity is a particularly important issue in the databases that I-FGM expects to deal with, in support of governmental agencies. Our databases may contain documents of different data type (images, text, multi-media files). Within each data type, another level of heterogeneity can occur. For example, images can occur in different forms such as photographs, satellite imagery, maps, etc. A straightforward method of dealing with this is to use separate retrieval methods for each data type and somehow combine their ranking results. This is a very ineffective method since the ranking measures used by the separate methods may share little or no semantic relationships. For example, it is difficult to decide whether an image of similarity x based on texture and color values is as relevant to users as a text of the same similarity value based on keyword matches. We resolve this problem by extracting the information from a document using a given retrieval method and then representing the semantic contents of the document in a common graphical structure called the **document graph**. A document graph (example in Figure 1) consists of nodes representing concepts, and edges representing relations between nodes. This representation extracts the main information contained in any given document.

The image retrieval method that we use with I-FGM requires certain characteristics as we alluded to in the previous section. First, it should be amenable to partial processing where information gleaned from each partial step is re-useable by the next partial step. Next, the similarity measure calculated from each partial step should be a good indicator of the final similarity value, which helps in designing resource allocation strategies. Also, the time taken to process an image with partial processing should not be significantly larger than one-step processing. Finally, the method should also be able to convert the visual content of images into document graphs. All of this will allow us to accept natural language queries so as to be

Figure 1. Document graph for the text "Workers at coal mine on strike"

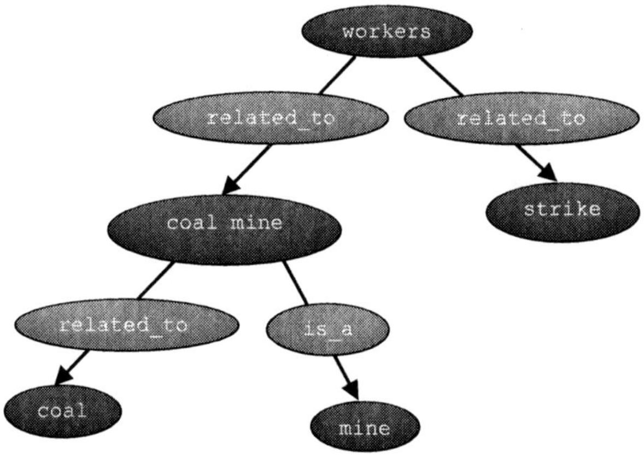

consistent with the text retrieval methodology already deployed within I-FGM.

A step-by-step representation of the retrieval process is depicted in Figure 2. When a new image arrives in the system, it is incrementally processed to extract its low-level features in the images. These features are compared with those images found in the concept library and matching concepts are then noted. Here, the **concept library** is a collection of well known concepts along with its annotation and an image feature vector representing its characteristics. The concept feature vector is modeled by a **machine learning** algorithm using a training set. The text annotations of these concepts are then combined to form the textual description of the image. The description is then converted into a document graph which is then compared with the document graph representation of the natural language query (query graph) and a similarity value is calculated. We now describe the steps of the image retrieval algorithm in detail.

Low Level Feature Extraction

Each image is represented by a 16 dimensional **feature vector** with each dimension representing a region of image. An image is said to have a maximum of 16 regions. This is borrowed from SIMPLIcity where it was found that 16 regions give good performance. Since we also use the same feature vector, we decided to use this value. Each region is represented by a six dimensional vector representing the color and texture information of the images. In order to extract the regions from an image, the image is incrementally processed with a sliding window. We use the LUV color space. For each window, a signature is calculated from the average values of the color and the 2x2 wavelet transform on the L component. Haar wavelets are used as they are computationally efficient and have good performance (Natsev, Rastogi, & Shim, 2004). The first three components of the signature are the average values of L, U and V values of the pixels in the window, respectively. The high frequency components of the wavelet transform form the remaining three components of the window signature. The signature of a window *w* is of the form:

$$h_w = \{l_w, u_w, v_w, m^1_w, m^2_w, m^3_w\}$$

where l_w, u_w, v_w are the average values of the pixel color in windows *w* and m^1_w, m^2_w, m^3_w are the high frequency components of the Haar wavelet transform of the L values in *w*.

Based on their signatures, the windows are clustered together using a clustering algorithm. We use the BIRCH (Zhang, Ramakrishnan, & Livny, 1996) **clustering** algorithm as it is one of

Figure 2. Image retrieval in I-FGM

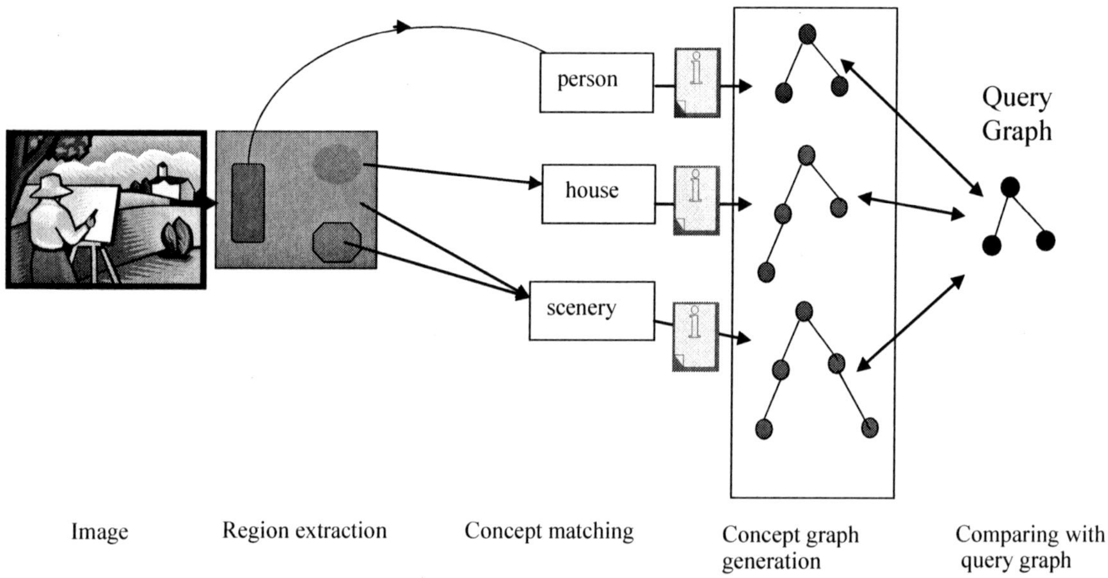

the most efficient clustering algorithms available. Each of the clusters form a region represented by its centroid. The area of each region is also calculated simultaneously. The regions are sorted according to its area and the signature of the largest region forms the first dimension of the image feature vector, the second largest region forms the second dimension and so on. Hence the image feature vector of an image x is represented by the vector:

$$f_x = \{l_{x,1}, u_{x,1}, v_{x,1}, m^1_{x,1}, m^2_{x,1}, m^3_{x,1}, \ldots, l_{x,16}, u_{x,16}, v_{x,16}, m^1_{x,16}, m^2_{x,16}, m^3_{x,16}\}$$

where $l_{x,i}$, $u_{x,i}$ $v_{x,i}$ are the average color values in the centroid for region i and $m^1_{x,i}$, $m^2_{x,i}$ $m^3_{x,i}$ are the wavelet transforms for the L color space in the centroid for region i.

Creation of the Concept Library

The library is created offline and this process is depicted in Figure 3. It consists of a set of concepts that are commonly found in the image databases that I-FGM is searching. Each concept is accompanied by a short textual description, which is generated manually. In our method the low level features of images are mapped to concepts in the library. The descriptions of the relevant concepts are then used to automatically generate the annotations for the images. This method of **automatic annotation** of images has less manual intervention than most other methods that generally require human generated metadata for each image. A classifier for each concept is generated by a machine learning algorithm based on logistic regression. A detailed description of the machine learning algorithm is presented below. A set of training images are used to create the classifier. The training images are of two types: images that represent the concept (positive training) and images that do not represent the concept (negative training). The image feature vector is extracted for each of these images and fed into the machine learning technique to create the classifier.

Image Matching

This process matches low level features of the images to high level concepts (Figure 4). For

Figure 3. Offline creation of concept library

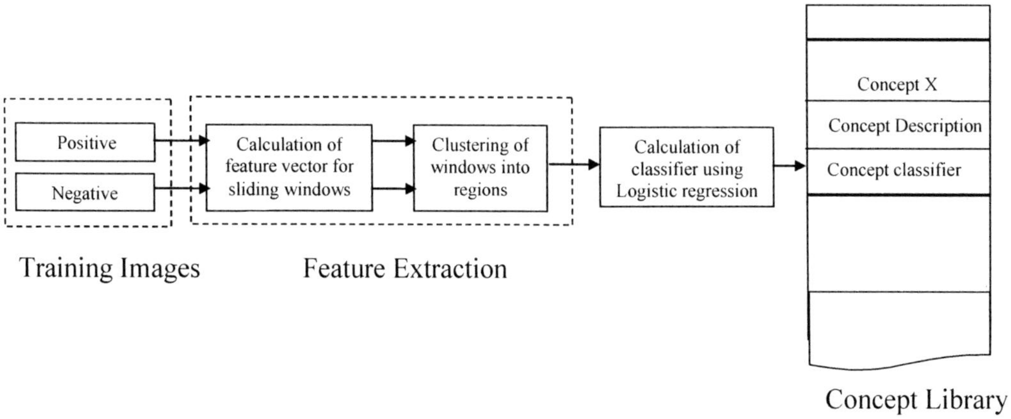

Figure 4. Extraction of relevant concept from the image

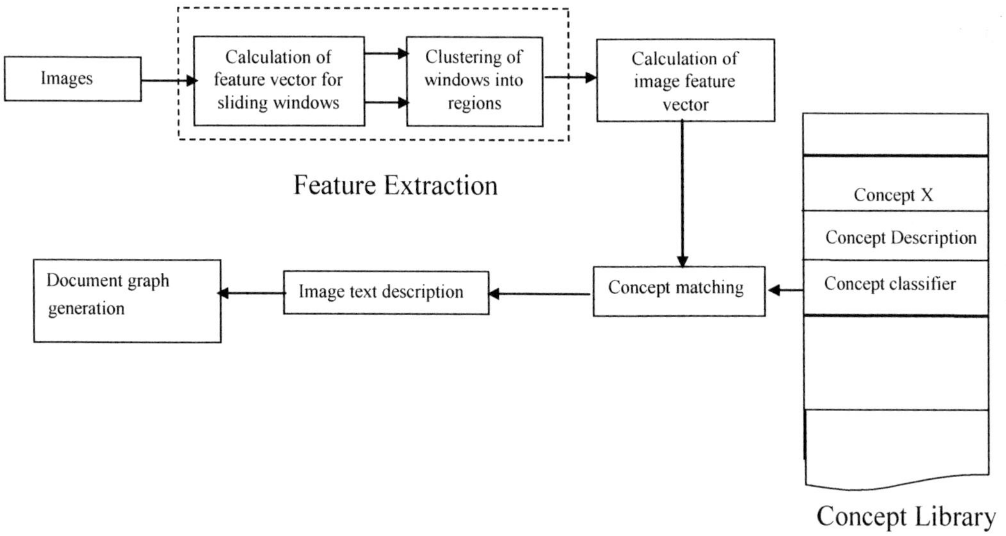

each image, we incrementally compute its feature vector. During each incremental step, the image feature vector for the portion of the image that has been processed is calculated and compared against the concept classifiers in the library. A machine learning algorithm determines if a particular concept is relevant to the image or not. If a concept is relevant, its concept annotation is stored. At the end of the matching phase, the annotations of all matched concepts are combined together to form the image description. The description is converted into a document graph and compared with the document graph of the query where the similarity is calculated.

Machine Learning Algorithm: Logistic Regression

Logistic regression (LR) is appropriate for matching concepts in the concept library with images because it can be modeled as a binomial classification problem. LR has been found to be appropriate for binary classification and can be improved to achieve fast speed and reliability

(Komarek, 2004). Some studies have compared LR with some other popular classifiers used in machine learning such as tree induction (Perlich et al, 2003), Naïve Bayesian classifier (Mitchell, 2005), and support vector machine (Vapnick, 1999). It has been found (Perlich et al, 2003) that LR performs better with small training data set while tree induction is better with a large data set. Naïve Bayesian classifiers require conditional independence among variables. Therefore, its application is limited, and in situations where such an assumption does not hold, LR is found to perform more accurately than Naïve Bayes (Mitchell, 2005). The loss function used in LR has been shown to be approximated by a support vector machine (Vapnick, 1999, Zhang et al, 2003). Algorithms based on LR have been used in CBIR (Ksantini, Ziou, Colin, & Dubeau, 2007) and in relevance feedback (Caenen & Pauwels., 2002) for image retrieval. Each concept is either relevant to the given image or not. The dependant variable (relevancy of the concept) can have two values: 0-not relevant and 1-relevant. The explanatory variables are the centroids of the regions in the image. The **classifier** for a particular concept is calculated by using positive and negative images. As mentioned before, the image vectors of each of these images are used to train the classifier. The training inputs are of the form:

$$t_j = \{l_{i,1}, u_{i,1}, v_{i,1}, m^1_{i,1}, m^2_{i,1}, m^3_{i,1}, \ldots, l_{i,16}, u_{i,16}, v_{i,16}, m^1_{i,16}, m^2_{i,16}, m^3_{i,16}, r_j\}$$

where $l_{x,i}$, $u_{x,i}$ $v_{x,i}$ are the average color values in the centroid for region i in the training image j. $m^1_{x,i}$, $m^2_{x,i}$ $m^3_{x,i}$ are the wavelet transforms for the L color space in the centroid for region i in the training image j:

$$r_j = \begin{cases} 0 & \text{for negative images} \\ 1 & \text{for positive images} \end{cases}$$

The logit function for an image vector x is given in Box 1, where α, β_i $(1 \le i \le 96)$ are weights calculated by the maximum-likelihood method from the training images. The logistic regression algorithm is implemented using the WEKA software (Witten & Frank, June 2005).

System Architecture

I-FGM has a flexible architecture based on a multi-agent system that enables it to quickly deploy and redeploy computational resources. It also provides plug-and-play facilities for rapid deployment of any new retrieval method. Based on functionality, I-FGM can be decomposed into the following components:

1. I-Forager
2. gIG-Soup
3. gIG-Builder
4. I-Matcher
5. Blackboard

A detailed description of the various components of I-FGM can be found in (Santos et al, 2005, 2006).

a. **I-Forager:** This component uses third party search tools to perform a first order filtering of the documents in the search space. In our prototype, three I-foragers are used to

Box 1.

$$g(x) = \alpha + \beta_1.l_{x,1} + \beta_2.u_{x,1} + \beta_3.v_{x,1} + \beta_4.m^1_{x,1} + \beta_5.m^2_{x,1} + \beta_6.m^3_{x,1} \ldots\ldots + \beta_{91}.l_{x,16}$$
$$+\beta_{92}.u_{x,16} + \beta_{93}.v_{x,16} + \beta_{94}.m^1_{x,16} + \beta_{95}.m^2_{x,16} + \beta_{96}.m^3_{x,16}$$

download potentially relevant images into the gIG Soup. Google, MSN and Yahoo are used in the I-Foragers. The query is sent to each of the I-Foragers and the top 50 results are downloaded into the gIG Soup. I-Forager calculates the first order similarity that is based on the rank returned by the search engines.

b. **gIG-Soup:** This component is the central data repository of I-FGM that holds the images as they are processed by I-FGM. The gIG-Soup is implemented using a NFS share directory to hold the image documents and a MySQL database that stores the document details such as image file name, similarity values and first order similarity. MySQL tables are also used to synchronize the working of the different components of I-FGM.

c. **gIG-Builder:** This component processes the document in the gIG-Soup into a document graph that is compared with the query graph to calculate its similarity. The gIG-Builders incrementally process the images and calculate the image feature vector. The feature vector is compared with classifiers in the concept library and matching concepts selected. The descriptions of the matched concepts are combined to form the text description of the concepts. Now that we have a text description of images, we can convert it into a document graph using the same method that we use for a text document (Santos et al, 2005, Santos et al, 2006). The image retrieval algorithm was described in detail in the previous sub-section. gIG-Builders select an image based on the priority values and calculate the signature of a certain number of windows, which is again dependant on the image priority. *8x8* pixel windows and sliding distance of 4 pixels are used. The feature vectors of the windows processed until that moment are clustered using the BIRCH **clustering** algorithm with a threshold value of 70. The centroids and areas of the clusters or regions are stored. The feature vector of the image is updated and compared with the classifiers in the library using the logistic regression algorithm. The text descriptions of the matched concepts are combined together to provide the text representation of the image.

d. **I-Matcher:** After the images have been converted into a document graph, it is compared with the query graph. The query graph is produced when the query is converted into a document graph. After comparison of the two graphs, a similarity measure is calculated. It is a numerical measure of how close the image is to the query. The **similarity** is given by the formula:

$$sim(q,d_i) = (\frac{n}{2*N} + \frac{m}{2*M}) * \rho$$

$$\rho = \begin{cases} 1 - \frac{C_1 - C_2}{L} & \text{where } C_1 \geq C_2 \\ 1 - \frac{C_1}{L} & \text{where } C_1 < C_2 \end{cases}$$

where q is the query graph, d_i is the document graph, n and m are the number of concepts and relation nodes respectively, of the query graph found in the document graph, and N and M are the total numbers of concept and relation nodes of the query graph. Two relation nodes are matched if and only if at least their parent and their child are matched. ρ is a probability measure of our confidence in the similarity. C_1 is the number of concepts matched to the image, C_2 is the number of possible relevant concepts, and L is the number of concepts in the concept library. We calculate C_2 from the number of concepts in the query graph. Since the concepts that are matched to the image are not always correct, we use ρ as a weight to the similarity value. For some images, the matched concepts are varied; for example "*dinosaur*", "*snowstorm*", and "*fruits*".

These images happen to have pixel characteristics found in all these concepts. By using a confidence measure, we are quantifying how sure the machine learning algorithms is about its matches. If the matches are small in number, those images have certain unique pixel characteristics that are found in only certain concepts. The confidence measure will be high for these images. For images that match a large number of concepts, we say that the machine learning algorithm is not so confident about its matches.
The priority value for the image is also calculated after each partial step. The priority function is used to determine the order in which the documents in the gIG Soup will be processed. This guides the allocation of computing resources. The amount of processing done during a particular step is also determined by the priority. The priority formula used is identical to the one in (Santos et al, 2006) except for the weights that were calculated for images, are used in the formula.

e. **Blackboard:** Since the documents are partially processed, its similarity values changes. In addition to this, the search space is dynamic. The documents having the top similarity values will change over time. Blackboard will display the most recent results in a rolling fashion. Such a display is essential when real time search results are required.

DISCUSSION

Results and Analysis

We validate the performance of our image retrieval algorithm in 3 steps. In the first set of experiments, we validate the ability of the logistic regression based machine learning technique to match image features to relevant concepts. We do this by comparing with another machine learning technique called C5.0 (Quinlan, 1993). C5.0 is an established data mining tool for discovering patterns that delineate categories, assembling them into classifiers, and using them to make predictions. It does automatic classification using decision trees. In the field of image classification, it has been used in classification of satellite imagery (Hurd, Civco, Gilmore, Prisloe, & Wilson, 2006) and protein crystallization (Zhu, Sun, Cheng, & Bern, 2004) images.

After we show the Logistics regression method to be an effective one in matching low level features in images, we proceed to the second step in our validation, i.e., validating the whole image retrieval algorithm. In our algorithm, we map regions in the image to known concepts. We now test if this matching is done effectively. We compare its performance with a previous prototype of I-FGM that implements WALRUS only. WALRUS is an established method and we have used WALRUS in I-FGM (Santos et al, 2007) to get good retrieval results. It may be noted that the concept based I-FGM is built on top of the WALRUS sub-system. If we can show that the precision of the concept based I-FGM is similar or better than the WALRUS based I-FGM, we can then conclude that matching of concepts and low level features is effective and thus validate our algorithm.

Finally, we have to validate whether the image retrieval algorithm coupled with the distributed processing approach of I-FGM helps in fast retrieval of images. We do this by comparing its performance with two control systems that represent traditional distributed methods.

Creation of Testbed

For conducting the experiments, an image testbed containing a sizeable number of images and a set of queries is created. We chose a scenario titled "Natural disasters" as disaster relief is one of the areas of E-government where quick retrievals are required in large and dynamic databases. We select a set of 5 queries from this scenario. They are:

1. Building damaged by hurricane Katrina
2. Firefighters fight wildfires
3. Heavy snow storms in the winter
4. Houses damaged by tornado
5. Houses damaged by tsunami

For each query, a testbed is created by running the 3 I-Foragers and downloading the top 50 results from each search engine.

Creation of Concept Library

Before the Concept Based I-FGM can be run, a **concept library** has to be constructed. Building a comprehensive library is difficult and time consuming. Instead, we tailor our library to contain concepts that are related to the "Natural disasters" scenario.

The library must also contain unrelated concepts to provide a fair assessment of our image retrieval algorithm. We use a set of 22 concepts listed in Figure 5. Each concept in the library consists of a brief concept description and the concept classifier. Examples of concept descriptions are shown in Figure 6. For each concept, two sets of images (20 each) representing the positive and negative images are used to train the classifier. These images are processed to extract its feature vector consisting of the centroids of its constituent regions. The feature vectors are used to train a classifier in Logistic Regression. Details about the Logistic regression technique are given in the previous sub-section. The concept library is stored in the memory of the gIG-Builders at the beginning of the experiment.

Validation of the Machine Learning Technique

In this section we validate the performance of Logistic Regression based machine learning technique implemented in the concept based I-FGM system by comparing it with C5.0. The existing studies in the machine learning community (Lim et al. 2000, Perlich et al, 2003) have shown that

Figure 5. List of concepts in the concept library

Beach	Damaged buildings	Cold weather	Dinosaur	Firefighter
Fires	Fruits	Tribal People	Snow Storm	Mud Slide
Mountains	Trees	Floods	Forest fires	Rainstorm
Tornado	Elephants	Flowers	Food	Tsunami
Hurricane	Katrina			

Figure 6. Examples of concepts and concept description in the concept library

	Concept	Concept description
1.	Beach	Beach has sand. Beach has lines with coconut trees. Beach has a blue ocean. People sunbath on the beach. Waves can be seen on the beach. People lie on the beach. People watch boats on the beach. There are boats on the beach. It is windy on the beach. People relax on the beach. People play on the beach.
2.	Damaged Buildings	Damaged buildings are caused by natural disasters. Damaged buildings are caused by flood, storm, and hurricane. Damaged buildings have damaged walls, leaking roots, broken doors, broken windows. Damaged buildings can also be caused by terrorism attack. For example, World Trade Center was damaged by terrorist attack.

LR performs competitively with other classifiers and performs better with small data sets than C4.5 (earlier version of C5.0). We would like to verify this finding on our own data set. The C5.0 algorithm was trained using positive and negative images for each concept in the concept library and classifiers were created. Our Logistic Regression (LR) technique and the C5.0 algorithm were used on the image testbed created for query 4: "Houses damaged by tornado". For each image the algorithm delivered matching concepts from the concept library. The relevant concepts for this query are "Damaged Buildings" and "Tornado". When the matched concepts of the two algorithms were compared, we observe that the LR technique matched the relevant concepts "Damaged Houses"

Figure 7. Concepts matched by the logistic regression and C5.0 algorithms

<table>
<tr><th rowspan="2"></th><th rowspan="2">Image</th><th colspan="2">Matching concepts</th></tr>
<tr><th>Logistic regression</th><th>C5.0</th></tr>
<tr><td>1</td><td></td><td>Damaged buildings,
Dinosaur, Fruits, Snowstorm, Mountains, Flood, Tornado,
Elephants
Flowers</td><td>Damaged-building,
Dinosaur, Elephant, Firefighter, Flood, Fruit, Rainstorm</td></tr>
<tr><td></td><td></td><td></td><td></td></tr>
<tr><td>2</td><td></td><td>Damaged buildings,
cold weather, dinosaur, fruits tribal people, food, mountains, trees, forestfires, rainstorm
tornado, flowers</td><td>Damaged-building,
Dinosaur, Elephants, Firefighter, Flood, Fruit, Rainstorm</td></tr>
<tr><td>3</td><td></td><td>Beach, Flood,
Damaged buildings,
Cold weather, Snowstorm, Mountains, Rainstorm,
Tornado,
Elephants</td><td>Beach
Damaged-building
Elephants
Flood
Mountains
Rainstorm</td></tr>
<tr><td>4</td><td>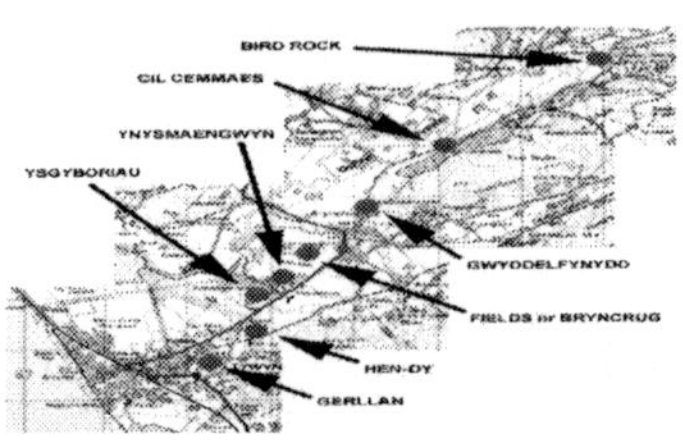
</td><td>Fruits, Trees, Tribal people, Snowstorm, Mountains, Forestfires, Elephants</td><td>Beach, Tree
Damaged –building,
Elephants, Flood, Rainstorm, Snowstorm</td></tr>
</table>

and "Tornado" for more relevant images than the C5.0 algorithm. This can be observed in the results tabulated in Figure 7. Due to space limitation, results for only 4 randomly picked images are displayed. Three of the images (1, 2 & 3) are relevant and the last one (4) is not relevant. For all the images, we see that LR method retrieves more matched concepts (marked in italics in Figure 7) than C5.0. It may be observed that most of the matched concepts of LR are also semantically similar. For example, for image 1 in Figure 7, two of the matched concepts are flood and rainstorm. Though non-relevant, they are semantically related to Tornado as they all belong to the class of natural disasters. For the relevant images 1, 2, and 3, the LR algorithm consistently matches the relevant concepts while C5.0 fails to match the concept "Tornado" to these images. Thus, we see that LR algorithm has a better performance than C5.0. In future work, user based relevance feedback will be used to refine the matches made by the machine learning algorithm. Thus we have validated the performance of the Logistic regression based machine learning technique implemented in our image retrieval algorithm.

Validation of Image Retrieval Algorithm

In this section, we will validate the image retrieval algorithm implemented in I-FGM. In the algorithm, we map the image features to high level concepts and obtain a textual description of the images. The document graphs are then generated from the text descriptions. The document graphs are then compared against the text query to determine the similarity measures. (The image algorithm was described in detail earlier.) We will compare the performance of the Concept-based I-FGM prototype with a purely WALRUS based I-FGM prototype that we developed in (Santos et al, 2007). By getting comparable or better results in Concept based I-FGM prototypes, we will show that using the concept mapping on top of WALRUS does not have an adverse effect on performance and we get just as effective results.

The WALRUS-based I-FGM prototype was the first step towards deploying image retrieval in I-FGM (Santos et al, 2007). It was developed to show that a regions based image retrieval algorithm like WALRUS can be easily incorporated into the I-FGM. The prototype has the same system architecture as the Concept-based I-FGM prototype. The image retrieval algorithm used in the WALRUS based I-FGM is identical to the Concept based I-FGM except for 2 differences: 1) WALRUS system uses query images instead of text queries, and 2) WALRUS system compares the regions of the query image with that of the search space images, instead of extracting concepts from images. I-matcher extracts the image feature vector from the query image and compares it with image feature vector of the search space image. The **similarity** measure used is:

$$Similarity(P,Q) = \frac{area(\cup_{i=1}^{n}(P_i)) + area(\cup_{i=1}^{n}(Q_i))}{area(P) + area(Q)}$$

Here P and Q represent the retrieved image and the query image respectively. The set of ordered pairs $\{(P_1, Q_1), \ldots, (P_n, Q_n)\}$ form a similarity region pair set for P and Q, where P_i is similar to Q_i and for $i \neq j$, $P_i \neq P_j$, $Q_i \neq Q_j$.

Both WALRUS-based and Concept-Based I-FGM prototypes are run with the testbed of 5 queries. **Precision** (Salton & McGill, 1983) is the performance metric that we use to compare the performance of the concept–based and WALRUS based I-FGM system. It is a commonly used metric in information retrieval and is defined as the ratio of the relevant documents (images) retrieved to the total documents (images) retrieved. In this chapter we use a slightly different definition: ratio of the relevant documents (images) among the top n retrieved documents (images). The two systems are run on each of the query testbed and the top 15 images for each query are analyzed to determine their relevance and finally calculate the precision.

Analysis of the Validation Results

The top 15 images retrieved by the WALRUS based I-FGM prototype for each query are analyzed to determine if they are relevant or not. We do this using certain criteria. For example, in query 1: "Building damage by hurricane Katrina", we only consider images that depict damaged buildings, especially on the coast as relevant images. The precision results obtained by the two systems for all the queries are tabulated in Figure 8. For lack of space we present the top 15 image results for only query 1 (Figures 9a,b). Each image is tagged as x.y where x is the name of the search engine that downloaded the image and y is the rank provided by it. The images deemed relevant are indicated by a check mark in Figure 9. A quick glance shows that the performances of the systems are comparable as they retrieve around the same number of relevant documents in each query. The Concept-based and WALRUS based systems win in two queries each (queries 1 & 3 for Concept-based system and queries 2 & 4 for WALRUS-based system) and has a tie for query 5. From these results, we can come to the conclusion that our Concept based image retrieval algorithm performs as well as WALRUS. It may be noted here that the concept mapping part of our current prototype is built on top of the WALRUS feature extraction sub-system. Relevant concepts are matched after the WALRUS sub-system extracts the regions in the images. The document graphs are then generated and compared with the query. We use this to provide a unified framework for heterogeneous data. Similar performance results for both WALRUS and Concept based IFGM show that the performance is not degraded when concepts matching are used with the feature extraction. This also leads us to conclude that the regions based feature extraction methodology can indeed be used to effectively map low level image features to higher level concepts.

Evaluation of Image Retrieval in I-FGM

In this section we will validate the effectiveness of I-FGM for image retrieval. We achieve this by comparing its performance with two other control systems that represent the traditional information and distributed processing paradigms.

The control systems differ from I-FGM only in the way the documents are chosen for processing. The control systems are baseline and partially intelligent systems. In the baseline system, the documents are chosen at random for processing. Each document is given the exact same chunk of time for processing in each step. In the partially intelligent system, the priority of a document is static and is equivalent to the first-order similarity. We use the image testbed created previously to conduct the simulation experiments. The images are processed by the gIG-Builders and the final similarity measures are recorded. The top *n* documents are selected as the target document set for each query.

Figure 8. Precision values attained by WALRUS based and Concept based I-FGM

	Precision	
	WALRUS-Based I-FGM	*Concept-based I-FGM*
Query 1	9/15	*10/15*
Query 2	10/15	*9/15*
Query 3	9/15	*11/15*
Query 4	13/15	*12/15*
Query 5	*10/15*	*10/15*

Figure 9(a). Precision results for Query1 using WALRUS-based I-FGM

The control systems and I-FGM systems are run on the testbed for each query. Two performance metrics calculated during each run are: 1) recall vs. time, and 2) document waiting times. **Recall** (Salton & McGill, 1983) is defined as the ratio of the relevant documents retrieved to the total number of relevant documents. We designate the top *x* documents selected by our image retrieval method as the set of relevant documents. We store the recall values for each control system at regular intervals throughout the period of simulation. The waiting time for a document is defined as the time spent in the gIG Soup before it is displayed on the blackboard. Since one of the goals of I-FGM is to get to the relevant documents as quickly as possible, the waiting time is an important metric.

Results and Analysis

As mentioned before, the control systems and I-FGM are run on the test beds of the 5 queries. The waiting times of relevant documents and recall values are monitored during the simulations.

It has the lowest waiting time for the most documents in queries 4 and 5. For query 3, it ties with baseline system to get the most number of documents in the shortest time. Overall, I-FGM

Figure 9(b). Precision results for Query1 using Concept-based I-FGM

is best in 3 queries, baseline in 2 queries and partial in one query.

We now carefully analyze the results of each query. In query 1 (Figure 10a), baseline system is the best performing system getting 6 out of the 11 documents the fastest. Partial comes second getting 4 documents and I-FGM is third with 2 documents. When we analyze the documents closely, we see that I-FGM performs poorly for this query for one primary reason. The similarity measure fluctuates, decreasing in one step and increasing in another.

In I-FGM, a priority function (used for selecting from the gIG-Soup) decreases the priority of an image when its similarity at a particular step does not increase proportional to the processing time in that particular step or when the similarity decreases. Documents with rapid fluctuations in similarity do not work well with this priority function. Although we used an initial set of experimental results to determine the weights in the priority function, more work needs to be done in formulating a better priority function. As we obtain more experimental results, the priority function will be refined and this will be part of future work. From the precision graph (Figure 10b), we see that I-FGM has a better **recall** for part of the simulation time. For query 2 (Figure 11a, b), partial system has lowest waiting times for 4 documents while I-FGM and baseline system comes second with 3 documents each. We can easily see why this is the reason. The relevant documents are highly ranked by the I-Foragers, i.e. they have a high expected first order similarity. Since the partial system processes the documents based only on the expected first order similarity, such documents are most likely to be picked by it quicker than the other systems. This is further helped by the fact that documents such as MSN.0 and Google.0 are small (around 2000 windows). But it may be noted that the performance of I-FGM is not much worse than partial as it gets only one document less than the partial systems.

For query 3 (Figure 12a, b), both I-FGM and baseline system perform the best, getting 4 documents each. Partial system comes in last with 1 document. When we analyze three documents (Yahoo.41, Google.53, Google.35), which is picked by baseline system the earliest, we see that these documents have a high similarity value after the first partial step itself. Since they are lowly ranked by the I-foragers, they have a low initial priority in the I-FGM system. Therefore I-FGM gets these documents only after a certain amount of simulation time has passed. Baseline system

Figure 10. (a) Document Waiting time-Query 1; (b) Recall Vs Time – Query 1

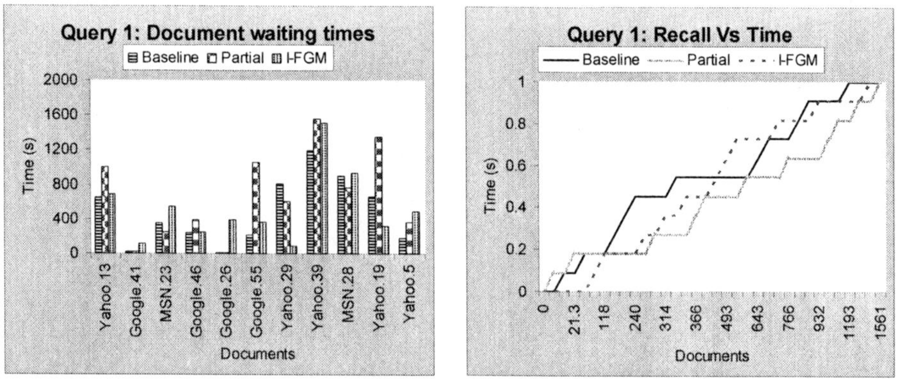

Figure 11. (a) Document Waiting time-Query 2; (b) Recall Vs Time – Query 2

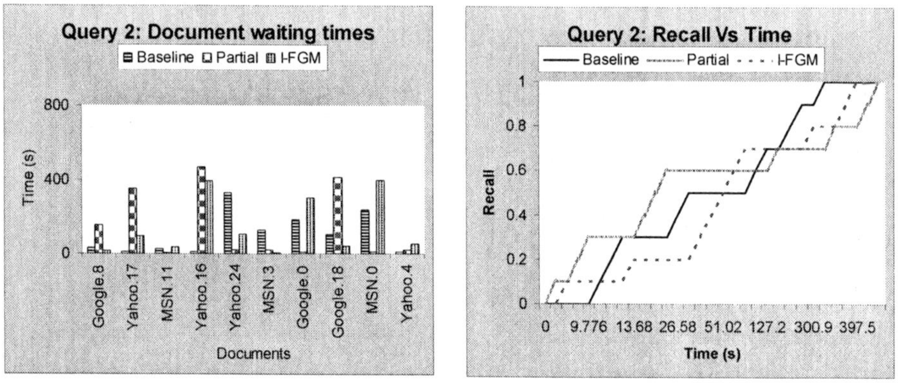

gets lucky by selecting these documents early. But since these documents give a high similarity value in the first processing step, they appear in the blackboard after the first processing step. I-FGM has better performance than baseline and I-FGM for queries 4 (Figure 13a, b) and 5 (Figure 14a,b). For query 4, I-FGM gets 5 out of the 8 relevant documents. Baseline system comes in second with 3 documents. In the recall graph also, I-FGM has a higher recall value than the other systems for

Figure 12. (a) Document Waiting time-Query 3; (b) Recall Vs Time – Query 3

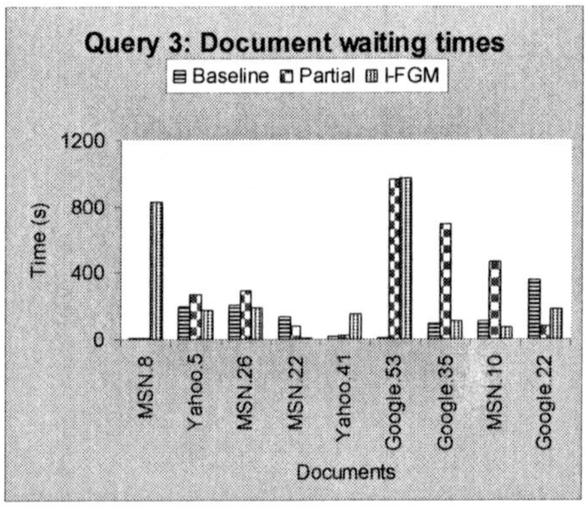

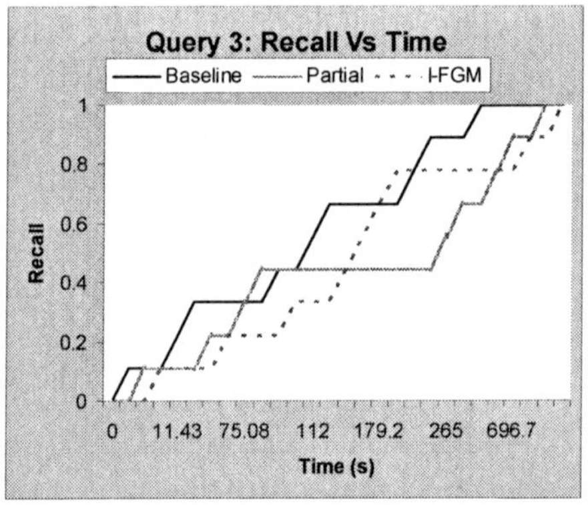

Figure 13. (a) Document Waiting time-Query 4; (b) Recall Vs Time - Query4

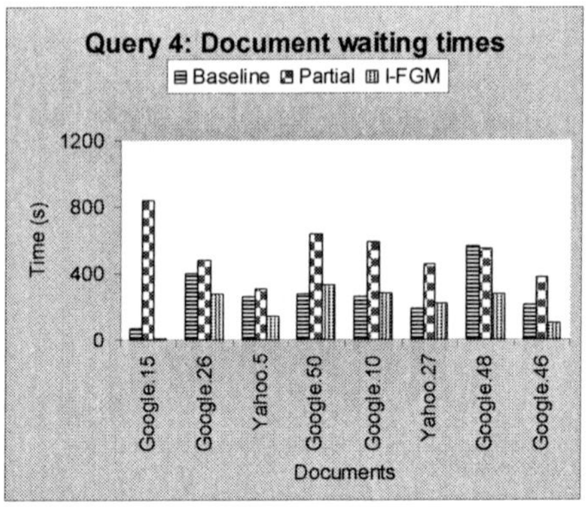

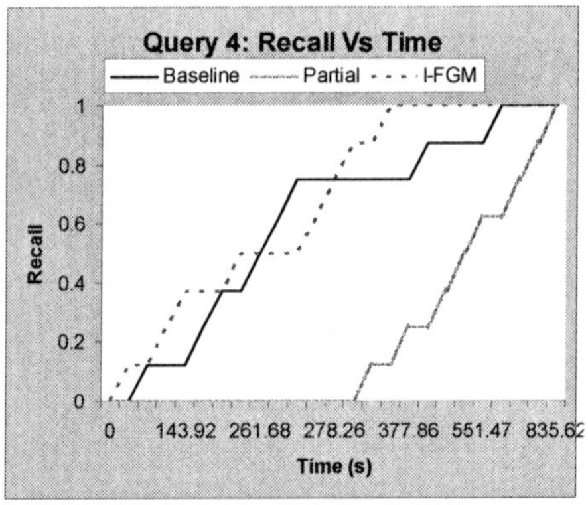

Figure 14. (a) Document Waiting time-Query 5; (b) Recall Vs Time - Query5

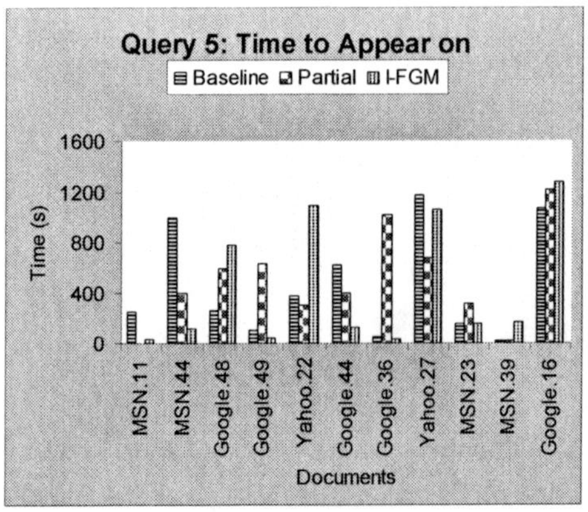

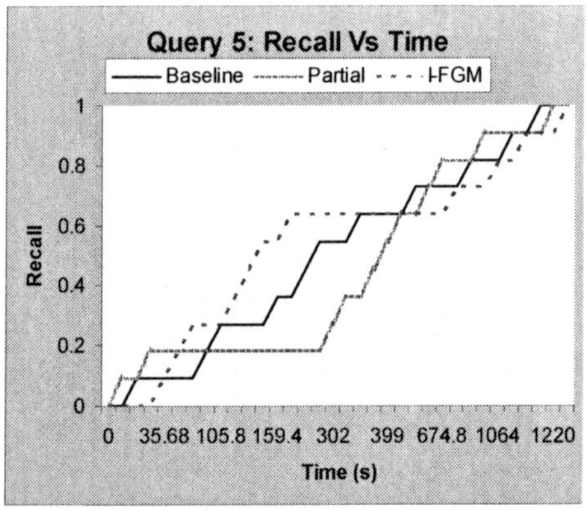

most of the simulation time. For query 5, I-FGM gets 5 documents out of 11 target documents. Partial and baseline tie for the second place with 4 each. In the recall graph (Figure 15b), I-FGM has a better recall than other system over the range (0.2-0.7). The similarity values for images can decrease over time (which does not happen in text retrieval) and fluctuate rapidly. These factors make the modeling of priority function for images a difficult task. Despite this, we have shown I-FGM to be better in the majority of queries, thus proving its feasibility as a quick and reliable retrieval method for images.

PRODUCTION-LEVEL SYSTEM

In the previous sections and in previous work, we demonstrated how the I-FGM framework can be used to retrieve text and image documents by conducting empirical studies on prototypes. But these prototypes were basic technology demonstrators, limited in scale by the small number of processors used. It could not handle multiple queries and each node could host one I-FGM process. Another important limitation was that the prototypes could handle only one type of document, either text or images but not both. An easily accessible, user-friendly interface that displays the real time results and the status of the internal processes in I-FGM system was also missing. In their current form, these prototypes cannot be deployed in the field. In order to validate its performance in real-life situation, we prepared an analyst-ready production level system. This system is built using 79 high end computing nodes. It has a user-interface that is available to the user via the Internet and can handle multiple queries from multiple users.

System Setup

The production-level system uses 79 nodes from a 100 node cluster. The nodes are high end Intel Pentium-D 2.8GHz 64-Bit dual processor servers connected by 1GBPS Ethernet links. Although I-FGM could be extended to all the 100 nodes, we achieved our performance goals using only 79 nodes. I-FGM components are implemented on the nodes as shown in Figure 15. In order to increase the variety of sources available to analysts, we added new I-foragers to search news and blog sources which are also important sources of real time information. In Figure 15, we have listed out all the search engines used in the I-Foragers, grouped under text and image headings. They are subdivided according to the specific type of documents. So text I-Foragers are divided up into blog, news and generic types. From Figure 15, we see that 35 and 31 nodes have been used as text and image gIG-Builders respectively. We used more text gIG-Builders because a typical query brings in more text documents than images and processing a text document is more computationally expensive. By simply scaling up the number of processors in the system from 20 to just 79 nodes, we are able to get meaningful search results within 10s of elapsed time. By implementing this system, we have demonstrated the scalability of the I-FGM framework to include more computing resources. We also show how the flexible architecture of I-FGM allows us to rapidly combine retrieval technologies, namely text and image retrieval. The implementation of the specific components is described in the earlier sections. Once a query is retrieved from the user, a set of processors pertaining to the different I-FGM components are activated in the corresponding nodes. I-foragers send the query to particular search engines and retrieve the results. The gIG Builder and I-matcher work towards processing the documents and determining its final similarity. These processes terminate when the documents for a query have been fully processed. The results are then displayed to the user through a User interface GUI that corresponds to the Blackboard component described in an earlier section.

Figure 15. Allocation of processors to I-FGM agents in Production-level Prototype

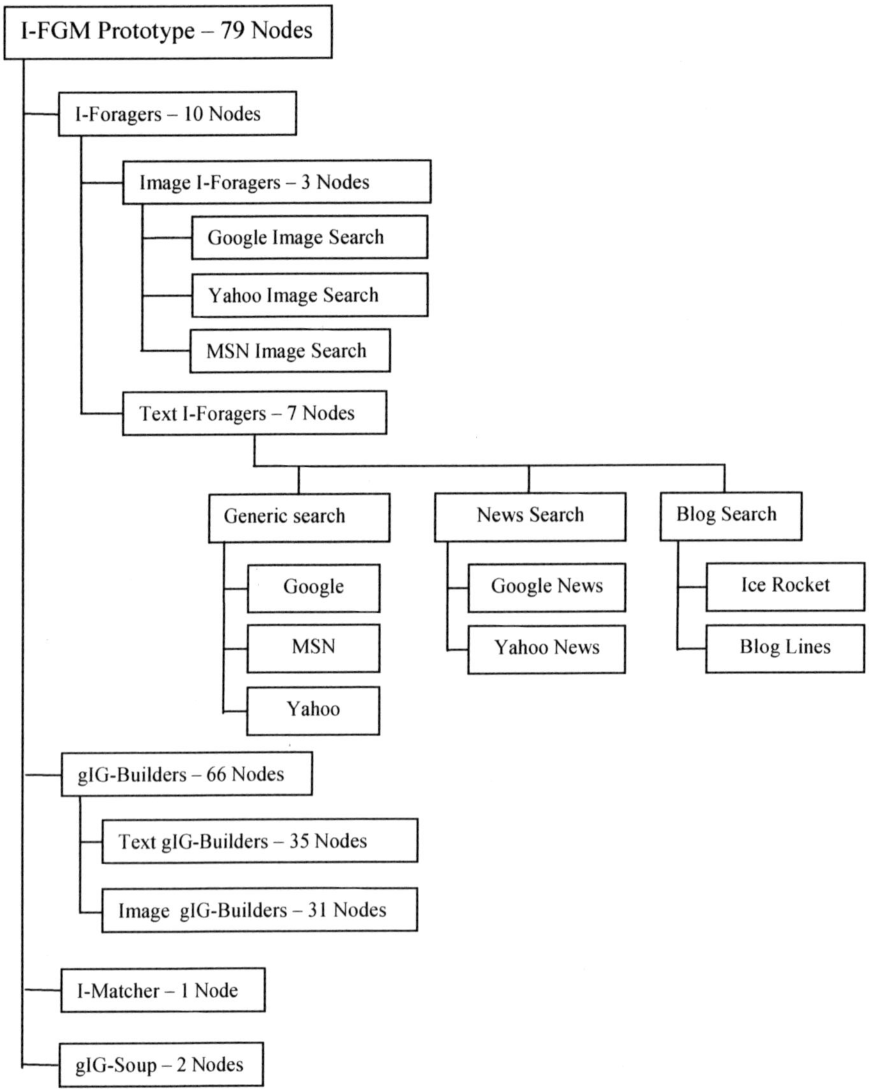

User Interface

One of the design criteria for the production system is that the users should be able to access it from any part of the world. Hence a web-based GUI using Java Server Pages (JSP) and Tomcat web server that is accessible via the Internet was designed. The user can use any Java enabled web browser to access this interface. The GUI, in addition to providing a place for the user to input the query and view the results, also displays the status of the documents in the search space as they are processed. The processed document graphs of individual documents can be viewed along with the status of the I-FGM processes. The different functionalities of the user interface are grouped together in different 'tabs'. These tabs are described in detail below:

1. **Search Results Tab** (Figure 16): The user enters the query in this tab and the top 10 text and image results are displayed side by

side. Each text result is accompanied by an automatically generated summary of the document along with a link to the full text. Each image result is displayed as a thumbnail with a link to the full image. The results are automatically updated as the documents are processed and more relevant documents are discovered. There is provision for the user to enter multiple queries and then cycle through the results for each of the query.

2. **Process Monitor Tab** (Figure 17): The analyst might be interested in the number of documents being foraged by a particular I-Forager. This is displayed in the Process Monitor tab. It also displays the document being processed by each gIG-Builder along with the percentage processed.
3. **gIG-Soup Monitor Tab** (Figure 18): This tab displays the status of the gIG-Soup and

Figure 16. Screenshot of Search Results Tab

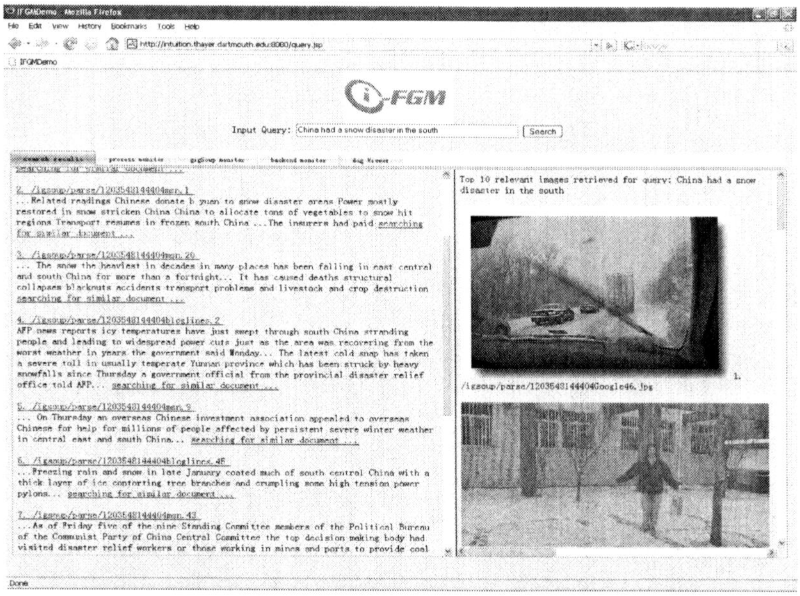

Figure 17. Screenshot of Process Monitor Tab

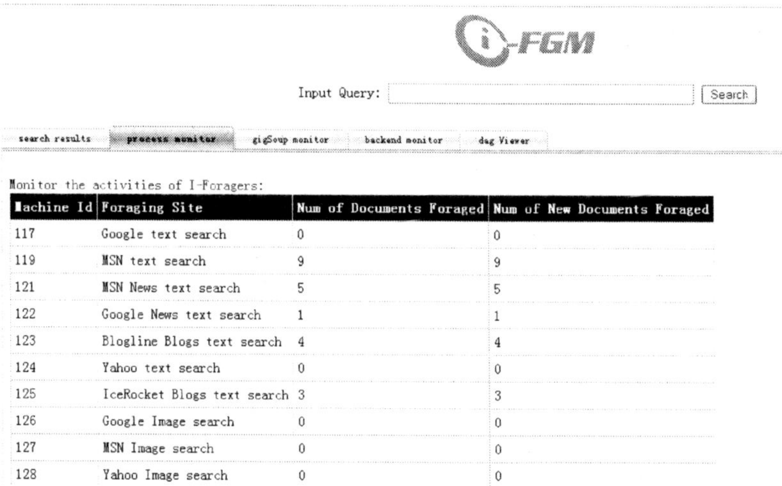

Monitor the activities of I-Foragers:

Machine Id	Foraging Site	Num of Documents Foraged	Num of New Documents Foraged
117	Google text search	0	0
119	MSN text search	9	9
121	MSN News text search	5	5
122	Google News text search	1	1
123	Blogline Blogs text search	4	4
124	Yahoo text search	0	0
125	IceRocket Blogs text search	3	3
126	Google Image search	0	0
127	MSN Image search	0	0
128	Yahoo Image search	0	0

the progress of processing of its documents. As described earlier, I-FGM incrementally processes the documents, allowing for efficient usage of the computing resources. gIG-Soup allows the user to monitor this dynamic process by graphically depicting documents as gradually darkening discs. The dark portion of a disc is equal to the portion of the corresponding document processed by gIG-Builders. The disc fills out as the processing of the document proceeds forward. There are separate section of discs for text and images. Additionally, newly foraged documents can be monitored separately as they are displayed using red discs.

4. **Backend Monitor Tab**: provides more details about the top ten results in the search results tab, such as the time it was foraged and the amount of time for which it was processed. This allows us to evaluate the processing efficiency of I-FGM and its ability to focus the computing resources on documents that are ultimately shown to be relevant.
5. **DAG Viewer Tab** (Figure 19): The text and image documents are converted into document graphs by the gIG-Builders. In order to view this internal representation of the documents, a DAG (Directed Acyclic Graph) viewer is implemented using the Scalar Vector Graphics (SVG) standard and the Adobe SVG Viewer plug-in. The list of documents is displayed in the left panel and the document graph for the document can be viewed by selecting it. The graphs can be zoomed in or out. If the document is not fully processed, then the partial graph is displayed.
6. **Image Concept Library Tab** (Figure 20): As mentioned in previous sections, the image concept library is designed to store a collection of well known concepts. The Image Concept Library Tab allows the viewing and modification of the entire concept library. The details of each concept such as title,

Figure 18. Screenshot of gIG-Soup Monitor Tab

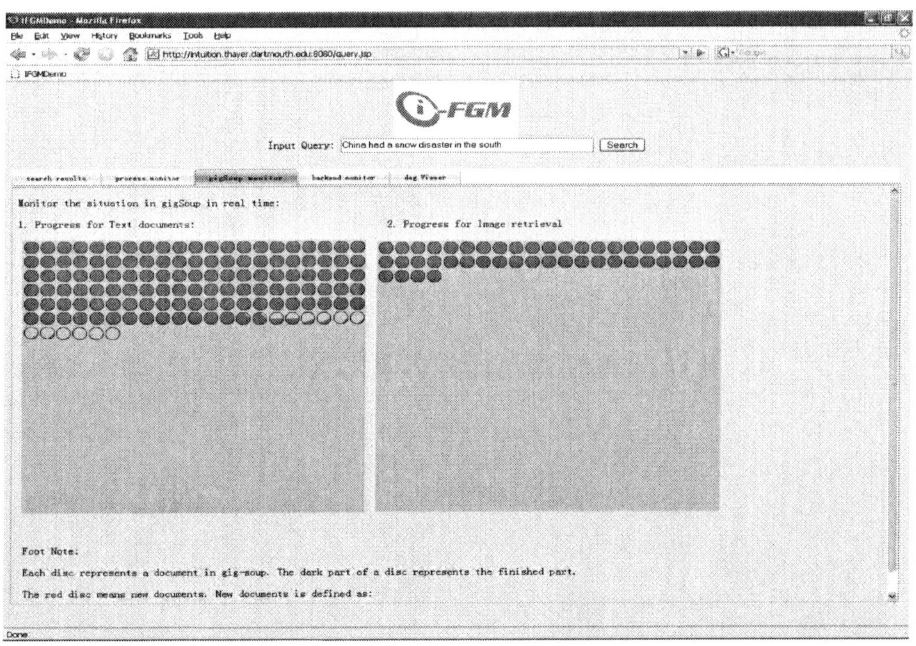

Figure 19. Screenshot of DAG Viewer Tab

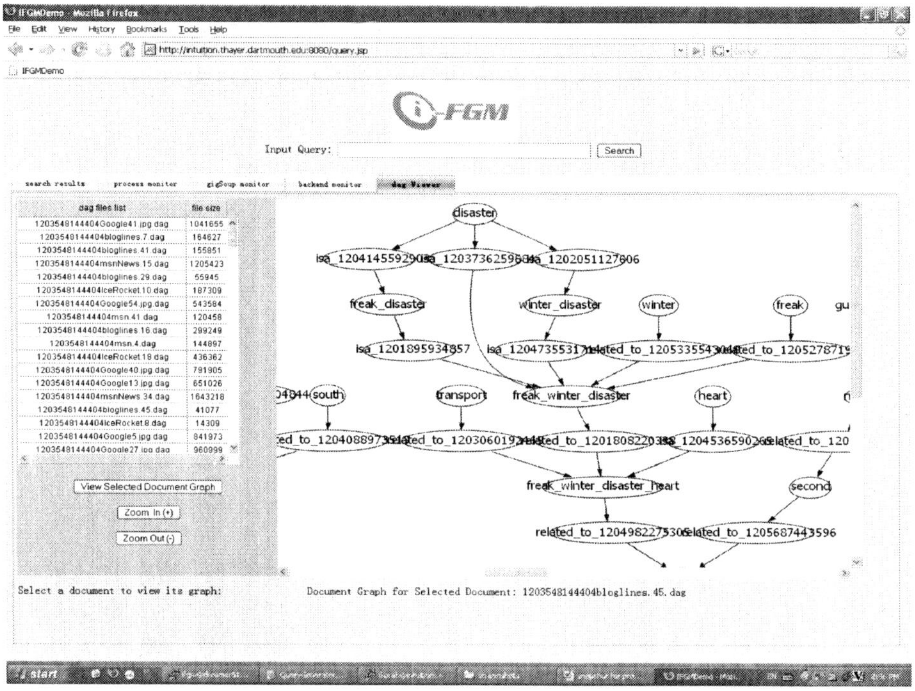

description can be changed by the user. Additionally, training images can be added or removed and a new classifier can be generated. The most important aspect of this tab is to enable the user to add new concepts. This will help the analysts to incorporate new themes into the concept library in lieu with his/her changing areas of interest.

In order to test the new system, we ran the system with a set of queries representing topics in a variety of scenarios such as natural disasters, terrorism, Iraq war, etc. They were chosen for the rapid pace of events in the scenarios and due to their relevance to typical analyst activities. In order to retrieve the image results for these scenarios, we built an image concept library consisting of 53 concepts pertaining to the topics we are interested in. The foragers brought in an average of 300 text documents and 50 images for each query. It took around 20 minutes to process all the documents completely for a query and we were able to get meaningful results displayed on the user interface in 10 seconds. Most of the top results were from blogs and news sources, validating their usefulness for analysts. The system was stress tested by running 10 queries by multiple users simultaneously on the system. For each query, the system invokes separate I-forager, gIG-Builder and I-Matcher processes in the nodes. Despite multiple I-FGM processes running on the nodes, time taken to process the documents and display relevant results was not affected. However, potential bottlenecks with the MySQL databases and the process invocation server were noted. Reducing the effects of these bottlenecks is left for future work.

CONCLUSION

In this chapter we designed and implemented an image retrieval algorithm based on mapping low level features of images to higher level con-

Figure 20. Screenshot of Image concept Library

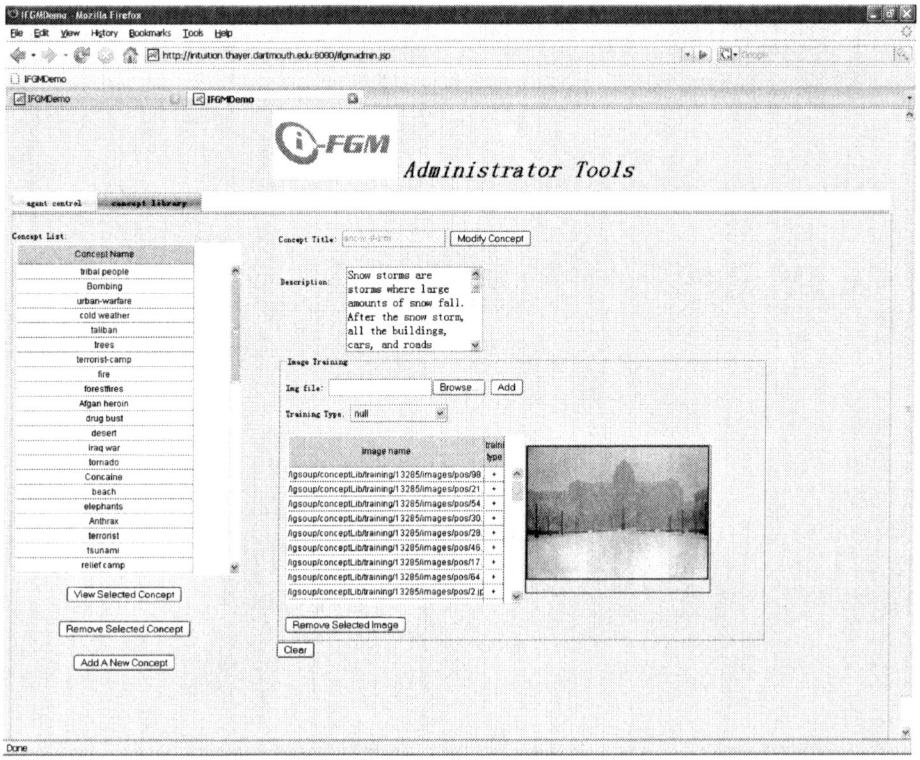

cepts. We validated this algorithm on I-FGM and showed that it can be used to represent the visual information of images as concepts and relations. Consequently, we also validated the methodology in I-FGM of providing a unified ranking for heterogeneous data types. I-FGM was also compared against two control systems to show that the image retrieval algorithm works well with partial processing and helps in faster retrieval of images. We also presented a deployable production-level system. This system shows the scalability of I-FGM with respect to adding computing resources, adding new sources of documents and bringing together different retrieval strategies under the same umbrella. The system has a functional GUI for interacting with analysts and also provides for simultaneous multiple queries by multiple analysts.

In the future, we plan to incorporate relevance feedback to allow users to give their inputs on the retrieval quality. Users can be asked explicitly to indicate which images and texts are most similar to what they are looking for. We may also observe the users' interactions with our system to infer implicitly which images pertain to their interests. These retrieved relevant images then will be used to modify the user's original queries by adding both textual and image information to them. This process will help guide the retrieval task so that it returns more relevant images to the user.

The work was supported in part by the National Geospatial Intelligence Agency Grant Nos. HM1582-04-1-2027 and HM1582-05-1-2042. This chapter updates and extends the previously published article by (Santos et al. 2008). We would also like to thank Dr. Qunhua Zhao for his various comments and advice in this project.

REFERENCES

Caenen, G., & Pauwels., E. J. (2002). *Logistic Regression Models for Relevance Feedback in Content-Based Image Retrieval.* Storage and Retrieval for Media Databases, San Jose, California, USA.

Carson, C., Belongie, S., Greenspan, H., & Malik, J. (2002). Blobworld: Image segmentation using expectation-maximization and its application to image querying. *IEEE Transactions on Pattern Analysis and Machine Intelligence,* 24(8), 1026-1038.

Daubechies, I. (1992). *Ten Lectures on Wavelets.* Philadelphia: SIAM.

Enser, P., & Sandom, C. (2003). Towards a comprehensive survey of the semantic gap in visual image retrieval. (LNCS, *2728,291-299*).

Hurd, J. D., Civco, D. L., Gilmore, M. S., Prisloe, S., & Wilson, E. H. (2006). *Tidal wetland classification from Landsat imagery using an integrated pixel-based and object-based classification approach.* Paper presented at the ASPRS 2006 Annual Conference, Reno, NV.

Kherfi, M. L., Ziou, D., & Bernardi, A. (2004). Image Retrieval from the World Wide Web: Issues, Techniques, and Systems. *ACM Computing Surveys, 36*(1), 35-67.

Komarek, P.(2004, May) *Logistic Regression for Data Mining and High-Dimensional Classification*, (Tech. report CMU-RI-TR-04-34). Pittsburg, PA: Carnegie Mellon University, Robotics Institute

Ksantini, R., Ziou, D., Colin, B., & Dubeau, F. (2007). *Logistic Regression Models for a Fast CBIR Method Based on Feature Selection.* Paper presented at the International Joint Conference on Artificial Intelligence.

Li, J., & Wang, J. Z. (2006). *Real-time Computerized Annotation of Pictures.* Paper presented at the ACM Multimedia Conference, Santa Barbara, CA.

Li, J., Wang, J. Z., & Wiederhold, G. (2000). *IRM: Integrated Region Matching for Image Retrieval.* Paper presented at the ACM Multimedia Conference, Los Angeles, CA.

Lim, T.S. Lim, Loh, W.Y. and Shih, Y.S. (2000). A comparison of prediction accuracy, complexity, and training time for thirty–three old and new classification algorithms. *Machine Learning,* 40, 203–228.

Ma, W. Y., & Manjunath, B. (1997). *NeTra: A Toolbox for Navigating Large Image Databases.* Paper presented at the IEEE International Conference on Image Processing.

Mitchell, T. (2005). *Generative and Discriminative classifiers: Naïve Bayes and Logistic Regression.* Retrieved from http://www.cs.cmu.edu/~tom/mlbook /NBayesLog- Reg.pdf

Natsev, A. (2001). *Multimedia Retrieval By Regions, Concepts, and Constraints.* Ph.D. Thesis, Duke University, Durham, NC.

Natsev, A., Chadha, A., Soetarman, B., & Vitter, J. S. (2001). *CAMEL: Concept Annotated iMagE Libraries.* Paper presented at the Storage and Retrieval for Image and Video Databases, SPIE, San Jose, CA.

Natsev, A., Rastogi, R., & Shim, K. (2004). WALRUS: A Similarity Retrieval Algorithm for Image Databases. *IEEE Transactions on Knowledge and Data Engineering, 16*(3), 301-316.

Perlich, C., Provost, F., and Simonoff, J. (2003). Tree Induction vs. Logistic Regression: A Learning-curve Analysis. *Journal of Machine Learning Research.* 4, 211-255

Quinlan, J. R. (1993). *C4.5: programs for machine learning.* San Francisco, CA: Morgan Kaufmann Publishers Inc.

Rui, Y., Huang, T., & Chang, S. (1999). Image retrieval: current techniques, promising directions and open issues. *Journal of Visual Communication and Image Representation, 10*(4), 39-62.

Salton, G., & McGill, M. (1983). *Introduction to Modern Information Retrieval*: McGraw-Hill.

Santos, E. Jr., Santos, E., Nguyen, H. Pan, L. and Korah, J. (2005). Large-scale Distributed Foraging, Gathering, and Matching for Information Retrieval: Assisting the Geospatial Intelligent Analyst. In *Proceedings of SPIE* (Vol. 5803, 66-77).

Santos, E. Jr., Santos, E., Nguyen, H. Pan, L., Korah, J. Zhao, Q., and Pittkin. M.(2006) I-FGM Information Retrieval in Highly Dynamic Search Spaces. In *Proceedings of SPIE.* (Vol. 6229, 1-12).

Santos, E., Jr., Santos, E., Nguyen, H., Pan, L., Korah, J., Zhao, Q., and Xia, H. (2007). Applying I-FGM to Image Retrieval and an I-FGM System Performance Analyses. In *Proceedings of the SPIE*: Defense & Security Symposium (Vol. 6560), Orlando, FL.

Santos, E., Jr., Santos, E., Nguyen, H., Pan, L., Korah, J., and Xia, H. (2008). *I-FGM as a Real Time Information Retrieval Tool for E-Governance.* Special Issue: E-Government Technologies for Managing National Secruity and Defense, *International Journal of Electronic Government Research,* 4(1), 14-25.

Smeulders, A. W. M., M. Worring, M., Santini, S., Gupta, A., & Jain, R. (2000). Content-based image retrieval at the end of the early years. *IEEE Transactions on Pattern Analysis and Machine Intelligence, 22*(12), 1349-1380.

Tsymbalenko, Y., & Munson, E.V. (2001). *Using HTML metadata to find relevant images on theWeb.* Paper presented at the Internet Computing, Las Vegas.

Vapnik, V. (1999). *The Nature of Statistical Learning Theory,* 2nd edition. Springer Verlag.

Veltkamp, R. C., & Tanase, M. (2000). *Content-Based Image Retrieval Systems: A Survey* (Technical Report No. UU-CS-2000-34): Dept. of Computing Science, Utrecht University.

Wang, J. Z., Li, J., & Wiederhold, G. (2001). SIMPLIcity: Semantics-Sensitive Integrated Matching for Picture Libraries. *IEEE Transactions on Pattern Analysis and Machine Intelligence, 23*(9), 947-963.

Witten, I. H., & Frank, E. (2005, June). *Data Mining: Practical Machine Learning Tools and Techniques* (Second ed.): Morgan Kaufmann.

Zhang, T., Ramakrishnan, R., & Livny, M. (1996). *BIRCH: an efficient data clustering method for very large databases.* Paper presented at the ACM SIGMOD International Conference on Management of Data, Montreal, Canada.

Zhang, J., Jin, R., Yang, Y., Hauptmann, A. G. (2003). Modified Logistic Regression: An Approximation to SVM and Its Application in Large-Scale Text Categorization, In *Proceedings of the Twentieth International Conference on Machine Learning* 2003. Washington DC.

Zhu, X., Sun, S., Cheng, S. E., & Bern, M. (2004). *Classification of Protein Crystallization Imagery.* Paper presented at the 26th Annual International Conference of IEEE Engineering in Medicine and Biology Society, San Francisco, California.

Chapter XVII
In-Stream Data Processing for Tactical Environments

Marco Carvalho
Institute for Human and Machine Cognition, USA

ABSTRACT

Data dissemination and information management technologies for tactical environments are quickly becoming major areas of research for both military and civilian applications. Critical to the problem is the need for fully distributed information management technologies that are efficient, adaptive and resilient. In this paper, we introduce and discuss a new strategy for tactical data dissemination and processing based on distributed online learning. Starting from a formal description of the problem we introduce our proposed solution and its theoretical properties. We also present and discuss a number of simulation experiments for different data dissemination scenarios, and conclude the work with a discussion on how such techniques may be applied to critical e-government environments under different assumptions of service availability and information release policies.

INTRODUCTION

Tactical networks are generally characterized as mobile ad hoc networks under policy and resource constraints. These types of network environments are commonly found in military and disaster recovery operations and represent a percentage of the types of environments where government agencies are required to effectively operate and collaborate.

Generally, the primary objective of tactical networks is to support fast formation of ad hoc groups and systems to share data, processing capabilities, and communication resources. One of the most critical and challenging problem in these types of environments is the distributed coordination of resource allocation for data distribution and processing. The decentralized and dynamic natures of tactical environments require resource coordination strategies that are distributed, efficient, and adaptive. Furthermore,

Copyright © 2009, IGI Global, distributing in print or electronic forms without written permission of IGI Global is prohibited.

coordination mechanisms are expected to be resilient to environmental changes and failures, with minimum requirements for maintenance and configuration.

Conceptually, the problem of dynamic resource allocation in tactical networks consists of finding and maintaining the best data distribution trees that together minimize the global utilization of resources for data processing and data transmission, while complying with policy constraints both at the levels of the nodes an network.

In this work we revisit a reinforcement learning-based strategy proposed by Carvalho (2006) for the resource allocation problem in tactical networks. The goal is to formulate the problem in a way that supports the application of a resource coordination protocol that will leverage from previously established localized learning techniques.

BACKGROUND AND PREVIOUS WORK

The resource allocation problem for data processing in mobile ad hoc networks can be generally classified into three main groups: (1) local data processing, (2) remote data processing, and (3) distributed (or in-stream) data processing. In each case, the goal is to allocate resources for data processing and distribution from a source node to multiple sink nodes requiring (possibly) different variations of the data.

In the first type of problems (i.e., local data processing), the source of the data is responsible for providing the necessary transformations required by each client. Similar to conventional client-server models, local data processing essentially allocates all processing to the data source (i.e., the server). The research focus on these types of problems is basically in the allocation of resources for data distribution (i.e., data routing).

Curran (2003) proposed a reinforcement learning-based algorithm for routing in ad hoc networks. The SWARM protocol is data agnostic, focused only on packet routing. When receiving a data packet, each node chooses the appropriate action (next hop) based on current policies. The work was later extended by Dowling, Curran, Cunningham, and Cahill (2004) who proposed the collaborative reinforcement learning-based routing protocol called SAMPLE, for mobile ad hoc networks. Chang, Ho, and Kaelbling (2004) have also proposed the use of reinforcement learning techniques for data routing in mobile ad hoc networks. Although the approach did not address tactical issues such as service decomposition and distribution, it did allow for interaction between data routing and node mobility. Peng and Deyun (2006) also leverage from reinforcement learning algorithms to improve quality of service (QoS) routing strategies. In his work, Peng proposes a heuristic-based algorithm that utilizes reinforcement learning to estimate best QoS routing paths from previous experience, reducing the number of QoS flood and probing packets for path maintenance in mobile networks.

Remote data processing problems try to identify a node in the network that is the best candidate for the data processing task. Like in the previous types of problems, the task of allocating resources for data processing is separate from the allocation of resources for data transmission in the network. For example, if a number of clients require data to be retrieved and processed from a server in the field, a remote data processing strategy will essentially identify a proxy node in the network (based on CPU, memory, and storage capabilities) to act as the point for data processing and re-distribution. Costs related with data transmission from the source to the proxy and from the proxy to each client are independently calculated.

In 2004, Baehni, Eugster, and Guerraoui proposed a data aware variation of conventional multicast protocols that took into account the nature of the data being transmitted when building the multicast trees. Other topic-based publish/subscribe systems such as such as TPS (Eugster, Guerraoui, & Damm, 2001) and JORAM (Maistre, 2003) also leverage from multicast protocols and the assumption of a clear hierarchy on data and events to build efficient multicast groups for topic-based data distribution. Similar approaches were also proposed by Katz and Brewer (1994), Chen and Schwan (2005), Carvalho and Breedy (2002), and others.

Most of the agent-based negotiation strategies or economical-model perspectives have also targeted remote data processing. Carvalho, Pechoucek, and Suri (2005), Pechoucek, Marık, and Stepankova, (2001), Kothari, Sabhash, and Zhou (2003), and Buyya, Stockinger, Giddy, and Abramson (2001), are all examples of such approaches.

Reinforcement learning techniques are also not new for remote data processing. They have been previously proposed for several data routing algorithms (Boyan & Littman, 1994; Choi & Yeung, 1996; Littman & Boyan, 1993; Miikkulainen & Kumar, 1999; Stone, 2000; Tao, Baxter, & Weaver, 2001).

A third and perhaps more interesting type of data processing in mobile ad hoc networks is distributed data processing. In these types of problems, a task is actually fragmented into sub-tasks that can be allocated to multiple nodes in the network in order to jointly minimize data processing and distribution costs.

The way in which tasks are fragmented and distributed (in-stream data processing) is a function of the capabilities of network nodes, topology, and policies. While a number of data-centric routing protocols such as SPIN-IT (Woodrow & Heinzelman, 2001) and Directed Diffusion (Intanagonwiwat, Govindan, & Estrin, 2001) have been proposed for data streaming in MANETs, the research on in-stream data processing is relatively new.

PROBLEM DESCRIPTION

For the purpose of this work, the formal description of the resource allocation problem is based on three concepts that, together, characterize the network environment and a task to be performed. These concepts are the network, the data-state transition (i.e., data transformation), and the data task.

The Environment and Task Description

The physical environment consists of a mobile ad hoc network represented by a network diagram. The network describes the current physical constraints of the system, both in terms of nodes (hosts) and communication (links) capabilities. The tasks, referred to as "data tasks" define both processing (data transformation) and transmission jobs to be accomplished by the network.

The Network Diagram

Definition 1: *A* ***Network Diagram*** *(NET) is defined as a graph structure NET (N,L) where* $N = \{ n_1, n_2, ..., n_n\}$ *is a set of vertices representing nodes (hosts) in the network and* $L = \{ l_1, l_2, ..., l_n\}$ *is a set of edges representing the communication links between nodes. Data transmission between nodes can only occur through a link* (l_i)*in the graph, and all links are assumed to be bi-directional and symmetric.*

There is a link-specific transmission cost factor (*tfactor*) associated with each edge, and a processing cost factor (*pfactor*) associated with each node (Figure 1). Communication edges are assumed to be symmetric so the same *tfactor* is valid for communications in both directions. At any given time, a node is aware of its current *pfactor* and the *tfactor* for the connected links. Both the *pfactor* and the *tfactor* are used to estimate the costs for processing and transmitting a data packet respectively.

A data transition diagram (Figure 1) essentially specifies (through a graph structure) all possible state transitions supported by a data type. An instance of a data type (i.e., a datum) can be duplicated, processed, or transferred between nodes. Examples of data types are video images (snapshots), documents, and sensor data-captures in general. Each data type in the framework has a finite, well-defined number of possible states and state-transition paths. A data type is fully described by a data state transition graph (*DST*), defined as follows:

Definition 2: *A* ***Data State-Transition Diagram*** *(DST) is a directed graph DST(D, F), where D* $= \{ d_1, d_2, ..., d_n \}$ *is a set of vertices representing all possible states that a datum can assume and* $F = \{f_1, f_2, ..., f_n\}$ *is a set of edges representing all functions* f_i *that can be applied on the data.*

The data information provided by the DST is static. It depends only on the data-type and it does not change in time or location in the network. Given an instance of a datum, every host in the network knows (or can obtain) the DST for the datum's data type. The proposed framework simultaneously supports multiple data types and data transactions competing for shared network resources.

Data Task Description

A data task is defined as a combined data processing and data transmission job assigned to a node in the network. It is constrained (in the context of this work) to a single source and potentially multiple destinations. A network node is capable of handling one data task at a time, but multiple data tasks can be simultaneously processed at multiple nodes in the network.

A data stream is a sequence of data packets that are individually processed. In this discussion a data task is defined as a task for handling a single data packet. A data stream implies a sequence of data tasks. To simplify the formal definition of a data task, the concepts of a source pair and a target pair will be first introduced.

Definition 3: *For a given NET(N,L) and DST(D,F), define a* ***Source Pair*** *sp(NET, DST) and a* ***Target Pair*** *tp(NET, DST) as tuples* $\langle n_i, d_j \rangle$ *where* $n_i \in$ N *and* $d_j \in$ D. *A* ***Target Pair Set,*** *denoted by* $TP = \{ tp_1, tp_2, ..., tp_h \}$, *is an unordered set of target pairs.*

To simplify notation, for discussions where a single data type is considered over a fixed (or temporarily fixed) network, the source pair (*sp(NET, DST)* $\langle n_i, d_j \rangle$) and the target pair (*tp(NET, DST)*

Figure 1. A NET (network) and a DST (data-state transition) diagrams

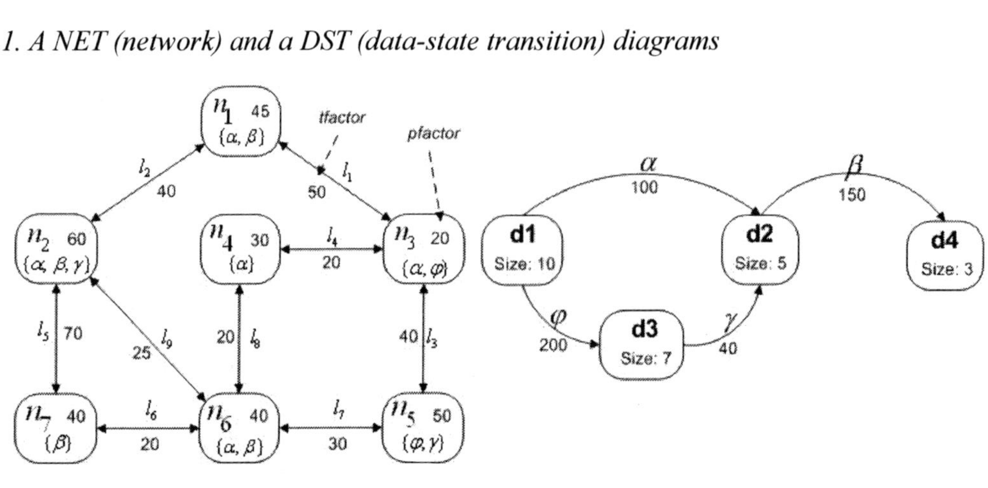

$= \langle n_k, d_k \rangle$) will be simply denoted as *sp* and *tp* respectively, under the implied assumption that $n_i, n_k \in$ N and $d_i, d_k \in$ D. Leveraging from the pervious definitions, a data task can be defined as follows:

Definition 4: *For a given NET(N,L) and DST(D,F), a* ***Data Task*** *is defined as a tuple dT(NET, DST) = ⟨sp, TP, phist⟩ where sp is a source pair sp(NET, DST) =* $\langle n_i, d_j \rangle$*, TP a target pair-set in (NET,DST), and phist an unordered set of nodes* $\{n_i\}, n_i \in$ N.

In a data task, the source pair identifies which node has which datum, and the set of target pairs defines the target nodes and the datum they should receive. A data task essentially specifies a source pair (node/datum) and a set of destination pairs (node/datum) as part of a task to be accomplished. To simplify notation, a data task *dT(NET, DST)* = ⟨*sp, TP, phist*⟩ is simply denoted as *dT* in contexts where a single data type *DST* and *NET* are considered. Furthermore, in order to facilitate the notions introduced in subsequent discussion, we should also define two auxiliary functions f_n and f_d as follows:

Definition 5: *Define a* ***Node Function****, denoted by* $f_n(\gamma)$ *for* $(\gamma = sp)$ *or* $(\gamma = tp)$*, as a function* $f_n(\langle n_i, d_j \rangle) = n_i$ *that returns the node* n_i *of the argument* γ.

Definition 6: *Define a* ***Datum Function****, denoted by* $f_d(\gamma)$ *for* $(\gamma = sp)$ *or* $(\gamma = tp)$*, as a function* $f_d(\langle n_i, d_j \rangle) = d_i$ *that returns the datum* d_j *of the argument* γ.

Both the node and the datum functions can be applied to a data task (*dT* = ⟨*sp, TP, phist*⟩), which is equivalent to applying the functions in the *source pair* (*sp*) of the data task. That is $f_n(dT = \langle sp, TP, phist \rangle) = f_n(sp)$ and similarly $f_d(dT = \langle sp, TP, phist \rangle) = f_d(sp)$.

A data task fully specifies the source node $sp = \langle n_i, d_j \rangle$ and the task to be performed. It is, by definition, assigned to the node $n_i = f_n(sp)$ specified in the source tuple ($sp = \langle n_i, d_j \rangle$) and can have an arbitrary finite size for the target pair set and the path history.

The path history (*phist*) rather than specifying part of the task, defines constraints on how the task can be handled or delegated. The *phist* essentially defines a blacklist for the tasks, that is, a list of nodes in the network that must not be relied upon for assistance with this specific task. A valid data task must satisfy two conditions:

a. All data d_j specified in the source pair ($sp = \langle n_i, d_j \rangle$) or target pairs $tp = \langle n_i, d_j \rangle \subset TP$ must be of the same data type. That is, all datum instances must be part of the same DST diagram. Furthermore, there must be at least one data transition path (in the DST graph) from the source datum $d_j = f_d(sp)$ and each of the data $dj = f_d(tp) \mid tp \in TP$.
b. None of the nodes specified in the target pairs must be part of the *phist* set, unless the task is defined as a *terminal task*. A terminal task is defined as follows:

Definition 7: *A* ***terminal task*** *is a data task dT = ⟨sp, TP, phist⟩ where the target pair set TP is a singleton* $\{tp\} \mid |\{tp\}| = 1$*, and the following conditions hold:* $f_n(sp) = f_n(tp)$ *and* $f_d(sp) = f_d(tp)$.

An example of a terminal task is $dT^{final} = n_1{:}\, d_1 \# n_1{:}\, d_1 \#\, phist$. Terminal tasks are *void* tasks that require no further processing or transmission of data. By definition, a non-terminal data task *dT* = ⟨*sp, TP, phist*⟩ assigned to node $sp = \langle n_i, d_j \rangle$ must be handled by that specific node, however, the concept of handling a task (as it will be described later) includes the notion of converting the task to another "equivalent" task (or a set of "equivalent" tasks) to be delegated to other nodes in the network.

For notational purposes, a data task can be represented as a single string, separated by '#' symbols to indicate each of the three elements of the tuple. For instance, the data task *dT* = ⟨*sp, TP,*

$phist\rangle = \langle(n_1, d_1), \{(n_2, d_3), (n_4, d_4)\}, \{n_0\}\rangle$, can be represented by the string $dT = n_1: d_1 \# n_2: d_3, n_4: d_4 \# n_0$. In this example, node n_1 is given datum d_1 and the task of ultimately delivering datum d_3 to node n_2 and datum d_4 to node d_4 (without relying on node n_0 (in *phist*).

In the general case, the string notation for the data task is defined as follows:

$dT = \langle sp,\ TP,\ phist\rangle$
$dT = f_n(sp): f_d(sp) \# \{f_n(tp_i): f_d(tp_i)\} \# \{n_j\} \mid tp_i \in TP \wedge n_j \in phist$

This notation will be extensively used for the description of the problems, simulations and results. The column symbols between nodes and datum types are optional in the notion and might be dropped when there is no risk of ambiguity, allowing for the task $n_2: d_1 \# n_3: d_2, n_4: d_2 \# n_1$, to be also represented as $n_2d_1 \# n_3d_2, n_4d_2 \# n_1$.

The State of a Node

A node $n_i \in N$ can be in one of two types of states: idle or active. The default state of a node is in idle. When a node receives a data task from one of its neighbors, it transitions from an idle to an active state (s_i^{active}). If the received task is a terminal-task (i.e., if it is addressed to the node itself), the node simply consumes the datum and immediately transitions to back to an idle state (s_i^{idle}). In this case, the node is not required to choose an action for handling the task.

If, on the other hand, the task received is non-terminal the node must choose an action that will locally handle the task. The local handling of task might involve data transformations or task delegation to one or more of its neighbors. After applying the selected action, the node state will transition to idle, and the node becomes ready to receive new data requests from its neighbors.

An **active state** of node n_i, denoted as s_i^{active}, is always equal to a *single data task* being handled by node n_i at the time, and is defined as:

$$s_i^{active} = dT = \langle sp, TP, phist\rangle \left|\left\{ \begin{array}{l} f_n(sp) = n_i, \text{ and} \\ dT_i \text{ is not a terminal state} \end{array}\right.\right. \quad (1)$$

An **idle state** of node n_i, denoted as s_i^{idle}, is always equal to a *set of data tasks* and defined as follows:

$$s_i^{idle} = DT \mid \forall dT_i \in DT \left|\left\{ \begin{array}{l} dT_i \text{ is a terminal state, or} \\ f_n(dT_i) \neq n_i \end{array}\right.\right. \quad (2)$$

where $DT = \{dT_0, dT_1, \ldots, dT_k\}$ is a finite (possibly empty) set of data tasks. Recall that $f_n(dT_i)$ is equal to $f_n(sp_i)$, where sp_i is the source pair of data task dT_i.

Actions

An *action* is defined as a transition from any active state (s_i^{active}) to an idle state (s_i^{idle}), as follows:

Definition 8: *For a given NET(N,L) and DST(D,F), an action* $a(s_i^{active})$, *or* $a(dT)$, *represents a state transition* $s_i^{active} \rightarrow s_i^{idle}$, *where* $s_i^{idle} = DT' = \{dT'_0, dT'_1, \ldots, dT'_k\}$ *and* $s_i^{active} = dT$ *is defined in Box 1.*

In Definition 8, $DST_{path}(d_i, d_j)$ denotes a path in $DST(D, F)$ connecting states d_i to d_j and indicates that a data conversion between the two states is theoretically possible.

Note that not all $s_i^{active} \rightarrow s_i^{idle}$ transitions constitute valid actions. For instance, the action $a_i(n_1 : d_1\#n_3 : d_2\#) = \{dT' = n_2 : d_1\#n_3 : d_2\# n_1\}$, corresponds to a state transition $dT \Rightarrow \{dT'\}$, that is, $(dT = n_1 : d_1\#n_3 : d_2\#) \Rightarrow \{(dT' = n_2 : d_1\#n_3 : d_2\# n_1)\}$. The results of this action is the state transition $s_i^{active} \rightarrow s_i^{idle}$ (and $s_i^{idle} \rightarrow s_i^{active}$) and the semantics is that node n_1 with datum d_1 and the task to deliver d_2 to n_3 (i.e. $dT = n_1 : d_1\#n_3 : d_2\#$) delegates the job to node n_2, providing it with datum d_1, that is, $\{(dT' = n_2 : d_1\#n_3 : d_2\# n_1)\}$. This is a valid action and it will result in having node n_2 responsible for the next move.

Box 1.

$$a(dT = sp, TP, phist) = DT' \begin{cases} (dT'_i)^{final} \vee f_n(sp) \neq f_n(dT'_i),\ \forall dT'_i \in DT' \\ (dT'_i)^{final} \vee f_n(dT'_i) \notin phist,\ \forall dT'_i \in DT' \\ \bigcup_{dT'_i} (TP_{dT'_i}) = TP_{dT},\ \forall dT'_i \in DT' \\ \exists DST_{path}(f_d(dT), f_d(dT'_i)),\ \forall dT'_i \in DT' \\ f_n(sp) \text{ is a neighbor of } f_n(dT'_i) \text{ in NET},\ \forall dT'_i \in DT' \end{cases}$$

Figure 2. An example of a valid action

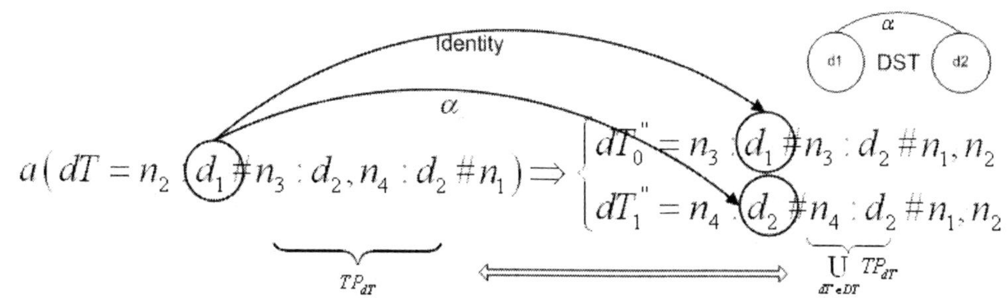

However, the action $a_j(n_1 : d_1\#n_3 : d_2\#) \Rightarrow \{dT' = n_2 : d_1\#n_5 : d_2\# n_1\}$ would be invalid because the "job" delegated to node n_2 (i.e. to deliver d_2 to node n_5) is different than the original job for which n_1 was responsible (i.e., n_3: d_2). Note that in the first case, the target pair-set is maintained through the conversion, which constituted a valid delegation of the task to a neighbor node thus a valid action. In the second example, the target pair-set was modified, which will result in a different outcome as node n_2 continues to handle the task.

Intuitively, in the first transition, the same data task (or an equivalent of it) is "delegated" to node n_2, which is now responsible for delivering datum d_2 to node n_3. In the second example, the target pair-set no longer includes the original task of delivering datum d_2 to node n_3. This constraint on the formation of the target pair set for a valid action is formally stated in the action definition (third condition in the list).

The example shown in Figure 2 satisfies all the conditions specified in the Definition 8. The example specifically highlights the fourth condition in the definition, that is, the required existence of a $DST_{path}(f_d(dT), f_d(dT'_i))$ in DST for all data transitions.

Note that the validation of the action relies solely on information available to node n_2. Aside from the list of neighbors (usually available to any node through the lower layer data link protocols) there are no assumptions or dependencies made on the capabilities of neighbor nodes.

Action Cost Estimation

In general, an action combines a data processing step with a data transmission. In its simplest form, an action simply consists on delegating the task to a neighbor node (data transmission) but it could also include local processing of the datum into one or more states.

The weights provided in both the DST and NET diagram allow for the cost estimation of both data transfer and data processing costs.

Equation 3, for instance, shows an example for cost estimation for a simple task ($dT = n_i d_k \# n_j d_p \# phist$) between two neighbor nodes n_i and n_j in a given environment.

$$Cost(a(dT)) = f_{st}(d_k, d_p) \cdot n_i^{pfactor} + d_p^{size} \cdot l_{i,j}^{tfactor} \quad (3)$$

Equation 3 shows the cost estimate for having node n_i (with datum d_k) deliver datum d_p to its neighbor node n_j (assuming that datum d_k can be converted to d_p through a function $f_{st}(d_k, d_p)$ available at n_i).

The equation considers that the data conversion from states ($d_k \rightarrow d_p$) happens at node n_i, before the transmission to node n_j. In this case, the data cost for the data conversion is given by $f_{st}(d_k, d_p) \cdot n_i^{pfactor}$, while the cost for the transmission is given by $d_p^{size} \cdot l_{i,j}^{tfactor}$.

Conversely, if the datum d_k was first transferred to node n_j to be then converted to d_p, the associated costs would be given by Equation 4, where the transmission portion is now weighted by d_k^{size}, and the processing cost by $n_i^{pfactor}$ (under the assumption that the transformation function $f_{st}(d_k, d_p)$ was also available at n_j).

$$Cost(a(dT)) = d_k^{size} \cdot l_{i,j}^{tfactor} + f_{st}(d_k, d_p) \cdot n_j^{pfactor} \quad (4)$$

Equations 3 and 4 produce exactly the same outcome at node n_j (i.e., datum d_p), however at different costs. An interesting decision to be made by node n_i is to determine which of the solutions (3) or (4) is the best (lowest cost) for the given task, namely, provide node n_j with datum d_p, without necessarily knowing the capabilities or data transformation costs of node d_j.

For a generalized action converting dT to a set $DT = \{dT'_0, dT'_1, ..., dT'_k\}$ (Equation 5), where $|DT| = k$, the overall costs consists in the sum of all transmission and data transformation tasks.

$$a\big(dT = \langle sp, TP, phist \rangle\big) \Rightarrow \{\langle sp'_0, TP'_0, phist' \rangle, \langle sp'_1, TP'_1, phist' \rangle, ..., \langle sp'_k, TP'_k, phist' \rangle\} \quad (5)$$

The data transmission sub-tasks are assumed to be independent from each other and their costs can be summed directly. The costs for the data conversion tasks, however, are estimated through a combined function $f_{st}(d_s, \{d_{sp0}, d_{sp1}, ..., d_{spk}\})$, where $d_{spj} = f_d(sp_j)$, that leverages from the commonality in the data. The data cost, in this case, can be estimated by Equation 6.

$$Cost(a(dT)) = f_{st}\left(d_s, \{d_{sp_0}, d_{sp_1}, ..., d_{sp_k}\}\right) n_j^{pfactor} + \sum_{j=1}^{k} \left(d_{sp_j}^{size} \cdot l_{i, f_n(sp_j)}^{tfactor}\right) \quad (6)$$

Figure 3. A sample data task for cost estimation

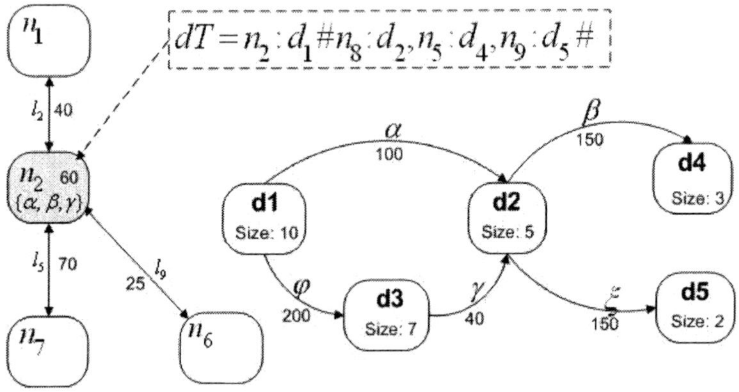

In Equation 2, the first term describes the combined costs for data processing while the second term aggregates all data transmission costs. The data processing costs are defined by the cost transformation of the minimum spanning tree from d_s(source) to $\{d_{t1}, d_{d2}, \ldots, d_{tp}\}$ (destinations), over the DST graph.

For example, consider the task shown in Figure 3. The graph shows only the local information available to the node, including its local neighbors and the DST for the data type described in the task.

If, given the state described in Figure 3, node n_2 chooses the action:

$$a(dT = n_2 : d_1 \# n_8 : d_2, n_5 : d_4, n_9 : d_5 \# n_2) \Rightarrow \begin{cases} dT'_0 = n_1 : d_2 \# n_8 : d_2 \# n_2 \\ dT'_1 = n_6 : d_4 \# n_5 : d_4 \# n_2 \\ dT'_1 = n_7 : d_5 \# n_9 : d_5 \# n_2 \end{cases} \quad (7)$$

The outcome of the action is shown in Figure 4. At the left side of the figure, the network graph shows the actual data transmissions from node n_2 to nodes n_1, n_6 and n_7, as defined in Equation 7.

At the right side of the Figure 4, the minimum spanning tree for the data conversion is shown over the DST diagram. The cost of the action is show in Equation 8 (see Box 2), where the $f_{st}(d_1, \{d_8, d_9, d_5\})$ is defined as the cost of the minimum spanning tree from d_1 to $\{d_2, d_4, d_5\}$.

In the general case the cost of an action $a(dT)$ is given by Equation 9:

$$Cost(a(dT) = DT') = f_{st}\left(f_d(dT), \{f_d(dT'_j)\}\right) f_n(dT)^{pfactor} + \sum_{j=1}^{|DT|}\left(\left(f_d(dT'_j)\right)^{size} \cdot l^{tfactor}_{f_n(dT), f_n(dT'_j)}\right)$$
$$, for \quad \forall dT'_j \in DT'sCost \quad (9)$$

The resource allocation problem consists of finding the best allocation of resources in the net-

Figure 4. The minimum spanning tree for data processing cost estimation

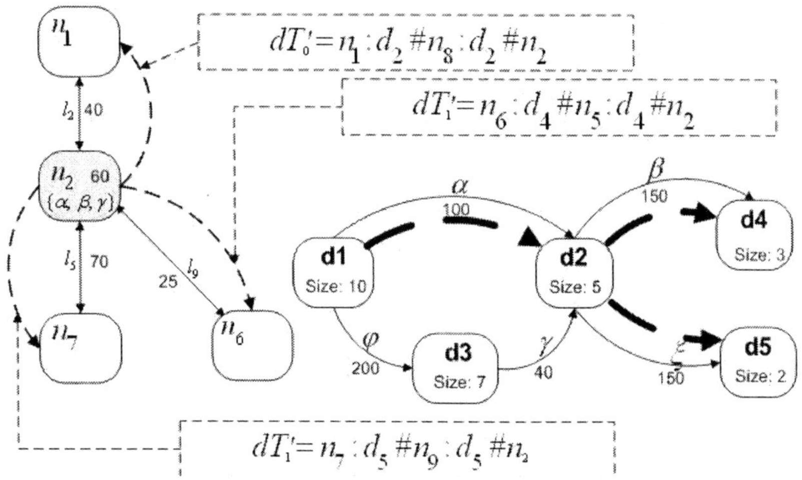

Box 2.

$$Cost(a(dT)) = f_{st}\left(d_1, \{d_2, d_4, d_5\}\right) \cdot n_2^{pfactor} + \sum_{j=1}^{|DT|}\left(\left(f_d(dT'_j)\right)^{size} \cdot l^{tfactor}_{2, f_n(dT'_j)}\right)$$
$$= f_{st}\left(d_1, \{d_2, d_4, d_5\}\right) \cdot n_2^{pfactor} + \left(d_2^{size} \cdot l_{2,1}^{tfactor} + d_4^{size} \cdot l_{4,6}^{tfactor} + d_5^{size} \cdot l_{2,7}^{tfactor}\right) n_7 \quad (8)$$

work that would realize the task successfully with the lowest possible cost ($\arg_A \min(TotalCost)$).

Each node has to make a local decision (that is not necessarily the best local choice) in order to allow for a global solution that will evolve to a minimum aggregate cost (in the optimum case).

Finding a solution for the resource allocation problem essentially consists of minimizing, at run-time, the global cost for all concurrent data requests in the network, that is, to solve the cost estimation problem in a dynamic environment. In practice, the problem consists of incrementally improving the cost estimate at each node, recognizing that the cost functions themselves are dynamic.

LEARNING STRATEGIES FOR THE RESOURCE ALLOCATION PROBLEM

For all practical purposes, the combinatorial nature of the resource allocation problem makes it very difficult to use strategies based on global information. Sub-optimal solutions are usually well accepted as long as they can be quickly identified and initialized to minimize latency.

One way to find the best action is to try each possibility and, through an exhaustive search identify which task would yield the lowest cost. There are, however, more efficient ways to choose the next action based on the incomplete experience acquired in early trials. Under certain constraints and assumptions, the problem can be reduced to a well known online learning problem in game theory known as the k-arm bandit problem.

The k-Arm Bandit Problem

The k-arm bandit problem proposed by Robbins (1952) defines a scenario where a gambler must choose one of "k" slot machines to place a bet. At each bet (which are assumed to have fixed value) the player pulls the arm of the slot machine and collects the reward in cash, if any. The objective of the game is to maximize the gains of the gambler over a fixed number of plays.

In order to achieve his/her goals in maximizing the gains, the gambler must be able to identify, as early as possible which of the machines gives the best odds for wining. Assuming, for now, that each arm returns its rewards based on a fixed pre-defined distribution that is unknown to the gambler, the challenge in the problem is to decide at each play, when to exploit a "known" distribution versus exploring a new one.

The dichotomy "exploration" and "exploitation" is a characteristic of most online learning problems and have been addressed in detail in the context of *Reinforcement Learning* by Sutton and Barto (1998), who enumerates a number of strategies for balancing exploitation and exploration for maximizing gains in the long run.

Among the strategies presented by Sutton and Barto (1998), two groups are of particular interest for this work, the ε-*greedy* and the softmax exploration strategies. The ε-*greedy* strategies essentially define a ε value that determines the ratio between exploratory and exploitative plays. It establishes that ε percent of the time, the gambler will not use its best known "arm" and will choose, instead, one of the other arms with equal probability.

Conversely, Softmax action selection strategies choose the next action (or "arm" to be played) through a probability distribution of the expected reward of all available arms. A very common distribution used for these types of strategies is the Gibbs or Boltzmann distribution. After a few plays, the probability of choosing arm "a" for the next play is proportional to the exponential of the accumulated observed for that action (Equation 10):

$$P_a(t) = \frac{e^{Q_t(a)/\tau}}{\sum_{b=1}^{n} e^{Q_t(b)/\tau}} \tag{10}$$

where $P_a(t)$ is the probability of choosing action (a) at play (t), $Q_t(a)$ is the accumulated rewards for action (a) up to time (t), and τ is a parameters known as the "temperature" for the distribution. The higher the temperature the more uniform-like the distribution will seem and the lower the temperature the greater will be the differences in the probabilities arising from differences in accumulated values.

Action Selection using SoftMax and ε-greedy Strategies

The selection of an action starts with a node first checking if the message is addressed to itself. If the node receiving the data task is listed in the target pair list it will first create a sub-task that is terminal.

For example, if node n_3 receives task $dT = n_3d_2$ # n_3d_4, n_2d_3 # *phist*, it must verify that the task is to be (at least partially) consumed by node n_3 itself, as it is listed in the target pair set. If there were no remaining nodes in the target pair set, the task would be completed and would no longer be forwarded. Node n_3 in that case would simply send a broadcast message announcing the success of the task, with the attached cost for handling the final conversion.

In the general case however, based on the received data task *dT* and the current set of neighbors, the selection of an action first requires the complete set of possible actions to be built for cost evaluation. The list of neighbor nodes is first pruned to remove any neighbors that are also listed in the *phist* of the data task. The remaining neighbors will be considered as candidates for receiving the task.

Consider for instance, the example shown in Figure 5, where node n_4 receives message n_4d_1# n_6d_2, n_7d_2 # n_1 from n_1 and that the transition between datum d_1 and d_2 is done through function α.

Figure 5 shows the list of all actions available to node n_4. The set of actions are created based on the received task n_4d_1# n_6d_2, n_7d_2# n_1 and the list of neighbors $\{n_1, n_2, n_6\}$ from which node n_1 was eliminated because it is listed in *dT*'s *phist*. The selection of an action will follow either an ε-

Figure 5. A list of possible actions

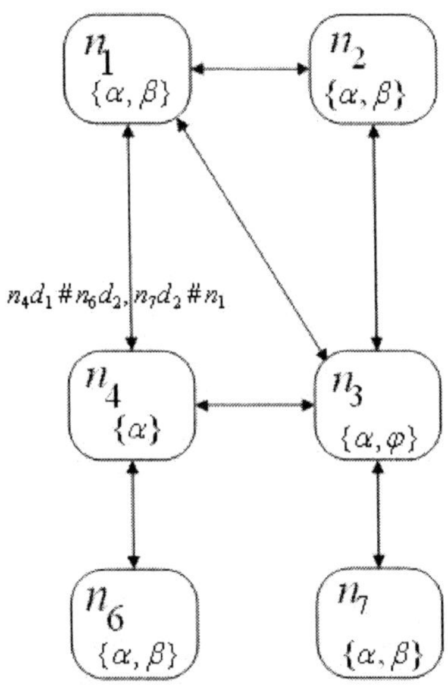

$$a_0(dT) = n_6d_1 \# n_6d_2, n_7d_2 \# n_1, n_4$$
$$a_1(dT) = (n_6d_1 \# n_6d_2 \# n_1, n_4)(n_3d_1 \# n_7d_2 \# n_1, n_4)$$
$$a_2(dT) = (n_6d_1 \# n_7d_2 \# n_1, n_4)(n_3d_1 \# n_6d_2 \# n_1, n_4)$$
$$a_3(dT) = (n_6d_1 \# n_6d_2 \# n_1, n_4)(n_3d_2 \# n_7d_2 \# n_1, n_4)$$
$$a_4(dT) = (n_6d_1 \# n_7d_2 \# n_1, n_4)(n_3d_2 \# n_6d_2 \# n_1, n_4)$$
$$a_5(dT) = n_3d_1 \# n_6d_2, n_7d_2 \# n_1, n_4$$
$$a_6(dT) = n_6d_2 \# n_6d_2, n_7d_2 \# n_1, n_4$$
$$a_7(dT) = (n_6d_2 \# n_6d_2 \# n_1, n_4)(n_3d_1 \# n_7d_2 \# n_1, n_4)$$
$$a_8(dT) = (n_6d_2 \# n_7d_2 \# n_1, n_4)(n_3d_1 \# n_6d_2 \# n_1, n_4)$$
$$a_9(dT) = (n_6d_2 \# n_6d_2 \# n_1, n_4)(n_3d_2 \# n_7d_2 \# n_1, n_4)$$
$$a_{10}(dT) = (n_6d_2 \# n_7d_2 \# n_1, n_4)(n_3d_2 \# n_6d_2 \# n_1, n_4)$$
$$a_{11}(dT) = n_3d_2 \# n_6d_2, n_7d_2 \# n_1, n_4$$

greedy or a SoftMax strategy, using the Boltzmann distribution. Even before receiving any feedback from neighbors, a prior can be estimated for the actions based on their local cost estimations. If there is absolutely no information about any prior probability for the actions, all tasks are considered equiprobable and the selection is based on a uniform random draw. The most likely scenario, however, is that node n_4 might have collected information reported by both nodes n_3 and n_6 either due to direct interactions with them in previous requests, or through promiscuously listening to messages from these nodes.

EXPERIMENTAL EVALUATION

The proposed algorithm was implemented and tested on a simulated network for several network topologies and data flows. The purpose of these tests was to verify the behavior of the algorithm, rather than benchmark its performance given that the current implementation is a not optimized and intended as a proof of concept version of the algorithm. In order to demonstrate and discuss the algorithm, a few scenarios were defined and simulated. In this section, we present some of our simulation results for different topologies and topology-change conditions.

The 4-Node Fixed Topology

The first simulation test is a fixed network with four nodes and a three-state data transition graph. Both the network topology (NET) and the DST diagram are shown in Figure 6. The figure also shows all costs associated with data processing (*pfactors, function costs*) and transmission (*tfactors, datum size*).

One single data stream was created for this test. The stream will consist of 10 tasks ($dT = n_1d_1 \# n_3d_2, n_4d_2 \#$) per second to the system (i.e., to node n_1) for a period of 120 seconds. The target nodes (target pair-set) for the task are nodes n_3(datum d_2) and n_4(datum d_2), with no processing capabilities (no functions available) as illustrated in Figure 6.

Nodes n_3 and n_4 will report (log) all successful tasks and their costs. A successful task, from a node's perspective, consists of having the specified datum delivered at the target node (i.e., receiving a terminal task). If both nodes report that the same task was completed (which can be matched by a task ID), then the overall task ($dT = n_1d_1 \# n_3d_2, n_4d_2 \#$) is said to have succeeded and the cost of completion is the sum of the costs from both n_3 and n_4.

Figure 7 shows the average aggregate cost results from four independent runs for each of

Figure 6. Four nodes network for test and DST

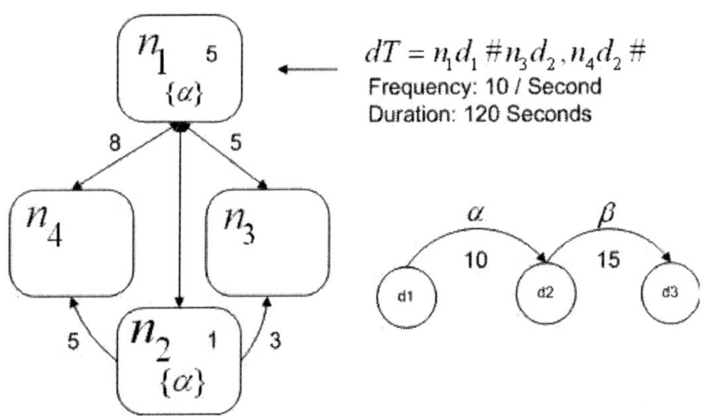

the policy selection strategies. Packet drops for each strategy are also shown in Figure 7.

In this example, the epsilon coefficient for the ε-greedy strategy is calculated at each iteration as the ratio of actions flagged as "unknown" and the total number of strategies available. Initially, with several unknown actions available the algorithm using an ε-greedy strategy will be more proactive on searching for new possibilities.

Out of 300 data tasks, the ε-greedy strategy lost an average of 28 tasks while Boltzmann lost nine tasks on average. Note that most of the loss in the ε-greedy occurs at the beginning of the process, while unknown actions are being explored.

The 4-Node Changing Topology

A more interesting scenario is when a change in topology occurs during the flow of a data stream. This example is shown in Figure 8, where the four node topology is used for the same scenario as the previous example.

In this case, however, node n_2 is initially removed from the topology and added at a later time. Figure 8 presents the average of four tests showing how the algorithms reacted to the insertion of the node in the topology. The time of the insertion was approximately the same in each run (dotted zone in the figure). In this example, both algorithms quickly detect the new neighbor and extend their set of available actions and find a better solution for the DDT.

The ε-greedy implementation, as expected fluctuates a little longer until it explores the new set of known solutions. Because the probability of exploration drops as new solutions become "known" (that is, recently tested), the curve stabilizes with the Boltzmann implementation after a while.

The costs, in both cases is the minimum cost available to in the network, the fact that the Boltzmann line at some point goes below that value (right after the addition of the node) indicates packets being dropped in some of the runs, resulting in a lower average cost.

The 7-Node Changing Topology

Another test involving the addition and removal of nodes is shown in Figure 9 for a 7-node topol-

Figure 7. Four node fixed topology Boltzman vs. ε-greedy

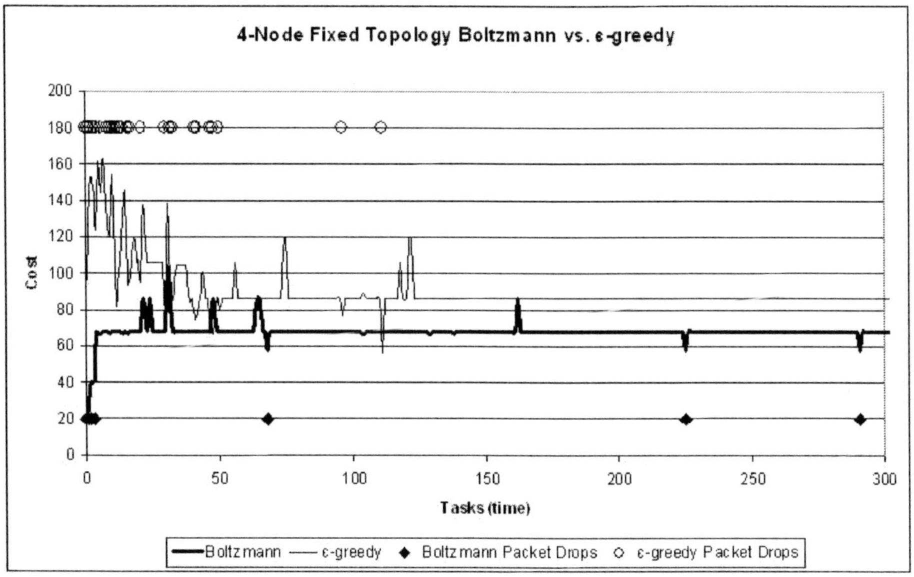

Figure 9. A 7-node network with changing topology

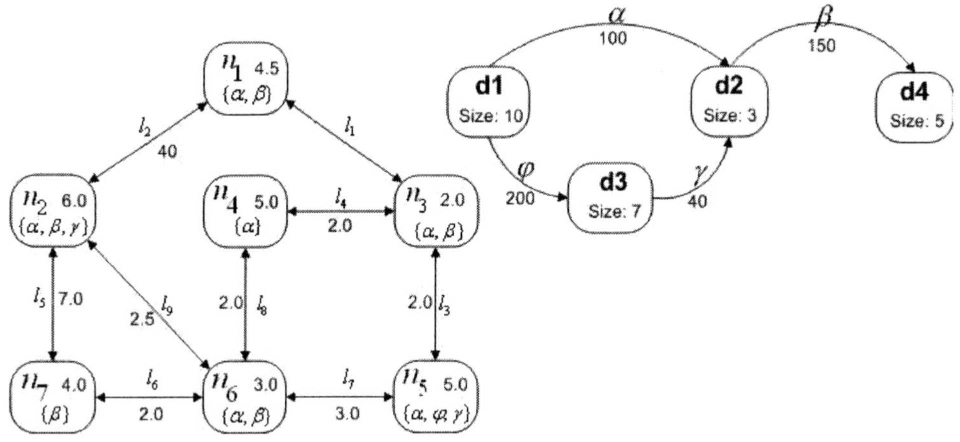

ogy and associated data task. The data stream in this example is given by $dT = n_1d_1 \# n_4d_2, n_3d_2\#$, injected in n_1 at a rate of 20 requests per second for 120 seconds.

In this simulation, the minimum cost path is through node n_3, which performs a transformation and then splits the stream to n_4 and n_3.

The resulting aggregate costs for the algorithm using both the Boltzmann and the ε-greedy strategies are shown in Figure 10.

At 20 requests per second, the horizontal axis in the figure provides an indirect measurement of "time." In this example, 30 seconds into the simulation, node n_3 is removed from the network (shown at the bottom of Figure 10) and the processing of the task is switched to flow through nodes n_2 and n_6.

Coincidentally in this case, this is also the shortest communication path for the flow, but in other simulations (not shown in this specific figure) if the processing cost of node n_6 increases, the transformation tasks starts happening at node n_2, as opposed to n_6. The effects of the removal of node n_3 are shown in detail in Figure 11.

Node 3 is added back to the network at time 60 (around 1200 in the x-scale) with a different set of edge costs. Note that both strategies move the processing flow back again to node n_3. Figure 12 shows in detail the recover to a lower cost configuration after node n_3 is re-added to the network.

CONCLUSION

In this article we have revisited and summarized the data distribution strategy for tactical environments proposed by Carvalho in 2006. The main contribution of this work was the design and proof-of-concept implementation of a novel approach for the resource allocation problem in tactical networks. In our approach, we leverage from pervious research on reinforcement learning and game theory to design a distributed algorithm for resource allocation that simultaneously addresses the requirements for resource constrained in-stream data processing in mobile ad hoc networks, an important capability for tactical environments.

The algorithm introduced in this work proposes the simultaneous allocation of resources for both data processing and data transmission in the network. This combined approach to the resource allocation problem differs from techniques commonly found in the literature that are: (1) centered at the application (or middleware levels) and rely

Figure 10. A 7-node network changing topology

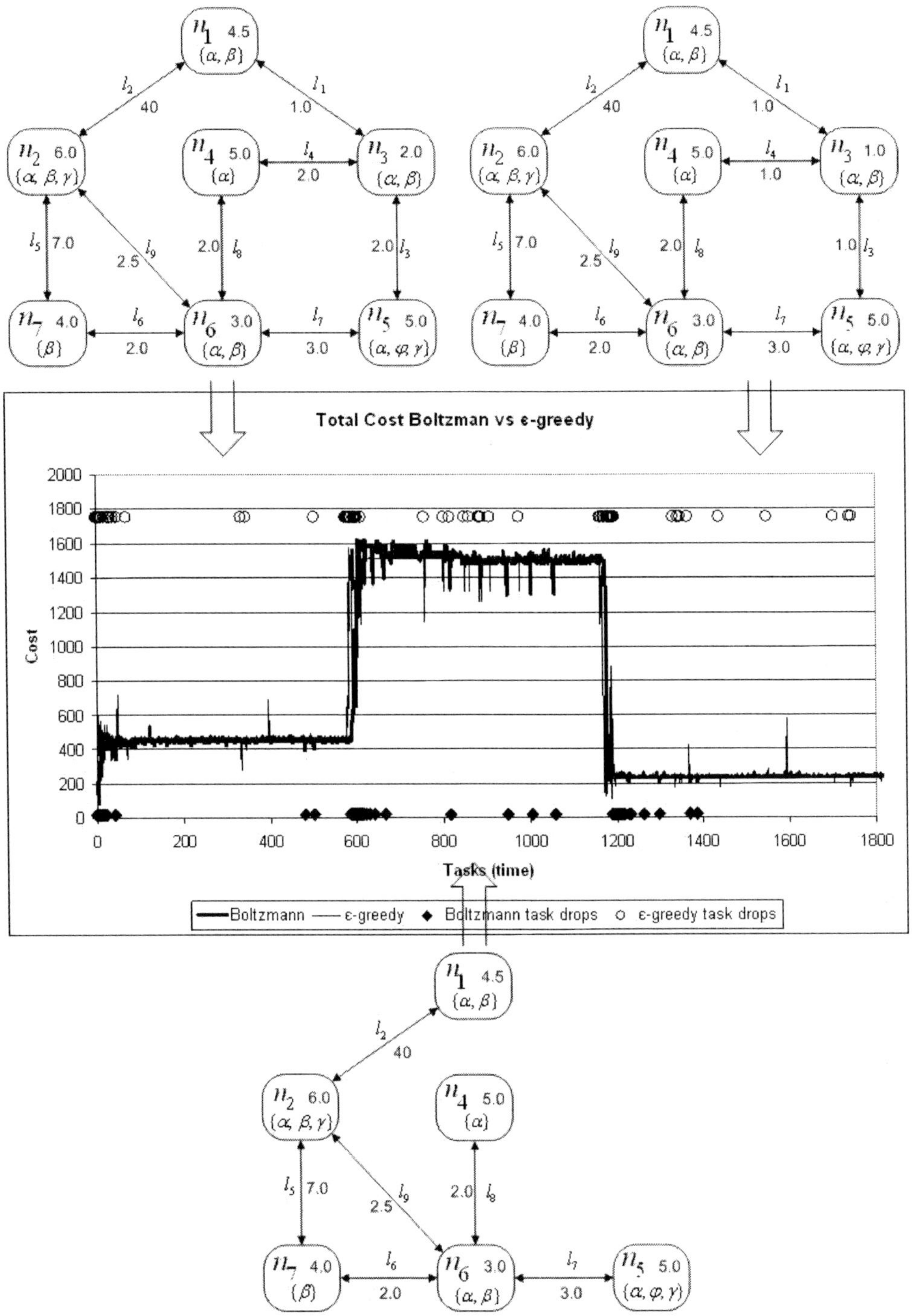

Figure 11. Removing node n3 from the 7-node topology

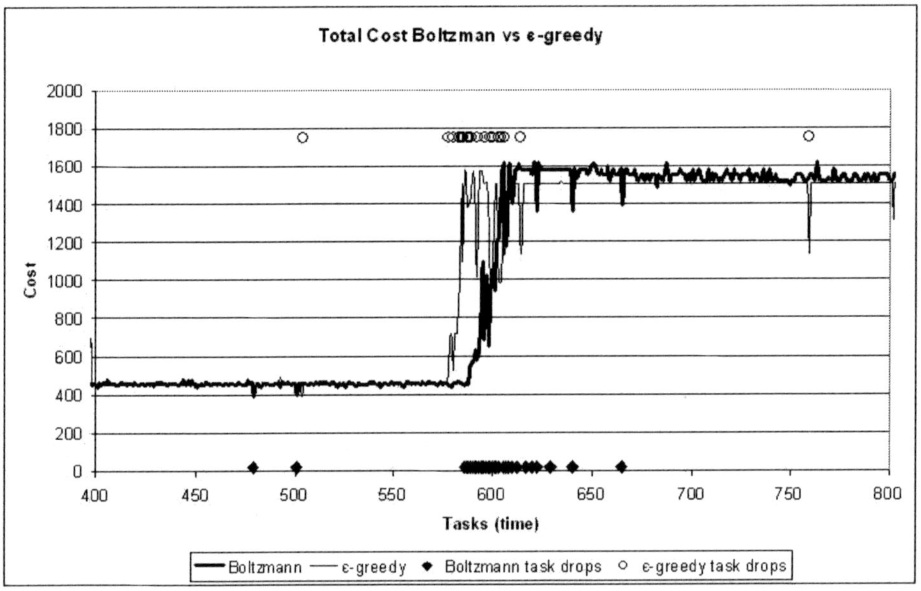

Figure 12. Re-inserting node n3 from the 7-node topology

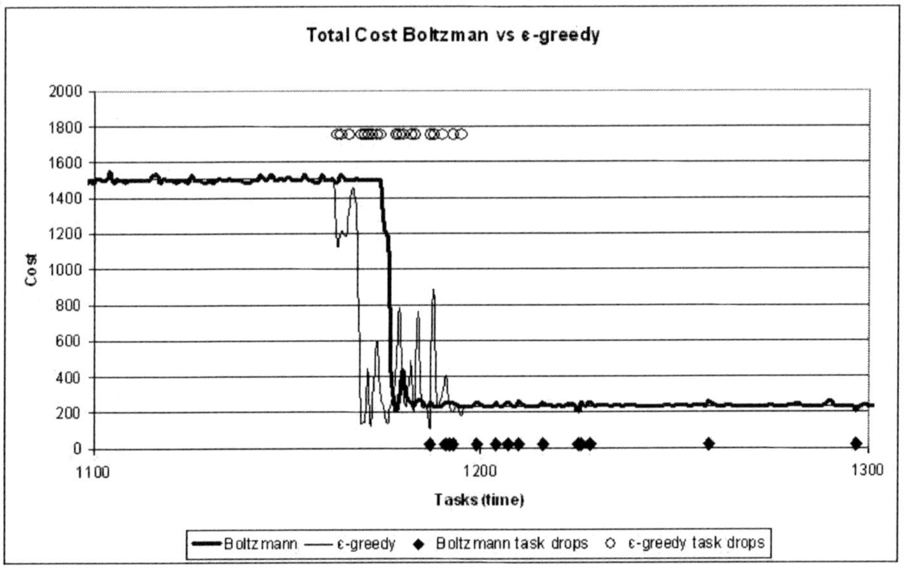

on models and estimates of the underlying communications framework for resource allocation or, (2) data-agnostic techniques centered at the network level that attempt to infer data processing requirements to better allocate routes.

In this work, the resource allocation problem was first defined and formally described in the context of an online learning in order to be mapped, under certain assumptions, to the well known k-arm bandit problem at the node level. From that formulation, two standard strategies for policy selection (ε-greedy and SoftMax) were slightly modified and integrated with the algorithm.

The resource allocation algorithm proposed in this work is reactive, efficient, flexible, and adaptive. The experimental results, although preliminary at this stage, have provided some evidence that the algorithm is capable of adapting to changes in both environment and task requirements. Further tests are necessary to validate the algorithm in large scale settings and benchmarking.

ACKNOLWEDGMENT

This work has been partially supported by the U.S. Army Research Laboratory under contract W911NF-04-2-0013, by the U.S. Army Research Laboratory under the Collaborative Technology Alliance Program, Cooperative Agreement DAAD19-01-2-0009, by the Office of Naval Research under grant N00014-03-1-0780, and by the Air Force Research Laboratory under Cooperative Agreement FA750-06-2-0064.

REFERENCES

Baehni, S., Eugster, P. Th., & Guerraoui, E. (2004, June). Data-aware multicast. In *Proceedings of the 5th IEEE International Conference on Dependable Systems and Networks (DSN '04)*.

Boyan, J. A., & Littman, M. L. (1994). Packet routing in dynamically changing networks: A reinforcement learning approach. *Advances in Neural Information Processing Systems, 6*.

Buyya, R., Stockinger, H., Giddy, J., & Abramson, D. (2001, August 20-24). Economic models for management of resources in peer-to-peer and grid computing. In *Proceedings of International Conference on Commercial Applications for High-Performance Computing,* Denver, CO. SPIE Press.

Carvalho, M. (2006). *Distributed resource coordination strategies for mobile ad hoc networks.* Unpublished PhD dissertation, Tulane University, New Orleans, LA.

Carvalho, M., & Breedy, M. (2002, October). Supporting flexible data feeds in dynamic sensor grids through mobile agents. In *Proceedings of the 6th International Conference in Mobile Agents (MA 2002),* Barcelona, Spain.

Carvalho, M., Pechoucek, M., & Suri, N. (2005, July). A mobile agent-based middleware for opportunistic resource allocation and communications. In *Proceedings of the Fourth International Joint Conference on Autonomous Agents and Multiagent Systems; Defense Applications of Multi-Agent Systems (DAMAS).*

Chang, Y., Ho, T., & Kaelbling, L. (2004). Mobilized ad-hoc networks: A reinforcement learning approach. In *Proceedings of the First International Conference on Autonomic Computing (ICAC'04)* (pp. 240-247).

Chen, Y., & Schwan, K. (2005, November). Opportunistic overlays: Efficient content delivery in mobile ad hoc networks. In *Proceedings of the 6th ACM/IFIP/USENIX International Middleware Conference (Middleware 2005).*

Choi, S. P. M., & Yeung, D. Y. (1996). Predictive q-routing: A memory-based reinforcement learning approach to adaptive traffic control. In *Proceedings of NIPS-8* (pp. 910-945).

Curran, E. (2003). *Swarm: Cooperative reinforcement learning for routing in ad hoc networks.* Unpublished MSc thesis, Trinity College, Dublin, Ireland.

Dowling, J., Curran, E., Cunningham, R., & Cahill, V. (2005, May). Using feedback in collaborative reinforcement learning to adaptively optimize MANET routing. *IEEE Transactions on*

Systems, Man, and Cybernetics—Part A: Systems and Humans, 35(3).

Duran-Limon, et al. (2000). *Context-aware middleware for pervasive ad hoc environments.* (Tech. Rep.). Project CORTEX.

Eugster, P., Th., Guerraoui, R., & Damm, C. H. (2001, October). On objects and events. In *Proceedings of the 16th ACM Conference on Object-Oriented Programming Systems, Languages and Applica-tions (OOPSLA 2001)* (pp. 131-146).

Intanagonwiwat, C., Govindan, R., & Estrin, D. (2000, August). Directed diffusion: A scalable and robust communication paradigm for sensor networks. In *Proceedings of the Sixth Annual International Conference on Mobile Computing and Networking (MobiCOM '00),* Boston, MA.

Katz, R., & Brewer, E. (1996). Wireless overlay networks and adaptiveApplications. In *Proceedings of MobiCom.*

Kothari, A., Sabhash, S., & Zhou, Y. (2003). Bandwidth-constrained allocation in grid computing. In *Proceedings of WADS.*

Littman, M., & Boyan, J. (1993). *A distributed reinforcement learning scheme for network routing* (Tech. Rep. No. CMU-CS-93-165).

Maistre, F. (2003). *JORAM.* Retrieved May 2005, from http://joram.ob-jectweb.org

Miikkulainen, R., & Kumar, S. (1999). Confidence based dual reinforcement q-routing: An adaptative on-line routing algorithm. In *Proceedings of the Sixteenth International Joint Conference on Artificial Intelligence* (pp. 758-763).

Pechoucek, M., Marık, V., & Stepankova, O. (2001). Towards reducing communication traffic in multi-agent systems. *Journal of Applied Systems, 2*(1), 152-174.

Peng, F., & Deyun, Z. (2006). *Hybrid optimize strategy based QoS route algorithm for mobile ad hoc networks.* Department of Computer Science and Technology, Xi'an Jiaotong University, Xi'an, China.

Robbins, H. (1952). Some aspects of the sequential design of experiments. *Bulletin American Mathematical Society, 55,* 527-535.

Stone, P. (2000). Tpot-rl applied to network routing. In *Proceedings of the 17th International Conference on Machine Learning.*

Sutton, R. S., & Barto, A.G. (1998). *Reinforcement learning: An Introduction.* Cambridge, MA: MIT Press/Bradford Books.

Tao, N., Baxter, J., & Weaver, L. (2001). A multi-agent, policy-gradient approach to network routing. In *Proceedings of the 18th International Conference on Machine Learning.*

Woodrow, E., & Heinzelman, W. (2001). *SPIN-IT: A data centric routing protocol for image retrieval in wireless networks.* Retrieved November 20, 2003, from http://www.ece.rochester.edu/~wheinzel/GroupWeb/papers/spin-it_icip02.pdf

This work was previously published in the International Journal of Electronic Government Research, Vol. 4, Issue 1, edited by M. Khosrow-Pour, pp. 49-67, copyright 2008 by IGI Publishing, formerly known as Idea Group Publishing (an imprint of IGI Global).

Chapter XVIII
AJAX in Development of Web-Based Architecture for Implementation of E-Governance

Dilip Kumar Sharma
G.L.A. Institute of Technology and Management, India

Gopalji Varshneya
G.L.A. Institute of Technology and Management, India

Ashwani Kumar Upadhyay
M. N. National Institute of Technology, Allahabad, India

ABSTRACT

This article analyzes the diffusion of a Web technology named AJAX in facilitating e-government architecture and enhancing its potential by enablement of modern Web features as democracy and collaboration. Flexibility needed for free flow of interactive collaboration, compatibility, and robustness is treated as vital in the chapter. Major enterprises that have created landmarks in terms of participation of individuals and enterprises, along with contemporary Web technologies, are also analyzed to consolidate priority of technologies befitting robust and sustainable Web architecture. Emphasis is on the point that a proper collaboration among private, public, and government entities can only be achieved by proper information dissemination and acceptance of competent Web technologies, AJAX being one of them. Features of AJAX such as sectional processing ability, speed, bridging, portability, and compatibility are viewed with criticality for practical establishment.

Copyright © 2009, IGI Global, distributing in print or electronic forms without written permission of IGI Global is prohibited.

INTRODUCTION

E-government means the use of information and communication technology to support the entire functioning of government. The most important aspect of proficient e-government includes improved efficiency, convenience, and better accessibility of services to public and government entities. Proficient e-government covers activities for organizing, managing, and controlling resources such as people, local government bodies, business organizations, and departments of state (like the legislature, judiciary, and government), through social, political, administrative, and economic arrangements that ensure sustainable development of entire country. The Canadian government's e-strategy is based upon a "user perspective" approach that determines the online offering and how information is organized and delivered to citizens (Canada, 2004). From a technological standpoint, the implementation of e-government implies e-enablement, interoperability, and semantic Web issues. So to provide information about government policies, programs, schemes, and products to targeted people with a user friendly citizen interface in local languages, multiple channels of communication, security of transactions, participating policy making processes, transparency in government activity, and open styles of functioning (Gupta, 2005), AJAX-based Web technology can be the best way. Designing such an application requires the consideration of elements such as ease of navigation, aesthetics, content, accessibility, and features such as personalization, customization, customer self-care, and data about communities. All these elements in combination will directly influence users' experience with the site, and ultimately their satisfaction and adoption.

Efficient realization of e-governments through the Web from a citizen's perspective is asserted by perceived usefulness along with the ease of its use (Mylene 2005). To achieve this, the government needs reliable Web technologies that are efficient, speedy, and support a transparent framework with disseminating information to the public and to other agencies that perform activities related to government administration. On the software level it is far more complex to manage all these aspects, and the technology named AJAX has noticeable features to quench this ever widening circle of responsibilities. E-administration, e-citizenship, e-servicing in an perfectly benefited e-state can only be achieved by developing futuristic framework of e-government with flexibility, absorption, and speed as few vital issues. AJAX has all of these software techniques and thus invites a liberal attitude with a need for initiating further research for implementation and fulfilling the requirement of efficiency in the huge and functionally complex nature of any governmental setup.

For the e-government set up there are two major challenges on an infrastructure level that are related to client server interaction. The first problem is related to the time parameter. The intention is to reduce the time consumed in processing the unique client request and providing the user with the liberty to do something else while the former request is being processed. The second parameter is about developing sophisticated framework for data passage. Discrete requests can be processed on an extensive scale at the same time and most of them will need both retrieval and postage. AJAX, which is being prominently deployed in most of today's successful service-oriented Web networks all over the world, is suggested for best results.

AJAX name is an acronym for asynchronous javascript and XML (extensible markup language) (Quin). The name was coined by Jesse James Garrett in February, 2005, from the adaptive path Web site (Garrett, 2005). It is a combination of existing technologies such as DHTML, CSS, JavaScript, DOM (Stenback, 2004), XML, XSLT, and XMLHttpRequest (Paulson, 2005). At present most dynamic Web interfaces are powered by JavaScript and wherever the need is expanding the booster of AJAX has become mandatory. The core component of AJAX is XML Http Request, which enables updating components of a Web page by sending and receiving information without page reloads.

AJAX can create an asynchronous request to the Web server by using the XMLHttpRequest object, which is initiated by JavaScript, and it calls a function to process the information that is fetched when the response is received. AJAX is known as a world of "No Page Refresh" and exceptionally endowed user interface as it is included in Windows applications (Asleson, 2005). In AJAX Web application server side processing is considerably decreased, hence AJAX has been accepted extensively in technologies deployed in managing airports, stations, chat portals, search engines, digital maps, different banking, and online buying-selling sites, and in prominent portals like Gmail, Google Maps, Hotmail, Yahoo!, and Rediffmail (where services to a large number of users is intended).

INITIATIVE OF AJAX BY COMPARING VARIOUS TECHNOLOGIES IN VIEW OF E-GOVERNMENT

Empirical evidence suggests that the quality of service generally plays a very important role in online business environments. It is extremely crucial to understand the needs of the user and tailor the service quality to cater those needs. Google's Taylor said his company will use AJAX as long as it likes what the technology offers. He explained, "We will use whatever technology platform provides the richest user experience possible" (Paulson, 2005). It is desirable that the framework developed is comprehensive, holistic, and above all meets the objectives for which it has been designed. The successful implementation of e-government depends upon the possibilities to obtain services through electronic channels such as the Internet that allows both submission and access of data related to government functioning. With an objective of developing a multilayered work platform consisting of unique hierarchy pertaining to various departments, the objectives of e-government can be thought of a network that has

- Transparency in operations
- A credible government-public interface that becomes an interactive forum
- Ease of information dissemination
- Access to all essential information for administration
- Enhanced participation of the people in decision making and program implementation
- A much more efficient service delivery system
- Community linkage

When the diffusion of advanced technologies to manifest a well-organized e-government is under consideration, it is imperative to look at all latest options available in the ever-growing field of IT. There are a lot of alternative technologies available to facilities for interactive Web development. In the following discussion of latest Web technologies, AJAX emerges as the best choice in technology that supports all the features needed in developing a complete e-government model.

Putting an Observant Eye on Other Contemporary Web Technologies that have Emerged Lately

XUL

XUL is a high-performance markup language for creating rich, dynamic user interfaces. It is part of the Mozilla browser and related applications, and is available in Mozilla browsers (like Firefox). XUL is comprised mainly of a set of high-performance widgets that can be combined to form more complex business applications and components. It allows the facility to build very sophisticated applications, but many developers report encountering insurmountable problems when using XUL to build complex interfaces.

- **Advantages:** High performance, fast, works with JavaScript, based on XML
- **Limitations:** Only compatible with Mozilla browsers.

XAML

XAML is a high-performance markup language for creating rich dynamic user interfaces. It is part of Avalon, Microsoft's next generation UI technology, and will be supported in future versions of the Internet Explorer browser. It is also XML-based and is supposed to allow the development of powerful UI, even in a Web page. XAML is probably Microsoft's response to other efforts like XUL and AJAX, but is also a natural progression of the convergence of RAD tools and the Web browser as an enterprise application platform.

- **Advantages:** High performance, robust, highly configurable.
- **Disadvantages:** Microsoft-only technology. Not executable on other platforms.

Java Applets

An Applet is a program written in JAVA that can be included on a Web page. These code snippets require the proprietary JAVA plug-in from Sun to run. They are written in a language that is ubiquitous and widely known, but are often jarringly slow-to-load components of Web-based applications.

- **Advantages:** Fast, supported on most platforms (with the Java plug-in)
- **Disadvantages:** Requires the Sun Java plug-in, which many organizations will not allow to be installed on workstations due to security concerns. Applets take a while to load when they first download.

Macromedia Flash and Shockwave

These are powerful presentation-layer frameworks. It is possible to use them to build Web-based user interface components and they are highly configurable.

- **Advantages:** Browser and platform compatibility, speed and flexibility, powerful development tools.
- **Disadvantages:** General distrust from enterprise software developers. Rare skill set required to do development with these components that most corporations do not have.

SVG (Scalable Vector Graphics)

A text-based graphics language that describes images with vector shapes, text, and embedded raster graphics. It can be integrated with XML data sources or SMIL (Synchronized Multimedia Integration Language). It has best interoperability with CSS and JavaScript.

- **Advantages:** Speed and flexibility.
- **Disadvantages:** Requires proprietary plug-in that many firms will not allow users to install. Rare skill set required to do development with these components that most corporations do not have. This language is still somewhat immature and developing.

AJAX (Asynchronous JavaScript and XML)

A set of native client-side browser technologies that can be combined to build powerful user interfaces and do asynchronous communication with business layer software on the server.

- **Advantages:** Powerful and has high level of browser and platform compatibility. No third-party platform (except for a browser) required for full compatibility. High interoperability with other Web-based components and code. AJAX uses the native browser scripting language.

- **Disadvantages:** Somewhat complex and can be quirky to do sophisticated development with, although the basic skill set necessary for interacting with components is quite common.

Considering the above an effective e-government assignment framework and technologies comparison can be viewed in Table 1.

AJAX allows updating to only a specific section of any Web page, hence the process consumes less bandwidth and increases the speed of interaction. This feature is also useful where broad band connections are not available. Quality of service and user satisfaction is assessed by the ease of delivering a Web presentation with full information, high speed, and low resource utilization. This makes AJAX most suitable for quality measures. It provides a clean and simple interface to the users with ease of access so that even a non-technical user can use the interface with full effect (Wilbert, 2002). An exception handling and error resolving technique can easily be implemented with the help of existing JavaScript library.

There is a security problem with AJAX if it is not implemented appropriately, so there is a need for proper understanding of the security

Table 1. Comparative study of contemporary technologies for Web interface

Government's View	Citizen/Business View	XUL	XAML	Java Applets	Flash	SVG	AJAX
1.Efficiency	Speedy Service	Best	Best	Medium	Medium	Medium	Best
2.Quality Of Service	Quality In Competitive Environment	Medium	Medium	Medium	Best	Medium	Best
3.Simplicity	User-Friendliness, Self-Service	Best	Medium	Best	Best	Best	Best
4.Transparency	Fair Trial / Audit Ability	Medium	Medium	Best	Best	Best	Medium
5.Ease Of Access To The Service	Availability And Simplicity	Less	Less	Less	Best	Less	Best
6.Mechanism For Problem Resolution and Exception Handling	Error and Exception Handling	Best	Best	Best	Medium	Medium	Best
7.Cost Effectiveness	Affordability, Value Proposition	Best	Best	Less	Less	Medium	Best
8.Manageability	Ease Of Control	Best	Best	Less	Less	Best	Best
9. Responsiveness	Interactivity	Best	Best	Less	Less	Less	Best
10.Scalability	Expandability	Best	Best	Less	Less	Less	Best
11.Provisions For Interoperability	Integration With Other Technology	Less	Less	Less	Less	Medium	Best
12.Security	Trust Consistency, Expectancy	Best	Best	Best	Best	Medium	Best
13.Extent Of The Use Of Open Source Application	Use Of Free Tools	Less	Less	Less	Less	Medium	Best
14.Integration / Collaboration	Convenience, Cost And Time Saving,	Less	Less	Less	Less	Less	Best

constraints. In AJAX the emphasis is only on components of Web pages so it provides scalable solutions apt for projects catering to a large number of clients. In view of cost consideration, application development cost with AJAX is quite high but its operational cost is low. There is no issue of interoperability because it is based on scripting language and XML. Commercial companies working around AJAX have been in the news recently with announcements that they will contribute to start an open source community which will contribute to the part of their product offerings. ClearNova is releasing ThinkCAP JX under the GPL license (Khatoikar, 2003).

The e-government framework is huge and complex, comprising every citizen and inviting almost all of the nation to participate and support, so the need for information exchange with appropriate classification and monitoring rights is abundant. Sites working on the largest databases across the world are using AJAX today to facilitate their further growth and to prevent blockages. They are engaging large teams of experts to do further research on AJAX for what it can and cannot give. This is ample evidence for AJAX suitability in the e-governance model. The prevalent use of AJAX technology and the rate of its acceptance suggest that in few years most Web-based service may use AJAX technology. The Web-based infrastructure of e-government is most suited for large scale distribution of information (Khatoikar, 2003) so care must be taken on all the parameters needed before of development. Before investing resources in AJAX based e-government system, one has to consider the following points:

Working and Current Market of AJAX

In a classical Web application, the user invokes a HTTP request to the Web server. Conventionally the server, after executing a process, returns an HTML page to the client, whereas in AJAX applications the request can be either for a GUI component, HTML segment, or even for data. After fetching data, the processing function can update any specific component of user interface using JavaScript (Andrew, 2002) and DOM (Stenback, 2004). As shown in Figure 1, AJAX is a client-side technology compatible with any server-side technology such as ASP.net, JSP, PHP, ColdFusion, and others. Figure 1 (a) shows a traditional Web application where user actions trigger an HTTP request to a Web server, which processes the request and returns an HTML page to the client. Additional requests lock up the application until the system updates the page.

Figure 1 (b) shows AJAX applications that create a JavaScript-based engine that runs on the browser. The engine intercepts user inputs, displays requested material, and handles many interactions on the client side. If the engine needs more data, it requests material from the server in the background, while letting the user continue to interact with the application climate.

Current Market Study to Consolidate Feasibility of AJAX for E-Governance

Hyper linking is the foundation of the Web. As users add new content, and new sites, it is bound in to the structure of the Web by other users discovering the content and linking to it. Much like synapses formed in the brain, with associations becoming stronger through repetition or intensity, the Web of connections grows organically as an output of the collective activity of all Web users.

Google Map

The spectacular facility of welcoming clients is displayed in the Google Map. This facility, where users can find the complete map of selected area, can be used for e-government projects where people are encouraged to put flags to mark their areas naming them by whatever regional attributes that they feel are significant to mention. This feature is called collaboration and can be used extensively in developing a powerful database containing the salient parameters related to the living standards of citizens of a country. In the e-government system volunteers literate in information technology will be employed by the government to feed all appropriate data for forming a useful database (Efstathopoulos, 2003).

Yahoo!

Yahoo!, the first great Internet success story, was born as a catalog, or directory of links, an aggregation of the best work of thousands, then millions of Web users. Yahoo! has since moved into the business of creating many types of content, and predominantly using technologies like Flash and AJAX.

eBay

eBay's product is the collective activity of all its users; like the Web itself, eBay grows organically in response to user activity, and the company's role is as an enabler of a context in which that user activity can happen. What's more, eBay's competitive advantage comes almost entirely from the critical mass of buyers and sellers, which makes any new entrant offering similar services significantly less attractive.

Rout

Powered by AJAX, Rout provides a common interface for message and data sharing. In reference to e-government projects this type of technology can be utilized for sharing public feedback in response to the working of the government to fulfill its needs and to judge the efficient running of projects and schemes in the view of public at large.

Amazon

Amazon sells the same products as competitors such as Barnesandnoble.com, and they receive the same product descriptions, cover images, and editorial content from their vendors. But Amazon has made a science of user engagement. They have an order of magnitude more user reviews, invitations to participate in varied ways on virtually every page, and even more importantly, they use user activity to produce better search results. While a Barnesandnoble.com search is likely to lead with the company's own products, or sponsored results, Amazon always leads with "most popular," a real-time computation based not only on sales but other factors that Amazon insiders call the "flow" around products. With an order of magnitude more user participation, it's no surprise that Amazon's sales also outpace competitors.

Wikipedia

Wikipedia, an online encyclopedia based on the unlikely notion that an entry can be added by any Web user, and edited by any other, is a radical experiment in trust, applying Eric Raymond's dictum (originally coined in the context of open source software) that "with enough eyeballs, all bugs are shallow," to content creation. Wikipedia is already in the top 100 Web sites, and many think it will be in the top ten before long. This is a profound change in the dynamics of content creation.

Google is investing for developing the AJAX technology. All of its major products like Orkut, Gmail, and latest beta version of Google Groups, Google Suggest, and Google Maps are AJAX applications. Other products like Flickr, Amazon's A9.com search engine, Yahoo! Maps, Wufoo, Zimbra, Hotmail, Rediff Mail, and Yahoo! Mail are depending on AJAX. This is not just another technology that works only in a laboratory but it works on applications of any size from the very simple, single-function Google Suggest to the very complex and sophisticated Google Maps.

The reason why Google and other sites are using this technique is the versatile uses of the XML feature for handling any interoperational system with perfect ease and unprecedented speed.

Salient Features of AJAX in View of Multi Functional Software Architecture

- **Local event-handling:** When there is a requirement of dynamic content loading and responsiveness, the server-based transportation of data can degrade the performance so in that case use of local facilities rather than via server request provides better performance. In such a case where local handling is sufficient, use of local caches is relevant.
- **Predictive download:** This technique allows pre-fetching of data in ideal network conditions. Note that this auxiliary information should ideally be downloaded after the main information has been loaded. AJAX based web interface can do this where a "background thread" might even be used to continuously monitor the user's local behavior, regularly pulling down information which might be useful.
- **Submission throttling:** This concept enables a web page to send request to the server without any user action after specific interval. The implementation of this can be easily achieved with the use of AJAX where an event fires after each time interval for fetching the data.
- **Periodic refresh:** Through this a web page is automatically updated after some interval this can be achieved with AJAX by sending 'get request' to server after each interval.
- **Drag-and-drop:** This can be implemented with the help of AJAX where drag event fires a request to the server and fetches the data required and update the component of page if required.
- **Browser-agnostic components:** For interactive presentation there is a requirement of DHTML but portability can suffer. Therefore encapsulation of units of DHTML activity into browser-agnostic components is derived from AJAX. A 'component' may simply be a JavaScript function with a bunch of if-statements, or a factory in an 'Abstract Factory' hierarchy, or a server-side, 'JavaScript Generation Object'.
- **Server-side code generation:** When the request processed by server and response is generated for the page update, there may be a chance of new component request so use of server-side framework to generate the HTML and associated JavaScript is more effective but server side AJAX processing and generation engine is still immature.

ADVANTAGES OF AJAX

Traffic to and from the server is reduced considerably because the small sections of Web page are downloaded each time separately so the bandwidth usage is most likely to decrease. This is due to the fact that through this technology there is no need for a post back to the server for rendering a complete HTML page. Exploiting modern

Web browsers' rich graphics capabilities transparency, shading, animation, Z-ordering, compositing, and so on to add more glitz and interactivity to the presentation of information with low bandwidth consumption (Garrett, 2005).

In a classic Web application, when the Web server sends a Web page to the browser it can use multiple connection threads to speed up delivery. However, this happens only for content between the <body> tags. All script and other files are transferred using only one connection thread, which diminishes overall performance. While working with AJAX one has to load just the basic scripts and CSS files, and then it requests the rest of the content through multiple connections. This increases overall performance.

Waiting time is reduced when the user submits a form. One does not have to wait for the entire page to be rebuilt and retransmitted by the server. Instead, only the relevant content changes and in noncritical cases, the visitor can still work while the data is being submitted.

If an error is encountered in the page section then other sections are not affected (if not logically linked) and the data already entered by the user is not lost. This way, only the specific part of the application fails to load and the remaining continues smoothly without causing head-aches for the users. This brings about a grace in functioning.

Limitations of AJAX

AJAX is quite complex for implementation. Developers should have expertise in JavaScript for implementing AJAX functionality because building a Web-based application that employs AJAX is more difficult than building it the classic way.

Because of its complexity an AJAX-enabled application requires more development time and costs. It is comparatively more difficult because the mixture of technologies needs special concern for every process to go smoothly.

Using AJAX to asynchronously load content into an existing page for updating only a small part of a page to the browser history and bookmarks will disable restoration of the exact page state. Also, clicking the back button in a browser might not have any effect as the URL (Tim, 2005) remains unchanged. To overcome these problems one must implement a way to save the current page state so that it can be restored later on when called from a bookmark or from the browser history.

AJAX is not meant to be used in every application. One of the main reasons for this is the fact that a search engine cannot index it so the developer has to keep in mind that the better idea is to distribute AJAX features within the application.

AJAX FOR FOSTERING WIDESPREAD COLLABORATION

The need for focusing on aspects of e-business and globalization while developing the infrastructure of e-government is critical. Investment of the home country in the foreign sector with enterprises like pharmaceuticals, software, and metal leading the way and vice versa is increasing day by day. Even the government sector has to keep an eye on all kinds of proceedings in the business sector, from mergers, acquisitions, expansions, share market, and valuations, to loans and debts of home companies in the foreign market, and these need to be carefully analyzed while framing treaties and policies at the governmental level to affect the economy of the country at its best and make way for enormous development of a country in terms of technique, intellect, and natural resources. The economy rests on the business and technical aspects of a nation, so the more e-government is capable of encouraging ideas like technology transfer and innovation management it will become more viable for its successful implication.

Discussion of Various Governmental Proceeding in View of AJAX

Through various departments, the government liquidates a large sum of money to promote, sustain, and foster development every year, and sometimes this money disappears because of lethargic functioning and corrupt nodes in the infrastructure. This can be checked only by a technology that welcomes frequent display of information to the public and can become a parameter of transparency. The technology will enable different levels of government on the basis of administrative power in relation to data feeding and access.

Major responsibilities of a well-organized government, like education, health, agriculture, telecommunication, public transport, and employment, for empowering the conditions of economy, security, and progress of a country, require a continuous interaction with the public both of rural and urban setups. The target of setting individual citizen records and establishing a channel by which they can convey their needs to the government requires a very advanced approach when it comes to techniques of information technology.

E-Forms

According to a May 2006 Gartner report (Gartner, 2006), with as many as 85%of business processes dependent on forms, shifting to e-forms could provide substantial savings in cost, time, and labor. Beyond the corporate sector, many state governments are also migrating to e-forms. Increasingly, e-forms products, such as IBM's Workplace Forms, are being built on AJAX. Support from AJAX enriches the user experience, streamlining the forms process by supplanting the traditional Web page loading on the server with an AJAX engine using JavaScript to communicate with the Web browser. AJAX also enhances working with E-forms by providing more a flexible development option via the Eclipse-based designer. Moreover, e-forms with AJAX support do not require expensive and time-consuming programming.

Improving Accessibility of AJAX Forms

Fortunately, there are some things that can be useful for increase accessibility of AJAX forms. Here are some recommendations.

- Inform the user at the top of the form that it requires JavaScript or detects JavaScript automatically and warns the user when it isn't available.
- Inform the user that the page is updated dynamically. This is especially important for screen reader users and will help them decide when to trigger a reread of the page.
- Make it possible to receive an alert when information is updated. This may not be practically possible depending on the complexity of the form but will help a screen reader user a lot. Alert boxes are read by the screen reader and are usually displayed together with a sound.
- Highlight recently updated areas for a short period of time. This will help sighted users understand what just happened. "The Yellow Fade Technique" can serve this purpose.

E-Business

Financial interaction through the Internet is already considered fast, convenient, and accurate because of various banks supporting this new system. Whether it is the matter of income tax return, payment of salary to government employees, transaction of money within or outside any government wing as railways, postal, telecom, electricity, and so on, or even the sensitive matter of dispersal of funds to various segments of government, the dream of efficient e-government is incomplete without monitoring financial transaction. When citizens and government departments interact financially by the means of Internet, the system supporting it undoubtedly will need to be efficient, secured, and comprehensive. Keeping in mind the united capacity of Java Script, CSS, and XML, a secured system for fund transfer and other financial transactions can be thought of for managing abundant confidential data to facilitate the targeted population (Medjahed, 2005).

Election

At the time of elections the major concern of the government is sharing information and establishing lawful proceedings of the voting process. These can be ensured by AJAX technology considering the amount of data transaction to be monitored with a specific client request from the server. Here the clients would be paid employees or volunteers of the e-government hierarchy who will have the power to report and access data.

Taxes

The collaboration feature of AJAX facilitates the epidemiological survey of a given huge chunk of population on the basis of a survey conducted by net educated volunteers in every field. In the department of taxation volunteers will be appointed to do a door-to-door survey recording the economic patterns of each citizen as a unit to the country's economy on the whole. With a well-maintained, complete, transparent overview of every individual's financial capacity there will be much fewer chances of tax theft, and AJAX has been time tested for its capacity of being uniquely directional in a multi-user environment.

Defence

Defence system have so many activities, from research, planning, management, execution, emergency management, troops distribution and arms management, and so forth, going on at the same time with security of data as a heartbeat of work. In such an environment satisfying the need of a multilayered and secured database on analysis of the patterns and needs for different regions is a task that requires immense feedback that is both organized and timely. These needs can be efficiently monitored by practical and effective real world technology such as AJAX.

Trade

A country's trade on all frontiers and sectors is a dynamic aspect with an incredible need of government to be informed about the economic distribution of resources in corporate world and its assessment with respect to the possibilities of growth in future. The role of technology in e-government and the management of the budget in relation to a country's economy with ways for cost-effective implementation itself needs immense research with a huge amount of data processing, validation, comparison, and synthesis. For this a capable front-end technology as AJAX is needed to encourage the mammoth task of recording, organizing, processing, and making the data accessible related to government's plans and policies intended for application in the world of trade and commerce.

Framing of Policies

Framing of policies needs an argumentative background of information that can be possible by means of a broader survey with large participation of citizens so that maximum amount of population is affected without conflicts or doubts regarding the demand of the public at large. Whether it be the health sector, education, or empowerment of poor by means of employment, all of these need epidemiological surveys for building up a large database. This goal can be very well realized by using AJAX technology, which provides the speed capable of supporting any level of work both in terms of quality and quantity.

Power of AJAX of Working at Lower Bandwidth Regimes

Proper implementation of public policies, transparency in funds, utilization of public benefit plans, law enforcement, rights and duties, and foreign relations in view of the present government's plans and policies have now been looked upon as being restricted to a intellectual section of urban population, but through AJAX one can think of encouraging the concept of mass involvement in such issues by giving citizens of a country in charge a sense of responsible for the country. Impact of IT is very nominal in rural areas, confirming very few awareness patterns. This is obviously an obstacle in all development processes related to IT. Planning to introduce new technologies with relevant infrastructure in rural areas is most essential and the reference of AJAX in bringing about an ease in this project is imperative.

Data in Table 2 is based on the findings of a survey conducted recently in rural India. It depicts the percentage of people accessing information on different subjects. It demonstrates the need of information even in rural India, where are people are presumed to be less information-hungry and detached from the main stream of thought relating to government functioning. Not to mention that a country's economy depends more on the contribution given by these people through agriculture, extraction of natural resources, labour required at dams, power plants, mines, refineries, and power projects, which are generally set away from urban land and need the cooperation and participation of such population.

AJAX comes as a rescuer in such situations in lesser bandwidth regimes. This technology, due to its portability and unique directional nature, remains productive at optimum levels. In rural areas other factors have to be considered as well questions like percentage of literacy, child mortality rate, and even line of poverty are still not resolved. But all of these circle and end up on the government's inefficiency to implement its projects. A proper communication channel for public interface enabling feedback can be a solution and a system based on a reliable database, Java script and AJAX can be the technical building blocks of such a dream.

AJAX AS A CONSTITUENT IN THE DEVELOPMENT OF SUSTAINABLE WEB ARCHITECTURE

The following reasons are presented in argument of sustainability of AJAX-based infrastructure:

- Efficient reach both in terms of accessibility and postage of data. Being an open source it has the power of flexibility and possibilities of continuous development. Providing maximum productivity at low budget restrictions.
- XML has always answered to the need of interoperability between systems and still continues as a promising technology in standards adopted in the future. Owing to the fact that AJAX is powered by XML it intrinsically represents all such advantages of XML arguing in favor of the sustainability of the system for which it is deployed.
- If a technology other than AJAX is used, it may prove to be multiple times more expensive in terms of time consumed and money spent. A major challenge for ICT projects has always been maintaining financial sustainability.
- Efficient handling of bulk data and active retrieval mechanisms, along with low bandwidth functionality, establishes cost effective system function contributing in increased sustainability.

Table 2. Frequency of access to information by the rural poor population in India (Cicchini, 2003)

Information accessed	Very often (%)	Quite often (%)	Seldom (%)	Never (%)
News/Politics	57.3	28.7	10.7	3.3
Entertainment	51.4	32.7	12.7	3.3
Health/Education	41.3	46.7	10.7	1.3
Training Programs	17.3	42.0	28.7	12.0
Agriculture/Markets	13.3	46.0	26.0	14.7
Welfare programs	11.3	31.3	41.3	16.0
Employment Opportunities	10.7	25.3	38.0	26.0

CONCLUSION

The target of making such an e-government model that is capable of realizing extensive government policies can be achieved only by deploying the latest technologies. Developing an infrastructure that not only facilitates secure financial transactions but also encourages administration to grass-roots collaboration is not at all an easy task. The role of AJAX has been appreciated in present Web-based technologies as far as democracy and accessibility are concerned. AJAX-based democracy in the context of e-government refers to development and functioning of an infrastructure that is by the people, for the people, and of the people. In such setups people have the power to incorporate features to facilitate desired objectives within the space in which they are allowed to do so. Latest Web 2.0 technology is known for the implementing democracy only because of its power of AJAX. Here the people are in capacity from the development phase of a facility-oriented technology and they are not just to avail services but also to participate in the development process as there is no one except these secluded groups themselves, each with diversified attributes, that would know all about their own demands with freedom of diffusing the technologies to fulfill them, integrating their own innovativeness into the pre-existing infrastructure. This interaction will solely be realized by the effective use of AJAX technology.

AJAX being already accepted in vast and distributed networks has gained the reputation of handling the largest networks. This very sole nature of AJAX to entertain the user request in its finite section of the Web page without disturbing rest of the page, enticing the user for an uninterrupted participation and wasting no time of the user when the screen is left either blank or waiting for the requested page to upload, is among one of the main reasons in support of AJAX. Speed due to XML is one another main reason behind the argument of its acceptance for e-government. At the user end AJAX has unbelieving flexibility to cater services along with potentiality for absorbing information from a very broad spectrum of beneficiaries involved in different levels inside the network. The AJAX bandwagon continues to reach the highest limits of acceptance both for building and availing conveniences and also fulfills the need of security of information in ever expanding infrastructure. From compatibility to effective collaborations, business transparency to scalability (in both general and ad hoc setups), the use of AJAX augments interaction and responsiveness of the Web page interface as just the requested section or the component is updated at a time. The user gets the feeling that working is instantaneous leveraging the client machine's processing power and temporal proximity by making the Web browser responsible for more aspects of the application execution (Smith, 2006). A major interactive feature of AJAX called collaboration is responsible for controlling parameters of rate, review, comment, tag, blog, and feed of a Web page (Edwards, 2005). This encourages participation and productivity of mass people in governmental activities.

ACKNOWLEDGMENT

All the companies/products/services names are used for identification purposes and may be the trademarks of their respective owners.

REFERENCES

Asleson, R., & Schutta, N. T. (2005). *Foundations of AJAX.* APress.

Cicchini, S. (2003). Tapping ITC to reduce poverty in rural India. *IEEE Technology and Society Magazine,* Summer.

Canada, P. (2004). *Government On-Line 2004, Public Works and Government Services* (68).

Edwards, C. (2005). How AJAX jacks-up Web app performance. *Information Professional, 2*(6), 10-11.

Efstathopoulos, P., Mammarella, M., & Warth, A. (2005). *The Meta Google Maps "Hack" University ofCalifornia, Los Angeles.* http://www.cs.ucla.edu/~pefstath/papers/google-meta-paper.pdf.

Gupta, M. P., Choudhari, R. D., & Banwet, D. K. (2005). Risk profile in e-governance. In *Project Proceedings International Conference on E-Governance.*

Galitz, W. O. (2002). *The essential guide to user interface design.* John Wiley & Sons Inc.

Garrett, J. J. (2005). *AJAX: A new approach to Web applications.* Retrieved July 26, 2006, from http://www.adaptivepath.com/publications/essays/archives/000385.php

InterAKT Support http://www.interaktonline.com/Support/Articles Accessed 28 July 2006

Khatoikar, A., & Garg, V. N. (2003). E-government: Issues in implementation and practices in India. In *Proceedings of the 22nd National IT Conference*, Colombo, Sri Lanka.

Medjahed B., & Bouguettaya A., (2005). A multilevel composability model for semantic Web services. *IEEE Transactions on Knowledge and Data Engineering, 17*(7), 954-968.

Mylene, M., & Buckman, R., (2005). New Web-based technology draws applications, investors. *Wall Street Journal* P. B1.

Quin, L. *Extensible Markup Language (XML).* Retrieved March 28, 2006, from http://www.w3.org/XML

Paulson, L. D. (2005). Building rich Web applications with AJAX. *IEEE Computer, 38*(10) 14-17.

Stenback, J., & Heninger, A. (2004). *Document Object Model (DOM) level 3 load and save specification.* Retrieved August 28, 2006, from http://www.w3.org/TR/DOM-Level-3-LS/

Smith, K. (2006). Simplifying AJAX-style Web development. *Microsoft, 39*(5), 98-101.

Tim, R., Fielding, T., & Masinter, L. (2005). *Uniform Resource Identifier (URI): Generic Syntax.* Internet Society. RFC 3986; STD 66.

W3C Web API Working Group. Retrieved 19 March 2006, from www.w3.org/2006/Webapi/

This work was previously published in the International Journal of Electronic Government Research, Vol. 3, Issue 3, edited by M. Khosrow-Pour, pp. 40-53, copyright 2007 by IGI Publishing, formerly known as Idea Group Publishing (an imprint of IGI Global).

Compilation of References

Abdorabo, A. (2004). E-Government and IP Symposium for the Arab Region, UAE – Dubai.

ACE Project. (2004). 'Focus on E-voting.' *Electoral Knowledge Network*. URL: http://aceproject.org/ace-en/focus/e-voting/ (Consulted 8/02/2008).

Adams, D. (2003, November 25). Democracy without sound grabs. *The Age*. Retrieved May 24, 2007, from http://www.theage.com.au

Adelaide City Council (2006). URL: http://www.adelaidecitycouncil.com/

Adkins, R. (2005). *Air Force Knowledge Now*. http://www.e-gov.com/events/2005/km/downloads/KM05_2-3_Adkins.pdf

Adner, R. (2006). Match your innovation strategy to your innovation ecosystem. *Harvard Business Review, 84*(4), 98-107.

Advertiser, 26 November 2005

AEC (2007). *Remote Electronic Voting for Overseas Australian Defence Force personnel*. Consulted at URL: http://www.aec.gov.au/Voting/e-voting/adf.htm (Consulted 8/02/2008).

AEC (2007). *Electronic Voting Trial for Electors who are Blind or Have Low Vision*. http://www.aec.gov.au/Voting/e_voting/low_vision.htm (Consulted 20-8-08).

Afuah, A., & Tucci, C. L. (2000). *Internet Business Models and Strategies*. Boston: McGraw-Hill, Irwin.

Agle, B.R., Mitchell, R.K., & Sonnenfeld, J.A. (1999). Who matters to ceos? An investigation of stakeholder attributes and salience, corporate performance, and ceo values. *Academy of Management Journal, 42*(5), 507-525.

Agre, Philip (2002). Real-Time Politics: The Internet and the Political Process. *Information Society* 18 (5), 2002, pages 311-331.

Ahituv, N. (1980). A systematic approach towards assessing the value of an information system. *MIS Quarterly, 4*(4), 61-75.

Ahuja, V. (2000). Building trust in electronic commerce. *IT Professional, 2*(3), 61-63.

Aichholzer, G., & Schmutzer, R. (2000, September 6-8). Organizational challenges to the development of electronic government. In *Proceedings of 11th International Workshop on Database and Expert Systems Applications* (DEXA'00), Greenwich, London, UK, pp. 379-383.

Ajzen, I. (1988). *Attitudes, personality and behavior*. Milton Keynes: Open University Press.

Ajzen, I. (1991). Theory of planned behavior. *Organizational Behavior and Human Decision Processes, 50*(2), 179-211.

Alavi, M., & Tiwana, A. (2002). Knowledge integration in virtual teams: The potential role of kms. *Journal of the American Society for Information Science and Technology, 53*(12), 1029-1037.

Alexandros, K., Panagiotis, S., Thanos, K., & Despina, P. (2005). A secure e-Government platform architecture for small to medium sized public organizations. Electronic Commerce Research and Applications, 4(2), 174-186.

Copyright © 2009, IGI Global, distributing in print or electronic forms without written permission of IGI Global is prohibited.

Allen, B.A., Juillet, L., Paquet, G., & Roy, J. (2001). E-governance & government on-line in Canada: partnerships, people & prospects. *Government Information Quarterly, 18*(1), 93-104.

Alt, R., & Zimmerman, H. D. (2001). Introduction to Special Section: Business models. *Electronic Markets, 11*(1), 3-9.

Amit, R., & Zott, C. (2001). Value creation in e-business. *Strategic Management Journal, 22*(6/7), 493.

Andersen, D. F., & Dawes, S. S. (1991). *Government information management: A primer and casebook.* Englewood Cliffs, NJ: Prentice Hall.

Andersen, K. V., Grönlund, Å., Moe, C. E., & Sein, M. K. (2005). Introduction to the Special Issue - E-Government in Scandinavia. *Scandinavian Journal of Information Systems, 17*(2), 3-10.

Anderson, B. B., Bajaj, A., & Gorr, W. (2002). An estimation of the relative effects of external software quality factors on senior is managers' evaluation of computing architectures. *Journal of Systems and Software, 61*(1), 59-75.

Annual Global Accenture (former Anderson Consulting: AC) Study Report, 2002.

Ara Irititja (n.d.) Archival Online Project- Stage 2. Consulted at URL: http:// www.irititja.com/ on 25/01/2008

Arbuckle, J. L. (1996). Structural equation modeling: Amos program. In *Proceedings of Eighth invitational research seminar on advanced issues in research analysis.* Case Western Reserve University.

Archer, N.P. (2005). An overview of the change management process. *E-government, International Journal of Electronic Business, 3*(1), 1.

Arcieri F et al. (2002). Experiences and issues in the realization of e-government services, Proc. of the 12th International Workshop on Research Issues in Data Engineering: Engineering E-Commerce/E-Business Systems, IEEE, New York (2002), pp. 143–148.

Arcieri, F. et al. (2004). A layered IT infrastructure for secure interoperability in Personal Data Registry digital government services, Proc. of the 14th International Workshop on Research Issues on Data Engineering: Web Services for E-Commerce and E-Government Applications (RIDE'04), IEEE, New York, pp. 95–102.

Argyris, C. (1982). *Reasoning, Learning and Action: Individual and Organiational.* San Francisco: Jossey-Bass Publishers.

Asleson, R., & Schutta, N. T. (2005). *Foundations of AJAX.* APress.

Audia, P.G., Locke, E.A., & Smith, K.G. (2000). The paradox of success: an archival and a laboratory study of strategic persistence following radical environmental change. *Academy of Management Journal, 43*(5), 837-853.

Austin, J. L. (1962). *How to do Things with Words.* Cambridge: Harvard University Press.

Australian Broadcasting Commission (2005), ABC Radio, 31 May.

Australian Broadcasting Commission (2008), ABC Radio, 6 February.

Australian Bureau of Statistics [ABS] (2003). *Socio-economic indexes for areas Australia 2001* (2039.0). Canberra: Commonwealth of Australia.

Australian Bureau of Statistics [ABS] (2007). *2006 Census of Population and Housing,* ABS, Canberra. Retrieved July 16, 2007, from http://abs.gov.au/websitedbs/d3310114.nsf/Home/census

Australian Bureau of Statistics [ABS] (2007). *Patterns of Internet Access in Australia,* Australian Bureau of Statistics, Canberra.

Australian Bureau of Statistics [ABS]. (2005, March 31). Internet activity survey [IAS]. Retrieved May 24, 2007, from http://www.abs.gov.au

Australian Capital Territory Electoral Commission (ACTEC). (2005). *Electronic Voting and Counting System Review.* Elections ACT, 2005 URL: http//www.elections.

act.gov.au/pdfs/election_04/2004electionreviewcomputervoting.pdf (Consulted 8/02/08).

Australian Department of Communications and the Arts (DCITA) (2005). Networking the Nation Program Project Funding List – South Australia: As at June 2005.

Australian Electoral Commission (AEC). (2005). *Australian Electoral Commission Annual Report 2004-5,* http://www.aec.gov.au/_content/What/publications/annual_report/2005/index.htm (Consulted 8-02-08).

Australian Local Government Association. (2004). *A Directional Roadmap for the Use of Electronic Technology by Councils.* Deakin, ACT: Australian Local Government Association.

Backus, M. (2001). E-governance in developing countries. *IICD Research Brief – No 1.*

Baehni, S., Eugster, P. Th., & Guerraoui, E. (2004, June). Data-aware multicast. In *Proceedings of the 5th IEEE International Conference on Dependable Systems and Networks (DSN '04).*

Bailey, J. (2007). *Local Council e-Consultation Guide.* Australia: Darebin City Council. Retrieved June 28, 2007, from http://www.darebin.vic.gov.au/Files/local_council_e-consultation_guide_2007.pdf

Bailey, J.E., & Pearson, S.W. (1983). Development of a tool for measuring and analyzing computer user satisfaction. *Management Science, 29*(5), 530-545.

Bajaj, A. and Ram, S. (2003). IAIS: A methodology to enable inter-agency information sharing in e-government. *Journal of Database Management, 14*(4), 59-80.

Bajaj, A., Tanabe, H., & Wang, C.-C. (2002). *XSAR: XML based search agent for information retrieval.* Paper presented at the AMerica's Conference on Information Systems, AMCIS, Dallas, TX.

Baker, G. (2003). Management Reform in Local Government. In B. Dollery, N. Marshall & A. Worthington (Eds.), *Reshaping Australian Local Government: Finance, governance and reform.* Sydney: UNSW Press.

Baldwin, C. Y., & Clark. K. B., (2000). Design Rules, The power of modularity. The MIT Press, Cambridge, Massachusetts.

Baligh, H.H. (1994). Components of culture: nature, interconnections, and relevance to the decisions on the organization structure.*Management Science, 40*(1), 14-28.

Balnaves, M., Walsh, L., & Shoesmith, B. (2006). E-Democracy: Media-liminal space in the era of age compression. In J. Weiss, J. Nolan, J. Hunsinger & P. Trifonas (Eds.), *International handbook of virtual learning environments* (pp. 1007 – 1023). Springer International Handbooks of Education, 14.

Bandura, A. (1986). *Social foundations of thought and action: A social cognitive theory.* Englewood Cliffs, NJ: Prentice Hall.

Barlow, S., Chen, P., Chimonyo, J., Lyon, A., & O'Loughlin, B. (2004). *eGovernance Practice and Potential in the Local Government Sector.* Paper presented at the The Australian Electronic Governance Conference, Centre for Public Policy, Melbourne University, http://www.public-policy.unimelb.edu.au/egovernance/ConferenceContent.html#nancyotis.

Barnes, S.J., & Vidgen, R.T. (2006). Data triangulation and web quality metrics: A case study in e-government. *Information & Management, 43*(6), 767-777.

Barney, D. (2000). *Prometheus Wired: The hope For Democracy in the Age of Network Technology.* Chicago: University of Chicago Press.

Barney, J. B. (1991). Firm resources and sustained competitive advantage. *Journal of Management, 17*(1), 99-120.

Barry, B. (2002). Social Exclusion, Social Isolation, and the Distribution of Income. In J. Hills, J. Le Grand & D. Piachaud (Eds.), *Understanding Social Exclusion.* Oxford: Oxford University Press.

Barua, A., Konana, P., Whinston, A. B., & Yin, F. (2001). Driving E-Business Excellence. *MIT Sloan Management Review, 43*(1), 36-44.

Baskerville, R. L., & Wood-Harper, T. (1998). Diversity in information systems action research methods. *European Journal of Information Systems, 7*(2), 90-107.

Batini, C., M.Lenzerini, & Navathe, S. B. (1986). A comparative analysis of methodologies for database schema integration. *ACM Computing Surveys, 18*(4), 323-364.

Bawden, Tania (2007). Exports in the digital era. Adelaide Now. *Advertiser,* 11 October 2007.

Bechhofer, S., Moller, R. & Crowther, P. (2003). The DIG Description Logic Interface. *Proceedings of 2003 International Workshop on Description Logic (DL2003), Rome, Italy,* 85–94.

Bekkers, V., & Homburg, V. (2005). *The information ecology of e-government.* Amsterdam: IOS Press.

Belkin, N. J., & Croft, W. B. (1987). Retrieval techniques. *Annual Review of Information Science and Technology, 22*, 109-145.

Benbasat, I., Goldstein, D.K., & Mead, M. (1987). The case research strategy in studies of information systems. *MIS Quarterly, 11*(3), 369-386.

Benson, T. (2002). E-Service Development Framework Primer. eGIF4 Project, 1.0b version. Office of the e-Envoy, Cabinet Office., UK.

Berman, S.L., Wicks, A.C., Kotha, S., & Jones, T.M. (1999). Does stakeholder orientation matter? The relationship between stakeholder management models and firm financial performance. *Academy of Management Journal, 42*(5), 488-506.

Berners-Lee, T., Hendler, J., & Lassila, O. (2001). The Semantic Web. *Scientific American, September.*

Bernhard, K., Jeroen, H., & Guenther, I. (2005). In principle: Towards an Open Architecture for e-government Identity Management, Working Paper No. 2504, ISSN: 1667-738X, Center for Technology and Innovation Management. Retrieved November 25, 2006 from http://www.cetim.org/wps

Beroggi, G. (2008). Secure and Easy Internet Voting. *IEEE Computer*, 41(2), 52-56.

Bertot, J.C., & Jaeger, P.T. (2006). User-centered e-government: Challenges and benefits for government Websites. *Government Information Quarterly, 23*(2), 163-168.

Billsus, D., & Pazzani, M. (1998). *Learning collaborative information filters.* Paper presented at the Machine Learning: Proceedings of the Fifteenth International Conference.

Blaha, M. R., & Premerlani, W. J. (1995). *Observed idosyncrasies of relational database designs.* Paper presented at the Second Working Conference on Reverse Engineering, Toronto, Canada.

Blair, M.M. (1995). *Ownership and control.* Washington DC: The Brookings Institution.

Blenkin, M., Rose, J., & Yue, N. (1996). Government Policies and Early Education: Perspectives from Practioners. *European Early Childhood Education Research Journal, 4*(2), 5-19.

BMM Australia (2007). *Audit of AEC's Electronic Voting Machine for Blind and Vision Impaired Voters.* http://www.aec.gov.au/Voting/e_voting/bvi_audit.htm (Consulted 20-2-08).

BMM Australia (2007). *Audit and Certification of a Remote Electronic Voting System for Overseas Defence Force Personnel.* http://www.aec.gov.au/Voting/e_voting/adf_audit.htm (Consulted 20/02/08).

Boatright, J.R. (2002). Contractors as stakeholders: Reconciling stakeholder theory with the nexus-of-contracts firm. *Journal of Banking and Finance, 26*(9), 1837-1852.

Boudriga, N. (2002). Technical issues in securing e-government. Proceedings of the IEEE International Conference on Systems, Man and Cybernetics, (2), pp. 392–397.

Bouwman, H., & MacInnes, I. (2006). *Dynamic Business Model Framework for Value Webs.* Paper presented at the 39th Annual Hawaii International Conference on System Sciences (HICSS2006), Hawaii.

Boyan, J. A., & Littman, M. L. (1994). Packet routing in dynamically changing networks: A reinforcement learning approach. *Advances in Neural Information Processing Systems, 6.*

Boyatzis, R.E. (1998). *Transforming qualitative information: Thematic analysis and code development.* CA: Sage Publication.

Bozeman, B., & Bretschneider S. (1986). Public management information systems: theory and prescription. *Public Administration Review*, Special Issue, *47*-487.

Bozeman, B., & Kingsley, G. (1998). Risk culture in public and private organizations. *Public Administration Review, 58*(2), 109-118.

Braendli, D. (2005). *The Scope of E-voting in Switzerland* [Conference paper, E-voting and Electronic Democracy: Present and the Future. An International Conference, Seoul, South Korea, March 17-18, 2005. URL: http://www.hallym.ac.kr/~icat/evoting2005/81ppt/braendli_paper.pdf (Consulted 25/08/05).

Bray, T. (1998). RDF and Metadata. Retrieved January 20, 2007 from http://www.xml.com/pub/a/98/06/rdf.html

Brisbane City Council (2007) *Participation Guidelines.* Brisbane City Council Website. Retrieved November 14, 2007, at http://www.brisbane.qld.gov.au/BCC:BASE:1190883272:pc=PC_1

Broughton, C. (2005). *Democracy and voting.* White Paper. Software Improvements, Australia, http://www.softwareimp.com.au/Common%20content/White%20Papers/votingDemocracy.pdf (Consulted 8/02/2008).

Brown, M. M., & Brudney, J. L. (2003). Learning organizations in the public sector? A study of police agencies employing information and technology to advance knowledge. *Public Administration Review, 63*(1), 30-43.

Brown, S. A., Massey, A. P., Weiss, M. M., & Burkman, J. R. (2002). Do I really have to? User acceptance of mandated technology. *European Journal of Information Systems, 11*(3), 283-295.

Bruijn, H. de, Heuvelhof, E. ten, & Veld, R., int (2002). *Process management: Why project management fails in complex decision making processes.* Boston: Kluwer.

Buchsbaum, T. M. (2005). *E-voting: Lessons Learnt from recent pilots.* Conference paper, E-voting and Electronic Democracy: Present and the Future. An International Conference, Seoul, South Korea, March 17-18, 2005. URL: http://www.hallym.ac.kr/~icat/e-voting2005/b-speakers.html. (Consulted 25/08/2005).

Burdess, N., & O'Toole, K. (2004). Elections and representation in local government: A Victorian case study. *Australian Journal of Public Administration,* 63(2), 66-78.

Buyya, R., Stockinger, H., Giddy, J., & Abramson, D. (2001, August 20-24). Economic models for management of resources in peer-to-peer and grid computing. In *Proceedings of International Conference on Commercial Applications for High-Performance Computing,* Denver, CO. SPIE Press.

Caenen, G., & Pauwels., E. J. (2002). *Logistic Regression Models for Relevance Feedback in Content-Based Image Retrieval.* Storage and Retrieval for Media Databases, San Jose, California, USA.

Caffrey, L. (1998). Information sharing between and within governments: A study group report. *London7 Commonwealth Secretariat*

Caldow, J. (2004). *E-Democracy: Putting Down Global Roots.* Institute for Electronic Government, IBM Corporation. URL: http://www-1.ibm.com/industries/government/ieg/pdf/e-democracy%20putting%20down%roots.pdf (Consulted 8/02/2008).

Calista, D.J. (1986). Reorganization as reform: the implementation of integrated human services agencies. In D.J. Calista (Ed.), *Bureaucratic and Governmental Reform,*(pp. 197-214). Greenwich, CT: JAI Press.

Caloyannides, M. et al. (2003). US e-government authentication framework and programs. IT Professional, 5(3), 16–21.

Campbell, A. E. & Shapiro, S. C. (1998). *Algorithms for ontological mediation* (Technical Report 98-2). University at Buffalo, The State University of New York, Department of Computer Science and Engineering, SNePS Research Group.

Campbell, A. E. (1999). *Ontological Mediation: Finding Translation Across Dialects by Asking Questions.* Doctoral dissertation, University at Buffalo, The State University of New York, Department of Computer Science and Engineering.

Canada, P. (2004). *Government On-Line 2004, Public Works and Government Services* (68).

Capling, Ann and Nossal, Kim Richard (2000). *Death of Distance or Tyranny of Distance? The Internet, Deterritorialisation and the Anti-Globalisation Movement in Australia.* Paper presented at the XVII Triennial World Congress of the International Political Science Association, Quebec City, 1 August 2000. Consulted at URL:http://rspas.anu.edu.au/ir/pubs/ir-cat.php#00/3 on 25/01/2008

Caroll, A.B. (1989). *Business and society.* Cincinnati: South-Western.

Carr, W., & Kemmis, S. (1983). *Becoming Critical: Knowing through action research.* Victoria: Deaking University.

Carrolton Technology Partners. (2006). http://www.louisianarebuilds.info

Carson, C., Belongie, S., Greenspan, H., & Malik, J. (2002). Blobworld: Image segmentation using expectation-maximization and its application to image querying. *IEEE Transactions on Pattern Analysis and Machine Intelligence,* 24(8), 1026-1038.

Carter, L., & Belanger, F. (2005). The utilization of e-government services: Citizen trust, innovation and acceptance factors. *Information Systems Journal, 15*(1), 5-25.

Carvalho, M. (2006). *Distributed resource coordination strategies for mobile ad hoc networks.* Unpublished PhD dissertation, Tulane University, New Orleans, LA.

Carvalho, M., & Breedy, M. (2002, October). Supporting flexible data feeds in dynamic sensor grids through mobile agents. In *Proceedings of the 6th International Conference in Mobile Agents (MA 2002),* Barcelona, Spain.

Carvalho, M., Pechoucek, M., & Suri, N. (2005, July). A mobile agent-based middleware for opportunistic resource allocation and communications. In *Proceedings of the Fourth International Joint Conference on Autonomous Agents and Multiagent Systems; Defense Applications of Multi-Agent Systems (DAMAS).*

Caudle, S.L., Gorr, W.L., & Newcomer, K.E. (1991). Key information systems management issues for the public sector. *MIS Quarterly, 15*(2), 171-188.

Ceccola, S. (2006). Defining service oriented architecture and examining semantic SOA. Web Report Accessed at: colab.cim3.net/file/work/SOACoP/2006_05_2324/SCeccola205242006.ppt, 2006.

Center for Collaborative Government. (2002, April). *Digital commons e-democracy, pilot - final report.* Canada: CEG.

Cerami, E. (2002). *Web Services Essentials.* California: O Reilly & Associates.

Chadwick, A., & May, C. (2003). Interaction between States and Citizens in the Age of the Internet: e-Government in the United States, Britain and the European Union. *Governance: An International Journal of Policy Administration and Institutions,* 16(2), 271-300.

Champy, J. (2002). *X-engineering the corporation: Reinventing your business in the digital age.* Warner Books.

Chandler, S., & Emanuels, S. (2002). Transformation not automation. In *Proceedings on the 2nd European Conference on E-Government*, Oxford, UK, (pp. 99-102).

Chang, I. C., Li, Y. C., Hung, W. F., & Hwang, H. G. (2005). An empirical study on the impact of quality antecedents on tax payers' acceptance of Internet tax-filing systems. *Government Information Quarterly, 22*(3), 389-410.

Chang, Y., Ho, T., & Kaelbling, L. (2004). Mobilized ad-hoc networks: A reinforcement learning approach. In *Proceedings of the First International Conference on Autonomic Computing (ICAC'04)* (pp. 240-247).

Chau, P. Y. K., & Hu, P. J. (2001). Information technology acceptance by individual professionals: A model comparison approach. *Decision Sciences, 32*(4), 699-719.

Checkland, P. (1991). From Framework through Experience to Learning: The Essential Nature of Action Research. Discussant's comments. In H.-E. Nissen & H. K. Klein & R. Hirscheim (Eds.), *Information Systems Research: Contemporary Approaches & Emergent Traditions.* Amsterdam: Elsevier.

Chen, P. (2002). Virtual representation: Australian elected representatives and the impact of the Internet. *The Journal of Information, Law and Technology, 3.* Retrieved May 24, 2007, from http://www2-test.warwick.ac.uk/fac/soc/law/ elj/jilt/2002_3/chen/

Chen, P. (2007) *Electronic Engagement: A Guide for Public Sector Managers* ANZSOG Monograph. Retrieved July 20, 2007, from http://epress.anu.edu.au/anzsog/engage/mobile_devices/index.html

Chen, P., Gibson, R., & Geiselhart, K. (2006). *Electronic democracy? The impact of new communications technologies on Australian democracy.* Report No. 6 for the Democratic Audit of Australia. Canberra, Australia: The Australian National University.

Chen, Y., & Schwan, K. (2005, November). Opportunistic overlays: Efficient content delivery in mobile ad hoc networks. In *Proceedings of the 6th ACM/IFIP/USENIX International Middleware Conference (Middleware 2005).*

Chen, Y.N., Huang, W., Chen, H M., & Ching, R.K.H. (2006). E-government strategies in developed and developing countries – an implementation framework and a case study. *Journal of Global Information Management 14*(1), January-March, 25-48.

Chesbrough, H., & Rosenbloom, R. S. (2002). The role of the business model in capturing value from innovation: evidence from Xerox Corporation's technology spin-off companies. *Industrial and Corporate Change, 11*(3), 529-555.

Chiang, R. H. L., Lim, E.-P., & Storey, V. C. (2000). A framework for acquiring domain semantics and knowledge for database integration. *The DATA BASE for Advances in Information Systems, 31*(2), 46-62.

Chircu, A.M., & Lee, H.D. (2003). Understanding it investments in the public sector: The case of e-government. In *Proceeding of American Conference on Information Systems (AMCIS)*, Florida, USA.

Choi, S. P. M., & Yeung, D. Y. (1996). Predictive q-routing: A memory-based reinforcement learning approach to adaptive traffic control. In *Proceedings of NIPS-8* (pp. 910-945).

Chong, A.(2004). Personal comment. Senior Research and Ethics Officer, Aboriginal Health Council of South Australia, September 2004.

Cicchini, S. (2003). Tapping ITC to reduce poverty in rural India. *IEEE Technology and Society Magazine,* Summer.

CISA (2008). *Nonprofit ICT Strategy Resources.* URL: http://www.communit.info/index.php/

CISA. *CommunIT Conference.* URL: http://www.connectingup.org

City of Holdfast Bay (n.d.) *State of the Environment Community Survey.* Consulted at URL: http://www.holdfast.sa.gov.au/surveys_forms.htm on 25/01/08

Clark, T. and Abbinga, P. (2004). *Enabling Independent and Empowered Participation in the Electronic Democratic Process by People with Disabilities.* [Conference paper]. E-Governance Conference, University of Melbourne. URL: http://www.visionaustralia.org.au/docs/services/jscelectoral.doc (Consulted 8/02/2008).

Clarkson, M.B.E. (1995). *A risk based model of stakeholder theory.* The Centre for Corporate Social Performance & Ethics, University of Toronto.

Clift, S. (2004). *DoWire - Democracies online newswire.* Retrieved May 24, 2007, from http://www.dowire.org/

Codd, E. F. (1970). A relational model for large shared databanks. *Communications of the ACM, 13*, 377-387.

Coe, A., Paquet, G., & Roy, J. (2001). E-Governance and Smart Communities. *Social Science Computer Review*, 19(1), 80-93.

Coleman, S., & Gøtze, J. (2002). *Bowling together: Online public engagement in policy deliberation*. London: Hansard Society.

Collis, B. (1999). Designing for differences: Cultural issues in the design of WWW-based course-support sites. *British Journal of Educational Technology, 30*(3), 201-215.

Collis, B., & Moonen, J. (2001). *Flexible learning in a digital world*. London: Kogan Page.

Commonwealth Scientific and Industrial Research Organisation (CSIROnd).Consulted at URL: http://www.csiro.au/csiro/content/standard/ps25q,,.html on 25/02/2008.

Community Information Strategies Australia Inc (CISA). URL: http://www.cisa.asn.au

*Compeau, D., Higgins, C. A., & Huff, S. (*1999). Social cognitive theory and individual reactions to computing technology: A longitudinal study. *MIS Quarterly, 23*(2), 145-158.

Connolly, D., Harmelen, F. V., Horrocks, I., McGuinness, D. L., Patel-Schneider, P. F. & Stein L. A.(2001). DAML+OIL (March 2001). *Reference Description*. Retrieved January 20, 2007 from http://www.w3.org/TR/daml+oil-reference

Cook, M.A. (1996) Building Enterprise Information Architectures. Reengineering Information Systems. Prentice Hall, New Jersey, USA.

Coonan, the Honorable Helen (2006). *ICT Driving Economic Growth*. DCITA, Media Release 7 March 2006. Consulted at URL: http://www.minister.dcita.gov.au on 8/03/2006

Coonan, the Honorable Helen (2006) *Estimating Aggregate Productivity Growth for Australia: The Role of Information and Communications Technology* and *ICT and Australian productivity: methodologies and measurement* [report], DCITA. Consulted at URL: http://www.minister.dcita.gov.au on 25/01/2008

Coonan, the Honorable Helen (2006). *$36.6 million for Backing Indigenous Ability*. DCITA. Consulted at URL: http://www.minister.dcita.gov.au on 25/01/2008

Coursey, D., & Bozeman, B. (1990). Decision making in public and private organizations: A test of alternative concepts of "publicness". *Public Administrative Review, 50*(5), 525-35.

Crabtree, J. (2001). *Whatever Happened to the E-lection: A survey of Voter Attitudes Towards new Technology During the 2001 Election*. http://www.egov.vic.gov.au/pdfs/electiondesigned1.pdf: iSociety

Crane, J. (2005). *Qualitative research methods*. Retrieved December 6, 2005, from http://web.isp.cz

Crawford, C.H, Bate, G., Cherbakov, L., Holley, K., & Tsocanos, C. (2005). Toward an On Demand Service-Oriented Architecture. IBM Systems Journal, 44(1), 81–108.

Crespigny, Robert Champion de (2006). Agility to prosper. *SA 2025 – My Vision for South Australia, Sunday Mail*, Feb. 12, 2006

Csetenyi, A. (2000, September 6-8). Electronic government: perspectives from e-commerce. *Proceedings of the 11th International Workshop on Database and Expert Systems Applications* (DEXA'00), (pp. 294-298). Greenwich, London, UK.

Cumming, J.F. (2001). Engaging stakeholders in corporate accountability programmes: A cross-sectoral analysis of UK and transnational experience. *Business Ethics: A European Review, 10*(1), 45-52.

Curran, E. (2003). *Swarm: Cooperative reinforcement learning for routing in ad hoc networks*. Unpublished MSc thesis, Trinity College, Dublin, Ireland.

Curtain, G., Sommer, M., & Vis-Sommer, V. (2003). The World of E-Government. In G. Curtain, M. Sommer & V. Vis-Sommer (Eds.), *The World of E-Government*. New York: The Haworth Press.

Cutlip, S.C., Center, A.H., & Broom, G.M. (1994). *Effective public relations*. Englewood Cliffs, NJ: Prentice-Hall, Inc.

d'Auray, M. (2003). The Dual Challenge of Integration and Inclusion: Canada's Experience with Government Online. In G. Curtain, M. Sommer & V. Vis-Sommer (Eds.), *The World of E-Government*. New York: The Haworth Press.

Darebin City Council (2005) 2005-2006 *Annual Report*. Retrieved 25 June 2007 from http://www.darebin.vic.gov.au/Files/Annual_Report.pdf

Darebin City Council (2006) 2005 *Household survey. Summary Report*. Retrieved 25 June, 2007, from http://www.darebin.vic.gov.au/Files/2005_Household_survey_summary_report.pdf

Darebin City Council. (2007). *Darebin eForum*. Retrieved May 24, 2007, from http://eforum.darebin.vic.gov.au/

Dario, G. (2005). *Research Report No. 7: Analysis of Informal Voting During the 2004 House of Representatives Election*. Canberra: AEC.

Darragh, I. (2003). *A step-by-step guide to successful Web consultations*. Canadian International Development Agency. Retrieved May 24, 2007, from http://www.pwgsc.gc.ca/econsultation/text/tools-e.html

Das, T. K., & Teng, B. S. (2000). A Resource-based Theory of Strategic Alliances. *Journal of Management, 26*(1), 31-61.

DataExchanger (2002). Pierre Audoin Conseil, "Guide comparatif EAI".

Daubechies, I. (1992). *Ten Lectures on Wavelets*. Philadelphia: SIAM.

Davidson, A. (1997). *From subject to citizen: Australian citizenship in the twentieth century*. Cambridge, UK: Cambridge University Press.

Davis, F. D. (1989). Perceived usefulness, perceived ease of use, and user acceptance of information technology. *MIS Quarterly, 13*(3), 318-340.

Davis, F. D., Bagozzi, P. R., & Warshaw, P. R. (1989). User acceptance of computer technology: A comparison of two theoretical models. *Management Science, 35*(8), 892-1003.

Davis, J.H., Schoorman, F.D., & Donaldson, L. (1997). Toward a stewardship theory of management. *Academy of Management Review, 22*(1), 20-47.

Defence Science and Technology Organisation (DSTO) (2007). *Adelaide Research Collaboration To Benefit Defence*. News Item, 28 November, 2007. Consulted at URL: http://www.dsto.defence.gov.au/news/5266/?print=true on 29/01/2008

Defence Science and Technology Organisation (DSTO). URL: http://www.defence_sa.com/html/infrastructure/dsto.htm

Defense Information Systems Agency- Net-Centric Enterprise Services. (2006). *Net-Centric Enterprise Services User Guide, Version 1.0/ECB 1.2*. http://www.disa.mil/nces /NCES_UG_Final_v1_0.pdf

Defense Information Systems Agency, Department of Defense. (2006). *Core Services - Net-Centric Enterprise Services*. http://www.disa.mil/main/prodsol/cs_nces.html

Deloitte Research (2000). *At the dawn of e-government: The citizen as customer*. Deloitte Consulting and Deloitte and Touche, New York.

DeLone, W.H., & McLean, E.R. (1992). Information system success: the quest for the dependent variable. *Information Systems Research, 3*(1), 60-95.

Demb, A., & Neubauer, F.F. (1992). The corporate board: Confronting the paradoxes. *Long Range Planning, 25*(3), 9-20.

Denman-Maier, E. & Parycek, P. (2003). Cross-cultural factors in global e-government. In Proceedings Of Electronic Government, (LNCS, Vol. 2739, 456-459). Berlin: Springer-Verlag.

Department of Communications, Information Technology and the Arts (DCITA) (2006). *Digital Inclusion*. Consulted at URL: http://www.dcita.gov.au/ie/community_co...social_impacts_of_ict/digital_inclusion

Department of Communications, Information Technology and the Arts (DCITA) (n.d.). *Networking the Nation: An Australian Government Initiative*. Consulted at URL: http://archive.dcita.gov.au/2006/06/networking_the_nation on 25/01/2008

Department of Defense. (2000). *Organizational Chart*. http://www.defenselink.mil/odam/omp/pubs/GuideBook/Pdf/DoD.PDF

Department of Homeland Security at Naval Post Graduate School. (n.d.). *Homeland Security Digital Library*. https://www.hsdl.org/

Department of Homeland Security. (2006). *History: Who Became Part of the Department?* http://www.dhs.gov/xabout/history/editorial_0133.shtm

Department of Homeland Security. (2006). *Special Report | Component approach aiding IT infrastructure consolidation*. http://www.gcn.com/print/25_17/41104-1.html

Department of Homeland Security. (2006). *Special Report | Forward Motion, Amid widely documented IT failures, security advances and infrastructure upgrades are gaining traction at DHS*. http://www.gcn.com/print/25_16/41076-1.html

Department of Premier & Cabinet (Western Australia). (2006). *Citizenscape*. Retrieved May 24, 2007, from http://www.citizenscape.wa.gov.au/

Department of Transport and Regional Services. (2005). *Local Government National Report*. Canberra: Department of Transport and Regional Services.

DHS (2007). U.S. Department of Homeland Security, *National Response Plan*. http://www.dhs.gov/xprepresp/publications, last accessed July 23, 2007.

Digital Bridge Unit (2007). *Review of Online Access Centres in Regional South Australia*. Information Economy Directorate, Government of South Australia. Consulted at URL: http://www.innovation.sa.gov.au/_data/assets/pdf_file/0006/7539/0706_OAC_Final_Report.pdf on 27/01/2008

Digital Bridge Unit (2007). *An Award winning project, Outback Connect in action*. Consulted at URL: http://www.innovation.sa.gov.au/ict/dbu/outbackconnect/whats_new on 25/01/2008

Ding, L., Kolari, P., Ding, Z., Avancha, S., Finin, T., & Joshi, A. (2005). *Using Ontologies in the Semantic Web: A Survey* (TR-CS-05-07). University of Maryland Baltimore County, Ebiquity Research Group.

Dizard, W. P. (2002). White House promotes data sharing. *Government Computer News, 21*(25), 12.

Dollery, B., Marshall, N., & Worthington, A. (2003). Introduction. In B. Dollery, N. Marshall & A. Worthington (Eds.), *Reshaping Australian Local Government: Finance, governance and reform*. Sydney: UNSW Press.

Donaldson, L., & Davis, J.H. (1994). Boards and company performance – research challenges the conventional wisdom. *Corporate Governance: An International Review, 2*(3), 151-160.

Donaldson, T., & Preston, L.E. (1995). The stakeholder theory of the corporation: Concepts, evidence and implications. *Academy of Management Review, 20*(1), 65-91.

Dooley, B.L. (2002). Telecommunications in India: State of the marketplace, *Faulkner Information Services* (February), Docid 00016872.

Dowling, J., Curran, E., Cunningham, R., & Cahill, V. (2005, May). Using feedback in collaborative reinforcement learning to adaptively optimize MANET routing. *IEEE Transactions on Systems, Man, and Cybernetics—Part A: Systems and Humans, 35*(3).

Drupal (2007). http://www.drupal.org, last accessed July 23, 2007.

Dubusson-Torbay, M., Osterwalder, A., & Pigneur, Y. (2002). E-business model design, classification, and measurements. *Thunderbird International Business Review, 44*(1), 5-23.

Duncan, G. T., & Roehrig, S. T. (2003). Mediating the tension between information privacy and information access: The role of digital government. In G. D. Garson (Ed.), *Public information technology: Policy and management issues*. Hershey, PA: Idea Group Publishing.

Duran-Limon, et al. (2000). *Context-aware middleware for pervasive ad hoc environments.* (Tech. Rep.). Project CORTEX.

Eardley A. et al. (2003) Methods for Developing Flexible Strategic Information Systems: Is the Answer Already Out There? In N. Patel (ed.) Adaptive Evolutionary Information Systems, Idea Group Publishing.

Edmiston, K. D. (2003). State and local e-government: Prospects and challenges. *American Review of Public Administration, 33*(1), 20-45.

Edwards, C. (2005). How AJAX jacks-up Web app performance. *Information Professional, 2*(6), 10-11.

Edwards, Grant (2006). Wireless ties up the city, Computers and Technology, p.96. *Advertiser*, 2/09/06

Efstathopoulos, P., Mammarella, M., & Warth, A. (2005). *The Meta Google Maps "Hack" University ofCalifornia, Los Angeles.* http://www.cs.ucla.edu/~pefstath/papers/google-meta-paper.pdf.

E-government Strategy. (2002 and 2003). US Federal Government, www.firstgov.gov.

Eisenhardt, K. M., & Santos, F. M. (2002). Knowledge-Based View: A New Theory of Strategy? In A. Pettigrew, H. Thomas & R. Whittington (Eds.), *Handbook of Strategy and Management* (pp. 139-164). London: Sage Publications.

Eisenhardt, K.M. (1989). Agency theory: An assessment and review. *Academy of Management Review, 14*(1), 57-74.

Eisenhardt, K.M. (1991). Better stories and better constructs. *Academy of Management Review, 16*(3), 620-627.

Electronic News, 4 May 2005.

Elgarah, W., & Courtney J.F. (2002, August 9-11). Enhancing the G2C relationship through new channels of communication: Web-based citizen input. In *Proceedings of 8th Americas Conference on Information Systems* (AMCIS 2002), (pp. 564-568). Dallas, TX.

Enser, P., & Sandom, C. (2003). Towards a comprehensive survey of the semantic gap in visual image retrieval. (LNCS, *2728,291-299*).

Eugster, P., Th., Guerraoui, R., & Damm, C. H. (2001, October). On objects and events. In *Proceedings of the 16th ACM Conference on Object-Oriented Programming Systems, Languages and Applica-tions (OOPSLA 2001)* (pp. 131-146).

European Communities. (2004). *Second Successful Use of Internet Voting During Swiss Federal Referendum* [newsletter]. European Commission, 02 December 2004 URL: http://europa.eu.int/idabc/en/document/3607/358. (Consulted 8/02/2008).

European Communities. (2004). *Internet Referendum Successfully Held in Switzerland* [newsletter]. European Commission, 28 September 2004. URL: http://europa.eu.int/idabc/en/document/3311/358. (Consulted 18/02/2008).

European Community. (2003). The role of e-Government for Europe's future, Communication of the European Commission. Retrieved December 15, 2005 from http://europa.eu.int/information_society/eeurope/2005/doc/all_about/egov_communication_en.pdf

Farkus, L. (2004). *Services and Metadata on Local Government Websites.* Canberra: Australian Local Government Association.

Federal Emergency Management Agency. (2006). http://www.fema.gov/hazard/hurricane/ 2005katrina/anniversary.shtm

Fernandes, D., Gorr, W., & Krishnan, R. (2001, August 3-5,). ServiceNet: An agent-based framework for one-stop e-government services. In *Proceedings of the 7th Americas Conference on Information System* (AMCIS 2001), (pp. 1590-1594). Boston.

Finin, T., Fritzson, R., McKay, D., & McEntire, R. (1994). KQML as an agent communication Language. *Proceedings of the 3rd International Conference on Information and Knowledge Management,* 456 – 463.

Fischer, E. A. (2001). *RL30773: Voting Technologies in the United States: Overview and Issues for Congress.* CRS Report for Congress, URL: http://www.ncseonline.org?NLE?CRSreports/Risk/rsk-55.cfm?&CFID=8946853&CFTOKEN=5583815 (Consulted 5/05/2005).

Foley, M., & McCulley, M. (1998). *JFC unleashed.* SAMS Publishing.

Forsythe, J. (1990). New weapons in drug wars. *Information Week, 278*, 26-30.

Foster, I and C. Kesselman, (Eds.). (2003). The Grid 2: Blueprint for a New Computing Infrastructure. San Francisco: Morgan Kaufmann Publishing, Inc.

Fotos, M. and Franklin, M. (2002). *Naïve political science and the paradox of voting.* Paper Prepared for the Annual Meeting of the Midwest Political Science Association, Palmer House Hilton, Chicago, April 25-28, 2002.

Foucault, M. (1991). Governmentality. In G. Burchell, C. Gordon, & P. Miller (Eds.), *The foucault effect: studies in governmentality* (pp. 87-104). Chicago: University of Chicago Press.

Freeman, R.E. (1984). *Strategic management: a stakeholder approach.* Boston: Harper Collins.

Frey, B.S. (1997). On the relationship between intrinsic and extrinsic work motivation. *International Journal of Industrial Organizations, 15*(4), 427-439.

Frooman, J. (1999). Stakeholder influence strategies. *Academy of Management Review, 24*(2), 191-205.

Fu, J. R., Chao, W. P., & Farn, C. K. (2004). Determinants of taxpayers' adoption of electronic filing methods in Taiwan: An exploratory study. *Journal of Government Information, 30*(5-6), 658-683.

Fustes, M. (2003). The unconstrained business. *Insight,* 3, 15-17.

Galbraith, J. R. (1977). *Organization Design.* Reading, Massachusetts: Addison-Wesley.

Galitz, W. O. (2002). *The essential guide to user interface design.* John Wiley & Sons Inc.

Ganek, A. G., & Corbi, T. A. (2003). The Dawning of the Autonomic Computing Era. IBM Systems Journal, 42(1), 5–18.

García, J. R. G., & Pardo, T. A. (2005). E-government success factors: Mapping practical tools to theoretical foundations. *Government Information Quarterly, 22*(2), 187-216.

Garrett, Elizabeth. (2001). Political Intermediaries and the Internet Revolution in Symposium, Internet Voting and Democracy, held at Loyola Law School in October, 2000. *Loyola of Los Angeles Law Review*, 34 (3). Consulted at http://llr.lls.edu/volumes/v34-issues3/garrett.pdf on 25/01/2008

Garrett, J. J. (2005). *AJAX: A new approach to Web applications.* Retrieved July 26, 2006, from http://www.adaptivepath.com/publications/essays/archives/000385.php

Gasmelseid, T. (2007). From Operational Dash Boards to E-Business: Multiagent Formulation of Electronic Contracts. International Journal of E-Business Research, 3(3), 77-97, July – September 2007.

Gasmelseid, T. (2007). Engineering multiagent systems. In M. Quigley (Ed.), *Encyclopedia of Information Ethics and Security*, 187-193. Idea Group Publishing, USA.

Geiselhart, K., Griffiths, M., & Fitzgerald, B. (2003). What Lies Beyond Service Delivery - An Australian Perspective. In G. Curtain, M. Sommer & V. Vis-Sommer (Eds.), *The World of E-Government.* New York: The Haworth Press.

Gelman, R. S. (1999). Confidentiality of social work records in the computer age. *Social Work, 44*(3), 243-252.

Ghoshal, S., & Moran, P. (1996). Bad for practice: A critique of the transaction cost theory. *Academy of Management Review, 21*(1), 13-47.

Gibson, C. F., & Nolan, R. L. (1974). Managing the four stages of EDP growth. *Harvard Business Review, 52*(1), 76-88.

Gibson, D., Kleinberg, J. M., & Raghavan, P. (1998). Inferring Web communities from link topology. In *Proceedings of ACM Hypertext '98*(pp. 225-234). Pittsburgh.

Gibson, Rachel and Stephen Ward (2002), Virtual Campaigning: Australian Parties and the Impact of the Internet, *Australian Journal of Political Science*, vol. 37, No.1, pp. 99-129.

Gillespie, D. F., & Glisson, C. (1992). *Quantitative methods in social work: State of the art. Binghamton, NY: Haworth Press.*

Glassey, O. (2001, June 27-29). Model and architecture for a virtual one-stop public administration. *The 9th European Conferences on Information Systems*,(pp. 969-976).

Glavinic, V. (2002). *Introducing XML to integrate applications within a company.* Paper presented at the 24th International Conference on Information Technology Interfaces, Zagreb, Croatia.

Golder, Wendy, Cleary, Jenny and Johnston, Ann (2006). *Outback Connect: Bridging the digital divide*. Refereed paper consulted at URL: http://www.regional.org.au/au/apen/2006/refereed/1/3059_clearyglover.htm?print=1 on 25/01/08

Golebiowska, J., Dieng-Kuntz, R., Corby, O. & Mousseau, D. (2001) . Building and exploiting ontologies for an automobile project memory. *Proceedings of the 1st international conference on Knowledge capture K-CAP,* 52 – 59.

Gonçalo, P. D., & José, A. R. (2006). A simple model and a distributed architecture for realizing one-stop e-government. Electronic Commerce Research and Applications, doi:10.1016/j.elerap.2006.02.001.

Goodman, M. A. (2001). CIA: The need for reform. *Foreign Policy in Focus, Special Report 13 F 2001*, 1-8.

Government Computing (2006), A New Era Dawns: Local Directgov Programme, May 2006

Government Computing Publication: March (2005)

Government Computing Publication: November (2005)

Green, P. (2004). *Electronic voting underway for ACT election.* Australian Capital Territory Electoral Commission. URL: http://www.elections.act.gov.au/media/media0413.html. (Consulted 8 08/2008)

Green, P. (2005). *Electronic voting and counting for elections for the Australian Capital Territory.* Paper presented at an International Conference on E-voting and Electronic Democracy: Present and the Future. March 17-18, Seoul [conference paper on line]. URL: http://www.hallym.ac.kr/%Eicat/e-voting2006/index.html (Consulted 8/02/2008).

Green, P. (2004). *Electronic voting and counting for elections for the Australian Capital Territory.* Paper presented at the International Conference on E-voting and Electronic Democracy: Present and the Future. March 17-18, Seoul. Consulted at URL: http://www.hallym.ac.kr/~icat/e-voting2005/81ppt/Phil%20Green.doc on 1/10/2005.

Greenley, G.E., & Foxall, G.R. (1998). External moderation of associations among stakeholder orientations and company performance. *International Journal of Research in Marketing, 15*(1), 51-69.

Gregory, R.J. (1999). Social capital theory and administrative reform: Maintaining ethical theory in public service. *Public Administration Review, 59*(1), 63-75.

Greunz, M., Schopp, B. & Haes, J. (2004). Integrating e-government infrastructures through secure XML document containers. Proceedings of the 34th Annual Hawaii International Conference on System Sciences (HICSS-34*)*, (2), p. 5004.

Griffiths, M. (2002). *Forming Audiences for E-Democracy: Government Policies, Portals and Pilots - and Citizen Literacies.* Paper presented at the 2nd European Conference on e-Government, St Catherine's College, Oxford.

Grönlund, A., & Horan, T. A. (2004). Introducing e-gov: History, definitions, and issues. *Communications of the Association for Information Systems, 15*, 713-729.

Grover, V., & Segars, A. H. (2005). An empirical evaluation of stages of strategic information systems planning:

Patterns of process design and effectiveness. *Information & Management,* 42, 461-479.

Guillaume, G. (1999). *L'empire de Réseaux.* Paris, France: Descartes & Cie.

Gupta, M. P., Choudhari, R. D., & Banwet, D. K. (2005). Risk profile in e-governance. In *Project Proceedings International Conference on E-Governance.*

Gupta, M. P., Kumar, P., & Bhattacharya, J. (2004). *Government online: Opportunities and challenges,* TMH, New Delhi.

Gupta, M., & Jana, D. (2003). E-government evaluation: A framework and case study. *Government Information Quarterly,* 365-387.

Haarslev, V. and Moller, R. (2003). Racer: An OWL Reasoning Agent for the Semantic Web. *Proceedings of the International Workshop on Applications, Products and Services of Web-based Support Systems, in conjunction with the 2003 IEEE/WIC International Conference on Web Intelligence,* 91-95.

Hacker, K.L., & van Dijk, J. (Eds.). (2000). *Digital democracy: Issues of theory and practice.* London: Sage Publications.

Hair, J. F., Tatham, R. L., Anderson, R. E., & Black, W. (1998). *Multivariate data analysis* (5th ed.). Englewood Cliffs, NJ: Prentice Hall.

Hamilton, S., & Chervany, N.L. (1981). evaluating information system effectiveness - Part I: comparing evaluation approaches. *MIS Quarterly, 5*(3), 55-69.

Haque, M.S. (2001). The diminishing publicness of public service under the current mode of governance. *Public Administration Review, 61*(1), 65-82.

Hasen, R. L. (1996). Voting without law. *Pennsylvania Law Review.* 144 (5), 2135-2179.

Hawley, J.P., & Williams, A.T. (1996). Corporate governance in the United States: The rise of fiduciary capitalism, a review of the literature. *Prepared for the Organization for Economic Cooperation and Development,* Paris, France.

Hayne, S., & Ram, S. (1990). *Multi-user view integration system (muvis)-an expert system for view integration.* Paper presented at the IEEE International Conference on Data Engineering (ICDE).

Hazlett, S. A., & Hill, F. (2003). E-government: The realities of using IT to transform the public sector. *Managing Service Quality, 13*(6), 445-452.

He, H. (2003). *What is service oriented architecture?* Retrieved from http://www.xml.com/pub/a/ws/2003/09/30/soa.html, 2006.

Hearst, M. (1998). Trends and controversies: information integration. *IEEE Intelligent Systems Journal* (Sept-Oct), 12-24.

Hedman, J., & Kalling, T. (2003). The business model concept: Theoretical underpinnings and empirical illustrations. *European Journal of Information Systems, 12*(1), 49-59.

Heeks, R. (2000). *Reinventing government in the information age.* London: Roultedge Press.

Heeks, R. (2002). *Understanding e-governance for development, i-government working paper Series.* Retrieved March 25, 2002, from http://idpm.man.ac.uk/idpm/igov11.htm

Heeks, R. (2003). Success and failure rates of e-government in developing/transitional countries: Overview. *E-government for Development,* Institute for Development Policy and Management, University of Manchester, UK.

Heintze, T., & Bretschneider, S. (2000). Information technology and restructuring in public organizations: Does adoption of information technology affect organizational structures, communications, and decision-making? *Journal of Public Administration Research and Theory, 10*(4), 801-830.

Hexmoor, H. & Sabaa, H. (2006) .Towards Semantically Coherent Collaboration. *Proceedings of the International Symposium on Collaborative Technologies and Systems* (pp. 264-269). IEEE Computer Society Washington, DC, USA.

Hill, L. (2001). A great leveller: Compulsory voting as a democratic innovation. In Marian Sawer (ed), *Elections Full Free and Fair*. Federation Press, Sydney.

Hill, L. (2002). On the reasonableness of compelling citizens to vote: The Australian case. *Political Studies*. 50(1), 80-101.

Hill, L. and Louth, J. (2006). Mobilising the youth vote and the future of British democracy. *Proceedings of the Australasian Political Studies Association Conference 2006*, University of Newcastle, http://www.newcastle.edu.au/school/ept/politics/apsa/PapersFV/Panel_Youth/Hill,%20Lisa%20&%20Louth,%20Jonathon.pdf

Hill, L. and Young, S.(2007). Protest or error? Informal voting and compulsory voting. *Australian Journal of Political Science*, 42 (3), 515-521.

Hillard, R. (2000). IEEE-std-1471-2000: Recommended Practice for Architectural Description of Software-Intensive Systems. Retrieved February 15, 2007 from http://standards.ieee.org.

Hiller, J., & Belanger, F. (2001). *Privacy strategies for electronic government e-government series*. Arlington, VA: PricewaterhouseCoopers Endowment for the Business of Government.

Hinton, C. (2001). *Seven keys to a successful enterprise GIS* (Report IQ Service Report, vol. 33, no. 3). Washington, DC: International City/County Management Association.

History Trust of South Australia. URL: http://www.history.sa.gov.au/

Ho, A.T-K. (2002). Reinventing local governments and the e-government initiative. *Public Administration Review*, *62*(4), 434-44.

Ho, J., & Pardo, T. A. (2004). *Toward the success of e-government initiatives: Mapping known success factors to the design of practical tools*. Paper presented at the 37th Hawaii International Conference on System Sciences (HICSS), organized by the College of Business, University of Hawaii at Manoa.

Hobsbawn, A. (2003, December 10). Phone a foreigner. *The Guardian*. Retrieved May 24, 2007, from http://society.guardian.co.uk/e-public/story/0,,1103283,00.html

Hofstede, G. (1980). *Culture's consequences: international differences in work-related values*. Newbury Park, CA: Sage Press.

Hofstede, G. (1991). *Cultures and organizations: Software of the mind*. London: McGraw Hill.

Hogarth, F. (2004, November 17-18). *Engaging communities online - A Queensland perspective*. Paper presented at the Australian Government Information Management Office [AGIMO] Seminar Enabling Government, Engaging Communities: An Online Perspective, Brisbane, Australia. Retrieved May 24, 2007, from http://www.agimo.gov.au/resources/events/2004/engage

Holden, S. H., Norris, D. F., & Fletcher, P. D. (2003). Electronic government at the local level: Progress to date and future issues. *Public Performance and Management Review*, *26*(4), 325-344.

Holkeri, K. (2003). *Case study – Citizen consultation and engagement: Share your views with US*. OECD. Retrieved May 24, 2007, from ccnm/gf/gov/pubg, 2

House of Representatives Standing Committee on Economics Finance and Public Administration. (2003). *Rates and Taxes: A Fair Share for Responsible Local Government*. Canberra: Commonwealth Government.

Howell, P (1986). The South Australia Act, 1834. in Jaensch, Dean (ed.) *The Flinders History of South Australia*, 1986, Wakefield, pp. 26-51 and URL: http://www.foundingdocs.gov.au/item.asp?dID=1

Huang, W., D'Ambra, J., & Bhalla, V. (2002). An empirical investigation of the adoption of egovernment in australian citizens: some unexpected research findings. *Journal of Computer Information Systems*, *43*(1), 15-22.

Huang, W., Siau, K. and Wei, K.K. (2004). *Electronic government: Strategic and implementations*. Hershey, PA: Idea Group Publishing.

Human Rights and Equal Opportunities Commission. (2007). *Electronic voting could decide election*. (Media

Release). http://www.hreoc.gov.au/about/media/media_releases/2007/91_07.html (Consulted 8/02/2008).

Hume, Ellen (2003). Resource Journalism: A Model for New Media. In Jenkins, Henry and Thorburn, David (eds.) *Democracy and new media,* Cambridge, Ma. MIT Press.

Hung, S. Y., Chang, C. M., & Yu, T. J. (2006). Determinants of user acceptance of the e-government services: The case of online tax filing and payment system. *Government Information Quarterly, 23*(1), 97-122.

Hungarian Algorithm (2007). http://en.wikipedia.org/wiki/Hungarian_algorithm, last accessed July 23, 2007.

Hunter, C. D. (2002). Political privacy and online politics: How e-campaigning threatens voter privacy. *First Monday, 2*(4).

Hurd, J. D., Civco, D. L., Gilmore, M. S., Prisloe, S., & Wilson, E. H. (2006). *Tidal wetland classification from Landsat imagery using an integrated pixel-based and object-based classification approach.* Paper presented at the ASPRS 2006 Annual Conference, Reno, NV.

IADB (Inter-American Development Bank) (2002). *E-governance; e-government. ICT for development.* Retrieved June 20, 2004, from http://www.iadb.org/ict-4dev/governance.htm

IBM. iTera Echo[2] High Availability for IBM iSeries, http://www.ibm.com

InfoDev and The Center for Democracy and Technology. (2002). *E-Government Handbook.* www.cdt.org/egov/handbook/

Information Age (2004). SeeBeyond empowers Sainsbury's transfomation. *Information Age,* B10-B11.

Information Age (2004). Understanding, implementing and managing core technologies, Information Age advisory series. *Information Age, 1*(3), 26.

Information Technology Council of South Australia. *Solution City Adelaide.* URL: http://www.solutioncity.com.au/

Innes, G. (2006). *In the National Interest,* interview with Peter Mares, 7 May 2006, Radio National. URL: http://www.abc.net.au/rn/nationalinterest/stories/2006/1630942.htm. (Consulted 8/02/2008).

Intanagonwiwat, C., Govindan, R., & Estrin, D. (2000, August). Directed diffusion: A scalable and robust communication paradigm for sensor networks. In *Proceedings of the Sixth Annual International Conference on Mobile Computing and Networking (MobiCOM '00),* Boston, MA.

InterAKT Support http://www.interaktonline.com/Support/Articles Accessed 28 July 2006

Interim Report of the Commission on Electronic Voting (IRCEV) (2004). *20-24, 29.* URL: http://www.cev.ie/. (Consulted 8/02/2008).

International Conference on E-government for Development (IceGD). Retrieved September 25, 2002, from http://www.palermoconference2002.org/en/home_a.htm.

Internode (2008). *Wireless Hotspots.* Consulted at URL: https://hotspot.internode.on.net/coverage/ on 24/02/2008

IRAS (2002). *Realizing our vision.* Singapore: Inland Revenue Authority of Singapore.

Irvine, C. E. (2000). Security issues for automated information systems. In G. D. Garson (Ed.), *Handbook of pPublic information systems.* New York: Marcel Dekker, Inc.

I-Ways (2005). E-government in the European union: online availability of public services. *I-WAYS, Digest of Electronic Commerce Policy and Regulation, 28,* 92–95.

Jackman S. and P. Brent. (2007). Rolls Close, Young People Still Under Represented. *Crikey,* October 29, 2007, http://www.mumble.com.au/misc/20071029_crikey_electoralroll.htm (Consulted 2-11-07

Jackson, N. (2002). State of the marketplace: e-government gateways. *Faulkner Information Services* (February), Docid 00018296.

Jaeger, P. (2002). Constitutional principles and e-government: An opinion about possible effects of federalism and the separation of powers on e-government policies. *Government Information Quarterly,* 357-368.

Jaeger, P.T. Assessing Section 508 compliance on federal e-government Web sites: A multi-method, user-centered, evaluation of accessibility for persons with disabilities. *Government Information Quarterly, 23*(2), 2006, pp.169-190.

Jain, A. and Patnayakuni, R. (2003). Public expectations and public scrutiny: an agenda for research in the context of e-government. In *Proceeding of American Conference on Information Systems (AMCIS),* August 2003, Florida, USA.

Janis, I.L. (1982). *Groupthink.* Boston: Houghton, Mifflin.

Janssen, D., Rotthier. S., & Snijkers K. (2004). If you measure it they will score: An assessment of international eGovernment benchmarking. *Information Polity, 9*,121–130.

Janssen, M., & Kuk, G. (2007). E-Government Business Models for Public Service Networks. *International Journal of E-government Research (IJEGR), 3*(3), 54-71.

Janssen, M., & van Veenstra, A. F. (2005). Stages of growth in e-government: An architectural approach. *The Electronic Journal of E-Government, 3*(4), 193-200. Retreived from www.ejeg.com

Janssen, M., Kuk, G., & Wagenaar, R. W. (2005). *A Survey of e-Government Business Models in the Netherlands.* Paper presented at the 7th International conference on Electronic commerce, Xi'an, China.

Janssen, M., Kuk, G., & Wagenaar, R. W. (2008). A survey of web-based business models for e-government in the Netherlands. *Government Information Quarterly, 25*(2), 202-220.

Järveläinen, J., Kestilä, T., Koskivaara, E., Pihlaja, P., & Salmela, H. (2006). *Adoption of IT in The Finnish Early Childhood Education.* Paper presented at the Well-being in the Information Society -seminar (WIS 2006) May 11-12, 2006, Turku School of Economics.

Jena–A Semantic Web Framework for Java. (n.d.). Retrieved December 4, 2006 from http://jena.sourceforge.net/index.html

Jenkins, C. 2006. Blind to lead way in E-voting. *Australian IT, The Australian.* July 25, 2006.

Jensen, M.C., & Meckling, W.H. (1976). Theory of the firm: Managerial behavior, agency costs and ownership structure. *Journal of Financial Economics, 3,* 305–360.

JMDT (2007). *JPEG Metadata Discovery Tool.* http://metadata.solers.com, last accessed July 23, 2007.

Joint Standing Committee on Electoral Matters (JSCEM). (2005). *The 2004 Federal Election: Report of the Inquiry into the Conduct of the 2004 Federal Election and Matters Related Thereto,* Canberra: The Parliament of Australia. URL: http://www.aec.gov.au/_content/why/committee/jscem/ (Consulted 8/02/2008).

Joshi, J. B. D., Ghafor, A., Aref, W. G., & Spafford, E. H. (2002). Security and privacy challenges of a digital government. In W. J. McIver & A. K. Elmagarmid (Eds.), *Advances in digital government, technology, human factors, and policy.* Norwell, MA: Kluwer Academic Publishers.

Joshi, J. et al. (2001). Digital government security infrastructure design challenges. Computer security 34 (2), 66–72.

Jowell, R.and A. Park. (1998). *Young People, Politics and Citizenship: A Disengaged Generation.* London: Citizenship Foundation.

Kaliontzoglou, A., et al. (2005). A secure e-government platform architecture for small to medium sized public organizations. Electronic Commerce Research and Applications, 4 (2), 174–186.

Kalloniatis, C, Kavakli, E, & Gritzalis, S. (2004). Security requirements engineering for e-government applications: Analysis of current frameworks. In *Proceedings Of Electronic Government,* (LNCS 3183, pp. 66-71).

Kalyanpur, A., Parsia, B., Sirin, E., Grau, B. C. & Hendler J. A. (2006) .Swoop: a web ontology editing browser. *Journal of Web Semantics,* 4(2), 144-153.

Kamel, Izzeldin. (2008). E-Banking and its impact on Sudanese Banking sector. Invited lecture, Management Forum, Jan 16, 2008, British Council, Khartoum, Sudan.

Kang, G. (2001). E-Racing E-Elections. *Loyola of Los Angeles Law Review*. 34 (3), 1155-1170.

Kangasharju, A., & Aaltonen, J. (2006). *Kunnallisen päivähoidon yksikkökustannukset: Miksi kunnat ovat niin erilaisia?* Government Institute for Economic Research. Available: <http://en.vatt.fi/file/vatt_publication_pdf/t119.pdf13.12.2006>

Kankanhalli, A., Tan, B.C.Y., & Wei, K.K. (2001, December 16-19). Seeking knowledge in electronic knowledge repositories: An exploratory study. In *Proceedings of the 22nd International Conference on Information Systems* (ICIS 2001)(pp. 123-134). New Orleans, LA.

Karyda, M., Balopoulos, T. , Gymnopoulos, L., Kokolakis, S., Lambrinoudakis, C., Gritzalis, S. & Dritsas, S.(2006) An ontology for secure e-government applications. *Proceedings of the first international conference on availability, reliability and security (ARES'06), 00*, 1033-1037.

Katz, R., & Brewer, E. (1996). Wireless overlay networks and adaptiveApplications. In *Proceedings of MobiCom.*

Kauppinen, S. (1995). *Päivähoidon ryhmäkokoselvitys [Group size evaluation of Day-care].* Helsinki: Stakes [The National Research and Development Centre for Welfare and Health].

Ke, W. & Wei, K. K. (2004) . Successful e-government in Singapore. *Commnications of ACM 47,* 95 - 99.

Kemmis, S., & McTaggart, R. (2000). Participatory Action Research. In N. K. Denzin & Y. S. Lincoln (Eds.), *Handbook of Qualitative Research* (Second ed.). Thousand Oaks, California: Sage Publications, Inc.

Kershaw, Alison (2007). *Playing Catch Up with the Digital Divide.* Paper presented at the 13th Australasian World Wide Web Conference (AUSWEB 2007), held at Coffs harbour, New South Wales, 30 June-4 July, 2007. Consulted at URL: http://ausweb.scu.edu.au/aw07/papers/refereed/kershaw/paper.html on 29 /01/2008

Khare, R., & Rifkin, A. (1997). XML: A door to automated web applications. *IEEE Internet Computing, 1*(4), 78-87.

Khatoikar, A., & Garg, V. N. (2003). E-government: Issues in implementation and practices in India. In *Proceedings of the 22nd National IT Conference*, Colombo, Sri Lanka.

Kherfi, M. L., Ziou, D., & Bernardi, A. (2004). Image Retrieval from the World Wide Web: Issues, Techniques, and Systems. *ACM Computing Surveys, 36*(1), 35-67.

Kim, E., & Lee, J. (1986). An exploratory contingency model of user participation and mis use. *Information and Management, 11*(2), 87-97.

King, Agnes (2006). Yes, Minister, IT needs you. *The Age*, 28 March 2006.

Kinos, J. (2006). Varhaiskasvatuksen keskeiset kehittämiskohteet ja -haasteet, *Puheenvuoroja varhaiskasvatuksen kehittämisestä.* (pp. 13-18): Opetusalan Ammattijärjestö OAJ.

Kinos, J., & Laakkonen, E. (2006). *Pienten lasten opettajat Varsinais-Suomessa. Selvitys lastentarhanopettajatilanteesta Varsinais-Suomen maakunnassa.* Turun yliopisto. Kasvatustieteiden tiedekunta. Available: <http://vanha.edu.utu.fi/tokl/LTO2006/LTO_VS_web.pdf13.12.2006>

Kirkman, G.S., Osorio, C.A. and Sachs, J.D. (2002). The networked readiness index: measuring the preparedness of nations for the networked world. In *The global information technology report: readiness for the networked world* (pp. 10-30). Oxford University Press.

Kisfalvi, V. (2000). The threat of failure, the perils of success and ceo character: sources of strategic persistence. *Organization Studies, 21*(3), 611-639.

Kiss, R. (2003). Reasserting Local Democracy. In B. Dollery, N. Marshall & A. Worthington (Eds.), *Reshaping Australian Local Government: Finance, governance and reform.* Sydney: UNSW Press.

Kleinig, Xanthe (2006). Principals are furious the Technology School of the Future has been scrapped. *Advertiser,* reported at *Adelaide Now.* Consulted at URL: http://www.news.com.au/adelaidenow/story/0,22606,20773414-5006353,00.html on 2/02/2008

Knoblock, C.A. & Ambite, J.L. (1997). *Agents for Information Gathering,* Software Agents. J. Bradshaw, (Ed.), MIT Press, Metlo Park, CA.

Knowlton, Brian (2006). U.S. voters overseas get a computerized helper. *International Herald Tribune,* 3/02/2006. Consulted at URL: http://www.iht.com/articles/2006/02/03news/vote.php

Knowlton, Brian. (2006). US voters overseas get a computerized helper. *International Herald Tribune.* Friday, February 3. URL: http://www.iht.com/articles/2006/02/03news/vote.php. (Consulted 8/02/2008).

Kolodner J. (1992). An Introduction to Case-Based Reasoning. *Artificial Intelligence Review,* 6(2), 3-24.

Komarek, P.(2004, May) *Logistic Regression for Data Mining and High-Dimensional Classification,* (Tech. report CMU-RI-TR-04-34). Pittsburg, PA: Carnegie Mellon University, Robotics Institute

Korotkiy, S. and Top L. (2006). Onto SOA: From Ontology-enabled SOA to Service-enabled Ontologies. *IEEE International Conference on Internet and Web Applications and Services,* 347-353.

Korupp, Sylvia and Szydlik, Marc (2005). Causes and Trends of the Digital Divide. *European Sociological Review, 21(4),* pp.409-422.

Kothari, A., Sabhash, S., & Zhou, Y. (2003). Bandwidth-constrained allocation in grid computing. In *Proceedings of WADS.*

Kretchmer, S., & Carveth, R. (2001). The color of the Net: African Americans, race and cyberspace. *Computers and Society,* September, 9-14.

Kruckeberg, D., & Starck, K. (1998). *Public relations and community: a reconstructed theory.* New York: Praeger, 52.

Ksantini, R., Ziou, D., Colin, B., & Dubeau, F. (2007). *Logistic Regression Models for a Fast CBIR Method Based on Feature Selection.* Paper presented at the International Joint Conference on Artificial Intelligence.

Kuk, G. (2003). Digital divide and quality of electronic service delivery in UK local government. *Government Information Quarterly, 20*(4), 353-363.

Labour Start. URL: http://www.labourstart.org/

Lacity, M., & Janson, M.A. (1994). Understanding qualitative data: A framework of text analysis methods. *Journal of Management Information System, 11*(2), 137-155.

Ladner, R., Petry, F. Gupta, K., Warner, E., Moore, P., & Aha ,D.(2008). Soft Computing Techniques for Web Services Brokering. *Soft Computing,* 12(11), 299-308.

Lambrinoudakis, C. et al. (2003). Security requirements for e-government services: a methodological approach for developing a common PKI-based security policy. Computer Communications, 26 (16), 1873–1883.

Lamont, J. (2006). *E-government: enhancing national security.* http://www.kmworld.com/Articles /ReadArticle.aspx?ArticleID=15806 (review)

LaPorte, T. M., Demchak, C. C., & de Jong, M. (2002). Democracy and bureaucracy in the age of the Web: Empirical findings and theoretical speculations. *Administration and Society, 34*(4), 411-446.

Larson, J. A., Navathe, S. B., & Elmasri, R. (1989). A theory of attribute equivalence in databases with application to schema integration. *IEEE Transactions on Software Engineering, 15*(4), 449-463.

Lawler, E.J., & Yoon, J. (1995). Structural power and emotional processes in negotiation: A social exchange approach. In R.M. Kramer, & D.M. Messick (Eds.), *Negotiation as a Social Process (*pp. 143-165). Thousand Oaks, CA: Sage.

Lawrence, A. (2004). From EAI to SOA. *Information Age, Infoconomy,* B8-B9.

Lawson, G. (1998). *NetState.* London: Demos.

Layne, K., & Lee, J. (2001). Developing fully functional e-government: A four-stage model. *Government Information Quarterly,* 18, 122-136.

Ledford, J. L. (2002). Establishing Best Practices for e-Government within the U.S. *Faulkner Information Services* (February), Docld: 00018275.

Lee, S. M., Tan, X., & Trimi, S. (2005). Current Practices of Leading e-Government Countries. *Communications of the ACM, 48*(10), 99-104.

Lenk, K., & Traunmuller, R. (2000, September 6-8).A framework for electronic government. In *Proceedings of the 11th International Workshop on Database and Expert Systems Applications* (DEXA'00),(pp. 71-277). Greenwich, London, U.K.

Lensink, Michelle, MP. URL: http://www.michellelensink.com

Li, J., & Wang, J. Z. (2006). *Real-time Computerized Annotation of Pictures.* Paper presented at the ACM Multimedia Conference, Santa Barbara, CA.

Li, J., Wang, J. Z., & Wiederhold, G. (2000). *IRM: Integrated Region Matching for Image Retrieval.* Paper presented at the ACM Multimedia Conference, Los Angeles, CA.

Li, W.-S., & Clifton, C. (1994). *Semantic integration in heterogeneous databases using neural networks.* Paper presented at the International Conference on Very Large Databases (VLDB).

Lim, E.T.K., & Tan, C.W. (2005, August 5-10). *What you think others think: Influence of presumed influence in e-collaborations.* Paper presented at the 65th Annual Meeting of the Academy of Management, OCIS Division, Honolulu, Hawaii.

Lim, M. (2002). Cyber-civic space in Indonesia: from panopticon to pandemonium? *International Development Planning Review,* 24(4), 383-400.

Lim, T.S. Lim, Loh, W.Y. and Shih, Y.S. (2000). A comparison of prediction accuracy, complexity, and training time for thirty–three old and new classification algorithms. *Machine Learning,* 40, 203–228.

Lindsey, D.H., Brass, D.J., & Thomas, J.B. (1995). Efficacy-performance spirals: A multilevel perspective. *Academy of Management Review, 20*(3), 645-378.

Littman, M., & Boyan, J. (1993). *A distributed reinforcement learning scheme for network routing* (Tech. Rep. No. CMU-CS-93-165).

Lovelock, and Ure. (2001). E-government in China. Retrieved from http://www.trp.hku.hk/publications/e_gov_china.pdf.

Lowndes, V., Pratchett, L., & Stoker, G. (2001). Trends in public participation: part 2 - citizen's perspectives. *Public Administration, 79*(2), 445-455.

Lumpkin, G. T., & Dess, G. G. (2004). E-Business Strategies and Internet Business Models: How the Internet Adds Value. *Organizational Dynamics, 33*(2), 161-173.

Ma, W. Y., & Manjunath, B. (1997). *NeTra: A Toolbox for Navigating Large Image Databases.* Paper presented at the IEEE International Conference on Image Processing.

Macdonald, I. (2001). *Local Government Receives Massive Networking the Nation Funding.* http://www.ministers.dotars.gov.au/im/releases/2001/july/m197_2001.htm: Media Release, Department for Regional Services, Territories and Local Government.

Macintyre, Clement (2005). Politics. In Spoehr, John (ed.), *The State of South Australia,* Wakefield, 2005

Mack, R., & Neilson, J. (1993). Usability inspection methods. *SIGCHI, 25*(1), 28-33.

Mackerras, M., and McAllister, I. (1999). Compulsory Voting, Party Stability and Electoral Advantage in Australia. *Electoral Studies,* 18, 217-233.

Magnuson, S. (2006). Homeland Security Mission Creates More Complications. *National Defense Magazine.* http://www.nationaldefensemagazine.org/issues/2006/August/HomelandSecurity.htm

Mahadevan, B. (2000). Business Models for Internet-based E-commerce. *California Management Review, 42*(4), 55-69.

Maistre, F. (2003). *JORAM.* Retrieved May 2005, from http://joram.ob-jectweb.org

Malone, T. W., & Crowston, K. (1990). *What is coordination theory and how can it help design cooperative work systems?* Paper presented at the Proceedings of the Conference on Computer-Supported Cooperative Work CSCW'90, , Los Angeles, California.

Mansell, M. (1993). Aborigines and the Constitution. *Human Rights Defender.* 2 (4), 27-28.

Marche, S., & McNiven, J. D. (2003). E-Government and E-Governance: The Future Isn't What It Used To Be. *Candian Journal of Administrative Sciences,* 20(1), 74-86.

Marchionini, G., Samet, H., & Brandt, L. (2003). Digital government. *Communications of ACM, 46*(1), 25-27.

Marks, E. & Bell, M. (2006). *Executives' Guide to Service-Oriented Architecture (SOA): A Planning and Implementation Guide for Business and Technology.* Wiley.

Markus, M.L. (1994). Electronic mail as the medium of managerial choice. *Organizational Science, 5*(4), 502-527.

Markus, M.L., & Robey, D. (1988). Information technology and organizational change: casual structure in theory and research. *Management Science, 34*(5), 583-598.

Markus, M.L., Tanis, C., & Fenema, P.C. (2000). Multisite ERP implementation. *Communications of the ACM, 43*(4), 42-46.

Martin, D.F., F. Morphy, W.G. Sanders and J. Taylor (2002). *Making Sense of the Census: Observations of the 2001 Enumeration in Remote Aboriginal Australia.* Research Monograph No.22, Centre for Aboriginal Economic Policy Research, Australian National University, Canberra: ANU E Press, available at http://www.anu.edu.au/caper_series/no_22/frames.php (Consulted on 8/02/2008).

Masood, S. (2002). The missing link. November 2002, 31-32.

Mathieson, K. (1991). Predicting user intentions: Comparing the technology acceptance model with the theory of planned behavior. *Information Systems Research, 2*(3), 173-191.

May, P. (2003). Amalgamation and Virtual Local Government. In B. Dollery, N. Marshall & A. Worthington (Eds.), *Reshaping Australian Local Government: Finance, governance and reform.* Sydney: UNSW Press.

McAllister, I and T. Makkai. (1993). Institutions or protest? Explaining invalid votes in Australian elections. *Electoral Studies* 12(1), 23-40.

McEachern, D. (2000). World's First Virtual Electorate. *Legislative Studies*, vol. 15, no. 1, Spring 2000, pp. 59-65

McFetridge, Duncan, MP. URL: http://www.duncanmcfetridge.com

McGregor, A. (2006). Personal email communication between Lisa Hill and Ms Anne MacGregor, Co-founder Southern Cross Group, 06/06/2006.

McGuinness, D. L. and Harmelen F. V. (Eds) (2004) .OWL Web Ontology Language Overview. Retrieved, December 4 2006 from http://www.w3.org/TR/owl-features/.

McNaughton, K. (1999). *Taxpayers reluctant to file over web, cnet.com.* Retrieved May 2, 2003, from http://news.com.com/2100-1017-223215.html?legacy=cnet

Mediadev (2002). Pourquoi et comment faire communiquer les applications. Livre blanc.

Medjahed B., & Bouguettaya A., (2005). A multilevel composability model for semantic Web services. *IEEE Transactions on Knowledge and Data Engineering, 17*(7), 954-968.

Medjahed, B. & Bouguettaya, A. (2005). Customized Delivery of E-Government Web Services. *IEEE Intelligent Systems*, 20(6), 77-84.

Medjahed, B. et al. (2003). Infrastructure for e-government web services. IEEE Internet Computing, 7 (1), 58–65.

Melville, N., Kraemer, K., & Gurbaxani, V. (2004). Information technology and organizational performance: an integrative model of it business value. *MIS Quarterly, 28*(2), 283-322.

Merkes, M. (2004, November 17-18). *Darebin eForum.* Paper presented at the Australian Government Information Management Office [AGIMO] Seminar Enabling Government, Engaging Communities: An Online Perspective. Brisbane, Australia. Retrieved May 24, 2007, from http://www.agimo.gov.au/resources/events/2004/engage

Merkes, M., Walsh, L. and Bailey, J. (2007). *Building Community Capacity Through eConsultation: Darebin eForum.* Paper presented at the Australian Social Policy Conference: Social Policy through the Life Course: Building Community Capacity and Social Resilience, 11-13 July 2007, Sydney NSW.

Merton, R.K., Fiske, M., & Kendall, P.L. (1990). *The focused interview: a manual of problems and procedures* (2nd ed.). New York: Free Press.

Michael Stevens (2002). Service-Oriented Architecture Introduction, Part 1. Retrieved April 26, 2005 from www.developer.com/design/article.php/1010451.

Miikkulainen, R., & Kumar, S. (1999). Confidence based dual reinforcement q-routing: An adaptative online routing algorithm. In *Proceedings of the Sixteenth International Joint Conference on Artificial Intelligence* (pp. 758-763).

Miles, M. B., & Huberman, A. M. (1994). *Qualitative data analysis: An expanded sourcebook.* Thousand Oaks, CA: Sage.

Milford, H.S. (2000). Racing to e-government: Using the internet for citizen service delivery. *Government Finance Review, 16*(5), 21-22.

Miller, A. George. (1995). WordNet: A lexical Database for English. *Communications of ACM* 38, 39-41.

Miller, J. A., Baramidze, G. T., Sheth, A. P. & Fishwick, P. A. (2004) . Investigating Ontologies for Simulation Modeling. *Proceedings of the 37th annual symposium on Simulation ANSS,* 55.

Milner, E. M. (2000). *Managing information and knowledge in the public sector.* New York: Routledge.

Minahan, T. (1995). Lack of interoperability delays import-export database. *Government and Computer News, 14*(10), 72.

Minnesota E-Democracy. (2004). *Minnesota e-democracy Web site.* Retrieved May 24, 2007, from http://www.e-democracy.org/

Mintzberg, H. (1996). Managing Government Governing Management. *Harvard Business Review, 74*(3), 75-83.

MIT (Department of Information Technology, Government of India), (2005), http://www.mit.gov.in, accessed during May-June 2005

Mitchell, R.K., Agle, B.R., & Wood, D.J. (1997). Toward a theory of stakeholder identification and salience: defining the principle of who and what really counts. *Academy of Management Review 22*(4), 853-886.

Mitchell, S. (2005). Step towards having our say electronically. *The Australian* 17/05/2005. URL: http://global.factiva.com/en/arch/display.asp (Consulted 8/02/2008).

Mitchell, T. (2005). *Generative and Discriminative classifiers: Naïve Bayes and Logistic Regression.* Retrieved from http://www.cs.cmu.edu/~tom/mlbook/NBayesLog- Reg.pdf

Mittu R., Guleyupoglu, S. Chang, C. Johnson, A. Dowdy, M. & Barlow, W. (2008). Unclassified Information Sharing in Stability, Security, Transition and Reconstruction Efforts. *International Journal of Electronic Government Research,* 4(1) , 36-48.

Monks, R.A.G., & Minow, N. (1995). *Corporate governance.* Blackwell, Cambridge, MA.

Monson-Haefel, R. (2004). *J2EE Web services.* Boston: Addison Wesley.

Moon, J.M. (2002). The evolution of e-government among municipalities: Rhetoric or reality? *Public Administration Review, 62*(4), 424-433.

Moon, M.J. and Norris, D.F. (2005). Does managerial orientation matter? The adoption of reinventing government and e-government at the municipal level. *Information Systems Journal, 15*(1), 43-60.

Moon, M.J., and Bretschneider S. (2002). Does the perception of red tape constrain it innovativeness in organizations? Unexpected results from simultaneous equation model and implications. *Journal of Public Administration Research and Theory, 11*(3), 327-52.

Moore, G. C., & Benbasat, I. (1996). Integrating diffusion of innovations and theory of reasoned action models to predict utilization of information technology by end-users. In K. Kautz & J. Pries-Hege (Eds.), *Diffusion and adoption of information technology* (pp. 132-146). London: Chapman and Hall.

Moore, R. (1999). Democracy and Cyberspace. In B. Hague & B. Loader (Eds.), *Digital Democracy: Discourse and Decision Making in the Information Age*. London: Routledge.

Morris, Dick (1999). *VOTE.COM.* Los Angeles, Renaissance Books

Morris, Dick (2000-1). Direct Democracy and the Internet in Symposium: Internet Voting and Democracy, held at Loyola Law School in October, 2000, and published in *Loyola Law Review*, Vol. 34:3 Consulted at URL:http://llr.lls.edu/volumes/v.34-issue3/morris.pdf on25/01/2008

Mousley, K. (2006). *Submission 84.* Submission to the Commonwealth Parliamentary Inquiry into Civics and Electoral Education, 16 June 2006. URL: http://www.aph.gov.au/house/committee/em/education/subs/sub084.pdf (Consulted 8/02/2008).

Mühl, F., & Krabina, B. (2003). Online One-Stop Government - Eine Integrierte Plattform: Ergebnisse des EU-Projekts eGOV. In Maria Wimmer (Hrsg.), Quo vadis e-Government? State-of-the-art 2003, Proceedings of eGOV Days 2003 OCG series, 165, pp. 156-165.

Muir, K. (2004, June). *Connecting communities with CTLCs: From the digital divide to social inclusion.* Report by the Smith Family. Sydney: the Smith Family.

Mylene, M., & Buckman, R., (2005). New Web-based technology draws applications, investors. *Wall Street Journal* P. B1.

NASSCOM (2005). Retrieved December 3, 2005, from http://www.nasscom.org

National ICT Australia Ltd (NICTA). Background: The Defence Science and Technology Organisation (2003) in Joint Media Release, *DSTO and NICTA sign agreement on ICT commercialisation,* Tuesday 9 December 2003. Consulted at URL: http://nicta.com.au/_data/assets/pdf-file/0004/NICTA_DSTO_agreement.pdf on 25/01/2008

National Security Agency. (n.d.). *Global Information Grid, Scope and Objectives.* http://www.nsa.gov/ia/industry/gigscope.cfm?MenuID=10.3.2.2

Natsev, A. (2001). *Multimedia Retrieval By Regions, Concepts, and Constraints.* Ph.D. Thesis, Duke University, Durham, NC.

Natsev, A., Chadha, A., Soetarman, B., & Vitter, J. S. (2001). *CAMEL: Concept Annotated iMagE Libraries.* Paper presented at the Storage and Retrieval for Image and Video Databases, SPIE, San Jose, CA.

Natsev, A., Rastogi, R., & Shim, K. (2004). WALRUS: A Similarity Retrieval Algorithm for Image Databases. *IEEE Transactions on Knowledge and Data Engineering, 16*(3), 301-316.

Navarra, D.D., & Cornford, R. (2003). A policy making view of e-government innovations in public governance. In *Proceeding of American Conference on Information Systems (AMCIS)*, Florida.

Navy PEO C4I & Space RAPIDS Team & Air Force ESC C2ERA Team. (2004). *Net-Centric Enterprise Solutions for Interoperability.* http://nesipublic.spawar.navy.mil/files/NESI-Overview-v1e.ppt

Nelson, R.R., & Winter, S.J. (1982). *An evolutionary theory of economic change.* Cambridge, MA: Harvard University Press.

Netcentric Enterprise Solutions for Interoperabilty (2006). *Netcentric Enterprise Solutions for Interoperability Part 5: Developer Guidance Version 1.3.* http://nesipublic.spawar.navy.mil/part5/releases/1.3.0/WebHelp/nesi_part5_v1_3.htm

New South Wales Government. (2005). *Community-builders.nsw*. Retrieved May 24, 2007, from www.communitybuilders.nsw.gov.au

Newcombe, T. (2000). Customer is king. *NetGov - Supplement to Government Technology*, 8-11.

Newell, S. J., Goldsmith, R. E., & Banzhaf, E. J. (1998). The effect of misleading environmental claims on consumer perceptions of advertisements. *Journal of Marketing: Theory and Practice, 6*(2), 48-60.

Nimmo, Dan and Sanders, Keith R (eds.), (1981). *Handbook of Political Communication,* Beverly Hills, California. Sage Publications

Nockleby, J. (2001). Why internet voting?. *Loyola of Los Angeles Law Review*. 34(3), 1023-1032.

Nolan, R. L. (1979). Managing the crisis in data processing. *Harvard Business Review, 57*(2), 115-126.

Nonaka, I., Reinmoeller, P., & Senoo, D. (1998). The "ART" of knowledge: Systems to capitalize on market knowledge. *European Management Journal, 16*(6), 673-684.

Norris, D., & Moon, M. (2005). Advancing e-government at the grassroots: Tortoise or hare? *Public Administration Review, 65*(1), 64-72.

Norris, P. (1999). Who surfs? New technology, old voters, and virtual democracy. In E.C. Kamarck, & J.S. Nye (Eds.), *Democracy.com? governance in networked world* (pp. 71-94). Hollis, NH: Hollis Publishing Company.

Norris, P. (2001). *Digital Divide: Civic Engagement, Information Poverty and the Internet Worldwide*. Cambridge & New York: Cambridge University Press.

Novak, Lauren (2007). Missing You…as MPs let young slip through Net. *Sunday Mail,* 12 August 2007

O'Malley, K., Higgins, P., Hayward, C., Watson, K., and Hilton, S. (2007). *E-Democracy in Bristol*. UK: Bristol City Council.

O'Neil, Michael (2005). Information reported at the *ICT Breakfast Forum for Solutioncity Adelaide Australia* members, 19 October 2005. Consulted at URL: http://www.solutioncity.com.au/ on 25/01/08

O'Rourke, R.(2005). *Homeland Security: Navy Operations -- Background and Issues for Congress*. http://www.history.navy.mil/library/online/homeland_security.htm

Oberle, D., Eberhart, A., Staab, S. & Volz, R. (2004). Application servers, enterprise computing and software engineering: Developing and managing software components in an ontology-based application server. *Proceedings of the 5th ACM/IFIP/USENIX international conference on Middleware*, 459 - 477.

Obrst, L., Wray, R. E. & Liu, H. (2001) .Ontological engineering for B2B E-commerce. *Proceedings of the international conference on formal ontology in Information Systems, 2001*, 117 - 126.

OECD. (2001). *Engaging citizens in policy-making: Information, consultation and public participation*. PUMA Policy Brief No. 10. Retrieved May 24, 2007, from http://www.oecd.org/dataoecd/45/25/35063274.pdf

OECD. (2001). *Starting Strong. Early Childhood Education and Care. Education and Skills*. OECD. Available: <http://caliban.sourceoecd.org/ vl=9220233/cl=12/nw=1/rpsv/cgi-bin/fulltextew.pl?prpsv=/ij/oecdthemes/99980029/v2001n7/s1/p1l.idx13.12.2006>

OECD. (2003). *Promise and problems of e-democracy: Challenges of online engagement*. OECD Report. France: OECD.

OECD. (2006). *Starting Strong II. Early Childhood Education and Care*. OECD Publishing. Available: <http://caliban.sourceoecd.org/vl=9220233/cl=12/nw=1/rpsv/cgi-bin/ fulltextew.pl?prpsv=/ij/oecdthemes/99980029/v2006n13/s1/p1l.idx13.12.2006>

Ojala, M. (1993). *IEA Preprimary Study in Finland 2. The use of early childhood settings*. Joensuu: University of Joensuu.

Oliver, C. (1997). Sustainable competitive advantage: combining institutional and resource-based views. *Strategic Management Journal, 18*(9), 697-713.

ONTOGOV project (2006). Retrieved December 30, 2006 from http://www.sciencedirect.com/science?_ob=RedirectURL&_method=externObjLink&_locator=url&_cdi=6902&_plusSign=%2B&_targetURL=http%253A%252F%252Fwww.ontogov.com%252F

OpenID (2007). *Open ID – Free Secure Identity*. http://www.openid.org, last accessed July 23, 2007.

Opetushallitus. (2000). *Esiopetuksen opetussuunnitelman perusteet [Core Curriculum for Pre-School Education].* Opetushallitus [The National Board of Education]. Available: <http://www.edu.fi/julkaisut/maaraykset/ops/esiops.pdf13.12.2006>

Orlikowski, W. (1993). Case told as organizational change: Investigating incremental and radical changes in system development. *MIS Quarterly*, *7*(3), 309-40.

Orr, G. (2004). *Australian Electoral Systems: How Well Do They Serve Political Equality?* Report prepared for the Democratic Audit of Australia. Report No.2, Australian National University.

Orr, G., Mercurio, B. and Williams, G. (2002). Australian Electoral Law: A Stocktake. *Election Law Journal*, 2 (3) 383-402.

Outback Areas Community Development Trust (OACDT). URL: http://www.oacdt.sa.gov.au/

Pablo, Z.D., & Pan, S.L. (2002, September, 2-4). A multidisciplinary analysis of e-governance: Where do we start? In *Proceedings of the 6th Pacific Conference on Information Systems* (PACIS 2002), Tokyo, Japan.

Pacific Bell (2002), *Pacific Bell/UCLA Initiative for 21st Century Literacies at the UCLA Graduate School of Education and Information Studies Re-evaluating the Bridge! An expanded Framework for Crossing the Digital Divide through Connectivity, Capability and Content, a Public Policy Roundtable*'. Los Angeles

Palmer, I. (2002). State of the world: E-government implementation. *Faulkner Information Services* (January), Docid 00018297.

Pan, S.L., Newell, S., Huang, J., & Wan, K.C. (2001, December 16-19). Knowledge integration as a key problem in an ERP implementation. In *Proceeding for the 22nd Annual International Conference on Information Systems* (ICIS 2001), (pp. 321-328).New Orleans, LA.

Paolucci, M., Soudry, J., Srinivasan, N., and Sycara, K. (2004). A Broker for OWL-S Web services. *Proceedings of the AAAI Spring Symposium on Semantic Web Services*, 562-567.

Papazoglou, M.P, & Georgakopoulos, D. Service oriented computing. *Communications of the ACM*, *46*(10), 25-28.

Pardo, T.A., & Scholl, H.J. (2002, January 7-10). Walking atop the cliffs: Avoiding failure and reducing risk in large scale e-government projects.In *Proceedings of the 35th Hawaii International Conference on System Sciences (HICSS 2002).* HI.

Pardo, T.A., Scholl, H.J., Cook, M.E., Connelly, D.R., & Dawes, S.S. (2000). *New York Atate central accounting system stakeholder need analysis*. Albany, NY: Central for Technology in Government.

Parkhe, A. (1993). Messy research, methodological predispositions, and theory development in international joint ventures. *Academy of Management Review*, *8*(2), 227-268.

Parkhomenko, O., Lee, Y. & Park, E. K. (2003). Ontology-driven peer profiling in peer-to-peer enabled semantic web. *Proceedings of the twelfth international conference on Information and knowledge management*, 564 – 567.

Parliament of Victoria. (2004). *Inquiry into electronic democracy* (Discussion Paper). Scrutiny of Acts and Regulations Committee, State of Victoria. Melbourne, Australia: Parliament of Victoria.

Parliament of Victoria. (2005). *Scrutiny of Acts and Regulations Committee, Inquiry into Electronic Democracy, Final Report, April 2005.* URL http://www.parliament.vic.gov.au/SARC/E-Democracy/Final_Report/ToC.htm (Consulted 8/05/06).

Parnell, Mark, MLC. URL: http://www.markparnell.org.au/

Paul, R. A.(2005). DoD Towards Software Services. *Proceedings of the 10th IEEE International Workshop on Object-Oriented Real-Time Dependable Systems* (WORDS'05), 3-6.

Paulson, L. D. (2005). Building rich Web applications with AJAX. *IEEE Computer, 38*(10) 14-17.

Pearce, J. (2002). Aussies vote for electronic polling: survey. *ZDNet Australia*. 17/12/2002. URL: http://www.zdnet.com.au/news/business/Soa/Aussies-vote-for-electronic-vouing-survey/0,139023166,120270740,00.htm (Consulted 8/2/2008).

Pechoucek, M., Marık, V., & Stepankova, O. (2001). Towards reducing communication traffic in multi-agent systems. *Journal of Applied Systems, 2*(1), 152-174.

Penfold, Liz, MP. URL: http://www.lizpenfold.com/

Peng, F., & Deyun, Z. (2006). *Hybrid optimize strategy based QoS route algorithm for mobile ad hoc networks.* Department of Computer Science and Technology, Xi'an Jiaotong University, Xi'an, China.

Perlich, C., Provost, F., and Simonoff, J. (2003). Tree Induction vs. Logistic Regression: A Learning-curve Analysis. *Journal of Machine Learning Research*. 4, 211-255

Pfeffer, J., & Salancik, G. R. (1978). *The External Control of Organizations - A Resource Dependence Perspective*. New York: Harper & Row.

Pfeffer, J., & Salancik, G.R. (1978). *The knowledge-doing gap: How smart companies turn knowledge into action.* Boston: Harvard Business School Press.

Pfeffer, J., & Sutton, R.I. (2000). *The knowledge-doing gap: How smart companies turn knowledge into action.* Boston: Harvard Business School Press.

Phythian, M., & Taylor, W. (2001). Progress in electronic service delivery by English District Councils. *The International Journal of Public Sector Management, 14*(7), 569-584.

Pickering, B.C. T., Dacey, P.,and Byrne, D. (2004). *Electronic Voting and Electronic Counting of Votes: A Status Report* [report]. AEC, 15 April 2004. URL: http://www.aec.gov.au/_content/what/voting/electronic_report/ (Consulted 8/02/2008).

Pihlaja, P., & Junttila, N. (2001). Julkishallinnon hajauttaminen - miltä päiväkodin lapsiryhmät näyttävät muutosten jälkeen? [Decentralisation of Public administration - how do child groups look like after changes in Day-care Centres]. *Varhaiskasvatuksen ammattilehti Lastentarha.*

Porter, M. E. (2001). Strategy and the Internet. *Harvard Business Review, 79*(3), 62-78.

Porter, M.E. (1992). Capital choices: Changing the way america invests in industry. *Research Report Presented to the Council on Competitiveness*, Co–sponsored by The Harvard Business School, Boston.

Poundstone, William (2008). A Paper Trail for Voting Machines. *New York Times.* URL: http://www.nytimes.com/2008/01/07/opinion/07poundstone.html, 7/01/2008 (Consulted 8/02/2008)

Prahalad, C.K., and Ramaswamy, V. (2000). Co-opting customer competence. *Harvard Business Review, 78*(1), 79-87.

Print, M, L. Saha, and K Edwards. (2004). *Youth Electoral Study: Report 1: Enrolment and Voting.* December 2004. URL: http://www.aec.gov.au/AboutAECPublications/youth_study_1/index.htm (Consulted 8/02/08.)

Provan, K. G., & Milward, H. B. (2001). Do Networks Really Work? A Framework for Evaluating Public-Sector Organizational Networks. *Public Administration Review, 61*(4), 414–423.

Prud'hommeaux, E. & Seaborne, A. (Eds.) (2007). *SPARQL Query Language for RDF.* Retrieved June 16, 2007 from http://www.w3.org/TR/rdf-sparql-query/

Pullen, S. and Minter Ellison Consulting. (2005). *Independent Review of the Northern Territory Electoral System: Final report and Recommendations.* Canberra: Scope.

Quin, L. *Extensible Markup Language (XML).* Retrieved March 28, 2006, from http://www.w3.org/XML

Quinlan, J. R. (1993). *C4.5: programs for machine learning*. San Francisco, CA: Morgan Kaufmann Publishers Inc.

Quinn, J.B., Anderson, P., & Finkelstein, S. (1996). Leveraging intellect. *Academy of Management Executive*, *10*(3), 7-27.

Rahimi, S., Carver, N. & Petry, F. E. (2005). A Multi-Agent Architecture for Distributed Domain-Specific Information Integration. In Ladner, R. & Petry, F. E., *Net-Centric approaches to intelligence and national security* (pp 129-148). New York: Springer US.

Rainey, G.W., & Rainey, H.G. (1986). Breaching the hierarchical imperative: The modularization of the social security claims process. In D.J. Calista (Ed.), *Bureaucratic and governmental reform*, (pp. 171-196). Greenwich, CT: JAI Press.

Rainey, H.G., Backoff, R.W., & Levine, C.H. (1976). Comparing public and private organizations. *Public Administration Review*, *36*(2), 233-244.

Ram, S., & Park, J. (2004). Semantic conflict resolution ontology (SCROL): An ontology for detecting and resolving data and schema-level semantic conflicts. *IEEE Transactions on Knowledge and Data Engineering*, *16*(2), 189-202.

Ram, S., & Zhao, H. (2001). *Detecting both schema-level and instance level correspondences for the integration of e-catalogs*. Paper presented at the Workshop on Information Technology and Systems (WITS).

Ram, S., Park, J., Kim, K. and Hwang, Y. (1999). *A comprehensive framework for classifying data- and schema-level semantic conflicts in geographic and non-geographic databases*. Ninth Workshop On Information Technologies And Systems (WITS), Dallas, TX.

Rann, Premier Mike (2007). *Update*. News Release, 24 January 2007, Government of South Australian. Consulted at URL: http://www.saplan.org.au/ on 24/01/2008

Rann, Premier Mike (2007). *Update*. News Release, 24 January 2007, Government of South Australian. Consulted at URL: http://www.saplan.org.au/images/TargetFactSheets/t4.2_target%20%fact%20sheet.doc on 23/02/2008

Rapoport, R. N. (1970). Three Dilemmas of Action Research. *Human Relations*, *23*, 499-513.

Rappa, M. (2002). *Business Models on the Web* [Electronic Version]. Retrieved 25 October 2006 from http://digital-enterprise.org/models/models.html.

Ratnasingham, P. (1998). The importance of trust in electronic commerce. *Internet Research: Electronic Networking Applications and Policy*, *8*(4), 313-321.

Raul, C. A. (2002). *Privacy and the digital state: balancing public information and personal privacy*. Norwell, MA: Kluwer Academic Publishers.

Reddy, M. P., Prasad, B. E., Reddy, P. G., & Gupta, A. (1994). A methodology for integration of heterogeneous databases. *IEEE Transactions on Knowledge and Data Engineering*, *6*(6), 920-933.

Reed, M. (2003). *Bridging the data gap*. Retrieved from http://www.digitalgovernment.org/news/stories/2002/1102/1102_dgrc_reed.jsp, 2006.

Relyea, H.C. (2002). E-gov: Introduction and overview. *Government Information Quarterly*, *19*, 9-35.

Rendleman, John (2007). Navy CIO approves open-source software use. *Government Computer News*. http://www.gcn.com/print/26_14/44462-1.html, last accessed July 23, 2007.

Rennie, G., & Hartley, J. (2004). *Show-Business for Ugly People? Media Politics and E-Democracy*. Paper presented at the The Australian Electronic Governance Conference, Centre for Public Policy, Melbourne University, http://www.public-policy.unimelb.edu.au/egovernance/ConferenceContent.html#nancyotis

Richard, E. (2004, August 4-6). *E-consultation: New roles for public servants*. Paper presented at the International Colloquium, Communication and Democracy: Technology and Citizen Engagement, Fredericton, New Brunswick, Canada.

Rights., U. S. H. C. o. t. J. S. o. C. a. C. (1984). *Domestic security measures relating to terrorism: Hearings*

(Congressional Hearings 98th Cong., 2nd sess.; Serial no. 51). Washington, DC: US Congress.

Robbins, H. (1952). Some aspects of the sequential design of experiments. *Bulletin American Mathematical Society, 55,* 527-535.

Ronaghan, S.A. (2002). *Benchmarking e-government: A global perspective-assessing the progress of the UN member states.* Report by the American Society for Public Administration [ASPA] and the United Nations Division for Public Economics and Public Administration [UNDPEPA]. New York: ASPA & UNDPEPA. Retrieved May 24, 2007, from http://unpan1.un.org/intradoc/ groups/public/documents/UN/UNPAN021547.pdf#search=%22%22Benchmarking%20E-governmen t%3A%20A%20Global%20Perspective%22%22

Rooksby, E., Weckert, J., & Lucas, R. (2002). The Rural Digital Divide. *Rural Society,* 12(3), 197-209.

Ross, J. (2003). Creating a strategic IT architecture competency: Learning in stages. *MISQ Quarterly Executive, 2*(1), 31-43.

Ross, J.W & Westerman, G. (2004). Preparing for Utility Computing: The Role of IT Architecture and Relationship Management. IBM Systems Journal, 43 (1), 5–19.

Ruby (2007). http://groups.drupal.org/node/2176, last accessed July 23, 2007.

Rui, Y., Huang, T., & Chang, S. (1999). Image retrieval: current techniques, promising directions and open issues. *Journal of Visual Communication and Image Representation, 10*(4), 39-62.

Rural Industries Research and Development Corporation. (2004). *Broadband adoption by agriculture and local government councils: Australia and the USA.* Barton, ACT: Rural Insustries Research and Development Corporation.

Salkowski, J. (2000). Thumbs down on E-voting until minorities go online. *Los Angeles Business Journal* via LookSmart's. URL: FindArticles@http://www.findarticles.com/p/articles/mi_m5072/is_17_22/ai_61894523/ (Consulted 8/08/2008).

Salmon, G. (2000). *E-Moderating: The key to teaching and learning online.* London: Kogan Page.

Salton, G., & McGill, M. (1983). *Introduction to Modern Information Retrieval*: McGraw-Hill.

Santos, E. Jr., Santos, E., Nguyen, H. Pan, L. and Korah, J. (2005). Large-scale Distributed Foraging, Gathering, and Matching for Information Retrieval: Assisting the Geospatial Intelligent Analyst. In *Proceedings of SPIE* (Vol. 5803, 66-77).

Santos, E. Jr., Santos, E., Nguyen, H. Pan, L., Korah, J. Zhao, Q., and Pittkin. M.(2006) I-FGM Information Retrieval in Highly Dynamic Search Spaces. In *Proceedings of SPIE.* (Vol. 6229, 1-12).

Santos, E., Jr., Santos, E., Nguyen, H., Pan, L., Korah, J., and Xia, H. (2008). *I-FGM as a Real Time Information Retrieval Tool for E-Governance.* Special Issue: E-Government Technologies for Managing National Secruity and Defense, *International Journal of Electronic Government Research,* 4(1), 14-25.

Santos, E., Jr., Santos, E., Nguyen, H., Pan, L., Korah, J., Zhao, Q., and Xia, H. (2007). Applying I-FGM to Image Retrieval and an I-FGM System Performance Analyses. In *Proceedings of the SPIE*: Defense & Security Symposium (Vol. 6560), Orlando, FL.

Sawer, M. (2001). Pacemakers for the world. In Sawer, M. (ed.) *Elections Full, Free and Fair,* Leichhardt: The Federation Press.

Saxena, A., & Wadhawa, S. (2004). E-business perspective of e-governance. In M. D. Gupta (Ed.), *Promise of e-governance: Operational challenges* (pp. 128-135). New Delhi: Tata-McGraw-Hill.

Schein, E.H. (1993). On dialogue, culture, and organizational learning. *Organizational Dynamics*, Autumn, 40-51.

Schiavo-Ocampo, S., and Sundaram, P. (2001). *To serve and preserve: improving public administration in a competitive world.* Manila, Philippines: Asian Development Bank.

Schmidt, M., Hutchison, B., Lambros, P., & Phippen, R. (2005). The Enterprise Service Bus: Making Service-oriented architecture real. IBM Systems Journal, 44 (4), 781-797.

Schneiderman, B., & Rose, A. (1996). Social impact statements: Engaging public participation in information technology design. In *Proceedings of The Symposium On Computers and The Quality Of Life*, (pp. 90-96).

Scholl, H. (2001). Applying stakeholder theory to e-government. In B. Schmid, K. Stanoevska-Slabeva, & V. Tschammer (Eds.), *Towards the e-society: e-commerce, e-business, and e-government* (pp. 735-747). MA: Kluwer Academic Publishers.

Scholl, H. J. (2006). Electronic government: Information management capacity, Organizational capabilities, and the sourcing mix. *Government Information Quarterly, 23*, 73-96.

Scholl, H. J., Klischewski, R., & Moon, J. M. (2005). Minitrack: E-government infrastructure and interoperability. Proceedings of the 38th Hawaii International Conference on System Science, IEEE.

Science, Technology and Innovation (2007). *Information Economy Directorate Highlights, STI, October 17 2007.* Consulted at URL: http://www.innovation.sa.gov.ay/ie/recent_highlights on 20/02/2008

Science, Technology and Innovation (2007). Centra Pilot. *STI-What's New*, STI, October 17 2007. Consulted at URL: http://www.innovation.sa.gov.au/ict/dbu/whats_new on 29/01/2008

Scope, (2004). Cited in *Scrutiny of Acts and Regulations Committee Victorian Electronic Democracy*, Final Report, May 2005. URL: http://www.parliament.vic.gov.au/sarc/E-Democracy/Final_Report/PartIII.htm, (Consulted 8/02/2008).

Scott, S.G., & Lane, V.R. (2000). A stakeholder approach to organizational identity. *Academy Of Management Review, 25*(1), 43-62.

Seaborne, A. (2004) .*RDQL – A Query Language for RDF.* Retrieved December 4, 2006 from http://www.w3.org/Submission/RDQL/

Sean McGrath and Conor O'Reilly (2004), A Service Oriented Approach to e-Government Architecture, Proceedings of the XML-Europe 2004, Amsterdam, The Netherlands. Retrieved November 22, 2006.

Searle, J. (1969). *Speech Acts: An Essay in the Philosophy of Language*. London: Cambridge University Press.

Seavey, A.C. (1996). Final thoughts on interesting times. *Journal of Government Information, 23*(4), 515-520.

Seddon, P.B. (1997). A respecification and extension of the delone and mclean model of IS success. *Information Systems Research 8*(3), 240-253.

Sheppard, B. H., Hartwick, J., & Warshaw, P. R. (1988). The theory of reasoned action: A meta-analysis of past research with recommendations for modifications and future research. *Journal of Consumer Research, 15*(3), 325-343.

Shilakes, C., & Tylman, J. (1988). Enterprise Information Portal. Merill Lynch.

Shleifer, A., & Vishny, R.W. (1996). *A survey of corporate governance, national bureau of economic research.* Working Paper 5554, Cambridge, MA.

Shostak, Arthur B. (2001), Today's Unions as Tomorrow's CyberUnions: Labor's Newest Hope. *Journal of Labor Studies*, April,2001. Consulted at URL: http://www.cyberunions.net/articles/article_shostak_1.htm on 25/01/2008

Siau, K. and Long, Y. (2005). Using social development lenses to understand e-government development. *Journal of Global Information Management*, (in press).

Silberschatz, A., Stonebraker, M., & Ullman, J. (1996). Database research: Achievements and opportunities into the 21st Century. *SIGMOD Record, 25*(1), 52-63.

Sirin, E., Parsai, B., Grau, B. C., Kalyanpur, A. & Katz Y. (n.d.). *Pellet: A Practical OWL-DL Reasoner.* Retrieved December 4, 2006 from http://mindswap.org/papers/PelletJWS.pdf

Smeulders, A. W. M., M. Worring, M., Santini, S., Gupta, A., & Jain, R. (2000). Content-based image retrieval at the end of the early years. *IEEE Transactions on Pattern Analysis and Machine Intelligence, 22*(12), 1349-1380.

Smith, K. (2006). Simplifying AJAX-style Web development. *Microsoft, 39*(5), 98-101.

Sneed, H. M. (2002). *Using XML to integrate exisitng software systems into the web.* Paper presented at the 26th Annual International Computer Software and Applications Conference, Los Alamitos, CA.

Snellen, I. (2000). Electronic commerce and bureaucracies. In *Proceedings of the 11th International Workshops on Database and Expert System Application*, (pp. 285-288).

SOAWorld Magazine News Desk. (2006). *ManTech Awarded Disaster-Mapping Contract From DHS.* http://webservices.sys-con.com/read/299259.htm

Solop, F. I. (2001). Digital democracy comes of age: Internet voting and the 2000 Arizona election. *PS: Political Science and Politics*. 34(2), 289-93.

South Australian Consortium for Information Technology and Telecommunications (SACITT). URL: http://www.sacitt.asn.au

South Australian Council of Social Services (SACOSS). *Strong Community, Healthy State*, (n.d.). URL: http://www.sacoss.org.au/strongcommunity/

South Australian Local Government Association (SALGA), (2004). *Building your Web Site.* Cited in O'Toole, Kevin, 'E-Governance in Australian Local Government: Spinning a Web Around Community?' (2007).Special Issue: E-Democracy in Australia: Practice and Innovation, *International Journal of Electronic Government Research*, Vol.3, No.4, October-December 2007. IGI Publishing, New York.

South Australian Policy Online (SAPO). *About South Australian Policy Online*. Consulted at URL: http://www.sapo.org.au/about/ on 25/01/2008

Southern Cross Group. (2006). *Primary Submission to the Joint Standing Committee on Electoral Matters Inquiry into Civics and Electoral Education*, 2006. 1.22. URL: http://www.aph.gov.au/house/committee/em/education/subs.htm. (Consulted 01/06/2006).

Sprecher, M. (2000). Racing to e-government: using the internet for citizen service delivery. *Government Finance Review, 16*, 21-22.

Stakes. (2005). *Varhaiskasvatussuunnitelman perusteet [National Curriculum Guidelines on Early Childhood Education and Care].* Stakes. Available: <http://www2.stakes.fi/varttua/vasu_/VASU-toinen%20painos.pdf13.12.2006>

Stamoulis D et al. (2003) A teleological Development of "Design-Decisions-Independent" Information Systems. In N. Patel (ed) Adaptive Evolutionary Information Systems, Idea Group Publishing.

Stampiglia, T. (1997). Converging technologies and increased productivity. *Health Management Technology, 18*(7), 66.

State Electoral Office, South Australia, (2003). *SEO South Australia, Annual Report 2002-2003.*

State Government of South Australia (2002). *Information Economy Policy Office*. URL: http://www.aoq.asn.au/papers/ie2002.pdf

State Government of South Australia (2004), 'Creating Opportunity: Moving Forward Together'. *South Australian Strategic Plan.* Consulted at URL: http://www.saplan.org.au/images/sa_strategic_plan_volume1a.pdf on 25/01/2008.

State Government of South Australia (2004). *Strategic Plan, Virtual Town Hall.* URL: http://www.stateplan.sa.gov.au

State Government of South Australia (2006), DFEEST, STI, Digital Bridge Unit. *Outback Connect.* URL: http://www.innovation.sa.gov.au/ie/dbu/outbackconnect

State Government of South Australia (n.d.). *ebizSA.* URL: http://www.innovation.sa.gov.au/ie/ebizsa/about_ebizsa consulted on 25/01/2008.

State Government of South Australia (n.d.). *The Virtual Electorate: Giving a voice to S A's 'Global Tribe'*. Consulted at URL: http://www.ie2002sa.gov.au/plan/default.html on 25/01/2008.

State Government of South Australia(2006). *David Unaipon Innovation Award*. Consulted at URL: http://www.innovation.sa.gov.au/ict/dbu/david_unaipon/home on 25/01/2008

State Government of South Australia, Department of Further Education, Employment, Science and Technology (DFEEST), Science, Technology and Innovation Directorate (STI). *Digital Bridge Unit*. URL: http://www.innovation.sa.gov.au/ict/dbu

State Government of South Australia, Science and Technology Innovation branch, South Australian Broadband Research and Education Network (SABRENet) (2005), *Media Release*. Adelaide, November 17, 2005. Consulted at URL: http://sabrenet.edu.au/ on 25/01/2008.

State Parliament of South Australia. URL: http:// www.parliament.sa.gov.au

Steimke, F., & Hagen, M. (2003). OSCI: a common communication standard for e-government. Lecture Notes in Computer Science, 2739, 250–255.

Stenback, J., & Heninger, A. (2004). *Document Object Model (DOM) level 3 load and save specification*. Retrieved August 28, 2006, from http://www.w3.org/TR/DOM-Level-3-LS/

Stevens, L (2007). *The In and Out of SOA, FedTech Technology Insights for leaders in Federal Government*. http://www.fedtechmagazine.com/article.asp?item_id=257

Stiglitz, J., Orszag, P., & Orszag, J. (2000). *The role of government in a digital age*. Retrieved April 16, 2002, from http://www.ccianet.org/digital_age/report.pdf

Stone, P. (2000). Tpot-rl applied to network routing. In *Proceedings of the 17th International Conference on Machine Learning*.

Stratford, J.S., & Stratford, J. (2000). Computerized and networked government information. *Journal of Government Information, 27*(3), 385-389.

Strauss, A.L., & Corbin, J. (1990). *Basics of qualitative research: Grounded theory procedures and techniques*. London: Sage.

Stringer, E. (2004). *Action Research in Education*: Prentice Hall.

Suh, B., & Han, I. (2003). The impact of customer trust and perception of security control on the acceptance of electronic commerce. *International Journal of Electronic Commerce, 7*(3), 135-161.

Sumner, Chris, (2003). Constitutional and Parliamentary Reform for South Australia. In Macintyre, Clement and Williams, John (eds.), *Peace, Order and Good Government*, Wakefield Press.

Sundaramurthy, C. (2000). Antitakeover provisions and shareholder value implications: A review and a contingency framework. *Journal of Management, 25*(5), 1005-1030.

Sundaramurthy, C., & Lewis, M. (2003). Control and collaboration: Paradoxes of governances. *Academy of Management Review, 28*(3), 397-415.

Surf Coast Shire (2007). Surf Coast Shire Eforum. Retrieved October 5, 2007, from http://eforum.surfcoast-directories.com/

Susman, G. I., & Evered, R. D. (1978). An Assesment of the Scientific Merits of Action Research. *Administrative Science Quarterly, 23*(4), 582-603.

Sutton, R. S., & Barto, A.G. (1998). *Reinforcement learning: An Introduction*. Cambridge, MA: MIT Press/Bradford Books.

Symonds, M. (2000). Government and the Internet - The Next Revolution. *The Economist*, June 24.

Symonds, M. (2000). The next revolution: After e-commerce, get ready for e-government. *The Economist*. Retrieved June 24, 2000, from http://www.economist.com/l.cgi?f=20000624/index_survey.

Tahinakis, P., Mylonakis, J., & Protogeros, N. (2006). The contribution of e-government to the modernisation of the Hellenic taxation system. *Electronic Government, an International Journal (EG), 3*(2), 139-157.

Tambouris, E. (2001). An Integrated platform for Realizing Online One-Stop Government: The eGOV Project. In: Proceedings of the DEXA International Workshop "On the Way to Electronic Government", IEEE Computer Society Press, Los Alamitos, CA.

Tan, C.W., Pan, S.L., & Lim, E.T.K. (2005). Managing stakeholder interests in e-government implementation: Lessons learned from a singapore e-government project. *Journal of Global Information Management, 13*(1), 31-53.

Tan, C.W., Pan, S.L., Lim, E.T.K., & Chan, C.M.L. (2005). Managing knowledge conflicts in inter-organizational project: an exploratory study of the infocomm development authority of singapore. *Journal of the American Society for Information Science and Technology, 56*(11), 1187-1199.

Tannenbaum, A.S. (1967). *Control in organizations*. New York: McGraw–Hill.

Tanriverdi, H. (2005). Information technology relatedness, knowledge management capability and performance of multibusiness firms. *MIS Quarterly, 29*(2), 311-334.

Tao, N., Baxter, J., & Weaver, L. (2001). A multi-agent, policy-gradient approach to network routing. In *Proceedings of the 18th International Conference on Machine Learning*.

Tapscott, D. (1995). *Digital economy: promise and peril in the age of networked intelligence*. New York: McGraw-Hill.

Taylor, M., & Kent, M.L. (1999). Challenging assumptions of international public relations. *Public Relations Review 25*(2), 131-144.

Taylor, S., & Bogdan, R. (1984). *Introduction to qualitative research methods*. New York: John Wiley & Sons.

Taylor, S., & Todd, P. A. (1995). Understanding information technology usage: A test of competing models. *Information Systems Research, 6*(2), 144-176.

Teece, D. J. (1998). Capturing Value from Knowledge Assets: the New Economy, Markets for Know-How, and Intangible Asset. *California Management Review, 40*(3), 55-79.

Teece, D. J., Pisano, G., & Shuen, A. (1997). Dynamic capabilities and strategic management. *Strategic Management Journal, 18*(7), 509-533.

Tennert, J.B., & Schroeder, A.D. (1999). Stakeholder analysis. *Presentation at the 60th Annual Meeting of the American Society of Pubic Administration*.

Terregov Project (2005). Retrieved October 20, 2005 from http://www.sciencedirect.com/science?_ob=RedirectURL&_method=externObjLink&_locator=url&_cdi=6902&_plusSign=%2B&_targetURL=http%253A%252F%252Fwww.terregov.eupm.net

The Federal Enterprise Architecture, Program Management Office web site (2005). Retrieved October 29, 2005 from http://www.feapmo.gov.

Thompson, C. S. (2002). Enlisting on-line residents: Expanding the boundaries of e-government in a Japanese rural township. *Government Information Quarterly, 19*(2), 173-188.

Thompson, J. D. (1967). *Organizations in Action*. New York: McGraw-Hill.

Thompson, R. L., Higgins, C. A., & Howell, J. M. (1991). Personal computing: Toward a conceptual model of utilization. *MIS Quarterly, 15*(1), 124-143.

Thorp, Dian (2006). e-Democracy. *IT Alive, The Australian,* May 4 2004.

Tim, R., Fielding, T., & Masinter, L. (2005). *Uniform Resource Identifier (URI): Generic Syntax*. Internet Society. RFC 3986; STD 66.

Timmers, P. (1998). Business Models for Electronic Markets. *Electronic Markets, 8*(2), 3-8.

Timson, Lia (2006). Victoria puts blind faith in electronic voting. *The Age*, November 14, 2006. Consulted at http://www.the age.com.au/news/technology/victoria-puts-blind-faith-in-electronic-voting/ on 8/02/2008

Traunmuller, R., & Wimmer, M. (2000, September 6-8). Process – collaboration – norms – knowledge: signposts for administrative application development. In *Proceedings of the 11th International Workshop on Database and*

Expert Systems Applications (DEXA'00),(pp. 1141-1145). Greenwich, London, UK.

Tricker, R.I. (1994). *International corporate governance*. Singapore: Simon & Schuster.

Tsymbalenko, Y., & Munson, E.V. (2001). *Using HTML metadata to find relevant images on the Web*. Paper presented at the Internet Computing, Las Vegas.

Turnbull, S. (1997). Stakeholder co-operation. *Journal of Co-operative Studies, 29*(3), 18-52.

U.S. Census Bureau. Government Organization: 1997 Census of Governments, Washington, D.C., 1999. Retrieved from http://www.census.gov/prod/www/abs/gc97org.html.

U.S. DoD (2007). U.S. Department of Defense, *DoD Directive 3000.05-Military Support for Stability, Security, Transition, and Reconstruction (SSTR) Operations*, http://www.dtic.mil/whs/directives/corres/html/300005.htm, last accessed July 23, 2007.

UK GovTalkTM (2004). Retrieved September 2006 from www.govtalk.gov.uk

UN (2002). *Benchmarking e-government: A global perspective, assessing the progress of the UN member states*. Division of Public Economics and Public Administration (DPEPA). Nettelafrica.org/doc/NetTel%20Safari@the%20Equator%20(Uganda%202003)/Benchmarkinge-govt.pdf

UN (2003). World public sector report: E-government at the crossroads, United Nations, New York.

UN (United Nations) and ASPA (American Society for Public Administration). (2001). *Global Survey of E-government*.

UNCTAD (2002). *Least developed countries at a glance*. United Nation Information Communication Technology Task Force.

United States Office of Management and Business. (2002). *Implementing the President's Management Agenda for E-Government*. http://www.usa.gov/Topics/Includes/Reference/egov_strategy.pdf

UNPAN, Benchmarking e-government (2002). A global perspective, United Nations Online Network in Public Administration and Finance, New York.

Vaduva, A., & Dittrich, K. R. (2001). *Metadata Management For Data Warehousing: Between Vision and Reality*. Paper presented at the International Database Engineering and Applications Symposium (IDEAS), Grenoble, France.

Valtioneuvoston periaatepäätös varhaiskasvatuksen valtakunnallisista linjauksista. (2002). Sosiaali- ja terveysministeriö. Available: <http://pre20031103.stm.fi/suomi/pao/varhais2/kasvatus.pdf13.12.2006>

Vapnik, V. (1999). *The Nature of Statistical Learning Theory*, 2nd edition. Springer Verlag.

Varshney, A. (2005). New frontiers of social policy. Proceedings of Arusha Conference. December 12-15, 2005. Retrieved December 1, 2006, from http://siteresources.worldbank.org/INTRANETSOCIALDEVELOPMENT/Resources/Varshney_Formatted.pdf

Vassilakis, C., Anya, S., Dimitrios, T., & Dimitris, G. (2005). A Blackboard-Oriented Architecture for e-Government Service Composition. Managing Modern Organizations with Information Technology. 309 – 312.

Veltkamp, R. C., & Tanase, M. (2000). *Content-Based Image Retrieval Systems: A Survey* (Technical Report No. UU-CS-2000-34): Dept. of Computing Science, Utrecht University.

Venkatesh, V, & Davis, F. D. (1996). A model of the antecedents of perceived ease of use: Development and test. *Decision Science, 27*(3), 451-481.

Venkatesh, V. (2000). Determinants of perceived ease of use: Integrating control, intrinsic motivation, and emotion into the technology acceptance model. *Information Systems Research, 11*(4), 342-365.

Venkatesh, V., Morris, M. G., Davis, G. B., & Davis, F. D. (2003). User acceptance of information technology: Toward a unified view. *MIS Quarterly*, 27(3), 425-478.

Vetere, G. and Lenzerini, M. (2005). Models for Semantic Interoperability in Service-Oriented Architectures. *IBM Systems Journal, 44*(4), 887-904.

Victorian Electoral Commission (VEC), 2007. *Report to Parliament on the 2006 Victorian State Election*, Section 6, Electronic Voting. http://www.vec.vic.gov.au/files/2006steteelectionreportSection6.pdf

von Hoffman, C. (1999). The making of e-government. *COI Enterprise Magazine* (November 15).

von Krogh, G. (1998). Care in knowledge creation. *California Management Review, 40*(3), 133-153.

W3C Web API Working Group. Retrieved 19 March 2006, from www.w3.org/2006/Webapi/

Walsh, L. (2006). The use of technology to extend e-government and citizen participation in Australia. In A. Anttiroiko & M. Malkia (Eds.), *Encyclopaedia of digital government*. Hershey, PA: Idea Group Reference.

Walsh, L. (2007). *Darebin eForum Evaluation Report*. Report commissioned by Darebin City Council. Centre for Citizenship & Human Rights, Deakin University, Melbourne Australia. Retrieved September 5, 2007, from http://www.darebin.vic.gov.au/Files/Darebin_eForum_Evaluation_090807.pdf

Walsh, L. (2007). A Case Study of Public Servants Engaged in E-Consultation in Australia. *The International Journal of Electronic Government Research* (IJEGR), 3(4), pp. 20-37.

Walsham, G. (1995). Interpretive case studies in is research: Nature and method. *European Journal of Information Systems, 4*, 74-81.

Wand, Y., Woo, C., & Hui, S. (1999, 11-12 December). *Developing Business models to Support information System Evolution.* Paper presented at the Ninth Workshop on Information Technologies and systems.

Wang, J. Z., Li, J., & Wiederhold, G. (2001). SIMPLIcity: Semantics-Sensitive Integrated Matching for Picture Libraries. *IEEE Transactions on Pattern Analysis and Machine Intelligence, 23*(9), 947-963.

Wang, Y. S. (2003). The adoption of electronic tax filing systems: An empirical study. *Government Information Quarterly, 20*(4), 333-352.

Watson & Mundy (2000). Electronic democracy: A strategic perspective. *Communications of ACM.*

Web Services, World Wide Web Consortium (2002). Retrieved July 25, 2006 from http://www.w3.org/2002/ws/

Webler, T., & Tuler, S. (2000). Fairness and competence in citizen participation – theoretical reflections from a case study. *Administration & Society, 32*(5), 566-595.

Weerakkody, V., Baire, S., & Choudrie, J. (2006). *E-government: A case for process improvement in the public sector.* Proceedings of the Hawaii International Conference on Systems Sciences (Hicss-39), January 2006.

Weerakkody, V., Janssen, M., & Hjort-Madsen, K. (2006). Realising integrated e-government services: A European perspective. *Journal of Cases in Electronic Commerce, 3*(2), 14-38.

Weill, P., & Vitale, M. (2001). *Place to Space: Migrating to E-Business Models*: Harvard: Harvard Business Press.

Wescott, C. (2002). *E-government in the Asia Pacific Region.* Retrieved March, 27, 2002, from http://www.adb.org/ Documents/Papers/E_Government/default.asp

Westphal, J. D. (1999). Collaboration in the boardroom: Behavioral and performance consequences of CEO-board social ties. *Academy of Management Journal, 42*(1), 7-24.

What is e-Government? (2007). http://www.wisegeek.com/what-is-e-government.htm

What is Jabber? (2007). http://www.jabber.org/about/overview.shtml, last accessed July 23, 2007

White, Trish, (2004). The State of ICT in South Australia: Collaborating To Work Fast and Smart. *Information Age*, 17/06/2004. Consulted at URL: http://www.infoage.idg.com.au/index.php on 25/01/2008.

Wimmer, M and Krenner, J. (2001). An Integrated Online One-Stop Government Platform : The Egov Project, 9th Interdisciplinary Information Management Talks. Proceedings of the Schriftenreihe Informatik, Universitätsverlag Trauner, Linz, pp. 329-337.

Wimmer, M, & Traunmueller, R. (2002). Towards an Integrated Platform for Online One-Stop Government. In: ERCIM News, Special Theme: e-Government, Issue 48, January 2002.

Wimmer, M. (2002). A European perspective towards online one-stop government: the eGOV project. Electronic Commerce Research and Applications 1 (1), 92–103.

Wimmer, M. and Bredow, B. (2002). A holistic approach to security aspects in e-government. Proceedings of the 35th Hawaii International Conference on System Sciences (HICSS-35), (5), p. 128b.

Wimmer, M., & Traunmuller, R. (2000, September 6-8). Trends in electronic government: managing distributed knowledge. In *Proceedings of the 11th International Workshop on Database and Expert Systems Applications* (DEXA'00), (pp. 340-345) Greenwich, London, UK.

Wimmer, M., Traunmuller, R., & Lenk, K. (2001). Electronic business invading the public sector: considerations on change and design. In *Proceedings of the 34th Hawaii International Conference on System Sciences.*

Witten, I. H., & Frank, E. (2005, June). *Data Mining: Practical Machine Learning Tools and Techniques* (Second ed.): Morgan Kaufmann.

Woodrow, E., & Heinzelman, W. (2001). *SPIN-IT: A data centric routing protocol for image retrieval in wireless networks.* Retrieved November 20, 2003, from http://www.ece.rochester.edu/~wheinzel/GroupWeb/papers/spin-it_icip02.pdf

World Bank (2005). *Definition of e-government.* www1.worldbank.org/publicsector/egov/definition.htm

World Bank. A definition of e-government. Retrieved 25 November 2006 from www1.worldbank.org/publicsector/egov

World Summit on the Information Society (2003-5). *Geneva-Tunis, FAQs.* Consulted at http://www.itu.int/wsis/basic/faqs.asp on 25/01/2008.

Yan, G., Ng, W. K., & Lim, E.-P. (2002). Product Schema Integration for Electronic Commerce-A Synonym Comparison Approach. *IEEE Transactions on Knowledge and Data Engineering, 14*(3), 583-598.

Yin, R. K. (1984). *Case study research: Design and methods.* Beverley Hills, CA: Sage Publications.

Yin, R.K. (1994). *Case study research: design and methods.* London: Sage.

Zetter, K. (2003). Aussies do it right: E-voting. *Wired News.* 3/11/2003. URL: http://www.wired.com/news/ebiz/0,1272,61045,00.html. (Consulted 8/2/2008).

Zhang, J., Jin, R., Yang, Y., Hauptmann, A. G. (2003). Modified Logistic Regression: An Approximation to SVM and Its Application in Large-Scale Text Categorization, In *Proceedings of the Twentieth International Conference on Machine Learning* 2003. Washington DC.

Zhang, T., Ramakrishnan, R., & Livny, M. (1996). *BIRCH: an efficient data clustering method for very large databases.* Paper presented at the ACM SIGMOD International Conference on Management of Data, Montreal, Canada.

Zhao, J. L. (1997). Schema Coordination in Federated Database Management: A Comparison with Schema Integration. *Decision Support Systems, 20*, 243-257.

Zhu, K., & Kraemer, K. L. (2005). Post-Adoption Variations in Usage and Value of E-Business by Organizations: Cross-Country Evidence from the Retail Industry. *Information Systems Research, 16*(1), 61-84.

Zhu, X., Sun, S., Cheng, S. E., & Bern, M. (2004). *Classification of Protein Crystallization Imagery.* Paper presented at the 26th Annual International Conference of IEEE Engineering in Medicine and Biology Society, San Francisco, California.

About the Contributors

Mehdi Khosrow-Pour, DBA, received his Doctorate in Business Administration (DBA) from the Nova Southeastern University (FL, USA). Dr. Khosrow-Pour taught undergraduate and graduate information system courses at the Pennsylvania State University – Harrisburg for 20 years where he was the chair of the Information Systems Department for 14 years. He is currently president and publisher of IGI Global, an international academic publishing house with headquarters in Hershey, PA and an editorial office in New York City (www.igi-global.com). He also serves as executive director of the Information Resources Management Association (IRMA) (www.irma-international.org), and executive director of the World Forgotten Children's Foundation (www.world-forgotten-children.org). He is the author/editor of over twenty books in information technology management. He is also the editor-in-chief of the Information Resources Management Journal, the Journal of Cases on Information Technology, the Journal of Electronic Commerce in Organizations, and the Journal of Information Technology Research, and has authored more than 50 articles published in various conference proceedings and journals.

* * *

Before joining the 'Electronic Voting and Electoral Inclusion: Implications for South Australia,' project as a PhD candidate in 2004, **Kate Alport** was a social researcher in the Centre for Internet Research, University of Adelaide and in the Anthropology Department at the South Australian Museum. She has a BA Hons in anthropology and an MA in international studies. Her areas of interest are social inclusion, social aspects of technology uptake and Indigenous issues. She is currently working at the Centre for Appropriate Technology in Alice Springs, Northern Territory.

William Barlow is the deputy director of the Integrated Information and Communication Technology (ICT) Support Directorate of the Office of the Assistant Secretary of Defense for Networks and Information Integration, Department of Defense Chief Information Officer (OASD(NII)/DoD CIO). His primary responsibilities include developing policy and guidance for information sharing in security, stability, transition and reconstruction operations between non-governmental and private organizations and the U.S. government. Prior to this position, he served as an information technology (IT) specialist (policy) in the Architecture and Interoperability Directorate where he developed policy and guidance for business, logistics and medical system's information support plans (ISPs).

Michael P. Dowdy is a senior systems analyst with Femme Comp Inc. (FCI) supporting the Integrated ICT Support Directorate, Office of the Assistant Secretary of Defense for Networks and Information

Copyright © 2009, IGI Global, distributing in print or electronic forms without written permission of IGI Global is prohibited.

Integration. He holds a Master's degree in security management from Webster University, St Louis, Missouri and a Bachelor's of computer science degree from Old Dominion University, Norfolk, Virginia. He is a retired U.S. Army Signal Corps officer, and graduate of the Army Command and General Staff College, the Army Systems Automation Officer Course, and the Marine Corps Command and Control Systems Course.

Suleyman Guleyupoglu is a principal scientist with the Advanced Engineering & Sciences, a division of ITT Corporation. He has been involved with online collaboration research since 2002. His other interests include expert systems, knowledge engineering, evolutionary algorithms and intelligent decision making. He holds MS/PhD degrees in engineering science & mechanics from The University of Alabama and an MBA degree from the University ofMaryland.

Bidyut Gupta received both his MTech and PhD degrees from University of Calcutta, Calcutta, India. He joined Indian Statistical Institute, Calcutta in 1982. In 1986, he was a visiting member of the faculty at the Computer Science Department, Colorado State University, Fort Collins. In 1988 he joined the Computer Science Department, Southern Illinois University, Carbondale, where at present he is a professor and the graduate program director. His research interest includes fault-tolerance in distributed systems, mobile computing, multi-agent systems, and routing in ad-hoc networks. He is a senior member of IEEE.

Before taking up her position as an associate professor of politics at the University of Adelaide, **Lisa Hill** taught at the University of Sydney, was a five-year fellow in political science at the Research School of Social Sciences, ANU, and a five-year ARC fellow at the University of Adelaide. Her current areas of interest are in political theory and issues in electoral behaviour and law, with a particular focus on compulsory voting. Recent publications include: 'Low Voter Turnout in the United States: Is Compulsory Voting a Viable Solution?' Journal of Theoretical Politics, 18 (2) 2006; 'Protest or Error? Informal Voting and Compulsory Voting' (with Sally Young), Australian Journal of Political Science, 42 (3), pp. 515-521, 2007; The Passionate Society: The Social, Political and Moral Thought of Adam Ferguson, Dordrecht: Springer Academic 2006 and The Politics of Women's Interests: New Comparative Perspectives (co-edited with L. Chappell) Oxford: Routledge, 2006.

Marijn Janssen is a director of education of the SEPAM (Systems Engineering, Policy Analysis and Management) and an associate professor at the Faculty of Technology, Policy and Management of Delft University of Technology. He holds a PhD (2001) in the field of management information systems and has been a consultant and information architect for the Ministry of Justice. His research is focused on ICT-service engineering of public service networks (e-government). He is particularly interested in intermediaries, like business process orchestrators, shared service centers and information brokers. His research is published in a large number of conference proceedings, book chapters, and international journals. More information: www.tbm.tudelft.nl/marijnj, he can be contacted at: m.f.w.h.a.janssen@tudelft.nl.

Jonna Järveläinen has worked as an assistant professor of information systems science at Turku School of Economics in Finland. She has lectured and researched in the areas of electronic business and electronic government. She has also supervised bachelor's and master's theses. She has published in International Journal of Electronic Government and Electronic Markets and several conference proceedings.

Timo Kestilä is doctoral student of information systems at the Turku School of Economics. Currently he is working as a researcher. He gained his master's in computer science at the University of Turku. He has over 20 years experience of different tasks in the information systems field. He has also worked as IS manager at the Finnish National Board of Taxes. His research interests are e-government and strategic information systems planning in an inter-organizational network. He has published in International Journal of Electronic Government.

Jarmo Kinos is currently an adjunct professor and senior lecturer in the Department of Teacher Education at the University of Turku. His main research interests and themes are in history, professionalism and the pedagogical practices of early childhood education. His latest research topic deals with the academization and scientification of ECE in Finnish universities. He has also worked as a kindergarten teacher in day-care centres. He has published in International Journal of Electronic Government.

John Korah is a doctoral candidate in the Department of Computer Science at the Virginia Polytechnic Institute & State University. He received his BE degree in electronics and instrumentation engineering from the Govt. College of Technology, Coimbatore, India. He has a Master's degree in electrical engineering from Virginia Tech. His research interests are focused on parallel/distributed computing, numerical algorithms, large scale network modeling/simulation and information retrieval. He also serves as a reviewer for the Journal of Supercomputing.

Eija Koskivaara is currently an assistant professor in the Department of Management at the Turku School of Economics. She obtained her doctoral degree in economics and business administration, majoring in information systems science. Her doctoral research focuses on continuous auditing and IS tools to support decision making. She is interested in creating an interactive virtual environment to support families and their well-being. She has published in International Journal of Electronic Government, Journal of Emerging Technologies in Accounting, Journal of Information Systems and Technology Management, Managerial Auditing Journal, and Journal of Operational Research Society.

George Kuk is an associate professor in strategy and information systems at the Nottingham University Business School. His research focuses on strategic dynamics, open source, knowledge networks and user innovation. He received his PhD in applied psychology from Nottingham University. He can be contacted at: g.kuk@nottingham.ac.uk.

Roy Ladner is the director of the Data Architecture and Administration Division at the Naval Meteorology and Oceanography Command. He serves as staff lead for the development and management of data and information that is needed to support the Naval METOC Command. He directs technical, programmatic and administrative aspects of the data and information life cycle to support all METOC and geospatial information and services information requirements for the Department of Navy Battlespace. Dr. Ladner also performs as the agent for the Command's navy-wide role as the functional data manager and also as co-lead for METOC data and information standardization across the Department of Defense.

Deqing Li is a graduate student in the Thayer School of Engineering at Dartmouth College. She received her BS degree in Internet and multimedia technology from Hong Kong Polytechnic University. Her research interests include artificial intelligence, information retrieval, intent inference and deception detection.

Clement Macintyre has degrees from Murdoch University and the University of Cambridge. He teaches politics at the University of Adelaide. In 2002-03 he was chair of the 'Panel of Experts' appointed by the South Australian Parliament to advise on the State Constitutional Convention held in 2003. He has expertise in European and Australian State and Federal politics and has recently published papers on South Australian political history and Australian constitutional arrangements. He is a regular media commentator on Australian state and federal politics.

Sean McCarthy works as a consultant for Femme Comp, Inc. (FCI) to the Department of Defense (DoD) CIO. He works to enable the DoD to more effectively communicate with non traditional participants during stability operations. Prior to coming to coming to the DoD he has lead and assisted the development of information systems to the Federal Aviation Administration (FAA) and the Federal Communications Commission (FCC). He holds a Bachelor's degree in economics from the University of Virginia and is working on a Master's degree on the management of information technology from the University of Virginia.

Ranjeev Mittu is head of the Intelligent Decision Support Section, within the Advanced Information Technology Branch of the Information Technology Division at the Naval Research Laboratory. His team is currently leading the development and integration of the ShareInfoForPeople portal, which is sponsored by the Office of Secretary of Defense (OSD) Networks and Information Integration (NII). He is a member of The Technical Cooperation Program, which is an international organization that promotes scientific collaboration among the US, UK, New Zealand, Australia and Canada. He holds a Master of Science degree in Electrical Engineering from The Johns Hopkins University in Baltimore, MD.

Hien Nguyen is an assistant professor at the Department of Mathematical and Computer Sciences at the University of Wisconsin-Whitewater. She received a PhD in computer science from the University of Connecticut in 2005. Her research interests include user modeling, information retrieval, collaborative information retrieval, recommender systems with a current focus on hybrid user model for improving a user's performance in information retrieval. Professional services and committee work include program committee for 2007 and 2006 IEEE International Conference on Systems, Man, and Cybernetics (IEEE SMC2007 and SMC2006). She also is a member of User Modeling-User Adapted Interactions Journal Special Reviewers Board. She also serves as a reviewer for User Modeling Conference (2007), IEEE Transactions on Systems, Man, and Cybernetics, Part B, Information Processing and Management, and AAAI 2006 (Poster).

Kevin O'Toole is an associate professor in the School of International and Political Studies at Deakin University where his major research is related to economic and social development in rural areas. His most recent work has focused on six areas: catchment to regional scale indicators of sustainability; integrating environmental, social and economic measures at local level; community governance; demand management for domestic water; comparative land use analysis; and evaluation of allied health retention in rural areas. Dr O'Toole has published over fifty journal and conference papers in recent years and is on the editorial panel of the journal *Rural Society* that reports on a range of issues in rural Australia.

Long Pan is a postdoctoral associate in the Laboratory for Computation, Information & Distributed Processing (LCID) at the Virginia Polytechnic Institute & State University. He received his PhD degree from CS department of Virginia Tech. He got his BS and MS degrees from the Automation Department of the Tsinghua University. His research interests are focused on SNA (social network analysis) on large and dynamic networks, SNA with culture infusion, parallel/distributed computing, data mining, and information retrieval. He is a member of IEEE, ACM, and INSNA. He serves as a reviewer for Journal of Supercomputing, and the International Conference on Parallel Processing (2007).

Fred Petry received the PhD in computer science from The Ohio State University in 1975. He has been on the faculty of the University of Alabama in Huntsville, Ohio State University and Tulane University and is currently with the Naval Research Laboratory. Dr. Petry has over 300 scientific publications including 115 journal articles/book chapters and 7 books written or edited. His monograph on fuzzy databases has been widely recognized as the definitive volume on this topic. He was selected as an IEEE fellow in 1996 for his research on the use of fuzzy sets for modeling imprecision in databases and in 2003 was made a fellow of the International Fuzzy Systems Association. In 2002 he was chosen as the outstanding researcher of the year in the Tulane University School of Engineering and in 2004 received the Naval Research Laboratory's Berman Research Publication award.

Päivi Pihlaja is a lecturer in special pedagogy in the Faculty of Education at the University of Turku. Her research interests lie in special education in early childhood and social relationships in special groups. She teaches special pedagogy, early childhood education and continuing professional development. She has also worked as a day-care teacher and as a coordinator in the Centre for Extensive Studies in Education at the University of Turku. She has published in International Journal of Electronic Government.

Shahram Rahimi is an associate professor and the director of undergraduate programs at the Department of Computer Science at Southern Illinois University Carbondale. He received his BS degree in computer engineering from National University of Iran (Shahid Beheshti), a MS degree in computer science and a MS degree in computer engineering from University of Southern Mississippi and his PhD degree from Center for Computational Sciences, Stennis Space Center. At the present he is the editor-in-chief for International Journal of Computational Intelligence Theory and Practice, the associate editor for Informatica Journal, and an editorial board member for several other journals. Dr. Rahimi's research interest includes distributed computing, multi-agent systems, and soft computing. He has over 110 peer reviewed journal articles, proceedings and book chapters in these research areas.

Pravab J. Rana received his BS degree from Nepal and his MS degree from Southern Illinois University. The subject of his thesis was Ontology Mediation in Multi-Agent Systems, directed by Dr. Shahram Rahimi.

Hannu Salmela is acting professor of information systems at the Turku School of Economics. His research interests include strategic planning of information systems, IT governance in inter-organizational networks and the use of IT in social and health services. He has conducted several collaborative action research projects on these topics with both private and public organizations. He has published in International Journal of Electronic Government, Journal of Strategic Information Systems, European Journal of Information Systems, International Journal of Public Sector Management, European Journal of Operational Research, and Information and Software Technology.

Eugene Santos, Jr. is a Professor of Engineering in the Thayer School of Engineering at Dartmouth College. He received his BS ('85) in mathematics and computer science from Youngstown State University, a MS ('86) in mathematics (specializing in Numerical Analysis) from Youngstown State University, as well as ScM ('88) and PhD ('92) degrees in computer science from Brown University. His areas of research interest include artificial intelligence, intent inferencing, information retrieval, automated reasoning, decision science, adversarial reasoning, user modeling, natural language processing, probabilistic reasoning, and knowledge engineering, verification and validation, protein folding, load balancing, virtual reality, and active user interfaces. He has served on many major conference program committees from intelligent agents to evolutionary computing. He is currently editor-in-chief for the IEEE Transactions on Systems, Man, and Cybernetics: Part B, an associate editor for the International Journal of Image and Graphics, and is also on the editorial advisory board for System and Information Sciences Notes.

Eunice E. Santos has BS and MS degrees in both mathematics and computer science, and received a PhD in 1995 from the University of California, Berkeley in computer science. Dr. Santos is the director of the laboratory for Computation, Information & Distributed Processing, and an associate professor in the Department of Computer Science at Virginia Polytechnic Institute & State University. Her research interests include parallel and distributed processing, computational science and engineering, intelligent systems, networking, and modeling & simulation. Dr. Santos has been awarded an NSF CAREER grant, the Spira Award for Excellence in Teaching in Engineering, and the Robinson Faculty Award. She is subject area editor for the Journal of Supercomputing and a member of the DARPA/IDA Defense Science Study Group.

Senior researcher **Jarmo Tähkäpää** is currently working at the Turku School of Economics as a lecturer in information systems science. His research interests focus on IS in the public sector and the health care environment, and his doctoral thesis was about managing the IS resource in health care. His teaching includes IS evaluation and qualitative methodologies, and he is also supervising master's and bachelor's theses. He has published in International Journal of Electronic Government.

Lucas Walsh is a researcher whose interests include the use of information and communication technologies in government and education. He has published internationally in these areas. During the last several years Lucas has held three Research Fellowships at Monash University, Deakin University and was postdoctoral research fellow in the School of Communications and Multimedia at Edith Cowan University. He has also worked for the international Baccalaureate Organisation and was a civil society delegate to the World Summit on the Information Society as a member of the WSIS Working Group for Education, Research and Academia, which deals both with online shared educational content (e.g. open course-ware) and with research related to education. In 2006, he was invited by the Darebin City Council to review its online consultation initiative and secured funding to develop a set of guidelines for public officials seek to implement their own online consultation strategies.

Huadong Xia is a graduate student in the Department of Computer Science at the Virginia Polytechnic Institute & State University. He received his BS degree in information science from Peking University and got his ME degree in computer science from the Chinese Academy of Sciences. His research interests include distributed computing, information retrieval and social networks analysis. He also serves as a reviewer for the Journal of Supercomputing.

Fei Yu is a graduate student in the Thayer School of Engineering at Dartmouth College. She received her BS degree in information technology from Hong Kong Polytechnic University. Her research interests include artificial intelligence, information retrieval, user modeling, natural language processing and intent inferencing.

Index

Copyright © 2009, IGI Global, distributing in print or electronic forms without written permission of IGI Global is prohibited.

H

I

K

L

M

N

O

P

R

S

T

U

V

W

X